50.00

ROMAN PAPERS

SIR RONALD SYME

(Photograph Alison Frantz)

RONALD SYME

ROMAN PAPERS

I

EDITED BY

E. BADIAN

OXFORD
AT THE CLARENDON PRESS
1979

Oxford University Press, Walton Street, Oxford OX2 6DP

OXFORD LONDON GLASGOW
NEW YORK TORONTO MELBOURNE WELLINGTON
KUALA LUMPUR SINGAPORE JAKARTA HONG KONG TOKYO
DELHI BOMBAY CALCUTTA MADRAS KARACHI
NAIROBI DAR ES SALAAM CAPE TOWN

Published in the United States by Oxford University Press, New York

© Oxford University Press 1979

British Library Cataloguing in Publication Data

Syme, *Sir* Ronald, b. 1903 Roman papers
  1. Rome — History
  I. Title II. Badian, Ernst
  337′ .008 DG209 79–40437
  ISBN 0–19–814367–2

Printed in Great Britain
at the University Press, Oxford
by Eric Buckley
Printer to the University

PREFACE

THE Editor owes thanks to many, and really adequate acknowledgement cannot be made here. But let me thank, first of all, the editors of the journals and collections in which these studies first appeared: whether or not they actually owned the copyright, they were courteous and helpful when approached about reprinting. (Copyright acknowledgement is made in the proper places throughout.) Next, I should like to thank D. K. Clift for preliminary work on an index, which incidentally led him to correct many minor slips in references, and the Loeb Classical Foundation at this university for a grant to Dr. Clift towards that work; my colleague G. W. Bowersock for help in reading, and suggesting bibliography on, some of these papers; an expert reader at the Oxford University Press who provided help of a quality rarely found among publishers' readers these days; and above all to Sir Ronald Syme himself, who helped in making the selection of works, was always willing to answer questions, and has for too long been patiently awaiting the result.

Most of the delay has been due to the project of an index of persons, embracing both this collection and two earlier ones, *Ten Studies in Tacitus* and *Danubian Papers*. These volumes will constantly have to be used together, and the latter has no index. The project turned out to be more difficult and time-consuming than had been thought. Dr. Clift's drafts provided a starting-point, but every major entry still needed several days of solid work (in some cases as much as nine or ten) before it was typed and ready for press. Since I could do such work only intermittently, it is understandable (though from the reader's point of view unfortunate) that the Press in the end decided not to wait until January 1979 for the completion of the project (the last batch of the first set of paged proofs of the text having reached me in October 1974). It is to be hoped that it will be made available at some future time, since it provides a key to the greater part of Sir Ronald Syme's work that will make fuller use of it possible—and that, of course, was the major purpose in bringing together the studies that form the present collection.

E. B.

CONTENTS

VOLUME I

VOLUME II

INTRODUCTION

THIS collection was originally intended to honour Sir Ronald Syme in the year of his seventieth birthday. It soon became apparent that this goal was optimistic, and circumstances have delayed its appearance until the seventy-fifth. The seventieth year was in any case properly marked by the volume of the *Journal of Roman Studies* (lxiii, 1973) dedicated to him, and I am at least dispensed from competing with the urbane Introduction to that volume by Fergus Millar. It is fitting too that the completion of Sir Ronald's third quarter-century should not only be distinguished by the completion of another major work, but be signified by the publication of what, in individual length though certainly not in aggregate importance, may be called his *Scripta Minora*.

These volumes include the greater part of Sir Ronald's writings up to 1970, and the choice was made by the Editor in consultation with Sir Ronald himself. However, the articles that, at the time when the selection was made, had already appeared in three separate volumes (*Ten Studies in Tacitus, Danubian Papers*, and *Emperors and Biography*) are omitted. The Bibliography at the end of Volume II, itself complete to 1970, gives full details on which of the articles and major reviews can be found in each of these volumes and in the present collection.

The text of the papers has not been altered, except that misprints and a few minor errors of fact have been corrected. Where Sir Ronald has over the years changed his mind, that must be left to be gathered from later publications, and this is where the Index was intended to be particularly helpful. Editorial additions are marked by square brackets, and the Editor is solely responsible for anything thus marked. These annotations (on the whole confined to articles and excluding reviews) are of two kinds. First, I have aimed at giving ample cross-references to Sir Ronald's other articles in this collection and in the other volumes listed above, and some cross-references to his major works; fewer, since those works are more easily accessible and particularly well indexed. This will help the reader not only in tracing occasional changes of interpretation, so as to make it clear when an older opinion ought not to be quoted as current, but in seeing the same problem treated and often further illuminated against a different background. Secondly, I have tried to refer the reader to some important later (and, very rarely, earlier) interpretations by other scholars, either adding support to views here expressed or presenting weighty arguments against those views. In particular, I have tried to cite all relevant evidence newly discovered. For technical reasons, nothing that appeared after 1974 could be systematically included, and coverage tapers off towards that date. This annotation inevitably had to be selective: with hundreds of articles appearing every year completeness could not even be aimed at, and it is realized that others would probably have chosen differently.

Various ways of arranging the material by subject-matter were originally considered, and similar volumes that have appeared in different countries were consulted for comparison. In the end it became clearer than ever how arbitrary all such classifications must be. They appeared to offer no advantage to compensate for what they inevitably lose. The simple chronological arrangement here presented can admittedly not be fully accurate, owing to differences in the actual speed of publication; nor can the selection be completely representative, since much in three major areas of Sir Ronald's work (Tacitus, Balkan Studies, and the *Historia Augusta*) had to be excluded. Yet, despite these limitations, it will at least enable the reader to follow, in a general way, the development of the ideas and the interests of an outstanding scholar. And this, surely, provides much of the charm, the *dulce*, of a collection such as this, just as the *utile* is provided by the union of what had been separated in time and place.

The movement that led from *The Roman Revolution* to Tacitus, Sallust, and the *Historia Augusta* as the main topics can now to some extent be followed; and so can the fact that no field that had once attracted Sir Ronald's notice was ever totally abandoned, even when his main interests changed. Few scholars, past or present, have been so successful at constantly extending their fields of interest rather than leaving one for another. The presence of certain major interests, pervading the whole of his work and varying only in proportion and alignment, is perhaps responsible for this, and they can be discerned as threads running through these studies and linking nearly all of them. Interest in administration and the process of government; in historical geography and topography; and interest in historiography, and in particular in the personality of the historian, gaining in importance—all these nourish and characterize Sir Ronald's practice of history. One might sum it up by the word 'prosopography' (which he gave to the *Oxford English Dictionary*), an art of which he is the outstanding and acknowledged representative.

Prosopography has suffered from some of its practitioners. In Sir Ronald's hands it is not the shuffling of index-cards or the movement of pieces on a game-board, sometimes known by that name and an easy target for those interested in other kinds of history. Nor is it confined to political interpretation in terms of personal association—it is not 'Namierization', whatever that term means, as some have charged without thorough acquaintance with the actual work. Indeed, Sir Ronald was forming and writing his kind of history before he had read Namier: its roots (if one wanted to indulge in *Quellenforschung*) are in quite a different tradition, the technique developed in nineteenth-century Germany, the historical depth English, and, above all, his own. In personal terms, his work is based on a profound interest in human beings and their relationships, against the background of their social environment in all its complexity. Those who like their history in terms of abstractions, or in terms of humanity viewed as material for statistical analysis, will find little to interest them in this collection. Not that ideas, or historical processes, are ignored—far from it. *The Roman Revolution* is about a social and political transformation; *Tacitus* is a portrait of a changing society and its government. Several of the studies in this collection investigate and dissect the process of social change as much as any treatise does, or a great historical novel. But unlike the former, they are about *people* who exemplify the process and embody it and, unlike the latter, they are about *real* people, brought to life, by rigorously controlled historical imagination, from the highways of well-known sources and the byways of esoteric documentation. Sir Ronald reminds us, in an age when it is often forgotten, that history in its true sense is a humanistic discipline. Not that philosophy or sociology are irrelevant; but in order to become history, they must be infused with living individual content.

It is difficult to sum up in a few words the contribution of one of the giants of scholarship and historiography. His major works by themselves suffice to secure him a place in the company of men like Niebuhr and Mommsen. But a large part of Sir Ronald's contribution is in fact contained in articles (some of substantial length), and although some of those dealing with particular fields have been collected, the true measure of his work has been difficult to appreciate. It is to be hoped that this collection will take its place beside the major works, supplementing them and adding further depth, instructing and delighting both those familiar with what is here reprinted and those who, while appreciating Sir Ronald's books, perhaps do not read many articles in journals and collections.

And in view of the fact that his rate and quality of publication has not decreased since the last items here included, we may hope for another volume before very long.

E. B.

Harvard University
December 1978

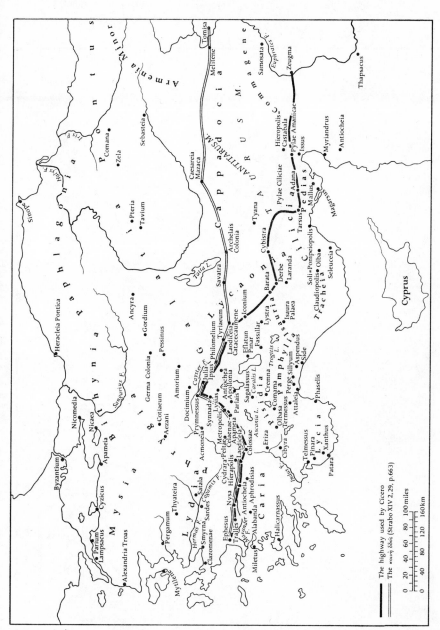

MAP 1. CILICIA

The highway used by Cicero
The κοινὴ ὁδός (Strabo XIV 2,29, p.663)

0   20 40 60 80 100 miles
0   40   80   120   160 km

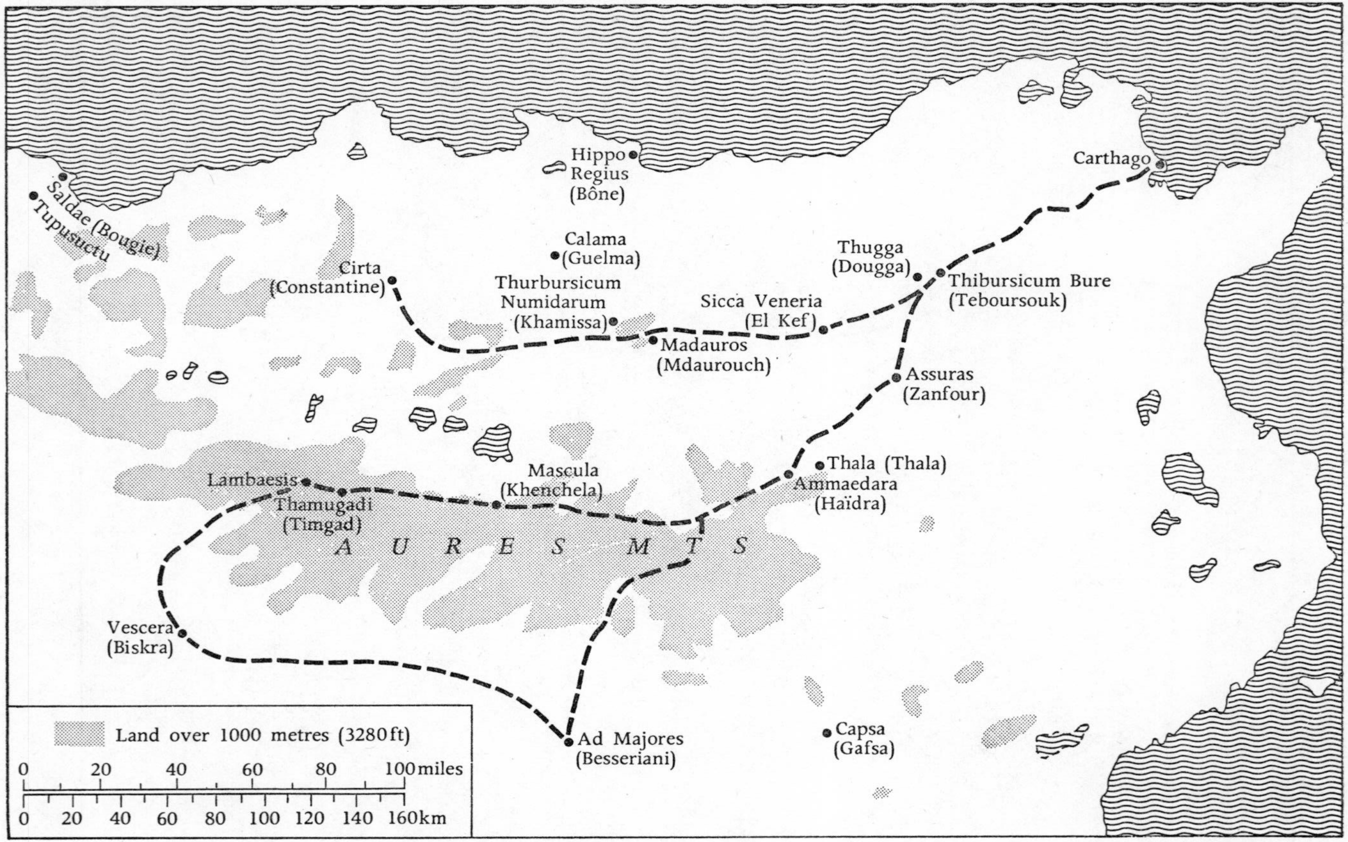

MAP 2. ROMAN NORTH AFRICA

Land over 1000 metres (3280ft)

Carthago

Thibursicum Bure
(Teboursouk)

Assuras
(Zanfour)

Thugga
(Dougga)

Thala (Thala)
Ammaedara
(Haïdra)

Capsa
(Gafsa)

Sicca Veneria
(El Kef)

Madauros
(Mdaurouch)

A U R E S   M T S

Hippo
Regius
(Bône)

Calama
(Guelma)

Thurbursicum
Numidarum
(Khamissa)

Masaula
(Khenchela)

Ad Majores
(Besseriani)

Cirta
(Constantine)

Lambaesis
Thamugadi
(Timgad)

Vescera
(Biskra)

Saldae (Bougie)
Tupusuctu

0   20   40   60   80   100miles
0   20   40   60   80   100   120   140   160km

I

The Imperial Finances under Domitian, Nerva, and Trajan[1]

THE work of the spade and the use of common sense have done much to mitigate the influence of Tacitus and Pliny and redeem the memory of Domitian from infamy or oblivion. But much remains to be done. The policy of this able and intelligent Emperor has been vindicated on the frontiers, but is still, in the matter of finance, condemned as extravagant and ruinous. Not only is this the view of those who, with the warrant of the senatorial tradition, see little in his reign but the dark night of despotism before the dawn of a new era of felicity—even a judicious historian like M. Gsell reproaches Domitian for not having done enough to restore the finances of the Empire, compromised as they had already been by Titus.[2] So the charge is not baseless; and it is more with sorrow than with surprise that we read at the beginning of M. Carcopino's elegant and ingenious paper, 'Les richesses des Daces et le redressement de l'empire romain', the emphatic statement, 'c'est un fait reconnu de tous que Domitien laissa derrière lui une situation financière obérée.'[3]

This way of looking at things at once renders inconsequent and unintelligible the financial policy of his successors—they make no economies worthy of the name, yet are none the less in a position to remit taxes and spend lavishly in peace and in war. How did they do it? The contradiction has sometimes been recognized but has never been explained. It is all very well to hail Nerva as a financial genius,[4] or with Paribeni to speak comforting words about the careful administration and personal economy of Trajan.[5] But Paribeni has not succeeded in convincing even himself of the

---

[1] [For a reply to the views here expressed, see C. H. V. Sutherland, *JRS* xxv (1935), 150 ff. Cf. also A. Garzetti, *Nerva* (1950), 60 ff.; G. Biraghi, *PP* vi (1951), 257 ff. Syme's view is reaffirmed in *Tacitus* (1958), 628–31.]

[2] *Essai sur le règne de l'empereur Domitien* (1894), 334.

[3] In *Dacia* I (1924), 28. [Cf., in reply to this, *Points de vue sur l'impérialisme romain* (1934), 73.]

[4] 'Seine Finanzverwaltung war mustergültig', *RE*, s.v. 'Cocceius', col. 143.

[5] *Optimus Princeps* i (1927), 153.

---

truth of this explanation.[1] One would therefore prefer, and one has a right to demand, fewer words and more facts. Carcopino might appear at first sight to have produced something solid. He has recently invoked the gold of Dacia—not the mines, which have sometimes been suggested as a motive for the conquest, but the hoarded treasures of the Dacian kings, which Trajan is deemed to have seized: for John the Lydian, on what should be good authority, namely that of Trajan's doctor Crito, records that after the conquest | Trajan brought back from Dacia enormous masses of gold and silver.[2] His figures are fantastic, and had always been dismissed as incredible, until Carcopino showed, on palaeographical grounds, how they could easily be reduced to something reasonable and acceptable. Carcopino may well be right, but that is not enough. Even if the gold of Dacia be admitted as a factor, it still remains to prove that there actually was a financial problem awaiting solution in the earlier years of Trajan's reign, and that it was solved in this way. Carcopino is therefore obliged to postulate that Trajan's reign should fall into two sharply defined halves, the first of embarrassment, the second of abundance, divided by the conquest of Dacia. Unfortunately this will not work: inquiry will show that the line cannot be drawn at the year 106 any more than it can at any other point.

We shall proceed to examine the evidence. In the first place it must be conceded that the more imposing of Trajan's constructions in Rome, the Forum and the Basilica, belong to the later years: this was natural enough. Four campaigns in Dacia absorbed time, attention, and money: Trajan reasonably postponed till after his victory the monuments that were to crown and commemorate it. It is surely an exaggeration to say of Trajan that, after 106, 'avec une intensité que n'avait éprouvée aucun des Flaviens, la fièvre du bâtiment le saisit à son tour'.[3] But where is the evidence? Most of the items of expenditure adduced by Carcopino in support of this statement belong to public works which must have been begun long before that date. Roads, harbours, and aqueducts are not made in a day or a year. The harbour of Civitavecchia was well on its way to completion when Pliny saw it (in 107?).[4] Nor can what Carcopino calls the draining of the Pomptine Marshes be admitted: the road, embankments, and bridges across the Pomptine Marshes are part of an elaborate programme of rebuilding the Via Appia and improving communications with Campania and the South which in any case took at least twelve years to complete; for it certainly goes back to Nerva, if not even to Domitian.[5] One

---

[1] At least he also says of Trajan (op. cit. ii 171) that 'le larghe vedute e le nobili ambizioni di lui segnavano vie più spaziose e più dispendiose alla politica finanziaria dell'impero'. Paribeni then goes on to suggest that Trajan, to meet these expenses, exploited imperial estates more intensively and debased the coinage.

[2] Joh. Lyd. *De Mag*. ii 28.   [3] Carcopino, op. cit. 30.   [4] Plin. *Ep*. vi 31.

[5] Cassius Dio (lxviii 15, 3) dates the completion of these works after the Dacian Wars,

could indeed suggest that a number of works for which we find a year of termination as late as 108 or 109, such as the Via Traiana, the Via Nova Traiana, the Aqua Traiana, were probably begun as much as four or five years earlier.[1] Nor has | Carcopino brought forward any reasons for his assigning to the second half of the reign the creation, both of all those bodies of *auxilia* that bear the name Ulpia, and of the two new legions II Traiana and XXX Ulpia.[2] As far as concerns the legions, everything points to their having been raised when and because they were needed, that is to say before or during the Dacian Wars.[3] Thus, much of Carcopino's evidence of increased expenditure in the years after the conquest of Dacia cannot be admitted. Similarly, remissions of taxes and generous *congiaria* are no new thing but are familiar features of either half of Trajan's reign.

It would thus appear that, whatever may be thought of the gold of Dacia, there is not enough evidence to prove that its influx marked a turning-point and left its traces in increased expenditure and diminished returns. Still less, on the other hand, are there to be found any indications of a financial stringency in the earlier half of Trajan's reign, where Carcopino's theory presupposes and demands them. He suggests that Trajan pursued the programme of economies inaugurated by Nerva and that the 'Economy Commission' (of which more later) continued to function: but there is no evidence at all to support this opinion,[4] and nothing more need be said. Nor can we let pass his statement that, apart from road-repairs and the new harbour at Ostia, the *Panegyric* of Pliny (delivered in the year 100) contains no allusions to the works of one of the greatest builders in the history of Rome.[5] It is to be regretted that Carcopino should not have scanned his *Panegyric* with a more vigilant eye. Pliny praises the Emperor, it is true, for his restraint in the matter of building; from the context,

and the inscription, *ILS* 5821, is of the year 109/10. *ILS* 280 and 285 expressly record Nerva as beginning, Trajan as finishing, parts of the work. In view of the great activity displayed by Domitian's successors on the Appia before Sinuessa, and in building a road from Puteoli to Naples, the Via Domitiana from Sinuessa to Puteoli should perhaps not be regarded as an isolated fragment. It was completed in 95 (Cassius Dio lxvii 14, 1). It is more than pure chance that not a single one of Domitian's milestones in the whole of Italy has survived, when we possess so many from Nerva's brief reign. Nerva could associate himself with Vespasian on a milestone, just as Trajan could make a dedication to Divus Titus (*ILS* 5819; *CIL* vi 946). But Domitian's memory had been condemned and his name suppressed. Most of the inscriptions relating to aqueducts, however, are less accessible than milestones, being on lead pipes: so we find that in Lanciani's collection 17 belong to Domitian, 1 to Nerva, 12 to Trajan (*I commentari di Frontino* (1880)).

  [1] *ILS* 291, 9496, 290.

  [2] He appears to assume (in any case wrongly, see *RE*, s.v. 'Legio', col. 1485) that the first mention of II Traiana occurs on an inscription of the year 109.

  [3] So Ritterling, *RE*, s.v. 'Legio'.

  [4] Certainly not in Plin. *Pan.* 62 and *Ep.* ii 1, 9, which he cites in his note.

  [5] It may be mentioned in passing that there are no adequate grounds for taking *Pan.* 29, 2 as an allusion to this harbour.

however, it is clear that he is referring especially to the private and personal buildings of Domitian, for he goes on to say of Trajan 'at quam magnificus in publicum es! Hinc porticus, inde delubra occulta celeritate properantur, ut non consummata sed tantum commutata videantur. Hinc immensum latus circi . . .'[1] So building was going on after all, and something more than the remodelling of the Circus Maximus of which other sources inform us.[2] It is not strange that Pliny does not find anything else to mention—Trajan had been in Rome only a short time, eighteen months at the most, and in any case neither Domitian nor Nerva seem to have left much that remained to be completed. There may indeed be some further items. Trajan may have repaired the Templum Divi Augusti,[3] but it is not easy to elicit from Martial the conclusion that he also completed the Ianus Quadrifrons of the Forum Transitorium.[4] Nor can it be taken as certain that the Baths of Trajan | were begun in the year 104.[5] Be that as it may, the early years of Trajan witnessed abundant activity in other branches. Nerva's programme of aqueducts was continued. When Frontinus was writing (in 98) the Anio Novus was being extended.[6] In 101–3 the course of the Tiber was regulated.[7] The harbour of Ostia is usually believed to have been begun in 103,[8] that of Civitavecchia cannot have been much later: and from an inscription of thanks set up to Trajan (when he was not yet Dacicus) it has been inferred that he was responsible for similar works at Terracina.[9] Nor were roads neglected in the first half of the reign. The rebuilding of the Appia across the Pomptine Marshes and from Terracina to Capua, the road from Puteoli to Naples, continue and complete the work of Nerva.[10] We notice also repairs on other routes— the Aemilia in 100, the Sublacensis in 103–5, the Latina in 105. In confirmation of this impression it might be remarked that most of the many milestones from roads in Spain and Numidia belong to the years before 106.[11] That is to say, whether we allow or not for the fact that between 98 and 106 Trajan had to think about the frontiers and his four great campaigns, the greatest since the days of Augustus, public works were by no means stinted, but went on, consistent and continuous, before and during, no less than after, the Dacian Wars.

But there is more than this. Already in the *Panegyric* there is never a hint of any financial stringency, but evidence on the contrary of a great outpouring of money, so much so that even Pliny must doubt and wonder

---

[1] *Pan.* 51.　　　　　[2] Cassius Dio lxviii 7, 2; *ILS* 286.　　　　　[3] Martial xii 2 (3).
[4] Paribeni, op. cit. ii 66 n. (Martial x 28 and 51).
[5] As Paribeni suggests, op. cit. ii 45.
[6] *De Aq.* 93.　　　　　　　　　　　　[7] *ILS* 5930; *CIL* vi 31550.
[8] The legend *Portus Traiani* appears on coins of the dates *cos. V* (103–11), and *cos. VI* (112).
[9] *ILS* 282. This might, however, refer to some other benefaction.
[10] See p. 2, n. 5.
[11] See the inscriptions quoted by Paribeni, op. cit. ii 126–7 and 142–4.

whether the Treasury can stand it.[1] We find not merely what is to be expected, loose and ample phrases about the Imperial munificence—we find also statements of fact. Trajan, while bestowing donative and *congiarium*, can at the same time renounce *aurum coronarium* and remit taxes. Moreover in the case of the *congiarium* special precautions are taken that none, not even the absent, should miss their share,[2] and that even infants —all children, says Pliny—should be admitted to the bounty.[3] Perhaps the *alimenta* were also extended—at least we must reckon under this head, or under that of a permanent admission to the *frumentationes*, the total of nearly 5,000 children which Pliny mentions in another place.[4] In view of this general impression of prosperity, there is every reason for believing that what was paid out in the way | of *congiarium* to the people and donative to the soldiers amounted to a large sum. The Chronographer of the Year 354 states that Trajan's *congiarium* was of 650 denarii.[5] If this figure represents a single *congiarium*, one might well expect it to be that which fell at the beginning of the reign: but, if every allowance be made and if it be assumed to be the total of the three *congiaria* that are attested on coins of Trajan's first decade, it is a monstrous total.[6] Moreover there had already been a change of Emperor, from Domitian to Nerva, and with it the inevitable *congiarium* and donative such a short time before. 650 denarii! Domitian had given in all 225 denarii in his reign of fifteen years, and Domitian, we are always told, was extravagant. But Domitian was a tyrant: Trajan was one of the good emperors and can therefore be commended for 'showing himself generous without continuing the evil practice of concessions to the idle populace'.[7]

In the face of all this expenditure the Treasury behaves in a most eccentric fashion: it turns a deaf ear to the advocates of stern economy,[8] refrains from pushing claims on debtors, refuses money, and even allows the mitigation of the *vicesima hereditatum* both to be carried a step further and to be made retrospective.[9] There is no trace of a shortage of money in the earlier years of Trajan, but adequate evidence to the contrary. The nearer

[1] *Pan.* 41, 1: 'nam mihi cogitanti eundem te collationes remisisse, donativum reddidisse, congiarium obtulisse, delatores abegisse, vectigalia temperasse, interrogandus videris, satisne computaveris imperii reditus.'

[2] *Pan.* 25, 3–4.

[3] *Pan.* 26, 3: 'omnes tamen, antequam te viderent adirentve, recipi, incidi iussisti.'

[4] *Pan.* 28, 4: 'paulo minus, patres conscripti, quinque milia ingenuorum fuerunt, quae liberalitas principis nostri conquisivit, invenit, adscivit. Hi subsidium bellorum, ornamentum pacis publicis sumptibus aluntur. . . .'

[5] Mommsen, *Ges. Schrift.* vii 574.

[6] Paribeni takes it to be that of 103 (op. cit. i 268), Carcopino that of 106 (op. cit. 31).

[7] Paribeni, op. cit. i 176.

[8] *Pan.* 41, 3: 'nunquam principibus defuerunt qui fronte tristi et gravi supercilio utilitatibus fisci contumaciter adessent . . . sed ad tuas aures cum ceteris omnibus tum vel maxime avaris adulationibus obstructus est aditus.'

[9] *Pan.* 40.

we get to the reign of Nerva and the time when Domitian is alleged to have bequeathed a bankrupt treasury, the more abundant does money seem to be.

Can the solution of the problem be found in the brief reign of Nerva? The difficulty of this has either been conveniently ignored or explained away in a very simple and unsatisfactory fashion. The following is, in brief, what may be called the accepted version. Nerva succeeds in September 96 to a dilapidated treasury, is obliged to find money, and therefore institutes an 'Economy Commission'. This works so well that, long before his sixteen months have run their full course, he is able to satisfy the goodness of his heart by remitting taxation and embarking on broad schemes of social and economic relief. It is perhaps unnecessary to point out that none of the ancient authorities, however unreliable they may be, is responsible for this pleasant little story: it is in the main a combination and manipulation of assumptions and inferences. It won't do. The only economies that can be attributed to the 'Economy Commission' are so trivial as to be laughable—the abolition of some sacrifices and horse races.[1] Nor were there other sources of money that can be deemed sufficient to restore the finances of the State, or were actually | exploited for that purpose and for that purpose only. All the gold and silver statues of Domitian were melted down, and did in fact produce large sums of money; but this procedure, like the demolition of his arches, was due, as is expressly stated, to detestation of him whose effigy or name they bore.[2] Cassius Dio, to be sure, mentions that there was a shortage of money;[3] but this is after some of Nerva's benefactions and not at the outset of his reign, when, if it had existed, it could so naturally and would so readily have been saddled upon Domitian. The selling of a part of the huge imperial patrimony—superfluous to a 'frugalissimus senex'—no doubt also provided funds.[4] But we are perhaps permitted to doubt whether Nerva was, like M. Aurelius, driven by bankruptcy to such extreme measures, and to regard it rather as something that was at the time useful and even necessary, a popular 'gesture'. It resembles his other exaggerated captation of popular favour, his calling the Palatine 'aedes publicae',[5] and was, like it, devised to make manifest to all men that, as Martial's jingle has it,

> non est hic dominus, sed imperator,
> sed iustissimus omnium senator.[6]

[1] Cassius Dio lxviii 2, 3. Zonaras (xi 19) alleges that gladiatorial contests were done away with.

[2] Cassius Dio lxviii 1, 1: μίσει δὲ τοῦ Δομιτιανοῦ αἱ εἰκόνες αὐτοῦ, πολλαὶ μὲν ἀργυραῖ πολλαὶ δὲ καὶ χρυσαῖ οὖσαι, συνεχωνεύθησαν, καὶ ἐξ αὐτῶν μεγάλα χρήματα συνελέγη.

[3] lxviii 2, 2.

[4] Cassius Dio lxviii 2, 2. Trajan also gave much away—'nec vero emendi tantum civibus tuis copiam praebes, sed amoenissima quaeque largiris et donas, ista, inquam, donas, in quae electus, in quae adoptatus es' (*Pan.* 50, 7).

[5] *Pan.* 47, 4.

[6] x 72, 8.

Not only was there no retrenchment worth speaking of—there was a pile of new expenses to be shouldered. Public works were not interrupted. In Rome, indeed, we know only of the existence of a building called Horrea Nervae,[1] and of the completion, or at least dedication, of the Forum Transitorium:[2] this is, no doubt, because there were no other buildings in course of completion at Domitian's death. On the other hand numerous milestones indicate extensive repairs of roads, an ambitious project of rebuilding the Via Appia and of driving a new road from Puteoli to Naples.[3] In the matter of the aqueducts a large programme was being carried out by the new *curator* Frontinus, both in general and by the extension of the Anio Novus and the Aqua Marcia.[4] Nor was it only that public works pursued their course unhampered. In other directions the government was generous, not to say lavish. In passing, one need only mention the institution of the *alimenta*, the agrarian law, the colonies, the privileges bestowed on cities, the various remissions of taxes and burdens that are recorded on coins.[5] | It is not surprising that tradition preserved from Nerva's reign the memory, not of a financial crisis, but of generosity and munificence.[6]

Is this rapid change from bankruptcy to abundance to be put to the credit of an 'Economy Commission' that makes no economies? The occasion, purpose, and actual results of the Commission will perhaps be revealed if the date of its institution can be discovered. It has always been assumed—and conveniently assumed—that it fell at the beginning of Nerva's reign, and had been called into being by the unhappy plight in which Domitian's misrule had left the finances. This is nowhere stated in the ancient authorities. Indeed, there is one very important piece of evidence that does not seem hitherto to have been given its full value.[7] Verginius Rufus, while rehearsing a speech of thanksgiving to Nerva, slipped and broke his thigh. From this followed a long illness, in the course of which—'etiam in hac novissima valetudine'—he felt that he was in danger of being nominated to serve on this Commission, which was then being set up by the Senate. The speech was clearly to have been delivered by Verginius in the course of his third consulate, which he held with Nerva as his colleague, either upon the occasion of entering upon that office on 1 January of the year 97, or when laying it down. And as commissions of this kind were recruited, not from magistrates in the exercise of their

---

[1] *ILS* 1627. [2] *CIL* vi 31213 = 953.

[3] For the details see *RE*, s.v. 'Cocceius', col. 148.

[4] *De Aq.* 88: 'sentit hanc curam imperatoris piissimi Nervae principis sui regina et domina orbis in dies et magis sentiet salubritas eiusdem aucto castellorum operum lacuum numero . . .'

[5] See Merlin, *Les revers monétaires de l'empereur Nerva*, or *RE*, s.v. 'Cocceius'.

[6] Aur. Victor, *Ep. de Caes.* 12, 4: 'iste quicquid ante poenae nomine tributis accesserat, indulsit, afflictas civitates relevavit,' etc.

[7] Pliny, *Ep.* ii 1.

ordinary functions, but usually from consulars of experience,[1] the institution of the 'Economy Commission' can hardly be placed at a date earlier
than six months from Nerva's accession on 18 September 96, and may
indeed, for all that any one can say to the contrary, belong even to a much
later date in that brief reign.[2] Its cause and occasion is, therefore, not
Domitian's empty treasury, but the lavish expenditure and general inefficiency of the new régime. We shall see that something of the kind was
certain to be necessary if we try to find out what the reign of Nerva was
really like. But this is not so easy: senatorial enthusiasm, backed by literary
genius, has so glossed and embellished the dawn of the new era of 'libertas
restituta' that a modern historian can be betrayed into saying that Nerva
passed away 'after enjoying a placid rule of sixteen months'.[3] There would
be better warrant for speaking of a period of anarchy such that before
long even a senator could rebuke Nerva and hint that there were, after all,
worse things than the despotism of Domitian,[4] an anarchy that continued
in extravagance and disorder and was already | on the edge of disaster[5]
when that weak old man, helpless and beleaguered in his palace, was
driven to associate in his discredited authority the commander of the army
that lay nearest to Rome.[6] Nerva was certainly a 'frugalissimus senex', but
the government of which he was the head, if it can be called a head, was
costly and ruinous and all but responsible for a great civil war. Its very
first days were disturbed and threatened. How had the assassination of
Domitian been received? 'Occisum eum populus indifferenter, miles
gravissime tulit statimque Divum appellare conatus est, paratus et ulcisci,
nisi duces defuissent: quod quidem paulo post fecit, expostulatis ad poenam
pertinacissime caedis auctoribus. contra senatus adeo laetatus est . . .'[7]
Senators exulted, as well they might, and theirs is the opinion that has

[1] Cf. Cassius Dio lv 6, 6; Tac. *Ann.* xv 18.

[2] Verginius' illness was long, and he died when Tacitus was suffect consul (Pliny loc.
cit.), at some time or other in 97, perhaps even in 98. [The true date is towards the end of
97; see F. Zevi, *LF* xcvi (1973), 137.] There is no definite evidence. Another statement of
Pliny (*Pan.* 58, 1), 'erat in senatu ter consul, cum tu tertium consulatum recusabas', may,
indeed, refer not to Verginius but to A. Didius Gallus Fabricius Veiento, and is therefore
inconclusive.

[3] B. W. Henderson, *Five Roman Emperors* (1927), 170. Nerva is a universal favourite with
historians. Paribeni can even speak of the indulgence that Nerva must have felt for the
caprices of Nero, and of his devotion to his eminent patron (op. cit. i 124).

[4] Cassius Dio lxviii 1, 3.

[5] *Pan.* 6, 3: 'ruens imperium super imperatorem'.

[6] With all deference to what Tacitus has told of the prophetic insight of Agricola
(*Agr.* 44), to what Pliny has proclaimed and posterity has believed of Trajan's virtues and of
his predestination to the purple, it may none the less be pointed out that there was another
factor—he commanded the army of Upper Germany and the quickest route into Italy:
within the preceding thirty years two men, Vitellius and Antonius Saturninus, had been
proclaimed Emperors at Mainz. In these critical days of the year 97 a civil war like that of
the year 69 was a prospect far from remote (cf. Pliny, *Ep.* ix 13, 11). [This view is fully
developed in *Tacitus* (1958), Ch. I.]

[7] Suet. *Dom.* 23.

come down to posterity: but they stood alone. It is all very well to suppose that Nerva (and Galba) 'were adopted by the Senate . . . as a palliative to the popular indignation aroused by their immediate predecessors'.[1] There was no popular indignation against Domitian—or against his murderers. The people took it quietly, as Suetonius says. What else could they do? Domitian had fed and amused them, but had stood no nonsense from them.[2] A fresh emperor, on the other hand, meant a fresh *congiarium*— and it was forthcoming. The mistake made by that other old man, Galba, was a grim lesson and was not forgotten.[3] Moreover, the people must be bribed and kept in a good humour. Some of the religious and social measures of Domitian were at once revoked.[4] In desperate subservience to the favour of the mob even the pantomimes, which he had abolished, were restored.[5] The Treasury showed itself indulgent to the point of weakness. Extra doles of corn are apparently what are commemorated on coins with the legend *Plebei urbanae frumento constituto*.[6] Something similar may be recorded in the mysterious notice in the Chronographer of the Year 354, 'funeraticium plebi urbanae instituit.' This last bounty amounted to $62\frac{1}{2}$ denarii a head, all but the total of a regular *congiarium*. Whether there was also a *congiarium* when Trajan | was adopted is not recorded; but it is not impossible. However that may be, the plebs received in cash from Nerva in sixteen months almost two-thirds of what they had got from Domitian in about as many years. It looks very much like bribery.[7] Likewise, too, with the whole of Italy. The benefactions of Nerva should not be taken as evidence that Domitian had neglected Italy and that his successor thereby restored a just balance: they rather prove that the Flavians had deserved well of Italy, as of the Empire as a whole.[8] Tradition has naturally exalted the work of Nerva and forgotten, or even suppressed, that of Domitian.[9] We may, indeed, if we so choose, attribute Nerva's good works to his 'loving and anxious care for the children of the poor'.[10] Such is a comforting and uplifting notion; but it is irrelevant. What was

[1] Mattingly and Sydenham, *The Roman Imperial Coinage* ii 221.

[2] Cf. Cassius Dio lxix 6, 1: ἐκέλευσε τοῦτο δὴ τὸ Δομιτιανοῦ κηρυχθῆναι 'σιωπήσατε'.

[3] As the Chronographer of the Year 354 tersely records, 'cong. promisit sed non dedit . . . decollatus foro iacuit.'

[4] The coin with the legend *Fisci Iudaici calumnia sublata* appears already in 96.

[5] *Pan.* 46. Trajan abolished them again, as Pliny says in his own happy phrase, 'utrumque recte; nam et restitui oportebat, quos sustulerat malus princeps, et tolli restitutos.'

[6] Mommsen (*Die röm. Tribus* (1843), 193) thought that this referred to a restoration by Nerva of the *frumentationes* which he had (conjecturally) abolished: this is not likely.

[7] And, as such, would have been properly denounced by historians, had it been the work of one of the 'bad Emperors'.

[8] Cf. Gsell, op. cit. 131: 'le gouvernement de Domitien eut des effets bienfaisants en Italie.'

[9] See p. 2, n. 5. There may be something in Asbach's suggestion that it was Domitian who really began the system of *alimenta* (*Römisches Kaisertum und Verfassung* (1896), Beilage I, 'Domitian als Begründer der Alimentationen').

[10] Henderson, op. cit. 174.

of immediate importance to the new régime was to outbid the Flavians. Hence the agrarian law, the *alimenta*, the founding of colonies, the mitigation of the *vicesima hereditatum*, the remission to Italy of the charges of the *cursus publicus*.[1] From the provinces we naturally have little evidence, though we find Nerva bestowing privileges and immunities on cities of the Greek East. It is not likely that the Flavian rule had been anything but popular:[2] but the provinces have no spokesman, save that Jew of Alexandria who, a hundred years later, celebrates Domitian as a Prince of Peace whom all men worship and gladly obey—a verdict the reverse of that of Pliny and Tacitus, and equally comprehensible.[3] Domitian's hand had lain heavy on senators:[4] the governors had to behave themselves, and the provinces rejoiced in Domitian's rule—as they had afterwards, under Nerva and also under Trajan, good reason to deplore his death.[5]

But from the civil population of Rome, Italy, and the provinces, if popularity was to be desired and to be sought, as it was sought, at all costs, there was at least no danger to be feared. It was otherwise with the soldiers: though a change of emperor had its charms, bringing with it as it did a fresh donative, it should not be forgotten how firmly professional pride and loyalty to their *imperator* were rooted in the breasts of the legionaries. The troops of Verginius Rufus were slow and reluctant to abandon even Nero, whom they | had never seen.[6] Domitian, on the other hand, had been with the troops more often than any reigning Emperor since Augustus; he had shown himself solicitous for their welfare, had raised their pay, and was no doubt popular with them. There was trouble ahead for the Emperor who had been made at Rome, the nominee of the Senate and protégé of the treacherous Imperial freedman Parthenius.[7] Only the accident that Dio Chrysostom happened to be at one of the Danubian garrison-towns has preserved for us a record of tumults such as probably broke out in other places as well.[8] And generals as well as soldiers were to be feared. The sinister legend 'Concordia exercituum', sure sign of anxiety for the loyalty of the troops, appears on the coinage; and some months later nobody knew which way the

[1] The evidence is conveniently summarized in *RE*, s.v. 'Cocceius', coll. 144–6.

[2] Cf. Gsell, op. cit. 155. Domitian's munificence is attested by the rebuilding of the Temple of Apollo at Delphi (*ILS* 8905), and by the repairing of the Stoa of Megalopolis (*AE* 1893, no. 128).

[3] *Or. Sibyll.* 12, 126.

[4] Suet. *Dom.* 8, 'magistratibus quoque urbicis provinciarumque praesidibus coercendis tantum curae adhibuit ut neque modestiores unquam nec iustiores extiterint; e quibus plerosque post illum omnium criminum reos vidimus.' Another passage, which panegyrists of Trajan's administration do not always quote, is *HA Alexander*, 64, 5.

[5] We may instance the scandalous leniency with which Marius Priscus was treated (Juv. i, 49). Compare Kahrstedt's vigorous protest, *Gnomon* vi (1930), 415.

[6] Tac. *Hist.* i 8: 'tarde a Nerone desciverant.'

[7] Eutrop. viii 1, 1; Aur. Vict. *Ep. de Caes.* 12, 2.

[8] Philostratus, *Vit. Soph.* i 7.

Governor of Syria was going to move.[1] It was clearly of urgent importance to pacify the resentment of the troops and purchase their acquiescence. A donative would, in any case, be customary and necessary—at
this critical time an inordinately large one: we infer that it was paid.
There is, indeed, no direct evidence on this point, but Pliny commends
Trajan because, on the occasion of *his* donative, he paid down to the troops
in cash only a half of the total sum.[2] This special and emphatic commemoration of what was surely nothing but a normal practice[3] calls for
some explanation—and a credible explanation can be found if it be
assumed that the last donative, that of Nerva, had been paid down at once
in cash. Nearer at hand there were the Praetorians to be reckoned with.
Their Emperor had been assassinated, with the connivance of their own
commanders, their loyalty had been betrayed and dishonoured. It is little
wonder that, as Suetonius records, 'miles gravissime tulit'. To appease them
a lavish donative must have been needed. It is, indeed, sometimes stated
that their resentment was due to their having received no donative, and
Nerva is heartily praised for not having bribed them.[4] This is hardly just
to the Praetorians—indeed, it is a gross misrepresentation of the evidence;
for they appear to have been pacified in some way or other after Domitian's assassination. They did not break out again till about a year later,
when, encouraged no doubt by the precarious plight of the new regime,
they demanded and extorted—not money, but the punishment of the
assassins of Domitian. That Emperor had cared for his soldiers and had
increased their pay, but he had kept them in hand. Even when he might
have been expected not to feel secure, he had not bribed them: the dona-
tive which he | gave them on his accession was no larger than that given
by Titus.[5] In our tradition, it is true, it usually appears to be 'bad Emperors' who buy the Praetorians—but it was not always so: M. Aurelius
and Verus lavished on them the monstrous sum of 5,000 denarii a head.[6]
Nerva must have remembered what had happened to Galba, who gave
no donative, and have acted accordingly. Naturally it is not recorded that
he bribed and bought the Praetorians: but it is proved by the course of
events.

Lavish expenditure had thus marked the first days of Nerva's reign.
Not merely were the very necessary donative and *congiarium* paid, and

[1] Pliny, *Ep.* ix 13, 11. Merrill dates this incident as late as the middle of the year 97
(*AJP* xxiii (1902), 404).

[2] *Pan.* 25, 2. Paribeni (op. cit. i 141) states that Trajan reduced the donative: this is
misleading.

[3] Vegetius ii 20.

[4] In *RE*, s.v. 'Cocceius', col. 139, we learn of the 'Unmut der Praetorianer gegen die
Mörder Domitians, dessen Tod ihre Hoffnungen auf ein ausgiebiges Donativum zu nichte
gemacht hatte.' Similarly Paribeni, op. cit. i 128. Yet Domitian's assassination made them
certain of a donative from his successor!

[5] Cassius Dio lxvi 26, 3.   [6] *HA Marcus* 7. 9.

paid in full, but every kind of fiscal generosity and tax-remission was practised. No doubt also quite a large amount of State money found its way into unauthorized pockets. After about six months of the new anarchy, increased expenditure and diminished revenue, whether or not in danger of reducing the State to bankruptcy, must at least have given senators grounds for alarm. The 'Economy Commission' can therefore be understood, in point of cause as in point of time, for what it really was, not a feeble and tardy attempt to fill a Treasury which Domitian had left empty, but a mild palliative to the extravagance of those who came after. It has been seen that nothing in the reign of Nerva can lend support to the belief that, as a consequence of Domitian's extravagance, the government found itself short of money. On the contrary, in order to present a consistent picture of the finance and policy of his successors, it will be advisable to assume that at his death the finances were in a healthy state, and that there was even a considerable store of gold in the Treasury.

Are there not, however, indications, and even positive evidence, that in his closing years Domitian was short of money? Such at least is almost an article of faith. Its source and value must therefore be investigated. It has on its side good authority—not the rampant turgidity of Pliny but a disinterested witness, Suetonius, who seems to be doing his best to present a reasonable and credible account of the character and policy of Domitian. The account will repay analysis: Suetonius notices a marked decline in the character and government of Domitian, apparently something real and not merely a reflection of that reaction to which popular opinion turns in time after the joy and hope that welcome a new ruler. He therefore seeks to find some cause for the change, and comes to the conclusion that Domitian was not so much naturally evil, but was driven to certain courses by the compulsion of circumstances. As Suetonius says, he became 'quantum coniectare licet, super ingenii naturam inopia rapax, metu saevus'.[1] It should be possible to determine at what time this change for the worse set in. | Suetonius, a little further on, after three chapters full of Domitian's good works, records that he did not abide in his career of clemency and restraint, but degenerated, descending to cruelty earlier than to rapacity.[2] This cruelty, the consequence of fear, seems to follow the great conspiracy and military revolt of Antonius Saturninus at the beginning of the year 89.[3] His rapacity therefore comes later; and we find that it coincides with the climax of the struggle with the Senate, the period 93–6, which Gsell calls the 'Reign of Terror'. This is significant: we know where we are, we can at once see on what grounds and with what evidence Domi-

---

[1] Suet. *Dom.* 3.
[2] Suet. *Dom.* 10: 'sed neque in clementiae neque in abstinentiae tenore permansit, et tamen aliquanto celerius ad saevitiam descivit quam ad cupiditatem.'
[3] Suet. *Dom.* 10: 'verum aliquanto post civilis belli victoriam saevior.'

tian could be called rapacious. Domitian, as we know, put senators to death and ruthlessly confiscated their goods. The inference which Suetonius has drawn, in his search for some kind of rational explanation of Domitian's cruelty, is of the *post hoc propter hoc* type—he killed them for their money. And this is the view that historians have accepted without hesitation.[1] But it is quite preposterous—Domitian's shortage of money and consequent rapacity is thereby made into the cause and motive of his struggle with the Senate, that struggle which was the main theme of a large part of his reign, though Suetonius strangely enough says never a word about it beyond giving a list of the victims. The struggle was political. Domitian fought the Senate and killed or exiled senators for reasons other than financial, for very good reasons. He had to face a continued opposition: the fact of repeated conspiracies is beyond doubt, but, as he himself once remarked, it was naturally not believed.[2] Domitian ruthlessly confiscated the goods of his enemies, not because this was the cause and motive of his proceeding against them, but because it was a most valuable weapon. A Flavian, son of Vespasian and grandson of the tax-gatherer from Reate, he had no need to learn this elementary lesson. He had wounded senators in their pride and prestige: being an *insidiosissimus princeps*, he could go still further and strike at their purses. Domitian knew what he wanted: but it is not surprising that Suetonius should have fallen victim to a misinterpretation of his motives. Again and again, in what passes for the history of the Roman Empire, an emperor's acts are assigned to motives either frivolous or sinister. Many details of Tacitus' portrayal of Tiberius at once suggest themselves. So too Suetonius: in the list of senators killed by Domitian occur the words 'ceteros levissima quaque de causa',[3] and the motives or alleged charges that he records bear him out to the full—if anybody believes that there were not adequate reasons behind the acts of what | Mommsen calls 'the sombre but intelligent despotism of Domitianus'.[4] This is precisely what made him more hated and feared than any of the rulers that had gone before. Tradition could brand him as a monster, never as a fool or a madman. No caprice or stupidity, no favourites or flatterers swayed his actions. His inflexible will carried out what his relentless logic had decided. In his duel with the Senate his rapacity is a weapon, not a cause or motive.[5]

The truth of this interpretation can be confirmed even from the literary

---

[1] It is explicit in Cassius Dio (lxvii 4, 5): ἃ δὴ τοῖς μὲν πολλοῖς ἐν ἡδονῇ, ὡς εἰκός, ἦν, τοῖς δὲ δυνατοῖς ὀλέθρου αἴτια καθίστατο. οὐ γὰρ ἔχων ὁπόθεν ἀναλώσει, συχνοὺς ἐφόνευσε—to say nothing of more recent writers.

[2] Suet. *Dom.* 21: 'condicionem principum miserrimam aiebat, quibus de coniuratione comperta non crederetur nisi occisis.'

[3] Suet. *Dom.* 10.   [4] *Ges. Schrift.* vi 544.

[5] Likewise are to be regarded the stern penalties that provided the sanction of his religious and social legislation. The ruthless exaction of the Fiscus Iudaicus (Suet. *Dom.* 12) is not a mere by-product of financial straits, but is rather something very much like persecution.

evidence. When Tacitus speaks of the Reign of Terror, he mentions the essential, and has nothing whatever to say about the rapacity of Domitian or any financial straits that may have been its cause.[1] As for Pliny, only once does he mention the possibility of filling an exhausted Treasury by confiscations.[2] And to him Domitian is the 'optimi cuiusque spoliator et carnifex'[3]—but Pliny never suggests that he acted as he did in order to raise ready cash. Domitian's sin of rapacity, *avaritia*, is the more abominable because superfluous—'detestanda avaritia illius, qui tam multa concupiscebat, cum haberet supervacua tam multa'.[4] He robs, not for his own use, but to deprive others:[5] and what he seizes he keeps.[6] The goods and the estates of the victims were not given away or sold in order to raise money, but remained in the Imperial possession[7]—a strange procedure, if he murdered and robbed from need of ready cash! It is not Domitian's extravagance that is remembered after his death and condemned: it is his *avaritia* which is rebuked in a rescript of Trajan[8] and becomes so firmly rooted in the senatorial tradition that Zonaras and Jordanes, who can hardly have had any external and independent evidence to support their opinions, can transfer it to another sphere and render it responsible for the revolt of the Nasamones and the Dacian invasion of Moesia.[9]

Domitian laid unsparing hands on the property of senators: and it was perhaps natural to assume that he did so in consequence of a shortage of money, the more so as Suetonius has failed to recognize, or perhaps hesitated to record, the war to the knife between Emperor and Senate. Can evidence of financial straits be found in anything else | that Domitian did? To provide support for his account of Domitian's financial exhaustion and consequent rapacity, Suetonius is obliged to invoke a remarkable story, to the effect that Domitian attempted to reduce the numbers of the army but desisted, finding that it yielded no solution of his pecuniary embarrassments and that it would weaken the Empire in face of the barbarians.[10] We must bear in mind that there is no evidence that he actually

---

[1] Tac. *Agr.* 44, 5: 'postremum illud tempus . . .'

[2] He says to Trajan: 'ut qui exhaustum non sis innocentium bonis repleturus' (*Pan.* 55, 5). And, to be sure, the Treasury did profit under Domitian—'locupletabant et fiscum et aerarium non tam Voconiae et Iuliae leges quam maiestatis singulare et unicum crimen eorum, qui crimine vacarent' (*Pan.* 42, 1). But Domitian was as serious and sincere in his political theory as he was in his religious and social legislation.

[3] *Pan.* 90, 5.   [4] *Pan.* 50, 5.

[5] *Pan.* 50, 2: 'quae priores principes occupabant, non ut ipsi fruerentur sed ne quis alius.'

[6] *Pan.* 41, 2: 'aliis quidem cum omnia raperent et rapta retinerent.'

[7] *Pan.* 50, 3. This property was restored, sold, or given away by Nerva and by Trajan.

[8] *Dig.* xlviii 22, 1: 'caput ex rescripto Divi Traiani ad Didium Secundum: scio relegatorum bona avaritia superiorum temporum fisco vindicata; sed aliud clementiae meae convenit.'

[9] Zon. xi 19; Jord. *Get.* xiii 76: 'Domitiano imperatore regnante eiusque avaritiam metuentes . . .' That is to say, these passages are not safe evidence for fiscal policy in the provinces.

[10] Suet. *Dom.* 12.

did any such thing: what we are given is a statement of intention never fully carried out and therefore to be regarded with suspicion.[1] Can we seriously credit a man of Domitian's intelligence—an intelligence which cannot be doubted or denied—with a notion at once so futile and so dangerous? Either of the two reasons assigned for his abandoning it would alone have been more than enough to prevent him from ever conceiving it. It looks very much as though Suetonius has got hold of one of those rumours that were assiduously fabricated in Rome, 'in conviviis et circulis', with a view to discrediting the Emperor with the troops: or the source of his story may lie in some savage witticism at Domitian's expense. He had increased the pay of the soldiers—but he had also, in grim fact, reduced their number: his Danube Wars had cost his Empire two legions.[2]

It is thus difficult to find any confirmation of the view that Domitian in his last years had fallen into a state of serious financial embarrassment which not merely affected but even determined his policy. The fact of a shortage of money cannot be established, but the causes which Suetonius assigned to it do seem, at first sight, quite reasonable and credible—'exhaustus operum ac munerum impensis stipendioque quod adiecerat'.[3] His buildings, spectacles, *congiaria*, and the increase of the pay of the soldiers must certainly have run away with quite a lot of money: but a closer examination of these items of expenditure will suggest conclusions very different from those that are commonly accepted. The pay of the soldiers had been raised by a third quite early in the reign, apparently in 84. This is no mere temporary largesse: such an irrevocable measure, such a permanent burden on the finances of the Empire, cannot have been undertaken without some justification and without some expectation of a continuous flow of revenue to meet it. Domitian's careful administration and the prosperity of the Empire satisfied this condition. Domitian, during his fifteen years, gave three *congiaria* of the modest total of 225 denarii a head:[4] Nerva and Trajan paid out at least $787\frac{1}{2}$ denarii in ten or eleven years, a fact which needs no further comment. The last of Domitian's *congiaria* had been paid at the beginning of the | year 93.[5] By then, too, his wars were over, and the last four years of his reign are years of unbroken peace. His buildings, however, both private and public, certainly demanded huge sums of money: but the money must have been there. The ancients worked mainly on a system of cash economy: there can hardly have been any question of running into debt and contracting large bills against future payment. The expenditure on a building must have been continuous and fairly consistent from the first brick to the last. Was, therefore, much

---

[1] Like the story of Caligula's intention of making his horse consul.
[2] V Alaudae and XXI Rapax, at least in the writer's opinion.
[3] Suet. *Dom.* 12.
[4] See the Chronographer of the Year 354.
[5] Martial viii 15, 4: 'et ditant Latias tertia dona tribus.'

being spent on building in the last years of Domitian? We learn, some-what to our surprise, that there was very little. The Palatine seems to have been completed towards 92,[1] the Templum Gentis Flaviae a year or so later.[2] The only constructions which can be dated to the last four years, 93–6 inclusive, are the Forum that Nerva was to dedicate and perhaps a triumphal arch.[3] Nothing else can be found, though it is precisely in the years 92–4 that Martial, in Books vii–ix of his epigrams, is most lavish of information about everything that concerns Domitian. The greater part of the imposing total of his building activities belongs to the earlier years of his reign, so far as there is any indication—and for a good reason. There are on the one hand the not inconsiderable works left incomplete when Titus died, the Flavian Amphitheatre, the Templum Divi Vespasiani, the Baths of Titus, the Arch of Titus; on the other, the rebuilding of the Capitol and the restoration of a number of edifices on the Campus Martius which had suffered in the great fire of the year 80, such as the Pantheon, the Iseum, and the Serapeum. Two other structures in the same region, the Odeum and the Stadium, will surely have been begun, if not before, at least quite soon after the institution of the Capitoline Games in 86, for the two branches of which, the aesthetic and the athletic, they were so clearly designed.[4] The Templum Castorum et Minervae must have been completed at least as early as the year 90.[5] The above list comprises by far the most important part of the buildings erected in Rome by Domitian.

There would, therefore, be better warrant for supposing that, had there been financial difficulties, they belonged to the earlier years of the reign. Titus, though his generosity has perhaps been | much exaggerated at his brother's expense, can hardly have exercised a beneficent influence on the finances of the Empire. His successor had at once to find money, not only for the regular *congiarium* and donative, only two years after the preceding one, but also to complete extensive buildings and repairs. Yet he appears to have found the money somehow, and to have been able to raise the pay of the troops into the bargain. Nay, more, he restored the coinage

---

[1] So Gsell, op. cit. 95.   [2] It is first mentioned in Martial ix.

[3] So at least Martial viii 65 has usually been interpreted. But I doubt whether it can be certainly established from the epigram that this arch was erected *after* Domitian's return (in January, 93) from his Suebo–Sarmatian War. Just such an arch, surmounted by two *quadrigae* of elephants, appears already on a bronze of the year 85, and again in 90–1. But an arch more or less is neither here nor there—especially in Domitian's reign (cf. the jest on the word ἀρκεῖ, Suet. *Dom.* 13).

[4] It is possible that they were completed or restored by Trajan: but another explanation could quite well be given of the passage in Cassius Dio (lxix 4, 1): τὸν δ᾽ Ἀπολλόδωρον τὸν ἀρχιτέκτονα τὸν τὴν ἀγορὰν καὶ τὸ ᾠδεῖον τό τε γυμνάσιον, τὰ τοῦ Τραιανοῦ ποιήματα, ἐν τῇ Ῥώμῃ κατασκευάσαντα, as of that in Pausanias which clearly ascribes to Trajan the Odeum—θέατρον μέγα κυκλοτερὲς πανταχόθεν (v 12, 6). This would not be the only sphere in which Trajan has usurped more than his due.

[5] *ILS* 1998.

and maintained it at a level of purity that it had seldom reached before and was never to reach again. There is no trace of a shortage of money in these earlier years of greatest expenditure.[1] Still less, we believe, is there in the *triennium* before his death. In the years 93–6 the finances must have been healthy and prosperous—the wars were over, the last *congiarium* paid, there was little building, there were no new or extraordinary expenses. We must postulate a full Treasury at Domitian's death, as at that of Tiberius: and such is in keeping with his character and policy: extravagance and inefficiency have their proper place in the anarchical reign of Nerva.

In this way and in this way alone can the financial policy of these emperors be understood. The causes of Domitian's impoverishment assigned by Suetonius, viz. buildings, donatives, and the increase of the military pay, though plausible, do not hold good when the accepted theory demands that they should, in the years 93–6; moreover, the evidence of its existence is either trivial, like the story of Domitian's attempt to reduce the strength of the army, or dangerously misleading, as when it is rendered responsible for Domitian's struggle with the Senate and for the severity of his social and religious policy. A financial stringency in Nerva's reign has its source, in point of time and in point of cause, in that reign itself; and in the earlier half of his reign Trajan was in no way embarrassed for want of money. Thus it matters little whether or not we succumb to the seductions of Carcopino: the gold of Dacia does not come into the question. Nor need we neglect facts or force them to fit those fair and empty phrases, the financial genius of Nerva and the economies of Trajan. The whole problem fades and dissolves before a just estimate of the policy of an Emperor whom Pliny called an *immanissima belua*, and whom Mommsen praised as 'one of the most careful administrators who held the imperial office'.[2]

[1] Suet. *Dom.* 9: 'cupiditatis quoque atque avaritiae vix suspicionem ullam aut privatus unquam aut princeps aliquandiu dedit, immo e diverso magna saepe non abstinentiae modo sed etiam liberalitatis experimenta.'
[2] *Provinces of the Roman Empire* (1886) i 108.

2

Pollio, Saloninus, and Salonae

A CALM has succeeded the clamour of the Virgilian Bimillenary, to be shattered all too soon by the commemoration of Augustus. In this brief interval there may be leisure to examine a question touching the career of Asinius Pollio and the history of the years 42–39 B.C. The Virgilian celebrations evoked two outstanding studies of the Fourth Eclogue, a poem dedicated to Pollio and written during—or perhaps just after—the consulate of Pollio (40 B.C.). Carcopino restated and sought to reinforce an opinion widely held in late antiquity among commentators of Virgil— the miraculous child of the poem was Saloninus, a son of Asinius Pollio: the child was born, he suggests, soon after the conclusion of the Pact of Brundisium, and shortly before the end of the year 40, while Pollio was still consul. At the time Pollio was at Salonae, on the coast of Dalmatia, which city his son's name commemorates.[1] Tarn, however, adopting and reinforcing the theory put forward by Slater in 1912, argued that the Fourth Eclogue shows traces of being an epithalamium in form, designed to celebrate the wedding of Antony and Octavia, the seal and bond of the Pact of Brundisium which was concluded in the autumn of the year 40 between the dynasts Antony and Octavian; Pollio, a friend and a partisan of Antony, acted as his plenipotentiary in the negotiations; the new epoch was thus introduced under the auspices of Pollio, 'te duce'; the child was the child to be expected from the marriage of Antony and Octavia;[2] it turned out in fact to be a girl.

This paper does not propose to discuss once again the identity of the perennial infant, human or divine: indeed, it is presented merely as a by-product of investigations into the history of Illyricum. It will have some relevance to that question, however, for an attempt will be made to show (1) that the city of Salonae, situated near Split, on the Dalmation coast, was not included in the province allotted to Pollio after the Pact of Brundisium; (2) that the child Saloninus did not derive his name from that city.

[1] J. Carcopino, *Virgile et le mystère de la IVe églogue* (1930).

[2] W. W. Tarn, 'Alexander Helios and the Golden Age', *JRS* xxii (1932), 135 ff.; cf. D. A. Slater, 'Was the *Fourth Eclogue* written to celebrate the marriage of Octavia to Mark Antony?' *CR* xxvi (1912), 114.

Classical Quarterly xxxi (1937), 39–48.

The connection of Pollio and his son with Salonae, a persuasion inherited from the ancient commentators, appears to be universally held. The majority of scholars believe that Pollio named his son to commemorate his capture of the city of Salonae. Pollio's capture of Salonae is recorded in manuals of literature, in general histories of Rome, and in special studies of Dalmatian affairs or of Roman provincial administration: it is accepted as a fact by the authoritative names of Groebe, Schanz–Hosius, Groag, Gardthausen, Tarn, Dessau, Zippel, Patsch, and Ganter.[1] Even Bennett in his acute study of the relations between Virgil and Pollio remarks that 'Saloninus quite obviously commemorates by his cognomen the taking of Salona'.[2] A small and distinguished minority, represented by Mommsen and Carcopino, is sceptical about a capture of Salonae:[3] but Carcopino maintains that Pollio spent the winter of the year | 40/39 at Salonae and named his son, born, it is argued, in 40, just before the end of the year, as a memorial of his sojourn.

A position so firmly fortified by time, numbers, and authority cannot be taken by a frontal assault; but it may collapse from within. If the evidence about Pollio's activities in the years 42–39 is examined to discover what light it throws upon his campaign beyond the Adriatic, after the Pact of Brundisium, it is seen to fall sharply apart into two classes. On the one side stand the historians and the *Acta Triumphalia*, evidence which though not abundant is unbiased and unequivocal: on the other, the scholiasts on Virgil and the scholiast (Porphyrio) on Horace's ode in honour of Pollio (ii 1). This testimony cannot be described as disinterested, for it is the fate of the scholiast that he must always be ready with an explanation. Now it is only the scholiasts that introduce Salonae in connection with Pollio and his son: the name of the Parthini, the native tribe over which Pollio in fact and officially triumphed, has escaped their notice. From the historians can be derived a simple and intelligible view of Pollio's campaign beyond the Adriatic: with the scholiasts enter confusion and error, locked in a close embrace.

To illustrate the sharp and complete distinction between these two classes of evidence it will be necessary to give a brief account of Pollio's movements, so far as they can be ascertained from the historians, in the years 42–39.

After Philippi it was decided, so we are informed by Appian, that Cisalpine Gaul should not be a province any more but should be united

---

[1] Groebe, in Drumann–Groebe, *Gesch. Roms* ii², 8 f. and *RE*, s.v. 'Asinius', col. 1592: Schanz–Hosius, *Gesch. der röm. Litt.* ii (1935), 25; Groag, *PIR*², A 1241; Gardthausen, *Augustus u. seine Zeit*, i 1, 236; Tarn in *CAH* x 49; Dessau, *Gesch. der röm. Kaiserzeit*, i 400 f.; Zippel, *Die röm. Herrschaft in Illyrien*, 223 ff.; Patsch, *Beiträge zur Völkerkunde von Südosteuropa*, v. i 55; Ganter, *Die Provinzialverwaltung der Triumvirn*, Diss. Strassburg (1892), 71 ff.
[2] H. Bennett, 'Vergil and Pollio', *AJP* li (1930), 341.
[3] Mommsen, *CIL* iii, p. 304; Carcopino, op. cit. 173.

to Italy.[1] But the change may not at once have been put into effect. In 41 and 40 B.C. the presence of Pollio in this region is attested—he had an army of seven legions, and for a time sought to prevent Octavian's general Salvidienus Rufus from marching from Italy to Spain.[2] The ancient commentators and biographers of Virgil bring the presence of Pollio in northern Italy into connection with the allotment of lands to veterans—plausibly, perhaps, though there is not a word of this in the historians, whose evidence suggests that he held a more important post than that of land-commissioner. The exact nature of Pollio's command, the extent of his competence and of his *provincia* are uncertain and, fortunately, irrelevant to the present inquiry.[3] Of his politics there is no doubt. The outbreak of hostilities in Italy between Octavian and the faction of L. Antonius during the year 41 B.C., which culminated in the siege of Perusia, placed Pollio, like the other Antonian army-commanders, in a cruel dilemma which was reflected in the indecision of their movements. After half-hearted attempts to relieve the doomed city, Pollio retired north-eastwards.[4] Perusia fell in February or March of 40 B.C. Pollio maintained himself for a time in Venetia, fighting against the generals of Octavian at Altinum and other places. From this point to his appearance at Brundisium in the autumn of the year, all is obscure. Our only definite information comes from Velleius, and it is scanty enough— 'Pollio Asinius cum septem legionibus, diu retenta in potestate Antoni Venetia, magnis speciosisque rebus circa Altinum aliasque eius regionis urbis editis, Antonium petens, vagum adhuc Domitium . . . consiliis suis illectum ac fide data iunxit Antonio.'[5] Pollio sought to join Antony. This he was able to do, for he won over to the cause of Antony the | Republican Domitius Ahenobarbus, whose fleet controlled the Adriatic. How many of his legions he was able to convey down the Adriatic is uncertain. However that may be, he is next heard of at Brundisium. He acted for Antony in concluding the famous Pact in late September or early October of the year 40.[6]

[1] Appian, *BC* v 3; cf. ibid. 21 and Dio xlviii 12,5.

[2] Velleius ii 76, 2; Appian, *BC* v 20.

[3] Carcopino (op. cit. 169) describes Pollio as governor of Cisalpine Gaul, Groebe (Drumann–Groebe ii 7) and Bennett (*AJP* li 328) say that he was Antony's legate in charge of the Transpadana. The terms 'governor' and 'legate' have a convenient vagueness. Cisalpine Gaul, to be sure, was to be reckoned a part of Italy after Philippi (cf. Appian, *BC* v 3, above, n. 1): yet even in the time of Augustus a proconsul is attested at Milan (Suetonius, *De Rhet.* 6). In the matter of Pollio's status in 41–40 B.C. I do not feel called upon to discuss the theory of J. Bayet ('Virgile et les "triumviri agris dividundis" ', *REL* vi (1928), 270 ff.) to the effect that Pollio was one of a board of three rotating land-commissioners, Pollio functioning in 41, Alfenus Varus in 40, and Cornelius Gallus in 39. Gallus, be it noted, was not a senator, but a man of equestrian rank. [*MRR* ii 372 is undecided on Pollio's status.]

[4] Appian, *BC* v 31–3; 35; 50.   [5] Velleius ii 76, 2; cf. Appian, *BC* v 50.

[6] As an indication of the date, Pais (*Dalle Guerre Puniche a Cesare Augusto* i 367 ff.) adduced

Pollio and Cn. Domitius Calvinus were the *consules ordinarii* of the year 40. The outbreak of the Perusine War had prevented Pollio from entering upon office on 1 January—indeed he may never have seen the city as consul. He may have accompanied the dynasts on their brief visit to Rome after the conclusion of the Pact of Brundisium—perhaps not. Appian states that from Brundisium Antony and Octavian at once dispatched their friends to deal with various urgent tasks.[1] But it is not certain that Pollio was one of these friends. However that may be, shortly before the end of the year a pair of suffect consuls was installed, namely L. Cornelius Balbus and P. Canidius Crassus.[2] For the date of the composition of the Fourth Eclogue this fact is of less importance than might be supposed. Whether Pollio laid down the consulate in October, November, or December, the whole year was reckoned, for purposes of dating, by the eponymous consuls, Pollio and Calvinus.[3] There would indeed have been no impropriety if the poem was composed—as perhaps it was—after the eponymous consuls had been replaced by others. The important fact is that the Treaty of Brundisium was signed, not merely while Pollio was still technically consul, but as a result of his mediation.

It may be that Pollio first visited Rome as consul; it may be that he laid down his consulate at once and was dispatched across the Adriatic from Brundisium to Dyrrachium. In any case, consul no longer, but proconsul, he went to one of Antony's provinces.[4] A tribe in the neighbourhood of Dyrrachium, the Parthini, had been giving trouble.[5] It was Pollio who suppressed them, as the *Acta Triumphalia* and the historian Cassius Dio attest.[6]

the inscription CIL x 5159, which records the setting up of a 'Signum Concordiae' on 12 October at Casinum, a veteran colony. Carcopino (op. cit. 123) seeks to fix the date of the Pact as 5 or 6 October.

[1] Appian, BC v 65: εὐθὺς ἐς τὰ ἐπείγοντα τοὺς φίλους ἑκάτερος αὐτῶν περιέπεμπεν. Appian does not mention Pollio here—only the sending of Ventidius against the Parthians. And it is not until a later passage (v 75) that he speaks of the dispatch of troops to the Balkans to deal with the Parthini. Further, Pollio's predecessor in Macedonia did not triumph until 1 January 39; cf. below, p. 22, n. 1.

[2] [*Inscr. It.* xiii 1, 504 f.]; Dio xlviii 32, 1: κἂν τούτῳ τούς τε στρατηγοὺς καὶ τοὺς ὑπάτους, καίπερ ἐπ' ἐξόδῳ ἤδη τοῦ ἔτους ὄντος, παύσαντες ἄλλους ἀντικατέστησαν, βραχὺ φροντίσαντες εἰ καὶ ἐπ' ὀλίγας ἡμέρας ἄρξουσιν. These words suggest that there was an interval after Brundisium when Pollio was still consul; so he may well have gone to Rome.

[3] Cf., e.g., Josephus, *AJ* xiv 389.

[4] Carcopino (op. cit. 175 ff.) argues that Pollio was still consul when he arrived at the other side of the Adriatic. This is necessary to his thesis—and it might be true. His attempt to prove that Pollio's colleague Calvinus was still consul when he had reached his province of Spain is not conclusive. The inscription CIL ii 6186 (Emporiae), 'Cn. Do[mitio] M.f. Cal[vino] cos. ite[r.], Apoll[. . .]', or coins with the legend 'cos. iter. imp.', do not prove this. 'Cos. iter.' is here a permanent title, not an indication of date. Compare ILS 42 (Rome), describing Calvinus as 'cos. iter. imper.' This inscription must date from 36 B.C. at the earliest.

[5] For their situation, see below, p. 22.

[6] [*Inscr. It.* xiii 1, 86 f., 568]; Dio xlviii 41, 7. Note also the existence of a person called

Many pangs would have been spared and many hypotheses stifled if scholars had cared to inquire which was in fact the province assigned to Pollio after the Pact of Brundisium, and what was its extent. The triumph which Pollio celebrated for his victorious campaign on 25 October 39 or 38 B.C. (for the year is missing) was recorded thus on the *Acta Trium-phalia*—'C. Asinius Cn. f. Pollio pro cos. an. [. . . . . .] ex Parthineis VIII K. Novem.'¹ The Parthini are described by Dio | and by Appian as an Illyrian people.² Florus calls the war 'Bellum Delmaticum' and to Horace the triumph is 'Delmaticus'.³ What more simple, therefore, than to describe Pollio's province as Dalmatia and leave it at that? A brief examination will suffice to dispel that airy assumption. The terms 'Illyrian' and 'Dalmatian' have a very general connotation. They are commonly employed in a geographical or an ethnical sense and are very far from being equivalent to the official administrative designation 'Illyricum'— that is, the Roman province beyond the Upper and Middle Adriatic lying between north-eastern Italy and Macedonia. Tribes described as 'Dalmatian' or 'Illyrian' extended a long way to the south-east, in Albania and southern Serbia, well into the province of Macedonia; and ethnically speaking, the boundary between 'Illyrian' and 'Macedonian' ran in the neighbourhood of the Lake of Ochrid. One of these Illyrian tribes was the Parthini. The Parthini are to be localized in the hinterland of Dyrrachium, in the modern Albania, as a contemporary authority, Caesar, indicates, and historians and geographers unequivocally testify.⁴ The exact status and area of Illyricum between the death of Caesar and the year 27 B.C. is a problem beset with peculiar difficulties. But of one thing we can be certain—the region of Dyrrachium did not belong to Illyricum in 39 B.C., but to Macedonia. The Pact of Brundisium established Scodra, not far from the mouth of the Drin, about forty miles north of Dyrra-

Asinius Epicadus, 'ex gente Parthina' (Suetonius, *Divus Aug.* 19), presumably a freed slave of Pollio.

  ¹ [*Inscr. It.* xiii 1, 86 f.]—there is no way of deciding whether 'an. [DCCXIIII]' or 'an. [DCCXV]' should be read. The *Fasti Barberiniani* (ibid., pp. 342–3) do not help.
  ² Dio xlviii 41, 7; Appian, *Ill.* 2; cf. Strabo vii 326.
  ³ Florus ii 25; Horace, *Odes* ii 1, 16.
  ⁴ Caesar, *BC* iii 11; 41; 42; Strabo vii 326: τῆς γὰρ Ἐπιδάμνου καὶ τῆς Ἀπολλωνίας μέχρι τῶν Κεραυνίων ὑπεροικοῦσι Βυλλίονές τε καὶ Ταυλάντιοι καὶ Παρθῖνοι καὶ Βρῦγοι; Appian, *BC* v 75: Ἰλλυρικὸν ἔθνος Ἐπιδάμνῳ πάροικον; Pliny, *NH* iii 145: 'a Lisso Macedonia provincia. gentes Partheni et a tergo eorum Dassaretae'; Pomponius Mela ii 3, 55; cf. further Cicero, *In Pisonem* 96; Livy xxix 12; xxxiii 34, etc. There are certain difficult problems connected with the Parthini. Appian (*Ill.* 16) mentions Pertheënetae among the tribes conquered by Octavian in 35–33 B.C.—i.e. north-west of the Drin (cf. Pliny, *NH* iii 143); and the existence of Parthini far in the interior of the Balkans, in western Serbia, has been inferred from the dedication to Juppiter Parthinus at Užice, *CIL* iii 8353; cf. Ladek, Premerstein and Vulić, *JŒAI* iv (1901), *Beiblatt* 157 ff. For another inscription (to 'I. O. Par.'), cf. ibid. 159 = *CIL* iii 14613. None the less, in view of the evidence of Caesar, Strabo, Appian, Pliny, and Mela, the Parthini proper are clearly to be localized in the hinterland of Dyrrachium. [Cf. J. J. Wilkes, *Dalmatia* (1969), 44; 165.]

chium, as the limit between the dominions of Antony and Octavian;[1] and this line was perpetuated as the boundary between the provinces of Macedonia and Illyricum under the Empire. Antony's man was dispatched to one of Antony's most important provinces—Macedonia. Pollio, then, was proconsul of Macedonia from late in 40 until October of 39 or 38. His predecessor in that command was L. Marcius Censorinus, who held a triumph 'ex Macedonia' on 1 January 39.[2]

So far so good. We turn to the commentators on Virgil and the trouble begins. It would be tedious as well as unprofitable to cite all the scholiasts, to trace their connection and filiation, to assess their varying degrees of ineptitude. *Crimine ab uno disce omnes.* Servius, on *Ecl.* iv 1 has the following explanation:

Asinius Pollio ductor Germanici exercitus, cum post captam Salonam, Dalmatiae civitatem, prius meruisset lauream, post etiam consulatum adeptus fuisset, eodem anno suscepit filium quem ex capta civitate Saloninum vocavit, cui nunc Vergilius genethliacon dicit. Quem constat natum risisse statim: quod parentibus omen est infelicitatis: nam ipsum puerum inter ipsa primordia perisse manifestum est.[3]

In the two matters where these divagations can be controlled, error is manifest. Pollio was not commander of the 'German army'; he did not hold a triumph before obtaining the consulate. Is the context of superior quality? What are we to make of the capture of Salonae, 'oppidum maritimum quod cives Romani fortissimi fidelissimique incolebant'?[4] The city of Salonae, where there was a *conventus civium | Romanorum*, had stood firm for Caesar in 48 B.C. against Pompeian generals and native Dalmatians: it was subsequently elevated to the rank of a colony, with the title of 'Colonia Julia Martia', by Octavian—if not by Caesar himself. Of the seizure of this important town by the Dalmatians and its recovery by Pollio there is no hint in the historians Appian and Dio, who followed quite good sources and who appear to be tolerably well informed about the historical transactions of these years. Moreover, in addition to Appian's *Civil Wars* there is Appian's *Illyrike*. Pollio's capture of Salonae is not impossible—but it would need better testimony than the scholiasts on Virgil and Horace.[5] The scholiasts, it will be recalled, are unaware of authentic pieces of history, like the campaign against the Parthini: in other respects they are contradictory as well as demonstrably erroneous.

---

[1] Appian, *BC* v 65; cf. Dio xlviii 28, 4.
[2] [*Inscr. It.* xiii 1, 86 f., 586.]
[3] Thilo–Hagen iii 1, 44. For the others, cf. Groag, *PIR*², A 1241; Carcopino, op. cit. 171 ff., and below, p. 25.
[4] *Bell. Al.* 43; cf. Caesar, *BC* iii 9.
[5] Apart from the Virgilian scholia, the only mention of a capture of Salonae is Porphyrio, on *Odes* ii 1, 15 f.: 'Salonas enim, Dalmatarum civitatem, Pollio ceperat'.

But though Pollio did not capture Salonae, might he not have made that town his headquarters during the winter of 40/39, before the campaign of the ensuing year? This is Carcopino's suggestion.[1] Yet here is a difficulty not to be surmounted by all the goodwill and all the ingenious arguments in the world. Pollio's province was Macedonia, his adversaries the Parthini, in the hinterland of Dyrrachium. Salonae (near Split) on the coast of Dalmatia was not in his province, but in Illyricum: it lies 250 miles away in a straight line across the sea, further by land and very difficult. To be sure, one is not entitled to postulate over-sharp divisions of province or competence. And Pollio may well have crossed the Drin and operated in Montenegro. Salonae is another question. To fit a capture of Salonae into a campaign against the Parthini, modern scholars have been driven to strange and questionable expedients. Ganter, in his detailed study of provincial administration in the triumviral period, treats the question at some length.[2] He supposes that it was Pollio's task after the Pact of Brundisium to conduct from northern Italy to Macedonia an army of eleven legions that had stood under Salvidienus Rufus in Gallia Transalpina (for thus he justifies the 'exercitus Germanicus' of Servius); Pollio took the 'safest way', through Venetia, Istria, Dalmatia, Illyricum to Epirus; the direction of his march is indicated by Virgil, *Ecl.* viii 6 f.; on the way he captured Salonae, but received no honour for a victory won in a province not his own, and that is why there is no mention of Salonae on the *Acta Triumphalia*. Against this reconstruction many objections could be urged; it will be enough to say that there is no evidence that Octavian bestowed an army of eleven legions upon an Antonian partisan, or likelihood that Pollio did not cross to his province of Macedonia from Brundisium. Another hypothesis betrays itself. Gardthausen, followed almost verbally by Groebe, lets Pollio defeat the Parthini behind Dyrrachium, after which 'the pursuit of the enemy brought the victorious army of Asinius Pollio beyond Scodra, the boundary of the provinces of Antony, as far as Salona, the conquest of which seems to have been the culmination of the war'.[3] A degree of mobility and endurance remarkable even in Balkan brigands!

It must be repeated that the distant city of Salonae was not in Pollio's province; and it is most unlikely that Octavian had entrusted to Pollio the control of one of his own provinces. It is a fact of fundamental importance for the interpretation of the history of these years and for the interpretation of the Fourth Eclogue, as Tarn has so forcibly argued, that Pollio was a partisan of Antony.[4] It will be recalled that he was assailed by Octavian in scurrilous verses: he made no reply, for sufficient reasons.[5]

[1] Carcopino, op. cit. 179.
[2] *Die Provinzialverwaltung der Triumvirn*, Diss. Strassburg (1892), 71 ff.
[3] *Augustus u. seine Zeit* i 1, 236; cf. Groebe, *RE*, s.v. 'Asinius', col. 1592.
[4] *JRS* xxii (1932), 153; cf. H. Bennett, *AJP* li (1930), 325 ff.
[5] Macrobius ii 4, 21.

Pollio was a loyal friend and a man of independent, not to say recalcitrant, |
temper. After his triumph he retired from public life. Later, under the
excuse of his earlier relations with Antony, Pollio refused to rally to the
'vaterländische Front' in the War of Actium.[1] It is to be regretted, but it
can well be understood, that history has preserved no record of the
private comments which these transactions elicited from a personality so
ferociously antisuggestible.

Pollio cannot be brought to Salonae as a conqueror or even for peaceful
hibernation in the winter of 40/39 B.C. Now the scholiasts are at one in
deriving his son's name from the name of that city.[2] Here agreement ends.
The simpler version, in the notes of Philargyrius, is that the boy was born
there.[3] The more pretentious version has variants. The Bern Scholia state
that he was born while Pollio was 'proconsul of Dalmatia':[4] according to
Philargyrius in another place he was born at the time of the capture of
Salonae.[5] The fullest account is that of Servius (on *Ecl.* iv 1, quoted above):
the boy was born in the year of Pollio's capture of Salonae and was named
in honour of that victory. Servius, be it noted, here makes the capture of
Salonae precede Pollio's consulate.

It would be presumptuous to adjudicate between 'authorities' so nicely
matched. The presence of Salonae in these precious variants is but an
inference from the name of Pollio's son. Given the name 'Saloninus' and
the fact that Pollio celebrated a 'Dalmatian' triumph, the scholiasts could
not help themselves. Had those commentaries not survived, the great
discovery of the capture of Salonae would perhaps have been reserved for
the 'Scharfsinn' of some scholar of the nineteenth century.

The inference from the name of Saloninus is not without parallel in
the melancholy annals of antiquarian ineptitude. The *Scriptores Historiae
Augustae* are most themselves when explaining names. Of the two rivals
of Septimius Severus, Albinus, they say, was named from his fair complexion, Niger (though also a blonde, we are gravely assured) from the
dusky hue of his neck. The emperor Antonius Gordianus was descended
from Trajan, while another emperor, (Claudius) Tacitus, was proud to
number among his ancestors the historian Cornelius Tacitus. Now
Gallienus had a son called Saloninus. The *Augustan History* leaps at the
inevitable—'de huius nomine magna est ambiguitas. nam multi eum
Gallienum, multi Saloninum historiae prodiderunt. et qui Saloninum,
idcirco quod apud Salonas natus esset, cognominatum ferunt.'[6] This

---

[1] Velleius ii 86, 4.   [2] For an account of these variants, see Carcopino, op. cit. 171 ff.
[3] Philargyrius on *Ecl.* iv 4 (Thilo–Hagen iii 2, 74).
[4] Schol. Bern. on *Ecl.* iv, *praef.* (Hagen, 775): 'Saloninus dictus a Salonis, civitate Dalmatiae; nam Pollio pro consule Dalmatiae constitutus progenuit eum.'
[5] Philargyrius on *Ecl.* iv 1 (Thilo–Hagen iii 2, 72): 'a Salona civitate quam eodem
tempore quo natus est pater eius expugnavit'.
[6] *HA Gallieni duo* 19, 2 f.

statement may be disposed of at once—the son was presumably named after his mother, Cornelia Salonina.

Reputations more securely established than those of the Virgilian commentators might tremble at being seen in the company of these drab and discreditable hacks. The confrontation shows up both parties.[1] Deeply rooted in these twin souls is the persuasion that people called Saloninus must derive their name from the Dalmatian city of Salonae. Yet 'Saloninus' is nothing more and nothing less than an impeccable derivation from the perfectly respectable gentile name 'Salonius'. 'Salonius', as the great authority Schulze has suggested, may originate from an Etruscan name.[2] | Salonii are attested at Vicetia in the Transpadana; and it is interesting to find that A. Caecina Alienus, who came from that town, had a wife called Salonina.[3]

The history of the name 'Saloninus' and of other names in '-inus' deserves study. Against the derivation from the city of Salonae, very powerful linguistic arguments can be adduced, as a reference to Wackernagel's paper on Latin 'Ethnika' will show.[4] Wackernagel has established the fact that Latin consistently avoids appending the suffix -inus to place-names the last consonant of which is intervocalic n.[5] Thus we never find forms like 'Cremoninus', 'Bononinus', etc. Wackernagel makes no mention of 'Saloninus': it is clear that he would have spurned the derivation from Salonae. That city, indeed, forms the adjective 'Salonitanus': 'Salonas' would also be acceptable, but it is very rare indeed.[6]

So much for the name. The same air of dubious authenticity hangs over the infant himself. The scholiasts are the earliest and only evidence for his existence.[7] Is this the solitary and redeeming piece of independent evidence which they supply about the poem—or is it not rather an occa-

---

[1] Cf. the penetrating remarks of Alföldi, 'The Numbering of the Victories of the Emperor Gallienus and of the Loyalty of his Legions', *NC*, series 5, ix (1929), 265: 'This is an imitation of the story of Saloninus preserved in the commentary of Virgil's *Fourth Eclogue*. . . . This connexion may perhaps reveal other threads from which the *Historia Augusta* has been woven.'

[2] *Zur Gesch. lateinischer Eigennamen*, 224. It is to be regretted that Schulze does not mention the name 'Saloninus'.

[3] *ILS* 968 (Vicetia: Salonia, the mother of a senator, probably a near relation of C. Salonius Matidius Patruinus); Tacitus, *Hist.* ii 20; cf. iii 8. For the name Saloninus, cf. also Martial vi 18, 1. It is perhaps worth mentioning that a soldier with the cognomen Saloninus (*CIL* iii 6300) was in fact of Dalmatian origin.

[4] J. Wackernagel, 'Zu den lateinischen Ethnika', *Archiv für lat. Lexikographie* xiv (1906), 1 ff. I am deeply grateful to Professor Fraenkel for this reference and for the consequent strengthening of my argument.

[5] Ibid. 9, 'Bei Stadtnamen, die als letzten Konsonanten ein zwischen-vokalisches *n*, *nn* enthalten, werden -*anus*, -*inus* durchaus verschmäht, ausschliesslich -*ensis* oder auch -*as* angewandt.'

[6] N. Vulić in *RE*, s.v. 'Salona', col. 2004, says 'Ethnikon: *Salonitanus*, daneben mehrfach: *Salonas*.' I can discover two examples of 'Salonas' (*CIL* iii 8831; vi 32895).

[7] I must thank Mr. Barber for emphasizing this fact.

sion for disquiet? According to Servius, the child smiled at birth and died almost at once—'quem constat natum risisse statim: quod parentibus omen est infelicitatis: nam ipsum puerum inter ipsa primordia perisse manife-stum est'.[1] How did he know? The identification of the child with a son of Pollio, rashly deduced from the poem, was made at an early date, to be sure. According to Servius, Asconius Pedianus was told by Asinius Gallus that he, Gallus, was the wonder-child.[2] It is not recorded what the scholarly and alert Asconius thought of this bold assertion. Further, there is no indication either that Gallus mentioned or that Asconius handed down the name of Saloninus in this connection. How did it come to the scholiasts?

Alföldi has drawn attention to the parallel with Gallienus' son Saloninus, also said to have been born at Salonae.[3] The reign of the emperor Gallienus witnessed much propaganda about the Golden Age, attested on the coins. To quote Mattingly, 'The coinage of Gallienus and his two sons, Valerian II and Saloninus, is full of the imagery of Virgil's Golden Age—the "Jupiter Crescens", the young prince whose youth is like that of Jupiter in Crete, the gods who watch over his growth ("Dei Nutritores"), the holy generation that is fit to inherit the new time ("Pietas Saeculi"). It seems more than probable that the Fourth Eclogue was taken to be, what Servius calls it, a "Genethliacon Salonini", or birthday piece for Saloninus, the little son of Pollio: it would naturally be applied then to the Saloninus of Gallienus.'[4]

Alföldi and Mattingly argue very plausibly that Messianic propaganda about Gallienus' son derived support from the legend about Pollio's child. Would it be too | rash to suggest that the fiction followed the reverse direction, that the identification of the miraculous child as Pollio's Salo-ninus, and the opportune discovery of that phantom infant, originate in the time of Gallienus? It will be recalled that there is no earlier and independent evidence for the existence of the child. The name certainly occurred in the family of Pollio—Saloninus, son of Gallus and stepson of the emperor Tiberius, is a figure of history:[5] Saloninus the son of Pollio is vouched for only by scholiasts. To be born and to smile at birth is the beginning—and the end—of Saloninus.

The infant perished 'intra ipsa primordia', says Servius. What did he

---

[1] On *Ecl.* iv 1 (Thilo–Hagen iii 1, 44), cf. above, p. 23.

[2] On *Ecl.* iv 1 (Thilo–Hagen iii 1, 46), 'quidam Saloninum Pollionis filium accipiunt, alii Asinium Gallum, fratrem Salonini, qui prius natus est Pollione consule designato. Asconius Pedianus a Gallo audivisse se refert hanc eclogam in honorem eius factam'.

[3] *NC*, s. 5, ix (1929), 265.

[4] 'Virgil's Golden Age: Sixth Aeneid and Fourth Eclogue', *CR* xlviii (1934), 164 f. The coins are, respectively, Mattingly and Sydenham, *Rom. Imp. Coinage* v 1, 117, no. 13; 127, no. 135; 119, no. 32.

[5] Tacitus, *Ann.* iii 75.

mean by this? Before the 'dies lustricus', that is the ninth day from birth, on which occasion a male child usually received its *praenomen*?[1] Blümner[2] states that the first eight days were called the 'primordia', citing Servius on *Ecl.* iv 1 (not a conclusive reference). Servius may, however, have been thinking of the first forty days—at least Philargyrius (on *Ecl.* iv 60) alleges that it is a fatal sign if a child smiles before the fortieth day. But it all matters very little, and it would perhaps be a frivolous antiquarianism further to inquire whether a child that died so young, 'intra ipsa primordia', had already been given a *cognomen*—for 'Saloninus' is not an inherited and inevitable *cognomen*.

One cannot deny outright the existence of Saloninus; and the name did occur in the family of Pollio, borne by his attested grandson. Fragments of recondite knowledge are sometimes preserved by the most miserable authorities. For example, the *Historia Augusta* derives the descent of the emperor Balbinus from the famous Cornelius Balbus.[3] A gross absurdity; yet it refers to him as 'Balbus Cornelius Theophanes', thus displaying curious learning, namely the little-known and authentic fact that Balbus was once adopted by Pompey's friend Theophanes.

Historical and linguistic evidences deprive the child Saloninus of all relevance, and even cast doubt upon his existence. Granted that there was a Saloninus and it was still desired to derive his name from the city of Salonae, the only device available is so weak that to mention it is to dispose of it at once. It has been shown that Pollio himself can hardly have been at Salonae in 40/39, when his province was Macedonia, not Illyricum. When do the scholiasts place the birth of Saloninus? The only evidence is tainted evidence. Servius in one place says at the time of the capture of Salonae, which he places before the consulate of Pollio;[4] in another place, apparently, in the year of Pollio's consulate.[5] Now the elder son Gallus might seem by his cognomen to commemorate Pollio's presence in Cisalpine Gaul in 41–40 B.C.;[6] and Gallus is said by Servius to have been born in the year preceding Pollio's consulate.[7] What of Saloninus? He *might* have been born at Salonae—his mother might have retired there for safety during the Perusine War (41–40 B.C.). Or Pollio himself might have visited that city between the spring and the autumn of 40, that is, between the end of the Perusine War and the Pact of Brundisium. Now, Pollio is last heard of near Altinum, vainly defending Venetia against the

[1] Macrobius i 16, 36; cf., for an amusing incident, Suetonius, *Nero* 6. The *cognomen* was often given much later in life.
[2] *Die röm. Privataltertümer*, 303 f.   [3] *HA Maximus et Balbinus* 7, 3.
[4] On *Ecl.* iv 1, quoted above, p. 23.
[5] At least he says that Gallus was born when Pollio was consul designate, above, p. 27, n. 2.
[6] Cf. Carcopino, op. cit. 169.
[7] On *Ecl.* iv 1, quoted above, p. 27, n. 2.

armies of Octavian.[1] By coming to terms with the master of the sea, Domitius Ahenobarbus, he was able to make his way to Antony and bring an ally with him. When cruising down the Adriatic, it is difficult to avoid putting in at Salonae. So Pollio might have visited Salonae after all—and named his son in memory of that town. If it were worth it, one could mention that Servius in one passage might appear to date Pollio's capture of Salonae to this time and occasion—'tunc Illyricum petebat, | expugnaturus Salonas et inde ad Orientem ad Antonium profecturus.'[2] The scholiasts were not aware that Pollio was on the eastern littoral of the Adriatic on two occasions—when on his way from northern Italy to join Antony before the Pact of Brundisium, and afterwards, in his province of Macedonia. This ignorance might be one of the reasons of their confusion.

But the scholiasts have done harm enough. Historical and linguistic evidence combines to banish, if not to abolish, the phantom child. *Ignorabimus*: it is only the scholiast that has an answer for everything. And by now it will be clear that those answers are erroneous, ignorant, and contradictory. About the Fourth Eclogue, they reproduce the opinions that the poem was written to honour either Saloninus, Pollio himself, or Octavian.[3] Of such vital facts as the Pact of Brundisium, the role of Pollio in the negotiation of that agreement, the marriage of Antony and Octavia, the relation in time between Pollio's consulate and Pollio's triumph, the name of the tribe from which that triumph was won, of all this they have no inkling. It is evident that no reliance can be placed upon their unsupported testimony; and nothing is gained by mixing bad evidence with good.

As for the identity of the miraculous child, the above observations may be held to tell against the view that it was Saloninus. Against that opinion the weightiest objections will remain those expressed by Tarn: and the poem itself betrays no hint that the consul invoked is about to become a father. But that question is really alien to the purpose of this paper.

To resume: the main points of the above argument are as follows: (1) Macedonia was the province assigned to Pollio after the Pact of Brundisium when he laid down his consulate; (2) Salonae did not belong to the province of the proconsul of Macedonia; (3) the only occasion in 40 B.C. when Pollio himself can have visited that city is before, not after, the Pact of Brundisium; (4) on linguistic grounds the name 'Saloninus' probably has nothing to do with Salonae; (5) Pollio may never have had a son called Saloninus.

---

[1] Velleius ii 76, 2; see above, p. 20.
[2] Servius on *Ecl.* viii 12 (Thilo–Hagen iii 1, 93).
[3] Philargyrius on *Ecl.* iv 1 (Thilo–Hagen iii 2, 72 f.): 'hanc eclogam scriptam esse aiunt in Asinium Pollionem, quidam in filium eius Saloninum, qui nomen accepit a Salona civitate, quam eodem tempore quo natus est pater eius expugnavit, sive in honorem Octaviani Augusti, sive Asinii Pollionis.'

APPENDIX: *Ecl.* viii 6–8

Tu mihi seu magni superas iam saxa Timavi
sive oram Illyrici legis aequoris—en erit unquam
ille dies, mihi cum liceat tua dicere facta?

As this passage, an address to Pollio, the unnamed patron addressed in the
Eighth Eclogue, has already been referred to twice, a brief attempt at elucidation may not be out of place. Servius states that the words were addressed to
Pollio 'qui tunc Illyricum petebat, oppugnaturus Salonas et inde ad Orientem
ad Antonium profecturus'.[1] Now Servius in another place (on *Ecl.* iv 1, quoted
above, p. 23) dates the capture of Salonae and Pollio's triumph before his consulate, as we have seen. A gross error in the matter of Pollio's triumph. More fortunate than Servius and his kin, a modern scholar can easily ascertain the true order
of events and the occasion and date of Pollio's triumph, viz. 25 October 39 or
38 B.C. It is therefore easy to understand these lines of Virgil: they were not
addressed to Pollio when he was on his way from northern Italy to a fictitious
capture of Salonae on the Dalmatian coast, as Servius and a modern scholar,
Ganter, suppose. That supposition is contradicted by internal evidence—Virgil
refers to Pollio's 'victorious | laurels' (12 f.), 'hanc sine tempora circum / inter
victricis hederam tibi serpere lauros.' The lines were therefore composed after
Pollio's victory over the Parthini in Macedonia, either in anticipation or in
celebration of the triumph which he earned. The poet, writing in vivid anticipation, imagines Pollio returning from Macedonia to northern Italy—he is already
(the word 'iam' is decisive here) crossing the cliffs of the river Timavus at the
head of the Adriatic, or is still sailing up the Dalmatian coast from Macedonia.
This interpretation is confirmed by a later echo of the phrase, when Virgil
describes Antenor's voyage up the Adriatic (*Aen.* i 244), 'fontem superare
Timavi'.

Not that Pollio did, as a matter of fact, return to northern Italy from Macedonia. But that is immaterial. The lines were written in northern Italy—or
rather, from the point of view of a man in northern Italy, in 39 or 38 B.C.[2]

[1] Servius on *Ecl.* viii 12 (Thilo–Hagen iii 1, 93). Yet Servius himself, commenting on
line 6 of that poem, takes it to refer to Augustus! He paraphrases 'ubi ubi es, O Auguste,
sive Venetiae fluenta transcendis', etc.

[2] [G. W. Bowersock, *HSCPh* lxxv (1971), 73 ff., dates the Eighth Eclogue to 35 B.C.
and takes the lines as addressed to Octavianus.]

3

Who Was Decidius Saxa?

I. *Caesar's New Senators*[1]

THE ancient evidence about the origin and social status of the new men
who were introduced into the Roman Senate by Caesar the Dictator is
neither abundant nor detailed, and prejudice might be suspected where it
cannot be proved. To take a parallel: it is evident that exaggerated opinions about the character of the Sullan Senate have been incautiously
adopted and slavishly perpetuated. Sallust speaks of 'gregarii milites' in
the Curia.[2] A careful examination of the composition of that body has
revealed the presence of only one man who had been a centurion, L.
Fufidius.[3] A salutary warning.

In Dio's account of Caesar's enrolment of 47 B.C. appear knights, centurions and 'lesser folk';[4] and in 45 B.C. soldiers and sons of freedmen were
admitted without discrimination.[5] As for the sons of freedmen, this was no
novelty, as Tacitus makes the Emperor Claudius observe on a famous
occasion—'libertinorum filiis magistratus mandare non, ut plerique falluntur, repens, sed priori populo factitatum est.'[6] Moreover, senators of this
origin are attested in the records of the last century of the Free State.[7] In
this respect, as in most, the establishment of the Principate marked no
violent | change: the proportion of senators of servile origin in the
Neronian Senate should not be measured by the interested assertions of
another Tacitean orator.[8]

Dio also speaks of centurions, an important topic.

[1] [For a fuller treatment see pp. 88–119 below.]   [2] Sallust, *BC* 37.

[3] H. Hill, 'Sulla's New Senators in 81 B.C.', *CQ* xxvi (1932), 170 ff. L. Fufidius is described
by Orosius (v 21, 3) as a 'primipilaris': on him cf. further Sallust, *Hist.* i 55 Maur.; Plutarch,
Sulla 31; *Sertorius* 12. [See, however, E. Gabba, *Athenaeum*, N.S. xxix (1951), 265 f.]

[4] Dio xlii 51, 5: τοὺς δὲ ἱππέας τοῦ τέλους τούς τε ἑκατοντάρχους καὶ τοὺς ὑπομείονας. If by τὸ
τέλος here Dio means only the *equites* of the eighteen centuries, the *equites Romani equo publico*,
it might be argued that other knights, not of this category, may wrongly be included by
Dio under the 'centurions and lesser folk'.

[5] Dio xliii 47, 3: καὶ προσέτι παμπληθεῖς μὲν ἐς τὴν γερουσίαν, μηδὲν διακρίνων μήτ᾽ εἴ τις
στρατιώτης μήτ᾽ εἴ τις ἀπελευθέρου παῖς ἦν, ἐσέγραψεν.

[6] Tacitus, *Ann.* xi 24.

[7] Cf. P. Willems, *Le Sénat de la république romaine* i 187 ff., 561. The censors of 50 B.C.
expelled such men and earned a reputation for severity: Dio xl 63, 4; Horace, *Sat.* i 6, 20 f.

[8] Tacitus, *Ann.* xiii 27: 'et plurimis equitum, plerisque senatoribus non aliunde originem
trahi.'

II. *Centurions*

Dio's remarks find vivid confirmation in Cicero's description of the Caesarian Senate—'in eo senatu, quem maiore ex parte ipse cooptasset, tot centurionibus suis inspectantibus'.[1] Further, the name of one of these men is known, C. Fuficius Fango, who governed Africa for Octavianus in 41 B.C.[2] L. Decidius Saxa, the provincial Roman who is the central theme of the present investigation, was either an ex-centurion or an equestrian officer. Others there were, but they are not so easily to be detected. Cicero becomes petulant about three Caesarians—'redeo ad Tebassos Scaevas Fangones: hos tu existimas confidere se illa habituros stantibus nobis?'[3] These men, Münzer deduces, were all senators.[4] This is not certain for Tebassus and Scaeva. The latter was a Caesarian centurion proverbial for valour and the type of his class;[5] and Tebassus was probably chosen by Cicero for ridicule because of his non-Latin name—compare the *gentilicium* 'Tebanus' and the Sabine word 'teba'.[6] That is to say, this is merely a collection of Caesarian types—perhaps, but not certainly, senators.

It might appear that the term 'centurion' explained itself. In the Roman army of the time of Sulla and Caesar a rigid distinction separated officers from the ranks. The normal centurion has begun service as a simple soldier, and centurions in service do not pass by promotion to the posts of *tribunus militum* or *praefectus equitum*.[7] These were restricted to Roman knights. So far so good. But three reservations commend themselves. First, in the early Principate the higher centurionate provides an avenue to the *equestris militia*. Now it is an offence against the facts of history as well as against historical method to argue upon the cheerful assumption that Augustus made all things new. Though rare, no doubt, this salutary innovation may, after all, have originated in the army of Caesar. The earliest example is, I believe, that friend of Augustus, T. Marius from Urvinum, 'ab infimo militiae loco beneficiis divi | Augusti ad summos castrenses honores perductus'.[8] The soldier, T. Marius, appears to have

---

[1] Cicero, *De div.* ii 23.

[2] Dio xlviii 22, 3: ἔν τε γὰρ τῷ μισθοφορικῷ ἐστράτευτο. πολλοὶ γὰρ καὶ τῶν τοιούτων εἰς τὸ βουλευτήριον, ὥσπερ εἴρηταί μοι, κατελελέχατο. CIL x 3758, an aedile of that name at Acerrae; Cicero, *ad. Att.* xiv 10, 2.

[3] *ad Att.* xiv 10, 2.   [4] *RE*, s.v. 'Fuficius', col. 200.

[5] Caesar, *BC* iii 53, etc. [Probably still a *primus pilus* after Caesar: see *ILLRP* 1116a.]

[6] For Tebanus, cf. *ILS* 973 (Amiternum). For the 'Pelasgian' word 'teba' in the Sabine country (Varro, *RR* iii 1, 6), cf. W. Schulze, *Zur Gesch. lateinischer Eigennamen*, 531; E. Norden, *Alt-Germanien* (1934), 107.

[7] J. N. Madvig, *Verfassung u. Verwaltung des röm. Staates* ii 505 f., 510 f. Of the three cases adduced by Kübler (*RE*, s.v. 'Equites Romani', col. 292) only one will do, L. Fufidius. Cf. M. Gelzer, *Die Nobilität der röm. Republik*, 2 [= *Kl. Schr.* i 20 f.]; H. Hill, *CQ* xxvi (1932), 170.

[8] Valerius Maximus vii 8, 6. Perhaps identical with the T. Marius Siculus (*CIL* xi 6058), who was *tr. mil. leg. XII*; cf. A. Stein, *Der röm. Ritterstand*, 160 f.

become a military tribune. Dio makes Maecenas warn Augustus against promoting to the Senate officers who had thus risen from the ranks.[1] Secondly, on retirement from the army, a centurion would not infrequently be in possession of the equestrian census; and so, as Cicero records, ex-centurions had served upon juries.[2] Thirdly, a specially favoured centurion of the early Principate is the man who temporarily divests himself of equestrian rank in order to enter the army—'ordinem accepit ex equite Romano'. The spirit of adventure and the lust of gain may well have drawn a few young knights—or at least younger sons of equestrian families—from the more military regions of Italy to the ranks of Caesar's legions. It would be rash to deny it. It might, therefore, be doubted whether all the men whom partial authorities designate as 'centurions' were humble and obscure in origin, or had passed without a break from the centurionate to the Curia.

Dio mentions a third class of new and undesirable senators, described as inferior in standing to knights and centurions (ὑπομείονες).[3] What class does he mean? A scribe—or ex-scribe—became quaestor during the dictatorship of Caesar.[4] Yet scribes might well be of equestrian rank.[5] Common soldiers?[6] But surely only through the centurionate, and perhaps with an interval after that. Fuficius Fango, who had risen from the ranks, was perhaps at one time in his life a municipal magistrate at Acerrae.[7] The 'gregarii milites' of Sulla (see above) were not elevated at one bound from the ranks to the Curia. Another example of this kind of misrepresentation can be discovered. A *lex iudiciaria* of M. Antonius provided that ex-centurions, whether they possessed the equestrian census or not, were to be eligible to serve on the jury-panels. Cicero therefore alleges that common soldiers are contemplated, and from a Gallic legion at that—'addo etiam iudices manipularis ex legione Alaudarum.'[8] Stories about soldiers and centurions must therefore be taken with a strong dose of caution.

III. *Provincials*

Dio has nothing to say of senators drawn from the provinces. A remarkable omission. Suetonius, recording Caesar's enrolment of aliens who lacked even the Roman citizenship until he granted | that status, has

---

[1] lii 25, 6.
[2] *Phil.* i 20: 'itaque viri fortissimi atque honestissimi, qui ordines duxerunt, res et iudicant et iudicaverunt.'
[3] xlii 51, 5.   [4] Cicero, *de Off.* ii 29.
[5] Cf. Gelzer, *Die Nobilität der röm. Republik*, 10 [= *Kl. Schr.* i 28].
[6] So Carcopino (*Histoire romaine* ii 2, 933), citing the case of Fuficius Fango.
[7] *CIL* x 3758; cf. Münzer in *RE*, s.v. 'Fuficius', col. 200. As the name is so uncommon, the aedile at Acerrae, if not this man, is surely at the least a close relation.
[8] Cicero, *Phil.* i 20; cf. xiii 3.

immortalized the Gauls who laid aside the trouser, a badge as well as a garment, to don the toga.

Divus Julius 76: civitate donatos, et quosdam e semibarbaris Gallorum, recepit in curiam.

Ibid. 80: peregrinis in senatum allectis, libellus propositus est: bonum factum: ne quis senatori novo curiam monstrare velit! et illa vulgo canebantur:

Gallos Caesar in triumphum ducit, idem in curiam.
Galli bracas deposuerunt, latum clavum sumpserunt.

Grave scholars have accepted these lampoons as substantially true—and have spoiled a good joke.[1] It is difficult to believe that Caesar went so far as to bestow senatorial rank on aliens who had only just received the Roman citizenship at his hands, more difficult still to divine his motive. It cannot have been a desire to degrade the prestige or dilute by an infusion of useless members the character of the body which, whatever form the constitution might take, was to supply the administrative hierarchy of the Empire.

Well may we regret that malicious interest has not preserved the names of any of these trousered aliens. It should be possible, however, to discover some indication of the origin and character of the senators who were branded with that derisive appellation.

In the first place, the province of Cisalpine Gaul. One of the favourite conventions of forensic and political oratory was the allegation of obscure birth or unsavoury pursuits: when such allegations are quietly examined, they commonly come down to very little. The father of the austere and cultivated L. Calpurnius Piso (*cos.* 58 B.C.) took to wife the daughter of a prosperous businessman from Placentia called Calventius. Now Placentia was an ancient and respectable colony of Cisalpine Gaul;[2] and there is no reason at all for regarding Calventius as a Celtic name. But this does not prevent Cicero from alleging that Calventius really came, not from Placentia, but from Mediolanum (formerly the capital of the Insubres) and describing Calventius as an Insubrian Gaul—'Insuber quidam fuit, idem mercator et praeco.'[3] Note the degrading profession of *praeco*. Not content with this, Cicero goes further—Calventius originally came not from Cisalpine Gaul at all, but from Gaul beyond the Alps;[4] and so Piso

---

[1] L. Friedländer, *Sittengeschichte* i[10] 107; E. Meyer, *Caesars Monarchie u. das Principat des Pompejus*[3], 463 f.: 'zahlreiche Ausländer, namentlich Spanier und Gallier, die eben erst, nach der Unterwerfung durch Caesar, das Bürgerrecht erhalten hatten und daher kaum Lateinisch konnten'; A. Stein, *Der röm. Ritterstand*, 208: 'halbbarbarische Gallier und Keltiberer', cf. 209, n. 1. See by contrast the crisp comments of Adcock, *CAH* ix 729 f.

[2] *In Pisonem*, fr. 9 = Asconius 2 (Clark, pp. 2 f.).

[3] *In Pisonem*, fr. 11 = Asconius 4 (Clark, p. 5). Cf. *in Pisonem* 26, 62: 'Mediolanensi praecone, avo tuo'.

[4] *In Pisonem*, fr. 10 = Asconius 3 (Clark, p. 4).

can be taunted with Gallic blood.[1] It might be doubted whether the enjoyment which these sallies afforded the orator and his audience bore any relation to their literal truth. On the contrary, perhaps, just as the well-known *gravitas* | and austere eyebrows of the same Piso gave zest and point to Cicero's accusations of unspeakable immorality. The appellation of the tribal name of Insubrian to men from the colonies and *municipia* of Cisalpina recurs in harsh words reported by Tacitus as uttered before Claudius in the imperial privy council—'an parum quod Veneti et Insubres curiam inruperint?'[2] The libel about Piso's ancestry will authorize the conjecture that some at least of the trousered Gauls were respectable citizens from Gallia Cisalpina. 'Est enim ille flos Italiae, illud firmamentum imperi populi Romani, illud ornamentum dignitatis.'[3]

Secondly, Gallia Narbonensis, a province early Romanized, and, along with Spain and the Cisalpina, remarkable for its contribution to the military and administrative hierarchy of the Principate. Apart from citizens of the Roman colony of Narbo, we must admit here men of Celtic origin, belonging to dynastic families that had received the Roman citizenship one or two generations earlier, for example from Cn. Domitius Ahenobarbus, who constituted the province *c.* 120 B.C., from C. Valerius Flaccus, proconsul *c.* 82–80 B.C., and from Pompeius Magnus.[4] The frequent occurrence of the three *gentilicia* Domitius, Valerius, and Pompeius in equestrian and senatorial families of Gallia Narbonensis under the Principate is no accident of statistics. Two examples will personify this class of civilized provincial: Caesar's friend, C. Valerius Procillus (or Troucillus), 'homo honestissimus provinciae Galliae', son of C. Valerius Caburus, 'princeps Helviorum',[5] and Pompeius Trogus (father of the historian). Pompeius Trogus was employed by the Dictator as a confidential secretary. His father, a Vocontian dynast commanding the cavalry of his tribe in the Sertorian War, had been rewarded with the Roman citizenship; an uncle went with Pompeius against Mithridates.[6] The adlection to the Senate of two or three men of this class would provide ample justification for lampoons. 'Fuit aliquando Bracata, nunc Narbonensis.'[7]

For Spain, the other source of Caesar's non-Italian senators, we are better informed. Two names are known. To them some scholars would add a third, the senator Titius, whose sons, the two young Titii Hispani, served as military tribunes in Africa in 46 B.C.[8] The *cognomen* may suggest,

---

[1] *Cum senatui gratias egit* 15; *in Pisonem* 53: 'bracatae cognationis dedecus'.
[2] Tacitus, *Ann.* xi 23.   [3] Cicero, *Phil.* iii 13.
[4] [See further E. Badian, *Foreign Clientelae* (1958), 309 ff.]
[5] Caesar, *BG* i 19, 47 and 53; vii 65.   [6] Justin xliii 5, 11 f.
[7] Mela ii 74; cf. Pliny, *NH* iii 31.
[8] *Bell. Afr.* 28: 'duo Titii Hispani adulescentes, tribuni legionis V, quorum patrem Caesar in senatum legerat.' His Spanish origin is accepted by Willems (*Le Sénat* i 596), Gelzer (*Die Nobilität*, 11 [= *Kl. Schr.* i 29]) and Carcopino (*Histoire romaine* ii 2, 933).

but does not prove, a Spanish origin. About L. Cornelius Balbus the Younger, quaestor in 43 B.C., there is no doubt.[1] His uncle, the Gaditane magnate who served Pompeius and Caesar so well, was apparently not put into the Senate by Caesar: he received the consulate from the triumvirs in 40 B.C. The nephew | acquired the Roman citizenship along with his uncle *c.* 72 B.C. The other man from Spain is L. Decidius Saxa, tribune of the plebs in 44 B.C. This person demands—and will repay—careful scrutiny.

IV. *L. Decidius Saxa*

Cicero several times in the *Philippics* refers with scorn and distaste to the Antonian partisan Decidius Saxa, whom Caesar had made tribune of the plebs.[2] Saxa was subsequently to command part of a Roman army in the campaign of Philippi, and perish in Syria at the hands of the Parthians (40 B.C.).[3] The three passages that describe him most fully are as follows:

Phil. xi 12: accedit Saxa nescio quis, quem nobis Caesar ex ultima Celtiberia tribunum plebis dedit, castrorum antea metator, nunc, ut sperat, urbis: a qua cum sit alienus, suo capiti salvis nobis ominetur.

Ibid. xiii 27: Saxam vero Decidium praeterire qui possum, hominem deductum ex ultimis gentibus, ut eum tribunum plebis videremus quem civem nunquam videramus?

Ibid. xiv 10: iam peritus metator et callidus decempeda sua Saxa.

Eduard Meyer, Arthur Stein, and other authorities appear to accept these allegations as true in a historical as well as in an oratorical sense, for they state that Decidius Saxa was a Celtiberian who had recently been given the citizenship.[4] Likewise Münzer, in Pauly–Wissowa, who says that Caesar brought the man from Spain to Rome and granted him the citizenship.[5] It will be well to discuss in order the legal status of Saxa before he entered the Senate, his origin, and his rank or profession.

Saxa served under Caesar in the campaign of 49 B.C.—'postero die Petreius cum paucis equitibus occulte ad exploranda loca proficiscitur. hoc idem fit ex castris Caesaris. mittitur L. Decidius Saxa cum paucis qui

---

[1] On him cf. especially Velleius ii 51, 3, 'ex privato consularis'—though some have thought that this phrase really applies to the uncle.

[2] *Phil.* viii 9 and 26; x 22; xi 12 and 37; xii 20; xiii 2 and 27; xiv 10.

[3] Dio xlvii 35, 2; xlviii 24, 3; xlviii 25, 2; Appian, *BC* iv 87; Velleius ii 78, 1; Livy, *Per.* cxxvii, etc.

[4] E. Meyer, *Caesars Monarchie*[3], 463 f. (quoted above), and 483; A. Stein, *Der röm. Ritterstand*, 209: 'ein eben erst mit dem Bürgerrecht beschenkter Keltiberer war z. B. L. Decidius Saxa, den Caesar gleich zum Volkstribunen für das J. 44 designierte'. Also P. Ribbeck, *Senatores Romani qui fuerint Idibus Martiis A.U.C. 710* (Diss. Berlin 1899), 33; G. Niccolini, *I fasti dei tribuni della plebe* (1934), 354.

[5] F. Münzer, *RE*, s.v. 'Decidius', col. 2271: 'darauf von Caesar mit nach Rom genommen, mit dem römischen Bürgerrecht beschenkt und für das nächste Jahr zum Volkstribun ernannt.'

loci naturam perspiciat.'[1] From the duties with which Saxa was entrusted it appears that he was either a centurion or an officer of equestrian standing:[2] in any case, a person of some value. He already has the three Roman names, including a *gentilicium* which is perhaps of central-Italian origin.[3] This disproves the theory of Münzer. Next, his origin. 'Ex ultima Celtiberia', says Cicero, and for the sake of an antithesis denies his citizenship —'ut eum tribunum plebis videremus quem civem nunquam videramus'. Is this true? It was a period of revolution, | social and political, when merit shot up like a meteor from origins obscure and often undiscoverable —to mention only Statilius Taurus, Tarius Rufus, P. Ventidius, the army-contractor, when an infant in Picenum captured and enslaved, but none the less praetor and consul in the year 43 B.C., Salvidienus Rufus, designate-consul for 39 B.C., though not a senator, M. Vipsanius Agrippa, ashamed of his own name Vipsanius, and consul at the age of twenty-five. 'Non mos, non ius', as Tacitus observes of this period.[4] But even so, wild Celtiberians do not command armies of Roman legions in the campaign of Philippi, and govern the province of Syria for M. Antonius. What is the narrow but necessary substratum of fact to Cicero's allegation that L. Decidius Saxa was a Celtiberian? That it need be but narrow emerges from the parallel quoted above, the designation of a Roman citizen from the colony of Placentia as an Insubrian or even as a Transalpine Gaul. A Spanish domicile, without any infusion of Spanish blood, would be enough for an orator: it is not safe to infer that Saxa was an alien born who had but recently received the Roman citizenship. We may therefore describe Saxa as a perfectly respectable Roman citizen from Spain, that is to say, 'Hispaniensis' rather than 'Hispanus': the distinction between the two words is none the less real for being commonly obscured. Balbus, a Gaditane lacking the citizenship by birth, is described by Velleius as 'non Hispaniensis natus sed Hispanus'.[5] Saxa served in Caesar's army as a centurion, perhaps even as an equestrian officer. Roman knights, indeed, were abundant enough in Spain at this time.[6] But this is not the place to quote the evidence for the extent and nature of Roman settlement in Spain, or the wide extension of the citizenship long before this date.[7]

[1] Caesar, *BC* i 66.
[2] Cf. the duty entrusted to P. Considius (*BG* i 21), probably a centurion of long experience.
[3] Compare the distribution of names in '-idius', '-iedius' and '-edius', demonstrated by Schulten ('Italische Namen u. Stämme', *Klio* ii and iii). The name Decidius is well attested in Campania—*ILS* 6038, 6363d, 6393; *CIL* x 360, 4090, 8124.   [4] Tacitus, *Ann.* iii 28.
[5] Velleius, ii 51, 3: 'non †Hispaniae Asiae† natus sed Hispanus'. *Hispaniensis*, Lipsius. The distinction between native-born and Spanish Roman appears clearly in Martial's words (xii, *praef.*): 'ne Romam, si ita decreveris, non Hispaniensem librum mittamus, sed Hispanum'.
[6] Cf. esp. *Bell. Al.* 56, for the census of Roman knights held by Q. Cassius Longinus.
[7] [On this, see E. Gabba, *Athenaeum*, N.S. xxxii (1954), 297–305.]

That is to say, no more than the Egnatius dubbed a Celtiberian by the poet Catullus[1] is Saxa to be held to be a newly enfranchised native of Celtiberia on the testimony of an unfriendly advocate; and 'Celtiberia' is perhaps no more than a libellous designation for a different and highly civilized region of Spain.

V. *Castrorum Metator*

Decidius Saxa is labelled by Cicero as a 'castrorum metator'. The phrase has sometimes been understood as a technical term, and Saxa has been joyfully hailed as the first known professional 'castrorum metator'.[2] Inquiry dissipates this convenient assumption—for what more convenient than a technical term to hide | behind? In the Roman army of the time of Caesar there is no trace of a separate corps of engineers, surveyors, or the like. The *praefectus fabrum*, divorced from the original function which the survival of the name indicates, has become a kind of chief of staff to a magistrate or a governor. 'Castrorum metator' is therefore a descriptive phrase, not an official title.

It accordingly remains to discover what officer chose the site and superintended the construction of a camp. In the time of Polybius, a tribune or some picked centurions;[3] in Caesar's campaigns there is but a single indication—on one occasion a centurion and some scouts are sent forward to find a suitable site.[4] For simplicity's sake it might be safest to assume that Saxa was a Caesarian centurion and leave it at that.[5] Another possibility is worth investigating—he may have been an officer of equestrian rank.

It is much to be regretted that there exists no adequate study of the equestrian officers of the Roman army in the Caesarian period.[6] The history of Roman civil and military institutions is the history of a slow growth and development. When one stage is missing from our tradition it can be inferred from what precedes or what follows. The origins of the *militia equestris* of the time of Augustus should be discernible a generation earlier, if one cares to look for them. An important equestrian officer of the Augustan army is the *praefectus castrorum*. But even here much is still obscure in the origin of this post; the functions and various employments

---

[1] 39, 17. The man is perhaps the Egnatius who wrote a poem *De rerum natura* (Macrobius vi 52, 12) and so the earliest Spanish Roman poet known by name; cf. F. Skutsch, *RE*, s.v. 'Egnatius', coll. 1993 f. For poets at Corduba, cf. Cic. *pro Archia* 26.

[2] A. Schulten, *RE*, s.v. 'Gromatici', coll. 1889, 1891.   [3] Polybius vi 41, 1.

[4] Caesar, *BG* ii 17.

[5] So Willems, *Le Sénat* i 594; Carcopino, *Histoire romaine* ii 2, 933.

[6] The career of C. Volusenus Quadratus (Caesar, *BG* iii 5; iv 21 and 23; vi 41; viii 23 and 48; *BC* iii 60) is suggestive. He cannot have been unique. [A beginning in J. Harmand, *L'Armée et le soldat à Rome de 107 à 50 avant notre ère* (Paris, 1967), Part II, ch. 3. Lists in Cl. Nicolet, *L'Ordre équestre à l'époque républicaine* i (Paris, 1966), 272–84.]

of the officer are a subject sorely in need of investigation.[1] It appears that one of the duties of the *praefectus castrorum* was to choose and delimit the camp. Vegetius says so: 'erat etiam castrorum praefectus, licet inferior dignitate, occupatus tamen non mediocribus causis, ad quem castrorum positio valli et fossae aestimatio pertinebat.'[2] Now Vegetius is himself the subject of problems of peculiar difficulty. Alone his statement would not avail. Two casual facts support it. In A.D. 7 at the great Battle of the Volcaean Marshes a *praefectus castrorum* is mentioned among the officers who fell,[3] and it is recorded that the Pannonians attacked the Roman army while it was making its camp.[4] In the time of Claudius a *praefectus castrorum* in Britain, in the company of legionary soldiers, is found laying out forts.[5]

Cicero describes Decidius Saxa as 'castrorum metator' and makes jokes about his 'decempeda'. Saxa was not a professional surveyor. All this might suggest that Saxa in some way more than other | centurions or officers was connected with castrametation. A certain Cafo is mentioned in the *Philippics* along with Saxa and never apart from him.[6] Cafo was probably an ex-centurion. Now the joke about castrametation is never made about Cafo. It might, therefore, appear that in Saxa we had the predecessor of the *praefectus castrorum* of the following generation.

But that is perhaps too much to hope. Closer scrutiny of the Ciceronian context will indicate that it may be safer to regard Saxa as an ex-centurion after all and will reveal the full significance of references to castrametation.

VI. *The Lex Agraria of June 44 B.C.*

Two land-bills were proposed and carried by the consuls M. Antonius and P. Cornelius Dolabella, the one in March or April, the second in June. Only the second concerns us here.[7] To execute its terms, which appear to have been pretty wide, a commission of seven was appointed, under the presidency of L. Antonius.[8] Of the *septemviri*, five members are known, the two consuls, L. Antonius, Caesennius Lento, and a certain Nucula. The other two lurk somewhere, hitherto undetected.[9] Yet they should be

---

[1] A. v. Domaszewski, *Die Rangordnung des röm. Heeres*, 119 ff., is not completely satisfactory on this point. [See now 2nd ed. (by B. Dobson, 1967), Add. Note by Dobson, p. xxxi.]

[2] Vegetius ii 10.   [3] Velleius ii 112, 6.   [4] Dio lv 32, 3.

[5] Tacitus, *Ann.* xii 38.

[6] *Phil.* viii 9 and 26; x 22; xi 12 and 37; xii 20. See further below.

[7] On the vexed questions concerning this legislation see Drumann–Groebe, *Gesch. Roms* i[2], 424 f.; Rice Holmes, *The Architect of the Roman Empire* i 16; J. D. Denniston, edn of Cicero, *Phil.* i–ii (Oxford, 1926), 94, 161 f.; M. A. Levi, *Ottaviano Capoparte* i 95 f.

[8] The principal evidence is Dio xlv 9, 1; Cicero, *ad Fam.* xi 2, 3; *ad Att.* xv 2, 2; xvi 3, 1; *Phil.* v 7 and 20 f.; vi 14; viii 26; xi 13.

[9] At least, according to Drumann–Groebe, *Gesch. Roms* i[2] 83; J. D. Denniston, edn of Cicero, *Phil.* i–ii, 94. Groebe suggests that C. Antonius, brother of the consul, was a member, citing *ad Att.* xv 9, 2 (which rather tells against it). Groebe, op. cit. 83 n., does not admit

discoverable among the Antonian rabble about whom Cicero is so generous of information.

Actors, male and female, says Cicero, were settled on lands in Campania.[1] What is the justification for this gibe? Apparently this, that one of the commissioners was a writer of mimes, the other had produced a tragedy.[2] The insinuation is that the commissioners made ample provision for themselves. Now Decidius Saxa and the inseparable Cafo are also stated by Cicero to have received lands in Campania;[3] further, they are given actors for neighbours,[4] and are vividly derided by Cicero as pugnacious and muscular centurions stationed among troupes of actors and actresses[5]—pretty strong but not certain evidence that Saxa had once been a centurion.

Were Saxa and Cafo merely the recipients of allotments? Hardly, for Saxa is described as skilled with the surveyor's rod and eager to display at the expense of Rome the art which he had learned in the camps.[6] Saxa, then, is the giver as well as the receiver of lands: | Saxa and Cafo are probably to be identified as the missing members of the 'divisores Italiae', the Commission of Seven. They were at their work when civil war broke out in the autumn of the year. To judge by Cicero's remarks, they appear to have enrolled veterans in Campania and led them northward to join Antonius for the War of Mutina.[7]

Saxa, but not Cafo, is derided as a 'castrorum metator'. Now Cafo looks like an ex-centurion—'veteranus Cafo, quo neminem veterani peius oderunt'.[8] On a rigid interpretation it might therefore be argued that Saxa with his especial function of castrametation had been, when in the army, something more than a centurion. This would perhaps be pressing a rhetorical text too far. Cafo is a nonentity, a pale shadow with no existence apart from Saxa. Cicero neglects Cafo, but spreads himself on the theme of Saxa. For obvious reasons. It was a richer theme. Saxa was a magistrate, Cafo perhaps not—at least Cafo is not mentioned among the senatorial partisans of Antonius.[9] Further, Saxa was not merely

---

Saxa, but remarks: 'Decidius Saxa wird Phil. XI, 12. XIV, 10 in einer anderen Beziehung ⟨metator und⟩ decempeda genannt' (*decempeda*, sic). [What we know is summarized *MRR* ii 332.]

[1] *Phil.* ii 101.   [2] *Phil.* xi 13.   [3] *Phil.* xi 12.   [4] *Phil.* xi 22.
[5] *Phil.* viii 26: 'Cafoni etiam et Saxae cavet, quos centuriones pugnacis et lacertosos inter mimorum et mimarum greges conlocavit.'
[6] *Phil.* xi 12; xiv 10, quoted above, p. 36.
[7] *Phil.* x 22: 'et sollicitant homines imperitos Saxae et Cafones, ipsi rustici atque agrestes', etc.; xi 22 and 37.
[8] *Phil.* xi 12.
[9] Cf. esp. *Phil.* xiii 26 ff. P. Ribbeck, *Senatores Romani qui fuerint Idibus Martiis anni A.U.C. 710* (Diss. Berlin, 1899), 46, reckons Cafo among Caesar's new senators. The name is absent from *RE*: it is almost certainly Etruscan; cf. W. Schulze, *Zur Gesch. lateinischer Eigennamen*, 137, 351.

an ex-centurion—he was born in Spain. To what cruel abuse excellent men from the provinces of Cisalpina, Narbonensis, and Spain were exposed, documentation has already demonstrated.

VII. *Conclusion*

The case of Saxa illustrates several branches of the technique of misrepresentation and provides a peg upon which to hang certain speculations about the military officers of the Caesarian period and the earliest unequivocally attested senators of provincial origin. Saxa, whatever his descent and whatever the proportions of Roman and Spanish blood in his veins, is more likely to be a Roman citizen by birth than a newly enfranchised native of Spain—'non Hispanus sed Hispaniensis', to invert Velleius' label for the Gaditane Cornelius Balbus.[1] He has been doubly unfortunate. He was defeated and killed by the Parthians. Had he been successful against the foreign enemy, he might have anticipated the Parthian triumph of that other *novus homo*, P. Ventidius: had he lived, he might have deserted Antonius for Octavianus and become one of the *principes viri* in the New State. But failure and death was the lesser of his misfortunes. In the year 44 B.C. Saxa was on the 'wrong side' in Roman politics. He stood by the consul Antonius. Had he joined the young Octavianus in raising an army in Italy 'privato consilio' and seducing from their sworn loyalty the legions of a consul, with what high-minded and patriotic fervour would not Cicero have | acclaimed a good citizen, even if born in Spain, even if the son of alien parents? The theme and the words were already there:[2]

Atque utinam qui ubique sunt propugnatores huius imperi possent in hanc civitatem venire, et contra oppugnatores rei publicae de civitate exterminari! neque enim ille summus poeta noster Hannibalis illam magis cohortationem quam communem imperatoriam voluit esse:

> hostem qui feriet, erit (inquit) mihi Carthaginiensis
> quisquis erit.

cuius civitatis sit, id habent hodie leve et semper habuerunt, itaque et civis undique fortis viros adsciverunt et hominum ignobilium virtutem persaepe nobilitatis inertiae praetulerunt.[3]

---

[1] Velleius ii 51, 3.   [2] Cicero, *pro Balbo* 51.

[3] The world of learning owes debts many and varied to Sir Henry Stuart Jones: it is the Camden Professor and historian of Rome that Oxford knows best. In Roman history, wherever knowledge may be deepened and however horizons may be widened, the transformation of the Roman State and the transition from Republic to Principate must ever claim the centre of interest. For this reason a paper concerning one of Caesar's partisans, a military man from Spain, may be offered as a tribute from the School of *Literae Humaniores*—and from one of the three Colleges with which Sir Henry's life in Oxford has been identified. [Volume xxvii of *JRS* was dedicated to Sir Henry Stuart Jones; this note appeared at the head of the original article.]

4

Pamphylia from Augustus to Vespasian

ON the authority of the historian Cassius Dio it was not uncommonly believed that Pamphylia constituted a separate province in the time of Augustus. Independent evidence, however, tells against this persuasion: in *Klio* xxvii (1934), the present writer sought to prove that Pamphylia was united with Galatia in a single provincial command;[1] and further, that this command was held, usually no doubt by legates of Augustus praetorian in rank, but on three occasions at least by men of consular standing, namely by L. Calpurnius Piso, by P. Sulpicius Quirinius, and by M. Plautius Silvanus, whom evidence literary or epigraphic connects with Pamphylia, with Galatia, or with both regions.

For the sake of simplicity and convenience it may be worth while to investigate briefly the further vicissitudes of Pamphylia down to the time when it was united with Lycia by Vespasian, a lasting change. The ancient evidence is ambiguous as well as scanty, and most modern authorities have refrained from considering as a whole the problem of the status of Pamphylia during the Julio-Claudian period. |

The first mention of Pamphylia after Augustus has reference to the year 43. Dio states that Claudius, when depriving the Lycians of their freedom, allotted them to the province of Pamphylia.[2] Most scholars have

---

[1] 'Galatia and Pamphylia under Augustus: the Governorships of Piso, Quirinius and Silvanus', *Klio* xxvii (1934), 122 ff. In a matter irrelevant to the main purpose of that paper, but arising from Dio's account of the dominions of King Amyntas (xlix 32, 3) and of their disposal after his death in 25 B.C. (liii 26, 3) the writer, in order to give a meaning to Dio's words, felt compelled to assume that the Pamphylian coast had not been a part of the Galatian kingdom of Amyntas. This appears to be false—Amyntas coined at Side in Pamphylia: see W. Wroth, *B.M. Cat. of Greek Coins, Galatia, Cappadocia and Syria* (1899), xviii; Head, *Historia Numorum*[2] (1911), 747. Dio states the existence of a separate province of Pamphylia before and after 25 B.C.—he is clearly in error, and, as already indicated (*Klio* xxvii (1934), 122), the contemporary Strabo should be followed in these matters. Strabo twice says that the Romans converted the whole of the Galatian kingdom into a province (xii 5, 1, p. 567, cf. xii 6, 5, p. 569). The opinion of L. R. Taylor and T. R. S. Broughton (*AJP* lv (1933), 127 f.; 139 ff.) that in the time of Augustus Pamphylia was attached to the province of Asia is refuted by the dedication to Plautius Silvanus at Adalia describing him as πρεσβευτὴν ἀντιστράτηγον Αὐτοκράτορος Καίσαρος Σεβαστοῦ (*SEG* vi 646, cf. *Klio* xxvii (1934), 139 ff.).

[2] Dio lx 17, 3: τούς τε Λυκίους στασιάσαντας ὥστε καὶ Ῥωμαίους τινὰς ἀποκτεῖναι, ἐδουλώσατό τε καὶ ἐς τὸν τῆς Παμφυλίας νόμον ἐσέγραψεν. Suetonius, *Divus Claudius* 25.

Klio xxx (1937), 227–31.

doubted the truth of this statement,[1] and refused to accept a province of Lycia–Pamphylia; their reason is that in A.D. 50 a procurator is attested in Pamphylia,[2] while Lycia, *c*. A.D. 58 at least, is governed by an imperial legate of praetorian rank, C. Licinius Mucianus.[3] The second of these points, however, is invalidated by an inscription discovered at Adalia shortly before the outbreak of the war of 1914: it proves that Mucianus governed Pamphylia as well as Lycia.[4]

Pamphylia and Lycia formed one province, under Mucianus *c*. A.D. 58. We may therefore suppose that Dio is correct in his view that Claudius joined the two regions in A.D. 43; the knowledge, for such I venture to think it can be called, that Galatia and Pamphylia were a single province in the time of Augustus explains what happened—Claudius severed Pamphylia from Galatia and united it with Lycia to form an entirely new province.

Was there a temporary interruption of this quite satisfactory union *c*. A.D. 50? An inscription of that year from Adalia records the repair of roads by an imperial procurator, M. Arruntius Aquila.[5] Does this justify the assumption that Pamphylia had been made a procuratorial province? At first sight it might appear so, until | one recalls that from similar evidence it was once inferred that the senatorial province of Bithynia was placed under procurators by Claudius, and, again, for a time by Vespasian. This was the opinion of Hirschfeld;[6] it involved peculiar difficulties and was rightly rejected by Brandis.[7] More recently, Seltman has shown that Bithynian coins of the same type and die bear indifferently the superscription of either Attius the proconsul or Junius Cilo the procurator (A.D. 54 or 55); likewise in A.D. 78, Naso the procurator and M. Salvidius Asprenas the proconsul.[8] The high rank and exceptional powers of the procurators

---

[1] E. Groag, *RE* iii ('Ti. Claudius Nero Germanicus'), col. 2795; C. Smilda, *Vita Divi Claudi*, 122; Dessau on *ILS* 215; A. Momigliano, *Claudius: the Emperor and his Achievement*, 111. Dessau (in his *Geschichte der römischen Kaiserzeit*) and *CAH* x express no opinion about the status of Pamphylia in the Julio-Claudian period; *CAH* xi (15, n. 3 and 590) is self-contradictory.

[2] Dessau, *ILS* 215: '[T]i. Claudius Drus[i f.] Caesar Au[g. G]erm[an]icus pontif. maxim[u]s, tr. po[t.] X., imp. XIIX, p.p., cos. desi[g.] V, [p]er M. Ar[ru]ntium Aqu[il]am procur. su[um] vias refecit.' (The Greek translation follows.)

[3] Dessau, *ILS* 8816 (Oenoanda). Pliny twice describes Mucianus as governor of Lycia (*NH* xii 9; xiii 88). He was perhaps the immediate successor of Eprius Marcellus, tried for extortion in A.D. 57 (Tacitus, *Ann.* xiii 33).

[4] *Mon. Antichi della R. Acc. dei Lincei* xxiii (1914), 214; *AE* 1915, 48. As follows: [Γά]ον Λικίνιον Μουκιανὸν πρεσβευτὴν Νέρωνος Καίσαρος Σεβαστοῦ Γε[ρμανικοῦ ἀν]τιστ[ράτηγον] . . . Kappelmacher (*RE* xiii, coll. 436 ff.) and Momigliano (*Claudius*) have neglected this piece of evidence.

[5] Dessau, *ILS* 215.

[6] *Die kaiserlichen Verwaltungsbeamten*² (1905), 374 f.; *Kleine Schriften*, 566 f.

[7] *RE* iii, coll. 527, 533.

[8] C. T. Seltman, 'The Administration of Bithynia under Claudius and Nero', *NC* Ser. 5, viii (1928), 101 ff.; cf. C. Bosch, *Die kleinasiatischen Münzen der röm. Kaiserzeit* ii 1, *Bithynien*, i 88 ff.

of the province of Bithynia–Pontus have been fully illustrated by a study of Rostovtzeff.[1] Now L. Antonius Naso, procurator in the senatorial province of Bithynia, superintends the construction of a road and sets up a milestone:[2] is it necessary to hold that the procurator who repaired roads in Pamphylia must have been the governor of that province? It may be that Pamphylia was a procuratorial province for a short interval. Lycia too? If not, the corollary would be that Lycia was either liberated again by the inconstant Claudius, or remained under an imperial legate—a tiny and peculiar province indeed. This is difficult to believe.

A simple solution emerges. Like Lycia, Pamphylia appears to be too small in area to constitute a separate province either under Augustus[3] or under his successors. Moreover, given the number of its cities, Pamphylia was singularly unfitted to be governed by a procurator. It follows that the man Arruntius Aquila who repaired the roads of Pamphylia was not praesidial procurator of Pamphylia, but financial procurator of Galatia.[4] Of the way in which administrative and financial provinces overlapped in the Roman Empire, there is abundant evidence. Upper and Lower Germany, for example, were comprised in the *provincia* of the procurator of Gallia Belgica. But it is not necessary to depart from Pamphylia in the search for a parallel. In the time of Hadrian, when Lycia–Pamphylia and Galatia were separate provinces, | governed each by an imperial legate, they belonged to the financial competence of a single procurator, as epigraphic evidence attests.[5]

It is therefore highly dangerous to assume that a procurator ever governed Pamphylia; and Lycia–Pamphylia was certainly a single province in 58, under an imperial legate. How long did this arrangement subsist?

In 55 Corbulo was appointed to a special command in the East, probably the province of Cappadocia–Galatia, formed specially for that purpose, and maintained, it is to be presumed, under his successor Caesennius Paetus in 61–2, a foreshadowing of the permanent Flavian arrangement. Groag has suggested that Pamphylia was attached to his province.[6] The evidence comes from Statius' panegyric of C. Rutilius Gallicus (*Silvae*, i 4, 76 ff.),

> hunc Galatea vigens ausa est incessere bello
> (me quoque), perque novem timuit Pamphylia messes
> Pannoniusque ferox arcuque horrenda fugaci
> Armenia et patiens Latii iam pontis Araxes.

[1] 'Pontus, Bithynia and the Bosporus', *PBSA* xxii (1916–18), 1 ff.
[2] Dessau, *ILS* 253.
[3] Cf. *Klio* xxvii (1934), 126.
[4] [Pflaum, *CPE* iii 1074, still lists him as 'Procurator Provinciae Pamphyliae (C)'.]
[5] *CIL* iii 431 = *ILS* 1449 '. . . proc. Lyc. Pamp. Galat. Paphl. Pisid. Pont.' Cf. *CIL* iii 7116, which adds Lycaonia.
[6] *RE* i A, coll. 1257 f.

Now Rutilius Gallicus is described on an Ephesian inscription as 'legatus (not 'legatus pro praetore') provinciae Galaticae',[1] and Groag infers that he was one of Corbulo's legates. This is pretty certain: but was Pamphylia a part of the province of Galatia–Cappadocia? One might doubt whether the testimony of Statius should be here pressed too closely, whether indeed Statius himself knew or cared about the exact territorial limits of Rutilius' official functions. About chronological order, we know that he did not worry, for Rutilius' command in Pannonia (as legate of XV Apollinaris, c. A.D. 54)[2] preceded, not followed, his service in Galatia. Furthermore, it is difficult to discern the purpose of attaching Pamphylia to Galatia at this time. Pamphylia and Galatia go quite well together, as under Augustus, likewise Cappadocia and Galatia, as under the Flavians; but Cappadocia–Galatia–Pamphylia is a rather unwieldy combination. In its favour there is no single and unequivocal piece of evidence. Moreover, as late as 58 we know that Pamphylia and Lycia were still united.[3]

Pamphylia next turns up in the year 69. 'Galatiam ac Pamphyliam provincias Calpurnio Asprenati regendas Galba per|miserat'.[4] There has been a change, and Lycia has been liberated. Who was the author of this innovation, Nero or Galba? The answer might appear to be simple, given the known ruinous generosity of Nero attested by his liberation of Hellas and his posthumous fame over all the East. But there is something that tells against Nero—the language of Tacitus. If Tacitus had said 'provinciam', instead of 'provincias', one would infer that Galatia–Pamphylia was already in existence as a single province when Calpurnius Asprenas was appointed. As Tacitus says 'Galatiam ac Pamphyliam provincias', it appears that the appointment of Calpurnius Asprenas made two provinces into one. It would follow that Galba, to combine Galatia and Pamphylia in the hand of one governor, had severed Lycia from its provincial partner and made it autonomous.

If so, this was the only change made by Galba in provincial administration with the exception of the transference of the Avantici and Bodiontici with their town of Dinia (Digne, Basses-Alpes) from the Alpes Maritimae to the province of Gallia Narbonensis.[5]

Whether made by Nero or by Galba, the change was ill-advised and transient. Vespasian deprived Lycia of liberty, a measure dated by Jerome to the year 73/4[6]—probably too late. As Vespasian required Galatia for

---

[1] Dessau, *ILS* 9499.   [2] Ibid., cf. *CIL* iii 4591.   [3] Under Mucianus.
[4] Tacitus, *Hist.* ii 9. Add perhaps the fragmentary inscription from Pisidian Antioch, published by Ramsay (*JRS* vi (1916), 134) and referred to this man by Groag, *PIR*² ii (1936), C 240. [*IRT* 346 registers Asprenas as governor of 'Galatia Paphlagonia Pisidia Pamphylia'—making the absence of Lycia certain.]   [5] Pliny, *NH* iii 37.
[6] Eusebius ed. Schoene, p. 159; Suetonius, *Divus Vespasianus* 8. [W. Eck, *ZPE* vi (1970), 71 ff., adduces persuasive arguments in favour of 74. He also (ibid. 65 ff.) argues for the presence of Sex. Marcius Priscus in Lycia as governor under Nero and Vespasian and rejects Suetonius' implication of its 'freedom'.]

the vast consular province of Cappadocia–Galatia, Pamphylia was left upon his hands. This meant the reconstitution of Claudius' province of Lycia–Pamphylia, by no means the only example of Vespasian's adoption of Claudian precedents.

If the above reconstruction is accepted, a clear and simple statement of the provincial permutations will emerge, namely, Galatia–Pamphylia from Augustus to Claudius with Lycia enjoying liberty; Lycia–Pamphylia from Claudius to Galba; under Galba a reuniting of Galatia and Pamphylia and liberation of the Lycian, temporary both and revoked by Vespasian.

5

The Origin of Cornelius Gallus[1]

C. CORNELIUS GALLUS requires brief introduction or none at all. A poet in his own right, the friend of Virgil and of Pollio, Gallus is enshrined for ever in literature—and in literary legend, for the inept fictions of Servius and his tribe will survive the most damaging of revelations, remembered even when refuted.[2] Not only that—Gallus is a conspicuous figure in the social and political history of the revolutionary age.

The first appearance of Gallus puts him at once in select and lettered company. Pollio describes him as a friend.[3] Gallus cut a dash in high society—the freedwoman Volumnia, commonly known as Cytheris, the most accomplished courtesan of the day, accorded for a time her favours and inspiration to the poet. But Gallus was not only a poet and a lover. His earliest adventures in war and politics from 43 B.C. to the War of Actium have left no mark in authentic historical record.[4] Pollio was a friend and adherent of Antonius; when Gallus turns up again, it is as one of the most prominent members of the faction of Octavianus. Active in the conquest of Egypt, he remained in the land as its first viceroy. His rule in Egypt, signalized by military exploits and the erection of magniloquent inscriptions,[5] was the cause—or at least the pretext—of his ruin.

[1] [See now J.-P. Boucher, *Caius Cornélius Gallus* (Paris, 1966), with discussion of the new readings of the Vatican Obelisk (cf. *AE* 1964, 255), pp. 33 ff. Cf. also *AE* 1968, 531.]

[2] W. B. Anderson and E. Norden may fairly be held to have demolished at last Servius' allegation that the second half of the Fourth Georgic was originally devoted to the laudation of Gallus ('Gallus and the Fourth Georgic', *CQ* xxvii (1933), 36 ff.; 'Orpheus u. Eurydice', *SPAW* (1934), 627 ff.), and the present writer cannot dissemble his conviction that the stories about Pollio's son Saloninus and Pollio's capture of the town of Salonae are merely 'gelehrte Namenfabelei'—and not so 'gelehrt' at that (*CQ* xxxi (1937), 39 ff. [above, pp. 19 ff.]). Norden's observations about the value of the scholia on the Latin poets are timely and trenchant: they will support scepticism about Virgil's estate and Gallus' role in its recovery (below, n. 4).

[3] *Ad. fam.* x 32, 5, 'etiam praetextam, si voles legere, Gallum Cornelium, familiarem meum, poscito.' Gallus is probably referred to in the earlier letter as well (31, 6).

[4] He may well have served on Pollio's staff in Gallia Cisalpina in 42–40 B.C.; but the details of his activity as a land-commissioner or the like, and his service in saving the farm of Virgil, explicitly but not always consistently related by the scholiasts and ancient lives of Virgil (Diehl, *Die Vitae Vergilianae*, 51 ff.; *PIR*[2] ii, C 1369), may not safely be invoked. For this reason I cannot follow the learned and elegant reconstruction of J. Bayet, 'Virgile et les "triumviri agris dividundis"', *REL* vi (1928), 270 ff.

[5] Dio liii 23, 5 ff.; *ILS* 8995 (Philae).

Classical Quarterly xxxii (1938), 39–44.

Threatened with prosecution or actually condemned, Gallus took his own life (27 or 26 B.C.).

All this is part and parcel of common knowledge. 'Gallus et Hesperiis et Gallus notus Eois.'[1] There is one fact, however, that does not seem to have received the attention that it deserves—the place of his birth. According to the Chronicle of St. Jerome (under the year 27 B.C.), the poet was born at Forum Iulii—'Cornelius Gallus Foroiuliensis poeta, a quo primum Aegyptum rectam supra diximus, XLIII aetatis suae anno propria se manu interficit.'[2] The notice, in so far as concerns Gallus' origin, is umimpeachable. Jerome derived most of his facts from Suetonius. His dates for the birth and death of literary figures, however, are sometimes his own.

Now comes a small difficulty. There were two places called Forum Iulii. When the name 'Foroiuliensis' is employed without qualification, which is meant, the naval harbour and colony of Roman veterans in Gallia Narbonensis (the modern Fréjus) or the *municipium* (Cividale di Friuli) in Italy beyond the Po? The first | choice should be for the former, without question or comment.[3] Yet some, in scruple praiseworthy but excessive, are unable to make up their minds;[4] and Camille Jullian, the historian of Gaul, in all the eight volumes of his massive work makes no mention of Gallus at all and by implication at least denies him a place among the Narbonensians illustrious in politics and in literature. Of the poets he writes, 'en dehors de Varron, la Gaule n'a donné aucun grand nom à la poésie durant les trois premiers siècles de l'Empire'.[5]

Exclusion is brutal, doubt a supererogation. Had it not given a name to a region of Italy (Friuli), who today would know of that obscure settlement of the 'Foroiulienses cognomine Transpadani', whom the statistical Pliny the Elder mentions only because he must, and damns in the same breath, 'quos scrupulosius dicere non attineat'?[6] On the other hand, the famous Narbonensian colony, 'vetus et illustris Foroiuliensium colonia', as Tacitus appropriately designates the home of his father-in-law,[7] neither receives nor requires any regional qualification. There could be no confusion.

Jerome, dating Gallus' death to 27 B.C., says that he was then forty-three years old. That is to say, he was born in 70 B.C., coeval with Virgil. The date should not be pressed too closely; and quiet scepticism in the face of precise chronology in matters that were never easy to ascertain, never widely made public—or of any real importance—will do nobody any harm. Thus there were even differences of opinion among ancient

---

[1] Ovid, *Am.* i 15, 29.   [2] *Chron.*, 188 Ol., p. 164 H.
[3] e.g. Schanz–Hosius, *Röm. Literaturgesch.* ii⁴ (1935), 170; *PIR*² ii, C 1369; F. Plessis, *La Poésie latine*, 290; Wight Duff, *A Literary History of Rome*² (1927), 550.
[4] C. Pascal, 'De Cornelii Galli vita', *RFIC* xvi (1887), 399; A. Stein, *RE*, s.v. 'Cornelius', col. 1343 and *Der röm. Ritterstand* (1927), 384.
[5] *Histoire de la Gaule* vi 147.   [6] *NH* iii 130.   [7] *Agr.* 4.

scholars about the year of birth of the Emperor Tiberius.[1] As for Gallus, the synchronism with Virgil may well excite suspicion; 70 B.C. was indeed an epochal year for students of Roman literary history.[2] It will further be recalled how the chronology of Lucretius was established with reference to the life of Virgil. But this is irrelevant. Gallus was born about 70 B.C., that is near enough. At that time the Roman colony of Forum Iulii had not yet come into existence. What is one to make of that?

The history of the site and its neighbourhood will provide an explanation. The date of the foundation of the veteran colony is not quite certain. Some, such as C. Jullian,[3] would take it back to the Dictatorship of Caesar, to 46 or 45 B.C. This is perhaps too early. The year 36 B.C., after the termination of the war against Sex. Pompeius, should not be at once excluded. However that may be, Kromayer argues (and most scholars since have followed him) that the colony was established soon after the Battle of Actium.[4] But this was not the beginning of Forum Iulii; the place owed its name and organization to Julius Caesar. It was one of those *fora*, or | market-places, without full municipal rights, which were so frequently established at suitable points along the great roads. Forum Iulii lacked a good natural harbour, it is true; but the site was of great strategic importance, on the main route from Italy to Spain, the environment fertile and attractive. It would be tempting to assume that there was some kind of settlement here or near by before Caesar's foundation, perhaps before the Roman conquest. So at least Jullian plausibly conjectures.[5] It is to be regretted that the neighbourhood can show as yet none of that archaeological evidence which makes the town of Glanum (Saint-Rémy de Provence) so unequivocal a document of the early Hellenization and early Romanization of Gallia Narbonensis.[6]

[1] Suetonius, *Tib.* 5.

[2] Jerome dates the death of Gallus to 27 B.C., Dio, however (liii 23, 5 ff.), to 26 B.C. It is sometimes assumed that Dio must be right here (R. Helm, 'Hieronymus' Zusätze in Eusebius' Chronik und ihr Wert für die Literaturgeschichte', *Philologus*, Supp. xxi 2 (1929), 60). But, given Dio's methods of composition, that is by no means certain. It is therefore unjustifiable to accept Jerome for the age of Gallus but not for the date of his death, and so put his birth in 69 or 68 (as Schanz–Hosius, *Röm. Literaturgesch.* ii⁴ (1935), 170). That surely misses the point of the alleged synchronism with Virgil. (I would assume that Jerome's original datum, whether right or wrong, was the year 27 B.C. Hence, given the synchronism with Virgil, the age of Gallus could be calculated.) Note also that one, but strangely only one, of the Virgilian scholiasts (Probus, *Ecl. praef.*) makes Virgil a 'condiscipulus' of Gallus—possibly true but not authentic.

[3] *Histoire de la Gaule* iv 31.

[4] J. Kromayer, 'Die Militärkolonien Octavians und Caesars in Gallia Narbonensis', *Hermes* xxxi (1896), 1 ff.; E. Kornemann, *RE*, s.v. 'Colonia', col. 529; E. Meyer, *Caesars Monarchie und das Principat des Pompejus*³ (1922), 488; A. Donnadieu, *La Pompéi de la Provence: Fréjus* (1927), 12 ff. [F. Vittinghoff, *Röm. Kolonisation* (1952), 160, accepting the conjecture that Caesar gave it Latin status.]

[5] *Histoire de la Gaule* ii 459: 'je crois Fréjus une station commerciale antérieure à la conquête.'

[6] P. Jacobsthal and E. Neuffer, 'Gallia Graeca', *Préhistoire* ii (1933), 1 ff.; P. de Brun,

At once the question arises, was Cornelius Gallus of native or of Italian extraction? The Romans founded a colony with full citizen rights at Narbo in 118 B.C.; and the province was invaded by Roman traders, businessmen, and bankers.[1] At the same time, the Roman citizenship spread among the natives, through patronage and gift of proconsuls, at a quite early date. The agency of C. Valerius Flaccus (82–80 B.C.) and of Cn. Pompeius Magnus is splendidly attested. Flaccus gave the franchise to Caburus, the chieftain of the Helvii: his son, C. Valerius Procillus (or Troucillus), a cultivated and admirable young man, was a friend of Julius Caesar.[2] A dynast of the Vocontii fought for Pompeius in the Sertorian War and was suitably rewarded; his son, Pompeius Trogus, was the private secretary of Caesar; his grandson took to writing history.[3]

When the Romans established a provincial colony, they often associated in the foundation certain of the better sort of the natives with grant of the citizenship.[4] In some places there were already Roman citizens to be found antedating the colony. Thus at Arelate the ancestors of Pompeius Paullinus probably go back before the Caesarian colony;[5] likewise, at Forum Iulii itself, the family of Cn. Iulius Agricola presumably possessed the franchise before 30 B.C., having received it from Caesar. It may be conjectured that the great-grandfather was a local dynast, Celtic or rather perhaps Celto-Ligurian, wealthy, civilized and respected, resident in the neighbourhood of Forum Iulii. Is the origin of Cornelius Gallus to be discovered in this class?

Nomenclature often helps. Gallus was the son of a Roman citizen, his full name being C. Cornelius Cn. f. Gallus.[6] His *cognomen* may suggest, but cannot alone prove, native extraction. What of the gentile name 'Cornelius'? It seems too common to be of any use. Sulla the Dictator liberated ten thousand slaves; and Cornelii were so frequent at Rome, says Cicero, that they could form a guild of their own.[7] Like the 'common soldiers' whom Sulla put into the Senate, the serried ranks of his freedmen exercise a baneful and perverse influence upon history; and the proportion

---

Assoc. Guillaume Budé, Congrès de Nîmes (1932), 136 ff.; H. Rolland, *Saint-Rémy de Provence* (Bergerac, 1934).

[1] *Pro Fonteio* 11, 13, 15, etc.

[2] Caesar, *BG* i 19, 47 and 53; vii 65. On the name, Procillus or Troucillus, cf. Rice Holmes's discussion, *Caesar's Conquest of Gaul*[2], 652.

[3] Justin xliii 5, 11 f. Caesar's secretary is perhaps, but not necessarily, the interpreter Cn. Pompeius (*BG* v 36).

[4] Tacitus, *Ann.* xi 24: 'cum specie deductarum per orbem terrae legionum additis provincialium validissimis fesso imperio subventum est.'

[5] Pliny (*NH* xxxiii 143) describes him as 'paterna gente pellitus'. If correct, and Pliny should have known, for he had served under Paullinus in Germania Inferior (he uses the word 'scimus' when describing the legate's silver plate), this means that Pompeius Paullinus of Arelate was of native extraction: an ancestor will have got the franchise from Pompeius.

[6] *ILS* 8995.

[7] Asconius, *In Cornelianam* 67 (Clark, p. 75).

of knights and senators of servile extraction in the first century of the Principate has been grossly exaggerated by prejudice or ignorance.[1] Hence it has | sometimes been stated as a fact that Cornelius Gallus was the son of a freedman.[2]

Gallus had been raised by the favour of Augustus from low estate, 'ex infima fortuna', as Suetonius says.[3] This looks bad. The statement has been accepted and enhanced by modern scholars.[4] What does it really amount to? Gallus is already in high society (Pollio and Cytheris) before he makes his way as a partisan of Octavianus. The term 'ex infima fortuna' is relative—it must be interpreted in its own context, with reference to the station of viceroy of Egypt, without precedent or parallel. But that is not all. If the social terminology of Roman literature is coolly examined, it is seen that allegations of humble and obscure origin, common enough even when there is no patent hostility or prejudice, are attached by convention to *novi homines* in virtue of their lack of previous distinction in public life.[5] Thus the first Pompeius to become consul at Rome is described as 'humili atque obscuro loco natus'.[6] Such disgusting upstarts of lowly or unknown antecedents usually turn out to be highly respectable Roman knights and municipal aristocrats of ancient standing and wealth—'domi nobiles'.

Cn. Cornelius the father of the poet need not be regarded as a freedman or a man of lowly station in society. But the question still remains: if native and not a Roman by birth, where did he get the name 'Cornelius'? When a foreigner acquired the franchise, he had to assume, officially at least, a *praenomen* and *nomen*. If he did not Latinize or translate his own family name, he might adopt the name of the proconsul or magistrate empowered by law (or usurping the right) to grant the citizenship. Hence the names of C. Valerius Caburus and (Cn.?) Pompeius Trogus. But not always; a Roman friend, patron, or benefactor might provide the gentile name of the new citizen. Thus the Sicilian P. Cornelius Megas, who received the franchise from Caesar, was so named to do honour to Cornelius Dolabella, as is expressly recorded.[7] Again, certain Roman

---

[1] Not to be believed is the speaker in Tacitus (*Ann.* xiii 27): 'et plurimis equitum, plerisque senatoribus non aliunde originem trahi.'

[2] F. Plessis, *La Poésie latine*, 290: 'c'est sans doute comme fils d'affranchi qu'il portait le nom de la gens Cornelia.'

[3] Suetonius, *Divus Aug.* 66: 'Salvidienum Rufum quem ad consulatum usque, et Cornelium Gallum, quem ad praefecturam Aegypti, ex infima utrumque fortuna, provexerat.'

[4] F. Plessis, op. cit. 290: 'd'une très humble origine'; *RE*, s.v. 'Cornelius', col. 1343: 'aus ganz ärmlichen Verhältnissen'; cf. E. Bickel, *Gesch. der röm. Lit.* (1937), 533. F. Skutsch, who nowhere mentions Gallus' Narbonensian origin, actually bases an argument upon his 'niedrige Herkunft' (*Gallus u. Vergil* (1906), 126).

[5] Cf. above all M. Gelzer, *Die Nobilität der röm. Republik*, 11 ff. [= *Kl. Schr.* i (1962), 29 ff.]

[6] Cicero, *In Verrem* ii 5, 181.

[7] Cicero, *Ad fam.* xiii 36.

gentile names were favoured for historical, sentimental, or social reasons.
Sicilians were in the habit of usurping the name Cornelius, possibly
a tribute to the Scipios, but largely because its very frequency baffled
detection and encouraged impostors—'quorum civis Romanus nemo erat,
sed Graeci sacrilegi iam pridem improbi, repente Cornelii'.[1]

The name 'Cornelius' seems quite hopeless as a clue. Light comes from
an obscure and kindred problem. L. Cornelius Balbus, the Gaditane magnate, certainly owed the citizenship to Pompeius.[2] Why then did he not
take the name of Pompeius, as did so many others? It is an old problem.
Some have invoked the Lex Gellia Cornelia of 72 B.C., which ratified
Pompeius' acta in Gaul and Spain. That is not very likely. There is more
to be said for the view propounded by Manutius centuries ago. Balbus, as
later emerges, was bound by especial ties of friendship and gratitude to
L. Cornelius Lentulus Crus.[3] The origin of the relationship is unknown
—but Lentulus may well have been with Pompeius in Spain at the time
of the Sertorian War.

On this principle and parallel, it remains to look around for a patron or
friend for the poet's father, called Cn. Cornelius. Not in vain. One has
the choice of | Cn. Cornelius Lentulus Clodianus, the Pompeian consul of
72 B.C., or Cn. Cornelius Lentulus Marcellinus (cos. 56). Both were legates
of Pompeius in the war against the pirates, and both may also have served
earlier under Pompeius, in Spain and Gaul. The one at least, Marcellinus,
was probably Pompeius' quaestor c. 74, to judge by coins.[4]

At the beginning of his special command in the West Pompeius seems
to have held authority over Gaul. Not only did he fight wars and make
dispositions on his way to Spain:[5] he wintered in Narbonensis in 77/6—
and even again in 74/3. It might therefore be conjectured that the parent
of the poet Gallus was a Narbonensian personage of some importance
who rendered service to Rome and her representatives, and who, befriended
by a Cn. Cornelius Lentulus, took the name of his patron when he
received the reward of the Roman citizenship.

To resume: if the foregoing argument is correct, Gallus was not of
colonial Roman or of freedman stock, but, like Caesar's friends Trogus
and Procillus, the son of a local dynast of Gallia Narbonensis. These men
came of a class that was eminently presentable and highly civilized, Greek
before they were Roman; they are the precursors of the famous Narbo-

---

[1] Cicero, In Verrem ii 3, 69.   [2] Cicero, Pro Balbo, passim.
[3] Cicero, Ad Atticum viii 15a, 2; ix 7b, 2; Velleius ii 51, 2.
[4] [Sydenham, CRR 752.] For Pompeius' legates in the Pirate War, cf. Appian, Mithr. 95.
[And see now J. M. Reynolds, JRS lii (1962), 97 ff.] The history of his relations with the
Cornelii Lentuli deserves investigation (cf. above for L. Cornelius Lentulus Crus).
[5] Cf. esp. Pro Fonteio 14, 'ex Cn. Pompei decreto'. Similarly, C. Valerius Flaccus was
active in both regions and triumphed 'ex Celtiberia et Gallia' (Granius Licinianus 39,
Bonn [= 31–2 Fl.])

nensian senators of the first century of the Empire. Caesar the Dictator admitted to the Roman Senate several members of this class, distinguished men and comparable to the Cornelii Balbi from Spain.[1] Their names have not been recorded. Nor are the Narbonensian senators known under Augustus. Cornelius Gallus, the Prefect of Egypt, helps to bridge the gap. A knight of such exalted rank is the social equal of senators, politically a greater power than most consuls in the revived and fraudulent Republic of Augustus. Gallus is a phenomenon but not a portent; he is remarkable but not unique.

Gallus and the other Narbonensians cast a vivid and convincing light upon a process otherwise forbidding because it is in the main impersonal, the Romanization of the provinces of the West, and help to fill out a thin and neglected chapter in the social and political history of provinces and Empire. No less conspicuous, no less solid, is the gain for the study of Latin literature. Of the two great Narbonensian poets, the one, Gallus, was native in origin, not colonial Roman. Perhaps also the other. P. Terentius Varro, the poet of the *Argonautica*, is given by some authors the *cognomen* 'Atacinus';[2] and Jerome states that he was born at the village of Atax in Narbonensis.[3] Now the Atax (Aude) is the river that runs by the colony of Narbo; the geographer Mela describes Narbo itself as 'Atacinorum Decimanorumque colonia'.[4] What is the explanation? We observe that Varro is nowhere called a citizen of the colony of Narbo. It is quite possible that he was, that 'Atacinus' is merely an unofficial, perhaps in origin familiar, depreciatory or poetical epithet applied to Varro to avoid confusion with the learned antiquary from the Sabine country, Varro Reatinus. If Jerome is right, however, and there really was a village called Atax, it may have been a native settlement in, or adjacent to, the territory of the colony of Narbo, into which it was subsequently incorporated with equal rights and full Roman citizenship.[5] Certainty cannot be obtained here. | Whatever be thought of 'Atax' and the adjective 'Atacinus', Varro himself *may* not have been a Roman citizen by birth. One would like to know how and from whom he acquired the name of P. Terentius Varro. Gallus' poems were highly Hellenistic; but

---

[1] Tacitus, *Ann.* xi 24, 'num paenitet Balbos ex Hispania nec minus insignis viros e Gallia Narbonensi transivisse?' On the social status and origin of Caesar's provincial senators, cf. *JRS* xxvii (1937), 127 ff. [above, pp. 31 ff.]. Saxa was probably of colonial Roman stock; not so the younger Balbus, the only other provincial recorded by name.

[2] e.g. Horace, *Sat.* i 10, 46; Quintilian x 1, 87.

[3] Jerome, *Chron.* under 82 B.C. (p. 151 H.): 'vico Atace in provincia Narbonensi.'

[4] Mela ii 75.

[5] As Mela's description of Narbo suggests. Jullian's view that Atax was a town-ward of Narbo (*Histoire de la Gaule* vi 145) is not very helpful. For doubts about the existence of a place called Atax, see F. Lenz, *RE*, s.v. 'Terentius', col. 692; on the name 'Atacinus', O. Hey, *Archiv für lat. Lexikographie* xiv (1906), 269, and J. Wackernagel, ibid. 10 'abweichend *Atacinus: Atax* als Ethnikon des bekannten Dichters; ich kann es nicht erklären'.

Varro, if Jerome be believed, did not learn Greek until the thirty-fifth year of his life.

Narbonensis can show two great poets, Varro and Gallus; and it will be recalled that the historian Cornelius Tacitus, who married the daughter of a senator from Forum Iulii, may himself be a Narbonensian—for certain indications point to that province or to provincial Italy, the land beyond the Po.[1] Once again the name 'Cornelius'—and no suspicion of freedman origin.

In the first century of the Roman Empire, Gallia Narbonensis stood in high repute—'agrorum cultu, virorum morumque dignatione, amplitudine opum nulli provinciarum postferenda breviterque Italia verius quam provincia.'[2] The convergent testimony of archaeology, history, and literature will demonstrate how deep lie the roots of this splendid efflorescence of Graeco-Latin civilization.

[1] Cf. M. L. Gordon, 'The *Patria* of Tacitus', *JRS* xxvi (1936), 145 ff. [and now Syme, *Tacitus*, Ch. XLV].

[2] Pliny, *NH* iii 31.

6

W. Weber, *Rom: Herrschertum und Reich im zweiten Jahrhundert*[1]

WILHELM WEBER'S first contributions to the history of the Antonines took the form of monographs on the sources, notably his *Untersuchungen zur Geschichte des Kaisers Hadrian* (1907) and the long and thorough study of the *Historia Augusta,* reviewing the work of O. Th. Schulz (in *Göttingische Gelehrte Anzeigen,* 1908). Thirty years have passed. Now, after extensive and sometimes remote researches into the world of ancient religions (above all those of the oriental lands) he reverts to the theme of earlier predilection and furnishes a broad survey of the Age of the Antonines, from Trajan to Commodus.

It is a 'popular' book, lacking tight organization and written in elevated and poetical language. Nor is it equipped with annotation or index. In fact, an expansion and remodelling of previous studies. The sections on Trajan and Hadrian derive from Weber's contributions to *Meister der Politik* (iii[1] 39 ff. = i[2] 199 ff.). Hadrian, that most versatile of emperors, now benefits from a third reincarnation. The four rulers Hadrian, Pius, M. Aurelius, and Commodus appeared barely three years ago, as a somewhat abridged English version, in the *Cambridge Ancient History,* vol. xi (1936), 294–392.

The conceptions which the author has formed and expressed are a matter of his own idiosyncrasy. And rightly so. History is not the mere collecting of facts: the exposition must be built up on some leading idea, or indeed on several, and be interpreted in their light. That is all the more necessary in a period devoid of striking transactions—or only on fragmentary record. Such is the Antonine Age, above all its heart and core, the uneventful reign of Antoninus Pius. A desperate problem for a historian. Weber adopts two principles for guidance: the religious evolution and the personalities of five rulers (along with the contrasts they afford).

The first of these principles represents a welcome innovation, all too often ignored or neglected in the past. Historians conceived their task narrowly, being satisfied with the mere factual framework, with the

[1] Stuttgart–Berlin, 1937.

Historische Zeitschrift clviii (1938), 554–61. Originally published in German; English version by the author. No references to the pages of the original text are given here.

details of warfare, finance, and administration. However that may be, certain religious and mystical beliefs, diffused ever more widely in this epoch, are not the whole of life in the Empire—and least of all in the governing class.

The second principle is in no way novel. It is an old friend, or rather an old enemy: namely the interpretation of imperial history through the characters and actions of the different emperors. To acquire a true under- standing of the Roman Empire, the fundamental need, the decisive approach, was to liberate men's minds from the spell of 'Kaiserbiographie'. That is, to see the Empire without the emperors. As Mommsen declared many years ago:

> Wer an die sogenannten Quellen dieser Epoche, auch die besseren geht, bemeistert schwer den Unwillen über das Sagen dessen, was verschwiegen zu werden verdiente und das Verschweigen dessen, was notwendig war zu sagen. . . . Die scharfen Abschnitte, welche in der landläufigen, durch jene Ober- flächlichkeit der Grundlage geirrten Auffassung die Regierungswechsel machen, gehören weit mehr dem Hoftreiben an als der Reichsgeschichte' (*Römische Gesch.* v⁴ (1904), 4).

That is to say, 'Reichsgeschichte' is not 'Kaisergeschichte'. It is something incomparably more important.

Caesar Augustus knew what he was about when he created a new form of government. It was his design to curb the free play of personality in the Commonwealth, and to introduce, in the place of political activity, the habits of duty and the routine of administration. Hence that depressing tone of history under the Caesars about which Tacitus raises complaint: 'nobis in arto et inglorius labor' (*Ann.* iv 32). The typical features of the Antonine period can be detected already in the first century.

With the process of time the character of the individual ruler forfeits influence more and more. It does not matter so much who is the Emperor. He may be a child or an imbecile, he may stay away from the seat of government—provided only that there should be a head, albeit nominal. Good emperors and bad, they lose the power to direct the machinery of State or arrest the stream of events (A. Alföldi, *JRS* xxvii (1937), 254 ff.).

By contrast, in the present book 'Kaiserbiographie' is brought back from banishment and installed with fresh adornments in the citadel of imperial Rome. The Trojan Horse imported a company of armed men: the belly of this creature is blown out with wind and words, it is full of corpses. History is concerned with people, living people. But what can be known about the Antonine rulers as people? To be sure, we possess their biographies, they belong to the 'better *Vitae*' in the *Historia Augusta*. Which is not saying much. All too often biography is impaired by the devices of rhetoricians, moralists, and propagandists, by the conventional figures of 'good' and 'bad' emperors set in sharp contrast. To establish a due balance it will often be expedient to rehabilitate bad emperors, however unattractive they may appear at first sight.

And in the end, human personality is a mystery. By good fortune or ill, Trajan has no extant biography. None the less, there is room for a certain suspicion that he was stylized, to represent the martial valour of old Rome. As Pliny says, 'vident enim Romanum ducem, unum ex illis veteribus et priscis' (*Pan.* 12, 1). Weber recognizes that there is something enigmatic about Trajan: 'Was Zeitgenossen auffingen, in Reden gestalteten, ist reizvoll, aber zuweilen nicht nah genug, doktrinär oder schwärmerisch und subjektiv' (p. 35). Indeed, the figure and portrayal of Trajan raises problems: 'Es scheint einfach und ist doch reich an Spannungen, es mutet römisch an und kann doch nur eine neue römische Gestalt sein, es will "ländliche Wahrheit" sein und ist doch zuerst prunkende Majestät, Kriegsherrlichkeit und völkervernichtender Zwang.'

His Trajan is in fact one of the best parts of the book. But, granted Weber's guiding idea, of what manner is the execution? These five rulers were all of provincial extraction. That is a theme that demands exacting scrutiny—and it is an exciting theme. How and why did they accede to the power? From one point of view it is accident that Trajan became emperor. But not from another: Trajan was a prominent member of the oligarchy of government, holding one of the great military provinces under a weak ruler when there was threat of civil war. Much nonsense has been talked about 'adoptive emperors'. As concerns Nerva's adoption of Trajan, Weber is inclined to dismiss that superficial and conventional notion, 'the choice of the best man'. With reason. How was the choice in fact decided? The sinister influence of that other Spaniard, Licinius Sura, may be suspected (cf. E. Groag, *RE* xiii, col. 475). There is some justification for speaking of a veiled *coup d'état*. Nerva's government was in an extremely difficult position. Nor would all contemporaries have regarded the elevation of Trajan as either natural or satisfactory. The attitude of the governor of Syria was dubious (Pliny, *Ep.* ix 13). It would have been worth mentioning that not long after there was no consular legate in Syria: a legionary legate, Larcius Priscus, carried out his functions (*ILS* 1055).

Weber emphasizes and illustrates the influence of the Spanish group that came to power with Trajan. Likewise, though not so strongly, the families from Narbonensis. Trajan's wife Plotina, he could have added, probably came from Nemausus (cf. *HA Hadr.* 12, 2); and Scaurianus and his son Gentianus, conjectured Narbonensian (E. Groag, *RE* v A, col. 669), deserve at least a mention.

That provincials accede to high office is (as Weber states) neither novel nor demanding an explanation, especially in view of the conspicuous role of Spain in the literature of the early Principate. Balbus, the man from Gades, became consul in 40 B.C. Now Balbus might be regarded as a resplendent exception. However, when one examines the civilization of Spain, and also of Narbonensis, in the last epoch of the Republic, Caesar's behaviour in admitting 'foreigners' to the Roman Senate appears in a different light—not a scandalous and unpardonable act of despotism. None of Caesar's Narbonensian senators is recorded by name, but we know their social stratum. They were men like Procillus, Trogus, and Gallus, of native aristocratic stock, not colonial Romans. Compare remarks in *JRS* xxvii (1937), 131; *CQ* xxxii (1938), 43 [pp. 31 ff., 47 ff. above].

That was long ago. What is the significance of provincial senators and rulers in the high prime of the Empire? Three questions have to be kept separate. First, in the blended ancestry of these men, what was the proportion between colonial and native? Second, what influence did that inheritance exert on mind, character, and comportment? Third, how far did Italians regard them as different, or as alien? It is by no means clear that Weber has put those questions to himself and examined them distinctly before he created his synthesis.

Like environment, the influence of race and extraction on character is of great importance. It would be folly to deny it. Folly also to deny the difficulties of a topic that offers such scope for cloudy thought and obscure language. The families of both Trajan and Hadrian came from Italica in the Spanish province of Baetica. Hadrian's ancestors, so he alleged, had settled there 'in the days of the Scipios', having come from Adria in Picenum.

One might incline to be sceptical about the pedigrees of old colonial families, in any age. However, let that pass. Hadrian's father married a woman from Gades. What conclusions shall one thence draw for the 'race' of Hadrian? What significance shall we assign to Spanish origin— at least in a geographical sense, over some seven generations? Weber writes:

> Kräften der Mitte und der Peripherie des Reiches, der Mischung von illyrisch-italischem und iberisch-afrikanischem Blut entstammte Hadrians Kraft. Der Ozean, die bald üppige, bald sonnverbrannte Ebene, der trägströmende Fluß der heimatlichen Landschaft am Südwestrand des Reichs hatten auf sein Geschlecht und seine Kindheit formend gewirkt (p. 228).

That looks impressive, and is vividly written. Is it convincing?

As concerns the boyhood of Hadrian, the climate and the landscape of Andalusia can have had no influence at all, if we believe, as is credibly stated, that he was born at Rome (*HA Hadr.* 1, 3), visited Italica only for a short time when he was about fifteen years old (ibid. 2, 1)—and never saw that city again. [Cf. pp. 617 ff., below.] And how explain the marked divergence in character between the two Spaniards, Trajan and Hadrian. Is it only the mother from Gades? And take another Spaniard, Marcus Aurelius, descendant of the Annii from Uccubi:

In der Familie erzählte man, und ein späterer Historiker hat, offenbar nachprüfend und weiterforschend, dies als berechtigt anerkannt, daß altitalisches Blut vom Sabiner Numa, dem frommen König Roms, und illyrisches vom alten sallentinischen König Malemnius, dem Gründer der kalabrischen Stadt Lopiae, in ihren Adern floß (p. 284).

Naturally, that comes from the *Historia Augusta* (*Marcus* 1, 6). Weber seems to accord credit, for on the same page he speaks of 'sabinisches Blut' in the veins of the Annii. It is a pity that we know of no ancient historian who recognized and held for proven the claim of the Annii to go back to Numa Pompilius, the Sabine king of Rome. One would know how to deal with him.

These two specimens will serve to illustrate the dangers of biography and genealogy when combined as a method of scholarly research. Concentration on the remote, obscure, and often (it must be confessed) highly dubious ancestry of the provincial emperors conceals the truth. It is simple enough. The political success of these men, and their personality, is not a direct consequence of their pedigree. Certainly, the Spaniards and the men from Narbonensis came rapidly to the fore. It was because they belonged to a successful group in the governmental oligarchy. What mattered was precisely education, wealth, and social rank. The Antonine Empire achieved a master-stroke in disguising the predominance of the rich under the mask and justification of ancient Roman standards of civic virtue in alliance with Greek culture.

For those reasons undue preoccupation with the origin and the ancestors of those emperors leads all too easily into error. Better, regard the governmental oligarchy as a whole. It is clear that, whatever be the ostensible form of government, Monarchy or Republic, there must be an oligarchy somewhere. The provincials, Trajan at the head, make their way in politics and seize the power because they are leading members of the oligarchy: wealth, rank, prestige. They are not the only members, nor do any divergences of education subsist, according to family or province. Antonine society is eminently cosmopolitan. As early as the year 94, a joint consulship was held by Valerius Asiaticus, of Celtic dynastic stock from Vienna of the Allobroges, and A. Julius Quadratus, a man from Pergamum. It is not at all likely that these two exhibited a notable difference in character, education, and social standing.

Since Weber attaches such great importance to the question of origin and pedigree, his views have here been discussed at some length. To turn to other matters. Trajan passed, as Weber shows, a large part of his career

on the periphery of the Empire: he had a feeling for space and distance, a
'Raumfantasie'. The historian should therefore emulate the emperor and
think in terms of geography. This author, however, is not exempt from
error. He maintains, for example, that after the Armenian campaign of the
year 114 a Roman army must have occupied Hyrcania and other regions
(p. 117). A glance at the map will excite doubt. Further, the frontier of
Germania Superior in the time of Hadrian is designated an 'Erdwall'
(p. 169); and the Brigantes in Britain are described as a people living to
the north of the Wall of Hadrian (p. 270).

There are other mistakes. It is alleged that there was a Parthian War
under Vespasian (p. 24). That cannot be. It is refuted by the express
testimony of a contemporary writer, namely Tacitus, who states that war
nearly broke out because of a false Nero (*Hist.* i 2, 1): that is to say, on
another occasion, presumably *c.* 88, under Domitian. Trajan is called
governor of Germania Superior shortly before the death of Domitian
(p. 27). Possibly correct—but the sole extant evidence states that he got
his command from Nerva (Pliny, *Pan.* 9, 5). Hadrian was hardly a nephew
of Trajan: the son of a cousin (*HA Hadr.* 1, 4). Further, Hadrian as
emperor visiting his home-town (p. 188): that is expressly denied by
Cassius Dio (lxix 10, 7).

This book does not always make the best selection of facts. Weber is
disposed to accept in a modified form the allegation of the miserable
Antiochene chronicler Johannes Malalas that the Parthians captured the
capital of Syria in the year 113/14. Further, we are twice vouchsafed the
information (pp. 149, 164) that in Hadrian's war no fewer than 580,000
Jews of military age perished in battle, to say nothing of the victims of
sieges and guerrilla warfare. The total of Palestinian population which
this figure implies would make Karl Julius Beloch turn in his grave.

The relative value to be attached to the different types of evidence is a
delicate question. For many tastes too much trust seems to be put in the
Historia Augusta and in coins, not enough in inscriptions. The standard
portrayal of Verus, a luxurious wastrel, is reproduced in this book. One
need not be desirous of a total rehabilitation—but what the *HA* reports
looks surprisingly like a rhetorical counterpart to the sanctified figure of
his imperial colleague, the philosopher M. Aurelius (cf. recently P.
Lambrechts, *L'Antiquité classique* iii (1934), 173 ff.). Also, one cannot take
quite seriously the emperor's injunction, when he came back to Italy in
176, that all soldiers should put on togas (p. 327, cf. *HA Marcus* 27, 3).
What a spectacle! Where did they get the togas? From robbing graves
(cf. Juvenal iii 172)?

The legends on coins are certainly a valuable source of information.
But what do they really have to tell us? All too often what the government wanted the people to believe. That is, not always the truth. It is nice

and edifying to read comforting legends like *Virtus Augusti, Felicitas, Fides Exercituum.* One needs valid evidence. Along with so much trivial or conventional material in the portrayal of Antoninus Pius information should have been supplied about the unsatisfactory behaviour of the governor of Hispania Tarraconensis (whatever it may have been) as recently disclosed: 'quod provinciam Hispaniam hostiliter [in]quietaverit' *NSA* 1934, 256). Moreover, the war in Britain towards the end of the reign: what is the point in adducing a mass of coins (none of them closely datable) with the usual optimistic legends and not mentioning an inscription that reveals an authentic and disturbing fact? The legions in Britain had to be strengthened with reinforcements from the army of Germania Inferior (*ILS* 9116).

The present work does not profess to provide a full and detailed account of warfare, politics, and administration. Nor does it quite succeed in being a social history. It is rather a grandiose synthesis of religious and intellectual currents during a whole epoch of the world's history. As such it must be judged. Many will value it, many not. The title and the author's name will excite high expectations and ensure without any doubt a wide circulation for the book. If a review is to furnish genuine criticism, and not a bare summary or standard appreciation, it must indicate, bold and clear, a number of defects both in the conception and in detail.

7

The Allegiance of Labienus

ILL fortune bore down the family of the Labieni, and an ill repute hangs over their memory. Q. Labienus, an ally of Saturninus, perished miserably, cut down in the Curia by good citizens. His nephew, T. Labienus, Caesar's legate in Gaul from the first campaign to the last, deserted to Pompeius Magnus at the outbreak of the Civil War, conveying promises which he failed to implement, was held in scant honour by his new allies, and met his death at Munda. The son of Caesar's marshal, a renegade styling himself 'Parthicus imperator', invaded the provinces of the Roman People and swept through Syria and Cilicia into Asia with an army of Parthian cavalry: he was defeated in battle and killed by Ventidius the Picene and the Marsian Poppaedius, generals of Antonius.

Little wonder, therefore, that the last Labienus of whom history has record, a vigorous orator towards the end of the reign of Augustus, was a sour and embittered character, refusing to emulate the docile troop of his contemporaries in their alacrity to profit from the new order in State and society.[1] 'Summa egestas erat, summa infamia, summum odium.' Labienus was truculent and ferocious. They called him 'Rabienus'. He also wrote history, in subject and treatment unacceptable to the government. When the Senate, solicitous for order, truth, and propriety, dutifully decreed that the offensive books should be consigned to public conflagration, the author retired to his family sepulchre, taking the manuscript with him, and put an end to his life.

In revulsion from the official or conventional history of the Principate of Augustus, it might be tempting to speculate about this much-neglected person, next to Cassius Severus the greatest orator of the opposition. More advantage, however, may emerge from renewed consideration of the life and career of the best-known member of the family, Caesar's marshal. It need not be done for mere rehabilitation or in the spirit of apology—there is no evidence that Labienus was a virtuous and amiable character.

The military man T. Labienus served with Caesar in Gaul for nine

[1] On the whole family of the Labieni, cf. Münzer, *RE* xii, coll. 257 ff. The principal evidence about the orator and historian T. Labienus is supplied by Seneca, *Controversiae* x, *praef.* 4 ff.

Journal of Roman Studies xxviii (1938), 113–25.

years, in rank and standing second only to the proconsul himself. He earned handsome recognition for merit in Caesar's dispatches and invidious enrichment, named beside the wealth of Mamurra | and the pleasure-gardens of Balbus.[1] Yet Labienus abandoned Caesar for Pompeius, for the oligarchs in the alliance of Pompeius, and for the cause of the constitution. Where is the reason to be sought?

Not in political principle. There was very little of it about at the time. A 'Rechtsfrage' there certainly was, as students know to their cost and sorrow. But it would be hazardous indeed to identify a 'Rechtsfrage' in Roman politics with a question of principle. What mattered was the 'Machtfrage'—would Caesar prevail, or would Cato, in the competition for the support and alliance of Pompeius Magnus?

To turn to the other extreme: was it a pure military calculation that induced Labienus, an experienced soldier, to change sides? That would be reasonable. Other contemporaries were coolly balancing the odds, with scant regard for the 'better cause'.[2] Labienus himself spoke with loud confidence to his new friends, expressing a low estimate of Caesar's military strength.[3] Furthermore, the whole strategy of Pompeius, distasteful if not inexplicable to many of his allies and associates, was simple and masterly. Caesar would be entrapped in Italy or entangled in a guerrilla war in Spain, while Pompeius returned to victory with all the armies and fleets of the eastern lands. Pompeius should have won.[4]

Yet the military calculation may not suffice to explain the conduct of Labienus. Personal grounds must be allowed due weight, friendship and loyalty, family feuds, or recent enmities. Neither Curio nor Caelius could have been on the same side as their personal enemies, Ap. Claudius Pulcher and Ahenobarbus. In this civil war many a man loathed the cause, but followed the friend, ally, or benefactor, as witness Pollio and Matius, on their own authentic and credible testimony.[5] Nor were all the partisans of Caesar possessed of Caelius' robust confidence in success.[6] Far from it: yet all the surviving legates of the Gallic Wars, save only Labienus and Cicero's brother, stood firm by their proconsul.[7]

Only one of the ancient sources assigns a reason for Labienus' behaviour —and it is a personal reason. Cassius Dio states that Labienus began to get

---

[1] *Ad Att.* vii 7, 6: 'et Labieni divitiae et Mamurrae placent et Balbi horti et Tusculanum?' On the theory that T. Labienus is to be identified with the 'Mentula' of certain poems of Catullus, cf. Tenney Frank, 'Cicero and the Poetae Novae', *AJP* xl (1919), 396 ff.

[2] As Caelius observed (*Ad fam.* viii 14, 3): 'illud te non arbitror fugere quin homines in dissensione domestica debeant, quam diu civiliter sine armis certetur, honestiorem sequi partem, ubi ad bellum et castra ventum sit, firmiorem, et id melius statuere quod tutius sit.'

[3] *Ad Att.* vii 16, 2; Caesar, *BC* iii 71, 4; 87, 7 ff.; *Bell. Afr.* 16, 1 f.

[4] Cf. E. Meyer, *Caesars Monarchie und das Principat des Pompejus*[3] (1922), 299 ff.; 309 ff.

[5] *Ad fam.* x 31, 3 (Pollio); xi 28, 2 (Matius).

[6] *Ad fam.* viii 14, 3; 17, 2.

[7] For the full list of his legates, cf. Drumann–Groebe, *Gesch. Roms* iii[2] (1906), 700f.

assertive; that Caesar would not brook his pretensions; that Labienus, offended and apprehensive, therefore deserted.[1] This view commends itself to the moderns. It has been | eloquently expounded by Mommsen. He writes: 'To all appearance Labienus was one of those persons who combine with military efficiency utter incapacity as statesmen, and who, in consequence, if they unhappily choose or are compelled to take part in politics, are exposed to those strange paroxysms of giddiness of which the history of Napoleon's marshals supplies so many tragi-comic examples. He may probably have held himself entitled to rank alongside Caesar as the second chief of the democracy.'[2]

Envy of Caesar, a noble, a patrician, and a statesman as well as a general, further, an overweening sense of his own merits and importance, all this will be conceded in Labienus. But the ultimate reason may lie elsewhere. It remains to investigate the origin and nature of his association with Caesar.

The year of Cicero's consulate opened with clear portents of trouble, among them a group of tribunes eager to exploit certain popular weapons or assert certain principles so as to embarrass the government. The land-bill of Rullus, perhaps a premature proposal, was indeed quickly abandoned by its authors. But before long the tribune T. Labienus re-enacted the *Lex Domitia*, thereby abolishing the Sullan and oligarchic practice of co-optation in the recruitment of the priestly colleges.[3] When the election to the office of *pontifex maximus* followed, the choice of the People fell upon the young patrician Caesar, ambitiously competing against two of the *principes civitatis*, Q. Lutatius Catulus and P. Servilius Vatia. Then came another assertion of the rights of the Roman People—and a warning to the government against the temptation to abuse the *Senatus consultum ultimum*. Nearly forty years before, a certain man called C. Rabirius had killed a Roman citizen, Saturninus. Labienus, satisfying a family feud, prosecuted Rabirius for *perduellio*, under an archaic form of law. It will not be necessary to discuss in detail this not altogether serious transaction:[4] sufficient that Labienus and Caesar were probably acting in concert.[5] Hence

---

[1] Dio xli 4, 4: αἴτιον δὲ ὅτι αὐτός τε καὶ πλοῦτον καὶ δόξαν περιβαλόμενος ὀγκηρότερον τῆς ἡγεμονίας διάγειν ἤρξατο, καὶ ὁ Καῖσαρ παρισούμενόν οἱ αὐτὸν ἰδὼν οὐκέθ᾽ ὁμοίως ἠγάπα. τήν τε οὖν μεταβολὴν μὴ φέρων, καὶ φοβηθεὶς ἅμα μὴ πάθῃ τι, μετέστη.

[2] *The History of Rome* v[2] (1901), 194 f. = *RG* iii 375. Also E. Meyer, *Caesars Monarchie*[3], 347; F. Münzer, *RE* xii, col. 266.

Adcock makes a further and very attractive suggestion—Labienus may have resented the advancement of M. Antonius (*CAH* ix 635). This young *nobilis* had held a military command in 52 and 51; and in 50 Caesar canvassed the Cisalpina for Antonius' election to an augurship (*BG* viii 50).   [3] Dio xxxvii 37, 1.

[4] On the whole question, cf. E. Meyer, *Caesars Monarchie*[3], 549 ff.; T. Rice Holmes, *The Roman Republic* i (1923), 452 ff.; E. G. Hardy, *Some Problems in Roman History* (1924), 110 ff.; J. Lengle, 'Die staatsrechtliche Form der Klage gegen C. Rabirius', *Hermes* lxviii (1933), 328 ff.

[5] Dio xxxvii 26 ff.; Suetonius, *Divus Julius* 12. He and L. Julius Caesar (*cos.* 64 B.C.) were

Labienus is commonly and conveniently regarded as one of Caesar's tribunes, a familiar category.

At this point it is expedient to stop for a moment. The earlier activities of Caesar are fatally open to misconception, being often read in the light of his later career as the clear foreshadowing of all that was to come after with inexorable consequence—the conquest | of Gaul, the rivalry with Pompeius, victory in civil war, and the establishment of the Dictatorship.[1] Similarly the Dictatorship of Caesar has been interpreted, not from itself or from the past, but from the future, as a world-monarchy based on divine right, levelling class and nation, in anticipation of Caracallus.[2] As Tarn so forcibly argues when discussing the historical background of the Fourth Eclogue, it is necessary to forget the future: in 40 B.C., people did not know about Augustus and the *Aeneid*.[3] So let it be with Caesar.

Much of the trouble is due to the prevalence, among writers ancient and modern, of biographic conceptions of history; and a large section of the period which, in political history, could—and should—be designated as the 'Age of Pompeius', is often narrated as the life and actions of Caesar. Hence an exaggeration of the importance of Caesar before his consulate. Strasburger has recently investigated the evidence for Caesar's earlier career.[4] He proves that precious little was known about it; that a number of trivial incidents have been unduly magnified in the light of subsequent history. Caesar was not scheming for the diadem from youth onwards—his actions should be interpreted in a more traditionally Roman and aristocratic fashion.[5] His ambition was that of the Roman noble, the consulate, sharpened by the fact that he came of a patrician house recently emergent from centuries of obscurity.

In the year when Caesar was elected *pontifex maximus*, the dominating factor in Roman politics was the absent Pompeius, in command of the provinces and armies of the East. Politicians in Rome competed for his favour, acting or pretending to act in his interests. Pompeius was a *popularis*, for what the term is worth; and Pompeius had used tribunes to get him power in defiance of the leaders of the governing oligarchy. Cicero's attitude is a valuable indication. He claims that his candidature for the consulate has the benevolent support of Pompeius;[6] and he argues that

the *duoviri* who tried the charge of *perduellio*. The name of Caesar is nowhere mentioned in Cicero's speech *Pro C. Rabirio perduellionis reo*. This need occasion no surprise: Cicero was aware of the danger of incurring a feud with an influential *nobilis*. Moreover, Caesar's role in the whole matter may not have been so very important after all: cf. below, p. 66.

[1] As by Mommsen and recently by Carcopino, *Points de vue sur l'impérialisme romain* (1934), 87 ff., and in his *Histoire romaine* ii 2: *César* (1936).

[2] Especially by E. Meyer, *HZ* xci (1903), 385 ff. = *Kl. Schr.* (1910), 443 ff.; *Caesars Monarchie*[3], 508 ff. For remarks in criticism of this view, *PBSR* xiv (1938), 1 ff. [below, pp. 88 f.].

[3] W. W. Tarn, 'Alexander Helios and the Golden Age', *JRS* xxii (1932), 154.

[4] H. Strasburger, *Caesars Eintritt in die Geschichte* (München, 1938).

[5] Ibid. 126 ff.   [6] *Comm. pet.* 51, cf. 5.

the bill of Rullus is detestable, being directed against the interests of the People's general. Pompeius was soon to return. In the meantime he sent home his legates to stand for office at Rome—and to further his own ambitions. He needed tribunes, praetors—and consuls, if possible.[1]

Among the most eminent of his allies were the two Metelli, Celer and Nepos, half-brothers of his wife Mucia.[2] Both had been | serving as his legates in the Mithridatic War.[3] Celer was elected praetor for 63, Nepos tribune for 62; and in the latter year the consular elections were postponed to permit the candidature of M. Pupius Piso, also a legate of Pompeius.[4]

Caesar had not chosen to seek political advancement and support from Pompeius by serving on his staff in the East. He preferred to remain in Rome, ensuring his praetorship and consulate through mastery of political intrigue, through favour of the populace. No act, however, of hostility towards Pompeius. If Caesar was helped by Crassus, that did not mean that his political allegiance was sealed and consigned once and for all. Certain historical sources indeed record actions of Caesar in Pompeius' interests or in concert with Pompeian agents. He is said, for example, to have spoken both for the *Lex Gabinia* and for the *Lex Manilia*. There is probably some exaggeration here.[5] Again, one source states that Caesar supported the tribunes Labienus and T. Ampius Balbus in their proposal to confer extravagant honours upon Pompeius, namely the right to wear the triumphal attire or a crown of gold on certain ceremonial occasions;[6] which might perhaps be doubted. Again, the measure of his responsibility for the prosecution of Rabirius may well have been exaggerated.[7] However that may be, the praetor Caesar was patently in alliance with the tribune Nepos at the beginning of 62 B.C. in various activities obnoxious to the government. Both were suspended. Nepos fled to Pompeius, with a pretext for war in defence of the tribunes' rights; but Caesar, through moderation, secured reinstatement.[8]

---

[1] For the list of his legates in the Pirate War and in the Mithridatic War, cf. Drumann–Groebe, *Gesch. Roms* iv² (1908), 420 ff.; 486.

[2] The relationship is attested by *Ad fam.* v 2, 6, cf. Dio. xxxvii 49, 3 (the divorce when Pompeius returned from the East).

[3] Dio xxxvi 54, 2 (Celer); Josephus, *BJ* i 127 (Nepos). Nepos had also been in the Pirate War: Appian, *Mithr.* 95.

[4] Dio xxxvii 44, 3. This was done despite Cato, cf. Plutarch, *Cato minor* 30; *Pompeius* 44, whose account of the whole affair is different but not inconsistent.

[5] According to Plutarch, Caesar supported the bill of Gabinius (*Pompeius* 25): in Dio, however (xxxvi 43, 2 ff.), it is the *Lex Manilia*. Strasburger (op. cit. 100 f.) suggests that they derive from a common source and produce, through an error somewhere, a doublet: there was only one speech by Caesar advocating the bill of a Pompeian tribune.

[6] Dio xxxvii 21, 4. Velleius, however (ii 40, 4), mentions only the tribunes who made the proposal. Note also Caesar's bill to take from Catulus and transfer to Pompeius the charge of restoring the Capitol: only in Dio (xxxvii 44, 1 f.). Compare the observations of Strasburger, op. cit. 102 f.

[7] As argued by Strasburger, op. cit. 119.

[8] Suetonius, *Divus Iulius* 16; Plutarch, *Cato minor* 27 ff.; *Cicero* 23, etc.

There is one small incident, however, touching the relations of Pompeius and Caesar that deserves a mention because it is commonly neglected. Caesar in 63 B.C. prosecuted C. Calpurnius Piso. Among the transgressions of Piso, when proconsul, had been the wrongful execution of a man from the Transpadana.[1] Everybody knows of Caesar's interest in Transpadani—and many are tempted to date his acquisition of their support far too early. Of greater moment at the time was the fact that Piso was an enemy of Pompeius. In his consulate (67 B.C.) Piso exhibited fierce opposition to the proposals of the Pompeian tribunes Gabinius and Cornelius;[2] and he | publicly announced that he would refuse to permit the election to the consulate of that 'seditiosissimus homo', M. Lollius Palicanus.[3] Further, Piso tried to prevent Pompeius from levying recruits in Gallia Transalpina.[4]

Whatever be thought of Caesar, Labienus certainly turns up in undistorted historical record as a close associate of Pompeian agents. Q. Metellus Celer, praetor in 63, terminated the last act of the comedy of Rabirius by the archaic and ludicrous device of lowering the red flag on the Janiculum.[5] Collusion, clearly. With whom? Surely not with Cicero, but with the prosecutor, Labienus. It had never been intended that old Rabirius should be put to death. Further, one of Labienus' colleagues in the tribunate, T. Ampius Balbus, was a fanatical Pompeian, at least at a later date, being then known as the 'trumpet of civil war'.[6]

At once the question arises—was Labienus a tribune in the pay and service of Pompeius? Labienus emerges in Roman politics as an ally of Celer, a predecessor of Nepos. Had he too been serving under Pompeius in the Eastern wars?

The allies of Pompeius in peace and war may roughly but conveniently be divided into two classes, distinguished in the main by the criterion of social eminence. In the first place, certain noble families such as the Cornelii Lentuli and the Caecilii Metelli, not bound by personal ties of allegiance, and able, if they liked, to sever relations without dishonour. The alliance with the Metelli, dating back to the days of Sulla and continuous for many years, though not altogether unequivocal, was severely strained when Pompeius on his return from the East divorced Mucia, the half-sister of Nepos and Celer, and was broken in 60 B.C., but repaired

---

[1] Sallust, *BC* 49, 1. For the date, cf. *Pro Flacco* 98.

[2] Dio xxxvi 24, 3; 39, 3; Plutarch, *Pompeius* 25 and 27; Asconius p. 58 Clark, etc.

[3] Valerius Maximus iii 8, 3.

[4] Dio xxxvi 37, 2. Piso, it is pretty clear, governed the Cisalpina and the Transalpina together; cf. also *Ad Att.* i 1, 2; i 13, 2, and the remarks of J. A. O. Larsen, *CP* xxvi (1931), 427 ff.

[5] Dio xxxvii 27, 3.

[6] *Ad fam.* vi 12, 3: 'tuba belli civilis'. His circumstantial report of certain alarming statements of Caesar the Dictator (Suetonius, *Divus Julius* 77) need not be taken too seriously in view of his known political allegiance.

again eight years later, when Pompeius' marriage to the daughter of
Q. Metellus Scipio foretold a new political alignment. With the Lentuli
his relations were not so significant—but quite verifiable.[1]

Secondly, his personal and almost feudal adherents, of municipal stock
from the towns of Italy, especially from Picenum, the region where the
Pompeii possessed large estates and wide influence, with the resources to
raise a private army.[2] The family itself is probably Picene in origin: the
root of the name 'Pompeius' is palpably Oscan, while the termination
probably indicates Etruscan influence | at some time in their history.[3] A
number of the friends and partisans of Cn. Pompeius Strabo are revealed
in his *consilium* at the siege of Asculum in 89 B.C., especially a group of
men belonging to the *tribus Velina*.[4] The Picene following of his son is a
topic that will repay investigation. For the purpose of the present inquiry,
it will be sufficient to mention two men whose antecedents are beyond
doubt—a politician and a soldier. The 'chattering Picene', M. Lollius
Palicanus, briefly designated by Sallust as 'humili loco Picens, loquax
magis quam facundus', was tribune of the Plebs in 71 B.C.:[5] he carried
through those negotiations with the army-commanders Pompeius and
Crassus which gave them the consulate and destroyed the constitution of
Sulla.[6] Palicanus hoped for the consulate of 66 B.C. and also of 64 B.C.,
but in vain.[7] L. Afranius achieved it in 60 B.C., a Picene of no personal
distinction who had served as a legate of Pompeius both in the Sertorian
War and in the East.[8]

Now T. Labienus was certainly a Picene.[9] He conferred benefits on

---

[1] Note, for example, Cn. Cornelius Lentulus Clodianus, consul 72 B.C., censor 70 B.C.,
and legate of Pompeius in the Pirate War (Appian, *Mithr.* 95); likewise Marcellinus, *cos.*
56 (ibid. and *SIG*[3] 750). Marcellinus had also been in Spain [Sydenham, *CRR* 752–3].
Further, it is quite likely that not only Balbus the Gaditane but also the parent of the poet
Gallus derived the *gentilicium* of 'Cornelius' from Lentuli active under Pompeius in the
provinces of the West, cf. *CQ* xxxii (1938), 42 f. [above pp. 51 f.].

[2] Plutarch, *Pompeius* 6; Velleius ii 29, 1; *Bell. Afr.* 22, 2, etc. Cf. M. Gelzer, *Die Nobilität
der röm. Republik* (1912), 77 f. [= *Kl. Schr.* i 96 f.].

[3] J. Duchesne, 'Note sur le nom de Pompée', *AC* iii (1934), 81 ff. [The tribe of the
Pompeii was Clustumina (L. R. Taylor, *Voting Districts of the Rom. Rep.* (1960), 244 f.),
and Picene origin is sometimes denied on the strength of this. But while origin from
within the *ager Picenus* assigned to citizens under the *lex Flaminia* is excluded (op. cit. 64),
and Clustumina does not occur in *Regio* V, we have no way of knowing whether all this
would be relevant to the case of an Italic family enfranchised by *c.* 200 B.C.]

[4] *ILS* 8888 [= *ILLRP* 515], cf. C. Cichorius, *Römische Studien* (1922), 130 ff., esp.
158 ff. It does not follow, of course, that every person on this list was a personal adherent
or permanent ally of the Pompeii. Among the names are 'C. Rabeirius C. f. Gal.' and
'L. Sergius L. f. Tro.' That is to say, Rabirius and Catilina.

[5] Sallust, *Hist.* iv 43 M.

[6] Pseudo-Asconius on *Div. in Q. Caec.*, p. 189 St.

[7] Valerius Maximus iii 8, 3; *Ad Att.* i 1, 1.

[8] Against Sertorius, Plutarch, *Sertorius* 19; Orosius v 23, 14. Against Mithridates, Plutarch,
Pompeius 34, etc.; Dio xxxvii 5, 4. A dedication to Afranius discovered near Cupra Maritima
makes his origin reasonably certain (*ILS* 878 [= *ILLRP* 385]).

[9] Cicero, *Pro C. Rabirio perduellionis reo* 22.

Cingulum, presumably the town of his origin:[1] a fact which the scholarly
Silius Italicus recalled when he required a Picene character in his historical
epic.[2] It would not be easy for such a man, 'humili loco', to make his
way, save as an adherent of the baronial house of Picenum—compare the
early life and early struggles of the 'muleteer' P. Ventidius, of a family
hostile to the Pompeii.[3] The possibility that the origin of Labienus brought
him into relations with Pompeius was indicated by Münzer, but nothing
more: he did not develop the theme.[4]

Of Labienus' life before his tribunate, only one thing is known. He
served as a military tribune under P. Servilius Vatia (*cos.* 79) in Cilicia.[5]
Caesar was also there. Hence a natural inference about the origin of their
political association. It has not been observed in this connection, however,
that Servilius' command lasted for four whole years, from 78 to 74,
whereas Caesar was with Servilius for only a brief space, returning to
Rome as soon as he heard of the death of Sulla.[6] Sulla died in the spring
of 78. |

Labienus, it may be guessed, for it is not recorded, was praetor in 61,
60, or 59 B.C. He turns up, a tried soldier, as Caesar's lieutenant in the
first campaign in Gaul. It will be presumed that, like other professional
military men of the age (one thinks of M. Petreius and L. Afranius), he
was already in possession of some military experience. How was it gained?
Labienus might have been a legate under Caesar in Spain (61–60 B.C.).
It is more natural to assume that he had served in the armies of Pompeius
in Spain or in the East. M. Petreius is first mentioned in 63 B.C. as a military
man, 'homo militaris'.[7] No detail of his earlier and intensive career, with
thirty years of service, has been preserved. It is quite fair to infer Pompeian
antecedents.[8]

The role and function of Labienus now become much more intelligible
—especially if the consulate of Caesar and his Gallic command are examined from the side of Pompeius, ignoring the unknown future which was
to reveal Caesar as a rival, not as an agent. In the first place, Pompeius
needed a consul. In 61 B.C. M. Pupius Piso, a witty and accomplished

---

[1] Caesar, *BC* i 15, 2.   [2] *Punica* x 34.

[3] For the fullest account of Ventidius, cf. Gellius xv 4. He was captured at Asculum in
infancy and led in the triumph of Pompeius Strabo. On certain Ventidii of Auximum,
enemies of the Pompeii, cf. Plutarch, *Pompeius* 6.

[4] Münzer, *RE* xii, col. 260: 'während seine Herkunft aus Picenum ihn in solche [sc.
Beziehungen] zu Pompeius bringen mochte.'

[5] Cicero, *Pro C. Rabirio perduellionis reo* 21.

[6] Suetonius, *Divus Julius* 3: 'meruit et sub Servilio Isaurico in Cilicia, sed brevi tempore.
nam Sullae morte comperta, simul spe novae dissensionis, quae per Marcum Lepidum
movebatur, Romam propere redit.'

[7] Sallust, *BC* 59, 6: 'homo militaris, quod amplius annos triginta tribunus aut praefectus
aut legatus aut praetor cum magna gloria in exercitu fuerat'.

[8] Münzer, *RE* xix, col. 1183. He may have been the son of the *primus pilus* Cn. Petreius
Atinas (Pliny, *NH* xxii 11).

fellow, had not been very effective. For the next year, better prospects: but Metellus Celer, helped forward to the consulate by Pompeius, now remembered a recent affront to the honour of his family and openly joined the enemies of Pompeius,[1] while the Pompeian soldier Afranius was a liability and a disgrace.[2] Hence the coalition of 60 B.C., formed with Crassus and Caesar to establish the domination of Pompeius.

To maintain his position, the dynast required provinces and armies, first of all Gallia Cisalpina, the key of Italy. 'Quid? hoc quem ad modum obtinebis? oppressos vos, inquit, tenebo exercitu Caesaris.'[3] To the consuls of the preceding year had been assigned by the Senate the two Gallic provinces.[4] Celer certainly did not leave Rome;[5] but it is quite likely that Afranius governed the Cisalpina as his consular province, till the beginning of 58 B.C.[6] However that may be, for the needs of Pompeius the Cisalpina was first in importance as well as the first province to be granted to his ally and agent, the consul Caesar. Gallia Transalpina was given subsequently.

Caesar's military experience as a commander of armies was | recent in date, of brief duration. That did not matter: the proconsul would be aided by men of great competence—legates, officers of equestrian rank, and centurions. It will be presumed that some of these were supplied by Pompeius, for Caesar himself had not yet had the time to acquire a large personal following. Among the earliest legates attested in the Gallic campaigns were Q. Titurius Sabinus, the son, it may be presumed, of a legate of Pompeius in the Sertorian War,[7] and Ser. Sulpicius Galba, who had recently seen service under C. Pomptinus in Gallia Transalpina:[8] the father of Galba had been present in the *consilium* of Pompeius Strabo at Asculum.[9] Not to mention T. Labienus.

[1] Dio (xxxvii 49, 1) states expressly that Celer was helped by Pompeius.
[2] Dio xxxvii 49, 3; *Ad Att.* i 18, 5, etc.
[3] *Ad Att.* ii 16, 2. The validity of this interpretation of a much-plagued passage need not here be discussed. [The phrase continues to be discussed. For detailed analysis (with earlier bibliography) see Chr. Meier, *Historia* x (1961), 79 ff.; and cf. L. R. Taylor, *Historia* xvii (1968), 187 f. Both these scholars agree with the view here advanced.]
[4] *Ad. Att.* i 19, 2.
[5] *Ad Att.* i 20, 5; Dio xxxvii 51, 2; xxxviii 7, 1. C. Pomptinus went on holding Gallia Transalpina for a time—how long, it is uncertain. A *supplicatio* for his victories was proposed or voted in 59 B.C., cf. *Schol. Bob.*, p. 149 St.
[6] Cf. M. Gelzer, 'Die Lex Vatinia de imperio Caesaris', *Hermes* lxiii (1928), 118; 135 [= *Kl. Schr.* ii 210; 225]. Indeed, it appears that Afranius celebrated a triumph, cf. Cicero, *In Pisonem* 58. This is not conclusive, however. For all that is known, Afranius might have governed Gallia Transalpina or one of the two Spanish provinces in the period 70–66 B.C. Compare M. Pupius Piso, who triumphed from Spain in 69 B.C.: Asconius p. 15 Clark. [Afranius' connection with Transalpina is confirmed by the occurrence of his—fairly rare —name there.]
[7] On Pompeius' legate, L. Titurius Sabinus (Sallust, *Hist.* ii 94 M), cf. Münzer, *RE* vi A, col. 1575.   [8] Dio xxxvii 47, 1.
[9] *ILS* 8888 [= *ILLRP* 515], cf. C. Cichorius, *Römische Studien* 138; Münzer, *RE* iv A, col. 768.

If Labienus was an old Pompeian partisan, his function in Gaul was not merely to lend to the proconsul his long military experience but, in a sense, to keep watch upon him in the interests of Pompeius and act as a check. In the autumn of the year 50 B.C. Caesar put Labienus in charge of Gallia Cisalpina.[1] This was dangerous—Caesar, if Hirtius is to be believed, was aware that Labienus was already being solicited by his enemies.[2] Given the political situation at Rome in this year and Caesar's well-authenticated desire to avoid the appeal to arms, his action might be interpreted as a 'gesture' to reassure Pompeius—and public opinion.

Hirtius assigns a precise reason for Caesar's conduct at this juncture. It must be quoted, likewise the sentence following:

T. Labienum Galliae praefecit togatae, quo maiore commendatione conciliaretur ad consulatus petitionem. ipse tantum itinerum faciebat quantum satis esse ad mutationem locorum propter salubritatem existimabat.[3]

The dependent clause in the first sentence is clumsy and ambiguous. In the first place, what is the subject of the verb 'conciliaretur'? Presumably 'Gallia togata', which region is to be induced to favour somebody's candidature for the consulate. Secondly, whose candidature is thus to be furthered by putting Labienus in charge of Cisalpine Gaul—Caesar's or Labienus'? Most scholars assume the former: that is because their heads are buzzing, their eyes dazzled, with the 'Rechtsfrage'. Mommsen, however, understood a prospective candidature of Labienus.[4] |

But that is not the whole trouble. The phrase is awkward and involved. Emendation has been resorted to. The standard editions of the *Bellum Gallicum* of Kübler, Meusel, Rice Holmes, and Klotz all accept a proposal of Kraffert, and make the sentence read as follows: 'T. Labienum Galliae praefecit togatae quo maior ei commendatio conciliaretur ad consulatus petitionem.'[5] So far so good. With this reading, the reference to Labienus'

---

[1] *BG* viii 52, 2.   [2] *BG* viii 52, 3.
[3] *BG* viii 52, 2, following the Oxford text and all the manuscripts except one (*Cod. Laurent. Ashburnham.* 33) not of the best, which gives 'maior et commendatior' for 'maiore commendatione'.
[4] *The History of Rome* v 194 = *RG* iii 375. As the English translation is obscure, it will be necessary to quote the German. 'Noch im J. 704 hatte Caesar ihm den Oberbefehl im diesseitigen Gallien übertragen, um theils diesen Vertrauensposten in sichere Hand zu geben, theils zugleich Labienus in seiner Bewerbung um das Consulat damit zu fördern.' It is to be regretted that Mommsen did not discuss and support his interpretation: he may subsequently have abandoned it. Münzer (*RE* xii, col. 266), referring to Mommsen's view, is inconclusive—'eine ganz sichere Deutung ist kaum zu geben'. But Münzer protests against the assumption that Labienus' candidature is 'unthinkable' merely because we have no record of his praetorship. Why should we? Labienus was not a prominent politician. Further, the praetorian *Fasti* cannot be recovered in entirety. Far from it. As many as five of the praetors of 59 B.C. are known by name, it is true; in 61 and 60, however, only one and four respectively. [See *MRR* ii 179, 183, 188 f.—not counting doubtful ones.]
[5] Namely the Teubner texts of Kübler and Klotz (1893 and 1927), Meusel's edition (Berlin, 1894), and Rice Holmes's annotated edition (Oxford, 1914). [There is a thorough

consulate is certain, on any reasonable and Latin use of Latin pronouns. It is therefore paradoxical and unfortunate that Rice Holmes should have argued that the pronoun 'ei' referred to Caesar and Caesar's consulate.[1]

Hence, if one follows the best modern texts of the *Bellum Gallicum*, there can hardly be any doubt. Perhaps the reading of the manuscripts could be defended after all, since Hirtius was not, in fact, a very elegant writer.[2] In any case, on either reading, the word 'ipse' at the beginning of the next sentence, referring to Caesar's own activities, as though by contrast, may perhaps be taken as an indication of the sense of the whole passage.

The text is in dispute. A brief glance at the social background of Roman political life will confirm the interpretation here adopted.[3] There is no likelihood that the low-born Picene commanded any great influence or even the beginnings of a *clientela* in Cisalpina, that his governorship of that region could win favour for Caesar, a noble and a consular. Caesar already possessed their votes; earlier in the year, when descending into the Cisalpina to canvass for the election to the augurship of his quaestor M. Antonius, he had commended his own candidature for the consular elections in 49 B.C.[4] To govern the Cisalpina was a favour and a benefit to Labienus, if the *novus homo* was to stand for the consulate. He needed a chance to spend money, exercise patronage, and capture votes: 'videtur in suffragiis multum posse Gallia.'[5] And why should the marshal not hope for the consulate? Labienus was better than Palicanus, not inferior to Afranius.

If Pompeius stood by Caesar and refused to sacrifice him to his enemies, then Caesar would be consul for a certainty in 48 B.C. With whom for colleague? Not Pompeius: the laurels of Gallic conquest | were an eyesore to the envious dynast, the splendour and the energy of Caesar a challenge and a rebuke. No: Pompeius would be absent in Spain or in Syria—or perhaps exerting his *auctoritas* on Roman politics from the suburban seclusion of his imperial palace in the Alban hills. The consul recommended by 'militaris industria' and by political allegiance was Labienus. As a dozen years before with Metellus Celer and Afranius, the Pompeian consular

---

discussion of this crux in the edition of Kraner–Dittenberger[18] (Meusel) (1960), 76 f., defending the manuscript reading, but at a loss to account for the facts it implies ('eine törichte Randbemerkung . . ., die in den Text geraten ist').]

[1] In his Oxford edition (1914): he there states that 'ei' must be given the meaning of 'sibi'. In *The Roman Republic* ii (1923), 327, the reference to Caesar's consulate is assumed without discussion.
[2] Klotz, *Cäsarstudien* (1910), 160, speaks of 'eine gewisse Plumpheit und Schwerfälligkeit des Ausdrucks'.
[3] Compare, for this purpose, the brief but fundamental study of Gelzer, *Die Nobilität der römischen Republik* (1912) [now in his *Kleine Schriften* i (1962), 17–135].
[4] *BG* viii 50.   [5] *Ad Att.* i 1, 2.

pair would be a *nobilis*, his political ally, and a *novus homo*, his personal adherent.

The claims of constitutional propriety, as they called it, or rather the jealous ambition of Pompeius and the infatuation of the chief men of the oligarchy, led by Cato, denied to Caesar the privilege he claimed of retaining his province and standing for the consulate in absence: he was driven to arms in defence of *dignitas* and *salus*. The year of Caesar and Labienus never occurred. The consular *Fasti* of the Roman People were spared for many years yet the dishonour of carrying a name with the alien and non-Latin termination of the type of 'Labienus'.[1]

The prospect of Labienus' consulate is merely hinted at, in passing, by a single author. But that author was a contemporary, a friend and confidant of Caesar the proconsul. There is no ground for distrust. Cicero, in letters written shortly after the outbreak of hostilities, has not anywhere chosen to append a note to the effect that Labienus was a Picene. Nor, for that matter, does any literary source reveal the origin of Afranius.[2] Likewise family relationships. Cicero does not insist on reminding his correspondents that C. Lucilius Hirrus was a cousin of Pompeius.[3] No historian or orator reports a small detail of great moment in Roman politics, the identity of the wife of Crassus' elder son: the mausoleum of Caecilia Metella stands as testimony.[4] Origins and kinship were known to everybody in an oligarchical society—and commonly assumed as known. Their transmission to posterity is often casual and precarious.

So it is with Labienus. In 50 B.C. his allegiance had become an important political factor. Unfortunately, there is no means of knowing what measure of confidence the enemies of Caesar felt in the desertion of Labienus, how far that expectation determined their decisions. The party of Caesar grew up in large measure with help from Pompeius—and later at his expense. Pompeius had a bad | name for dropping his partisans when once they had served his purpose or on a change of political alliance. When Pompeius was seen to be returning to his old Sullan connections, the result was a movement of enemies of the dominant oligarchy in the direction of Caesar. The proconsul became a political dynast who could

---

[1] On names of this type, extending from Etruria eastwards to Picenum and the Sabine country, cf. W. Schulze, *Zur Gesch. lateinischer Eigennamen* (1904), 109 f. They may be discovered among obscure Roman senators in the second century B.C. The first consul with a name ending in '-ienus' was L. Passienus Rufus (4 B.C.). Earlier candidates had been unlucky, namely C. Bellienus 'qui consul factus esset, nisi in Marianos consulatus et in eas petitionis angustias incidisset' (Cicero, *Brutus* 175) and the ill-starred partisan of Octavianus, Q. Salvidienus Rufus, *cos. des.* for 39 B.C.

[2] There is only the inscription *ILS* 878 [= *ILLRP* 385].

[3] On this interesting character and the precise degree of his relationship to Pompeius, cf. C. Cichorius, *Römische Studien*, 67 ff.; Münzer, *RE* xiii 1642 ff.; A. B. West, 'Lucilian Genealogy', *AJP* xlix (1928), 240 ff.

[4] *ILS* 881.

hope to rival Pompeius—by patronage he had attached to himself towns and whole provinces, senators, knights, and soldiers. Gaul, both Transalpine and Cisalpine, had been won over from the *clientela* of Pompeius to his own. A large number of Caesar's supporters, Roman or provincial, were former adherents of Pompeius. It now became a question which side they would choose if it came to civil war. For the most part they stood by Caesar. There were men from Picenum among them, such as L. Minucius Basilus.[1]

Not so Labienus. His communications may have encouraged Pompeius to press for war—a brief and easy war. In December of 50 B.C. Pompeius spoke with contempt of Caesar's military strength.[2] He may have fancied that the proconsul's victories in Gaul were largely the work of the Picene military man trained in his own school; and Labienus was soon to assert in person the poor quality of Caesar's troops.[3]

Whatever the odds that Labienus might desert, Caesar in 50 B.C., though conciliatory, was quite on his guard. Labienus had only one legion under his control. When Labienus left Caesar, he was able to carry hardly any troops with him—no legions, but only auxiliary cavalry.[4] His desertion, no doubt highly distasteful to Caesar (who makes no mention of it in his narrative of the Civil War) and a momentary encouragement to Caesar's enemies, had little influence on the course of operations and issue of the war.[5]

Labienus is mentioned by Cicero in the same breath with Afranius and Petreius. 'Afranium expectabimus et Petreium; nam in Labieno parum est dignitatis.'[6] All three were to fall in battle for the Republic, or rather for the cause of Pompeius. In social origin, in career and loyalty, Labienus clearly belongs with the Pompeian military men, Afranius the Picene and Petreius the son of a centurion from the Volscian country.[7] |

So much for the marshal Labienus. The last member of the family

---

[1] Caesar's legate L. Minucius Basilus was certainly Picene. Originally known as M. Satrius, and described as 'patronus agri Piceni et Sabini' (Cicero, *De off*. iii 74), he was adopted by his maternal uncle, whose name he took. Note 'L. Minucius L. f. Vel.' in the *consilium* of Pompeius Strabo and 'L. Minicius L. f.' on an inscription from Cupra Maritima (*ILS* 5391). On this man, cf. C. Cichorius, *Röm. Studien*, 175 f.; Münzer, *RE* xv, col. 1947. Another Picene, first occurring in historical record as a legate of Caesar in the Civil Wars, was L. Nonius Asprenas (Cichorius, op. cit. 170; Münzer, *RE* xvii, col. 865): the founder of a family of long duration and high distinction—they intermarried with the Calpurnii Pisones.

[2] *Ad Att*. vii 8, 4: 'vehementer hominem contemnebat et suis et rei publicae copiis confidebat.'

[3] *Ad Att*. vii 16, 2; Caesar, *BC* iii 71, 4; 87, 2 ff.; *Bell. Afr.* 16, 1 ff. According to Dio (xli 4, 2 f.), Labienus revealed Caesar's military plans to Pompeius.

[4] *Bell. Afr.* 19, 4 etc.

[5] Cicero was enthusiastic at first, calling Labienus a ἥρως (*Ad Att*. vii 13, 1) and a 'vir magnus' (ibid. vii 13a, 3), but soon cooled off (ibid. viii 2, 3).

[6] *Ad Att*. viii 2, 3.

[7] Pliny, *NH* xxii 11, cf. Münzer, *RE* xix, col. 1182.

recalled with passion his Pompeian loyalties—'animus inter vitia ingens et ad similitudinem ingeni sui violentus, qui Pompeianos spiritus nondum in tanta pace posuisset.'[1] There were 'Pompeiani' of very different types in the Principate of Augustus; and the word itself is ambiguous. As the Latin language lacked a single word to express the meaning of 'Republican' or 'anti-Caesarian', the term 'Pompeianus' was called into service. Republicanism, of course, was highly respectable in the Principate of Augustus. As for Pompeius Magnus, however, his violent, illegal, and treacherous career resembled far too closely that of the ruler of Rome to make a complete rehabilitation anything but uncomfortable. Pompeius was not a true champion of the Republic. Still, Pompeius, though unedifying in his life, had become sanctified by dying for the Republic against Caesar; and Caesar was a 'bad man', politically suppressed by the heir to his name and power.

Hence the historian Livy could be called 'Pompeianus' by Augustus; which was not meant, or taken, for a rebuke.[2] Very far from it. Livy praised the leaders of the Catonian faction, the champions of *Libertas*; and he wrote generously of Pompeius, defending his memory against the attacks of Sallust. Augustus and Livy are both Pompeians, sham ones. But there were still genuine Pompeians in the time of Augustus, mindful of the ties of personal loyalty, either to the house of Pompeius or to the cause which took its name from Pompeius, good men who treasured *fides* and *pietas*. The truculent orator Labienus was one of them. Another was Ti. Claudius Nero (*cos.* 13 B.C., *cos. II*, 7 B.C.). The consequences of his return to power in A.D. 4 are soon apparent on the consular *Fasti* which reveal, along with a cluster of *novi homines*, the names of certain distinguished Pompeian families.[3]

To resume. The hypothesis that the ostensible renegade was an old Pompeian partisan will not only explain his behaviour when compelled to choose between Caesar and Pompeius or illuminate his earlier activities as tribune in the year of Cicero's consulate: it will confirm, if confirmation be needed, the fundamental importance in Roman political life of patronage and ties of personal allegiance, of *fides* and *amicitia*.

[1] Seneca, *Controversiae* x, *praef.* 5. This passage should suffice to prove what is nowhere explicitly stated, that the orator belonged to the same family as the great marshal and his son, the 'Parthicus imperator'.

[2] Tacitus, *Ann.* iv 34: 'Titus Livius, eloquentiae ac fidei praeclarus in primis, Cn. Pompeium tantis laudibus tulit ut Pompeianum eum Augustus appellaret; neque id amicitiae eorum offecit.'

[3] A brief indication about the *novi homines*, PBSR xiv (1938), 7 [below, p. 94]. It will hardly be necessary to emphasize the value and significance of this evidence about Tiberius. F. B. Marsh, however, appears to deny the influence of Tiberius on the choice of consuls in the period A.D. 4–11 (*The Reign of Tiberius* (1931), 43 f., cf. 67), for inadequate reasons. His conception of Tiberius is therefore peculiarly vulnerable. [P. A. Brunt, *JRS* li (1961), 71 ff., after elaborate analysis, denies that A.D. 4 marks a turning-point or that Tiberius' influence can be detected.]

8

M. Durry, *Pline le Jeune:*
Panégyrique de Trajan[1]

THE solitary speech surviving from three whole centuries of post-Ciceronian Latin oratory has had a long time to wait for an adequate commentator. Monstrous neglect, one might think. Yet there is some excuse. Many scholars have expressed a marked and personal distaste for Pliny's masterpiece. 'Ein höchst unerfreuliches Produkt', says the grave and judicial Schanz; and Schiller spoke of 'Bombast und fast byzantinische Kriecherei'. Not only is the subject repulsive—an official theme with repetitive and ingenious praise of the head of the government: the style of the orator, technically perfect and palatable in small doses, soon becomes tedious through preciosity and unrelenting pursuit of the pointless epigram and forced antithesis.

Marcel Durry deserves praise not only for scholarship but for courage and goodwill. He has produced an edition and commentary of the *Panegyricus*, complete with an introduction examining the character and circumstances of the speech (pp. 1–79), nine brief appendices on historical points (pp. 232–46), a bibliography and four indexes. This should turn out to be a very serviceable piece of work.

The *Panegyricus* is an example of a definite literary type, namely the *actio gratiarum* of a consul. Pliny spoke his thanks when entering office on 1 September, A.D. 100. The speech which L. Verginius Rufus (*cos. III*, 97) was rehearsing when he slipped and broke his thigh may likewise have been intended for the first day of office. But that is not quite certain: we know that the oration of another consul, Fronto, came near the end of his consular term (p. 25 N). As it stands, the *Panegyricus* would take three hours to declaim. That is terrible. As F. A. Wolf observed long ago, 'enecuisset principem novus consul si ita dixisset ut scripsit.' Moreover, Pliny himself testifies to the fact that these *gratiarum actiones* were often very brief indeed (*Ep.* iii 18, 6). The solution is clear, and few have disputed it—not a patient Princeps imitating Augustus for hours and hours ('recitantes et benigne et patienter audiit'), but a subsequent amplification

[1] Paris, 1938.

by the proud author. How much was added? The topic is attractive. Durry refuses to follow or to reproduce the lengthy inquiries of Dierauer and Mesk. He is content to indicate certain passages as probable additions, for example the strenuous military career of the young Trajan (*Pan.* 13–15), the purple patch about famine in the land of Egypt (30 f.), the horrid and deserved fate of the delators (55), the unexceptionable family life of the new Emperor (81 ff.). But these are only examples. The process of deflating the *Panegyricus* would have to be very drastic and could not escape being arbitrary.

One type of subsequent insertion is naturally of peculiar interest, namely the anachronism, for it may both prove decisively the fact of rewriting and reveal the date of final publication. As may well be believed, the speech has been minutely scrutinized for clues of this kind. Precious little emerges. Yet there are two points that deserve discussion. A number of scholars, including recently Paribeni and Carcopino, are disposed to discover in the *Panegyricus* (29, 2) a reference to the construction of Trajan's great harbour at Ostia. Durry follows them (pp. 10 ff. and in his note on *Pan.* 29, 2). He denies, it is true, that the speech contains references to events later than the year 101; but he holds that the *Portus Traiani* may well have been begun as early as 101. Against that possibility, as a possibility, there is of course no argument. But more evidence is needed. A great fuss has been made about nothing at all. It will suffice to quote the passage in order to show that Pliny says not a word about any precise harbour-works, but is simply extolling, with comparison of Pompeius, the beneficent and inevitable influence of the new regime upon commerce and communications. It runs as follows: 'nec vero ille civilius quam parens noster auctoritate, consilio, fide reclusit vias, portus patefecit, itinera terris, litoribus mare, litora mari reddidit diversasque gentes ita commercio miscuit ut, quod genitum esset usquam, id apud omnes natum videretur.'

Not Ostia therefore, but sheer generalities. The other point concerns foreign and military policy. Trajan came to Rome for the first time as Emperor in the course of the year 99 after making a tour of the northern frontiers, passing from Rhine to Danube. He had embarked upon no warlike operations whatsoever. The encomiast therefore sets | about belauding the moderation of the Emperor, his magnificent refusal to cross the river Danube to the Dacian bank—'magnum est, imperator Auguste, magnum est stare in Danubii ripa' (16, 2). Then, all of a sudden, a complete change of tone and attitude. The panegyrist of peace becomes a prophet of war—he sees conquest and a triumph, a real triumph, no Flavian fraud. 'Accipiet ergo aliquando Capitolium non mimicos currus nec falsae simulacra victoriae, sed imperatorem veram ac solidam gloriam reportantem.' There follows a clear reference to Decebalus, the king of the Dacians, a description of the pomp of a Roman triumph, the hope even that the military emperor may earn the *spolia opima*. Surely an insertion, celebrating Trajan's triumph at the end of the Dacian War (A.D. 102)? But that would be a hasty inference. As Durry shows, there is no need to believe these lines written any later than the early months of the year 101, when war was afoot. One could perhaps go further. There is no inherent contradiction between praising an emperor for keeping the peace at the moment and prophesying war and victory later on. Though not initiated into the military plans of Trajan, Pliny need have possessed no peculiar insight if he believed that an emperor trained in the practice of arms and eager to justify the elevation of a *vir militaris* would have his war sooner or later—and it would be a *Bellum Dacicum*. Two years earlier, when Tacitus wrote his *Germania*, he showed that he had formed a fair estimate of the character of Trajan. He interrupts his narrative to recount the relations of Roman and German from the days of the Cimbri to the second consulate of Trajan: 'tam diu Germania vincitur.' It looks as though Tacitus expected wars and conquests from the new emperor. He was right—but it was a mistake to anticipate laurels from Germany. Perhaps his historical studies had misled him—he did not realize that the Danube had recently and suddenly become much more important than the Rhine.

So much for the date of the *Panegyricus* and kindred problems. The literary *genus* to which the speech belongs has many ancestors and a distant past. In Latin literature, Durry points to three valuable documents that have survived, three significant stages in the growth of monarchy, namely the *Pro Marcello* of Cicero, Velleius' praises of Tiberius and the tract *De Clementia* which Seneca composed for the guidance of his imperial pupil—and for publicity. Instructive parallels can be adduced from all three: one of the best is *Pro Marcello* 5 = *Pan.* 14, 1 and 15, 1. Given the complete absence of orations or other monuments of 'Kunstprosa' in the thirty years after Seneca's death, one should draw illustrations from all possible sources. Durry refers briefly to epigraphic laudations. There is one literary parallel that he has missed. Pliny's account of the military career of Trajan deserves to be supplemented, and can perhaps be illuminated, by Statius' poetical *encomia* of the life and works of two *viri militares*, Rutilius Gallicus and Vettius Bolanus (*Silvae* i 4 and v 2). That Statius is a poet, Pliny an orator, is beside the point. Anything that emphasizes the literary—and perhaps the spiritual—kinship of Pliny and Statius is of value. Certain of Pliny's epistles, elegant essays on trifling themes, could have been versified: the *Silvae*, conversely, turned into prose. In the *Panegyricus*, Pliny points out that Jupiter now has leisure for his celestial offices, having furnished Trajan to be his vice-regent on earth—'tantum caelo vacat postquam te dedit qui erga omne hominum genus vice sua fungeretur' (80, 4). Not very different, despite the word 'deus', is Statius on Domitian (*Silvae* iv 3, 128 f.):

> en! hic est deus, hunc iubet beatis
> pro se Iuppiter imperare terris.

Official orators on solemn public occasions find it easy as well as expedient to eschew originality and to suppress inconvenient facts. There is usually a *corpus* of received truth to hand—'sagesse des nations et salut des orateurs'. Pliny is no exception—the *Panegyricus* is bristling with platitudes. Durry has set himself the task of collecting and classifying these pearls of traditional wisdom (pp. 35–9). Some of them are splendid, for example 'cum sint odium amorque contraria' (68, 7). Another is described by Durry as the solitary example of its kind—'sunt diversa natura dominatio et principatus' (43, 3). Surprising if true: one would have thought that the antithesis between | 'principatus' and 'dominatio' was both implicit and expressed in all the official 'ideology' of the Empire, not only as long as there was a public opinion to be respected or cajoled, but long after the words had ceased to have any meaning at all. Compare the history of *Libertas*. Even in the third century, emperor or usurper has the effrontery to call himself 'vindex libertatis'.

If poverty of thought cannot quite be disguised, it may at least be excused by splendour of language and variety of expression. Durry proceeds to examine vocabulary, syntax, and style of the *Panegyricus*. He finds a number of neologisms—some insignificant. (Durry quotes 'pantomimus' and 'donativum'; but the former is attested as early as Seneca the Elder, *Suas.* ii 19; and certain others cannot have been inventions of Pliny.) The poetical colouring is laid on bright and thick, antithesis is tediously frequent. Hence a curious baroque style, prolix yet precious, repetitive but now and then neat and concise. A linguistic study of this kind is not merely valuable but essential—and that not for the sake of Pliny only. 'C'est une chance pour Pline, dans ce jeu un peu sinistre des engloutissements et des survivances, que le *Panégyrique* soit un des rares textes où nous puissions toucher, avant Tacite, le germe de ce qui fait Tacite unique. Une comparaison entre le *Panégyrique* et l'œuvre de Tacite s'impose' (p. 60). Diverse in character and attainments, Tacitus and Pliny enjoyed a community of studies and friends, they exchanged their writings in draft. It should be possible to discover some traces of their association: among Roman men of letters it was an amiable and laudable practice to honour a forerunner or a friend by taking over or echoing some of his characteristic phrases. So Pliny, as might be expected, imitates the *Agricola* more than once. But Tacitus did not disdain to borrow from his friend. 'An excidit trucidatus Corbulo?' (*Hist.* ii 76, 7) surely derives from 'an excidit dolori nostro modo vindicatus Nero?' (*Pan.* 53, 4).

Moreover, the *Panegyricus*, in vocabulary and expression, yields certain remarkable anticipations of the *Annals* (pp. 63 ff.).

One point of contact with the *Histories* looks pretty clear at first sight —Pliny's remarks upon adoption (*Pan.* 7 f.) and Galba's speech delivered when adopting Piso (*Hist.* i 15–17). The parallel between Galba and Nerva was not hidden from contemporaries (cf. *Pan.* 8, 5): it was perhaps closer than they cared—or dared—openly to admit. So we have two accounts of a similar situation, two variations on the one theme. To which belongs priority in time, to Tacitus or to Pliny? The question has been debated at some length: Wölfflin and Mesk argue for Tacitus, Hohl for Pliny. Durry concludes that there is not much in it—simultaneity and common sources rather than direct imitation. Pliny proclaims that the adoption of Trajan saved Nerva and saved the Empire—'atque adeo temere fecerat Nerva, si adoptasset alium' (8, 5). Tacitus' theme is rather different—more sophisticated and at the same time more honest. He makes Galba demonstrate that monarchy is inescapable—but it must be a constitutional monarchy. Whether Tacitus needed to derive inspiration and arguments from the historical work of Pliny's uncle, *A fine Aufidi Bassi*, as Durry is inclined to believe (pp. 62 f.), is another question. Not even Pliny would have needed to do that.

To turn to the commentary. It is literary and linguistic rather than historical; and at times a little too full in its illustration or explanation of silver Latinity where there can surely be no real difficulty to students who are so far advanced as to wish to read—or need to read—the *Panegyricus*. The evidence of coins could be more copiously invoked to illustrate the official meanings of words and the nature of the programme advertised by the government. Mattingly, by his frequent quotation of the *Panegyricus* when discussing the coinage of Nerva and Trajan, shows how effectively the two sources can be combined (*BMC, R. Emp.* iii (1936)). Indeed, many chapters in Pliny's speech could be given coin-legends for their headings. But there is no mention of Mattingly in notes or bibliography. Charlesworth's two papers are omitted (*HTR* xxviii (1935) and xxix (1936)): the same writer's valuable lecture, *The Virtues of a Roman Emperor: Propaganda and the Creation of Belief* (1937) perhaps came too late for notice—and for profit. Two dissertations published in 1935 on subjects highly relevant to the *Panegyricus* and to Trajan would also have helped, namely L. Berlinger, *Beiträge zur inoffiziellen | Titulatur der röm. Kaiser* (Diss. Breslau), and A. Hennemann, *Der äussere und innere Stil in Trajans Briefen* (Diss. Giessen). Again, reference to the very voluminous and not always accurate work of Paribeni, *Optimus Princeps*, will not preclude the need to turn from time to time to *CAH* xi for the history of the reigns of Nerva and Trajan.

The notes suffer visibly from the lack of consultation of the works indicated above. Pliny describes Trajan as 'castus et sanctus et dis simillimus princeps' (1, 3): this is a place for pretty full annotation. On the word 'dominus' (2, 3, etc.) both Charlesworth (*HTR* xxviii 135) and Last (*CAH* xi 412) could be mentioned. 'Tuo saeculo' (40, 5) calls for illustration from Pliny's letters to Trajan (x 1, 2; 3, 2)—to say nothing of Trajan's own phrase 'nec nostri saeculi est' (x 97, 2). Trajan was a soldier, acceptable to the troops—'quotus enim quisque cuius tu non ante commilito quam imperator?' (16, 5). It is worth nothing that he liked to use the word 'commilito' himself in letters (x 20, 1; 53; 101; 103) and in rescripts (*D.* xxix 1, 1). Pliny speaks of the 'quies' of his own tribunate (95, 1). Now the word is almost a technical term (cf. *AJP* lviii (1938), 7 f., on the *quietis cupido* of Cornelius Fuscus), and should be explained, not merely by the absence of those *tribunicii furores* so common and so deplorable under the Free State, but by the parallel of the tribune Agricola, 'quiete et otio' (*Agr.* 6, 3). On linguistic points, the expression 'habeantque muneris tui' (75, 5) turns up in Tacitus (*Ann.* xiv 55), 'id primum tui muneris habeo'; and 'fluminibus immensis' (16, 5) simply means the Danube—there is no point in mentioning tributaries of that river, and those the least important; similarly another plural of majesty, 'cum legiones duceres' (14, 3), where it is quite erroneous to say 'le pluriel est justifié par le fait que la légion était complétée par les *auxilia*'; the emotional position of the patriotic adjective deserves a note in the passage 'Romanae aquilae, Romana signa, Romana denique ripa' (82, 4). Finally, a phrase in the very first sentence of the speech is described as a hexameter, and the opening words of the *Annals* of Tacitus are adduced in support. The hexameter is 'patres conscripti, maiores instituerunt'. Even if the first syllable of the first word were long in quantity, which it is not normally, though Silius Italicus could write 'virtutis patrum' (*Punica* x 69), it would still be doubtful whether this collocation of syllables could profitably be regarded as a verse. It is quite fortuitous.

On the historical side, the notes are rather meagre in places. A complete and exhaustive commentary is not called for and can be dispensed with, if the right and relevant references are briefly indicated: in this case the explanatory matter could have been made at once more precise and more up to date. To take the intense and varied military career of Trajan (14 ff.), a section to which one is tempted to prefix Statius' remarks about Rutilius Gallicus:

> mox innumeris exercita castris
> occiduas primasque domos et sole sub omni
> permeruit iurata manus; nec in otia pacis
> permissum laxare animos ferrumque recingi.

Trajan served as a military tribune 'per stipendia decem' (15, 3). That is portentous and unprecedented. In explanation it is not enough to say, 'les cursus mentionnent ceux qui durent deux ans, ce qui est rare': it would be more useful to mention the fact that the longest total of service attested apart from Trajan is in three legions, as P. Aelius Hadrianus (*ILS* 308, (cf. *HA Hadr.* 2, 2 and 5) and the younger L. Minicius Natalis (*ILS* 1029 and 1061). Unlike many young men, including Pliny, Trajan took a serious view of his military tribunate—'neque enim prospexisse castra brevemque militiam quasi transisse contentus'. The exactest comment can be derived from the *Agricola* (5, 1)—'nec Agricola licenter, more iuvenum qui militiam in lasciviam vertunt', etc. During some of his ten *stipendia*, Trajan served in the army of his father, the legate of Syria. An inscription (*ILS* 8970) records the *ornamenta triumphalia* of the parent, Pliny a 'Parthicus laurus' of the son (14, 1): indeed, the son is made responsible for the honouring of his father (89, 3), by a distasteful exaggeration. It would have been well to point out that there can be no question of a real *Bellum Parthicum*, as Paribeni | (who is referred to here), W. Weber, and others have believed, in flat contradiction of the clear testimony of a conscientious historian contemporary with the events (Tacitus, *Hist.* i 2, 1). Pliny commends Trajan for learning the art of war in the camps and not from a 'Graeculus magister' (13, 5). The parallel cited is Juvenal iii 78, the omniscient and esurient Greek. That is hardly the point here. What Pliny is thinking about can better be illustrated by Marius' sneer at the generals who, 'postquam consules facti sunt, et acta maiorum et Graecorum militaria praecepta legere coeperint: praeposteri homines' (Sallust, *BJ* 85, 12). Nor would it be alien to the theme to mention the treatise on tactics of the Greek Onasander, dedicated to the Roman senator, Q. Veranius—who succumbed within a year of assuming command in the ferocious province of Britain (Tacitus, *Agr.* 14, 3), for all his reputation, easily won perhaps, of *severitas* (*Ann.* xiv 29, 1).

There is a certain looseness in the explanation of administrative terms. A province garrisoned by one legion cannot be called a *provincia inermis* (as is stated in the note on 19, 1); nor must the legionary commander in such a province necessarily be the governor. Tarraconensis refutes both assertions. Again, it is by no means correct to say that 'le titre complet de ce gouverneur d'une province impériale était *legatus pro praetore*' (9, 2). Nor is it enough to state that Trajan was appointed by Nerva as governor of one of the two Germanies (5, 2), probably Germania Superior (9, 2). No discussion is needed—Germania Superior is reasonably certain. The note on 9, 5, 'ad exercitum miserit', is also inadequate.

If the *Panegyricus* be regarded as a valuable historical source, there is all the more reason to pounce upon and interrogate those facts which Pliny mentions only vaguely or for misrepresentation. Pliny is a peculiar kind of distorting mirror for the history of Domitian. 'Decertare cupere cum recusantibus' (16, 2) is probably a reference not merely general and derogatory but precise and definite, namely to Domitian's campaign against the Germans of Bohemia in the spring of the year 89. The frozen Danube (12, 3) deserves for elucidation something more than a passage of Ovid (*Tristia* iii 10), if the Dacian incursion into Moesia, the opening of Domitian's wars, actually took place in the winter of 85/6, as many believe, though not for cogent reasons. About the character of Domitian's wars and the merits of his frontier policy there cannot fail to be dispute and debate. But in the matter of 'falsae simulacra victoriae' (16, 3) one might take leave to doubt whether Couissin can, or could have, 'corroboré les dires des anciens en étudiant les trophées de l'époque'. It is not a matter that could be decided by study of the monumental effigies of history.

The 'Économy Commission' established by Nerva is also a topic of contention. If one admits, following Paribeni, that it continued its activities under Trajan (note on 62, 2), it is only fair to state that there is no evidence at all one way or the other. It can also be argued that it lapsed when its cause and occasion came to an end, the chaotic and extravagant rule of Nerva. Trajan, as the evidence of his coin-legends indicates pretty clearly, did not regard himself as inheriting and continuing the policy of Nerva (cf. *BMC, R. Emp.* iii, p. lxix).

A few more points, of subordinate value. Pliny refers to holy men and buffoons at the banquets of Domitian—'peregrinae superstitionis ministeria aut obscaena petulantia mensis principis oberrat' (49, 8). The former are clearly ministrants of the cult of Isis, about the Flavian predilection for which a little more might have been said: the strange funeral banquet of Domitian (Dio lxvii 9) perhaps belongs here. About buffoons, no evidence save that Domitian on an occasion of state had by him a dwarf with whom he held converse, asking if he could guess for what reason Mettius Rufus was going to be appointed Prefect of Egypt (Suetonius, *Dom.* 4). Trajan is praised for his refusal of statues of silver and gold (52, 3): the judicious advice of Maecenas would here be in place (Dio lii 35, 3). Pliny urges very strongly that commendations from the provinces should be given preponderant weight in the granting of honours at Rome—'volo ego, qui provinciam rexerit, non tantum codicillos amicorum nec urbana coniuratione eblanditas preces, sed decreta coloniarum, decreta civitatum adleget' (70, 9). Tacitus makes Thrasea | Paetus pronounce the contrary opinion, protesting against the insolence of provincials: 'nobis opinio decedat, qualis quisque habeatur, alibi quam in civium iudicio esse' (*Ann.* xv 20, 4).

Certain historical problems find mention in the appendices (pp. 231–45), among them the consular *Fasti* of the year 100, containing an enigmatic *ignotus* who was consul for the third time, succeeding Frontinus. No suggestion is offered. The gap must remain. As for Spurinna, there is no evidence that he had been given a second consulate by Nerva, as is here stated. Apart from the *ignotus* and one other suffect consul, the list appears to be complete. Perhaps one should insert either Ti. Julius Ferox (cf. Pliny, *Ep.* ii 11, 5) or M. Pompeius Macrinus Theophanes (proconsul of Africa in 116 or 117). [For the consuls of 100, see now below, pp. 256 f.].

The career of the elder Trajan is also discussed. Durry presents (from *Milet* i 5, 53 f.) a more recent version of the inscription of his career than Dessau gave (*ILS* 8970). The milestone from Aracha near Palmyra, of the year 75, could have been mentioned (*AE* 1933, 205): it helps, be it ever so slightly, the dating of his governorship of Syria. Then follows a page about the date of his death. Strack argued, for a purely numismatic reason, that he did not die until 112, the year in which coins of his consecration appear. That theory coolly overrode the testimony of Pliny. The orator imagines an amicable debate conducted in a higher sphere between Nerva and Trajan's father on the topical theme of adoption. Nerva is described as 'Divus': as for the parent by blood, 'sed tu, pater Traiane, nam tu quoque, si non sidera, proximam tamen sideribus obtines sedem' (90, 2). That should have been clear enough—when Pliny delivered his speech, the parent Trajan was dead but not deified. It did not require the evidence of the *Fasti Ostienses*, with their record of the events of 112, to prove that 'Traianus pater' did not die in that year.

What one is provided with is very useful; yet one is tempted to ask for an appendix, however brief, on the career of Pliny between 90 and 100, especially in view of what he himself says about his position in the last years of Domitian—'si cursu quodam provectus ab illo insidiosissimo principe antequam profiteretur odium bonorum, postquam professus est substiti' (95, 3). Did Pliny halt in his career? Whatever date one adopts for Pliny's praetorship, 93 or 95 (Mommsen and Otto respectively), possibly even 90 or 91 (for Harte's theory should be noticed (*JRS* xxv (1935), 51 ff.), there is still the prefecture of the *aerarium militare* to be accounted for, hence the suspicion that the orator has been guilty of an 'inexactitude embarrassante', to call it by no other name. That was common form after Domitian's death. Pliny says that Trajan had been passed over by Domitian, 'praeteritus est a pessimo principe qui praeteriri ab optimo non poterat' (94, 3). Which may well be true. If so, it conflicts emphatically with Durry's hypothesis that Trajan held high commands on the Danube in 91–6 (p. 17): the 'inexactitude' should have been pointed out. Knights as well as senators did their best to cover up their services to the Flavian dynasty. It is to be regretted that we do not possess the explanation which Titinius Capito, a man who wrote biographies of the victims of despotism in the right and safe season and kept statues of Brutus, Cassius, and Cato in his mansion, was in the habit of publishing to a complaisant audience: he was a high secretary of state, continuous under Domitian, Nerva, and Trajan (*ILS* 1448).

What then, in the end, is the use and value of the *Panegyricus*? The paucity of literary sources for the period counsels us to cherish what little we have. But not with uxorious indulgence. There is a large question indeed, how far any official speech can be true. Undue reliance on the *Panegyricus* will make it more and more difficult to discover what the reign of Nerva was really like. Pliny, to magnify Trajan, admits quite a lot—'concussa res publica ruensque imperium super imperatorem' (6, 3). There is much more that could be said. The adoption of Trajan was not due merely to inspiration from Juppiter Optimus Maximus (cf. the pertinent observations of E. Groag, *RE* xiii, col. 475); and we learn precious little about the attitude of the provincial armies and their commanders, the arbiters of empire and beneficiaries of the great secret first revealed in the year 68, but well known all along, ever since Pompeius and Caesar. The fact that for a time in 97 or 98 there was no consular legate in Syria (*ILS* 1055), combined with a | stray notice in Pliny (*Ep.* ix 13, 10 f.), is enough to invite, and to justify, conjecture (cf. *Philologus* xci (1936), 238 ff.).

Nor do we really know very much about the character of Trajan. 'Dès avant son adoption, on l'avait distingué. Agricola présageait son élévation; flatterie après coup? non, puisque Nerva, qui appartenait au même milieu que le beau-père de Tacite, le choisit entre tous spontanément. Dès qu'il succède à Nerva, on l'appelle *Optimus*; flatterie encore? Non, puisque le *cognomen* survivra à la joie du couronnement' (p. 20). Now Trajan was a quite distinguished person, the son of a father who had been one of the strongest supports of the Flavian dynasty; of the army-commanders, he was probably the best available; and he turned out to be a very capable and highly acceptable emperor. Still, behind the official and necessary façade of the soldier-emperor, just, modest, and *civilis*, there is something discordant and elusive, as Weber has done well to point out (*Rom: Herrschertum u. Reich im zweiten Jahrhundert*, p. 35). Nor will the language of Trajan's letters and edicts reveal as much as might be hoped, if one believes, as is not altogether paradoxical, in the existence of a regular chancellery-style, brief, firm, and clear, owing not a little to the 'neue Sachlichkeit' of the Flavians.

Not indeed that the personal and individual note of an emperor may not be detected from time to time in official documents. For example, there is preserved by Pliny a rather woolly and unsatisfactory edict of Nerva, the descendant of a family of jurists (*Ep.* x 58): it is followed by a crisp and admirable rescript addressed to a provincial governor, in good chancellery-style. Emperor was substituted for emperor but the system of government and the administrative personnel did not change so very much. Titinius Capito was the secretary *ab epistulis* under Domitian, Nerva, and Trajan: it will not be fancied that this man was compelled to transform his prose-style twice in two years.

These considerations need not be taken to mean that one should despise the *Panegyricus* as a historical source. The document must be examined with care, interpreted with caution. Compare the remarks above about Ostia and about the death of Trajan's father. Another example: Weber has recently stated that Trajan 'must' have been despatched to the Rhine shortly before the death of Domitian (op. cit. 27); compare also Paribeni (op. cit. 84). That is dead against Pliny (9, 5, cf. 94, 4): it was Nerva who sent him there. Above all, the speech is not merely an encomium of Trajan—it is a kind of senatorial manifesto in favour of constitutional monarchy, as Durry neatly demonstrates (pp. 21–4). Yet even here, it is not indispensable—one can go a long way with the brief speech of Galba (in Tacitus' *Histories*) or coin-legends for company.

The chief value of the *Panegyricus* is that it furnishes a document for linguistic and literary history—and a monument, by contrast, to the solitary genius of Tacitus. The *Panegyricus* is good of its kind. How good? 'Enfin, le recueil des *Panegyrici* ne se serait pas ouvert avec le discours de Pline, s'il avait eu quelque prédécesseur digne de lui être comparé' (p. 33). This may be true, but looks a little bit like an argument from silence. Pliny's speech is the first official panegyric that we have. There must have been others before it, of some merit; for the century had witnessed an abundance of eloquent consuls and loyal servants of the government, animated with due measure of pride in their work or with literary vanity. That bad man, Eprius Marcellus, could have turned out a fine speech on the necessity for monarchy and tolerance, if we believe Tacitus—'ulteriora mirari, praesentia sequi; bonos imperatores voto expetere, qualescumque tolerare' (*Hist.* iv 8, 2). Or, in Pliny's own time and entourage, what of the oration of Verginius Rufus, delivered in his third consulate under Nerva? We know, it is true, nothing of the oratorical accomplishments of this old gentleman. Did Pliny perhaps lend his eager talent and help to compose a speech for his guardian? No matter: when Pliny wrote, the formulae and the themes of the *gratiarum actio*, the 'ideology' of the Empire and the grand antithesis between 'principatus' and 'dominatio', had been in existence for a very long time.

To sharpen the necessary contrast between good emperors and bad, no device was too trivial, no sophistry too transparent. Domitian abolished pantomimes: permitted | again by Nerva, they were forbidden by Trajan. Pliny was equal to the theme—'utrumque recte; nam et restitui oportebat, quos sustulerat malus princeps, et tolli restitutos' (*Pan.* 46, 3). The government is always right. It is indeed fitting that Pliny should stand at the head of the *Panegyrici veteres*. They even surpass him in the technique of 'utrumque recte', or 'having things both ways'. Only Gibbon can do justice. 'When Maximian had reluctantly abdicated the empire, the venal orators of the times applauded his philosophic moderation. When his ambition excited, or at least encouraged, a civil war, they returned thanks to his generous patriotism and gently censured that love of ease and retirement which had withdrawn him from the public service.'

The *Panegyricus* may perhaps be regarded not merely as the heir of a long tradition but as a herald and symbol of the intellectual and spiritual poverty of the period that was to follow, a condition not solely due to despotic government or to any repression of free speech: there was nothing worth writing about. Pliny was alarmed at the state of contemporary youth, observing rebelliousness and dangerous originality—'statim sapiunt, statim sciunt omnia, neminem verentur, imitantur neminem atque ipsi sibi exempla sunt' (*Ep.* viii 23, 3). He need not have worried. These dynamic young men (if they really existed) were soon to become dreary and representative figures, leaders of state and society in a dead season, the blessed Age of the Antonines.

9

Caesar, The Senate, and Italy*

I. *Caesar's Policy and Intentions*

THE central and revolutionary period of Roman history runs from the tribunate of Tiberius Gracchus to Augustus' seizure of sole power and establishment of a constitutional monarchy. Caesar's heir prevailed through the name of Caesar—'puer qui omnia nomini debes'; and he perpetuated the name, as title, cult, and system, to distant ages. Yet Augustus as Princeps did not invoke Caesar's rule to provide precedent and validity for his own. Quite the reverse. What rank and role in the transformation of the Roman State should therefore be assigned to the Dictatorship of Caesar—mere episode or cardinal moment and organic part?

The problem is large, the debate continuous and acute.[1] During the last generation, opinions about Caesar's imperial policy and the shape which he intended to give to the Roman State have ranged to the widest extremes, roping in for parallel or contrast the figures of Sulla, Pompeius, and Augustus. Eduard Meyer's contribution was impressive—even dominant for a time.[2] He regarded Caesar as the heir to the world-empire of Alexander: it was Caesar's design to establish a 'Hellenistic monarchy', depress Rome, elevate the provinces, and rule by right divine, king in name and title, as well as in fact, of all the world. The Caesar of Carcopino's swift and splendid narrative stands in the same line, more Mommsenian perhaps and more Roman, but hardly less absolutist and theocratic.[3]

But the other side has not lacked advocates, especially among English scholars. The caution of Pelham and of Rice Holmes induced them to reasoned doubt and suspension of judgement; and Rostovtzeff was firmly |

* [See also pp. 31 ff. above. *The Roman Revolution* should be consulted throughout, for a view of this subject in its historical context. T. P. Wiseman, *New Men in the Roman Senate 138 B.C.–A.D. 14* (1971), gives a detailed prosopographical analysis of Italian and provincial senators in this period.]

[1] About the whole question there must now be consulted Gagé's valuable paper: 'De César à Auguste: où en est le problème des origines du principat', *RH* clxxvii (1936), 279 ff. It is not only a *compte-rendu*, but an original contribution.

[2] 'Kaiser Augustus', *HZ* xci (1903), 385 ff. = *Kl. Schr.* (1910), 443 ff.; *Caesars Monarchie u. das Principat des Pompejus* (1919; 3rd ed. 1922).

[3] 'La royauté de César', *Points de vue sur l'impérialisme romain* (1934), 89 ff.; *Histoire romaine* ii (1936), *César.*

Papers of the British School at Rome xiv (1938), 1–31.

sceptical about 'Caesar's monarchy'.[1] More recently, Adcock has made the most thorough-going attempt to refute the theories of Meyer: Caesar's position 'was no more royal than it was divine'.[2]

When the exegetes are at variance, the books must themselves be ambiguous and Sibylline. Most of the evidence about the acts and policy of Caesar the Dictator is either hostile or posthumous: statements of alleged intention are removed for ever from proof or disproof. Caesar's purpose to have himself proclaimed king stands on no firmer testimony than his rumoured design to transfer the capital of the Empire from Rome to Alexandria or to Ilium.[3] The enemies of the Dictator were assiduous both in the fabrication of rumours and in the engineering of 'incidents'. Again, Caesar may well have said that Sulla was a fool to resign the Dictatorship: a reasonable opinion—but we have only the word of T. Ampius Balbus, a notorious and fanatical Pompeian.[4] But open and avowed Pompeians are clearly not the most insidious enemies. Caesar's heir acquired for himself the name, the halo, and the partisans of Caesar. After exploiting the Caesarian cause in his revolutionary period, Augustus politically suppressed the memory and person of Caesar, or revived it only to point the contrast between *Dictator* and *Princeps*. Livy was not the only 'Pompeian' in the Principate of Augustus. What Virgil and Horace say—or rather, what they do not say—about Caesar the Dictator is also a reflection of official history.

The worst is yet to come. As a man and as a statesman, Caesar is a tremendous and dominating figure. Hence a double danger for history. In the first place, if history be regarded as the record of great men (to the neglect of their allies, associates, and partisans), they may easily become types, as so often in Greek historical biography, mere lay-figures, harmonious and complete in shape and member. Artistic and logical consistence extends from characters to policy, act, and system. Thus did Eduard

[1] Pelham, *Essays on Roman History* (1911), 25 ff.; Rice Holmes, *The Roman Republic* (1923) iii 336; Rostovtzeff, *Soc. and Ec. History of the Roman Empire* [2nd ed. (1957), 27 f.].

[2] *CAH* ix 718 ff. [The debate continues. On Caesar as a god-king, see, e.g., A. Alföldi, *Studien über Caesars Monarchie* (1953); G. Dobesch, *Caesars Apotheose* (1966); H. Gesche, *Die Vergottung Caesars* (1968); S. Weinstock, *Divus Iulius* (1971). For an assessment in terms of the contemporary evidence, see H. Strasburger, *Caesar im Urteil seiner Zeitgenossen*, 2nd ed. (1968).]

[3] Suetonius, *Divus Iulius* 79, 4, on which Meyer (*Caesars Monarchie*[3], 521) remarks, 'zweifellos durchaus zutreffend': it has been taken fairly seriously by Mommsen, *Reden u. Aufsätze*, 173 f., and Warde Fowler, *Roman Essays and Interpretations*, 216 ff. (referring to Horace, *Odes* iii 3, 37 ff.). There is no indication that Suetonius believed what he retails as rumour ('varia fama percrebruit').

[4] 'Nec minoris impotentiae voces propalam edebat, ut Titus Ampius scribit, *nihil esse rem publicam, appellationem modo sine corpore ac specie. Sullam nescisse litteras qui dictaturam deposuerit. debere homines consideratius iam loqui secum ac pro legibus habere quae dicat*' (Suetonius, *Divus Iulius* 77). Carcopino (*Points de vue*, 94) can hardly be right in assigning these utterances to Caesar's early years. Both content and context are against that. On the political sentiments of T. Ampius Balbus, cf. esp. Cicero, *Ad fam.* vi 12, 3.

Meyer set out avowedly to depict Caesar's monarchic rule as the counterpart to the Principate of Augustus.[1] His conception derived from a false and schematic contrast between two men and two systems, which he enhanced as he developed his thesis by producing an additional foil to Caesar—namely Pompeius and the 'Principate of Pompeius'. | Hence Pompeius emerges in startling relief as the precursor of Augustus. But Meyer's Republican Augustus is a highly dubious character, best given up altogether. To be sure, Augustus could claim Pompeius as a forerunner[2] —but better not. The parallel between his own rise to power, a period of history neither edifying nor 'constructive' in a constitutional sense, but palpably real and remembered, and the violent, illegal, and treacherous career of the young Pompeius was too close to be comforting. Again, to invert Meyer's values, Caesar is closely akin to Pompeius as a political dynast, Augustus to Caesar as an absolutist ruler. It therefore becomes advisable to reassert the continuity between Caesar and Augustus[3]— which cannot be done if the Triumviral period is omitted.

Secondly, teleological and 'progressivist' theories of history may be responsible for the creation of a Caesar who is artistically convincing or ideally satisfying . . . but no more than that. Caesar may indeed, if it helps, be described as the heir of Alexander and forerunner of Caracallus in a united world of which Rome is only the capital, no longer the mistress, with Italy depressed to the level of the provinces. Caesar certainly has his place in the long process of which that is the logical end and development: so have Pompeius and Augustus. Caesar should be left in his own time and generation, neither praised for superhuman prescience of a distant future nor blamed for blind precipitance to snatch an unripe fruit. Nor, in his own generation, does it follow that Caesar saw the end from early youth, willed it and strove for it—namely sole power undivided and the establishment of monarchy by right divine, succeeding where Sulla is deemed to have failed.

Given these hazards of evidence and conception, the task might appear hopeless, best abandoned. So Pelham many years ago, in revulsion from Meyer's theories when they were first adumbrated—'it is safer to resign ourselves to a frank confession that we have no satisfactory clue to Caesar's views for the future, even assuming that he had been able to form any.'[4] Certain difficulties arise from terminology, convenient words that are deplorably formal and abstract, such as 'Hellenistic Monarchy'. Again, 'divine honours' may lead to a confusion of thought.[5] In truth, they pre-

[1] *Caesars Monarchie*[3], vi (preface), 'die Monarchie Caesars darzustellen als Gegenbild zu dem Prinzipat des Augustus'.

[2] Cf. J. Gagé, *RH* clxxvii (1936), 324, 336.

[3] Cf. J. Gagé, ibid. 342; also M. A. Levi, *RFIC* lxiii (1935), 404 (review of *CAH* x). Levi's excellent *Ottaviano Capoparte* (1933) helps to bridge the gap.

[4] *Essays on Roman History*, 27.   [5] Cf. esp. Nock, *CAH* x 489.

suppose neither divinity nor royalty. 'Rex' and 'regnum' are traditional weapons of the Roman political vocabulary, applied to any exercise of exorbitant power. Caesar certainly behaved as a 'rex'. But Caesar no less than Augustus knew that the title of 'king' is not indispensable to monarchic rule.

Perhaps the formulation is defective. 'Non rex sed Caesar.' It may be | expedient to turn from the grandiose and alluring topic of Caesar's aims and intentions and examine with care the recorded acts of Caesar's Dictatorship: 'Dictator Caesar', as Roman posterity termed him. The authentic testimony of his own sayings and writings is of paramount value. Wickert has acutely invoked the *Bellum Civile*.[1] In this work (which contains much more than military history) Caesar convicts his enemies of unconstitutional behaviour, demonstrates that the constitution cannot work—and presents his own apology for not restoring it. Further, Caesar's insistence upon 'clementia' is deliberate and revealing—he sets himself above all parties, like a monarch, treating his enemies as subjects whom it would be pointless and unprofitable to destroy. Wickert's arguments carry conviction—but even so do not bring the final proof that Caesar was bent on establishing despotism rather than some form of constitutional and 'Augustan' rule. Nor should they be taken to suggest any antithesis to Augustus.

Above all, Caesar's time was short. He assumed the title and powers of Dictator, loathed though they were from memories of Sulla, to preclude opposition, delay—and perhaps the veto. After a Civil War, the ordering of the Roman State could not but be arbitrary in act and unsatisfactory in result.[2] After his three years' absence in the Balkans and the East, the situation might have altered. But speculation would be unprofitable. Certain of the acts of the Dictatorship, especially the increase in the number of magistrates and total of the Senate, demand renewed investigation. Bitterly unpopular with contemporaries, these measures have provided definite evidence in support of extreme views about Caesar's rule and future policy; and, though the fact has been ignored or disputed, they had a continuous and lasting effect upon the Roman State, being perpetuated for ten years (or more) under the Triumvirate, masked perhaps and retarded by Augustus but not abolished. The constitution never recovered.

II. *Italians in the Senate*

But this is not all. Under the Principate of Augustus, Italy emerges into history as a unit with common language, sentiments, and institutions, not quite a nation in the modern sense (for the Roman People transcended the

---

[1] L. Wickert, 'Zu Caesars Reichspolitik', *Klio* xxx (1937), 232 ff.

[2] [It now seems likely that Caesar was at one time *dictator rei p. constituendae*: see L. Gasperini, *Studi pubblicati dall'Istituto Italiano per la Storia Antica* xix (1968), 381 ff.]

geographical bounds of Italy), but still something that may with convenience and propriety be termed a nation, if only to show how different Italy had been two generations earlier. The process of the unification of Italy was long and arduous. Some of the most effective agents were involuntary or unconscious. Such were Sulla and the Triumvirs, working through proscription, confiscation, | and colonies. In so far as the transformation of Italy was not the work of time and slow impersonal influences, two measures, being matters of official policy and organization, may from time to time be attached to definite individuals and definite moments in history.

First, the extension and regularization of municipal institutions. This was the logical result of the liquidation of the Bellum Italicum and grant of the Roman franchise to all Italian communities. But even the nominal and formal uniting of Italy did not take effect all at once. The subject has recently been investigated in an original but over-schematic fashion by Rudolph, who makes startling claims for Caesar, by no means easy to substantiate.[1] The subject is large, and cannot be discussed here: on any account the role of Caesar in municipal legislation is evident and important.

Secondly, by composition and recruitment the Senate of Augustus is representative of Italy as a whole, not merely Latium with the Sabine country, Umbria, Etruria, and Campania, but the 'Italia' that rose against Rome in 91 B.C., and the new Italy of the North, till recently a province in status. As with the linguistic and municipal unification of Italy, time and circumstance have worked undetected. Yet definite agents may be invoked. How much was due to Caesar the Dictator? Here, as so often in Roman history, both Cicero and Augustus stand in the way.

Cicero claimed to be the peculiar representative of the towns of Italy; he had many friends and wide influence among the 'homines municipales ac rusticani'.[2] It is not surprising that his adherents contrived to get votes of the local senates passed in order to bring pressure upon opinion at Rome and secure the orator's restoration from exile. Italy carried him back on her shoulders, so he boasted—and his enemies remembered.[3] Earlier than that, in the oration for P. Sulla, he had spoken in moving tones for 'tota Italia', for the municipal men—and for himself, answering the personal attack of the patrician Manlius Torquatus who described him as a 'rex peregrinus'. Cicero inquires, 'quam ob rem qui ex municipiis veniant peregrini tibi esse videantur?'[4] Further, if Cicero be a 'pere-

---

[1] H. Rudolph, *Stadt u. Staat im römischen Italien* (1935): on his main thesis, cf. especially Sir H. Stuart Jones, *JRS* xxvi (1936), 268 ff.; M. Cary, ibid. xxvii (1937), 48 ff.; R. Meiggs, *CR* xlix (1935), 235 ff.   [2] *Comm. Pet.* 31. He did not need Quintus' advice here.
[3] 'Sallust', *In Cic.* 4, 7; Macrobius ii 3, 5 (a joke of Vatinius—'unde ergo tibi varices?').
[4] *Pro Sulla* 23. This important passage invalidates an argument of Rudolph, *Stadt u. Staat*, 158.

grinus', what of the others 'qui iam ex tota Italia delecti tecum de honore
ac de omni dignitate contendent?'[1] Cicero speaks of candidates for office
as being chosen from the whole of Italy; and there were certainly masses
of municipal men in the Senate of his time. None the less, some of the
peoples of Italy, such as the Paeligni, perhaps also | the Marsi and Marru-
cini, had not yet sent a senator to Rome. Now Cicero was indefatigable
in deed as well as word to support the interests of his friends from the
towns, in money matters and in law-suits. For example, he defended in
the courts Caelius and Plancius, bankers' sons both; he may well have
helped them in their official careers. These men came from Tusculum and
from Atina respectively.[2] But one cannot discover any body of municipal
partisans (especially from those Italian peoples whose inclusion alone can
justify the phrase 'tota Italia') who owed admission to the Senate to
Cicero's patronage; still less can the *Fasti* show a *novus homo* whom
Cicero helped forward to the consulate. Cicero regarded himself as all
the representation that Italy should require among the *principes civitatis*.
Nor will it be a convincing view that Cicero's own political speeches and
tracts, though sagacious as well as eloquent, exercised any influence on the
recruitment of the Senate during his life-time—or later.

Augustus is another matter. An active political and military leader in
the period of the Revolution, he began with a small and undistinguished
personal following in 44 B.C. (hardly any senators, still less *nobiles* or
consulars), which in time captured the Caesarian party and enlisted most
of the Republicans and Antonians, until no other party of consequence
was left in the State. His earliest adherents had been Roman knights of
municipal extraction like Salvidienus, Agrippa, and Maecenas: loyal to his
revolutionary origin, to his equestrian partisans, and to the 'Italia' which
he had done so much to create, Augustus as Princeps, while ostensibly
restoring the Republic and reviving the *nobiles* of Rome as allies in his
monarchic, dynastic, and matrimonial policies, was careful to provide
for continuous and easy recruitment of the Senate from the municipal
aristocracy of Italy.

Augustus' acts and aims can be established in different ways. The
Emperor Claudius when censor proposed to admit to the Senate certain
notables of Gallia Comata. Looking about for precedents to commend
this liberal policy, he appealed to the respectable authority of Augustus
and Tiberius. It was their wish, he said, that the best men from the towns
of Italy should have a seat in the Roman Senate. 'Sane novo m[ore] et
divus Aug[ustus av]onc[ulus m]eus et patruus Ti. Caesar omnem florem

---

[1] *Pro Sulla* 24.
[2] *Pro Plancio* 19 ff. (Atina). On the hypothesis that Caelius Rufus came from Tusculum,
cf. Münzer, *RE*, s.v. 'Caelius', col. 1267. There was an important family of Caelii here
(*CIL* xiv 2624, 2627); and the consul of A.D. 17, C. Caelius Rufus, was aedile at Tusculum
(*CIL* xiv 2622).

ubique coloniarum ac municipiorum, bonorum scilicet virorum et locupletium, in hac curia esse voluit.'[1] | Excellent, unimpeachable testimony, so it might appear. An Emperor should have known what he was talking about—and so should his audience, the Senate. There are also facts.

Q. Varius Geminus, so his epitaph records, was the first man from all the Paelignians to become a senator at Rome.[2] To be sure, he owed that rare distinction to young Ovid's wilful abandonment of the senatorial career and surrender of the *latus clavus*. But the lack of Paelignian senators is remarkable enough—and should prompt inquiry about the representation in the Senate of other Italic peoples. There is no doubt that Augustus promoted many men from small towns and remote parts of Italy. The study of senatorial prosopography and of Italic nomenclature supplies palmary examples of dim persons with fantastic names, pre-eminent among them all Sex. Sotidius Strabo Libuscidius from Canusium.[3] Not Augustus only: when Tiberius returns to a share in the control of public affairs in A.D. 4, the result is seen in an accession to the consular *Fasti* of *novi homines*[4]—which is in no way alien to Claudian tradition and to the character of Tiberius. It will suffice to mention two pairs of brothers, the Vibii from Larinum in Samnium, the Poppaei from Picenum; and Papius Mutilus, of a dynastic Samnite house.[5]

So far so good. The imperial orator asserts that the policy of Augustus (and of Tiberius) was an innovation—'sane novo more'. What is one to make of that? Were there, then, no representatives of Italy and the *municipia* in the Senate before Augustus? Surely there were. Cicero urged against the patrician Torquatus the presence of many municipal rivals for honours—'ex tota Italia delecti'.[6] Again, when rebutting Antonius' slurs

---

[1] *ILS* 212, col. ii, *init*. For the interpretation, see especially H. M. Last, *JRS* xxii (1932), 232 (review of Momigliano, *L'opera dell' imperatore Claudio*) and *JRS* xxiv (1934), 59 ff. (review of Carcopino, *Points de vue sur l'impérialisme romain*). As there emphasized, the primordial meaning of the phrase 'coloniae et municipia' is 'the towns of Italy' (but in antithesis, be it noted, not to the provinces, but to Rome); and though the phrase can be extended to cover communities in the provinces (e.g. *ILS* 214), the context in the *Oratio Claudi Caesaris* is against that. For the class of men referred to by Claudius, note the phrase 'equites et viri boni ac locupletes' used by Cicero's brother (*Comm. Pet.* 53).

[2] *ILS* 932.

[3] *ILS* 5925. Of the two family names which he bears, each is found only at Canusium: Sotidius, *CIL* ix 349 and 397; Libuscidius, 338, 348, 387, 6186. See W. Schulze, *Zur Gesch. lateinischer Eigennamen*, 236 and 359, for the evidence about each name, separately impressive: if combined, the result is almost incredible.

[4] [*Contra* P. A. Brunt, *JRS* li (1961), 71 ff.]

[5] C. Vibius Postumus (*cos. suff.* A.D. 5) and A. Vibius Habitus (*cos. suff.* A.D. 7) certainly came from Larinum, cf. *CIL* ix 730: earlier members of the family are mentioned in Cicero's speech for their fellow-townsman A. Cluentius Habitus, namely Sex. Vibius and C. Vibius Capax (*Pro Cluentio* 25 and 165). C. Poppaeus Sabinus and Q. Poppaeus Secundus, consul and consul suffect respectively in A.D. 9, presumably came from the small town of Interamna Praetuttianorum in Picenum (cf. *ILS* 5671 and 6562). Papius Mutilus is no doubt a descendant of the Samnite leader of the Bellum Italicum (cf. H. M. Last, *CAH* x 455): but he is not a novel or unique phenomenon.   [6] *Pro Sulla* 24.

upon the origin of his protégé, the young Octavianus, Cicero exclaims, 'Why, we all come from *municipia*!'¹ Rhetorical exaggeration, perhaps; but facts support the orator. On the other hand, Claudius' remarks are also rhetoric, though not such good rhetoric. The fragments of Claudius' speech are distinguished neither for relevance nor for veracity. The Emperor did not need to make out a good | case for his proposal. No sooner the speech delivered, a *senatus consultum* was passed, without discussion.

In the matter of imperial policy about senators from the provinces, that speech is by no means a safe guide. Claudius mentions by name not a single one of the excellent Narbonensians at that time present in the Roman Senate.² A different approach is therefore indicated—to find out first of all what senators there were of provincial origin and interpret the speech, like any other oratorical or governmental pronouncement, in the light of established facts. Likewise the 'novus mos' of Augustus.

Claudius alleges an innovation. But even if senators from the *municipia* had been rare and infrequent before (which is not proved), they must have become exceedingly common when Caesar added 300 new members or more to that august assembly. Yet Claudius says nothing of Caesar's work in what survives of the speech. Caesar might have been mentioned just before, in the part now lost. But that is not likely: Claudius' phrase 'novo more divus Augustus' clearly denies to Caesar any part in the process and policy of admitting Italy to the Senate of Rome.

The deliberate omission of Caesar is both comprehensible and instructive. Caesar was not a useful precedent—indeed, officially, his Dictatorship did not exist, for it was not 'res publica constituta', but merely an unhappy and not very long episode in an era of anarchy. The same conception appears in Tacitus. From the third consulate of Pompeius in 52 B.C. (or perhaps rather from the outbreak of the Civil War, for he is vague here) down to the sixth consulate of Augustus, he reckons a period of revolution—'exim continua per viginti annos discordia, non mos non ius.'³

Like the years of the Triumvirate, the Dictatorship might conveniently be blotted from official history in the interests of a government that sought to mask its authentic and unedifying origins by asserting continuity with the respectable and Republican past. On a partisan and arbitrary theory of constitutional law, the acts and transactions of twenty years of crowded history did not exist. But they had happened: the work of the Revolution

¹ *Philippic* iii 15, 'videte quam despiciamur omnes qui sumus e municipiis, id est omnes plane: quotus enim quisque nostrum non est?'
² Such as Cn. Domitius Afer, a consular, and Domitius Decidius, the father-in-law of Agricola, in high favour with the government, to judge by his promotion (*ILS* 966): Claudius speaks only of Valerius Asiaticus—'dirum latronis nomen'—and his brother, the one dead, the other expelled, and the Roman knight L. Vestinus.
³ Tacitus, *Ann.* iii 28.

was not undone—many of the principal agents of violence and illegality survived to pass with easy and superficial metamorphosis into the supporters and ministers of the 'Republic' of Augustus. Augustus is the heir of Caesar: but not that only. He is also the heir of Octavianus. But such formulations, in appearance personal and definite, are really abstract and delusive. Neither his revolutionary career | nor his constitutional rule is historically intelligible without the party he led, the party with whose mandate and support he prevailed and governed.

This is no place to develop that theme. But a cursory examination of the composition of the Senate during the Revolution may help to restore and vindicate the continuity of history.

III. *The Size of the Roman Senate*

Caesar the Dictator augmented the size of the Senate, in various ways, briefly as follows. In 49 B.C. he secured restitution for some at least of the victims of political justice, condemned under the third consulship of Pompeius;[1] and now or later other 'calamitosi homines', among them senators expelled by the censors of 50 B.C., returned to public life. A large number of men acquired senatorial rank through standing for magistracies, often with dispensations—for this mode of entry was less invidious than direct adlection. Even Sulla submitted the list of his new senators to the approval of the People. The tribunate as well as the quaestorship was used to provide entry (as for Pollio, *tr. pl.* in 47 B.C.), a proceeding which had a popular and 'democratic' appearance.[2] Like Sulla, Caesar also increased the total of certain magistracies. How many quaestors were elected for the years 48–5 B.C. is not recorded. In 44 there were certainly forty;[3] and the same number were chosen in advance for 43.[4] This may have been intended for permanence: the tribunate was not touched (naturally enough), and only two aediles were added. These magistracies could not therefore have been made compulsory in a senatorial *cursus honorum*, which is not surprising. The number of praetors, however, was doubled, rising from ten to fourteen in 45 and to sixteen in 44 and 43;[5] and Cassius Dio clearly indicates sixteen as a regular and familiar figure.[6] Some change was long due here. Two consuls and eight praetors in the system of Sulla were designed to furnish the promagistrates to govern ten provinces. By

---

[1] Caesar, *BC* iii 1, 4—note that Caesar (deliberately) mentions only the men condemned under the domination of Pompeius—'illis temporibus quibus in urbe praesidia legionum Pompeius habuerat'.

[2] And even under Augustus and as late as Claudius the tribunate can be used as a method of entry to the Senate for men who have not held the quaestorship (Dio liv 30, 2; lvi 27, 1; lx 11). Note also the inscriptions, *ILS* 916 and 945; *AE* 1925, 85.

[3] Dio xliii 47, 2.   [4] Dio xliii 51, 3.   [5] Dio xlii 51, 3; xliii 47, 2; 49, 1; 51, 4.
[6] Dio xliii 49, 1.

the outbreak of the Civil War the total of provinces had increased to
fourteen: Caesar was clearly budgeting for eighteen, in permanence.[1]

But these measures were not enough, if Caesar was to satisfy the
aspirations of his partisans and create a strong and efficient Senate. In
virtue of dictatorial | powers he revised the roll of the Senate three times,
in 47, 46, and 45, adding new members.[2] The proportion of his nominees
who entered the Senate by this means cannot be discovered. There is only
one definite statement about the size of Caesar's Senate—according to
Cassius Dio, 900 after the revision of 45 B.C.[3]

Three hundred is the conventional total of the Senate before Sulla: that
number, or its multiples, turns up in the various and controversial accounts
of the proposals of C. Gracchus and of Livius Drusus concerning jury-
courts and senators. According to Appian, Sulla twice added 300 members
to the Senate, in 88 and in 81. His account has been disputed—the first
addition is merely a doublet of the second, or, though authentic and
actually voted, it was never carried out.[4] The compromise does not really
save much of Appian: why doubt that Sulla would have wished before
departing to the East to strengthen the Senate by including certain of his
equestrian partisans? It would take no time at all. Three hundred, however, a figure familiar in its rotundity, may be excessive. But this is not all.
It will not do entirely to omit from calculation the adlections made by the
censors of 86 B.C. under the domination of Cinna.[5] Hence, though Appian
again records 300 in 81 B.C., it is impossible to determine closely the
number of new senators then created by Sulla. The wastage of the preceding decade had been considerable. Orosius and Eutropius reckon at
200 the casualties of the Bellum Italicum and the Civil Wars.[6] To that
should perhaps be added the natural deaths of ten years and expulsions by
Sulla. Therefore, despite the additions in 88 and 86, he may have required
as many as 300 new senators in 81: hardly the 500 which Carcopino
postulates, as though the history of the Senate in the previous decade
could be explained merely by subtracting 200 casualties from the total of
the pre-Sullan Senate.[7]

However that may be, after Sulla 600 is a reasonable total, automatic-
ally supplied by the twenty quaestors of the new ordinance. There appears

---

[1] As shown by Mommsen, 'Die Zahl der röm. Provinzen in Caesars Zeit', *Ges. Schr.*
iv 169 ff.

[2] Dio xlii 51, 5; xliii 27, 2; 47, 3.   [3] Dio xliii 47, 3.

[4] Appian (*BC* i 59, 267; 100, 468), as interpreted by E. G. Hardy, 'The Number of the
Sullan Senate', *JRS* vi (1906), 59 ff.; cf. H. M. Last, *CAH* ix 209 (cf. 286) and O'Brien
Moore, *RE*, s.v. 'Senatus', col. 686. Carcopino (*Histoire romaine*) omits the *lectio* of 88.

[5] P. Willems, *Le Sénat de la république romaine* (1885), i 403 ff.; H. Bennett, *Cinna and
his Times*, Diss. Chicago (1923), 43 f. A *lectio* was certainly held in 86; cf. Cicero, *De domo
sua* 84.   [6] Orosius v 22, 4; Eutropius v 9, 2; cf. H. Bennett, op. cit. 35.

[7] [See E. Gabba's notes on the passages cited in his commentary on Appian, *BC* i
(2nd ed., 1967).]

to have been a definite total fixed by law—or rather perhaps by custom.[1] In the years 81–75 the tribunate, excluding its holders from higher office, was not much in competition among the more reputable or the more ambitious. Yet it is not certain that Sulla had repealed the *Plebiscitum Atinium*.[2] Therefore | certain individuals may have entered the Senate without having held the quaestorship. The practice is attested before Sulla[3]—and long afterwards. Members of this class were probably to be found amongst the senators expelled by the censors of 70 B.C. They removed no fewer than sixty-four persons, of whom seven are known by name.[4] Despite that purge, in 61 B.C. the censors, when completing their rolls and admitting—or rather retaining—all ex-magistrates, found that they had to exceed the legal total.[5] The Senate after Sulla in the seventies may also have been well above 600—perhaps nearer 700; likewise the Senate at the outbreak of the Civil Wars. (See further below, p. 104, on this topic.) One of the censors of 50 B.C., Ap. Claudius Pulcher, is said by Dio to have been very strict, expelling not merely all freedmen's sons, but also many quite respectable persons.[6] Only two names are known, however, Sallust and Ateius Capito, and that in a period rich in prosopographical information: there may be some exaggeration in the severity alleged.

Dio rates the Senate as augmented by Caesar in 45 B.C. at 900. It is difficult, however, to estimate precisely how many new senators were added by the Dictator, for here again there are the casualties of the Civil Wars and natural deaths to be deducted—and deducted from an existing total which may well be as high as 650. Further, it is possible that Dio's basic figure was not 900, but, once again, the familiar and almost traditional 300, added to an assumed 600. If so, the total of Caesar's Senate will be lower than 900, perhaps only 800. Either figure harmonizes with what is known of the Senate of the Triumviral period, when it had risen to over 1,000—under a system compared with which the Dictatorship of Caesar was regarded as an age of gold.[7] Hence, to preserve distances, one might be tempted to adopt the lower figure for the more respectable Senate of Caesar. On the other hand, there are the many casualties—the proscriptions, Philippi, and Perusia.

---

[1] Dio xxxvii 46, 4.

[2] This may seem improbable, but is admitted by Lengle (*RE*, s.v. 'tribunus', col. 2489). The *Plebiscitum Atinium* (Aulus Gellius xiv 8, 2) gave ex-tribunes a seat in the Senate. On the date of this important measure, cf. P. Willems, *Le Sénat* i 228 ff. (*c.* 119 B.C.?); J. Carcopino, *Histoire romaine* ii 338 f. (103 B.C.?). [*MRR* i 458 f., 500 f.]

[3] C. Norbanus was tribune before being quaestor: F. Münzer, 'C. Norbanus', *Hermes* lxvii (1932), 220 f.

[4] Livy, *Per.* xcviii; for the names, P. Willems, *Le Sénat* i 417 ff.

[5] Dio xxxvii 46, 4; ὑπὲρ τὸν ἀριθμόν.

[6] Dio xl 63, 4: πάντας μὲν τοὺς ἐκ τῶν ἀπελευθέρων, συχνοὺς δὲ καὶ τῶν πάνυ γενναίων; Horace, *Sat.* i 6, 20 f.   [7] Dio xlvii 15, 4: ὥστε χρυσὸν τὴν τοῦ Καίσαρος μοναρχίαν φανῆναι.

Let it then be taken that 300 or 400 men entered the Senate under the Dictatorship, through magistracies or by adlection. Had the Republic endured, there would in any case have been about 100 new senators in the period 48–44 B.C.—namely, the quaestors of each year. What manner and sort of men were the remainder? |

IV. *Caesar's New Senators*

About Caesar's partisans, old senators as well as new, the testimony of his enemies has been dominant. All too easy and convenient the antithesis between legitimate government and rebellious proconsul, between the party of all virtuous and patriotic citizens and the gang of adventurers, morally and (worse than that) socially reprehensible. As everybody knows, Caesar's adherents were a 'colluvies':[1] there were among them men who had actually been expelled from the Senate or condemned in the law-courts, thus forfeiting senatorial rank. Given the nature of justice at Rome in the last age of the Republic, indignation is out of place. The disgrace of men like Gabinius and Sallust is evidence not so much of crime and immorality as of the power of their enemies. The opponents of Caesar represented the party in power, namely the dynast Pompeius and a group of noble families (the Scipios, the Metelli, the Lentuli, and the Marcelli) allied with the constitutionalist faction of Cato, which for long had striven against the domination of Pompeius, but which now saw a chance to assert the Republic by destroying Caesar as a lesson to his rival. The antithesis does not lie between senators and non-senators. Caesar's party, though in a sense anti-senatorial, possessed many members of high distinction, sons of noble families. Above all, the patricians. Münzer has drawn attention to the significance of Caesar's alliance with the Aemilii and the Servilii.[2] There were other patricians on his side. But this is not the place to investigate Caesar's senatorial following.

The reproach of ignoble and disgusting origin bears heavily upon Caesar's new senators. The evidence is various, convergent, and consistent, ranging from sober history to invective and lampoon.[3] His nominees included soldiers, centurions, scribes, sons of freedmen, and aliens newly enfranchised.[4] The consensus of antiquity has bemused the moderns. Not only have these charges been believed and repeated with hardly a word

---

[1] Cicero, *Ad Att.* ix 10, 7; cf. ix 18, 2 (νέκυια).

[2] *Römische Adelsparteien u. Adelsfamilien* (1920), 347 ff., esp. 358.

[3] The most important is as follows: Dio xlii 51, 5; xliii 27, 2; 20, 2; xlvii 3; xlviii 22, 3; Suetonius, *Divus Iulius* 76, 3; 80, 2; Cicero, *Ad fam.* vi 18, 1; *De div.* ii 23; *De off.* ii 29; *Phil.* xi 12; xiii 27; Seneca, *Contr.* vii 3, 9; Macrobius ii 3, 11.

[4] The most definite description of their status comes from Dio xlii 51, 5: τοὺς δὲ ἱππέας τοῦ τέλους τούς τε ἑκατοντάρχους καὶ τοὺς ὑπομείονας; xliii 47, 3: μηδὲν διακρίνων μήτ᾽ εἴ τις στρατιώτης μήτ᾽ εἴ τις ἀπελευθέρου παῖς ἦν. Dio says nothing of provincials, a remarkable omission.

anywhere of caution or scepticism[1]—they have even been improved upon. Cicero had spoken of senators who had once been *haruspices*:[2] Dessau gravely states that there were mercenaries and gamblers in Caesar's Senate.[3] Extreme and unwarranted opinions uttered about Sulla's Senate (there were com|mon soldiers there too) should be a warning. More than that, an examination, however cursory, of the categories and vocabulary of Roman politics, with the repeated and ridiculous motive of obscure origin alleged against highly respectable Roman knights and municipal aristocrats, shows what it means—namely, lack of distinction in public life, that is to say, lack of senatorial rank. A page of Gelzer would almost suffice in lieu of discussion.[4]

About common soldiers, the less said the better. Neither soldiers nor centurions will have been promoted directly from the ranks to the Curia. Centurions were not all 'rustici atque agrestes';[5] if their family and origin were not already reputable enough for municipal honours, legionary service might enhance their fortune and status.[6] They would then often be in possession of the equestrian census, and therefore, having risen in social status, eligible for the jury-panels or for the *equestris militia*.[7] The equestrian officers of this period are an important and neglected part of social history. One of Sulla's ex-centurions is known to have entered the Senate by standing for the quaestorship—namely, the notorious L. Fufidius, 'honorum omnium dehonestamentum'.[8] Of the centurions with whom Caesar swamped the Senate, one at least is clearly attested, C. Fuficius Fango;[9] another was perhaps L. Decidius Saxa, though he may have been an equestrian officer.[10]

---

[1] L. Friedländer, *Sittengeschichte* I[10], 107; E. Meyer, *Caesars Monarchie*[3], 463 f.; A. Stein, *Der röm. Ritterstand*, 208; J. Carcopino, *Histoire romaine* ii 933; H. Dessau, *Gesch. der röm. Kaiserzeit* i (1924), 18; cf. 94. Cf., however, Adcock, *CAH* ix 729 f., a welcome exception.

[2] *Ad fam.* vi 18, 1.

[3] *Gesch. der röm. Kaiserzeit* i (1924), 94: 'Landsknechte waren unter ihnen und Spieler.'

[4] *Die Nobilität der röm. Republik* (1912), 11 [= *Kl. Schr.* i 28 f.].

[5] Cicero, *Phil.* x 22—perhaps a typical term for centurions.

[6] C. Fuficius Fango, or a member of his family, was an aedile at Acerrae (*CIL* x 3758); and N. Granonius was quattuorvir at Luceria at some stage in his career, perhaps between two centurionates (*ILS* 2224).

[7] On the jury-panels, cf. Cicero, *Phil.* i 20. On ex-centurions passing into the *equestris militia*, note, under Augustus, T. Marius Siculus (Val. Max. vii 8, 6 with *CIL* xi 6058), cf. A. Stein, *Der röm. Ritterstand*, 160 f., and on the whole question of centurions, R. Syme, *JRS* xxvii (1937), 129 [above, pp. 32 f.]; to which add, from the triumviral period, L. Firmius (*ILS* 2226). L. Septimius, the assassin of Pompeius, had been a centurion and is described by Caesar as 'tribunus militum' (*BC* iii 104, 2)—but that was at Alexandria. The subject is large and important—and calls for more thorough investigation than can here be given.

[8] Sallust, *Hist.* i 55 Maur., cf. Orosius v 21, 3 ('primipilaris'); Plutarch, *Sulla* 31; *Sertorius* 12.

[9] Dio xlviii 22, 3: ἐν τε γὰρ τῷ μισθοφορικῷ ἐστράτευτο. Cf. Cicero, *Ad Att.* xiv 10, 2.

[10] Cicero, *Phil.* xi 12; xiii 27; xiv 10 etc. On Saxa, cf. R. Syme, 'Who was Decidius Saxa?' *JRS* xxvii, 1937, 128 ff. [above, pp. 31–4]. It is not certain whether Cafo (an ex-centurion never mentioned apart from Saxa) was also a senator, ibid. 135 f. [= 39 f.]. Tebassus and

A certain Cornelius, a scribe under the Dictatorship of Sulla, became *quaestor urbanus* under Caesar.[1] No outrage here—scribes might well be of equestrian standing: more than a century earlier an ex-scribe became praetor, governed a province, and celebrated a triumph.[2] The scribe Cornelius, quaestor in 44 B.C., is sometimes taken for a freedman of Sulla —but this is unlikely, as his name is Q. Cornelius, not L. Cornelius. Like the soldiers and centurions of Sulla, the 10,000 slaves whom he liberated and endowed with his name exert a pervasive and baneful influence.

As for the sons of freedmen, no law in Rome barred them from the | magistracies. Their presence in the Senate was no novelty of the Empire, as many wrongly believed—the Emperor Claudius once had to remind his audience that it was also Republican practice.[3] Such intruders were not accorded a friendly welcome. One at least was among the victims of the purge of 70 B.C.—but he was treated gently.[4] Twenty years later Ap. Pulcher made a clean sweep. It is not surprising that this class of undesirable senator should turn up again in the Senate under Caesar, under Augustus,[5] and, more frequently no doubt but hardly in alarming preponderance, during the first century of the Empire.[6]

Less familiar to their Roman contemporaries than freedmen's sons, more exciting and momentous as an historical phenomenon, are the provincials.[7] But the innovation should not be exaggerated. Every Roman citizen (except a freed slave) was eligible for magistracies. Despite the respectable authority of scholars like Zumpt and Mommsen, it is difficult to maintain that there was any such thing as a 'ius honorum'. Nor could there in law be any distinction between the Roman who inherited the franchise and the new citizen, between the colonial Roman and the

Scaeva (Cicero, *Ad Att.* xiv 10, 2) were probably not, ibid. 128 [= 32]. Scaeva is merely a type of Caesarian centurion—in fact, *the* type (*BC* iii 53). [Cf. *ILLRP* 1116a.]

[1] Cicero, *De off.* ii 29 (without the name); cf. Sallust, *Hist.* i 55 Maur.: presumably the Q. Cornelius who was *quaestor urbanus* in 44 (Josephus, *AJ* xiv 219).
[2] M. Gelzer, *Die Nobilität der röm. Republik*, 10 [= *Kl. Schr.* i 28]. Cicereius, an ex-scribe, was praetor in 173 B.C. (Val. Max. iii 5, 1; iv 5, 3). The *Fasti triumphales* from Urbisaglia [*Inscr. It.* xiii 1, 338 ff.] also attest his origin.
[3] Tacitus, *Ann.* xi 24: 'libertinorum filiis magistratus mandare non, ut plerique falluntur, repens, sed priori populo factitatum est.'
[4] Cicero, *Pro Cluentio* 132: 'negat hoc Lentulus; nam Popilium, quod erat libertini filius, in senatum non legit, locum quidem senatorium ludis et cetera ornamenta relinquit et eum omni ignominia liberat.'
[5] T. Annius Cimber, 'Lysidici filius' (Cicero, *Phil.* iii 14), may be one of Caesar's new senators. It is not certain when M. Gellius, suspect of servile extraction (Plutarch, *Cicero* 27), entered the Senate. A freedman's son C. Thoranius (? Toranius) is attested in the Senate in 25 B.C. (Dio liii 27, 6).
[6] The Tacitean orator (*Ann.* xiii 27) exaggerates wildly when he says, 'et plurimis equitum, plerisque senatoribus non aliunde originem trahi.'
[7] Suetonius 76, 3, cf. 80, 2. Neither Dio nor Cicero mentions this. Yet a strong hint in Cicero (*Ad fam.* ix 15, 2): 'cum in urbem nostram est infusa peregrinitas, nunc vero etiam bracatis et Transalpinis nationibus.'

Roman citizen of foreign extraction. A provincial senator even earlier than the Dictatorship of Caesar could cheerfully be admitted—the more so as a large part of Italy had only recently ceased to be foreign.[1]

From Spain Caesar brought in two men, the younger Balbus, 'non Hispaniensis natus sed Hispanus',[2] of the dominant family in Gades, and the military man L. Decidius Saxa, termed a wild Celtiberian by Cicero, but probably, as the name indicates, of Italic and colonial stock;[3] and possibly a third senator, if it could be taken as certain that the father of the two young military tribunes, the Titii Hispani, came from Spain.[4] |

Caesar's Gallic senators were an easy target for ridicule and lampoons assailing the national trouser and since perpetuated in sober history. It remains to track them down. Certainly they were not chieftains from Gallia Comata, the region recently conquered by Caesar, though the popular verse ran 'Caesar Gallos in triumphum duxit, idem in Curiam'. Excellent men from Gallia Cisalpina may even have been thus derided and traduced, for that land was still a province in status.[5] Narbonensis, however (or Gallia Bracata), is their proper home. Caesar's Narbonensians would demand a special chapter to themselves, which may be thought surprising, for the name of none of them happens to be known. But their class and type can be determined—not so much Roman colonists as native dynasts whose families had received the Roman citizenship from proconsuls a generation or two before. To this class belong Caesar's friend C. Valerius Procillus (or Troucillus), his secretary (Cn.?) Pompeius Trogus, Helvian and Vocontian respectively[6]—and probably C. Cornelius Gallus as well.[7] These men are the forerunners of the illustrious

---

[1] A Spanish origin, from Sucro, was alleged against Q. Varius, tr. pl. 90 B.C., 'propter obscurum ius civitatis Hybrida cognominatus' (Val. Max. viii 6, 4, cf. iii 7, 8; Asconius, In Scaur. 20 (p. 22, Clark); Quintilian v 12, 10; Auctor de viris illustribus 72). Further, Verres' quaestor Q. Caecilius may have been of Sicilian origin (Div. in Q. Caec. 39; Pseudo-Asconius, p. 98, Or. = Stangl ii 185). F. Münzer, RE, s.v. 'Caecilius', col. 1231, says 'ein Sicilier von Geburt'; cf. also Tenney Frank, 'On the Migration of Romans to Sicily', AJP lvi (1935), 61 ff.

[2] Velleius ii 51, 3. Balbus was quaestor in 44 B.C. His uncle was elevated, it appears, not by Caesar, but by the Triumvirs, becoming consul in 40 B.C.: cf. Pliny, NH vii 136.

[3] Cf. JRS xxvii (1937), 132 [= above, p. 37]. To the evidence about nomenclature there given add the proscribed Samnite Cn. Decidius (Cicero, Pro Cluentio 161; Tacitus, Dial. 21).

[4] Bell. Afr. 28, 2: 'duo Titii Hispani adulescentes, tribuni militum legionis V, quorum patrem Caesar in senatum legerat.' The cognomen 'Hispanus' is not certain evidence. In favour of Spanish origin, however, cf. now Münzer, RE, s.v. 'Titius', col. 1557.

[5] Compare Cicero on the maternal grandfather of L. Piso (interpreted in JRS xxvii (1937), 130 f. [above, pp. 34 f.]). Caesar naturally championed men from the Transpadana. L. Hostilius Saserna (from Verona?) may be one of his new senators; cf. Münzer, RE, s.v., col. 2514. We have it only on the authority of the scholiast on Horace, Sat. i 3, 130, that P. Alfenus Varus (cos. suff. 39 B.C.) came from Cremona.

[6] Cf. JRS xxvii (1937), 131 [above, p. 35]. On the family of Procillus, see Caesar, BG i 19, 4; 47, 4 and 53, 5; vii 65, 1; on the problem of his name, cf. T. Rice Holmes, Caesar's Conquest of Gaul[2], 652. For Trogus, Justin xliii 5, 11 f.

[7] On the hypothesis that his father Cn. Cornelius was a Gallic notable who received the

Narbonensians who emerge as consuls three generations later under Caligula, D. Valerius Asiaticus from Vienna and Cn. Domitius Afer from Nemausus; and after them the next attested consul is Pompeius Paullinus —all three, it will readily be presumed, of native extraction, recalling Roman proconsuls by their family names.[1]

Provincial or freedman stock and ex-centurions, these newcomers were negligible, a tiny fraction at the most. No doubt there were many dubious and unsatisfactory characters in Caesar's Senate, as will be expected of any government that follows a Civil War, as under Sulla and under Augustus: it demands a singular faith in human wickedness and folly to believe that all were like that. Caesar the Dictator was certainly high-handed in his methods; but it will not seriously be contended that he deliberately filled the Senate with the criminal, the ignoble, and the incompetent in order to discredit utterly the governing class of imperial Rome.

It is stated by Cassius Dio that Caesar added to the Senate men lower in | standing than Roman knights.[2] That is hard to believe: it may well be doubted whether any of his new senators (*ex hypothesi* the partisans of a generous politician), whatever their origin, were so badly off as to lack the equestrian census, no large sum of money or beyond the rational expectation of a successful centurion or one of the lesser *publicani*.

It requires no special pleading, no exaggerated scepticism, no act of faith to believe that Caesar's candidates and nominees belong to the class of Roman knights—officers in the army, business men or country gentry, the flower of Italy.

A small dose of prosopography will be salutary. Indeed, the neglect of this prophylactic may be largely responsible for the prevalence of exaggerated opinions about the social status both of Caesar's senatorial partisans and of his new senators. Certain histories of the Caesarian period, while recording or even transcribing ancient scandal and ancient jests about these unfortunates, refrain from names altogether, or, if mentioning individuals, give a few only and the most scandalous, as though typical.

---

franchise from a Cn. Cornelius Lentulus, either Clodianus (*cos.* 72) or Marcellinus (*cos.* 56), cf. R. Syme, 'The Origin of Cornelius Gallus', *CQ* xxiii (1938), 39 ff. [above, pp. 47 ff.].

[1] As Paullinus is described by Pliny as 'paterna gente pellitus' (*NH* xxxiii 143), an ancestor was probably a native dynast of Arelate or its vicinity who received the citizenship from Pompeius. Paullinus was suffect consul *c.* A.D. 54. The thesis about Narbonensian senators here adumbrated is strengthened by the presence of municipal aristocrats with names like 'L. Domitius Axiounus' and 'Pompeia Toutodivicis f(ilia)' on early inscriptions of Nemausus (*ILS* 6976 f.). Narbonensis was very much under the protection of the Domitii. They lost it to Pompeius, Pompeius to Caesar. [The first consul from Narbonensis may have been P. Memmius Regulus (*suff.* 31): see *Tacitus* ii 787 and cf. E. Badian, *Foreign Clientelae* (1958), 317 f. Perhaps also indirectly due to a Pompeian connection, although the Memmii are difficult to sort out.]

[2] Dio xlii 51, 5: τοὺς ὑπομείονας; compare also lii 42, 1 (on the state of the Senate in 27 B.C. after the Civil Wars): πολλοὶ μὲν γὰρ ἱππεῖς, πολλοὶ δὲ καὶ πεζοὶ παρὰ τὴν ἀξίαν ἐκ τῶν ἐμφυλίων πολέμων ἐβούλευον.

Thus Meyer names only Decidius Saxa and a certain C. Curtius, an impoverished person from Volaterrae.[1] Carcopino is more generous, though not from benevolence to Caesar and Caesar's men:[2] yet even Carcopino provides only the three Spaniards, Balbus, Saxa, and Titius, and two other characters: C. Fuficius Fango, whom he describes as a 'common soldier' (Fango can have been that no longer when quitting the army), and P. Ventidius, 'ancien muletier' (of which more later).

Now, it is quite impossible to establish accurately the names of even a half of Caesar's Senate. Even before the outbreak of the Civil War, with abundant evidence and fewer disturbing causes, only about two-thirds of the senators are known by name. Willems drew up the list of the Senate of 55 B.C., establishing just over 400 names, which happens to coincide very closely with the largest totals of senators recorded as present in the Curia in that period.[3] But over 200 names are lost beyond recall. Ribbeck emulated Willems for the year 44 B.C.[4] He was able to present just under 300 attested names. Going further, through various descending categories of probability, including senators attested as alive in 51–45 B.C., and certain characters active shortly after 44 B.C., who may, or may not, have been of senatorial rank, he was able to go as high as the number 475. Even if | Ribbeck's figures were accepted one and all, there would still be some 400 unknown and anonymous Caesarian senators. Ribbeck's work is neither complete nor impeccable; but it will serve for rough approximations.

Exact statistics are excluded; and there are many uncertainties of detail. Thus Willems, who discusses the *lectio senatus* of 50 B.C., includes among the senators before the outbreak of the Civil War, on an estimate of the length of their careers, certain men who may well have been first admitted to stand for honours by the Dictator—for example three of the praetors of 44 B.C. (namely, C. Turranius, M. Vehilius, and M. Cusinius).[5] Again, Ribbeck notes as indubitable Caesarian senators certain characters like the mysterious M. Lurius, who does not turn up till 40 B.C., and C. Volusenus Quadratus, who may never have been a senator at all.[6] On the other hand, given the anonymous 200 and more before the outbreak of the Civil War, certain individuals lacking record until the Dictatorship or the Triumviral period may have been in the Senate all the time, discreet

[1] *Caesars Monarchie*[3], 463 f.　　　　　　　　　　　　　　[2] *Histoire romaine* ii 933.

[3] *Le Sénat* i 427 ff. In 61 B.C., excluding magistrates, about 417 (Cicero, *Ad Att.* i 14, 5); likewise in 57 B.C., 415 (Cicero, *Post red. in senatu* 26); in 49 B.C., 392 (Appian, *BC* ii 30, 119).

[4] P. Ribbeck, *Senatus Romanus qui fuerit Idibus Martiis anni A.U.C.* 710, Diss. Berlin (1899).

[5] Willems, *Le Sénat* i 565 ff. These are very obscure personages, the first senators known of their families.

[6] M. Lurius, an admiral serving for Octavianus in Sardinia in 40 B.C. (Dio xlviii 30, 7) and commanding the right wing at Actium (Velleius ii 85, 1), is otherwise unknown. C. Volusenus, Caesar's experienced equestrian officer (*BG* iii 5, 2 etc.; *BC* iii 60, 4), certainly deserved senatorial rank. There is no evidence that he received it.

and unobtrusive. Thus L. Vinicius from Cales, consul suffect in 33 B.C.—
apparently the same person as the tribune of the plebs in 51 B.C., but never
heard of since then.[1] Nor will it be forgotten that some of Caesar's partisans, such as Pollio, would perhaps have won a seat in the Senate if the
Republic—that is to say, the domination of Pompeius—had not been
superseded by the Dictatorship of Caesar.

These hazards must be reckoned with. Failing completeness, it may be
useful to call up certain representative names of Roman knights who
supported Caesar. The financial interests were heavily on his side, as is
convincingly demonstrated by the complaints, alike of the Pompeians
and of the more revolutionary of Caesar's own partisans. Cicero and
Caelius have left the record of their opinions. Among Caesar's associates
and intimates were to be found personages like Balbus the millionaire
from Gades and, seldom separated from Balbus, the familiar Oppius
(probably a member of a banking family). These men were not introduced into the Senate by Caesar—they were more useful outside. But
other financiers coveted standing and repute as well as wealth and influence. L. Aelius Lamia, an old friend of Cicero, whose cause he had championed, now entered the Senate. Lamia is described as 'equestris ordinis
princeps'.[2] The same term is applied to C. Curtius, the 'fortissimus et
maximus publicanus':[3] his son, C. Rabirius Postumus, the prince and
paragon of all the bankers, heir to the virtues and to the wealth of his
parent, | was an ardent Caesarian, and became a senator, even hoping for
the consulate.[4] These men belonged to the class whose interests Cicero
had never failed to support, whose virtue and patriotism he never tired
in acclaiming. Let the panegyrics which Cicero lavished on Roman
knights be admitted as well as the sneers and vilification of the obscure
origin of Caesar's senators. There is not much to choose between them
for veracity.

With Lamia and Rabirius in the Senate, 'concordia ordinum' was
carried a stage further than Cicero intended when he advocated that respectable ideal. What of 'tota Italia'?

V. *Tota Italia*

Mommsen, in no way disposed to depreciate the role of Caesar as a
national Italian statesman, none the less seems to underestimate the influence and the adherents he could command in Italy. 'In Italy proper, on

---

[1] Cicero, *Ad fam.* viii 8, 6.
[2] Cicero, *Ad fam.* xi 16, 2. He became aedile in 45 B.C. (*Ad Att.* xiii 45, 1).
[3] Cicero, *Pro C. Rabirio Postumo* 3.
[4] *Ad Att.* xiii 49, 2. The identity of C. Rabirius Postumus and the Caesarian Curtius has
been argued (and I think proved, despite the doubts of Vonder Mühll, *RE* s.v. 'Rabirius',
coll. 25 ff.) by Dessau, *Hermes* xlvi (1911), 613 ff.

the other hand, the influence of Caesar was not even remotely to be compared to that of his opponents . . . the mass of the burgesses naturally . . .
beheld . . . in Cato and Pompeius the defenders of the legitimate Republic,
in Caesar the democratic usurper.'[1] Meyer goes further, and states that
Caesar was not popular in Italy.[2] No evidence is adduced in support of
this opinion: it is refuted by the course of events.

The middle class in Italy was naturally averse from war; the solid virtues
so often commended by Cicero now crumble and rot before his eyes,
turning into crass materialism.[3] Not only apathy, but distrust. What sort
of champion of the constitution was Pompeius? and what was the constitution? Though Caesar by invading Italy was technically the 'aggressor',
many honest and non-political men, quite unable to disentangle the
'Rechtsfrage' between Caesar and the Senate—and not regarding it as
very relevant—saw in the action of the government at Rome nothing
more than a fraudulent and violent attempt of the oligarchy to entrap and
destroy the proconsul who had conquered the Gauls—'tantis rebus gestis',
as they said at Auximum, if we are to believe Caesar.[4] Pompeius had
boasted that he needed but to stamp with his foot in Italy: he knew better
in his heart. His decision to abandon Italy, concealed for a time and most
disconcerting to many of his senatorial followers, was a rational calcula-
tion—he could not hold Italy. Likewise Caesar's invasion, | five cohorts
against the world, was not as rash as it appeared: it was political strategy.

But in certain regions of Italy, precisely where lay Caesar's line of
invasion, Rome and the 'legitimate government of Cato and Pompeius'
were regarded, not merely with distrust, but even with distaste. In
Picenum, Cingulum fell, though owing benefits to Labienus;[5] Auximum,
which honoured Pompeius as its patron,[6] welcomed the proconsul of
Gaul. At Sulmo of the Paeligni the townsfolk streamed forth to greet
Caesar's man, M. Antonius. To be sure, we have Caesar's account of this;
and Caesar was skilled at presenting his own case in the narrative of the
Civil War. But it all seems very reasonable. The contrary would surprise.

The peoples of central Italy from Picenum through the Apennine lands
down to Samnium and Lucania rose in arms against Rome in 91 B.C., for
liberty and justice. Crushed or submitting, they were by no means satisfied, still less reconciled. They had not been fighting for the Roman

---

[1] *The History of Rome* (Engl. transl. 1901), v 200.

[2] *Caesars Monarchie*[3], 347, 'bei der römischen Nation dagegen, in dem gesunden Teil der
Bevölkerung Italiens, konnte Caesar im Kampf gegen die Republik kaum irgendwo auf
Sympathien hoffen.'

[3] *Ad Att.* viii 13, 2: 'nihil prorsus aliud curant nisi agros, nisi villulas, nisi nummulos suos';
ibid. vii 7, 5; viii 16, 1.

[4] *BC* i 13, 1: for 'tantis rebus gestis', cf. Suetonius, *Divus Iulius* 30, 4.

[5] *BC* i 15: for the Picene origin of Labienus, cf. Cicero, *Pro C. Rabirio perduellionis reo* 22;
Silius Italicus, *Punica* x 32; [and see above, pp. 62 ff.].

[6] *ILS* 877 [= *ILLRP* 382].

franchise; and the *Lex Julia* may perhaps be regarded not so much as a measure to satisfy legitimate aspirations as the offer of a guaranteed amnesty to weaken the insurgents. Alternately encouraged and thwarted by Roman politicians in the previous generation, the Italians were to be cheated further; for it was not intended that their votes should have any effect in Rome. In the end, at the cost of a civil war, the Italians were distributed honestly over all the tribes; but even by 70 B.C. many, it is clear, had not cared to register at all—the roll of that year shows only 900,000 citizens.[1] But not among the Italici only burned resentment at damage and defeat. Etruria and Umbria had been strong for the cause of Marius. They were mercilessly punished by Sulla. Volaterrae and Arretium did not forget. Now Caesar never forswore his Marian traditions and connections, but took every opportunity to recall, revive, and exploit them, eulogizing Marius, replacing his trophies, and championing the sons of the proscribed. It is not always clear what meaning and content should attach to the term 'Popularis';[2] but the adherents of that party, if such it can be called, followed Caesar when Pompeius deserted it, returning to his Sullan connections. Caesar kept faith and never dropped an ally. Three examples—Vatinius, Gabinius, and a certain Sulpicius Rufus are found on his side.[3]

It may therefore be held not merely as plausible but as certain that Caesar | had a great following in Italy. At his coming all the enemies of Sulla and Pompeius, all the victims of Roman domination, took heart again. In Picenum the Pompeii had great estates and influence—hence many enemies, mindful of Pompeius' father, Pompeius Strabo, a brutal and treacherous character, and the violent beginnings of his own career. Nor did Pompeius improve matters by threatened appeal to Sullan precedents—'Sulla potuit, ego non potero?' Caesar's clemency by contrast was insidious and effective; and Italy was averse from war. But in addition to Italian apathy, one may surely assume in many regions active hostility to Rome, nourished on the memories of the Bellum Italicum, the sufferings of Etruria, and the desolation of Samnium.

The extension of the Roman franchise after the Bellum Italicum had no immediate effects. Nor will everybody say of Sulla, constructive statesman though he was, that 'de l'Italie, "expression géographique", il

---

[1] Livy, *Per.* xcviii. Some have been shocked by this low figure. It is quite credible, as Tenney Frank shows, 'Roman Census Statistics from 225 to 28 B.C.', *CP* xix (1924), 333 f. [See T. P. Wiseman, *JRS* lix (1969), 69 f.; P. A. Brunt, *Italian Manpower 225 B.C.–A.1. 14* (1971), 6–8, 91–9.]

[2] [See Chr. Meier, *RE*, s.v. 'Popularis'; J. Martin, *Die Popularen in der späten Republik* (Diss. Freiburg, 1965).]

[3] P. Sulpicius was married to a Iulia (Val. Max. vi 7, 3, cf. Münzer, *RE*, s.v. 'Iulius' (no. 544), col. 893). One would be tempted to conjecture a relationship with the democratic tribune of 88 B.C.

suscita la réalité d'une patrie'.[1] That passionate identity of interest and sentiment which we call a nation was of slow birth in Italy. One cannot but suspect that it has sometimes been dated much too early by modern scholars, with the result that the profound difference between Italy in Cicero's day and the Italy of Augustus has been obscured.[2] Cicero's re-iteration of 'tota Italia' is a deception. Old feuds and old loyalties were not forgotten. An integral national patriotism did not emerge until the War of Actium, or perhaps after that affair, created by the menace (real or imagined) of a foreign enemy, the propaganda of Octavianus, and the national policy of Augustus; for his Principate transformed into a reality what in 32 B.C. had been in large measure fraud and violence, the sworn and sacred union of 'tota Italia'.

It remains to look about for Caesar's allies among the Italici, peoples at war with Rome only forty years before. For demonstration, it will not be necessary to investigate and tabulate by origin and domicile all the members, real or supposed, of Caesar's Senate; and it would demand undue space, detail, and controversy to trace here the subsequent history of all the families that provided the insurgent leaders of the Bellum Italicum.[3] Three significant figures will suffice for illustration.

Herius Asinius, *praetor Marrucinorum*, fought and fell in the cause of Italia.[4] His grandson, C. Asinius Pollio, a friend and partisan of Caesar, entered the Senate under the Dictatorship (*tr. pl.* 47 B.C.) and became consul | in 40 B.C. Another consul of the revolutionary period was the notorious and proverbial P. Ventidius (*cos. suff.* 43 B.C.). Captured at Asculum, the infant Ventidius had been led in the triumph of Pompeius Strabo.[5] Cicero and Plancus called him a muleteer;[6] so did his soldiers, but in friendly ribaldry when Ventidius entered Rome to assume the consulate.[7] That is to say, before acquiring senatorial rank, Ventidius had been a Roman knight engaged in the department of supply and transport for Caesar's army.[8] Ventidius the muleteer is a familiar character: not so widely known is the fact that there was a family of Ventidii at Auximum in Picenum, holding office there.[9] The young Pompeius expelled them

---

[1] Carcopino, *Histoire romaine* ii 476.

[2] e.g. M. P. Charlesworth, *CAH* x 83: 'the statesmanship of two generations before had produced out of civil war a people and made a nation of what had once been a city.' F. B. Marsh (*A History of the Roman World from 146 to 30 B.C.*, 423) likewise anticipates when saying that the Social War 'welded the population of Italy into a single nation.' Note the firm observations of Last in this matter, *CAH* x 425–8. [See now the careful assessment by P. A. Brunt, *JRS* lv (1965), 97 ff.]

[3] I hope to treat this subject elsewhere [see *Rom. Rev.*, *passim*]. [4] Livy, *Per.* lxxiii.

[5] Dio xlix 21, 1 f.; Aulus Gellius xv 4; Velleius ii 65, 3; Pliny, *NH* vii 135; Val. Max. vi 9, 9.

[6] Cicero, *ap.* Pliny, *NH* vii 135; *Ad fam.* x 18, 3 (Plancus). [7] Gellius xv 4, 3.

[8] Cf. M. Gelzer, *Die Nobilität der röm. Republik*, 11 [= *Kl. Schr.* i 29 f.]

[9] Plutarch, *Pompeius* 6 (referred to by Gelzer, but not by other modern historians of the period): καὶ τοὺς πρωτεύοντας αὐτῶν ἀδελφοὺς δύο Οὐεντιδίους ὑπὲρ Κάρβωνος ἀντιπράττοντας διατάγματι μεταστῆναι τῆς πόλεως κελεύσας κ.τ.λ.

when raising his private army for Sulla. Now, it cannot be proved that
Ventidius himself came from Auximum and belonged to that respectable
family of municipal aristocrats; but it is quite possible. Another neglected
fact falls into line here. Ventidius shattered and destroyed the Parthian
armies in Cilicia and Syria, led by Pacorus and young Labienus, a Pompeian partisan from Cingulum in Picenum. Serving with Ventidius as
quaestor or legate was a certain Poppaedius Silo.[1] There can be no mistake
here: this man must be a member of the dynastic Marsian family which
provided the impulsion to the Bellum Italicum—and was largely responsible for that war being called 'Bellum Marsicum'.[2] Q. Poppaedius Silo,
the famous Marsian, was a personal friend of Livius Drusus—and associated with the Samnite Papius Mutilus as consul of the new state of Italia.

The aristocracy of Italy is strongly in evidence on the side of Caesar,
families that could claim a history as old as that of the patriciate of Rome
but conventionally liable to the shameful rebuke of municipal origin—
'municipalia illa prodigia', so Florus terms the leaders of the Italian insurgents.[3] The entry of this class into the governing aristocracy of Rome is a
topic of tremendous historical importance. The Paeligni, as we know,
could not show a senator before Augustus. But Pollio may well be the
first senator from the Marrucini, Poppaedius from the Marsi, unless the
excellent L. Staius Murcus, legate of Caesar in 48 B.C., is a Marsian—he is
certainly a central Italian of some kind or other.[4] |

Certainty lies out of reach. There may have been Marsians and Marrucini, local rivals and enemies of the dynastic families of the Poppaedii and
the Asinii, in Sulla's Senate or soon after him.[5] As for the great Samnite
house of the Papii Mutili, a member became consul under Augustus in
A.D. 9—but the Papius who was tribune in 65 B.C. may have belonged to
it.[6] The evidence is defective: more than 200 senators of Cicero's day are

---

[1] Dio xlviii 41, 1. On 'Poppaedius', the true form of the name, see W. Schulze, *Zur Gesch. lateinischer Eigennamen*, 367. It is not stated, it is true, that this man acquired senatorial rank from Caesar; he might only have held the quaestorship after Caesar's death.

[2] Strabo v 4, 2, p. 241: Μαρσικὸν δὲ ὠνόμασαν τὸν πόλεμον ἀπὸ τῶν ἀρξάντων τῆς ἀποστάσεως καὶ μάλιστα ἀπὸ Πομπαιδίου. Cf. 'dux et auctor' (Florus ii 6, 10).

[3] Florus ii 6, 6.

[4] Cf. F. Münzer, *RE*, s.v. 'Staius', coll. 2136 ff. Note the inscription (*ILS* 885 [=*ILLRP* 444]) from Introdacqua near Sulmo. Münzer suggests that this may well be his home ... but there were no Paelignian senators before Augustus (*ILS* 932). Dolabella's legate M. Octavius Marsus (Cicero, *Phil.* xi 4; Dio xlvii 30, 5) could also raise a claim. [L. R. Taylor, *Voting Districts of the Roman Republic* (1960), suggests Ventidius came from Asculum, Staius perhaps from Bovianum Vetus (pp. 264, 255 f.).]

[5] A certain C. Urbinius was quaestor in Spain under Metellus Pius (Sallust, *Hist.* ii 70 Maur.): an Urbinia married Clusinius, a Marrucine (Quintilian vii 2, 26), and Pollio was concerned in a famous law-suit, defending her heirs against a man who alleged that he was the son of Clusinius.

[6] Indeed, the notorious Milo was a Papius by birth; he was adopted by his maternal grandfather, T. Annius of Lanuvium (Asconius, *In Milonianam* 47 = p. 53 Clark). [But Milo came from an aristocratic Lanuvine family of Papii: see Asc. 31 Cl. and cf. Sydenham,

lost to name and knowledge, deserving for the most part the label of 'homo novus parvusque senator'.[1] For this reason one must be careful not to exaggerate the role of Caesar in bringing into the Senate men from the country towns of Italy. Comparison with the composition of the Senate both before his Dictatorship and after will be useful for guidance.

VI. *Sulla's Senate*

Sulla's new senators have also come in for abuse, ancient and modern.[2] The more perverse allegations about their origin and class should never have been accepted. It is clear that they were Roman knights; and there will be reason to recognize the broad-minded liberality of Sulla,[3] even when we hold that he could hardly have acted otherwise. But what kinds of knights? that is the question: a sharp divergence of opinion can be detected. Carcopino, neglecting the additions of 88 and 86, produces a mass of 500 people with whom Sulla swamped a depleted Senate of 100 members, chosen purposely from non-senatorial families.[4] This is excessive. But Hill appears to go to the other extreme. Taking the evidence of Appian and Livy, he supposes that, except for a few rare individuals of the category of Afranius and Petreius, Sulla's nominees were drawn from the eighteen centuries of the *equites equo publico*, which were composed, for the greater part, of the sons and relatives of senators.[5] Other knights he wishes almost wholly to exclude, because of Sulla's well-known hostility to the businessmen. But this view depends upon a complete and therefore unreal antithesis between Senate and Knights, as though they were identical with the parties | of Sulla and of Marius. As with the Knights, so with Italians. Sulla hated Samnites: he killed a large number of them. But certain Samnites he favoured. Minatus Magius, a dynast of Aeclanum, chose the Roman cause and helped Sulla at the siege of Pompeii. He received the franchise, his sons the praetorship at Rome.[6] Not only this—there is that

---

CRR 773, 964 ff. The tribune probably belonged to this family rather than to that of the Papii Mutili.]

[1] *Bell. Afr.* 57, 4.

[2] Dion. Hal. v 77, 5: ἐκ τῶν ἐπιτυχόντων ἀνθρώπων. Sallust, *BC* 37, 6: 'quod ex gregariis militibus alios senatores videbant.' The 'gregarii milites' are an exaggeration for ex-centurions, on which see above, p. 100. Livy, *Per.* lxxxix and Appian, *BC* i 100, 468 tell a different story.

[3] H. M. Last in *CAH* ix 286.

[4] J. Carcopino, *Sylla ou la monarchie manquée* (1931), 65: 'évitant à dessein les familles sénatoriales'; *Histoire romaine* ii (1935), 455.

[5] H. Hill, 'Sulla's New Senators in 81 B.C.', *CQ* xxvi (1932), 170 ff. Livy (*Per.* lxxxix) describes the Senate as being recruited 'ex equestri ordine', Appian (*BC* i 100, 468), ἐκ τῶν ἀρίστων ἱππέων. This evidence is not the only support for Hill's thesis—he made an extensive prosopographical examination. [Improved by E. Gabba, *Athenaeum*, N.S. xxix (1951), 262 ff.]

[6] Velleius ii 16, 2: 'cuius illi pietati plenam populus Romanus gratiam rettulit, ipsum viritim civitate donando, duos filios eius creando praetores, cum seni adhuc crearentur.'

remarkable and ignored character Statius the Samnite, who had fought against Rome—and then, by reason of his valour, wealth, and family, was made a senator at Rome.[1] Here perhaps we have one of Sulla's senators of 88 B.C., a renegade rewarded for deserting in time the Italian cause.

Schur has argued that it was the policy of Sulla to revitalize the Roman Senate by bringing in the municipal aristocracy of Italy.[2] This is reasonable enough, though Schur gives no examples. Among the 300 or more new senators may be included, in addition to Sulla's own partisans, certain renegades from the lost causes of Marius and of Italia. Statius is a case in point. What can be discovered of the composition of the Senate in the generation after Sulla?

The evidence is not only incomplete, but fortuitous. Odd persons with peculiar, if not unique, names turn up in the most varied connections. For example, the *Senatus Consultum de Oropiis* reveals the unknown senator Voluscius.[3] The brothers Caepasii, small-town orators, appeared from nowhere and captured the quaestorship.[4] Such a name had never been heard of before. Fidiculanius Falcula was a grand name for Cicero to play with, not merely because its bearer was disreputable—'senator populi Romani, splendor ordinis, decus atque ornamentum iudiciorum, exemplar antiquae religionis, Fidiculanius Falcula'.[5] Nor should we require the testimony of Asconius to assure us that Cicero in the speech *Pro Cornelio* leapt with alacrity upon the name of M. Terpolius (*tr. pl.* 77 B.C.).[6]

Most significant are the conclusions to be derived from the nomenclature of the non-Latin regions of Italy, as revealed especially in the masterly and comprehensive work of Wilhelm Schulze[7] and the valuable studies of other students—especially, for this purpose, the prosopographical articles of Münzer. Willems long ago drew attention to the gentile names ending in *-enus* and | *-ienus*, which appear in the Roman Senate as early as the second century B.C.[8] The termination indicates Etruria, Umbria, or

---

[1] Appian, *BC* iv 25, 102: Στάτιος δὲ ὁ Σαυνίτης, πολλὰ Σαυνίταις ἐν τῷ συμμαχικῷ πολέμῳ κατειργασμένος, διὰ δὲ περιφάνειαν ἔργων καὶ διὰ πλοῦτον καὶ γένος ἐς τὸ Ῥωμαίων βουλευτήριον ἀνακεκλημένος.

[2] W. Schur, 'Homo novus', *BJ* cxxxiv (1929), 54 ff.

[3] *SIG*³ 747 [= Sherk, *RDGE* 23], 10: on the name, W. Schulze, *Zur Gesch. lateinischer Eigennamen*, 523. [Perhaps Volscius.]

[4] Cicero, *Brutus* 242 (cf. *Pro Cluentio* 57): 'eodem tempore C. L. Caepasii fratres fuerunt, qui multa opera, ignoti homines et repentini, quaestores celeriter facti sunt, oppidano quodam et incondito genere dicendi.' W. Schulze, op. cit. 351, gives only one other example of this name, *CIL* iii 14045. The first consul with a name terminating in '-asius' is Sex. Vitulasius Nepos (A.D. 78).

[5] *Pro Caecina* 28.

[6] Asconius, *In Corn.* 72 (p. 81 Clark): 'contemptissimum nomen electum esse . . . apparet.'

[7] *Zur Gesch. lateinischer Eigennamen* (1904).

[8] *Le Sénat* i 181; Schulze, op. cit. 104 f.

the Sabine and Picene lands. Again, there are the endings *-idius, -edius,* or
-iedius. Adolf Schulten has demonstrated their origin from the Osco-
Sabellian regions and studied their distribution.[1] Names of this kind are
thickest in the heart of the Apennines, in the territories of the Marsi and
Paelignians.

Names of the two types here mentioned, though not common, are not
rare in the Senate of Cicero's day—and, as they belong to obscure persons,
were no doubt more frequent among the 200 unknown senators. A certain
C. Vibienus perished from wounds received in a riot stirred up by
Clodius;[2] and an elderly one-legged senator of Pompeian sentiments called
Sex. Teidius discovered the body of the murdered demagogue.[3]

In this matter, the Senate of Caesar does not show a perceptibly higher
proportion. But the evidence is imperfect: it cannot therefore be invoked
to produce valid statistics. It is evident that there must have been a large
number of obscure and worthy senators of municipal origin in the Senate
after Sulla, not only from Latium, Campania, and the Sabine country,
but also from Umbria, Etruria, and Picenum. (The central highlands,
however, as has been indicated, were hardly represented at all.) It was
not difficult for the municipal man to enter the Senate: but he could hardly
hope for the consulate, which was practically the monopoly of a small
minority, the *nobiles.* Hence in tracing the emergence of alien elements
at Rome the consulate provides an instructive guide. Münzer has demonstrated the significance of certain consulates held by men with names of
palpably non-Latin terminations of various types, viz. M. Perperna (130),
C. Norbanus (83), C. Carrinas (*suff.* 43) and P. Alfenus Varus (*suff.* 39):[4]
one should perhaps add T. Didius or Deidius (98), P. Ventidius (*suff.* 43)—
and L. Passienus Rufus (4), for Octavianus' friend Q. Salvidienus Rufus,
cos. des. for 39, did not survive to take office.

The consulates under Caesar's Dictatorship (48–44 B.C.) show nothing
novel or alarming. They were nine in number, five *nobiles* and four *novi
homines:*[5] of the latter all had been in the Senate before the outbreak of the
Civil War, all had served as his legates in Gaul. This fact cannot utterly
refute, but it may help to invalidate, extreme and schematic views about
the social standing of Caesar's new senators. On the whole they will
have brought | no revolutionary change, for good or for evil, to the lower
ranks of that body, save by the infusion of partisans from the Italia of
90 B.C., as attested in the three significant characters of Pollio, Poppaedius,

[1] 'Italische Namen u. Stämme,' *Klio* ii (1902), 167 ff., 440 ff.; and iii (1903), 235 ff.
[2] Cicero, *Pro Milone* 37 (cf. S. H. Rinkes, *Mnemosyne* x (1861), 216).
[3] Asconius, *In Mil.* 28 (= p. 32 Clark); cf. Plutarch, *Pompeius* 64.
[4] Münzer, *Röm. Adelsparteien u. Adelsfamilien,* 47 f.
[5] Viz. (excepting Caesar and including Dolabella, *cos. suff.* 44) *nobiles*: P. Servilius
Isauricus, M. Aemilius Lepidus, Q. Fabius Maximus, M. Antonius, P. Cornelius Dolabella;
novi homines: Q. Fufius Calenus, C. Trebonius, P. Vatinius, C. Caninius Rebilus.

and Ventidius, and by the handful of worthy Roman citizens from the provinces of the West.

VII. *From Caesar to Augustus*

Pompeius was no better than Caesar, so Cicero confessed in despondency and Tacitus with cool and bitter scepticism about the ostensible champions of constitutional government.[1] Had Pompeius prevailed there might not, it is true, have been any great increase in the total of the Senate. The governing oligarchy might have checked him. More than that, the greater number of equestrian partisans from Italy and the provinces whom he might have wished to promote had already been seduced by his Marian and 'democratic' rival. In the past Pompeius had furthered the interests of his partisans, inherited and acquired, in Picenum. Hence Lollius Palicanus, Afranius, and others.[2] But he can have had few friends among the defeated peoples of the Bellum Italicum: there was indeed a Paelignian, a certain Attius,[3] who would no doubt have attained senatorial rank. As for the clientèle which Pompeius had built up for himself in the provinces of the West, he would perhaps have been defrauded of suitable material here for his new senate; for so many of his adherents had been won over by Caesar—as witness the Balbi and others.[4]

It was not Caesar but the Triumvirate that depressed beyond recovery the dignity of magistracies and of Senate. A character in a play produced under the Dictatorship professed himself dazed and speechless when he saw six aediles in the place of the traditional four;[5] and Cicero became shocked and petulant about sixteen praetors—'magistratus levissimus et divulgatissimus'.[6] He was spared the sight of sixty-seven praetors in a single year.[7] Caesar, by a *Plebiscitum Antonium* of the beginning of 44 B.C.,

[1] Cicero, *Ad Att.* viii 11, 2: 'dominatio quaesita ab utroque est'; Tacitus, *Hist.* ii 38; *Ann.* iii 28.

[2] M. Lollius Palicanus, *tr. pl.* 71, was 'humili loco Picens, loquax magis quam facundus' (Sallust, *Hist.* iv 43 M.): he thought of standing for the consulate in 67, Val. Max. iii 8, 3. As for Pompeius' man Afranius (*cos.* 60 B.C.), note the inscription *ILS* 878 [= *ILLPR* 385] (between Asculum and Cupra Maritima). Further, one might assume with some confidence that T. Labienus began, as he ended, in loyalty to Pompeius. [See above, pp. 62 ff.] The Picene following of the Pompeii can clearly be detected in the *consilium* of Pompeius Strabo at Asculum ([*ILLRP* 515]): cf. C. Cichorius, *Röm. Studien*, esp. 157 ff.

[3] Caesar, *BC* i 18, 1.

[4] The elder Balbus got the citizenship from Pompeius; so did the Vocontian dynast, father of Caesar's secretary Trogus; and Cornelius Gallus' father may have owed it to a Cn. Lentulus in the service of Pompeius in Gaul and Spain (cf. *CQ* xxxii (1938), 39 ff. [above, pp. 47 ff.]). Gallus first emerges into authentic history as the friend of the Caesarian Pollio (Cicero, *Ad fam.* x 32, 5).

[5] Laberius, *ap.* Gellius xvi 7, 12:

> 'duas uxores? hercle hoc plus negoti est, inquit cocio:
> sex aediles viderat.'

[6] *Ad fam.* x 26, 2.   [7] Dio xlviii 43, 2 (38 B.C.).

reserved the right of designating the consuls and half of the other magistrates.[1] Caesar | had appointed suffect consuls in 45 B.C., and he intended that Dolabella should take his place when he departed to Macedonia. But he did not intend that the consulate should be other than annual, as witness his designations for the two years following. The Triumvirs changed that, rising even to six consuls in 34 B.C. and eight in the year following. Though Augustus restored annual consuls and a semblance of free election, the names on the consular *Fasti* and the record of certain significant incidents in the early years of his Principate (such as the grant of the consulate to Cn. Piso in 23, though he had apparently not held the praetorship)[2] show how firm and undisputed his control really was.

The most disreputable individuals entered the Senate not under Caesar, but after his death. Such at least the ancient evidence indicates, especially Suetonius—'erant enim super mille, et quidam indignissimi et post necem Caesaris per gratiam aut praemium adlecti, quos orcivos vulgus vocabat.'[3] Antonius naturally takes the blame for that, and the posthumous working of Caesar's intentions, real or forged. Cicero in the *Philippics* mentions a certain senator, Asinius, who, he alleges, crept into the Senate after Caesar's death.[4] So the charge is not baseless. However that may be, Cicero does not expressly render Antonius responsible for a senatorial adlection either in the *Philippics* or in his correspondence—which is surprising, if the consul Antonius had behaved in an outrageous or even in a questionable fashion. That is to say, the most definite kind of testimony, the contemporary and the hostile, is silent. It will be readily conceded that the actions of the Triumvirate were open to more damaging criticism than was the consulate of Antonius. Only one adlection is definitely recorded, in 39 B.C., when familiar categories of undesirables—namely, soldiers, provincials, sons of freedmen, and slaves—were admitted to the Senate:[5] it is also stated that men lower in rank than knights had become senators.[6] Definite and alarming tales of this period are also recorded, escaped slaves standing for magistracies and being elected—or recognized in time and carried off by their masters.[7]

However that may be, despite the proscriptions (though that measure, being mainly a capital levy, was directed especially against knights) and

---

[1] Dio xliii 51, 3; Suetonius, *Divus Iulius* 41, 2; Cicero, *Phil.* vii 16.
[2] Tacitus, *Ann* ii 43 [*PIR*², C 286].   [3] Suetonius, *Divus Aug.* 35, 1.
[4] Cicero, *Phil.* xiii 28: 'apertam curiam vidit post Caesaris mortem: mutavit calceos: pater conscriptus repente factus est.' For other statements about new senators after Caesar's death see Appian, *BC* iii 5, 17; Plutarch, *Antonius* 15. Yet nothing about this in Cicero's criticism of Antonius' management of the *acta* of Caesar (e.g., where one might expect it, in *Phil.* i 24—'de exilio reducti a mortuo' etc.).
[5] Dio xlviii 34, 4: ἔς τε τὸ βουλευτήριον πλείστους ὅσους οὐχ ὅτι τῶν συμμάχων ἢ καὶ στρατιώτας παῖδάς τε ἀπελευθέρων, ἀλλὰ καὶ δούλους ἐνέγραψαν.
[6] Dio lii 42, 1.
[7] Dio xlviii 34, 5; Jerome, *Chron.*, Ol. 284, p. 158 H; *Digest* i 14, 3.

the Battle of Philippi, by far the most terrible carnage of the Civil Wars,[1] the Senate | after Actium had swollen to a total of more than 1,000.[2] In 28 B.C. Octavianus and Agrippa, in virtue of censorial powers, conducted a revision of the list of the Senate.[3] One hundred and ninety 'unworthy members' were induced to depart by moral suasion of different kinds. What was the true point and character of this painless purge?

The pretext and official claim is manifest and suspect. 'Undesirables' had entered the Senate in a period of anarchy: only a purified and reputable Senate could receive from Octavianus' hand the restored Republic, only a strong government could guide and rule. In the conventional and prevalent view about the low social status of Caesar's senators, it is perhaps natural that they, or such few of them as still survived, should be regarded as the principal victims of the purge of 28 B.C.[4] Yet if lack of social distinction be regarded as the original sin, the Caesarians were surely less vulnerable than the packed partisans of ten years' triumviral despotism.

But that is not the point. What, in the eyes of Octavianus and his adherents, were the qualities desirable in the senator of the future? What were the defects that disqualified? The answer is simple. Lack of the fortune necessary to keep up a senator's station—and lack of loyalty to the victor of Actium or of protection from the more powerful of his allies.

In 32 B.C. more than 300 senators had fled from Italy with the consuls Ahenobarbus and Sosius, espousing the cause of Antonius and the constitution.[5] Some may have returned with Plancus and other renegades, a few perished at Actium, or were executed after the victory. What was the fate of the remainder? Octavianus after Actium confiscated for the needs of his veterans the lands of Italian communities.[6] It may well be that a number of Antonian senators, contemptuously pardoned, and not formally stripped of their status—for there had been no *lectio senatus*—were now persuaded to give up a position which they had forfeited by their past conduct, whether or not they had been mulcted of their estates.

It is evident that the purge was not directed against men of 'obscure origin', real or alleged. Certain of the scandalous upstarts, such as Ventidius the Picene and Saxa the Roman from Spain, were dead. But the Senate still retained the alien-born Balbus from Punic Gades, the Picene Tarius Rufus 'infima natalium humilitate',[7] and many another, the pillars of the new order—not to mention M. Vipsanius Agrippa and T. Statilius Taurus, the | greatest of them all. The Revolution was triumphant

---

[1] Velleius ii 71, 2; 'non aliud bellum cruentius caede clarissimorum virorum fuit.'
[2] Suetonius, *Divus Aug.* 35, 1; Dio lii 42, 1.   [3] Dio lii 42, 1–3.
[4] e.g. 'Caesarian interlopers', M. Hammond, *The Augustan Principate* (1933), 22 and 116.
[5] Over 700 senators fought on Augustus' side in the War of Actium (*Res Gestae* 25, 3); but the total of the senate was over 1,000 (Suetonius, *Divus Aug.* 35, 1; Dio lii 42, 1).
[6] Dio li 4, 6.   [7] Pliny, *NH* xviii 37.

and consolidated. 'Magis alii mores quam alii homines', to invert a familiar phrase.

After the purge the Senate still numbered about 800 members. With the return to constitutional government in 28 and 27 B.C., magistracies resumed their Republican total and functions, the only change, so a government writer alleges, being the raising of the praetors from eight to ten.[1] The number was not kept, rising on one occasion at least to sixteen:[2] Tiberius regarded twelve as normal and Augustan.[3] As for the consulate, Augustus intended at first that it should be annual: it was not until 5 B.C. that suffect consuls became a regular institution.

The contrast with Caesar's Dictatorship is greater in show than in substance, to be explained largely by the fact that Caesar, coming to power in and through civil war, had to carry out changes in a swift and drastic fashion. Augustus after Actium found himself in a happier situation. The Revolution had gone so far—and all his partisans had been so adequately rewarded—that it was both easy and expedient to call a halt and pose as the champion of restoration; 'cum . . . novis ex rebus aucti tuta et praesentia quam vetera et periculosa mallent.'[4] Not that there was, however, or could be, a real reaction. Twenty years of social change cannot be undone so long as the authors of the process—and its beneficiaries —remain in power.

Caesar's Senate of 900 was a disgusting and unwieldy body, never intended, it has been alleged, to work as an efficient organ of government. In point of size the restored and purified Senate of 28 B.C. was not any more manageable; and this was the Senate which, in the view of some authorities, recovered and exerted its ancient functions as well as its dignity and prestige in the first and most 'constitutional' period of the primacy of Augustus. So the Senate endured for a decade. In 18 B.C. Augustus reduced its total to 600.[5] It is stated by Dio that he would have wished to go further, to 300, that is to say, to the Senate before Sulla— which can hardly be taken seriously, save as a threat to those who were dissatisfied at this modest reduction, and as a profession of Republican ideals. Yet, even so, the Augustan Senate was now probably above 600. Twenty quaestors in Sulla's system were held to be adequate to supplement a Senate of that size: yet it appears that that number was exceeded in the generation following. It is not certain whether Sulla's quaestors were intended to hold that office in their thirtieth year. It has been suggested that he established the age of thirty-seven.[6] | If so, the prescription was certainly neglected in the generation of Cicero—to take only the

---

[1] Velleius ii 89, 3.   [2] Dio lvi 25, 4.   [3] Tacitus, *Ann* i 14.
[4] Tacitus, *Ann.* i 2.   [5] Dio liv 13 f.
[6] Cf. Mommsen, *Staatsrecht* i³ 568 f. Against this, however, cf. J. Carcopino, 'La naissance de Jules César', *Mélanges Bidez* (1934), 35 ff., esp. 60 f.

examples of Cicero and of M. Antonius. If the age of thirty be assumed as the statutory minimum, Augustus reduced the term by five years, a change which can plausibly be dated to the early period of his Principate.[1] This would be equivalent to raising by one-sixth the normal expectation of a senator's life, and hence the total of the Senate. From the middle period of Augustus' rule onwards a Senate of at least 700 members may plausibly be deduced. The contrast with Caesar's 900 (if they were so many) becomes illusory.

What of that other convenient contrast, the social status of senators under Dictatorship and revived Republic? As for consuls, Caesar's appointments have been mentioned already, five *nobiles* and four *novi homines*. The Triumvirate, however, set a high premium on the latter class. The Augustan consuls in the first decade of the new dispensation show no appreciable change from the Triumviral proportion; with the year 18 B.C. and after, a change, which, however, may be due less to considered policy than to circumstances and 'demographic' accidents—a whole generation of young *nobiles* was now growing up, the sons of the defeated and proscribed, claiming the consulate as of hereditary right.

The composition of the Senate as a whole, however, must have shown a decline of social distinction: many noble families had perished utterly in the revolutionary period. On the other hand, the purge of 28 B.C., while removing some 200 senators, affected only a fraction of the accessions of the preceding twenty years; for, allowing for the many casualties of the period, if the Senate at the time of Actium numbered over 1,000, these cannot on any reckoning have been less than 700. Moreover, Augustus deliberately fostered the steady recruitment of the Senate from the equestrian order; and it may be presumed that his policy was followed, if not indeed extended, by the Claudian Tiberius, who, like Caesar, was a patrician and a liberal.

VIII. *Conclusion*

Falling short of a complete catalogue of names and origins, for it is not to be had, the above brief and imperfect sketch, by mentioning here and there a few significant names, may none the less suggest that certain changes in the | recruitment of the Roman Senate were not as abrupt and scandalous as has sometimes been fancied; and that such changes, however

---

1 The provision is attested as early as 24 B.C. in the dispensation accorded to Tiberius, of five years, permitting him to be quaestor in his twentieth year: Dio liii 28, 3. Its origin may belong to an earlier date (29–8 B.C.?). Likewise the reduction by ten years in the age required for the consulate. L. Calpurnius Piso (*cos.* 15 B.C.) was certainly consul in his thirty-third year. Also Ahenobarbus (*cos.* 16 B.C.)? He had been aedile in 22 B.C. (Suetonius, *Nero* 4), therefore perhaps quaestor in 24 B.C.

brought about, could not be arrested, and were not in fact annulled. The Senate of the generation after Sulla must have contained a great mass of municipal men—who by the nature and condition of their being do not impress their deeds and personality on the records of history, but are casually preserved, if at all—for more than 200 have faded into deserved oblivion. Republican history is the history of the *nobiles*.

Yet one part of Italy still lacked its due place in the life of the Roman State, the Italia of 90 B.C. Whatever be thought of the ambitions of Caesar, whatever be the judgement of his rule and policy, one fact remains. In supplementing the Senate, Caesar brought in, among other 'municipal' adherents, excellent men from the Italici, the aristocracy of those peoples. The Dictator perished, but the Dictatorship was perpetuated by Triumvirate and Principate, and his work was not undone. Augustus was not, as Claudius alleged, an innovator, the author of a 'novus mos'; though no reactionary, he would perhaps have been shocked by the language as well as by the policy for which his grand-nephew invoked the blessing of his precedent.

Like Claudius, Augustus could not have appealed to Caesar. It is time to redress the balance. Yet justice to Caesar should not pass into extravagant laudation or countenance any reversion to the schematic contrast or facile antithesis between statesmen and policies which it is the object of this paper to deprecate. By the time of Augustus, the Senate of Rome may be described as representative of all Italy, containing as it did 'omnem florem ubique coloniarum ac municipiorum, bonorum scilicet virorum et locupletium'. The familiar and laudable term 'representation' may engender error and anachronism. Augustus was no doubt glad to see in his Senate men from every part of Italy; he even toyed with the idea of allowing town-councillors to record their votes in absence for elections at Rome.[1] But senators were not chosen to represent a region. They made their way as individuals, men of wealth, merit, and loyalty, or as members of an order in society, the propertied classes; which is evident also for the imperial Senate of the Antonines, with its imposing ranks of local aristocrats from the provinces, east and west, the successors of the Italian 'boni viri et locupletes'. It was not for abstract reasons that Pompeius gave the Roman franchise to local dynasts in Gaul and Spain and promoted partisans from Picenum, that Caesar brought into the Senate adherents from the Italici and even provincials. Loyal in the past, | these men would be useful in the future.[2] The creation of 'tota Italia', however satisfying and

---

[1] Suetonius, *Divus Aug.* 46.

[2] And to a Roman it was no 'novus mos' to bring in *novi homines*—'neque novus hic mos senatus populique Romani est putandi quod optimum sit esse nobilissimum' (Velleius ii 128, 1), a phrase which suitably illustrates the observation of the Emperor Claudius (*ILS* 212, col. ii *init.*).

indeed 'inevitable' to the student of political theory, was not the product of abstract speculation applied to human affairs, but the work of time and circumstance, violently accelerated by Civil War and confiscation, by Dictatorship, and by Revolution.[1]

[1] For valuable improvements in form and substance, the writer is deeply in the debt of Professor H. M. Last and of Mr. R. Meiggs.

10

Observations on the Province of Cilicia

I. *Cilicia: Area and Function*

THE Roman province of Cilicia is an elusive entity.[1] Naturally enough, given its origin and its name. Beginning in the year 102 B.C. as the maritime command of M. Antonius against the pirates of the southern coast of Asia Minor, this *provincia* usurped at once the title of Cilicia,[2] and before long acquired territory and permanence.[3] 'Cilicia' is the most ambiguous of terms; and Cilicians can dispute with Phrygians the claim to widest extension among the peoples of Asia Minor. In the loose language of geography or of ethnography, Cilicia can denote both the coast eastward from Pamphylia in the direction of Syria and the interior to the north, covering parts of Pisidia, Lycaonia, and even Cappadocia.[4] Any pirates or brigands in those territories could without impropriety be called 'Cilices'. Yet in the beginning and for nearly forty years, the regions of Cilicia proper, both the rough and the smooth, lay outside the limits of the Roman province. | 'Pamphylia' would have been a more correct designation: and 'Pamphylia' is attested.[5]

After Sulla's reorganization of Asia Minor, the province of Cilicia extended some way to the north from the coast of Pamphylia through

---

[1] On the history of the province under the late Republic, see Marquardt, *Röm. Staatsv.* i² (1882), 379 ff.; W. M. Ramsay, *A Historical Commentary on St. Paul's Epistle to the Galatians* (1899), section 11: 'Origin of the Province Galatia', 103 ff.; H. A. Ormerod, 'The Campaigns of Servilius Isauricus against the Pirates', *JRS* xii (1922), 35 ff.; id., *CAH* ix 354 ff.; D. Vaglieri, *Diz. ep.* ii 1 (1900), s.v. 'Cilicia', coll. 225 ff.; A. H. M. Jones, *The Cities of the Eastern Roman Provinces* (1937), 64 f.; 132 ff.; 202 ff. My debt to the last-named work is considerable and continuous. [On the whole subject-matter of this article see now D. Magie, *Roman Rule in Asia Minor* (1950).]

[2] *SEG* iii 378 (*c.* 100 B.C.: Delphi), B, § 7 f.: τήν τε Κιλικίαν διὰ ταύτας τὰς αἰτίας κτλ. [M. Antonius: *MRR* i 568 ff.]

[3] It was when governor of Cilicia in 92 B.C. that Sulla made dispositions in Cappadocia and marched to the Euphrates (Appian, *Mithr.* 57). [The date should be 96/5 B.C.: see E. Badian, *Studies in Greek and Roman History* (1966), 157 ff.]

[4] To Herodotus, the Halys flowed διὰ Κιλίκων (i 72); and the 'Eleventh Strategia' of Cappadocia was Cilician (Strabo xii 1, 4, p. 534). The usage went back to very early times. For Cilicia with the meaning of Lycaonia, cf. also Appian, *BC* v 75, 319; *Mithr.* 75.

[5] Cicero, *In Verrem* ii 1, 93; Athenaeus v, p. 213a. [On Cilicia proper, see M. V. Seton-Williams, *AS* iv (1954), 121 ff.]

Pisidia towards Phrygia and Lycaonia: how far, it is uncertain.[1] P. Servilius (*cos.* 79 B.C.), proconsul of Cilicia from 78 to 74, was active on the northern side of the Taurus. His conquest of the Oroandeis and Isaurians perhaps presupposed—and certainly produced—direct Roman control over Lycaonia. Isauria in its earliest and restricted sense, namely the region about Isaura Vetus and Isaura Nova, could quite properly be described as a part of Lycaonia.[2] The direction of Servilius' line of march is uncertain;[3] but even Servilius did not annex either Cilicia Tracheia or Cilicia Pedias. About the territories northwards, in the hinterland, precision is baffled by the confusion of a period of wars. Finally, however, Pompeius made a settlement which aimed, so it may be presumed, at some permanence. Abolishing the kingdom of the Seleucids, or rather recognizing its extinction, he added Syria and Cilicia Pedias to the empire of Rome. Hence a new province, Syria (64 B.C.): but Pedias was attached to the existing province of Cilicia, which, enlarged on this flank, now lost whatever Phrygian territory it may previously have embraced. |

Phrygia as a whole was divided by the Romans into three dioceses or *conventus*. The principal and assize-cities were Laodicea ad Lycum, Apamea, and Synnada. The earlier history of Roman Phrygia is very obscure: after Pompeius' settlement, the three dioceses were certainly united to the province of Asia in the years 62–56 B.C.[4] In those six years

---

[1] Marquardt (op. cit. 381) and V. Chapot (*La Province romaine proconsulaire d'Asie* (1904), 78 f.) suggest that when Cn. Cornelius Dolabella was proconsul, in 80–79 B.C., his province included two of the dioceses of Phrygia (Apamea and Synnada): Laodicea certainly lay outside it, as emerges from *In Verrem* ii 1, 72 ff. Cicero's description of the province is vague and rhetorical—'Lyciam, Pamphyliam, Pisidiam Phrygiamque totam' (*In Verrem* ii 1, 95). 'Tota Phrygia' is not enough to prove that the two dioceses of Phrygia then belonged to the province of Cilicia. According to A. H. M. Jones, *The Cities*, 132, 'only those parts adjacent to Pisidia', i.e., only Phrygia-towards-Pisidia? Cilicia received its first consular governor in 78 B.C., P. Servilius; in 74 his successor was L. Octavius (*cos.* 75), who died almost at once. The operations of Servilius north of the Taurus surely presuppose the control of a wide extent of territory to the east of the province of Asia.

[2] Strabo xii 6, 2, p. 568. On the different meanings of 'Isauria', cf. W. M. Ramsay, *JRS* vii (1917), 277 ff. Ultimately it came to comprise Cilicia Tracheia.

[3] For a full discussion, H. A. Ormerod, *JRS* xii (1922), 35 ff. Ormerod argues that Servilius invaded Isauria from the direction of the Pamphylian coast, crossing the Taurus. Yet he might have come from Phrygia, from the west or north-west. A few years later Q. Marcius Rex (in 67 B.C.) marched 'per Lycaoniam cum tribus legionibus in Ciliciam' (Sallust, *Hist.* v 14 M). He may even have passed through Cilicia and reached Antioch; cf. G. Downey, 'Q. Marcius Rex at Antioch', *CP* xxxii (1937), 144 ff. (drawing upon Malalas, p. 225 Bonn). [See B. Levick, *Roman Colonies in Southern Asia Minor* (1967), 22 f.]

[4] W. H. Waddington, *Fastes des provinces asiatiques* i (1872), 57 ff. This emerges from certain details about the proconsulates of L. Valerius Flaccus and Q. Tullius Cicero (62–58 B.C.). Further, coins: C. Fabius and T. Ampius Balbus were proconsuls of Asia in 58–57 and 57–56 respectively (Waddington, 57 ff.). Cistophori of Fabius were minted at both Apamea and Laodicea, of Ampius at Apamea (*B.M. Cat.*, *Phrygia*, xxxiii, lxxiv f.). Cistophori of Ephesus show that both Fabius and Ampius were proconsuls of Asia (*B.M. Cat.*, *Ionia*, 67). The dating, given correctly by Waddington, is reversed by the B.M. catalogues

the history of Cilicia, however, is a complete blank. The name of not a single proconsul has been preserved—a deplorable loss for Roman political history, for these men, like the earliest governors of Syria, would almost certainly be adherents of Pompeius.[1] It has even been conjectured that Pompeius at first united Syria and Cilicia into one province:[2] improbable, but not altogether absurd—at least until 58–57, when Gabinius became proconsul of Syria. There is no indication at all that Gabinius exercised authority over Cilicia.

However that may be, with the year 56 comes a change, stability for six years, ascertainable boundaries, and an abundance of information. The evidence is quite clear—in 56 B.C. a wide region of the interior, namely the three dioceses of Laodicea, Apamea, and Synnada, was detached from Asia and assigned to Cilicia.[3] The island of Cyprus had already been annexed in 58; | the status of Lycia is uncertain.[4] The Roman province of Cilicia, with a coastline running from the Swallow Islands to the Gulf of Alexandretta, now extended northwards in a great sweep to the southern marches of Bithynia, taking in Dorylaeum and Midaeum, thence south-eastwards, fronting in turn Galatia, Cappadocia, and Commagene, to Mount Amanus and the boundary with Syria: it embraced the regions

and by V. Chapot, *La Province romaine proconsulaire d'Asie*, 78. That T. Ampius Balbus was proconsul in 57–56 is proved by Cicero, *Ad fam.* iii 7, 5: cf. also i 3, 2. [In fact the dating in *B.M. Cat.* is correct and accepted by Syme, *CP* 1 (1955), 130. Ampius' date is 58–57, Fabius' 57–56.]

[1] Appian, *Syr.* 51, reveals the governors of Syria in 64–58 B.C., namely, M. Aemilius Scaurus, L. Marcius Philippus, and Cn. Cornelius Lentulus Marcellinus. Scaurus was Pompeius' stepson; and Pompeius' relations with the Lentuli at different times are an instructive study—for an example, cf. *CQ* xxxii (1938), 42 f. [above, pp. 51 ff.]. For a former legate of Pompeius having Syria in prospect as his province, see the next footnote.

[2] D. Vaglieri, *Diz. ep.* 226. He points to the fact that the tribute of Cilicia and of Syria was assessed on the same scale. No proof. Nor has he noticed Cicero, *Ad Att.* i 16, 8 (July 61 B.C.): 'Pisonem consulem nulla in re consistere umquam sum passus, desponsam homini iam Syriam ademi.' This was M. Pupius Piso, legate under Pompeius in the East and consul in 61 B.C. (cf. esp. Dio xxxvii 44, 3). Note further Josephus (*AJ* xiv 79), who says that Pompeius left a garrison of two legions in Cilicia. [Cilicia was demonstrably a praetorian province in 58: see E. Badian, *JRS* lv (1965), 115.]

[3] Cistophori of the three proconsuls P. Cornelius Lentulus Spinther, Ap. Claudius Pulcher, and M. Tullius Cicero, coined at Apamea and at Laodicea (*B.M. Cat.*, *Phrygia*, xxxiii and 72 f.; lxxiv and 281 f.). The omission of the three dioceses from a Milesian inscription enables it to be dated pretty closely ([Sherk, *RDGE*, no. 52]). The transference of these regions explains the sense in which a proconsul of Cilicia could be regarded as the successor of a proconsul of Asia—'quid? Appius Lentulo, Lentulus Ampio processit obviam, Cicero Appio noluit' (*Ad fam.* iii 7, 5; cf. i 3, 2). Hence the change belongs to the year 56 B.C. Cicero himself refers to the three *conventus* as 'haec mea Asia' (*Ad Att.* v 21, 8). [But see E. Badian, *JRS* lv (1965), 118: 'Ampio' is an emendation and *Ad fam.* iii 7, 5 is not good evidence.]

[4] Presumably autonomous. Lycian troops in Cicero's army (*Ad Att.* vi 5, 3) prove nothing. They may come from the Milyas, a part of his province, or from Lycia as 'free' allies of the Roman People.

known as the Milyas, Pamphylia, Pisidia, the three dioceses of Phrygia, Phrygia-towards-Pisidia, Phrygia Paroreios, Lycaonia, Cilicia Tracheia, and Cilicia Pedias.

It was clearly convenient that the proconsul of Cilicia should go to Tarsus by land and have occupation by the way, holding assizes at Laodicea, Apamea, and Synnada.[1] That is not, however, the whole truth or sole reason for the transference of Phrygia to Cilicia. The enumeration of territories as set forth above reveals the nominal area, but disguises the essence and nature, of the province of Cilicia. A *provincia* is a function or a sphere of action rather than a definite region subject to regular organization. Now just as Macedonia may with propriety be regarded as the Via Egnatia and Narbonensis as the Domitia, so Cilicia in the years 56–50 B.C. is the highroad from western Asia to Syria. Very precisely so: save for his military operations on the borders of Cilicia Pedias, the proconsul Cicero hardly strayed from the road at all. He did not need to—the assize-towns were on it, all the way from Laodicea to Tarsus.

There are two main routes from west to east in Asia Minor, for the traveller must pass either north or south of the wide stretch of salt desert in the middle. Ever since the fall of the Hittite power, the southern route was the more important: indeed, it is the very nerve and backbone of any imperial state that holds both Syria and western Asia Minor. The central and inevitable section, ap|proached on the eastern side from Burnt Laodicea, where the high roads from Melitene and from the Cilician Gates of necessity came together, ran through Phrygia Paroreios (the depression some sixty miles in length between the mountains of the Emir Dağ on the north and the Sultan Dağ on the south). Towards this funnel also converged routes from the west, from Ephesus and from Sardis, and from the north, through Dorylaeum, all meeting in the plain of the Cayster, at the western entrance of Paroreios—a district the strategic importance of which is revealed by the name of Ipsus.[2] Hence the main road from the west to Syria, after passing through Paroreios, proceeds by Burnt Laodicea to Iconium, thence to the Cilician Gates. Cities of immemorial antiquity like Celaenae, Thymbrium, Tyriaeum (or Tyraeum) and prediluvial Iconium, and Seleucid foundations with significant names, such as Apamea (which is also Celaenae), the two Laodiceas, and Philomelium, indicate something of its early history. Indeed, as has recently been demonstrated in the decisive disposal of an old problem, this was precisely the Persian Royal Road.[3] Xerxes probably followed it, marching from the Cilician Gates to Celaenae; and, conversely, Cyrus the Younger setting out from Celaenae, after a detour northwards into Phrygia, soon

---

[1] W. M. Ramsay, *A Historical Commentary on St. Paul's Epistle to the Galatians*, 107.
[2] [On the site of Ipsus (mod. Sipsin) see M. H. Ballance, *AS* xix (1969), 143 ff.]
[3] W. M. Calder, 'The Royal Road in Herodotus', *CR* xxxix (1925), 7 ff.

rejoined the road of his 'Anabasis' and entered Phrygia Paroreios.[1] Further, this route was evidently the vital line of communications for the Seleucid monarchs in their policy of conquering and controlling Asia Minor. They also developed an alternative way to Apamea, going south of the Sultan Dağ through Phrygia-towards-Pisidia and linking their colonies of Antioch and Apollonia.[2] The purpose of these foundations was not merely to provide protection against the Pisidian mountaineers: a southern route, in any case useful, became necessary when the Gauls arrived and menaced the central section of the Royal Road.

The military function of the Roman province of Cilicia now becomes evident. By its northerly extension towards Bithynia, | Cilicia covers Asia completely from the eastern side, takes in the backward regions and spares the need of a garrison in Asia. The proconsul of the military province of Cilicia has under his charge a long frontier and three vassal-states, Galatia, Cappadocia, and Commagene. Hence the personal ties which Cicero and M. Brutus (the son-in-law of another proconsul, Ap. Pulcher) contracted with the Galatian Deiotarus. Not only that: the governor moving along the central road has another frontier to guard, for all along the south, from Pisidia eastwards, stretches the wild region of the Taurus, held by intractable brigand-tribes or petty dynasts nominally subject to Rome and intermittently submissive. Of the people of the Isaurians, no word since they yielded a *cognomen* to P. Servilius: their kinsmen the Homonadenses (or however they may be spelled), a 'Cilician' tribe in the region around Lake Trogitis, have not yet emerged into notoriety. About Cilicia Tracheia, complete obscurity, save that the ancient Teucrid dynasty of priest-kings continued at Olba; and even in Pedias there was a vassal-king, Tarcondimotus, with his capital at Hieropolis-Castabala.[3]

Cn. Cornelius Dolabella (80–79) was followed by two proconsuls of consular rank, first P. Servilius (78–74), and then L. Octavius (*cos.* 75), who died almost at once; and Cilicia was the province originally assigned to Lucullus: his successor there in 67 was also a consular, Q. Marcius Rex. During this period—and subsequently under the Republic—no consular ever held Asia by itself as his province. These facts will suffice to demonstrate that Cilicia was the paramount military province.

Then Pompeius assumed a special command and after Pompeius there is a mysterious gap in knowledge for six years (62–56)—no mention of

---

[1] Namely, near Καΰστρου πεδίον (? Ipsus), whence he marched to Thymbrium and Tyriaeum (Xenophon, *Anabasis* i 2, 11 ff.).

[2] On the importance of this route, cf. W. M. Ramsay, 'Military Operations on the North Front of Mount Taurus', *JHS* xl (1920), 89 ff.; 'Geography and History in a Phrygo-Pisidian Glen', *GJ* lxi (1923), 279 ff.; 'Res Anatolicae III', *Klio* xxxii (1930), 243. [See B. Levick, op. cit., ch. II.]

[3] The evidence for these Cilician dynasts is arranged and discussed by A. H. M. Jones, *The Cities*, 202 ff. [G. W. Bowersock, *Aug. and the Greek World* (1965), 46 ff.].

Cilicia, no governor named. But from 56 to 50, a series of three consulars
—P. Cornelius Lentulus Spinther, Ap. Claudius Pulcher, and M. Tullius
Cicero: all three were hailed by the army of Cilicia with the title of
imperator. The enlarged Cilicia was clearly designed to be the most important of all the eastern provinces: the change made in 56 B.C. perhaps
has some relevance | to Roman political history. Cilicia would have
retained that rank but for the ambition of Crassus and his war against the
Parthians, which brought Syria into prominence and primacy.[1]

The repartition of the eastern lands into Roman provinces and assize-
districts was often arbitrary and inconsequent. Strabo complains that the
Romans introduced confusion by cutting across ethnic units for administrative purposes.[2] With justice: there were many perplexing and anomalous conglomerates. In the course of time, a change might come for the
better, as when Galatia and Cappadocia, joined by Vespasian, were separated by Trajan, or when Cilicia, south Lycaonia, and Isauria were united
in one province by Pius. But not always. Claudius created, and Vespasian, after a brief intermission, made permanent the province of Lycia–
Pamphylia.[3] A fictitious unity—each half retained its own individuality
and its own provincial assembly. Provincial boundaries were largely
unreal: they might be ignored by the provincial assemblies (κοινά), as in
Lycia–Pamphylia, Pontus, and elsewhere, or by the fiscal arrangements
of the central government, as almost everywhere.[4]

Cilicia began as a maritime command and turned into the *provincia* of
a proconsul moving backwards and forwards along a continental road.
Motley and composite the province certainly was. But it was neither
paradoxical nor ridiculous—it corresponded with notorious facts of
geography and of history. Being such, Cilicia might have persisted. Yet,
almost at once, it was reduced in area and degraded in standing. It lost
the three dioceses of Asia in 49 B.C. Cicero was the last governor of consular rank. Ten, or perhaps even six years after his proconsulate, the
province of Cilicia, diminishing by degrees, had ceased to exist as a
separate entity. It is the purpose of the present essay to investigate the
vicissitudes of the province in its last age—and also, for the sake of |
clarity and completeness, to indicate in what manner, not so long after,
a new province emerged which, bearing a different name, yet embraced
most of the area and answered to several of the functions of the old Cilicia.

[1] [See Badian, op. cit. (p. 122, n. 2), showing that the change was in fact decided on in
58, when Gabinius received Syria.]
[2] Strabo xiii 4, 12, p. 628: εἰς δὲ τὴν σύγχυσιν ταύτην οὐ μικρὰ συλλαμβάνει τὸ τοὺς Ῥωμαίους
μὴ κατὰ φῦλα διελεῖν αὐτοὺς ἀλλὰ ἕτερον τρόπον διατάξαι τὰς διοικήσεις, ἐν αἷς τὰς ἀγοραίους
ποιοῦνται καὶ τὰς δικαιοδοσίας.
[3] Dio lx 17, 3; Suetonius, *Divus Claudius*, 25: cf. *Klio* xxx (1937), 227 ff. [above, pp. 42 ff.].
[4] For example, the financial procurator of Galatia, active at Attaleia, in Pamphylia,
under Claudius (*ILS* 215). Note also a procurator of Cappadocia and Cilicia under Nero
(*JRS* ii (1912), 99 = *AE* 1914, 128), of Cilicia and Cyprus under Hadrian (*AE* 1935, 167).

Ambiguity of terminology and inadequate evidence render the whole subject obscure and intricate. Clearness can be won only at the cost of laborious detail—and tedious repetition. The inquiry does not concern Cilicia alone—it derives its origin from an attempt to establish the date of a group of Cicero's letters in the thirteenth book of the collection *Ad familiares* (43–6 and 73–4). They are six in number, and they still float unanchored within the limits of fifteen years. That is a large space of time.

II. *The Proconsul Philippus* (Cicero, *Ad fam.* xiii 73–4)

Cicero commends to the proconsul, Q. Philippus, the two financiers, L. Oppius and L. Egnatius (*Ad fam.* xiii 74); later, when Philippus has returned to Rome, Cicero duly thanks him for his services in the matter, but goes on to express his concern for a certain Antipater of Derbe, with whom Philippus is 'very angry'. Cicero intercedes on behalf of the sons of Antipater, hostages in the possession of Philippus (ibid. 73).

On the interpretation of these two letters depends the dating of four others, relating either to Oppius and Egnatius or to the officials to whom they are commended (ibid. 43–6). Oppius, it is stated, was established at Philomelium. He there had charge of the interests of L. Egnatius Rufus.[1] The central problem is this—was the proconsul in question, namely Q. Marcius Philippus, governor of Asia or of Cilicia? and at what date?

Conjectures have ranged widely, from 58 B.C., or even earlier, down to 44 B.C. Asia has been supported by powerful advocacy. Klebs and Cichorius suppose that Philippus was proconsul of Asia about 54 B.C.;[2] and Münzer seems disposed to accept that opinion.[3] Among the commentators on Cicero, O. E. Schmidt, in Mendelssohn's edition, dated the whole group of letters shortly before the | year 58.[4] Sjögren, in the recent Teubner edition, is content to follow the precedent set by Mendelssohn.[5] Tyrrell and Purser put the two letters to Philippus in 55 and 54;[6] at a later place in their edition, however, they show signs of wobbling, but lack courage to desert the earlier date.[7] Tyrrell and Purser were unable to form a clear opinion. Quite recently, however, a definite thesis and claim to finality: L. A. Constans, the scholarly editor in the Guillaume Budé series, has argued that Q. Marcius Philippus was proconsul of Asia precisely in 45–44 B.C., between the governorships of P. Servilius Isauricus

---

[1] *Ad fam.* xiii 43, 1. This is the only letter of the group which gives the *cognomen* of L. Egnatius.
[2] E. Klebs, *RE* i, col. 2513; C. Cichorius, *Römische Studien* (1922), 168 f.
[3] *RE* v, col. 1999; xiv, col. 1580; xviii, col. 738.
[4] M. Tulli Ciceronis Epistularum Libri Sedecim (Leipzig, Teubner, 1893), 449.
[5] Leipzig, Teubner, 1925.
[6] Vol. ii, no. 128 = *Ad fam.* xiii 74; no. 165 = 73.
[7] Vol. vi, nos. 918 f. = *Ad fam.* xiii 43 f.

and C. Trebonius.[1] Carcopino regards the problem as solved.[2] Likewise, K. Springer in the latest report for Bursian—'Verfasser beweist unwiderleglich, daß er 45–44 Proconsul von Asien war.'[3] In the face of high authority and strong conviction it would not be dishonourable to capitulate. But this is not a prosopographic frolic, a mere matter of nailing down a solitary stray proconsul. Much more than that is at stake: there may still be time to arrest the formation of a dogma. As Münzer has lately indicated, the whole question stands in need of renewed investigation.[4] Was Philippus proconsul of Asia or of Cilicia, and when was the whole group of letters *Ad fam.* xiii 73–4 and 43–6 in fact written?

In the first place, wishing to have Philippus in Asia in 45–44, Constans must thence expel P. Servilius Isauricus (*cos.* 48). Not so easy. This man, appointed proconsul by Caesar in 46 to set in order a shattered province, has left abundant testimony of his manifold activities—so far, no fewer than fourteen inscriptions have come to light.[5] Now Caesar's *Lex de provinciis* prescribed two years as the normal tenure for a governor of consular rank;[6] examples show that the rule was kept,[7] and it has generally been assumed | that P. Servilius held his province from 46 B.C. until the summer of 44 B.C. In truth, there is no definite and dated evidence that he continued to govern Asia in 45–44: but Constans is hardly justified in dismissing the considered opinions of Münzer as merely 'une affirmation sans preuve'. Persons of some consequence can easily escape historical mention, it is true—for example, there is no record at all of the consular Cn. Domitius Calvinus (*cos.* 53), an eminent Caesarian, from the Ides of March to the campaign of Philippi, and after that, nothing more for two years. P. Servilius, however, was not a general but a politician. Had he been at Rome in the spring and summer of 44, he should have been heard of. From ambition and for the consulate, Servilius had deserted kinsmen and allies, espousing Caesar's cause: Caesar's removal liberated his loyalties and his energies. Being married to a half-sister of M. Brutus, and thus becoming the brother-in-law of Cassius and of Lepidus, he stood between the parties, true to none but himself—a sinister and disquieting personage. Münzer has demonstrated beyond dispute how important a factor he was in the politics of the years 44 and 43.[8] If P. Servilius returned from Asia in the late summer of 44 B.C., his presence was soon felt. In the Senate on

---

[1] L. A. Constans, 'Observations critiques sur quelques lettres de Cicéron', *RPh* lvii (1931), 247 ff.
[2] In his review of the Budé edition (vol. i (1934)), *JS* 1936, 111.
[3] K. Springer, 'Cicero, Briefe 1929–1933', Bursian, *Jahresberichte* cclx (1938), 55.
[4] *RE* xvii (1936), col. 1054.
[5] F. Münzer, *Römische Adelsparteien u. Adelsfamilien* (1920), 356 ff.; *RE* ii A, coll. 1778 ff.
[6] Dio xliii 25, 3.
[7] W. Sternkopf, 'Die Verteilung der röm. Provinzen vor dem mutinensischen Kriege', *Hermes* xlvii (1912), 321 ff., esp. 324 ff.
[8] *Röm. Adelsparteien*, 356 ff., esp. 364.

2 September he supported Cicero in an attack on the policy of the consul, M. Antonius.[1]

But there are other and positive reasons that preclude the governorship of Asia by Philippus, not merely in 45 B.C. but in any year. So far, in the main, the opinions of Ciceronian commentators have been mentioned or discussed. Against them stands, impressive and coherent but seldom admitted, the testimony of scholars whose principal care has been the history and administration of the eastern provinces. Bergmann a century ago, in his pioneer study, Waddington, Sir William Ramsay, and others have taken it as self-evident that Philippus was a proconsul of Cilicia, assigning his governorship to a late date, towards 44 B.C.[2] The issue turns upon two points, upon Derbe and upon Philomelium. | The more important first.

III. *Antipater of Derbe*

Tyrrell and Purser describe Antipater as an unknown Greek of Derbe; nor is Constans any more precise—'ce personnage, ainsi que ses fils, était venu de Derbe en Asie, sans doute pour y faire des affaires, et ce furent elles qui, précisément, leur donnèrent l'occasion de mécontenter le gouverneur.' A persistent disinclination to discover who Antipater really was. Yet Antipater is mentioned three times by Strabo.[3] He was a local dynast in south Lycaonia, holding Derbe and Laranda, both places of some consequence. How and when he gained Laranda is not recorded: it is quite likely that he was already in possession of that stronghold when Cicero was proconsul. On 1 September 51 B.C., Cicero set out for Iconium, making for Cybistra and the Cilician Gates.[4] The shortest route south-eastwards, passing through the vicinity of Barata, is deficient in water and unsuitable for an army. Cicero will have chosen instead the longer road to Cybistra: it bent southwards, by way of Lystra, Derbe, and Laranda. It is the fairest of conjectures that he then met and was entertained by that Derbene towards whom he later acknowledged ties of friendship and hospitality.[5] Derbe lies athwart a main road to the

---

[1] Cicero, *Ad fam.* xii 2, 1.

[2] R. Bergmann, 'De Asiae Romanorum provinciae praesidibus', *Philologus* ii (1847), 641 ff.; W. H. Waddington, *Fastes* i (1872), 23; W. M. Ramsay, *Galatians* (1899), 108. Also V. Chapot, *La Province romaine proconsulaire d'Asie* (1904), 80, and L. W. Hunter, *JRS* iii (1913), 89.

[3] Strabo xii 1, 4; 6, 3; 8, 9 (pp. 535, 569, 679).

[4] For details and dates, cf. the careful study of L. W. Hunter, 'Cicero's Journey to his Province of Cilicia in 51 B.C.', *JRS* iii (1913), 73 ff., esp. 87 f.

[5] *Ad fam.* xiii 73, 2: 'cum Antipatro Derbete mihi non solum hospitium, verum etiam summa familiaritas intercedit.' On this, see esp. L. W. Hunter, *JRS* iii (1913), 89. Hunter was dissatisfied with current opinions in this matter. He wrote: 'The whole question of the dating of this group of letters deserves treatment in a separate paper as there are many misconceptions and at least one grave error in the accepted statements on the subject of Antipater and his relations with Cicero.' Hunter's conjecture about the route followed by

Cilician Gates.[1] Likewise Laranda, with an additional strategic advantage
—Laranda is the starting-point of several routes across the Taurus, the
most important of which, commemorated by Barbarossa's last journey,
entered Tracheia by way of Coropissus, thence running to Seleucia ad
Calycadnum and the sea. Of the condition and status of Cilicia Tracheia
at this time, nominally subject to Rome, nothing at all | is recorded:
between Pompeius and Antonius, a complete void. In any case, no single
or central authority. Antipater, holding the vantage points of Derbe and
Laranda, may well have extended his rule a long way southwards into
Tracheia, encroaching at the expense of the decadent Teucrid dynasty
of Olba.

Strabo calls Antipater a brigand.[2] The man of Derbe belongs to a
recognizable class—resourceful individuals who seize power in troubled
times, found principalities in regions difficult of access, and are tolerated
of necessity by the central government or even enlisted in the service of
public order. Such was Cleon from Gordiucome, the robber-chief in
Mysian Olympus, who stood loyal to Rome when Q. Labienus and the
Parthians swept over Asia (40 B.C.): Cleon was recognized and rewarded
by Antonius, more nobly still by Augustus, who conferred upon him the
lucrative priesthood of Pontic Comana.[3] Cleon seems to have been an
authentic brigand. Some, however, of the petty princes of Asia Minor
could boast a reputable origin, going back to the old aristocracy of the
land, priestly and dynastic families which had been there from the beginning. So perhaps Tarcondimotus, the son of Strato, ruler of Hieropolis–
Castabala, who gave military aid to the proconsul Cicero and who later
assumed the title of king, no doubt by gift of Antonius—his name is
theophoric and echoes back to the days of the Hittites, recalling Tar-
khundaraba, king of Arzawa.

Tarcondimotus fell in battle, fighting for Antonius in the War of
Actium, and Cleon perished in his first month at Comana through im-
piety, or at least through a surfeit of illicit pork. Like the antecedents, the
precise transgressions of Antipater are unknown. In the end, after a long
career of impunity, he was attacked and killed by Amyntas, the king of
Galatia, at some time later than 36 B.C., probably after the Battle of
Actium.

Cicero can be confirmed: Cicero himself says: 'iter mihi faciendum per Lycaoniam et per
Isauros et per Cappadociam arbitratus sum' (*Ad fam.* xv 2, 1). This points very clearly to
the road through Lystra and Derbe. (Isaura Nova is perhaps, as Ramsay has argued, to be
localized at Dorla, between these two towns.) According to Strabo, Derbe was situated
on the flank of Isauria—τῆς δ' Ἰσαυρικῆς ἐστὶν ἐν πλευραῖς ἡ Δέρβη (xii 6, 3, p. 569).

    [1] [On Derbe see M. Ballance, *AS* vii (1957), 147 ff.; xiv (1964), 139 ff.]
    [2] Strabo xii 1, 4, p. 535 (λῃστής). Derbe was his τυραννεῖον (p. 569).
    [3] Strabo xii 8, 9, pp. 574 f., gives a circumstantial account of his career and fate. [See
G. W. Bowersock, *Augustus and the Greek World* (1965), 48 f.]

So far the scanty literary record, the combined testimony of Cicero and of Strabo. A neglected inscription falls into line and confirms the power and influence of Antipater. A community in the border-zone of Lydia and Phrygia, probably Temenothyrae, set up a memorial of the friendly services rendered by Antipater of Derbe, the son of Perilaus, in a matter between them and the | Roman government.[1] There is no clear indication of date; and the wording of the inscription does not prove that Antipater himself either visited Rome, or even attended in person at the transaction, in the presence of the Roman consuls, to which the fragmentary inscription refers just before its mention of the good deeds of Antipater. It is clear, however, that an embassy had been sent from Temenothyrae to Rome—or perhaps to the 'legitimate' Pompeian government at Thessalonica in 49 B.C., when, under the menace of requisitions in the Civil War, the communities of Asia would stand in need of powerful defenders.[2]

Over all the East, kings and tetrarchs, dynasts and cities were in the *clientela* of Pompeius Magnus; they conducted or dispatched contingents to help him in the war. Loyalty to Pompeius could cover or justify private aggrandizement. Deiotarus the Galatian was the greatest of the vassal-kings. The confusion after Pharsalus and Caesar's long delay in Egypt gave him freedom to encroach upon his neighbours, whether or no his suppression of Castor Tarcondarius belongs to this date.[3] Antipater, it may be conjectured, | owed the title, if not the original possession of his principality to Pompeius. He was up to no good in the years 49–47; and

[1] *IGR* iii 1694, reproduced integrally from the text of J. Keil and A. v. Premerstein, *Bericht über eine zweite Reise in Lydien* (*Denkschr. der k. Ak. in Wien, phil.-hist. Klasse* liv (1911), 135, no. 248):

> [. . . .]ονει[. .]
> [. . .]ιων καὶ ἔστησεν παρόντων καὶ τῶν ὑπάτων. ἐ[πεὶ]
> [Ἀντ]ίπατρος Περιλάου Δερβήτης πολλὰς ἀποδείξ[εις]
> [παρέ]σχηται τῆς πρὸς ἡμᾶς εὐνοίας ἐν παντ[ὶ καὶ-]
> [ρῶ]ι τοῖς [. . . . . τ]ῆς πισ[τῆς]
> [πρ]οθυ[μίας . . . .]πολε[. . . .]
> [. .]νομο[. . . . .] καὶ ιερε[. . .]

The inscription was found at Uşak ('bei der Moschee Buldaily-Djamissi im Hofe der Medresse') but, like others from this site, may have been brought from elsewhere. Whether Uşak is or is not the ancient Temenothyrae is here irrelevant: for a discussion, ibid. 133 f. Keil and Premerstein assume that Antipater had visited Rome and entered into relations with influential persons before the time of Cicero's proconsulate of Cilicia: but that is only an inference from the words, 'non solum hospitium, verum etiam summa familiaritas', of the letter *Ad fam.* xiii 73, 2, which they date to *c.* 54 B.C. But that date cannot stand. They are right, however, in pointing out that the subject of the verb ἔστησεν in l. 2 can hardly be Antipater, for he is mentioned, with his full name, at the very beginning of the following sentence. They suppose that the community which recorded its gratitude to Antipater was either Temenothyrae or Acmonia.

[2] Compare the exemption from military service accorded to the Jews by the consul Cn. Cornelius Lentulus Crus, then in Asia (Josephus, *AJ* xiv 228, etc.). Both consuls, however, were later at Thessalonica together (Dio xli 43, 2).

[3] Strabo xii 5, 3, p. 568.

Caesar will have been 'very angry' with Antipater, just as he was with Deiotarus.[1] Hence the taking of hostages by the proconsul of Cilicia. Philippus might have been proconsul of Cilicia in 44 B.C.: he was probably the first proconsul of that province to be appointed by Caesar, in 47, soon after the termination of the Alexandrian War (see further below, p. 136).

The lord of Derbe and Laranda was a formidable factor, given the strategic importance of his principality in relation to the high road from Asia to Syria; the extent and nature of his influence with the Roman government (i.e. with Pompeius?) is shown by the gratitude of a distant community like Temenothyrae. Antipater was perhaps a more reputable character than Cleon the brigand—his father Perilaus bore a fine Macedonian name and showed historical sense in choosing an appellation for his heir (centuries earlier, Antipater the Macedonian had a son called Perilaus).[2] By kinder fate or by a nicer calculation in crime and treachery, Antipater might have survived to win a regal title and earn the gratitude of Rome's rulers as an agent of the imperial peace, to pass into history as the peer and equal of Herod and of Amyntas. No doubt but that he was endowed with some at least of the requisite qualities—'dignus ille quidem omni regno', as Cicero said, extolling another friend of Cilician days, the crafty and murderous Deiotarus.[3]

IV. *Philomelium: Asia or Cilicia?*

L. Oppius was resident at Philomelium.[4] He there had charge of the interests of L. Egnatius Rufus, a Roman knight who did business in Asia and in Bithynia as well. Cicero professes himself to be under the deepest obligation to Egnatius. The nature of the | services rendered by the financier might be conjectured: it happens to be recorded. During the Civil War both Cicero and his brother, in need of ready cash, expected to get a loan from Egnatius.[5] It will be presumed that they were not disappointed. The letters to the proconsul Philippus (and certain others as well) therefore convey the express testimony of Cicero's gratitude—and, more important for the question under debate, an indication of the date at which they were composed.

---

[1] Caesar's firm language on their first confrontation is vividly recorded in *Bell. Al.* 68. Caesar then restored his royal title. But that was not the end of the trouble. Brutus championed the cause of Deiotarus at Nicaea and so did Cicero later in Rome. Cicero then, addressing Caesar, says, 'non enim iam metuo ne illi tu suscenseas' (*Pro rege Deiotaro* 35). The same verb describes Philippus' feelings about Antipater of Derbe—'ei te vementer suscensuisse audivi et moleste tuli' (*Ad fam.* xiii 73, 2).

[2] Plutarch, *De frat. amore* 15, p. 486 A. (*RE* on 'Perilaus' ignores the parent of Antipater of Derbe.)

[3] *Ad Att.* xiv 1, 21.   [4] As stated in *Ad fam.* xiii 43, 1 (and only there).

[5] *Ad Att.* vii 18, 4; x 15, 4; xi 3, 3; xii 18, 3; 30, 1 f.; 31, 2.

The town of Philomelium (Akşehir) was a foundation of the Seleucid period.¹ It lay on the northern flank of the Sultan Dağ, beside the Lake of the Forty Martyrs, in the middle of Phrygia Paroreios. The extension of that region from west to east along the main road is given by Strabo, namely from Holmi (near Ipsus) to Tyriaeum.² Paroreios was bounded on the west and north by the Synnadic diocese, on the south-west by Phrygia-towards-Pisidia, on the east by Galatia and by Lycaonia. As indicated above, a number of routes converge at the western end of Paroreios and unite to form the central link of the road from Asia to Syria. For administrative purposes, the region could have been joined either with Asia or with Cilicia. Under the Empire, it belonged to the province of Asia:³ not necessarily so under the Republic.⁴

The earliest history of Paroreios in the Roman period, as of other inland regions, is naturally obscure. Philomelium itself first turns up in the year 70 B.C. Cicero is arguing about the requisitioning of corn by provincial governors: as a hypothetical example, he imagines people from Philomelium being commanded to bring corn to Ephesus.⁵ This would imply that Philomelium was in the province of Asia; and it has sometimes been taken as | proof. Yet if two of the three dioceses of Phrygia belonged to the province of Cilicia,⁶ it is evident that Philomelium, which lies further east along the main road, must also have been in Cilicia. Again, in 62–56, when all three dioceses were attached to Asia, it is by no means certain that Philomelium went with them. Philomelium was old Phrygian land—but so, for that matter, was Pisidic Phrygia and Lycaonia as far to the south-east as the ancient city of Iconium. Neither of these regions was ever joined with Asia, so far as is known.⁷

In the years 56–50 Philomelium was inevitably a part of Cilicia, for the three Phrygian dioceses were then in Cilicia. Further, Cicero held assizes there, as is clearly stated—and, what is more remarkable, the assizes for Lycaonia.⁸ This fact has not always been noticed: it is perhaps an indica-

¹ The name recalls the Seleucid general, Philomelus; and a certain Lysias, son of Philomelus, was a local dynast in Phrygia (for the evidence, Stähelin, *RE* xiii, coll. 2531 f.; Ruge, ibid. xix, coll. 2520 ff.). Hence another city, called Lysias: on the site, J. G. C. Anderson, *JHS* xviii (1898), 107; W. M. Ramsay, *CB* i 754.

² Strabo xiv 2, 29, p. 663 [from Artemidorus]. On the region cf. W. M. Ramsay, *The Historical Geography of Asia Minor*, 139 f.; J. G. C. Anderson, *JHS* xviii (1898), 109 ff.; W. M. Calder, *JRS* ii (1912), 237 ff.

³ Pliny, *NH* v 95: 'hos includit Lycaonia in Asiaticam iurisdictionem versa, cum qua conveniunt Philomelienses, Tymbriani, Leucolithi, Pelteni, Tyrienses.'

⁴ As stated by A. H. M. Jones, *The Cities*, 64; 391. Cf., however, Ramsay, *CB* i 341; 428, and *Galatians*, 108; V. Chapot, op. cit. 80.   ⁵ *In Verrem* ii 3, 191.

⁶ Ramsay, *CB* i 341; V. Chapot, op. cit. 78 f. See also above, p. 121, n. 1.

⁷ Antioch might, it is true, have belonged to the province of Asia for a brief period, from 49 or 47 to 39 B.C.: there is no evidence.

⁸ *Ad fam.* iii 8, 6: 'quod isdem diebus meus conventus erat Apameae, Synnade, Philomeli, tuus Tarsi.' Cf. ibid. xv 4, 2; *Ad Att.* v 20, 1. In the spring of the next year he held the assizes for the whole of his province (excepting Cilicia Pedias and Cyprus) at the one

tion of the standing connections of Philomelium and of Phrygia Paroreios with the territory to the south-east. In the year after Cicero's departure, the three dioceses reverted to Asia. But not the region of Phrygia Paroreios. Just as previously, before 56 B.C., it need not have shared in the vicissitudes of Phrygia, so now Paroreios along with Philomelium, the capital of the Lycaonian *conventus*, presumably remained in Cilicia. Hence a man resident at Philomelium is recommended to the good offices of Q. Philippus. The theory that Philippus was proconsul, not of Cilicia but of Asia, is seen to have rested upon a pair of treacherous supports—an incautious assumption touching Philomelium and pure ignorance about Antipater of Derbe. In any case, Philippus must be a proconsul of Cilicia between 47 and 44 B.C. It will now be possible to assign a date to the kindred group of letters of recommendation. |

V. *The Letters* Ad fam. *xiii 43–6*

The first pair of these epistles (43–4) commend L. Oppius in person and the interests of the absent L. Egnatius Rufus to a Roman official. About the date, no reasonable doubt: the greater part of the second (44) is identical, not merely in substance but in words, with the first letter to Philippus (74). About the recipient, a difficulty. All the manuscripts of the first letter bear the address 'Quinto Gallo': for the second, some have 'Gallo', others 'Gallio'.[1] Rather than assume an otherwise unknown Quintius, or rather Quinctius, many scholars prefer to follow the opinion of Manutius and choose Quintus Gallius.[2] If so, which Q. Gallius? Not, as some suppose, the aedile of 67 B.C.[3] Given the approximate date as fixed by the synchronism with Philippus, it would have to be Q. Gallius, praetor in 43 B.C. This man was accused of conspiring against the life of Octavianus in August or September of that year; he disappeared, under dark rumours incriminating the young consul.[4] His standing would make it a reasonable conjecture that he had served under Philippus in Cilicia, either as quaestor or as legate.

The next two letters (45–6) are addressed to a certain Appuleius, given

place, Laodicea—'Idibus Februariis, quo die has litteras dedi, forum institueram agere Laodiceae Cibyraticum et Apamense, ex Idibus Martiis ibidem Synnadense, Pamphylium (tum Phemio dispiciam κέρας), Lycaonium, Isauricum' (*Ad Att.* v 21, 9). Cf. W. M. Ramsay, *JRS* xii (1922), 151: 'In Cicero's time and use the Isaurican conventus had Iconium as its centre, while the Lycaonian conventus looked to Philomelion as its meeting-place. The editors of Cicero's letters mis-state the facts and misrepresent history in respect of those two conventus.' They are not the only culprits.

[1] For the *apparatus*, cf. the editions of Mendelssohn and Sjögren.
[2] e.g. Vonder Mühll, *RE* vii, col. 671. A Quinctius Gallus is, however, not impossible, cf. Münzer, *RE* xviii, col. 738, pointing to the inscription *CIL* i² 1820, which mentions a Q. Quinctius Q. f. Gallus.
[3] Asconius, 78 f. (p. 88 Clark).
[4] Appian, *BC* iii 95, 394; Suetonius, *Divus Aug.* 27, 4.

in the first of them the title of 'proquaestor'.[1] The first of them concerns, as usual, the operations of Egnatius Rufus. But not this time through his agent at Philomelium: it is his slave Anchialus and his interests in the province of Asia—'Anchialum servum negotiaque quae habet in Asia.'[2] The subject of the second letter is a freedman, L. Nostius Zoilus, beneficiary along with Cicero in a will. |

In the first place, the province of which Appuleius was quaestor. Not necessarily the same as that of Philippus and of Q. Gallius, for L. Oppius, resident at Philomelium, does not occur here. Not Cilicia, therefore, as some have supposed,[3] but Asia. For the date, at first sight a wide margin seems possible, between 51 and 44. The activities of the financier L. Egnatius Rufus were not confined to the provinces of Cilicia and Asia, but extended to Bithynia. We find him recommended to the good offices of Silius, governor of Bithynia–Pontus in 51–50 B.C.[4]

If the identity of Appuleius were fixed, that might help. Now in the winter of 44–43 B.C. the retiring quaestors of Syria and of Asia, C. Antistius Vetus and M. Appuleius, handed over the funds at their disposal to M. Brutus.[5] Appuleius had presumably served as quaestor under P. Servilius. (Trebonius' quaestor is known—he was the young P. Lentulus Spinther.)[6] Further, this M. Appuleius might be, as Groag has conjectured, no other than M. Appuleius, *cos.* 20 B.C., the son of that obscure Sex. Appuleius who married the elder Octavia, step-daughter of L. Marcius Philippus and half-sister of Octavianus.[7] If M. Appuleius, attested as the retiring quaestor of Asia in 44 B.C., were the same person as Appuleius the proquaestor in Cicero's letter of recommendation, there would follow an interesting conclusion. The pair of letters, *Ad fam.* xiii 45–6, would clearly be the latest in date of the whole book.[8] But that is too much to

---

[1] That is to say, either a quaestor with his term prorogued or a legate acting as quaestor.

[2] The word 'Asia' can, of course, be applied to the three Phrygian dioceses—'iter igitur ita per Asiam feci ut etiam fames qua nihil miserius est, quae tum erat in hac mea Asia (messis enim nulla fuerat), mihi optanda fuerit' (*Ad Att.* v 21, 8); but that is irrelevant here, for precisely in the years in which this letter must fall (49–44 B.C.), Cicero's Asia no longer belonged to the province of Cilicia. Therefore, on any count, Appuleius must be the quaestor of Asia.

[3] M. Bülz, *De prov. Rom. quaestoribus*, Diss. Leipzig (1893), 62 f.; F. Sobeck, *Die Quaestoren der röm. Republik*, Diss. Breslau (1909), 69.

[4] *Ad fam.* xiii 47.

[5] Cicero, *Phil.* x 24; xiii 32; Appian, *BC* iii 63, 259; iv 75, 316; *Epp. ad M. Brutum* i 7, 2.

[6] *Ad fam.* xii 14 f. (29 May 43 B.C.). He regarded himself as governor of Asia after Trebonius' death, adopting the title 'proquaestor pro praetore'.

[7] *PIR*[2], A 959. Fonteius and Fonteia, father-in-law and wife respectively of the quaestor M. Appuleius, are honoured on inscriptions of Ephesus (*GIBM* iii 547, 2–3). Groag identifies as one person (1) the quaestor of 44 B.C., (2) the quaestor of the inscriptions, (3) the consul of 20 B.C.

[8] That is, unless the letter to C. Sextilius Rufus, quaestor in charge of Cyprus (*Ad fam.* xiii 48), were to be dated as late as the beginning of 43 B.C., which would be highly questionable (see below, p. 141, n. 6).

hope for. It may be tempting, but it is not necessary to identify Appuleius the proquaestor with the better-known M. Appuleius. There are too many Appuleii in this period. The proquaestor Appuleius might be the elder of the two brothers, namely | Sex. Appuleius (*cos.* 29 B.C.)—or even their father. Yet again, there was a P. Appuleius, tribune in 43 B.C., an old associate of Cicero—'meorum omnium consiliorum periculorumque iam inde a consulatu meo testis, conscius, adiutor' (whatever that may be worth).[1] This man could easily have been quaestor of Asia in 47 or 46. For dating, the years 51–44 are theoretically available. Yet, on a strict but reasonable interpretation, given the very close resemblance in phraseology between the first letter to Appuleius and the first to Q. Gallius, these letters should belong to the time and period when Q. Philippus was proconsul of Cilicia. Appuleius will have been quaestor of Asia under Cn. Domitius Calvinus (48–47)—and proquaestor after his departure in the winter of 47–46, before the arrival of the proconsul P. Servilius.[2]

As this section has already wandered far into the intricacies of prosopography, it will not be an alarming divagation now to speculate also about Philippus the proconsul of Cilicia.

VI. *The Identity of Q. Philippus*

Given the *cognomen*, he was pretty clearly a Marcius. Now in this generation a multiplicity of Marcii are discovered in official positions in the eastern provinces, namely men with the *cognomina* Rex, Philippus, Figulus, Crispus, and Censorinus. Q. Philippus is evidently a near relative of that L. Marcius Philippus (the son of the famous censor) who governed Syria for two years (62–60 B.C.) in the interests of Pompeius, after Scaurus, the stepson of Pompeius, and before Marcellinus, with whom he held the consulate in 56 B.C.[3] Like his father before him, L. Philippus was a crafty person, solicitous for personal survival in times of civil strife. He was in relations with Pompeius, with Cato—and with Caesar, whose niece Atia he married in 58 B.C., on the death of her husband C. Octavius, thereby acquiring three step-children. The matrimonial tie furnished a respectable pretext for neutrality in the Civil War: his son, tribune in 49 B.C., was active in Caesar's interests,[4] and became praetor in 44.

Q. Philippus is either the brother or the nephew of the consul | of 56 B.C. Cichorius observed that Q. Marcius Q. f. Pap. was present in the *consilium* of Cn. Pompeius Strabo at Asculum in 89 B.C., a young man, to judge by his position on the list.[5] Cicero also served at Asculum. Now

[1] Cicero, *Phil.* xiv 16. Further, the proscribed Apuleius (Appian, *BC* iv 46, 195) may be different from any of the Appulei here mentioned.
[2] For the date, see below, p. 137.
[3] Appian, *Syr.* 51. Appian gives no *praenomen*.   [4] Caesar, *BC* i 6, 4.
[5] *ILS* 8888 [= *ILLRP* 515 (improved text)]; cf. C. Cichorius, *Römische Studien* (1922), 168 f.

Cicero, interceding for the captive sons of Antipater, appealed to an old friendship with Q. Philippus—'pro vetere nostra necessitudine'.[1]

For this reason, Cichorius identified the two men. He suggested that Q. Marcius L. f. Philippus was praetor in 56, proconsul of Asia in 55–54.[2] But Cilicia, it has been shown, was the province of Philippus. There is a way out—the appeal to personal friendship might apply no less to the son of a man who had been with Cicero at Asculum. Caesar sometimes employed fairly elderly men to govern provinces and command armies, it is true. More conspicuous the very young in high favour and high office. Caesar frequently placed quite important provincial commands in the charge of quaestors or ex-quaestors (compare, in the following section, Sex. Julius Caesar, Q. Cornificius, and C. Antistius Vetus). Therefore, Q. Philippus may well be the son of Cicero's 'Kriegskamerad'; hence, a young man about the same age as his cousin (*tr. pl.* 49), and governor of Cilicia with the rank and title of *quaestor pro praetore* or *quaestor pro consule*.

Some scholars, accepting Cilicia, have put Philippus in 45 or 44 B.C.[3] Whichever be the year, a conflict will then arise with the existing evidence. Neither year is completely ruled out—we know so little, and strict proof is precluded. But 47–46 is available and accords with the evidence. In justification, it will be necessary to dissect and review a tangled chapter of provincial history under the dictatorship of Caesar.

VII. *Cilicia and Syria, 48–44 B.C.*

After the battle of Pharsalus, Caesar, hastening to Egypt in pursuit of Pompeius, left the three provinces of Asia, Bithynia–Pontus, | and Cilicia under the charge of the consular Cn. Domitius Calvinus.[4] For how long, it is not quite clear. Calvinus was with Caesar in the Bellum Africum.[5] Hence his tenure of all three provinces has sometimes been made to run from the autumn of 48 B.C. to the spring of 46.[6] Now according to Cassius Dio, Caesar, after his victory over Pharnaces at Zela, himself before departing to Italy made certain arrangements in Pontus and left the rest to Calvinus.[7] The author of the *Bellum Alexandrinum*, however, does not

[1] *Ad fam.* xiii 73, 2.

[2] *Römische Studien*, 168 f. C. Claudius Pulcher, however, praetor in 56 B.C., was proconsul of Asia precisely in 55 B.C. (Waddington, *Fastes*, 31 f.; Münzer, *RE* iii, col. 2856).

[3] Bergmann, Waddington, and Ramsay, above, p. 128, n. 2. Also Hölzl, *Fasti praetorii* (1876), 94 f., who, adopting 45, has perpetuated the conjecture that Philippus was praetor in 46. [Stella Maranca, *Fasti praetorii* (1926), assigned the praetorship to 'paulo ante 44' (p. 336; cf. 363).]

[4] *Bell. Al.* 34, 1: 'Asiam finitimasque provincias'. Cilicia is not definitely mentioned, but Calvinus sent an officer there to get troops (ibid. 34, 5). Syria might also have been under his charge: there is no record about it.   [5] *Bell. Afr.* 86, 3; 93, 1.

[6] E. Letz, *Die Provinzialverwaltung Caesars*, Diss. Strassburg (1912), 76 ff.

[7] Dio xlii 49, 1.

mention Calvinus in this context, but states that Caesar left two legions in Pontus under Coelius Vinicianus.[1] That man might therefore have been chosen as an independent governor. Possibly Caesar divided Bithynia and Pontus: however it be, C. Vibius Pansa apparently governed Bithynia in 46 B.C.;[2] and P. Servilius was the successor of Calvinus in Asia in that year, presumably from spring or early summer.

Even if Calvinus held both Bithynia–Pontus and Asia until the beginning of 46, the same would not follow for Cilicia. Cilicia at this time was not contiguous with Bithynia–Pontus—and it had problems of its own. After the Alexandrian war, Caesar came to Syria and to Cilicia in the summer of 47 B.C. on his way to Pontus and made certain dispositions affecting those provinces.[3] In Syria Caesar appointed as governor a young kinsman, the quaestor Sex. Julius Caesar.[4] It may be presumed that he did not neglect Cilicia either, but likewise gave it a governor of its own at last, namely Q. Marcius Philippus (also a relative, being the brother or nephew | of the husband of his own niece). On his journey northwards, Caesar encountered Deiotarus and rebuked him for unsatisfactory behaviour during the Civil War.[5] Another vassal of Rome, Antipater the son of Perilaus, was taken to task by the proconsul of Cilicia—for Caesar did not go anywhere near Laranda and Derbe.

The successor of Philippus in the spring or early summer of the next year is known, thanks to the acute investigations of Ganter.[6] It was a correspondent of Cicero, the poetical and accomplished Q. Cornificius, quaestor in 48, praetor probably in 45.[7] When Cornificius set out from Rome, the African campaign was imminent; Cornificius, however, was going to a peaceful command.[8] Before long, he had a war upon his hands. The Pompeian Q. Caecilius Bassus, encouraged by reports of Caesar's ill success in Africa, raised an army, joined battle with the governor of Syria, won over his legion, and had him assassinated.[9] The death of Sex.

---

[1] *Bell. Al.* 77, 2. As Dessau observes, the inscription of M. Coelius Vinicianus (*ILS* 883 [= *ILLRP* 402]) omits this command: but may it not be the post of *pr. pro cos.* there given?

[2] Cistophori of Apamea and of Nicomedia bearing his name, *B.M. Cat. Pontus, etc.*, 109; 152, there wrongly dated to 48–7 instead of to 47–6; cf. Th. Reinach, *RN* 1891, 374, n. 1. Pansa cannot have remained long in Bithynia, for he was back in Rome by the early autumn of 46 B.C. (Cicero, *Ad fam.* vi 12, 2; *Pro Ligario* 1; 7).

[3] *Bell. Al.* 66, 1 ff.: 'ipse eadem classe qua venerat proficiscitur in Ciliciam. cuius provinciae civitates omnes evocat Tarsum, quod oppidum fere totius Ciliciae nobilissimum fortissimumque est. ibi rebus omnibus provinciae et finitimarum civitatium constitutis', etc.

[4] *Bell. Al.* 66, 1; Dio xlvii 26, 3.   [5] *Bell. Al.* 68.

[6] F. L. Ganter, 'Q. Cornuficius', *Philologus* liii (1894), 132 f.; the letters here relevant are *Ad fam.* xii 17–19.

[7] The date of the praetorship is not established. There are difficulties about 47, which Hölzl (*Fasti praetorii*, 86) adopts. Münzer, *RE* iv, col. 1625, inclines to 45.

[8] *Ad fam.* xii 18, 1: 'in summum otium te ire arbitrabar et ab impendentibus magnis negotiis discedere.' Cf. ibid. xii 17, 1.

[9] Dio xlvii 26, 3 ff.; Josephus, *AJ* xiv 268; Appian, *BC* iii 77, 312 ff. = iv 58, 250 ff.; Livy, *Per.* cxiv.

Caesar belongs to midsummer, probably July, of the year 46 B.C.[1] After this, Bassus seized the strong place of Apamea and made it his base. Caesar did not at once send out a special general to deal with Bassus, but entrusted Syria and the conduct of the war to Cornificius, who had already arrived in Cilicia.[2] Thus Syria and Cilicia were united under one command. But not for long. No military operations of Cornificius are recorded: in the next year it is C. Antistius Vetus who fights against Bassus and his Parthian allies.[3] Cornificius will then have left his province at the end of the year 46—perhaps to assume the praetorship at Rome.

It is not at once apparent who were the officials in charge of Cilicia and of Syria in the year 45. Fortunately, there is one valuable piece of evidence —a dispatch written by C. Antistius Vetus on | the last day of December 45 B.C., addressed, it may be presumed, to Caesar, and in the possession of Balbus who showed it to Cicero. Vetus had succeeded in investing Bassus at Apamea when the Parthians turned up and raised the siege: for this he blamed Volcacius.[4]

Three alternatives present themselves. Volcacius was proconsul of Syria, or (like Cornificius for a few months towards the end of 46) proconsul of Syria and Cilicia combined together, with Antistius serving under him as quaestor; or else, Volcacius was proconsul of Cilicia, Antistius an independent governor, holding Syria. The third is to be preferred— Antistius, and he alone, is mentioned by Dio in his full account of the operations of the year 45 B.C. in Syria against Bassus;[5] and it is Antistius who composes the dispatch to the central government. Hence we have C. Antistius Vetus, quaestor and governor of Syria. Volcacius, about whom he complains, was in charge of a neighbouring army and province, that is, Cilicia.[6] A man called Volcacius was praetor in 46,[7] presumably to be identified with L. Volcacius Tullus, *cos.* 33 (the son of the consul of 66). If this account is accepted, there is no room for Q. Philippus in Cilicia in 45 B.C., nor is 44 free from difficulties. Indeed, there may have been no separate province of Cilicia in 44 (below, pp. 139 f.).

After Antistius, the next governor of Syria was L. Staius Murcus in 44 B.C. The date of his arrival is uncertain—perhaps quite early in the

---

[1] Ganter, *Philologus* liii 137.

[2] *Ad fam.* xii 19, 1: 'bellum, quod est in Syria, Syriamque provinciam tibi tributam esse a Caesare ex tuis litteris cognovi.'

[3] Dio xlvii 27, 2 ff.; cf. Cicero, *Ad Att.* xiv 9, 3.

[4] Cicero, *Ad Att.* xiv 9, 3 (18 April 44 B.C.): 'et Balbus hic est multumque mecum, ad quem a Vetere litterae datae pridie Kal. Ianuar., cum a se Caecilius circumsederetur et iam teneretur, venisse cum maximis copiis Pacorum Parthum; ita sibi esse eum ereptum, multis suis amissis, in qua re accusat Volcacium.'   [5] Dio xlvii 27, 2 ff.

[6] So W. Sternkopf, 'Die Verteilung der röm. Provinzen vor dem Mutinensischen Kriege', *Hermes* xlvii (1912), 330 f. Volcacius is omitted from D. Vaglieri's list of governors of Cilicia in *Diz. ep.* Neither of these writers mentions Q. Marcius Philippus at all.

[7] *Ad fam.* xiii 14, 1.

year.[1] According to Appian, he summoned to his aid Marcius Crispus, the governor of Bithynia, who came to Syria with | an army of three legions.[2] Some, distrusting Appian, would infer a mistake and suppose Crispus really to have been governor of Cilicia.[3] That is possible; but the hypothesis that there was a northern army-command at this time in Bithynia–Pontus would fit in very well with what can be surmised about the distribution of the armies and about Caesar's frontier and foreign policy in the East—and it is accepted by Mommsen.[4] Caesar had left two legions in Pontus after the battle of Zela; and he proposed, we are told, to invade the Parthian dominions by marching through Armenia Minor.[5] Hence the need for an army and a base in the north. Sixteen legions is given as the total of the army which Caesar was to lead against the Parthians.[6] This is not a special striking force, a field army, but simply the total of the legions in Macedonia and in the eastern provinces in 44 B.C.[7]

Q. Marcius Crispus was an experienced military man.[8] He was proconsul of Bithynia–Pontus in 45 B.C., the successor of Pansa and the predecessor of Tillius Cimber: in the spring of 44 he marched with his army to Syria—no doubt a cause of vexation to the Liberators when they found that Cimber, like Trebonius, was to succeed to an unarmed province. There were no legions in either Bithynia or Asia when those proconsuls arrived.

Murcus and Crispus with six legions conducted operations against Bassus in 44 B.C. and soon shut him up in Apamea. The quaestor C. Antistius Vetus stayed there until late in the year: on his way back to Rome he handed over his moneys to M. Brutus. In 45 B.C. Marcius Crispus had certainly been governor of Bithynia: in 44 he *may* have held the title of proconsul of Cilicia.[9] Again, either Philippus or some unknown person could have been proconsul, without an army. Yet it is possible that Cilicia

[1] According to Appian (*BC* iii 77, 316 = iv 58, 253) he was sent against Bassus by Caesar. In another place, a certain Murcus is mentioned among the people who tried to claim credit for being in the plot to murder Caesar (*BC* ii 119, 500). The identification with L. Staius Murcus is accepted by Sternkopf, *Hermes* xlvii (1912), 336 f., and by Münzer, *RE* iii A, col. 2137. There are difficulties in the whole story. However that may be, Sternkopf and Münzer both assume that Murcus was governor of Syria in 44 B.C., as successor to C. Antistius Vetus. Josephus (*AJ* xiv 270; 279) states quite definitely that Murcus was governor of Syria.

[2] Appian, *BC* iii 77, 316: ἐπεκαλεῖτο Μάρκιον Κρίσπον ἡγούμενον Βιθυνίας, καὶ ἀφίκετο αὐτῷ βοηθῶν ὁ Κρίσπος τέλεσιν ἄλλοις τρισίν; cf. iv 58, 253. Sternkopf, *Hermes* xlvii (1912), 330 f., accepts this. So too Münzer, *RE* iii A, col. 2137; xiv 1555 f.

[3] E. Schwartz, 'Die Vertheilung der röm. Provinzen nach Caesars Tod', *Hermes* xxxiii (1898), 186, followed by E. Letz, *Die Provinzialverwaltung Caesars*, Diss. Strassburg (1912), 84.

[4] *Ges. Schriften* iv 162 f.　　　　　　　　　　[5] Suetonius, *Divus Iulius*, 44.

[6] Appian, *BC* ii 110, 460.

[7] Namely, six in Macedonia, three in Egypt, the Syrian legion formerly under Sex. Julius Caesar and the two three-legion armies commanded by Murcus and Crispus in 44 B.C.　　　　　　　　　　　　　　　　[8] Cicero, *In Pisonem* 54.

[9] Sternkopf, *Hermes* xlvii (1912), 332, barely admits this possibility.

and Syria | were united under Staius Murcus—who will have commanded that army which in the previous year Volcacius had failed to bring to the help of Vetus. Compare the position of Cornificius in 46 B.C.

In any case, the junction of the two provinces was probably contemplated for the next year. Late in March or early in April 44 B.C., the consul Dolabella was allotted Syria as his province; his colleague Antonius received Macedonia. At the beginning of June, however, Antonius, while retaining at his disposal the six Macedonian legions (or rather four or five of them), took in exchange both Gallic provinces, the Cisalpina and Comata. Further, the tenure of the consular province was prolonged to five years.[1] Dolabella fell short of Antonius in resource, in prestige, and in power. He could not expect so formidable a province. But even so, Syria alone might appear an inadequate portion. In 47 B.C. Caesar had left there only one legion as garrison. Moreover, the Parthian danger threatened both provinces and made a single command desirable. It may therefore be conjectured that Syria, the consular province of Dolabella, was to include Cilicia: Cilicia, indeed, had now been much reduced in area, namely to Pedias and Lycaonia (see below).

A hazardous guess, perhaps, but confirmed by attested official terminology in the next year. Cassius, reaching Syria earlier than Dolabella in the winter of 44–43, induced the armies at Apamea, besiegers and besieged, to join him. In the record of the seizure of the provinces of the East by Cassius, there is no mention of Cilicia as a separate entity or of any proconsul. In the Eleventh Philippic (*c.* 6 March) Cicero proposed that Cassius should be recognized as legitimate proconsul of Syria in the place of Dolabella; further, he was to exercise *imperium maius* over the provinces of the East—'ut imperandi in Syria, Asia, Bithynia, Ponto ius potestatemque habeat'.[2]

The province of Cilicia has come to an end. Before tracing the stages of its decline and extinction and the transference of its peculiar functions to other administrative units, it will be well | to set out in the form of a table the list of governors of Cilicia and of Syria in this dark and troubled period:

	Cilicia	Syria
47/6?	Q. Marcius Philippus	Sex. Julius Caesar
46	Q. Cornificius	
45	L. Volcacius Tullus	C. Antistius Vetus
44	?	L. Staius Murcus
43	P. Cornelius Dolabella	
	C. Cassius	

---

[1] On the complicated problems of this legislation see the convincing arguments of Sternkopf, *Hermes* xlvii (1912), 357 ff.

[2] Cicero, *Phil.* xi 30. The proconsuls Q. Marcius Crispus and L. Staius Murcus and the legate A. Allienus are mentioned by name.

VIII. *The Abolition of Cilicia*

In 49 B.C., under the Pompeian government of the East, the three dioceses of Phrygia were transferred to Asia. C. Fannius was governor of Asia: his cistophori were minted at Laodicea and Apamea as well as at Ephesus.[1] That would prove only two of the three dioceses, it is true. But Cicero, writing in 46 to the proconsul P. Servilius, confirms the transference of all three.[2] The territorial diminution of Cilicia proceeded apace. According to Cassius Dio, Caesar at Alexandria offered Cyprus to Arsinoe.[3] This account has been doubted.[4] It is in no way incredible; and it is likely enough, on any theory, that after the termination of the Alexandrian War, Caesar granted this old Ptolemaic possession to Cleopatra. An Egyptian general, Sarapion, is attested in possession of the island in 43 B.C.[5] There is no indication of Roman administration at all in the intervening period, unless the mysterious quaestor C. Sextilius Rufus be dated to 47 B.C.[6]

At Tarsus, in the summer of 47, Caesar made various arrangements about Cilicia.[7] Now in 43 B.C., P. Spinther, Trebonius' quaestor and acting-governor of Asia after the death of Trebonius, expressly states that Side in Pamphylia is a part of his province.[8] When had it been severed from Cilicia? Perhaps in 49 B.C., when the three dioceses went, perhaps by Caesar in 47. How much of the hinterland from Pamphylia northwards was also attached to Asia, for convenience and to provide through-communications, has not been recorded.

---

[1] *B.M. Cat. Phrygia*, xxxiii (Apamea); lxxiv f. (Laodicea); *Ionia* (Ephesus), 68.

[2] *Ad fam.* xiii 67, 1; 'ex provincia mea Ciliciensi, cui scis τρεῖς διοικήσεις Asiaticas adtributas fuisse.'   [3] Dio xlii 35, 5.

[4] A. Bouché-Leclercq, *Histoire des Lagides* ii (1904), 193: on p. 213, n. 4, however, he states that Caesar gave to Cleopatra the possession and revenue of Cyprus.

[5] Appian, *BC* v 61, 262; cf. v 9, 35. Hence it is not necessary to put off her occupation of Cyprus until a grant made by Antonius much later (Dio xlix 32, 5; 41, 2).

[6] Cicero, commending to C. Sextilius Rufus all the people of Cyprus and especially the Paphians, refers to ordinances made by P. Lentulus and by himself and describes Sextilius' position thus—'cum primus in eam insulam quaestor veneris' (*Ad fam.* xiii 48). It has been supposed that he was quaestor of Cilicia early in 46 (before the arrival of the governor of the province Q. Cornificius), by Ganter, *Philologus* liii (1894), 55, and by Sternkopf, *Hermes* xlvii (1912), 331. The language of Cicero, however, suggests that he was an independent governor of Cyprus. When? Possibly in 49 B.C. under the Pompeian government of the East, perhaps, as indicated in the text, in 47–6. There is a further complication —he must be the same man as the Sextilius Rufus commanding a detachment of the Republican fleet off the coast of Cilicia in the summer of 43 B.C. (*Ad fam.* xii 13, 4; also perhaps Dio xlvii 31, 4, who calls him Λούκιον 'Ροῦφον; cf. Münzer, *RE* ii A, col. 2037). But it would be difficult to date the letter as late as 43 B.C., on the hypothesis that C. Sextilius Rufus was a governor of Cyprus then appointed by the Republicans after they had recovered the island from Cleopatra's general (Appian, *BC* v 9, 35). None of the letters of that book (*Ad fam.* xiii) are likely to be quite so late. [See E. Badian, *JRS* lv (1965), 113 ff.: 49 B.C is most probable.]

[7] *Bell. Al.* 66, 2.

[8] *Ad fam.* xii 15, 5: 'usque Sidam, quae extrema regio est provinciae meae'.

As has been indicated above, Cilicia was united with the province of Syria in 44 B.C., perhaps under L. Staius Murcus, or, at latest, under his successor, P. Dolabella. The last clearly attested separate governor of Cilicia was L. Volcacius Tullus in 45. Antonius, it is true, might have revived a separate province of Cilicia (i.e. Pedias and Lycaonia) after Philippi. If so, it has left no trace of its existence; and no proconsul of Cilicia is mentioned at the time of the Parthian invasion in 40 B.C. The union of Syria and Cilicia in one province is not expressly recorded by any of the ancient authorities until the governorship of C. Sosius in 38–36 B.C.:[1] it might, however, be postulated for his predecessors under Antonius' government of the East, the 'Celtiberian' and the 'muleteer', namely L. Decidius Saxa (40 B.C.) and P. Ventidius in 39 and 38.

The enlarged province of Syria proceeded to divest itself of more and more Cilician territories as it contracted to a manageable area. Antonius, wise and courageous in his generosity, gave over to the vassals of Rome many regions that were difficult to police | or unproductive to exploit. According to Appian, in 39 B.C. Amyntas, the secretary of Deiotarus the Galatian, received Pisidia for his dominion; Polemo, son of Zeno of Laodicea, Cilicia:[2] as usual, the term 'Cilicia' is deplorably vague. In this context it appears to cover Lycaonia, for Strabo definitely states that Polemo's capital was Iconium.[3] There is no reason to doubt this. Further, a point of interest: Philomelium, which had remained a part of Cilicia after 50 B.C., was perhaps now assigned to the province of Asia, where it remains ever after.[4]

Therefore, as early as 39 B.C., the province of Syria is reduced to Syria with Cilicia Pedias—for Cilicia Tracheia can hardly be regarded as provincial land. In any case, in 36 B.C., Tracheia was transferred to Cleopatra, so it is recorded.[5] This cannot have been a large area—it was limited on the north by the domain of Antipater of Derbe, on the east by the principality of Olba, where Antonius recognized the rule of Aba as queen, and by the maritime possessions of King Tarcondimotus, namely Elaeussa and Corycus.[6]

The status of Cilicia Pedias under the early Principate is nowhere expressly stated—Dio's often anachronistic account of the division of the provinces in 27 B.C. gives no help.[7] Some have found the problem trouble-

---

[1] Dio xlix 22, 3: τὴν ἀρχὴν τῆς τε Συρίας καὶ τῆς Κιλικίας.   [2] BC v 75, 319.
[3] Strabo xii 6, 1, p. 568. On this meaning of 'Cilicia', cf. Appian, *Mithr.* 75; on Polemo's dominion, W. M. Ramsay, 'Lycaonia', *JŒAI* vii (1904), Beiblatt, 65 f.
[4] Pliny, *NH* v 95. Yet, as Strabo says that Amyntas held certain parts of Phrygia Paroreios (p. 569), the transference might not have taken place till his death in 25 B.C.
[5] Strabo xiv 5, 6, p. 671; A. H. M. Jones, *The Cities*, 209; 438.
[6] On these dynasties, cf. now especially A. H. M. Jones, *The Cities*, 203 ff.; 209. Corycus and Elaeussa belonged to Tarcondimotus, as may be inferred from Dio liv 9, 2.
[7] Dio liii 12, 7: ἡ Συρία ἡ κοίλη καλουμένη ἥ τε Φοινίκη καὶ Κιλικία καὶ Κύπρος καὶ Αἰγύπτιοι ἐν τῇ τοῦ Καίσαρος μερίδι τότε ἐγένοντο. It is evident that Syria, Cilicia Pedias, and Cyprus

some, conjuring up nebulous theories of a separate Cilicia or a Cilicia united in one province with senatorial Cyprus.[1] To discover the truth, one needs only to glance back to the Triumviral period. Indeed, for most ideas, acts, and institutions of the Principate, the source and model lies there. Octavianus made war upon the Queen of Egypt, the ally of Antonius; and he alleged against his rival for power a shocking charge, that he had | surrendered provincial dominions of the Roman people to the kings of the East. After his victory, Octavianus maintained for the most part the *acta* of Antonius, whether they concerned Roman provinces or vassal-states (save that in Egypt he became king himself). In 27 B.C. the area of territory in Asia under direct Roman government was smaller than at any time since the ordinances of Pompeius.

Therefore, the extent and character of Syria under the Principate may easily be discovered—it is simply the Antonian province of Syria. There is indirect confirmation at an early date. Shortly after Actium, M. Valerius Messalla Corvinus (*cos.* 31 B.C.) was appointed proconsul of Syria:[2] if the verses of his protégé, the poet Tibullus, with the mention of Cilicians, the Taurus, and the river Cydnus, are of any value, they indicate that Pedias belonged to his province.[3] It will not be forgotten, however, that the principality of Tarcondimotus in Pedias around Hieropolis–Castabala was soon revived,[4] and that Tracheia as a whole continued for a century to be ruled by kings—by the monarchs of Galatia, Cappadocia, and Commagene in turn. Ruler and title might vary—their function was the same. Cilicia Pedias remained a part of the province of Syria until the beginning of the reign of Vespasian. Antiochus IV, ruling over Commagene and Cilicia Tracheia, was deposed in A.D. 72. Commagene was added to Syria. Tracheia was now joined with Pedias in a new imperial province, governed by legates of praetorian rank.

For more than a century there had been no province bearing the name of Cilicia. The old Cilicia under the late Republic was a large but not anomalous province, with a function of its own—especially in the six years when it contained Phrygia, corresponded with the main road from Laodicea by Philomelium, Iconium, and the Cilician Gates to Tarsus, and was the most important command in the East, calling for three consular proconsuls in succession. Cilicia, gradually shrinking in area, was merged into Syria. In the meantime a new entity arose, lopped of Phrygia in the

will have formed one province until 22 B.C., when Cyprus was given to the Senate (Dio liv 4, 1). Syria, Phoenice, and Cilicia (but not Cyprus) retained a common provincial assembly, *IGR* i 445.

[1] W. E. Gwatkin, *Cappadocia as a Roman Procuratorial Province*, Univ. of Missouri Studies, v (1930): refuted by J. G. C. Anderson, *CR* xlv (1931), 189 f.
[2] Dio li 7, 7. The precise date of his governorship has been debated—and is here irrelevant.
[3] Tibullus i 7, 13 ff.
[4] Dio liv 9, 2 (20 B.C.).

west and of Pedias in the east, but incorporating the central portions of the old province of Cilicia, namely Pamphylia, Pisidia, Pisidic Phrygia, Isauria, | Lycaonia, and (for a time) Tracheia, and answering to the main function of that institution. Its area and history may now be summarily indicated, if only to round off the present inquiry and substantiate its principal contention.

IX. *Conclusion: Galatia*

Cilicia lapsed to Syria and Syria soon discarded its acquisitions, retaining only the region of Pedias, which was commended by the respectable ties of geography and of history. Rome had broken the power of the Hellenistic monarchies, bringing thereby anarchy over all the East and trouble upon herself. It became expedient to restore these kingdoms or devise an equivalent. It was not the strength but the weakness of the vassal states that menaced the security of the Roman rule, as was evident during the Parthian invasion of 40 B.C. Hence the measures taken by M. Antonius— the strengthening of Egypt, the last survivor of the monarchies founded by the generals of Alexander, the choice of new men regardless of dynastic claims in the eastern principalities, and even the creation of entirely new kingdoms. Polemo, Herod, Archelaus, and Amyntas were the rulers chosen by Antonius—and bequeathed to Augustus.[1]

Antipater the son of Perilaus, lord of Derbe and Laranda, was not among them. Had he been loyal to Rome, it was his duty to lend help against the Parthians when they broke through the Cilician Gates in 40 B.C. A robber-prince is more likely to have been treacherous than incompetent. Treacherous, that is to say, to the Caesarians. Antipater had presumably been an adherent of Pompeius, and the Parthians were led by a Pompeian, young Labienus. Yet Antipater still continued in possession of his domain—too strong perhaps to be molested. Polemo, ruler of Lycaonia in 39–36, left him alone, as did Amyntas at first.

Amyntas came gradually to possess the largest of all the vassal kingdoms in Asia Minor. In 39 B.C. he was granted Pisidia. Three years later, after the death or deposition of Castor, the grandson of Deiotarus, Galatia proper (the territory of the three Galatian tribes) was added to his kingdom and 'parts of Lycaonia and Pamphylia' | as well[2]—for Polemo vacated his Lycaonian tetrarchy to become king over Pontus and Armenia Minor. In the War of Actium, Amyntas deserted Antonius at a suitable moment, just before the final decision. Confirmed by the victor in possession of his realm, like all the more important vassals except Cleopatra, the

---

[1] W. W. Tarn, *CAH* x 69 f.; 114. [For a discussion of M. Antonius' measures in the East, see H. Buchheim, *Die Orientpolitik des Triumvirn M. Antonius* (1960); for Augustus' preservation, on the whole, of Antonius' arrangements, G. W. Bowersock, *Augustus and the Greek World* (1965), esp. 42 ff.]   [2] Dio xlix 32, 3.

ostensible cause and head of the war, Amyntas received augmentation of territory, namely that part of Cilicia Tracheia that had been assigned to Egypt since 36 B.C.[1]

The extent of his dominion is made reasonably clear by various references in a contemporary writer.[2] With one exception—Strabo says nothing whatever about the coast of Pamphylia. Hence doubt and confusion. But Amyntas coined at Side in Pamphylia.[3] The area of his kingdom of Galatia can therefore be established—from the coast of Pamphylia and Tracheia northwards to the marches of Bithynia and of Paphlagonia, eastwards from the province of Asia to the frontiers of Cappadocia, of Commagene, and of the province of Syria.

As the kingdom of Galatia included the unsubdued or uncertain regions of the Taurus, namely Pisidia, Isauria, and the interior of Tracheia, it corresponded in function with the late-Republican province of Cilicia, with this difference: instead of extending from west to east along the highway from Asia to Syria, definable almost entirely in terms of that historic route, the Galatian kingdom lay athwart it, on a north-to-south axis, a geographical perversity. It was the duty of Amyntas to control, conquer, and pacify the southern mountain zone, regions that no empire yet had subjugated. He set about his task with spirit and with vigour. In the west he | captured Cremna, a stronghold of the Pisidian hill-country, and killed its tyrant: on the eastern flank he suppressed Antipater of Derbe. The central region baffled him. He attacked the tribe of the Homonadenses and slew their tyrant, only to perish subsequently in an ambush (25 B.C.).[4]

Rome annexed. Augustus might now have revived the province of Cilicia, leaving the Galatians under a king. He chose instead to maintain the existing boundaries, though recent in origin and enclosing a fantastic conglomeration of territories. Amyntas' kingdom—the whole of it, so Strabo clearly states—was made a Roman province.[5] Pamphylia had

---

[1] Strabo xiv 5, 6, p. 671.

[2] In Strabo xii 5, 3–7, 3, pp. 568–71; also xiv 5, 6, p. 671 (Tracheia).

[3] B.M. Cat. Galatia, Cappadocia and Syria (1899), xviii; Head, *Historia Numorum*² (1911), 747. This proves that the coast of Pamphylia belonged to Amyntas' kingdom; cf. *Klio* xxx (1937), 227 [above, p. 42]; A. H. M. Jones, *The Cities*, 413. Strabo nowhere records the status of the cities of Pamphylia; and Dio, stating that Amyntas received 'parts of Pamphylia' (xlix 32, 3), both implies that some of Pamphylia lay outside his kingdom and appears to believe in the existence of a separate province of Pamphylia (liii 26, 3—his account of what happened after the death of Amyntas). For these reasons the present writer, in an earlier essay, was moved to deny that Amyntas held the coast of Pamphylia: *Klio* xxvii (1934), 122 ff. A mistake. The inaccurate passage in Cassius Dio (liii 26, 3) has been the cause of persistent errors. Emendation to produce sense, as there suggested (*Klio* xxvii 125), is no remedy. It may now be taken as pretty certain, on various and converging evidence, that both Amyntas' kingdom of Galatia and the Roman province, its successor, included the coast of Pamphylia. See further n. 5.   [4] Strabo xii 6, 5, p. 569.

[5] Strabo xii 5, 1, p. 567: νῦν δ᾽ ἔχουσι ῾Ρωμαῖοι καὶ ταύτην καὶ τὴν ὑπὸ τῷ Ἀμύντᾳ γενομένην πᾶσαν εἰς μίαν συναγαγόντες ἐπαρχίαν. Compare p. 569 (on Sagalassus). Dio's account

belonged to Amyntas; and there was never at any time a separate province of Pamphylia.[1] Like Cilicia Pedias, it was too small to stand alone. Pamphylia could have been joined to Asia—but it was not. It now belonged to Galatia and it stayed with Galatia until Claudius, depriving the Lycians of their autonomy, separated Pamphylia from Galatia and created a new province, that of Lycia–Pamphylia.[2]

The Roman province of Galatia, or Galatia–Pamphylia as it may for convenience be designated, began in 25 B.C. Cilicia Tracheia, however, a region peculiarly suited to be ruled by kings, passed, perhaps at once, to Archelaus of Cappadocia.[3] |

Galatia–Pamphylia was a frontier-province of the first importance. On north and east it marched with the dependent kingdoms of Paphlagonia, Pontus, and Cappadocia: in the south it possessed a military zone. Therefore the province might have been given a permanent garrison of legions. But Augustus could not spare the troops. None the less, there were legions in Galatia more than once during the Principate of Augustus, drawn, it will be guessed, from the armies of Syria and Egypt. The Roman governors inherited the duties that had been fatal to Amyntas. The first imperial legate was M. Lollius, of praetorian rank.[4] On at least three occasions, however, the existence of consular legates may be surmised: they were L. Calpurnius Piso (*cos.* 15 B.C.), P. Sulpicius Quirinius (*cos.* 12 B.C.), and M. Plautius Silvanus (*cos.* 2 B.C.).[5] Consular legates in Galatia need not arouse disquiet or scandal—the hierarchy of imperial provinces and

runs: καὶ οὕτω καὶ ἡ Γαλατία μετὰ τῆς Λυκαονίας ῾Ρωμαῖον ἄρχοντα ἔσχε τά τε χωρία τὰ ἐκ τῆς Παμφυλίας πρότερον τῷ Ἀμύντᾳ προσνεμηθέντα τῷ ἰδίῳ νομῷ ἀπεδόθη (liii 26, 3, on which cf. *Klio* xxvii, 125 [also above, p. 42]). Jones points out that Dio's account is best explained by his inability to conceive that a Roman province of Pamphylia did not exist (*The Cities*, 403). Under 11 B.C. and under A.D. 43 he speaks of such a province, wrongly (liv 34, 6; lx 17, 3). Jones also adduces Pliny, *NH* v 147, where the community of the Actalenses (i.e. Attaleia) is reckoned in with Galatia. This question will hardly need to be discussed afresh.

[1] Compare the preceding note. Pamphylia had been added to the province of Asia (Cicero, *Ad fam.* xii 15, 5), probably by Caesar in 47 B.C. That the same assignment held for the time of Augustus has been argued recently by L. R. Taylor and T. R. S. Broughton, *AJP* lv (1933), 127 f.; 139 ff. They did not, however, examine fully the problem of the area of Amyntas' kingdom or refer to the inscription from Attaleia honouring Augustus' legate, M. Plautius Silvanus (*SEG* vi 646, cf. *Klio* xxvii 139 ff.).

[2] Dio lx 17, 3; Suetonius, *Divus Claudius* 25. The procurator attested on a milestone at Attaleia in A.D. 50 (*ILS* 215) is not a governor of Pamphylia, but simply the financial procurator of Galatia–Pamphylia whose *provincia* survived the severance of Pamphylia; cf. *Klio* xxx (1937), 227 ff. [above, pp. 43 f.]. [The date of the organization of the province of Galatia has been debated. See Levick, op. cit. 193 f., firmly supporting 25 B.C. On the extent of the province, ibid. 29 ff.]

[3] Strabo xiv 5, 6, p. 671 (cf. xii 1, 4, p. 535): Strabo's reasons are adequate—ἐδόκει πρὸς ἅπαν τὸ τοιοῦτο βασιλεύεσθαι μᾶλλον τοὺς τόπους ἢ ὑπὸ τοῖς ῾Ρωμαίοις ἡγεμόσιν εἶναι τοῖς ἐπὶ τὰς κρίσεις πεμπομένοις, οἳ μήτ᾽ ἀεὶ παρεῖναι ἔμελλον μήτε μεθ᾽ ὅπλων.

[4] Eutropius vii 10, 2.

[5] For the evidence and for arguments in support of this theory, see *Klio* xxvii 122 ff. It is accepted in the main by J. G. C. Anderson, *CAH* x 270 ff.; 877 f.

their division into consular and praetorian was the result, not of a single act in the month of January 27 B.C., but of a long process. At first Augustus divided as he pleased the different regions comprised in his *provincia,* west and east. His legates might be either praetorian or consular: it depended upon the nature of the tasks or the standing of the men available. There is quite clear evidence, for example, for the two Spanish provinces in the years 27–19 B.C.[1]

There was much to be done in Galatia. The full history of it all is lost —it was never written. The visible results were half a dozen military colonies, a road—or rather, a series of roads—and a pacified land.[2] This was not the work of one man or of one campaign. In 13 or 12 B.C., L. Calpurnius Piso is attested in Pamphylia:[3] he was called away to suppress a great insurrection in | Thrace. At some date between 12 B.C. and A.D. 1, P. Sulpicius Quirinius subjugated at last the land of the Homonadenses— a necessary but not an urgent task.[4] Under the year A.D. 6 the historian Cassius Dio records an Isaurian War that otherwise would never have been known:[5] it may be presumed that M. Plautius Silvanus terminated that war. Like Piso some twenty years earlier, he brought an army from the East for service in the Balkans (A.D. 7).[6] Silvanus is honoured by an inscription of Attaleia in Pamphylia which describes him as πρεσβευτὴν ἀντιστράτηγον Αὐτοκράτορος Καίσαρος Σεβαστοῦ.[7]

---

[1] *AJP* lv (1934), 315 ff.; cf. also *JRS* xxiv (1934), 125 (on praetorian or consular pro-consuls in Macedonia) [= *Danubian Papers* (1971), 52].

[2] The credit, not merely of illuminating and enlarging, but very precisely of discovering, this notable chapter of Anatolian and of imperial Roman history belongs to Sir William Ramsay (see especially 'Studies in the Roman Province of Galatia, I. The Homonadeis and the Homanadensian War', *JRS* vii (1917), 229 ff.). The present writer regrets that he should be compelled to disagree about Quirinius and about the status of Galatia in the time of Augustus. [On Roman roads in Galatia see I. W. Macpherson, *AS* iv (1954), 111 ff.]

[3] Dio liv 34, 6: also *Anth. Pal.* vi 241 (a helmet presented to Piso by Pylaemenes— presumably the son of Amyntas, cf. *OGIS* 533). *Anth. Pal.* xi 424, written by a Piso, concerns Galatia.

[4] Tacitus, *Ann.* iii 48; Strabo xii 6, 5, p. 569. The acephalous *elogium* from Tibur (*ILS* 918) is best omitted. It may belong to Quirinius: if so, it cannot in itself prove that he was twice governor of Syria, i.e., not only when he held a well-authenticated census after the annexation of Judaea in A.D. 6, but also at an earlier date. [See *Rom. Rev.* 400 f. and *Akten des VI. Internationalen Kongresses für griechische und lateinische Epigraphik* (1973), 585 ff. (suggesting Piso the Pontifex as the subject of the *elogium*).]

[5] Dio lv 28, 3. The precise tribe involved cannot be known, for Dio is probably using 'Isaurian' in the wide sense of his own day, referring to Cilicia Tracheia and its hinterland, not merely to the region about Isaura Vetus and Isaura Nova, not far from Derbe. Perhaps a resurgence of the Homonadenses?

[6] Velleius ii 112, 4.

[7] *SEG* vi 646, cf. *Klio* xxvii 139 ff. The supporting (but superfluous) inference there drawn from the presence of the name Silvanus, [ἐπὶ Σ]ιλουανο[ῦ], on the inscription of the Sebasteion at Ancyra (*OGIS* 533) is probably incorrect. Further, the four names occurring at intervals on the inscription are perhaps not those of high priests, who had taken names from the governors, but represent the governors themselves, as argued long ago by Rostovtzeff, *Mélanges Boissier* (1903), 418 ff.

Galatia, a large subject, may not suitably be discussed here. Among other things, however, an attempt has been made to assert and demonstrate a continuity in function, though not precisely in area, between Cicero's province of Cilicia, the kingdom of Amyntas, and the Augustan province of Galatia. Not, indeed, that that is a novel or alarming contention. It was stated forty years ago by Sir William Ramsay in a most convincing fashion.[1]

The present essay, dedicated to Mr. Buckler and written for a volume of which Professors Calder and Keil are the editors, is intended as the acknowledgment, however summary and imperfect, of a great debt due to the learned company of scholars whose labours have illuminated the history and antiquities of Anatolia.

---

[1] In his *Historical Commentary on Galatians* (1899).

I I

M. Gelzer, *Caesar der Politiker und Staatsmann*[1]

MANY have essayed to write the biography of Julius Caesar. The subject is important, the events exciting; and the facts are presumed to be known. Therefore the enterprise might appear to be easy as well as popular and remunerative. Very different is the origin of the present volume. This historical biography has certainly not been composed in the belief that others have already done the work, even though it be tedious to compare their results, as Pliny the Younger said when he described one form of the writing of history, 'parata inquisitio sed onerosa collatio'.

On the contrary we have here set forth in a clear and orderly fashion the mature opinions of a scholar who has devoted a lifetime to the independent study of Roman antiquities. Not only that. An interval of twenty years has permitted him to revise his views, to sharpen his conclusions. In 1921 a volume entitled *Julius Caesar* heralded a collection called *Meister der Politik*. Since then Matthias Gelzer has made notable contributions to the study of the Caesarian period, for example, the articles on Crassus, Lucullus, and Catilina in the encyclopaedia of Pauly–Wissowa. This volume is therefore not merely an enlarged new edition, the justification for which is to be found in those detailed articles: it should be described, discussed, and appraised as an entirely new work.

It is a good book. One would expect it to be. Designed to ensnare that elusive creature, the educated reader, it extorts the admiration of the professional student, even to the point of making him forget, for a time, his passion for footnotes, appendices, and quotations in the language of the subject. The matter is scrupulously chosen and tidily arranged, the exposition lucid, the style simple, concrete, and unpretentious. Caesar would have approved. But Caesar was not only an exemplar of *imperatoria brevitas*. He was also a literary purist; and the language of this book sometimes causes discomfort, for example: 'der in der Senatstaktik wenig routinierte Haudegen Afranius' (p. 78). The author is not arguing a thesis; and remembering that history is narrative, not research, disputation, and the passing of judgments, he lets the facts speak for themselves.

[1] Munich, 1941.

Something has been lost in the process. Gelzer discards personal detail and plausible or instructive anecdotes. Caesar is therefore depersonalized. We miss not only the tall, wiry man with a clear complexion and lively dark eyes: the avid and passionate aristocrat is also toned down. Not enough is reproduced of Caesar's own assertion of Caesar's *dignitas*; and characteristic utterances like that recorded by Pollio at the battle of Pharsalus—'hoc voluere'—are omitted; likewise Caesar's rebuke to the people of Corduba, 'even if he perished, Rome had legions that could tear down the heavens.' Still, we have much to be thankful for. Bombast and mysticism are absent. Wilhelm Weber, who depicted in a peculiar fashion the emperors of the Antonine dynasty, might have felt impelled to turn his attentions to the first of the Caesars: perhaps he has already done so.

The book keeps close to its central theme and purpose—'der Politiker und Staatsmann'. The wars are well and clearly narrated, but military matters are kept in due subordination to politics. What emerges in a most convincing fashion is Caesar's skill as a politician, his grasp of means and ends in any given operation (see especially Gelzer's summing-up, p. 346). It is patent in his earliest acts, in the intrigues and alliances of his mature years, in the final triumph over his adversaries, even though he was baffled at the last by a situation not of his own desiring and quite beyond his control; for to speak of Caesar's political genius does not mean that he had seen all and planned all from the outset, namely civil war, military autocracy and sole rule. Caesar's intelligence was lucid and logical. But the Goddess he worshipped was Fortuna. Who knows but that this opportunist might not, at some stage of his career, have changed his colours, like other politicians who had to begin with the opposition before they could make their way forward and finish, respected as well as successful, in the front ranks of the dominant oligarchy? Perhaps it would not have been too late when in 60 B.C. Caesar, returning from Spain, sought both a triumph and a consulate and was rebuffed by the *factio optimatium*, Cato in the forefront. However that may be, the language that may be used to welcome and justify the political conversion of a *popularis* is well attested; for it was employed by Cicero when speaking of Caesar a few years later—'qui si ex illa iactatione cursuque populari bene gesta re publica referunt aspectum in curiam atque huic amplissimae dignitati esse commendati volunt, non modo non repellendi sunt, verum etiam expetendi' (*De prov. cons.* 38).

So much in general. Which aspects of the subject will the student of Roman history scrutinize most carefully, having in mind recent work on the Caesarian period? In the first place, the social and political background. So abundant and so excellent is the historical evidence for the last age of the Roman Republic, for the thirty years between the dictatorships of Sulla and of Caesar, that the | likelihood of any considerable misapprehension about the true character of Roman public life might appear to be excluded. This is not so. Presumptions based upon the parliamentary theories and practices of the nineteenth century have long been dominant and die hard, especially in the Anglo-Saxon countries. If, however, proper attention is paid to the structure of society in ancient Italy and to the character of political terminology at Rome, the truth is evident enough. Conditions were feudal rather than parliamentary; and political terms tend to be emotional phrases or partisan appellations—as Sallust was there to tell us. But, unfortunately, the arguments and the language of Cicero conserved their influence; the researches of Fustel de Coulanges were insufficiently regarded by many Roman historians; and Gelzer's own study, *Die Nobilität der römischen Republik* (1912) [now in *Kleine Schriften* i], small in bulk but a marvel of neatness and lucidity, was not enough to dispel error. In the present volume the extra-constitutional bases of power at Rome stand out clearly (pp. 1–31).

Despite election by the People, a procedure which the political theorists of antiquity consider to be aristocratic as well as democratic (for the terms are not contradictory), an oligarchy ruled, based on the great families whether of patrician or of plebeian origin. The *nobiles*, in Gelzer's definition, are the descendants of consuls; and public policy is directed by the leading men of consular rank, the *principes*, as they are often designated. But their power does not really rest upon votes and speeches—it derives from personal influence and personal ties of allegiance, from the fundamental institution of *clientela*. As the dominion of Rome, transcending Italy, embraces the provinces, so do the *clientelae* of politicians and generals. After Italy, whole nations and provinces are dragged into Roman quarrels, and the last survivor in the line of the 'monarchic faction leaders' (Appian, *BC* i 2, 7) becomes by the force of events ruler over all the nations. One *princeps* displaced the *principes*. It is a long process —and highly instructive. One of the leading actors was Cn. Pompeius Strabo, the father of Pompeius Magnus (p. 30). This is a conception very different from the fancied competition of rival parties of *Optimates* and *Populares*. In a sense there was a party of *Optimates*—their identity can often be established, their habits observed. Cato, for example, was not only a man of principle or a ferocious defender of the honour and the interests of his own class: he stands at the centre of a complicated system of family alliances between the leading *nobiles* in the oligarchy of government. As Cicero so pertinently remarked, 'cum autem certi propter divitias aut genus aut aliquas opes rem publicam tenent, est factio, sed vocantur illi optimates' (*De re publica* iii 23). On the other hand, there was no party of *populares* (p. 24): the term 'popularis' is applied to individuals, to measures, to policies (cf. especially Cicero, *In Cat.* iv 9). Naturally enough the leaders of the opposition to the *factio optimatium* will tend to be, not hardy democrats from the plough or the shop, but nobles of dynastic family; and conversely, in defending its station and interests, the dominant oligarchic party will use from time to time both men and methods that can be called 'populares'.

For the guidance of the general reader—and others as well—a little more might have been said about the social and political role of knights in this period. What was the real and effective difference between knights and senators? There is room for debate. Rostovtzeff asserted that in the time of Augustus a sharp line of demarcation was drawn between the two orders. This opinion cannot be substantiated. There was then, it is true, a senatorial census, which apparently had not existed under the Republic; and there were certain visible and vestimentary marks of distinction. But the essential fact is this—the two orders belong to the same social class: the difference resides in *dignitas*. Similarly in the last age of the Republic. In a Senate which numbered over 600 members the *nobiles* were a minority. For the rest, many of the less flamboyant senators, belonging to the type of 'homo novus parvusque senator', derive their origin from equestrian families and differ from knights not in wealth, habits, or influence, but only in *dignitas*. Conversely, many knights who could easily have entered the Senate preferred to shun the career of honours. For adequate reasons. The Empire had its 'equitum Romanorum praevalida nomina' (Tacitus, *Ann.* xii 60). So had the Republic. They are conspicuous among the allies and agents of the great party-leaders. Hence, behind the façade of the Constitution, men of equestrian rank play an important political role. Nor is evidence wanting of the high social presentability of knights: the sons of the *nobiles* do not disdain to frequent their tables, marry their daughters, and inherit their fortunes. The case of Cossutia, omitted by Gelzer, is relevant enough. This wealthy heiress was Caesar's betrothed until it was ordained that he should marry Cornelia, Cinna's daughter (Suetonius, *Div. Jul.* i 1). The Cossutii were engaged in the production of works of art in Greece. The earliest known member of the family is the architect D. Cossutius, employed at Athens on a considerable task by the king Antiochus Epiphanes (*RE*, s.v. 'Cossutius', coll. 1673 f.; J. Hatzfeld, *Les Trafiquants italiens dans l'Orient hellénique* 228). Perhaps the Cossutii belonged to the faction of Marius—compare the Granii, a commercial family of Puteoli, whose Marian and Caesarian allegiance is splendidly attested. In their marriage-alliances the Julii were clearly looking out for wealth or political influence, not mere social distinction. Caesar's aunt was the wife of Marius; and one of his sisters married M. Atius Balbus (Suetonius, *Div. Aug.* 4, 2): | the marriage, which cannot fall later than 78 B.C., may have some political utility. The other sister appears to have been the wife in succession of a Pinarius and a Pedius. The Pinarii were a patrician *gens* of prehistoric, not to say fabulous, antiquity. Compare L. Pinarius Natta, attested as *pontifex* in 57 B.C. (Cicero, *De domo sua* 134). But it is not clear that all Pinarii of this age could establish a claim to patrician descent. As for the Pedii, there is instructive evidence. Persons bearing this name are attested in the Italian commercial colony at Delos, and it is possible that the Pedii were of non-Latin origin, having only attained the franchise after the *Bellum Italicum* (*RE*, s.v. 'Pedius', col. 38).

It is the same with the significance of the patriciate in this age, for strange views find public expression. An authoritative manual, after cursorily identifying the *optimates* with the whole senatorial order, goes on to speak of the patricians as though they were synonymous with *nobiles* (*CAH* ix 777). This obscures the fact that the *nobilitas* was of mixed origin, patrician and plebeian, the older element being far from dominant in the amalgam. Another chapter in the same volume, referring to the poet Lucretius, of whose origin nothing is known, states, 'he was no doubt a patrician' (*CAH* ix 746). To label him an Umbrian, as does Piganiol (*La Conquête romaine*[3] (1940), 457), is a conjecture, to be sure, but not a misconception. In the matter of the patriciate, rigorous definition is attainable as well as profitable. There were few patricians left in the ranks of the *nobilitas*; only twelve of the patrician *gentes* are represented on the Consular Fasti after the Hannibalic war; they steadily diminished in numbers and in importance, and they had to fight tenaciously for survival, for the *factio optimatium* was based upon the dynastic houses of the plebeian nobility. Caesar, highly conscious of his patrician origin, appealed to descent from kings and gods in his contests with Popillii, Lutatii, Domitii, and what not: the *plebs* of Rome understood. Nor was Caesar unmindful of the historical claims of his peers. Caesar, like Sulla before him, was eager to revive the patriciate; he has his due place between Sulla and Augustus. Various decayed patricians joined his following, and a Fabius Maximus, the first since 116 B.C., got the consulate from him. What Caesar's dictatorship announced, his heir's Principate achieved, the renaissance of the patrician nobility: no fewer than ten *gentes* are represented on the Fasti during the reign of Augustus. The Postumii were gone for good; but Quinctii and Furii revive after a century's decay, and a Quinctilius emerges, descended like the Julii from the nobility of Alba Longa, 'illustri magis quam nobili ortus familia', as Velleius (ii 117, 2) significantly remarks. But the renaissance of the patricians was brief and illusory: they perished in the murderous embraces of the dynasty of the Julii and Claudii.

In fact, the earliest notice about the young Julius Caesar is relevant to his patrician origin. At some time after the death of Cornelius Merula

(87 B.C.), possibly as late as 84 B.C., he was designated for the office of *flamen Dialis*, but not actually inaugurated, though this is stated by Gelzer (p. 32), and by others. They might appeal to Velleius Paterculus and to Plutarch, but the language of Suetonius does not prove it: furthermore a reputable source attests the fact that the priesthood lay vacant for seventy-five years, that is to say, 87–11 B.C. (Tacitus, *Ann.* iii 58). What happened is surely clear enough: *nominatio* by the *pontifex maximus* had occurred, but, for some reason or other, the ceremony of *inauguratio* had been postponed. One might be tempted to ask, where was the attraction for a young man of parts. The taboos with which the office was hedged normally debarred its holder from public life—though the recent fate of Merula was a warning example. Again, the fact that the *flamen Dialis* might not divorce would surely bother a man in the game of marriage alliances and dynastic politics. Gelzer, speculating on the matter, inclines to invoke the influence of a powerful mother and a pious aunt—for Caesar's father had just died (p. 33). Perhaps they thought this would be the way to keep the young man safe and inactive in a murderous period: despite the double alliance with the faction of Marius and Cinna, they could hope for protection from influential relatives in the party of Sulla. The tenure of the priesthood was for life, but a resolute man could presumably get out of it, even if *inauguratio* had taken place, by contemplating a corpse, eating beans, or perpetrating some other enormity. In the course of the Hannibalic War a Claudius is known to have resigned—'quod exta perperam dedit, flamonio abiit' (Livy xxvi 23). Otherwise C. Julius Caesar might have left no deeper trace in the history of Rome and the world than did other patricians such as P. Scipio, the feeble son of the great Africanus, who was also *flamen Dialis*—or Caesar's own first cousin Sextus, of whom nothing is recorded save the fact that he was *flamen Quirinalis* (Cicero, *De haruspicum responso* 12). The Julii, it will be recalled, were an ancient sacerdotal family, worshipping as a *gens* the enigmatic deity Vediovis (*ILS* 2988 [= *ILLRP* 270]): it was proper for a patrician, whatever his religious or philosophical beliefs, to possess an exact knowledge of ritual, as witness the writings of the consulars L. Caesar and Ap. Pulcher; and Caesar himself was something of a sacerdotal expert, as he demonstrated, not merely by the prosecution of Rabirius, with its archaic procedure and horrid penalty, but many years later when he ordained that two mutinous soldiers be sacrificed by a priest and their heads be hung upon the Regia. This feature in Caesar's character has often been neglected, not least, be it noted, by those who argue that Caesar intended to establish for himself an autocracy on a religious basis. |

The evidence about Caesar's early life down to the year which saw him *pontifex maximus* and praetor elect (63 B.C.) presents a cardinal problem in historical study, relevant to things more important than the mere details of Caesar's career. How much was in fact remembered and recorded? How much was artistically fabricated so as to stand in harmony with the acts of the consul, proconsul, and dictator, with the supposed intentions of the autocrat—and with the character of the tyrant? We all know how Sulla, with a suitable prescience, observed that there was many a Marius in that young man; how the statue of Alexander the Macedonian at Gades moved Caesar to angry tears; how in that city he dreamed a dream portending monarchy. Retailed with faith, or at least with affection, by many biographers and historians, several of the familiar anecdotes are quietly jettisoned by Gelzer.

Some details, it is true, are unimpeachable, such as are attached to the names of persons. Suetonius is far and away the best authority: yet even the testimony of Suetonius, when purified of tale and fable, can be sensibly augmented from other sources. For example, both Velleius and Plutarch mention Caesar's relations with the Antistii Veteres, father and son. These authors also furnish the name of the governor of Asia in 74 B.C., M. Juncus (perhaps M. Junius Juncus, the husband of Rutilia Polla, *CIL* vi 3837; if so, perhaps a distant connection of Caesar). That name also occurs in the significant fragment of Caesar's speech *Pro Bithynis* quoted by Aulus Gellius (*NA* v 13, 6); therefore it is probable that only the survival of the speech has preserved the name of Juncus and introduced it to the historical tradition. Suetonius records Caesar's election as *tribunus militum*, that is to say, to one of the twenty-four tribunates in the first four legions of the traditional consular levies. The office of *tribunus militum* ranked as a minor magistracy (cf. the *Lex Acilia* and Cicero, *Pro Cluentio* 148), and had perhaps by now been entirely divorced from service in the field. Plutarch says that Caesar's election followed a sharp contest with a certain C. Popillius (*Caesar* 5), a unique detail. This person presumably belongs to the dynastic plebeian house, now in decay, which had produced, along with other unprepossessing characters, the consul of 132 B.C., odiously remembered for his treatment of the followers of Ti. Gracchus. Very few Popillii were left, no doubt a relief to their contemporaries, as it is a convenience to students of prosopography. This C. Popillius is perhaps to be identified with the senator Popillius Laenas who held converse both with Caesar and with the conspirators on the Ides of March (Plutarch, *Brutus* 15 f.), but he is not necessarily the C. Popillius who was *tr. pl.* (*ILS* 5800 [= *ILLRP* 465a], ? 68 B.C.). The Popillius Laenas who killed Cicero is certainly a different person. Another detail, garbled in Plutarch but confirmed by Asconius, is the prosecution of C. Antonius (76 B.C.); and it is Velleius who informs us that Caesar, when absent in the East, was elected *pontifex* in place of his kinsman, the deceased Cotta (C. Cotta, *cos.* 75 B.C.). Cotta died late in 74 B.C.

In general the sources show a tendency to concentrate on familiar episodes, such as 'Caesar and the Pirates'; and Plutarch on that topic confuses and combines Caesar's two sojourns in the Eastern lands (80–78 and 75/4–74/3 B.C.). On the second occasion Caesar went out in the winter of 75/4 B.C., but apparently did not stay long: he returned to Rome on hearing that he had been chosen *pontifex*. Common to all sources is a dearth of information about the interval between Caesar's return from the East (74/3 B.C.) and his quaestorship in Hispania Ulterior (? 69/8 B.C.). The only indication of political activity comes from Suetonius (*Div. Jul.* 5, 1–2), and it is scanty enough. Suetonius says that in his military tribunate Caesar helped the agitation for restoring the power of the tribunes of the *plebs*: he also supported with success the *lex Plotia de reditu Lepidanorum*. As narrated by Suetonius, the two actions appear to fall in the same year. However that may be, the date of the *Lex Plotia* is uncertain, perhaps as late as 70 B.C. (cf. *CAH* ix 896), but surely not later. One would expect the election to the military tribunate to fall shortly after Caesar's return (i.e. in 73, for 72): he had something to back up his candidature with, namely, the suppression of pirates, the protection of provincials from the troops of Mithridates—and aspersions on the capacity of M. Juncus.

Was this the sum of his political activity? The speech in defence of Cn. Decidius, the proscribed Samnite, perhaps belongs to these years (cf. Tacitus, *Dial.* 21, 6, corrected by means of Cicero, *Pro Cluentio* 161). Perhaps also the publication of the speech *Pro Bithynis*—for, if it was originally delivered abroad before the proconsul Juncus, how did it get known to, and quoted by, later writers at Rome? (It is possible, however, that the speech belongs to a later date. Gellius, quoting from it, refers to the 'auctoritas C. Caesaris, pontificis maximi'. But that is not conclusive for the dating.) These two speeches could easily have had considerable political importance: they will not have been to the liking of the Sullan oligarchy, vindicating as they did the victims of the established order. Similarly the brush with Popillius may have evoked some expressions of political significance—otherwise, how and why did the occasion, trivial in itself, pass into historical record? No other election of a *tribunus militum* is known in this period save that of Cato, if indeed the word used by Plutarch, ἀποδειχθείς, could be so interpreted: Cato served as a real military tribune, in Macedonia | (*Cato minor* 9). It would be Caesar's way to show up the social pretensions as well as the political record of unpopular oligarchic families. Perhaps the Popillii, like other plebeian *gentes*, had a fraudulent pedigree. Their very name betrays non-Latin origin. If the Pomponii asserted descent from Numa Pompilius, the Sabine king of Rome, history could no doubt have been invented, and philology invoked, with equal validity, for the Popillii.

It was about this time that, if we are to believe Carcopino, the young patrician conceived the splendid and precise ambition to which he was to consecrate the rest of his life—'ce plan, César l'a conçu aux environs de sa trentième année, sans que personne, d'abord, s'en aperçoive autour de lui' (*Histoire romaine* ii 2: *César* (1936), 602 [= ² 642]). Notice also, 'au seuil de sa carrière historique, il a franchement découvert le but théocratique et royal qu'il lui assignait' (ibid. 609 [= ² 649], with reference to the funeral oration delivered over his aunt Julia). Carcopino states that men at the time were unaware of Caesar's design. If this is so, how do we know about it?

Gelzer does not accept any such prescience or predestination in the early career of Caesar (p. 36); and he is impervious to mere anecdotes. None the less he has allowed himself to be influenced by tendentious accounts of certain of Caesar's acts, real or alleged. For example, Caesar's canvassing in the towns of Italia Transpadana on his way home from Spain after his quaestorship was interpreted as a revolutionary venture—'ad audendum aliquid concitasset, nisi consules conscriptas in Ciliciam legiones paulisper ob id ipsum retinuissent' (Suetonius, *Div. Jul.* 8). Gelzer believes in the truth of this allegation—'Caesar . . . hoffte auf eine bewaffnete Erhebung' (p. 43). Yet this was the man who, we are told, would have nothing to do with the rising of Lepidus, considering it a silly business (Suetonius, *Div. Jul.* 3, 2). Caesar's purpose was surely to extend his *clientela* in the Transpadana. Was it then that he made the acquaintance of a certain Valerius of Verona—and of another Valerius, of Milan, in whose house he once ate asparagus (Plutarch, *Caesar* 17)? Anyhow, when a few years later a man from the Transpadana had been wrongfully punished by a proconsul, he knew where to look for help (Sallust, *Bell. Cat.* 49, 2). In so far as we know Caesar, he is reluctant to use violence unless he has a legal position, an army, and an emotional plea.

The same argument applies to the belief that late in December 66 B.C. Caesar and Crassus were involved in a plot to seize power after assassinating the consuls and a part of the Senate. Suetonius cites certain authorities implicating Caesar (see below). Sallust, however, says nothing of Crassus and Caesar, but gives the prime role to Catilina. Gelzer, accepting the main facts from these alternative accounts (including the precise dates which Sallust assigns to the two attempts which were postponed, namely 1 January 65 B.C., and 5 February), combines them both so as to produce a plot of Crassus, Catilina, and Caesar (p. 49). And, of course, the (subsequent) sending of the quaestor Cn. Piso to Spain is invoked. The true character of certain political intrigues—or abortive demonstrations—at this time will never be known. As for Piso, it may well be that a simple piece of political jobbery engineered by Crassus has been accorded a sinister and portentous interpretation; and Piso did not survive to give his own version. In general, an instructive lesson emerges. Those modern accounts which make most of this 'conspiracy' need to explain, or cannot help betraying, the remarkable contrast between the magnitude of the enterprise so explicitly attested, and its trivial outcome. For example, we are told that 'the rashness of the conspirators in inviting detection was matched by their luck in escaping punishment' (*CAH* ix 478). This saves everybody's face. Catilina was especially lucky, for on New Year's Eve, he had been 'observed to be making overt preparations for some kind of foul play' (ibid. 477). As for the intended victims, one of them, L. Manlius Torquatus, seems to have borne no malice (Cicero, *Pro Sulla* 81). The other consul of 65 B.C. was L. Aurelius Cotta. According to Carcopino, Caesar, lacking both the rancour and the illusions of Crassus, was very properly reluctant to have a kinsman murdered. Therefore, first of all he had the attempt postponed, for he was waiting for the news of Piso's rising in Spain, and then, on 5 February, caused it to fail by refusing to give the agreed signal: in the meantime he had heard of Piso's death (op. cit. 612). This dating of the affair of Piso is wilful—it presupposes that Piso must have gone to Spain before 1 January 65 B.C. (which contradicts the sources): the time taken in winter by his journey to Spain and by the message of his death must be reckoned. Caesar in 45 B.C. got from Rome to Saguntum in seventeen days, but that was exceptional—'multis itineribus nocte dieque confectis cum celeri festinatione' (*Bell. Hisp.* 2, 1).

That is not the only rotten joint in the ramshackle edifice. Caesar, of course, has the monopoly of humanity and discernment. What of M. Crassus? The eminent consular, who was probably thinking about his candidature for the censorship, wanted to do other things with the Senate, not massacre it. That would have been a pity—he commanded such influence in the high assembly (Plutarch, *Pompeius* 22). Historians who make much of the sinister and fruitless designs of Crassus in this period seldom stop to notice that he was marrying one of his sons to a Metella, the other to a Cornelia, the heiress of the last surviving branch of the Scipiones. Even Gelzer's article on | Crassus in Pauly–Wissowa omits these facts. One of these days the unpretentious truth may emerge—Crassus was a conservative politician.

But it all matters very little. To look at the evidence of the 'original authorities' adduced against Caesar by Suetonius is enough—'meminerunt huius coniurationis Tanusius Geminus in historia, Marcus Bibulus in edictis, C. Curio pater in orationibus' (*Div. Jul.* 9, 2). We do not know that the historian Tanusius was less prejudiced than the rancorous Bibulus, whereas Curio's inaccuracy was pathological. Composing a dialogue with the dramatic date of Caesar's consulate he referred to subsequent events of Caesar's proconsulate; and professing that he had never even entered the Senate in that year, depicted himself leaving the Curia along with his son (Cicero, *Brutus* 218). 'Non tali auxilio.'

Caesar was presumably working with Crassus in the year of his aedileship (65 B.C.). What had been his relations with the absent Pompeius, who was the dominant factor in the politics of the city? Suetonius says nothing; but Plutarch states that he supported the *Lex Gabinia* (67 B.C.), Cassius Dio the *Lex Manilia* (66 B.C.). Most scholars, including Gelzer, accept and combine the two notices. Yet perhaps there is a doublet: perhaps the tradition preserved only a vague memory of one speech on behalf of a Pompeian tribune's proposal. Plutarch, not in his *Caesar*, but elsewhere, be it noted (*Pompeius* 25), says that Caesar was the only senator to support the *Lex Gabinia*. This statement, accepted by Gelzer (p. 44), and by Carcopino (*César*, 560), is surely an exaggeration. Likewise Carcopino's estimate of Caesar's power and influence at this time: 'Pompée, proclamé grâce à lui le magistrat en chef de la République' (ibid. 605 [= 2nd ed., 645]). Clearly, if the young Caesar in these years was powerful enough to bestow on Pompeius the armies and fleets of the Republic, why doubt that he could frustrate a revolution and prevent a massacre of the Senate?

In the common and canonical interpretation most of the activities recorded or inferred of both Crassus and Caesar in the years 65–63 are dismal failures. It is alleged that they were seeking to gain control of armies and provinces, or to seize power in Rome, against Pompeius Magnus. All in vain. The 'conspiracy' of 66/5 B.C. collapses because Crassus changes his mind, or Catilina gave the signal too soon, or Caesar not at all . . . or for some other reason. Crassus proposes the enfranchisement of the Transpadani: he is thwarted by Catulus, his colleague in the censorship. Again Crassus wishes to annex Egypt, with Caesar as his agent, but the *optimates* are too strong. The grandiose and impressive agrarian bill of Rullus is brought to nothing by the eloquence of the consul Cicero; and the miserable Rabirius, indicted for the murder of Roman citizens, is not condemned after all to be crucified on a barren tree.

On the other hand the influence and prestige of Crassus and of Caesar do not appear to have been depressed by these accumulated defeats; and Caesar sweeps on triumphantly in his career, not merely to praetorship and consulate: the people chose him *pontifex maximus*. That is to say, Caesar got certain highly desirable things. Perhaps he did not take the abortive proposals quite as seriously as his biographers do. In truth these ostensible failures are evidence of political craft. They demonstrated to the Transpadani, to the knights, and to the Roman *plebs* precisely who were their friends—and who were their enemies, namely Catulus and the *optimatium conspiratio*, as Suetonius calls them (*Div. Jul.* 11, 3).

Early in 63 B.C., after the prosecution of Rabirius, which was surely designed only as a demonstration, Caesar and the tribunes his allies gave the government a real shock. Labienus re-enacted the *Lex Domitia*, and (whether for that reason or not) Caesar came before the People as candidate for the office of *pontifex maximus*. The order of events as given by Dio and Suetonius is of some importance. It is kept by Gelzer, whereas the *CAH* and Carcopino have abandoned it, for inadequate reasons. Caesar's success was a historical event: by bribery and by popular favour a man of mere aedilician rank prevailed against the *principes*. Caesar's rivals were the two senior consulars, namely, P. Servilius Isauricus and Q. Lutatius Catulus—for nobody took notice of an Etruscan relic called Perperna (*cos.* 92 B.C.). Gelzer states that the office had hitherto only been held by the most distinguished consulars (p. 57). One should, however, recall the choice of that remarkable young man, P. Licinius Crassus, in 212 B.C., not to speak of a recent event: Cn. Domitius Ahenobarbus (*cos.* 96 B.C.) got himself elected in 103 B.C. The election of Caesar was a blow to others beside Catulus. The son of Ahenobarbus, kinsman of Catulus and bright hope of the *factio optimatium*, saw his *urbana gratia* being usurped by a dangerous rival.

What was the precise value of the supreme priesthood to Caesar? Gelzer does not discuss the matter. Others have—and have misconceived it. For example, Carcopino says that Caesar 'en avait modifié la nature et accumulé le dynamisme. Il s'en était saisi comme du levier spirituel à soulever l'État' (*Points de vue sur l'impérialisme romain* (1934), 114). This opinion is specious and fragile. Caesar was certainly interested in ritual, and desirous of maintaining (and exploiting) the State religion; but one looks in vain for evidence of a change in the nature and significance of the | office of *pontifex maximus*; and in any case long absence from Rome (presumably also a part of the future autocrat's precise programme) would severely limit his ritual or spiritual operations. A lot of accumulated dynamism must have been frittered away during Caesar's proconsulate. Being *pontifex maximus* meant for Caesar what it meant for Metellus who preceded him, and for Lepidus who followed—it was primarily an emblem of political success and a channel of political patronage. Finally the patrician had recaptured the supreme priesthood from the plebeian *nobiles*: they had held it for nearly seventy years.

The year that saw Caesar *pontifex maximus* and praetor designate confirmed and enhanced his importance in Roman politics; the famous speech in the debate about the accomplices of Catilina revealed skill as well as audacity. At the same time it evoked the earliest surviving and authentic contemporary opinion. Cicero accepts Caesar as a *popularis* and, perhaps with veiled irony, hails him as a sincere and sensible *popularis*—'intellectum est quid interesset inter levitatem contionatorum et animum vere popularem saluti populi consulentem' (*In Cat.* iv 9). No less instructive are the Caesarian terms of the appeal to Caesar 'sicut ipsius dignitas et maiorum eius amplitudo postulabat' (ibid.). The patrician's public boast

98] Caesar der Politiker und Staatsmann

of descent from kings and gods (Suetonius, *Div. Jul.* 6, 2) had no doubt
been heard more than once: it was highly relevant to his disputes with
members of the plebeian nobility; and Caesar's predilection for his own
dignitas finds repeated attestation (especially in the *Bellum Civile*). In the
last resort, it is personal justification for taking up arms.

It would be difficult to stop this man becoming consul: the opponents
could only block the triumph claimed by the proconsul for his exploits
in Spain. Caesar had worked with Crassus: at the same time he had co-
operated, in 63 B.C., with certain Pompeian tribunes in vexing the government. He might therefore seem destined to bring the two together. It is
surprising that the alliance of the dynasts was kept secret for so long.

Caesar began his consulate with words of deadly conciliation, showing thereby his special talent for putting his enemies morally in the
wrong (p. 91). Only gradually were revealed the complete and menacing
programme, the spirit and methods of the new consul. Gelzer analyses
the two agrarian bills and generously appraises them (p. 84), and he
carefully distinguishes between the status of the two provincial commands voted to the consul (pp. 11 f.), namely, the one by the *Lex Vatinia*,
the other by a *senatus consultum*. Further, Gelzer maintains that Caesar
acquired effective control of the province of Cisalpina (with Illyricum)
from the day on which the *Lex Vatinia* was passed—'er besaß jetzt
nämlich während seines Consulats eine starke militärische Macht in
Italien' (p. 101). This theory, however, is not necessary to explain either
the evidence or the situation.

Alive to the heightened significance of Gallia Cisalpina in view of the
menace of the Dacians in the Danubian lands, Gelzer none the less holds
that Caesar had his eye on Transalpina from the outset. A point of some
importance is the meaning of 'Caesaris exercitus' (especially in Cicero,
Ad Att. ii 16, 2). It has been much debated. Was it the army of Gallia
Cisalpina, or was it Caesar's *clientela* in Rome and in Italy, above all the
colonists established in Campania in virtue of the agrarian legislation of
59 B.C.? Gelzer (p. 94) maintains the latter view, as laid down in his
article, *Hermes* lxiii (1928), 113 ff., despite the appropriateness of the reference to the army of Cisalpina which dominated Italy and was the effective
guarantee for the future maintenance of the laws passed in Caesar's consulate. Now Cicero, in the letter referred to, represents Pompeius as
saying 'oppressos vos tenebo exercitu Caesaris'. Speaking for himself, the
dynast could refer without dishonour to the garrison of the Cisalpine
province as 'Caesaris exercitus'; for, whoever had proposed in the Comitia
that extraordinary command, and whoever was to hold it, the intention,
the will, and the power was that of Pompeius Magnus: it was an expression
of his *auctoritas* or *potentia*. On the other hand, that same Magnus, who

M

had celebrated triumphs over three continents, was not going to describe his own veterans, his own clients, as 'exercitus Caesaris'. This, be it said, is irrelevant to the question whether the phrase could, or could not, in other contexts, denote the personal following of Caesar.

Caesar's consulate would have marked a date in history even if Caesar had never survived to conquer Gaul and the whole world. For a century programmes of reform, whoever were their real authors, or intended beneficiaries, had been championed by tribunes. Now, however, Caesar revived the consular power as a weapon of direct political action. When a superior demagogue became tribune he was dangerous enough; as consul he was formidable. Moreover, after his consulate, he could extend his *clientela* from the urban or Italian *plebs* to the soldiers and the provinces.

Caesar's earliest acquaintance with the provinces was gained in the course of his two sojourns in the Eastern lands, where the family was known—his father had been proconsul of Asia; and the special interest of the Julii in the city of Ilium had already received epigraphic commemoration | (*ILS* 8770). Caesar had served on the staffs of the governors of Asia and of Cilicia; he had contracted, or rather perhaps renewed, ties of friendship with the royal house of Bithynia, and had subsequently championed the Bithynians, regarding them as his clients; again, he had prosecuted Dolabella and Antonius, in defence of the Macedonians and the Greeks. The record is consistent and instructive. But the Eastern lands never saw Caesar again for twenty-five years. His quaestorship was the turning point. It opened his eyes to the importance of the provinces of the West, namely, the two Spains and the two Gauls, as sources of military and political power. But the time had not yet come to exploit those sources. After his quaestorship Caesar decided not to serve as mere legate to a provincial governor—or even advance his prospects, as did other nobles, in the campaigns of Pompeius Magnus—but make certain of his praetorship and consulate through *urbana gratia*. Now at last, in 59 B.C., the patrician demagogue had acquired, from the alliance of Pompeius, the means to steal his *clientela* in the two Gauls and emulate his military glory. This was clear enough to contemporaries, not least to Pompeius, mortified at seeing a political agent develop into a rival magnate: Crassus had less reason for displeasure. The crisis in the relations of the three dynasts which broke out in 56 B.C. was provoked by Pompeius, so Gelzer holds, but ended more to the advantage of Caesar (p. 134).

Gelzer neatly traces, step by step, and with due interrelation of events in Gaul, especially in the year 52 B.C., the development in the Roman political situation that ended with the appeal to arms. The dexterity of Caesar is finally evident in Curio's seductive proposal, which was based on equity rather than on legality—both dynasts should resign their armies for the sake of the Commonwealth (p. 204). It will hardly be expected that one should hold here long discourse about what is called the 'Rechts-frage'. As Cicero observed in the speech *Pro Marcello*, 'erat quaedam obscuritas'. Gelzer, however, seems to have defined it too clearly and too rigidly: he hardly seems to recognize the possibility that, at one stage, Caesar might well have wished to become consul in some year earlier than 48 B.C. When Caesar's command was prolonged in 55 B.C. did he or his allies imagine that the conquest of Gaul could last so long? And did Caesar contemplate so long an absence from Roman politics? The law, it is true, prescribed an interval of ten years between consulates. But what was the law? A generation that had seen an *eques Romanus* become consul, and had recently seen that same person consul without colleague, ought not to have been shocked by—and could hardly have found arguments against—a proposal to remit a year or two in favour of the conqueror of Gaul with his powerful and popular claim, 'tantis rebus gestis', to say nothing of the support and approval of Pompeius Magnus.

Be that as it may, Magnus at last decided for—or was captured by—the party of Cato, which wished to destroy or abase both dynasts in convenient order of priority. Caesar had no wish for war, but was left with no alternative; and the defeat of his adversaries was not the most difficult of the tasks that confronted him.

In fact, next in interest to the social setting of the period and to the proper interpretation of the early career of Julius Caesar will be placed the question of the last acts and ultimate intentions of the Dictator. These are all kindred topics. If Caesar is unduly magnified at the expense of his rivals, his allies, or the whole *nobilitas*, the results are commonly seen to be the same whether his earliest or his last period is discussed, namely, a logical and theoretical construction, a monster not a man. Ed. Meyer, for example, created a Caesar aspiring to establish at Rome a 'Hellenistic Monarchy' (*Caesars Monarchie und das Principat des Pompejus*, 1919; 3rd ed. 1922), in perfect contrast to the principates of Pompeius and of Augustus, which are alleged to be kindred in nature.

But that premature 'Hellenistic Monarchy', which Adcock has pertinently criticized (*CAH* ix, 718 ff.), is perhaps ceasing to be fashionable, and the 'principate' of Pompeius, loudly acclaimed for some years, seems to have lost its prestige: a notion of the nature of Augustus' rule more realistic than that of Ed. Meyer is long overdue. Those constructions, based as they are upon sharp and schematic contrasts of men and policies, obscure the steady development of autocracy at Rome, a process in which Caesar follows Pompeius as a military dynast—and Augustus betrays, even when he does not acknowledge, his Caesarian antecedents. However that may be, Carcopino's Caesar, monarchic and theocratic in ambition from his youth, unswerving until the goal is attained, also seems too perfect to be genuine. Gelzer shuns the name of Hellenistic monarchy, and he is averse from schematic constructions. But even Gelzer, while discarding many fables or theories, seems willing to swallow a handsome portion of the modern legend of Caesar (see below).

Caesar's actions were more revolutionary than his intentions. As he had not wished to make war upon his own class, conciliation was a prime necessity, to be attempted without delay. At first with some success—Brutus, never a Pompeian, gave up that cause after the battle of Pharsalus and agreed to govern a province for Caesar; the behaviour of Ser. Sulpicius Rufus, a neutral, was also | significant; and Caesar's attitude towards M. Marcellus may have encouraged hopes of genuine concord. But the atmosphere at Rome was unhealthy (p. 318). It was soon poisoned by pamphlets and controversy about Cato. Caesar's ferocious rejoinder gave the lie to his *magnitudo animi*. His *clementia* remained a fact, no less distasteful for that. Certain of the Republicans had refused pardon; and Brutus now showed where his true allegiance lay by divorcing his wife and marrying Cato's daughter. Caesar was not liked or trusted by the *nobiles*. As Gelzer remarks, there was something sinister about him—'so war etwas Unheimliches in seinem Wesen' (p. 348). Men remembered his past all too clearly, his arrogance and his bitter personal feud with a respected consular like Catulus—and the satisfaction which, like a true aristocrat, he took in his feuds: compare his reported remark in the Senate, 'invitis et gementibus adversariis adeptum se quae concupisset, proinde ex eo insultaturum omnium capitibus' (Suetonius, *Div. Jul.* 22, 3). We know how a sensible and moderate man like Ser. Sulpicius Rufus regarded the situation—'cogita, quemadmodum adhuc fortuna nobiscum egerit: ea nobis erepta quae hominibus non minus quam liberi cara esse debent, patriam, honestatem, dignitatem, honores omnes' (*Ad fam.* iv 5, 2). Nor, as the days passed, did there come any sign or guarantee of a restoration of normal government. Caesar knew how to use the language, as when he indignantly rebuked a Galatian tetrarch—'a man of his calibre ought to have known where stood the *res publica* and who was consul' (*Bell. Al.* 68, 1); and of course he had taken up arms not only in defence of his own *dignitas* but also to 'rescue the *res publica* from the domination of a faction'. But there was no word of Rome or the Republic in his letter to Metellus Scipio, only 'quietem Italiae, pacem provinciarum, salutem imperii' (*BC* iii 57, 4).

To whom was Caesar to turn? The Dictator occupied a lonely eminence—'so wurde es, je höher er stieg, immer einsamer um ihn' (p. 299). Gelzer emphasizes and perhaps exaggerates Caesar's lack of reputable allies from the ranks of the aristocracy, stating that otherwise he could scarcely have chosen men like Antonius, Lepidus, and Dolabella (p. 329; cf. 262, where a list of his senatorial supporters is given). Of the leading men in the Senate, the consulars, many had perished, especially those of the opposing side. For example, of the ten consulars who, so Cicero claimed, crossed the seas with the army of the Republic, only two were now alive (Cicero himself and Ser. Sulpicius Rufus). Yet it might be doubted whether the situation was quite as bad as that. The Pompeian consulars ('quos cives, quos viros', says Cicero) were not really an impressive collection, and, save in years and standing, not conspicuously preferable to certain of the young *nobiles* in the following of Caesar.

Though Caesar had defied the government and had invaded Italy, perhaps the support he could count on was both more considerable and more reputable than Gelzer would allow. Among his followers Caesar numbered both the impoverished and the wealthy. Gelzer says nothing of Caesar's supporters in the towns of Italy, where Sulla and the system of Sulla had many enemies—compare the local aristocrats in the party of Catilina, 'multi ex coloniis et municipiis, domi nobiles' (Sallust, *Bell. Cat.* 17, 4). Significant above all are the peoples and the families that had fought for Italia against Rome only forty years before, as witness Pollio, whose grandfather had fallen in battle as leader of the Marrucini. Again, the bankers in the party of Caesar deserve especial note: they can hardly have regarded him as a dangerous revolutionary. It is one of the merits of Gelzer's book that he recognizes that the problem of Caesar's party does exist—though he does not discuss it fully, except with reference to Caesar's senatorial following and to Caesar's staff in Gaul (pp. 151 f.). The latter group forms an interesting collection of people, Oppius, Balbus, Mamurra, Hirtius, and Cn. Pompeius Trogus, the Vocontian—at least three of them, be it noted, inherited from Pompeius Magnus. The staff of the proconsul developed into the cabinet of the Dictator. That was just the trouble. On the other hand, Roman nobles, curtailed of pride and privilege, did not contemplate with equanimity a future in which they were to be ministers of an autocrat instead of his allies and equals. Caesar's breach with his own class was tragic and comprehensible (p. 329).

The present irked both him and them. The autocrat's task had become too much for him. Perhaps he hoped to evade it by going to the wars, without having set in order the Roman State. Nothing much seems to have been done—otherwise would the liberators have thought that the simple removal of the tyrant would be sufficient to restore the Republic? Nor, when the *acta* of Caesar's dictatorship are quietly scrutinized, do they give any clear indication of his intentions—and who after all could know his intentions?

For the rest, the 'evidence' commonly turns out to be gossip or propaganda. Suetonius reports the rumours that L. Cotta was to propose in the Senate that Caesar be given the title of *rex*, for a Sibylline oracle foretold that the Parthians could only be conquered by a king (*Div. Jul.* 79, 3).

Gelzer accepts the oracle and assumes that it was Caesar who set the sacred apparatus in motion. (So also Carcopino, *César*, 1005 [=² 1045].) This is far from certain. Indeed, those who discover truth in what Suetonius describes as a rumour do not attach sufficient importance to the testimony of a contemporary. Cicero denies that Cotta was going to proclaim any such oracle—'Sibyllae versus observamus, quos | illa furens fudisse dicitur. quorum interpres nuper falsa quidem hominum fama dicturus in senatu putabatur eum, quem re vera regem habebamus, appellandum quoque esse regem, si salvi esse vellemus' (*De Div.* ii 110). That is to say, Cicero is evidence for the contemporary existence of the rumour; he may, or may not, be taken to confirm the genuineness of the oracle, but his testimony proves that Cotta was not going to propose that anything should be done about it.

Gelzer also believes in the genuineness of alleged senatorial decrees to the effect that the dignity of *pontifex maximus* should be hereditary in Caesar's family, that he should personally have the right of dedicating the *spolia opima* in the temple of Jupiter Feretrius, as though he had slain a hostile leader with his own hand (p. 332). Both proposals seem highly unhistorical. As for the *spolia opima*, they only became relevant to the prestige of the ruler of Rome when a proconsul of Macedonia claimed them in 29 B.C., thereby infringing the martial monopoly of the new Romulus. Similarly, the rumour that Caesar intended to remove the capital of the Empire from Rome to the Eastern lands, to Ilium or to Alexandria (Suet. *Div. Jul.* 79, 3) presumably arose at some time or other in the twenty years after his death. Meyer accepted the report as a true indication of Caesar's designs, and Gelzer describes it as 'nicht unglaubhaft' (p. 339). Alexandria was in fact, for a time, the second capital of the Roman Empire, under Marcus Antonius the Triumvir; and the fear that the seat of empire might be transferred eastwards is attested by Livy in the speech of Camillus, by Horace (*Odes* iii 3, 57 ff.), and by Virgil (*Aen.* xii 828)—'occidit, occideritque sinas cum nomine Troia.' Whether Caesar, however, entertained such a design is another question. Many things tell against it, not merely the argument which some invoke, namely, his grandiose plans for rendering the city of Rome both beautiful and habitable.

If the rumours of the ancients and the logical constructions of the moderns are both dismissed, is enough left to explain why Caesar was assassinated? It would appear so. Gelzer holds that the title of *dictator perpetuus* possessed in public law the full meaning of *rex* while avoiding the odious word (336); and in the language of Roman politics, Caesar's position could fairly enough be described as *regnum*—compare Cicero's remark quoted about 'eum quem re vera regem habebamus'. It is therefore paradoxical to suppose that Caesar, who had a healthy contempt for names and forms, demanded the appellation when he had the substance. 'Vis imperii valet, inania tramittuntur.'

In truth, Caesar's position had become such that some of his own followers could not stand it. The sentiments and the actions of resentful Pompeians or stern Republicans call for no elucidation; and Brutus would certainly have killed Pompeius had Pompeius become an autocrat. Significant and decisive is the behaviour of Caesarians like D. Brutus and C. Trebonius. Caesar fell, but the party, the methods, and the system prevailed in the end. A military monarchy, albeit with an aristocratic and traditionalist colouring, was substituted for an oligarchy deriving from popular election. The two political classes in ancient Rome, namely, the nobility and the *plebs*, were stripped of their privileges for the benefit of the non-political orders in Italy and in the provinces.

About certain points of detail and matters of controversy, scholars will wish to learn Gelzer's opinion; for it will have to be reckoned with. The year of Caesar's birth is a vexed question—and very important, concerning as it does the age-limits in the official career of a senator: was it 102, 101, or 100 B.C.? Gelzer decides for 100, firm against the authority of Mommsen and the blandishments of Carcopino. The precise relationship of Caesar's mother to the three brothers Cotta (Gaius, Marcus, and Lucius) is nowhere recorded. Some, like Carcopino, assume that they were her brothers. This seems too close for comfort. It is more likely that they were her cousins (p. 32), as Münzer supposed. Some of the family ties that were invoked or exploited in Roman politics were pretty thin— compare the remote genealogical relation between Caesar and Mamercus Lepidus Livianus (*cos.* 77 B.C.), who, along with the Aurelii Cottae, protected the young man from the anger of Sulla. Even Münzer had some trouble in establishing it (*Römische Adelsparteien,*'313). It runs through the Rutilii. Certain closer connections by blood or marriage have already been indicated or discussed. Caesar lost his first wife Cornelia when he was quaestor, just before his departure to his province. On his return he married Pompeia, whose grandfathers were Q. Pompeius Rufus and Sulla. An astute move. While asserting and exploiting at every point the various links with the defeated party of Marius and Cinna, Caesar was careful to keep his hands free for independent political action. Another connection might also serve, that with Pompeius' kinsman M. Atius Balbus (see above). In 59 B.C. Caesar's daughter Julia was given in marriage to Pompeius Magnus, as a seal and pledge of the new alliance. She had previously been betrothed to a certain Servilius Caepio, as we are informed by Suetonius and by Plutarch. Unfortunately this man's *praenomen* has not been preserved. Münzer's theory is exciting and seductive: he supposes that this Servilius Caepio is no other than Marcus Brutus,

who in fact bore the official name of Q. Caepio Brutus, | derived, he
assumed, from adoption by his maternal uncle Caepio (presumably Q.
Servilius Caepio), who died in 67 B.C. Gelzer does not accept this identification. He believes that the Q. Servilius Caepio who adopted Brutus
was another person of the same name, precisely the Caepio who was
to have married Julia in 59 B.C. (p. 93, cf. *RE*, s.v. 'Iunius (Brutus)', col.
976). This intricate subject calls for renewed investigation. In any case the
sources are explicit about Brutus' family—his mother Servilia had only
one brother, namely, that Servilius Caepio who died in 67 B.C. while
Cato was serving as a military tribune in Macedonia. Another Servilius
Caepio will have to be discovered or invented if Münzer's identification
is to be rejected.

Caesar's marshal Labienus is a character of some historical interest.
Gelzer mentions their common military service in 78 B.C. under P.
Servilius in Cilicia (p. 55), but does not allude to Labienus' origin from
Picenum, which would justify the hypothesis that he owed something—
perhaps a great deal—to the patronage of Pompeius. Another point about
Labienus. A vexed passage ([Caesar,] *BG* viii 52, 2) has usually been taken
to refer without doubt to Caesar's second consulate. It can, however,
and perhaps should, attest a candidature of Labienus (cf. the arguments
adduced in *JRS* xxviii (1938), 121 ff. [above, pp. 71 ff.]). Gelzer appears
to share this view, for he writes 'Labienus, welchen der Imperator damals
über Gallia citerior gesetzt hatte, damit er von dort bequem seine Bewerbung um das Consulat betreiben könne' (p. 204). It is to be regretted that
Gelzer has not been fuller and more explicit: the prospect of a double
candidature of Caesar and Labienus, supported by Pompeius Magnus,
must surely have loomed large in the hopes and fears and intrigues of the
year 50 B.C.

As for the two *Epistulae ad Caesarem senem* attributed to the historian
Sallust, Gelzer accepts both of them as genuine, assigning them (in the
received order) to 46 and to 50 B.C. respectively (p. 201, cf. 294). That is a
question that would take too long to debate. The so-called *Lex Julia
municipalis* is regarded as of minor importance (p. 305). Gelzer is also
careful not to make too much of Cicero, *De re publica*. The child Ptolemy
Caesar, whom some called Caesarion, is here stated to have been born
in the year 47 (p. 275), and the authenticity of his parentage seems wholly
to be accepted (p. 338) despite the cogent arguments of Carcopino, highly
plausible on both points. Gelzer believes that the main purpose of the
intended polygamous proposal of the tribune C. Helvius Cinna in 44 B.C.
was to legitimize that infant. But the proposal does not stand on firm
ground: Cinna was not long in a position to affirm or deny anything, for
he perished on the day of Caesar's funeral. Further, without according
undue credence to the testimony of Oppius, put up by Octavian to deny

the Caesarian parentage of Cleopatra's son, one can believe that the importance of both mother and son has been exaggerated. Gelzer calls her 'das dämonische Weib' (p. 275), but he does not go so far as Ettore Pais, according to whom Cleopatra revealed to Caesar in a most convincing way the glamour and the utility of 'Hellenistic Monarchy'. He would never have known about it otherwise.

The size and composition of the governing oligarchy is a topic of central importance. Gelzer states that the post-Sullan Senate comprised 450 members (p. 38). Surely this is too small. The highest attested attendance is about 415, in 61 B.C., excluding magistrates (Cicero, *Ad Att.* i 14, 5; cf. for 57 B.C., the same figure, approximately, *Post red. in senatu* 26). To that sum must also be added persons occupied in the provinces on business, official or private, absentees, and valetudinarians. Again, the action of the censors of 70 B.C., who expelled no fewer than 64 senators, presupposes a high total. The question is relevant to Caesar's augmentation of the high assembly. Some have fancied that by raising the Senate to 900 the Dictator deliberately proposed to impair the usefulness as well as the prestige of both Senate and senator (for example, Carcopino, op. cit. 932 f. [=² 973 f.]). Gelzer (p. 306) does not fall a victim to this tendentious simplification of history. Nor, among Caesar's new senators, does he admit trousered Gauls and wild Celtiberians. The Gauls, it need hardly be added, came from the Cisalpine and Transalpine provinces (that is to say, Gallia Togata and Gallia Bracata), not from Gallia Comata; and the alleged Celtiberian L. Decidius Saxa is an Italian (cf. *JRS* xxvii (1937), 127 ff. [above, pp. 31 ff.]). The ancient evidence demands the most exacting scrutiny—just as, in any period of history, the language of social prejudice and political misrepresentation: compare Gelzer's own general remarks (*Die Nobilität der römischen Republik* 10 ff. [= *Kl. Schr.* i 29 ff.]). Gelzer here states that ex-centurions and people of even less reputable origin were to be found among the new senators—'auch verdiente Centurionen und Leute noch geringerer Herkunft' (p. 282). What does this mean? If an ex-centurion possessed the equestrian census, as well he might (cf. Cicero, *Phil.* i 20), why should he not become a senator? But who are the social outcasts, lower even than centurions? Presumably scribes and sons of freedmen. Yet these people had been seen before. An ex-scribe had been praetor in 173 B.C. (Val. Max. iii 5, 1; iv 5, 3); and no law of Republican Rome debarred the son of a freedman from standing for magistracies— as an imperial scholar once observed, 'priori populo factitatum est' (Tacitus, *Ann.* xi 24, 7). If Caesar's new senators engross all the discredit, | inadequate justice is done to the nominees of Sulla, of the Triumvirs— and of Augustus (see further, *PBSR* xiv (1938), 12 ff. [= above, pp. 88 ff.]).

This is not the place to discuss in full the precise significance of the extravagant honours that in antiquity might be privately or officially paid to eminent or powerful men, a subject frequently misunderstood. Nor can the allegedly 'divine honours' paid to Caesar the Dictator here be investigated. Gelzer is sober and reserved. But one cannot help thinking that he accords undue gravity to the placing of statues of Caesar in the temples of Quirinus and of Clementia (pp. 323, 333; cf. Carcopino, op. cit. 999 [=² 1039]). That was nothing new. A century earlier M. Marcellus (*cos.* III 152 B.C.) had put statues of his grandfather, his father, and himself in the temple of Virtus et Honos. He seems to have escaped censure. But this is not all. Gelzer even believes (p. 332) that Cassius Dio (xliv 4, 4) and Appian (*BC* ii 106) are reporting facts when they say that statues of Caesar were to be set up in all temples at Rome and also in the *municipia*. As for the temple of Clementia, which Dio says was common to Caesar and that goddess (xliv 6, 4), it must be recalled that in fact it was a temple dedicated to *Clementia Caesaris*; and, whatever the precise definition of the functions which Marcus Antonius was to exercise as *flamen*, nothing had been done about it before Caesar's death; therefore this may be one of the extravagant honours declined by Caesar. Exaggeration, anachronism, and misconceptions can be detected in certain reports of these matters, above all in Cassius Dio, who is so much more explicit than Suetonius, a fact not altogether to his credit. If the truth could be ascertained, it would be instructive to compare the position of Caesar's heir after the battle of Actium with that of Caesar the Dictator, especially in respect of extraordinary powers and honours.

Marcus Antonius is not a popular character; but it is surely not worth repeating that on two occasions he plotted to murder Caesar (p. 314). P. Cornelius Dolabella (*cos. suff.* 44 B.C.) is said to have been under thirty (p. 325). This is a watering-down of Appian, who gives the age of the consul as twenty-five (*BC* ii 129)—surely an exaggeration, in spite of the contempt which Caesar showed for constitutional forms, and the favouritism he extended to young men of patrician families. If genuine, the detail must have supplied damaging evidence of Caesar's *regnum*; yet no other source mentions it. Finally, Octavian appears as designate for the post of *magister equitum* after Lepidus in 44 (p. 325).

Errors of fact or of typography will creep into the most careful piece of workmanship. One could not expect to find many here. On p. 41 M. Cotta is described as the author of a *lex iudiciaria* in 70 B.C.: it was his young brother Lucius, *cos.* 65 B.C. On p. 207 is quoted in German the vital passage where Caesar (*BC* i 4, 4) complains that Pompeius had disloyally come to terms with their common enemies: for 'Freunden' read 'Feinden'. The index is drawn up on a salutary principle, according to family names. Unfortunately it is inaccurate in a dozen instances. Some of them are dangerously misleading. Vagueness about *gentilicia*, a characteristic of the untutored in every age, has been known to produce deplorable results.

Readers of Shakespeare's tragedy will recall one of the jollier scenes, where the poet Cinna, vainly protesting, is torn to pieces by angry citizens. He was C. Helvius Cinna, of Brixia: they thought he was a Cornelius Cinna, a noble and a patrician at that. In this index the name of the unhappy poet is doubly disguised—he is called 'Helvetius Cornelius Cinna'.

It will not be necessary further to insist upon the quality of Gelzer's work in general or upon the solid and singular merits of this biography of Julius Caesar: the reviewer regrets only that, being confined in a distant city and lacking books, especially Strasburger's study of the early years, he may not have been able to accord it the treatment it deserves.

12

REVIEW

W. Hoffmann, *Livius und der Zweite Punische Krieg*[1]

I F Livy has been unduly neglected in England during the last generation, the same cannot be said of certain other countries. After Soltau and Kahrstedt, Klotz applied himself to the investigation of Livy's sources, and operated upon the historian with the traditional knife, or axe, unrelenting. The patriarch of *Quellenforschung* has recently summarized, though not quite in the form of an epitome, the results of many separate and scattered studies, and has produced a comprehensive work, *Livius und seine Vorgänger* (Neue Wege zur Antike, Reihe 2, 9–11, Leipzig, 1940–1). The method he adopts bears primarily upon the origin and validity of historical statements: it may have little to tell about the historian himself. In the meantime a younger generation, turning aside from these austere delectations, from dogma, dispute, and nihilism, prefers to analyse the literary technique of Livy and endeavours to situate him more precisely in his spiritual environment.

Heinze's patient and subtle inquiry, *Virgils epische Technik* (1903), was an inspiring model. The subjects are related. Livy, so safe doctrine holds, is a sort of prose-Virgil. Hence various essays, for example Burck, *Die Erzählungskunst des T. Livius* (1934), and Hellmann, *Liviusinterpretationen* (1939). But Heinze's method is not so remunerative when applied to Livy. By the nature of things a historian is more severely restricted in his choice and arrangement of material than is an epic poet, however scholarly the latter may be, however respectful of tradition. The literary interpretation attempts to grasp and portray the Augustan historian as a *Gesamterscheinung*, or something of the kind. A laudable aspiration. But the 'new approach', or the latest formula, may well prove a disappointment and send one gladly back to Hippolyte Taine. Burck makes much of a Peripatetic school of writing, with Livy as its Latin representative. Concept and execution have been briskly handled by R. Jumeau—'tant d'esprit de système, si peu de sens de la réalité et une si grande confusion' (*REA*

[1] *Hermes*, Einzelschriften, Heft 8, Berlin, 1942.

Journal of Roman Studies xxxv (1945), 104–8.

xxxviii (1936), 68). Nor does the *interpretatio Augustea* so much in vogue seem able to produce a satisfactory picture of an individual set against the background of his epoch: compare the brief and pertinent remarks of Momigliano on Hellmann, *JRS* xxxiii (1943), 120. That there should now exist a lengthy disquisition entitled *Die Religiosität des Livius* (G. Stübler, 1941, 215 pp.) will not perhaps be a comfort to everybody. Is there such a subject? Bayet, a sane and alert scholar, assumes that Livy is fundamentally sceptical: 'la préoccupation morale tient chez lui la place du sentiment religieux' (in the Budé edition of Book i (1940), p. xxxix).

In fact, what tends to emerge from certain recent studies is only that familiar and representative figure, 'Livius der augusteische Mensch'. The manuals know him of old, and the pedagogues—and he now comes in handy to recommend the alliance between moral regeneration and ordered government.

The present inquiry advocates a middle path between aesthetics and surgery. What Hoffmann proposes to demonstrate is not just the extent of Livy's debt to his predecessors but how, by transfusing and interpreting his material, the historian discloses his own distinctive qualities, above all his relation to the Roman past. For this purpose it is not enough to concentrate upon a single book or an episode. A broad survey is required. At first sight the earlier books might seem attractive, as offering for comparison the narrative of Dionysius of Halicarnassus. This, he points out, is delusive. It is not at all certain that the Greek, Livy's contemporary, is a safe guide to the understanding of | Roman annalists. For one thing, the fellow is too wordy. His rhetorical amplifications dilute the Latin sources. Livy is far closer to them. (Compare Klingner's observations, in criticism of Burck, *Gnomon* x (1934), 578—or, for that matter, C. Peter long ago, *RhM* xxix (1874), 513 ff.) Hoffmann, therefore, prefers a later section of the Livian corpus (and, it might be added, one which permits something better than a comparative study in the field of historical romance). His choice falls upon the Second Punic War. This has the advantage of securing Polybius' company for part of the way, down to Cannae, with subsequent fragments of great value: hence the opportunity to draw a general distinction between Greek and Roman conceptions of history. Moreover, the earliest of the Roman historians, Fabius Pictor, can be discerned through Polybius—and, through Livy, Coelius Antipater becomes tangible, less than three generations subsequent to the events he recorded. Finally, the subject, 'bellum maxime omnium memorabile quae unquam gesta sint' (Livy xxi 1, 1). Not only the greatest of all wars ever, but close to the heart of the patriotic historian. The struggles with Etruscans, Gauls, and Samnites, for all the contemporary relevance of a theme such as the uniting of Italy or a providential hero like Camillus, 'Romulus ac parnes patriae conditorque alter urbis' (v 49, 7), could not hope to compete; and though his readers might be impatient to get on to 'haec nova', the exciting but deplorable history of the Civil Wars, Livy knew what was good for them, the war which brought out the supreme virtues of the Roman People and provided the moral justification for empire.

In an age that encouraged almost any manifestation of exact learning, the third decade of Livy was much belaboured. Gymnasial programmes begot an infinite tedium. A renewed study needs to justify itself.

Hoffmann points to the artistic unity of Books xxi–xxx, in episodes and as a group. In marked contrast are the books that follow—here Livy appears to be quite incapable of mastering and shaping the narrative. What with Polybian material, archaic strata, and annalistic accretions, falling apart at sight, the dissector has easy game. What is the reason— the complexity of the history or the inadequacy of the historian? In the developed unity of Books xxi–xxx Hoffmann detects the hand of Coelius Antipater. Not unreasonably. Many have done so since Peter (C.), in a programme some eighty years ago. Coelius wrote a monograph on the War, in seven books, *c.* 120 B.C. The later annalists, Quadrigarius, Valerius Antias, and Tubero, do not appear to have treated the subject in any way so fully.

The inevitable prelude, a discussion of the causes of the War, at once suggests a comparison not to the credit of Roman historians. From Thucydides the Greeks had learned to understand clashes between sovereign states as more or less normal phenomena, proceeding from a discoverable series of causes and 'incidents'. The Roman found it difficult to see Rome's wars as anything but a conflict between right and wrong. Even Polybius seems to have been influenced by the conception which he found in Fabius Pictor. Livy, as might be expected, comes out with a simple explanation, the revengeful ambition of one man, Hannibal, supported by a perfidious government. We are invited to admire the penetration of Polybius; he had 'den Krieg aus der in beiden Staaten ruhenden Dynamik hergeleitet und damit eine Tiefenschicht blossgelegt, wie sie nur aus griechischem geschichtlichem Denken heraus möglich war' (p. 15). Perhaps this is an overvaluation of Polybius. Livy's preoccupation with the personal and the concrete does not mean that he was entirely superficial.

Hoffmann goes fully into the intricacies of the question—a reviewer does not have to follow him. It would have been helpful, however, if Hoffmann had briefly stated his own view of the truth about Rome's relations with Saguntum, treatywise or otherwise, before Hannibal attacked that city. Not everyone has Polybius at his fingers' ends—or can keep him there, for Polybius' exposition is lacking in clearness and in logic. Nor, on the other hand, can the problem be simply put and simply disposed of, in the manner of Piganiol—'selon la version de Polybe, que les modernes suivent unanimement, Rome avait conclu alliance avec Sagonte: on discute seulement sur le point de savoir si cette alliance est antérieure au traité conclu en 226 entre Rome et Carthage' (*La Conquête romaine*[3] (1940), 184).

Livy, as is well known, gets himself into a mess about Saguntum—and actually admits that his chronology is wrong (xxi 15, 3 ff.). As for Polybius, the valuable pieces of information provided in the course of his disquisition seem to have rendered many critics blind to the imperfections of his account (note especially iii 30, 3 f.). The relevance (if any) of the undertaking made by Hasdrubal in 226 or 225 B.C., not to make conquests beyond the Ebro, is nowhere explained. The reader who approaches the text with an open mind about most things, including Spanish geography, can hardly help assuming that Saguntum lies north of that river, not a hundred miles to the south. Polybius, the great thinker, preserves his reputation—and the miserable Appian is denounced for plainly stating that Saguntum is north of the river.

It is a welcome relief to turn to the story of the War. It opened with a series of military defeats, | a problem for the patriotic annalist. It was not enough to lay the blame on 'political' generals like Flaminius and Varro, even though Varro could be socially incapacitated into the bargain, as a butcher's son. The saving remedy was to exalt the steadfastness in evil days of the Roman Senate—and of Q. Fabius Maximus. As Hoffmann shows, the material discrepancies between Polybius and Livy in their accounts of Fabius' dictatorship after Cannae are not serious (p. 36). But Livy concentrates upon the personality of Fabius—not strategy but moral qualities. Everything else is subsidiary: Hannibal and Minucius Rufus are reduced to the role of lay figures.

The War went on, the luck began to turn—and Scipio emerged. That the Scipio of Polybius is flat and schematic is no new discovery. Yet Hoffmann's observations deserve to be read. Polybius explains everything about Scipio Africanus. Livy, however, shows a truer understanding of human character—and, in the matter of Scipio's religious beliefs, scores heavily by leaving the question open. A comparison of the speeches put into Scipio's mouth on the occasion of the mutiny in Spain also turns to the advantage of the Roman historian: it exhibits a 'tiefe Deutung des Verhältnisses von Einzelmensch und Staat' (p. 88). In this superior comprehension is manifested the working of recent political experience at Rome.

The salient chapter of the book is devoted to Livy's treatment of the confrontation of two national heroes, Fabius and Scipio. The one saved Rome, but the other won the War. The contrast is patent—not merely two strategies but two epochs. 'Zwei Zeitalter treffen in Fabius und Scipio aufeinander. Altes und Neues, Bindung und Freiheit stehen sich gegenüber' (p. 126). It rises to an artistic culmination in Fabius' speech 'de provinciis consularibus' and Scipio's firm but temperate answer (xxviii 40, 1 ff.).

Now the whole incident is at once seen, as history, to be superfluous. Elected consul for 205 B.C., Scipio had already been allotted Sicily as his province (xxviii 38, 12), so in effect the decision had been given in favour of the invasion of Africa. It is generally agreed that the scene is some annalist's elaboration. The confrontation of the two *principes* also appears in Plutarch. There the old man is represented in an odious light, dominated by φιλοτιμία, and sparing no device to thwart or discredit his young rival—he even tries to incite the other consul, the *pontifex maximus* P. Crassus, to canvass for the command in Sicily (*Fabius* 25). Livy's handling of the situation is highly illuminating. Livy does not invent on a large scale. He feels bound to follow what he regards as an adequate source, mentioning discrepancies now and then. But he reserves the right to interpret, to colour, and to harmonize. In this instance he has certainly toned things down. Both Fabius and Scipio come off very creditably. Both were right, only Fabius is a little out of date. Livy has displayed consummate understanding: 'wieder greifen wir seine Fähigkeit, Gegensätze, die noch seinen Vorgängern als unüberbrückbar gelten, dank einer tieferen Einsicht in die Vielgestaltigkeit des Geschehens auszugleichen und zu versöhnen' (p. 93). Contemplating this reconciliation, this 'higher synthesis', one is tempted to add, 'magnanimi heroes, nati melioribus annis', or, likewise with emphasis on the second member of the phrase, 'concordes animae nunc et dum nocte premuntur'. The history that will reveal Fabius as a *veterator* as well as a *cunctator* has yet to be written.

Hoffmann also attempts, as the subject seems to invite, a delineation of Coelius Antipater—welcome, for the annalists are dim figures—even if it does not carry one very far. Coelius, writing under the influence of Hellenic enlightenment (which was not only rational but rhetorical), was yet not wholly emancipated from Roman tradition. He therefore seems consigned to a populous and inevitable limbo, the 'age of transition'. Commonplaces will therefore serve. Coelius is a reputable character when one passes to the annalists of the Sullan and Caesarian periods, vile *epigoni* who, lacking sympathy for the grandeur of ancient days, transferred to the earlier history the discord and the degradation of their own times (p. 125). Yet even the 'later annalists' cannot entirely deface the picture. The better tradition was too strong for them, and Livy showed good sense in going back to Coelius Antipater for his principal source. Yet Livy is not just a copyist, or an improver of fair copies. He transcends Antipater and emerges supreme. 'Keiner seiner Vorgänger und keiner der Späteren hat das Ewige römischer Leistung in solcher Tiefe geschaut' (p. 127).

With this appreciation of Livy, the unique apostle of Rome's greatness, who shall quarrel? The conclusion might be reached without undue exertions—and maintained, even if some of the author's arguments are convicted of imperfect validity.

Livy produced a classical and conventional narrative of the Second Punic War. A similar fate has since befallen a subsequent period of Roman history, precisely the epoch spanned by the life of T. Livius of Patavium (born in 59 B.C., or perhaps in 64 B.C.). Hoffmann does not seem aware of this disturbing factor. His assessment of Roman history in the last century B.C., especially the impact of certain powerful individuals, as contributing in a most significant fashion to Livy's conception of Africanus, is therefore vulnerable. He succumbs to a fallacy, assuming that Caesar possessed for contemporaries that peculiar and exclusive uniqueness with which the modern world has invested | him, to the obscuration of other dominant figures in the series of the dynasts. On Caesar's behalf he can, it is true, appeal to Mommsen, notably on one count. Mommsen showed that the speech attributed to Ti. Sempronius Gracchus in Livy's account of the attacks on the Scipiones is anachronistic—'castigatum enim quondam ab eo (*sc.* Scipione) populum ait, quod eum perpetuum consulem et dictatorem vellet facere; prohibuisse statuas sibi', etc. (Livy xxxviii 56, 12, cf. *RF* ii 502 ff.). In these exceptional honours which Scipio is alleged once upon a time to have deprecated, Mommsen saw a reference to Caesar, and, be it noted, not merely in general, but precisely datable to the spring of 49 B.C.: Livy's source, he held, was a pamphlet, deriving not from extremist enemies of Caesar, but from 'sensible Liberals'. Taking this well-known thesis as proved, perhaps without close scrutiny, Hoffmann sets out for further discoveries. The Livian confrontation between Fabius and Scipio is alleged to contain numerous features which point to its having originated in the fifties or the forties of the last century B.C.; further, certain characteristics of Cato Uticensis have been applied to Fabius, and the whole scene has been worked up as an 'anticipation' of the Sallustian antithesis between Cato and Caesar (p. 91).

This is not at all convincing. Was it left to some annalist of Caesar's day to invent the contraposition? Klotz, referred to by Hoffmann, assigns it to Valerius Antias, which is not quite so bad. But why not Coelius Antipater himself, whom Cicero describes as an 'exornator rerum' (*De oratore* ii, 54)? The procedure could perhaps be justified on Thucydidean or on Polybian principles. There was surely strong opposition to Scipio from elder statesmen in 205 B.C., even if only a rearguard action by rancorous conservatives. Nobody may have recorded the scene—but then, let it be retorted, what is there to guarantee the authenticity of Scipio's speech to the mutineers, as retailed by the irreproachable Polybius (xi 25 ff.)?

In Livy's account of the senatorial debate Fabius protests vigorously.

A consul, he says, should not employ his army as an instrument of selfish ambition, he ought to regard himself as a servant of the Republic—'ego . . . P. Cornelium rei publicae nobisque, non sibi ipsi privatim creatum consulem existimo, exercitusque ad custodiam urbis atque Italiae scriptos esse, non quos regio more per superbiam consules quo terrarum velint traiciant' (Livy xxviii 42, 22). The criticism can, of course, be applied to Caesar (so Hoffmann, p. 91). What about Sulla and Pompeius?

Again, let Pompeius only be taken as relevant for parallel with Scipio. In Plutarch's *Life*, Fabius argues that it is dangerous to trust one man's luck: εἰπὼν δὲ τὸ μνημονευόμενον, ὡς ἐπισφαλές ἐστι πιστεύειν ἀνδρὸς ἑνὸς τύχῃ τηλικαῦτα πράγματα, χαλεπὸν γὰρ ἀεὶ εὐτυχεῖν τὸν αὐτόν (*Fabius* 26, 3). It looks as though the argument about fortune was adopted, and further developed with hypocritical solicitude, by Catulus when opposing a bill to confer special powers on a notoriously lucky general: it was promptly countered, for the People cried out with one voice that, if Pompeius perished, they would still have Catulus (Cicero, *De imperio Cn. Pompei* 59 etc.). The τόπος was neither recent nor novel. Hoffmann in fact concedes in another context (pp. 73 f.) that such an argument would not have been anachronistic to the setting of the Second Punic War, for it occurs in Ennius (*Ann.*, fr. 289 Vahlen): 'haudquaquam quemquam semper fortuna secuta est'. The strange thing is this: it is not employed by the Livian Fabius. Which might—or might not—repay speculation.

There are other features of Pompeius, especially in his early career, that suggest a close parallel with Scipio—youthful ambition, the claims of the superior individual, and the appointment of a *privatus cum imperio* to conduct war in Spain. Some might also be tempted to invoke Pompeius' later policy, his marriage with Cornelia, the daughter of the last of the Scipiones: superfluously, nor is the label of 'Pompeianus' which Augustus applied to Livy (Tacitus, *Ann.* iv 34) here of relevance. But Pompeius and Caesar were soon eclipsed in the eyes of Livy's contemporaries by the man of destiny himself, the 'divinus adulescens'. Yet one finds that Octavianus is omitted from an evaluation of the influence of recent history upon Livy and, in particular, upon Livy's conception of Scipio Africanus. This is most unfortunate. The fact that biographies of Scipio were written by Oppius and by Hyginus (Gellius, *NA* vi 1, 2) deserves exploitation.

The times changed quickly, and Augustus transcended Octavianus. Scipio's address to the mutineers is quoted by Hoffmann (p. 102) to show how Livy regarded the relation between the individual and the State. Perhaps one can go further. Surely the passage is startling and contemporary, not merely 'Augustan' but something that might (or should) have been said by the Princeps himself; and it suggests a comparison between Caesar and Caesar Augustus. The Dictator, rebuking the people of Hispalis, appealed to the military might of Rome: did they not know

that even if Caesar were killed Rome had armies that could tear down the
heavens (*Bell. Hisp.* 42, 7)? In contrast, Scipio according to Livy (xxviii
28, 11)—'si ego morerer, mecum exspiratura res publica, mecum casurum
imperium populi Romani erat?'

The words are there. To insist would be superfluous. Yet, for the sake
of completeness, it might be added that the way to deal with soldiers, and
the language to be employed, was a theme of | acute and present concern.
Caesar had cowed them with the appellation of 'Quirites'. The Scipio of
Livy hestiates whether to call his men citizens, soldiers, or foemen—
'cives? qui a patria vestra descistis? an milites? qui imperium auspiciumque
abnuistis', etc. (xxviii 27, 4). The passage was recalled by Tacitus in
Germanicus' speech to the mutineers on the Rhine. Now Octavianus after
Actium confronted and tamed the turbulent legions: 'divus Augustus
vultu et aspectu Actiacas legiones exterruit' (Tacitus, *Ann.* i 42). The
soldiery were surely not the only ones to be impressed. Civilians (and
historians) had had enough of the exigencies of the military: compare the
contemporary testimony of Cornelius Nepos (*Eumenes* 8, 3).

One matter remains, fundamental to the estimate of Livy's historical
methods. Livy has been given the credit for toning down and for
sublimating, in a moral and patriotic fashion, the discord between Fabius
and Scipio that had been invented by a recent, a very recent, annalist.
This is not altogether fair to Livy. He was probably dealing with a well-
established and plausible tradition; and he did not modify it unduly.
An illuminating—and disquieting—parallel ought to be quoted, namely the
feud between Cato the Censor and Scipio. The sources followed by Livy
suppressed the fact that Cato had served as quaestor under Scipio in
205 B.C.—and had quarrelled with his chief, as Plutarch and Nepos report.
Such at least is the explanation of Münzer, *Hermes* xl (1905), 50 ff., esp.
68 ff. Not all are ready to accept it—perhaps malicious invention had
been at work, projecting Cato's enmity into the past. However that may
be, expurgation is elsewhere clear enough. A fabricated predecease of
Scipio precludes the ultimate animosities and covers up the events of 185
and 184 B.C.—in some sources at least. The history had been properly
'arranged' before Cicero wrote his *Cato Maior*. Compare especially, for
cooked chronology, Cato's assertion about the date of Africanus' death,
Cato 19: 'anno ante me censorem mortuus est.' Hence perfect harmony.
Cato actually parades as an old family friend (ibid. 77): 'ego vestros patres,
tu, Scipio, tuque, Laeli, viros clarissimos mihique amicissimos' etc. 'No
less bland, pious, and benevolent is the same Ciceronian Cato when
alluding to his own conduct as censor. He expelled from the Senate L.
Flamininus, but only because he had to: 'invitus feci' (ibid. 42). This is not
the old bulldog himself, the πανδακέτης of the notorious epigram, but a
decayed dachshund. Livy found the right phrase for Cato's attacks upon

Africanus—'adlatrare magnitudinem eius solitus erat' (xxxviii 54, 1). Livy also recounted the precise enormities committed by Flamininus, referring to Cato's speech (xxxix 42, 5 ff.), and mentioning names, 'Philippum Poenum, carum ac nobile scortum'. Valerius Antias followed an expurgated version, and so did Cicero, extenuating the guilt of Flamininus—and contradicting the testimony of Cato.

Livy deserved well of the Republic. But he was not responsible for these deliberate perversions of history. The devil's work had already been done.

13

REVIEW

H. Siber, *Das Führeramt des Augustus*[1]

To the understanding of the rule of Caesar Augustus there are many obstacles. Not merely biography and the worship of success. Fashions and predilections such as the imperial cult, the constitutional settlements, Cicero's *Republic*, and Augustus' *Res Gestae* can be incriminated, as Momigliano points out when discussing the *Cambridge Ancient History*, vol. x (*JRS* xxxiv (1944), 109). That critic announces good tidings—those who traffic in mystical incantations will find the market apathetic. The jurists are a tougher tribe, with Mommsen's prestige at their back and all the force of Roman tradition. Emancipation requires effort. Anton von Premerstein broke the spell when he demonstrated the extra-constitutional sources of Augustus' supremacy, disclosing the party leader, the head and centre of a vast *clientela* (*Vom Werden und Wesen des Prinzipats*, ABAW, N.F. xv (1937)). But the liberator was enmeshed again. He argued that the Princeps in 27 B.C. received from Senate and People a general mandate of express formulation, an official 'cura et tutela rei publicae'; and he wished to elevate *auctoritas* into a juridical concept.

Dr. Siber, a jurist by profession, defends his own Penates. The reaction from Mommsen, he maintains, has gone too far if, overriding the plain testimony of the sources, it expels jurisprudence and installs extraneous notions. Sociological phenomena are not the same thing as public law—and they are not an adequate substitute for it either. Which is all very proper. The Roman habit of mind was legal and conservative. Though the constitution of the Republic was highly vulnerable, being in the main unwritten, the reformer or revolutionary had to reckon with custom, rule, and precedent. To get round the law you must know what the law is. Augustus claimed that his predominance rested upon a lawful basis—and in truth, as the First Citizen held the best cards, he had every reason to insist on the rigour of the game. Let the attempt, therefore, be made to define the powers of Caesar Augustus with the nicest precision of thought and language.

[1] Leipzig, 1940.

One of the instruments of rule contrived by the Princeps was peculiar and elusive, the *tribunicia potestas*. Tacitus calls it the 'summi fastigii vocabulum' (*Ann.* iii 56), and the general tendency is to rate it very high indeed. Yet Augustus seems not to have realized all the potentialities of the device until 23 B.C., when, discarding the consulate, he required a basis of authority inside the city for his dealings with Senate and People. The utility of *tribunicia potestas* is evident—power divorced from office. At the same time a large part of its value may be symbolical. It is not too great a strain on the imagination to conceive that a constitutional monarchy could have evolved without this resource, that the history of the Principate might have gone on much as we know it. But not without *imperium*. The command over provinces and armies was essential from the beginning.

In January 27 B.C. the Senate voted to Augustus, now consul for the seventh time, certain powers for a period of ten years, and the *senatus consultum* was duly confirmed by a *lex*, as Cassius Dio indicates: τὴν μὲν οὖν ἡγεμονίαν τούτῳ τῷ τρόπῳ καὶ παρὰ τῆς γερουσίας τοῦ τε δήμου ἐβεβαιώσατο (liii 12, 1). The nature and definition of the grant is a subject of perennial debate, a long history in itself, a track well beaten. Merely to pass where the great pachyderms have stamped and trumpeted is no merit. Credentials will be closely scrutinized. Has the author a talisman, or at least a prophylactic; is his contribution a new approach, or, failing that, a judicious compendium of respectable opinions?

In the 'first constitutional settlement', Siber distinguishes three elements. First, there is a military *imperium* which he describes as 'namenlos'—that is, apparently, not tied to any province or group of provinces—embracing all armies wherever stationed throughout the Empire (pp. 21 f.), and consequently running in Italy, outside the *pomerium* of Rome (p. 37). But, secondly, the *imperium* also carries civil authority in the imperial | provinces—'eine gleichfalls ausschließliche bürgerliche Gewalt über die Kaiserprovinzen' (p. 31). Lastly, on Augustus is conferred the right to make war and peace—for life (p. 21).

As for procedure, Siber suggests that the *senatus consultum* did not name any provinces, but left the choice to the discretion of Augustus; they were specified in the *lex*. Why should this be? Cicero's drafts for Brutus and for Cassius in 43 B.C. define the provinces in which the Liberators are to exercise *imperium* (*Phil.* x 25 f.; xi 30). The items enumerated above, with further details into the bargain (as set out on p. 53), would make a cumbersome *lex*. Siber appeals to the phraseology of Roman laws, diffuse, wooden, and pedantic (pp. 53 f.). Perhaps it is. Yet Cicero's proposals about 'extraordinariae potestates' are not clumsy, but clear and precise. Too high a standard, somebody may object, 'not Tully, Ulpian serves his need'. However, there were surely some people in the inner councils of the Caesarian party with diplomatic experience and skill in drafting, not least Munatius Plancus, the grand old man whose congenial duty it was to sponsor the title 'Augustus'. If the recent disturbances were detrimental to style and scholarship (note the defective orthography of an ex-consul who wrote 'ixi' for 'ipsi' and lost his job, Suetonius, *Divus Aug.* 88, 2), they may also have put long-winded legal pedantry out of fashion. These comments are strictly relevant: as will hereafter emerge, the powers conveyed to Augustus by Senate and People could have been formulated with elegance and concision.

With a ponderous *lex satura* on his hands if not on his conscience, Siber must next explain how the *imperium* of the Princeps was modified and extended by the 'second settlement' four years later. He conjures up two *imperia* vested in the same person—that of 27 B.C., purely military but not proconsular, and that of 23 B.C., which was proconsular, confined to the senatorial provinces, and not military (p. 38).

Siber's doctrine is open to criticism in general and in particular. First, the right to make peace and war, depending on one interpretation of Strabo xvii 3, 25, p. 840. Siber goes to Pompeius Magnus for precedent, to a provision of the *lex Gabinia* (Appian, *Mithr.* 97). For all that it helps he might adduce the *lex Trebonia* as well (Dio xxxix 33, 2). The *acta* of Magnus were subject to ratification by Senate and People, whereas the theory deduced from Strabo appears to vest sovranty in the Princeps—especially if it was a life-long grant. Kolbe has argued very forcibly on the other side: 'Von der Republik zur Monarchie', in the volume *Aus Roms Zeitwende* (*Das Erbe der Alten* xx (1931), 39 ff., esp. 49 f.). Nor is Siber's counter-attack (p. 21) carried home. It may be added that explicit formulation was unnecessary in 27 B.C., even were such a life-long prerogative not entirely repugnant to the conventions so carefully respected when Republican government was restored. This argument, be it noted in passing, constitutes an objection to Premerstein's interpretation of ἐσαεὶ καθάπαξ (Dio liii 32, 5), and to his theory that *imperium* was granted for life in 23 B.C. (op. cit. 233: accepted in *Rom. Rev.* 336). Compare the remarks of H. M. Last, *JRS* xxviii (1938), 213; xxxiii (1943), 104.

Siber postulates various types of *imperium*. One of them is a military *imperium* valid in Italy. He touches on the Praetorian Guard (p. 37). Something might have been said about army commanders in Northern Italy during the conquest of the Alpine lands in the early years of the Principate. Here was a use for that *imperium*, Augustus having been appointed (on Siber's theory) commander-in-chief of all armies everywhere. Reflection will suggest, however, that it was not required. In the system of a Republic, real or nominal, the Senate, without violation of public law, can send out a magistrate or promagistrate with *imperium*—compare practice in the War of Spartacus or the military mandates assigned in 63 B.C. (Sallust, *BC* 30, 3 ff.). Or the Transpadana might be temporarily allotted to the *provincia* of a proconsul of Illyricum, as presumably when P. Silius Nerva operated against the Camunni and Venostes in 16 B.C. (Dio liv 20, 1 f.). A proconsul happens to be attested in the North, L. Piso, sitting in justice at Mediolanum (Suetonius, *De rhet.* 6). On that occasion a Transpadane orator made protest: Italy was again being reduced to the condition of a province. What might not have been said about a permanent military *imperium* that embraced the whole land from the Alps down to Rhegium? |

The main weight of Siber's argumentation is massed in support of an empire-wide *imperium* in 27 B.C., defined as exclusively military and needing to be supplemented by a purely civil *imperium* in the imperial provinces. The military *imperium*, he affirms, is not proconsular. He derives it from the extraordinary commands in the last generation of the Free State—though not from all of them: the laws of Gabinius and Manilius for Pompeius, but not the proconsulate of Spain under the *lex Trebonia* or Julius Caesar's command in Gaul. The validity of the distinction between *imperium* as 'proconsular' and *imperium* as 'purely military' will need to be established.

Siber starts with a pair of proofs that augur ill for his operations. He quotes Tacitus' account of the transference of Macedonia and Achaia from the Senate to the Princeps in the second year of Tiberius' reign: 'Achaiam ac Macedoniam onera deprecantis levari in praesens proconsulari imperio tradique Caesari placuit' (*Ann.* i 76). As these provinces are then liberated from *imperium proconsulare*, it follows that only senatorial provinces were normally subject to it, not imperial: therefore Caesar's *imperium* over Caesar's provinces is not proconsular. The proof fails. The phrase simply means 'government by proconsuls'. Tacitus abhors technical terms. The second proof matches the first. The consul Pompeius, we are told, swore a solemn oath that he would *never* accept a province, and he kept the oath. Therefore his *imperium* under the bills of Gabinius and Manilius were not proconsular (p. 27). The deduction is false. What Pompeius said in 70 B.C. has no bearing on his behaviour three or four years later, and what he said was 'se in nullam provinciam ex eo magistratu iturum' (Velleius ii 31, 1).

Siber's criterion appears to be of this nature: when a man governs a single province his *imperium* both is, and is called, *imperium proconsulare*: 'zum Wesen des prokonsularen Imperium gehörte die Beschränkung auf die einzelne Provinz' (pp. 26 f.). Quite different are other commands abroad, like that of M. Antonius (*pr.* 74 B.C.) or Pompeius' successive mandates against the Pirates and against Mithridates—'die Imperien des

Antonius und des Pompeius waren nicht prokonsular, weil sie die Grenzen des auf eine bestimmte Provinz beschränkten Prokonsulates überschritten' (p. 27). This is not all. A further step is taken, insidiously or unconsciously. Pompeius' *imperium* is not only not proconsular, it is purely military (ibid.). And so the *lex Manilia* does not make him governor of certain eastern provinces. Magnus is an army commander active in provinces without governors—'das rein militärische Imperium des Pompeius von 66 in den statthalterlosen asiatischen Provinzen'.

The doctrine is not convincing. Siber maintains that both Pompeius and his *legati* possessed only military competence—'sie waren also wie er selbst bloß Offiziere' (p. 28). On the same page he cannot help conceding to the legates the rank of 'legatus pro praetore' because of Cn. Lentulus Marcellinus (*SIG³* 750). That explodes the argument. Even if the occupations of a *leg. pro pr.* happen to be mainly military (compare Labienus under Caesar, *BG* i 21, 2), he shall not be dismissed as a mere 'Offizier', or, to use another misleading term, 'Feldlegat'. As for the Mithridatic War, Dio says that Magnus had the provinces of Cilicia and Bithynia (xxxvi 42, 4). Siber affirms that Dio is in error. Yet what more natural than to suppose that Pompeius in 66 B.C. inherited Cilicia from Q. Rex, Bithynia from Glabrio? A minor point tells in favour of Dio. More circumspect than certain recent historians, he does not assign the province of Asia to Magnus. Already in 69 B.C. the Senate had decided to remove Asia from the *provincia* of Lucullus (Dio xxxvi 2, 2), and governors of Asia are known in the period of Pompeius' eastern command.

A primary question arises. What is a province? Siber operates with rigidly delimited territorial units. Not so the Romans. The employment of the term *provincia* will help to obviate confusion. A *provincia* is not the same thing as a province; and the character of *imperium* exercised abroad is not affected by the presence or absence of provincial organization and definite frontiers. Siber calls Q. Metellus (*cos.* 69 B.C.) proconsul of Crete (p. 29). Therefore, presumably, he concedes *imperium proconsulare*. But Crete, though Metellus' *provincia*, was not yet a Roman province. Neither was Achaia, which his authority seems to have covered (Cicero, *Pro Flacco* 63). Nobody is | going to pretend that the *imperium* of Q. Metellus belongs to a special category, distinct from that of other proconsuls.

It is time to abbreviate the discussion. Nobody denies that in fact and in history it makes a huge difference whether an *imperium* embraces a peaceful land or a *provincia maxime triumphalis*, whether its operation is tied to a narrow region or ranges over a wide area, whether the tenure is brief in duration or prolonged for a stretch of years. The roots of the Empire are properly discerned in the Republic, in the *extraordinariae potestates* of Pompeius—and of Caesar the proconsul. That is not a legitimate basis for juridical discriminations. Still less can it be used to support an exclusively military *imperium* contrasted with the *imperium* of magistrate or pro-magistrate. All sorts of *provinciae* could be created. Similarly *imperium* exercised outside the city remains in essence unchanged if it is held by a magistrate proceeding to his province in virtue of a normal (or abnormal) allocation, or by a *privatus*, if a *lex* confers an extraordinary command or if the Senate less obtrusively produces the same result. Siber, and others, neglect Lucullus. He began with Cilicia, but soon got Asia, then Bithynia. Also, by the way, this proconsul probably had *legati pro praetore* under him: compare the inscription of C. Salluvius Naso (*ILS* 37 [= *ILLRP* 372]).

And now to end the matter. Siber points out that Cicero nowhere defines the authority of Pompeius Magnus under the laws of Gabinius and Manilius as proconsular (p. 27). The consequence is more deadly than he could have imagined. Cicero does not designate the *imperium* of provincial governors in that fashion either. It is *consulare imperium* (cf., for example, *In Pisonem* 38, 56, etc.). In fact, 'imperium proconsulare' is not only not a technical term in Republican writers—they never use it at all (Mommsen, *Staatsrecht* ii³ 647).

There is no mystery. If, going by the plain meanings of words and by the law of Rome, a 'proconsul' is the exact equivalent of a 'consul' (in the sphere *militiae*, for he does not occur *domi*), then a proconsul's competence is without impropriety called 'consular', or, for that matter, just *imperium*. Siber's discovery of a new category, 'nameless' *imperium*, evaporates.

It might be urged that Sulla's ordinances modified the whole relation between urban magistracies and provincial commands. Proof, however, is required, how far the Dictator went beyond the regularization of current practice. Siber's formulation suggests a decisive change, 'daß Sulla die bisher den Konsuln zustehende einheitliche Heerführung in mehrere über die in den einzelnen Provinzen stehenden Heere verzettelte und die Teilimperien den promagistratischen Statthaltern übertrug' (p. 26). It looks as though the author misunderstands the situation before Sulla as well as after Sulla. Proconsuls and propraetors were no novelty. They had been in command of armies for many, many years, though lacking the auspices, so Cicero asserts (*De div.* ii 76). Cicero is not just referring to an innovation of Sulla the Dictator; and Sulla himself had governed Cilicia after his praetorship (Plutarch, *Sulla* 5). In the last age of the Free State the normal governor is a promagistrate. But a magistrate may depart to his *provincia* long before the twelve months of his office in Rome have elapsed, cf. H. M. Last, *CAH* ix 294 f., and, for a list of examples, J. P. V. D. Balsdon, *JRS* xxix (1939), 63. Siber is aware that no law debarred a consul from commanding an army, yet he does not seem prepared to admit that he can govern a province. As for the consuls of 74 B.C., Lucullus and Cotta, he states that they did not have 'prokonsularisches Imperium'. They had only military command, as consuls, 'als solche gegen Mithridates geschickt'. The distinction is unreal. What matters is the difference between *imperium domi* and *imperium militiae*. Lucullus takes up his *provincia* while still consul and continues it as pro-consul, with an identical *imperium*. On Siber's theory, Lucullus, being consul, may command an army in the East but is not permitted to govern his province: the latter *imperium* only assumes shape and force, myster-iously, during the night of 29 December 74 B.C., when the *imperator* is in camp somewhere near Cyzicus.

The fact that Augustus held the consulate continuously from 27 to 23 B.C. impedes the attempt to define the nature of his *imperium*. If, on Republican precedent, a consul | may hold a province, why should not Augustus rule his *provincia* as consul? Hence the view of Pelham (*Essays* (1911), 68): 'nor was it only as a domestic magistracy that Augustus held the consulship during the first five years of his principate. He was consul, but with a "province" which embraced more than half the empire. By holding this imperium with its wide area as consul, he ranked at once as chief magistrate of the state, without no less than within Rome.' This theory, though technically impeccable, involved a strained and antiquarian interpretation of consular powers. The precedent for the Princeps' *im-perium* of 27 B.C. lies in the extended commands of a proconsular charac-ter. Whereas the *imperium militiae* is identical whether its holder be consul or proconsul, a distinction might be drawn, even though Augustus' tenure of the consulate between 27 and 23 B.C. masks its operation and seems to render the question academic or theological. It might be prefer-able to say that Augustus governed his province 'while consul' rather than 'as consul'. When he was assigned his *provincia* for ten years, it can hardly have been expected that he would continue as perpetual consul all that time; and his resignation of the consulate in 23 B.C. did not entail a surrender of the *provincia*. The *imperium* of 27 B.C. would not have been impaired in itself, had the First Citizen decided not to be elected consul for 26 B.C. with Taurus as his colleague.

Augustus adopted the obvious formula for combining civil authority and military power, namely the consulate and a *provincia*. It is an attempt to be on both sides of the *pomerium* at the same time—and not completely successful. In 23 B.C. he has to get a permanent dispensation. The *lex* of 27 B.C. might suggest a question of some interest to the student of Roman constitutional theory. Did the Princeps thereby and at once enter into complete control over his provinces? He had resolved to withdraw Spain, Gaul, and Syria from government by proconsuls, to administer those regions himself, through *legati*; he may now have requested the Senate to instruct the proconsuls to depart—or he may have waited until he set out *paludatus* and crossed the sacred precinct, perhaps even longer. Augustus left Rome in the summer, intending to go to Gaul and Spain. From Gaul Messalla triumphed in September, but the retiring proconsul of Spain, Sex. Appuleius, did not hold his celebration until the following January. These were not dangerous men. Neither was M. Cicero (*cos. suff.* 30 B.C.), governor of Syria about this time. The proprieties were no doubt respected.

Though absent, Augustus retained in his grasp the supreme magistracy. What interpretation he put upon consular prerogative in the years 27–23 B.C., it is impossible to say. Previously, since he had resigned the title of Triumvir, it had constituted his sole legal link with the *res publica* (apart from tribunician powers, not yet fully exploited). Now, however, the Republic having been restored, he had no more *potestas* than any of his colleagues in magistracy (*Res Gestae* 34). The historian Tacitus deliberately refuses to see any change in 27 B.C., but implies the same behaviour before and after the 'first constitutional settlement'—'posito triumviri nomine consulem se ferens', etc. (*Ann.* i 2). Being consul, Augustus had a share in the direction of public policy, though it may be too much to say that he 'could control through consular *imperium* the proconsuls abroad' (*Rom. Rev.* 315). The notion of a consular *imperium maius* which those words might appear to support is hazardous and perhaps unnecessary. Anyhow, there is no evidence. A pronouncement of Cicero's on public law has long held the field—'omnes enim in consulis iure et imperio debent esse provinciae' (*Phil.* iv 9). The context is instructive—a sophistical attempt to demonstrate that M. Antonius is not really a consul, and a dishonest suppression of Antonius' claim to the province of Gallia Cisalpina (which was based on a *lex*, not on consular prerogative, cf. *Rom. Rev.* 162).

Whatever the value of the consulate in law or in fact, Augustus soon saw that he could do without it. In 23 B.C. a dispensation enabled him to retain his proconsular *imperium* after entering the *pomerium*; his powers were extended to cover the public provinces in the form of *imperium maius*; and he now proceeded to convert the *tribunicia potestas* into an instrument of civil authority. More than adequate compensation, it should appear, for what he lost by surrendering the consulate. These arrangements are the decisive act in the establishment of the constitutional monarchy.|

By contrast, the powers of 27 B.C. are simple and summary—consulate and proconsulate. The Princeps took a *provincia*. As it did not comprise the totality of the armed provinces, for Africa, Illyricum, and Macedonia remained under proconsuls, Augustus was not in law commander-in-chief of the Roman army (compare especially Kolbe's arguments). Nor is there any case for an *imperium maius* of 27 B.C. over the public provinces (despite Premerstein, op. cit. 231, reviving Mommsen's view). The *imperium* of Augustus differed from that of other provincial governors, not in essence but in fact, by the extent and duration of his mandate.

Simple also was the formulation. Premerstein's theory that a definite *cura et tutela rei publicae* was now conferred (op. cit. 117 ff.) lacks plausibility because it lacks necessity. Caesar Augustus was certainly a guardian and protector of Rome and the Empire. The notion is familiar and contemporary, being attested by the poet Horace and by inscriptions. It provided a link with military heroes, with Romulus now high in favour —men might recall 'patriae custodem' in Ennius—and with C. Marius, 'custode civitatis atque imperii vestri' (Cicero, *Post red. ad Quirites* 9). Nobody can have doubted, friend or foe, that the leader of the Caesarian party, given his power and prestige, intended to pose and act as 'protector', at the very least. The *senatus consultum* which proposed and defined Augustus' *provincia* may well have said something about his cardinal virtues—they were now to be advertised on a golden shield in the Curia —virtues which, having rescued Rome from the foreign enemy, were requisite to preserve the Empire in the days of peace. Compare the preamble of Cicero's proposal for Brutus—'cum Q. Caepionis Bruti pro consule opera consilio industria virtute, difficillimo rei publicae tempore,' etc. Further, Brutus is instructed to guard and preserve his *provincia*— 'utique Q. Caepio Brutus pro consule provinciam Macedoniam Illyricum cunctamque Graeciam tueatur defendat custodiat incolumemque conservet' (*Phil.* x 26). None the less, it must be observed that, whereas such edifying sentiments might properly be expressed in a *senatus consultum*, they are less congenial to the form of a *lex*; if the Senate, when decreeing a *provincia* for Caesar Augustus at the same time enounced, as cause and justification, the protection of that *provincia*, or even added suitable remarks about the Empire in general, it did not thereby actually vote a 'cura et tutela rei publicae' or create a new office.

Premerstein's notion of a comprehensive mandate in 27 B.C. (with, be it noted, *imperium maius* over the public provinces) appears to give an undue extension both to the prerogative of the Princeps and to the sphere of written law. If Premerstein strains belief, Siber provokes incredulity. He presents Augustus not with one *imperium*, but with two—a universal command of all armies and a civil authority valid in the imperial provinces. The attempt to set up a juridical distinction between a proconsul's *imperium* and an exclusively military *imperium* in the last age of the Republic has already been dealt with. Applied to Augustus, it involves all sorts of clumsy complications (see further below).

A spurious refinement of doctrine masks real confusion. It baffles Latin as well as sense. If the contemporaries of Cicero and of Augustus could conceive a distinction between civil and military *imperium* when exercised in the provinces by a mandatory of Senate and People, how would they have expressed it?

The *imperium* of 27 B.C. can be called just *imperium*, without adjectival qualification. Indeed, the clause defining the *provincia* could dispense with the word altogether. Compare the *SC* for Cassius—'senatui placere C. Cassium pro consule provinciam Syriam obtinere' (Cicero, *Phil.* xi 30). In this case *imperium* is named only when it has to be specified as *maius imperium*—'ut imperandi in Syria Asia Bithynia Ponto ius potestatemque habeat utique, quamcunque in provinciam eius belli gerendi causa advenerit, ibi maius imperium C. Cassi pro consule sit quam eius erit qui eam provinciam tum obtinebit cum C. Cassius in eam provinciam venerit' (ibid.). This does not mean that the modern term 'proconsular *imperium*' need be deprecated or discarded. It is in no way misleading, for the development of constitutional practice had gradually severed the command of armies and provinces from the urban magistracies. In fact, a law of 52 B.C. enjoined that severance, a law re-enacted by Augustus, perhaps quite early in his Principate (Dio puts it in 27 B.C., but that is not proof). There were advantages in this procedure that did not escape the managers | of patronage at Rome—'(ut) per paucos probati et electi in provincias mittantur' (Caesar, *BC* i 85, 9).

If this explanation be accepted, the 'first constitutional settlement' is not a proper subject for lengthy and intricate disquisitions. The real complexity is discovered beyond the law and the constitution, in the things unspoken and undefined. As the *res publica* could be managed and exploited there was every reason for setting up the mechanism again. The arrangements of 27 B.C. look like a summary improvization—the minimum of powers requisite. If so many matters were deliberately left undefined, what did it matter for the present, so long as the Caesarian party held together? Disputes about the constitution are not the sequel to civil war, but rather the prelude.

In the *Res Gestae* there is no word or hint about the *provincia* conferred in 27 B.C. or the extended and comprehensive *imperium proconsulare* of 23 B.C. How account for the omission? Though Augustus was not composing a treatise on constitutional law, he was at least proclaiming the legality of his rule, and in one respect, *auctoritas*, expounding an official doctrine about the nature of his primacy in the Roman State. Siber suggests that, since the dominant note in the *Res Gestae* is the establishment of peace, it was appropriate that the author of the document should emphasize, not the military *imperium*, but the tribunician powers as the emblem of supreme authority (p. 70). That is not the impression the *Res Gestae* make on every reader. If the Princeps extols peace, he has much to say about the work of pacification, the many wars, the advance of the

Roman frontier everywhere; nor does he shrink from the term 'exercitus meus'. Some other reason must be sought. Perhaps in a narrow and formal conception of the res publica as 'senatus, magistratus, leges'. Supposing the author of the Res Gestae to circumscribe his relation to the Republic, confining it to magistracies or magisterial powers in the city, one might adduce a justification for the omission of authority outside that sphere, over provinces and armies: compare Cicero's view of the Roman State in his Republic. Or it might be said that, having continuously exercised imperium since his extraordinary propraetorship of 43 B.C. (unless it be for the calendar year 32 B.C., when he was no longer Triumvir and not yet consul again), Augustus did not choose to catalogue all subsequent modifications in the scope and tenure of his imperium. Whatever be the force of these reasons or excuses, it is not evident that the First Citizen can be acquitted of a reticence that amounts to duplicity: 'est et fideli tuta silentio merces', as an Augustan poet remarks. Control of provinces and armies, first usurped then legalized, is the basis of power: the 'truest explanation', and therefore least advertised. (Augustus confesses, however, to the private army of his first usurpation (Res Gestae 1); and he must surely have shunned overt and pointless mendacity about the legal duration of the Triumvirate (ibid. 7).)

The problems of imperium in the early Principate are not restricted to the head of the government. What of proconsuls, especially if they happen to command armies? Siber maintains that a proconsul possesses no military competence, only civil; if a proconsul of Africa commands an army, it is in virtue of his being at the same time a 'military legate' of Augustus, and only his high rank in society saves him from being so designated— 'der dann für dies militärische Kommando sein Feldlegat war und nur wegen seiner hohen bürgerlichen Stellung als Prokonsul, in Africa sogar mit konsularem Rang, nicht so genannt wurde' (p. 23, cf. 32, 85). The notion makes havoc of Roman public law. The legal disparity between a proconsul and a legate of Augustus is clear and fundamental. Juridically, indeed, the proconsul is the equal of the Princeps in the period 27–23 B.C. Now the proconsul becomes in effect reduced to the position of a legate after the imperium maius of 23 B.C. That is another question. An unfortunate tendency persists to confuse the distinction between law and fact: compare brief observations on proconsuls of Macedonia and legates of Moesia in JRS xxxv (1945), 110.

Siber mentions Africa. He omits to notice that proconsuls regularly governed other military provinces, Illyricum and Macedonia, until the one was taken over by the Princeps and the other surrendered its legions to the new command in Moesia. Siber describes | the situation of Africa as transitional. Rather, a vestigial remnant, preserving one of the most

valuable clues to the arrangements of 27 B.C. If the restoration of constitutional forms had any meaning, it meant that proconsuls had the same
imperium as before. Even after 23 B.C. two of them hold triumphs, Atratinus in 21, Balbus in 19, but then no more. They can still for a time be
hailed *imperator*, for example, Passienus Rufus (*ILS* 120), but are not
regarded as fighting under their own auspices; cf. the formula on the
inscription from Lepcis Magna [*IRT* 301]: 'auspiciis Imp. Caesaris Aug. /
pontificis maxumi, patris / patriae, ductu Cossi Lentuli.' Tiberius Caesar
even held that a proconsul would be within his rights in granting military
decorations (*Ann.* iii 21). One may doubt whether his predecessor had
generally been so liberal.

Tiberius when Princeps assumed only one imperatorial salutation, 'imp.
VIII', for the victory of Germanicus in A.D. 16 (Tacitus, *Ann.* ii 18) and
shared by the prince as 'imp. II'. Augustus' earlier record showed one
nasty episode. In Dio's account (li 25, 2) he takes the title of *imperator* from
M. Licinius Crassus, the proconsul of Macedonia, for himself (hence
presumably 'imp. VII'). This was pure usurpation, not to be justified even
by triumviral practices—and he was no longer Triumvir, but only consul.
The need for some constitutional regulation became patent (on the
significance and consequences of this incident, cf. esp. Groag, *RE* xiii,
coll. 283 ff.). Siber suggests that, subsequent to 27 B.C., the Princeps may
well have assumed salutations for the victories of proconsuls, perhaps IX
between 25 and 15 B.C.) for Atratinus, XVI (between A.D. 2–3 and 6)
for Passienus Rufus (pp. 87 f.). This is not very likely. If Atratinus, why
not the more notorious exploits of Balbus in the distant land of the Garamantes? A third case transcends refutation. Late in the reign of Augustus
a proconsul of Asia carried out 300 executions in one day, so at least
Seneca alleges (*De ira* ii 5, 5). This massacre, so Siber infers in all serious-
ness, points to an insurrection that had to be suppressed by imperial
troops: hence perhaps 'imp. XX' (p. 99).

The *imperium* of proconsuls need not cause any embarrassment. Less
amenable is derivative ('abgeleitetes') *imperium*, as Siber calls it: it is an
innovation, it admits variations, and the evidence is not always adequate.
As indicated above, it is juridically vicious to describe a proconsul commanding troops as an imperial legate. Still, it might happen that one of
Caesar's legates is accorded proconsular *imperium*.

Siber propounds the following principles (pp. 84 f.). 'Derivative' *imperium* derives from Augustus' purely military *imperium* of 27 B.C. over
all the armed forces. Its purpose is always military, it contains no civil
competence, its holders fight under their own auspices, and are exclusively
members of the imperial family (among them being reckoned Agrippa
and Augustus' stepsons Tiberius and Drusus). To be distinguished from
such *imperia*, however, is a *proconsulare imperium* bestowed on younger

members of the dynasty. This the author defines as a 'fictitious' *imperium*. Proconsuls of Africa were also specially granted it, in order to enable them to hold a triumph (p. 85, cf. 31). Further, 'dies fiktive war seit 27 das einzige "proconsulare imperium", das noch militärische Natur hatte' (p. 31).

The subject is far too vast and intricate to be discussed in this place. But the term 'derivative *imperium*' is a bad choice to describe powers which the Senate confers. The reviewer cannot conceal misgivings about Siber's postulates, argumentation, and conclusions. To take one example only, Agrippa. Siber will not allow him any kind of special *imperium* before 13 B.C., not even when he was active in the East from 17 to 13; and the grant of 13 B.C. is purely military, making him 'nächst Augustus höchster Befehlshaber der ganzen bewaffneten Macht ausserhalb Italiens' (p. 91). It must be conceded that the evidence for Agrippa's powers before 13 B.C. is deplorably scanty, that one assumes, for example, an *imperium* in the period 23–18 B.C. mainly because of his eminence and the variety of his operations (Syria 23 B.C., Gaul and Spain 20–19 B.C.). The attempt might have been made to argue that Agrippa did not receive proconsular *imperium* as early as 23 B.C., that he was employed as and where convenient as the senior *leg. Aug. pro praetore*, in virtue of the Princeps' prerogative in managing his own *provincia*. Here as elsewhere Strabo's phrase is useful guidance, κατὰ τοὺς καιροὺς πολιτευόμενος (viii 3, 25, p. 840; cf. iii 4, 19 f., p. 166 and iv 1, 1, p. 177, in reference to provincial boundaries).[1] Moreover the Princeps through *auctoritas* could give | special instructions or wide powers to his legates: compare the 'secreta mandata' to L. Piso (Seneca, *Ep.* 83, 14) or the position of L. Vitellius in A.D. 36 (Tacitus, *Ann.* vi 32). But Siber does not make the attempt, which in any case would conflict with reasonable deductions from Cassius Dio (liii 32, 1; liv 11, 6), and would become futile for the years 17–13 B.C. That the Senate voted Agrippa a triumph in 14 B.C. (Dio liv 24, 7) surely indicates proconsular *imperium*. Siber seems quite unaware of the evidence for Agrippa's intervention in the senatorial provinces in the East—to mention only several passages from Josephus or the letter to the town council of Argos (*AE* 1920, 82 [= Sherk, *RDGE* 63]).

Special *imperia* need fresh and full investigation. They will perhaps be found to baffle any single formula or systematic classification. Nor, touching the portion of Caesar, is it legitimate to start with cut-and-dried categories of provinces, according to the grades and hierarchies of consular and praetorian. Rather should one think of Caesar's *provincia* developing gradually into a system of provinces, Caesar's legates gradually becoming

---

[1] [An *imperium aequum* (to that of provincial governors) now seems to be attested for 23 B.C.: see E. W. Gray, *ZPE* vi (1970), 227 ff. Gray argues (following Dio) that it was left *aequum* when renewed in 18 B.C. and made *maius* in 13.]

governors of the imperial provinces. Hence many possibilities in this little-known period of transition. At the same time it is not advisable to multiply administrative anomalies or special commands—one need only recall the paradoxical consequences of the opinion that denied to P. Sulpicius Quirinius the governorship of Galatia merely because he was consular in standing.

A final observation on *imperium*. In the course of this discussion it has been taken as axiomatic that *imperium* conferred by the sovran body carries both civil and military authority, inseparable by its very nature. The purely military *imperium* of which some scholars are so fondly enamoured might, however, be discovered in the early Principate, but at a lower level. Besides 'legati Augusti pro praetore' there are 'legati Augusti' in the provinces of Caesar. This way lies the development of the post of 'legatus legionis'—it is not so described on inscriptions before the reign of Tiberius, the earliest example being *ILS* 940. Similarly an equestrian officer can hold command as 'pro legato' (*ILS* 2677 f.; *AE* 1938, 173). Perhaps the title of a legionary commander in Egypt was, strictly speaking, 'praefectus pro legato'.

Whatever may be the validity of Siber's doctrines about public law, they are all too often impaired by insufficient precision or by forced interpretations. He accepts Dio's statement that Julius Caesar was voted the *praenomen imperatoris*, transferable to his descendants (Dio xliii 44, 2 f.). Like the similar provision concerning the office of *pontifex maximus*, this item will not command general acquiescence. Caesar's heir, in fact, began to put 'Imp.' before his name in 38 B.C.—with dubious right, so Siber contends, for his triumviral power did not stand in the succession of Caesar's dictatorship (p. 30). This is all beside the point. The phenomena deserving attention are the use of 'Imp.' for Pompeius Magnus as a kind of *cognomen*, without numerical qualification (e.g. *ILS* 877 [= *ILLRP* 382]), and the way in which a *cognomen* could be transferred into a *praenomen*, as when Magnus' son took to calling himself 'Magnus Pompeius Pius' (*ILS* 8891 [= *ILLRP* 426]). 'Imperator Caesar' looks like a powerful overbid. It need not be added that this nomenclature has no juridical significance. [See below pp. 361 ff.]

Siber affirms that the Caesarian leader did not drop the title of Triumvir until 30 B.C. (p. 19). Bright hopes of new radiance shed around an old crux are rudely extinguished. Siber argues from Tacitus' phrase 'posito triumviri nomine consulem se ferens', etc. (*Ann.* i 2). But Tacitus in this impressionistic description of the gradual consolidation of Augustus' legal authority after the military victory is deliberately eschewing dates. Not to indicate a precise point in time, but to convey a deadly innuendo, that is his aim—'having resigned the title (but not the powers) of Triumvir, and professing to be (merely) consul'. The historian is elsewhere misinterpreted (pp. 100 f.). From *Ann.* i. 31, the author infers that A. Caecina (*cos.* 1 B.C.) is a legionary legate. Rather hard on the eminent and experienced consular, who had previously commanded the army of Moesia; and the fine testimony to his 'quadraginta stipendia' (*Ann.* i 64) is turned against him, to demonstrate an unsatisfactory career—'als Zeichen schlechten Fortganges seiner Laufbahn.' This being so, no confidence can be felt in Siber's views about the precise nature of Germanicus' command on the Rhine in these years. Lastly, Velleius makes a statement | of some interest concerning the restoration of Republican government in 27 B.C.— 'imperium magistratuum ad pristinum redactum modum' (ii 89, 3). Siber interprets this as the replacement of nomination (under triumviral practices) by election (p. 80). That is not the meaning of the Latin.

Dr. Siber came as no novice to these pursuits. An earlier contribution in the same series, *Zur Entwicklung der römischen Prinzipatverfassung* (1933), will perhaps be recalled, further 'Cäsars Diktatur und das Prinzipat des Augustus', *ZRG* lv (1935), 99 ff. The bibliography also discloses articles of the year 1939 on Augustus' matrimonial legislation and on Tiberius' reform of the elections. The present inquiry proclaims 'exaktes Staatsrecht' and 'klare römische Rechtsbegriffe' (p. 1), but the reader goes away unsatisfied. Precision is not there, that precision which might have been a delight for its own sake, even though it cannot pronounce a valid verdict on the rule of Caesar Augustus. Ready for legal subtleties, or for the extremity of verbal refinements, one is confronted with impracticable complications. Yet simplicity, economy, and elegance are said to be the distinctive qualities of classical Roman law (F. Pringsheim, *JRS* xxxiv (1944), 60 ff.).

Despite grave misconceptions about the character of Roman public law and disturbing errors of detail and Latinity, Siber works his way towards a not unsatisfactory estimate of the Principate: Augustus, while preserving all the institutions of the Free State, gradually built up something new and permanent, an unfettered 'Führeramt' (pp. 73 f.). Further, the Princeps' constitutional dispositions were not just a sham and a delusion (the only *arcanum imperii* Siber allows is Egypt, though not perhaps for the better reason). Who, indeed, was there to deceive, and who wanted the authentic Republic? We know the senators of 27 B.C. or can divine them, the victors in civil war and survivors of a revolution—the innocence of Plancus or the tender scruples of Statilius Taurus. And the later generation that grew up in the years of peace was not so much simple-minded as easy-going and averse from awkward questions. Velleius Paterculus parades the restored Republic with ceremonial language, 'prisca illa et antiqua rei publicae forma revocata' (ii 89, 4). He deals in form, not substance. Siber condones Velleius as an 'etwas primitive Soldatennatur'

(p. 71). Which does less than justice to Velleius' family and attainments—old municipal aristocracy, now senatorial in rank (not for the first time), and he knew all the tricks.

At the end it must be asked, if the author's conclusion about the Principate is acceptable—a synthesis between Republic and Monarchy, but in fact monarchic—was it worth the labour and all the intricate choreography 'in quadriviis et angiportis'? The thing was known. 'To resume, in a few words, the system of the Imperial government, as it was instituted by Augustus, and maintained by those princes who understood their own interest and that of the people, it may be defined as an absolute monarchy disguised by the forms of a commonwealth. The masters of the Roman world surrounded their throne with darkness, concealed their irresistible strength, and humbly professed themselves the accountable ministers of the senate, whose supreme decrees they dictated and obeyed' (Gibbon, *Decline and Fall*, Ch. III).

The descendants of Romulus created, or inherited, a conception of *imperium* generous and grandiose in its simplicity. Whereas in various branches of legal science the *gens togata* produced experts and professors, it knew no class or category of constitutional lawyers. 'Staatsrecht', to Voltaire at least, is something peculiarly Germanic—'ce que l'on appelle en Allemagne *l'étude du droit public*, pour laquelle la nation germanique est si renommée' (*Siècle de Louis XIV*, Ch. II). At Rome the relation of Caesar Augustus to Senate and People can be defined without pains and contortions. The true problem lies elsewhere, not in texts and formulae, but in the facts of power and the movement of history—the origin of Augustus' supremacy, the growth and composition of the Caesarian party, the manner in which the ruler's authority was conceived, expressed, and exerted at different times and in different lands over the wide earth. The theme is given by the combination in one person of *princeps*, *imperator*, *basileus*.

14

E. H. Clift, *Latin Pseudepigrapha*
A Study in Literary Attributions[1]

IN every age the principal criteria of authenticity are the stylistic and the historical. They do not always bring certainty, for we do not know enough about either style or history. If a different approach can be devised, or a subsidiary method, so much the better—and what could be more promising than to investigate the conditions in which books were made, published, and preserved, to ascertain the restraints upon forgery or erroneous ascriptions? Dr. Clift takes for her main theme the public libraries of Augustan Rome. Those institutions surely operated for the best, sifting, verifying, rejecting.

The first chapter, neatly put together and attractively written, is devoted to libraries and literary interests in the Roman world. From the private collectors of books in the late Republic the narrative passes easily by way of Varro, that transitional character, whose services were enlisted by Julius Caesar, to Pollio, who seems to have inherited the plan (and may have acquired some of the material: at least Varro complained of books disappearing in the proscriptions), and thence to Augustus and the monarchy, with two magnificent establishments, one on the Palatine, the other in the Portico of Octavia. Contemporaries were no doubt impressed, even though Strabo may omit the libraries from his account of the monuments and amenities of the City. About the subsequent history of the metropolitan collections various details are preserved. Some of the most picturesque come from the *Historia Augusta*. There is a delicious and impudent fabrication in the preface of the *Vita Aureliani* (1 f.), where the Prefect of the City, Junius Tiberianus, in amiable discourse with the biographer, incites him to write history without scruple, for he will have many illustrious companions in mendacity, 'habiturus mendaciorum comites, quos historicae eloquentiae miramur auctores', and offers him access to ineffable treasures, 'curabo autem ut tibi ex Ulpia bibliotheca et *libri lintei* proferantur'.

Dr. Clift eschews this fable, but is not consistently on the alert. She

[1] Baltimore, 1945.

succumbs (p. 32) to the lure of the 62,000 volumes in the possession and enjoyment of the younger Gordian (*HA Gord.* 18, 2 f.), the volumes which, in an immortal phrase, 'attested the variety of his inclinations'. Moreover, 'Flavius Vopiscus', one of the six ostensible authors of the imperial biographies, seems to get both his credentials and his existence accepted, for his testimony about the collection in the Domus Tiberiana is invoked—'The age of Vopiscus is the last certain date for the survival of the library' (p. 26).

In a review of a book that deals with authorship and authenticity, a cursory reminder about the *Historia Augusta* may not be out of place. For the rest, the material here summarized about municipal and provincial libraries serves to illustrate the day-to-day life under the Empire, or rather the pursuits of the leisured classes. Students are familiar with Pliny's foundation at Comum, though cheated of the inaugural address; and Ephesus displays as the most imposing of its ruins the edifice which Aquila the consular consecrated to the memory of his father, but did not live to complete. It may come as a surprise to learn of a library at Dertona (not generally recognized as one of the 'cultural centres' of northern Italy) as early as 22 B.C. It should be recalled that there is some doubt about the date, '[M. Claudio Mar]cel[lo et L. Ar]runtio,' as supplemented in *CIL* v 7376: compare the caution of G. E. F. Chilver, *Cisalpine Gaul*, 88. Indeed, the year might well be A.D. 77, with the suffect consuls C. Arruntius Catellius Celer and M. Arruntius Aquila (*CIL* x 8038).

What the metropolis got from the provinces (including the Transpadane zone of northern Italy) in the way of books, erudition, and enlightenment can hardly be overestimated. Which among the great names in imperial literature is not provincial? Their fame is secure. Minor agents will not be despised. M. Valerius Probus from the colony of Berytus in Syria has captured attention. Aspiring to a military career, but unable to secure nomination as a centurion, he fell back on philology. The early classics, neglected at Rome, were read in the schools of Berytus—'durante adhuc ibi antiquorum memoria necdum omnino abolita sicut Romae' (Suetonius, *De gramm.* 24). Probus therefore went to the texts, and emended them. The influence of Probus has been variously estimated, sometimes exaggerated. Leo was disposed to believe that Probus had a great deal to do with the revival of Plautine studies in the early Empire. Dr. Clift deprecates the concentration on one man's work, reasonably enough. She prefers to attribute a change of taste to 'the influx of provincials into Rome during the Flavian era', with especial emphasis on the adlection of provincials into the Senate by the Emperor Vespasian (p. 70). This is a large subject, and the precise timing of provincial influences is a highly delicate operation. In so far as literature is concerned, the new senators under the Flavian dynasty are perhaps a symptom rather than a

cause. Provincials were already well ensconced. Seneca and Domitius
Afer are dominant figures in the Rome of Claudius and Nero. They look
like innovators, not archaists. Not but what the general run of colonial
Romans or Romanized provincials may have cherished a predilection for
the ancient classics. Transpadane and provincial Italy was commonly
extolled as a haven of sound tradition. One of Pliny's friends had a trained
wife who turned out *epistulae* reminiscent of the early dramatists—
'Plautum vel Terentium metro solutum legi credidi' (*Ep.* i 16, 6).

The chapter on 'Plautine Pseudepigrapha' (pp. 40–78) is a fair and full
statement of a problem that exercised scholars in antiquity. Twenty-one
plays of Plautus survive, apparently the canon set up by Varro of the
indubitably genuine. But Varro did not disdain to plead for others, and
Gellius in the second century affirms that more than 130 'Plautine' plays
were in circulation (*NA* iii 3, 11). Thirty-four titles have been recorded,
and they form the subject of this chapter, which terminates with a table
arranging them in four categories of merit, the probable, the possible, the
doubtful, and the spurious. It will be noted that in several particulars the
author differs from the judgement of Varro. For example, the *Boeotia* is
only 'possible'. Varro approved of the play, and Gellius had read it.
Hence a certain perplexity. Varro's opinions about the Plautine corpus,
it is argued, had much weight in determining which plays were admitted
to the two Augustan libraries. Yet, we are told, 'Varro's lists, however,
are not conclusive for us, though presumably they were for many Romans'
(p. 65). If that is so, then surely acceptance by the Roman libraries
becomes an imperfect criterion of authenticity—and the general thesis of
the book receives no corroboration.

We are on safer ground with 'Republican prose of doubtful authenticity' (pp. 79–122) and 'Augustan Pseudepigrapha' (pp. 123–50), for most
of the material here discussed is extant. Many readers will turn first to the
Appendix Vergiliana. They will not be startled to find that Dr. Clift,
responsive to recent tendencies and domestic examples, is highly conservative. Her statement that most of the poems 'are now considered
authentic' (p. 125) will no doubt cause muttering in certain quarters, but
as the exposition is unduly compressed for the complexity of the subject
—less than | six pages—it would not be reasonable to insist or dispute.
'Republican prose', however, touches many historical questions, method
as well as substance. It is a great convenience to have the evidence about
so many disputed writings, from Appius Claudius down to Sallust, carefully digested and clearly set forth in a single study. Dr. Clift impugns
nothing that is now accepted by the general consensus of the learned
world. If it should appear no longer necessary to defend the letters of
Brutus and the *Commentariolum Petitionis*, it may be salutary to recall that

these admirable compositions were under sharp fire in the old hybristic days. How far should the reaction go, and what are the standards to be? As the *Commentariolum* and the Sallustian *Epistulae* are here brought into the same dicussion, the confrontation may be instructive. The *Commentariolum* is secure—or at least the value of this admirable and contemporary treatise on electioneering would not decline even if some unpredictable chance revealed that it was not written by Quintus Cicero, but, let it be supposed, by Atticus. The loss would be trifling—an interesting detail about Quintus. Much more turns upon the *Sallustiana*. Dr. Clift is all for salvage. Here and elsewhere her operations will have to be carefully scrutinized. The following points may be singled out.

Speeches purporting to have been delivered by Scipio Africanus and by Ti. Sempronius Gracchus are involved in the notorious imbroglio about the attacks on the Scipiones. Livy had his doubts about these documents—'si modo ipsorum sunt quae feruntur' (xxxviii 56, 5), and Cicero stated that no composition of Africanus survived—'nulla enim eius ingenii monumenta mandata litteris' (*De off.* iii 4). Such testimony takes a lot of getting over, and most scholars have been content to assume forgery, exercising their fancy about its date and purpose. The speech attributed to Ti. Gracchus had an especial fascination, by reason of certain anachronisms that might be significant: it referred to a refusal of extravagant honours by Scipio Africanus—perpetual consulate, dictatorship, statues, etc. (Livy xxxviii 56, 12). Mommsen saw a hint of Julius Caesar and supposed that the oration was a pseudepigraphic pamphlet of 49 B.C. (*RF* ii 502 ff.), whereas Ed. Meyer argued for 44 B.C. (*Caesars Monarchie*[3], 531 ff.). The Caesarian theory has not infrequently been taken as proved in works of derivative erudition. De Sanctis, however (*RFIC* N.S. xiv (1936), 189 f.), threw out the suggestion that the speech originated in the time of Sulla: composed by a 'Sullan annalist' as a part of his history, it was excerpted from the body of the text and put into separate circulation. That might, or might not, be so. Who can tell? Nor is a failure among scholars to reach unanimity about the origin of a doubtful story sufficient to rehabilitate a suspicious document. Dr. Clift turns the tables on them a little too completely, and succeeds in what few can have attempted, in redeeming Livy from his own scepticism—'Since all attempts to explain these two speeches as forgeries fail, since, furthermore, they are historically plausible and Livy could produce a version of the Scipionic trials which would accord with them, there seems to be a reasonable certainty that they were genuine' (p. 87). Dr. Clift does not feel any qualms about the whole story of Ti. Gracchus' intervention. If Plinio Fraccaro was right (*Studi storici* v (1911), 259 ff., esp. 312 ff.), nothing avails—the speech is bogus because the situation it presupposes is bogus.

The *pièce de résistance* is provided by the *Sallustiana*, namely the pamphlet *In Ciceronem* and the two *Suasoriae* or *Epistulae* entitled 'Ad Caesarem senem de republica'. The method is that of many other scholars, to establish the 'dramatic date' of each document, to argue that it is also the actual date, and thence to infer, with the help of stylistic or historical criteria, that only Sallust and nobody else could have composed them at that date. Thus the *Invective* is put in 54 B.C., for it conforms to the historical situation and contains no reference to any damaging transactions in Cicero's career subsequent to that year. Dr. Clift's further observations seem to be impaired by a *non sequitur*, perhaps by several—'Because Quintilian furnishes ancient authority for the attribution of the *Invective* to Sallust and the date of its composition seems to have been the year 54 B.C., which makes it more unlikely that the false attribution of the pamphlet to Sallust during his lifetime would remain undetected, the work may be accepted as genuine' (p. 97). It must, on the contrary, be asked, how can we conceivably know that the speech was assigned to Sallust *in Sallust's lifetime*, that is, before 35 B.C.? In fact, all there is to go on is Quintilian's attribution (*Inst. Or.* iv 1, 68) and the 'dramatic date', 54 B.C. The field is still open, and it could still be contended (though hardly proved) that the *Invective* belongs to 54 B.C., with Sallust for its author (though there is no evidence for his hostility towards Cicero at this early date), or, for that matter, L. Piso, as Reitzenstein and Schwartz suggested once upon a time, *Hermes* xxxiii (1898), 87 ff.

There is no reason why the *Invective* should not belong a generation or two later. An elaborate attempt to put it in the years 35–30 B.C. has recently been made by O. Seel, 'Die Invektive gegen Cicero', *Klio*, Beiheft xlvii (1943), 153 pp. This exhaustive discussion of three pages of Latin text cannot be regarded as wholly satisfactory. Seel claims to prove that the *Invective* uses the *Philippics* of Cicero, the Sallustian *Epistulae*, and probably the *Bellum Catilinae*; the author, a crafty fellow, arranged his material with fiendish ingenuity—'mit skrupelloser Raffinesse' (p. 99); and he wrote | as a deliberate propagandist, in the interest of Octavian (pp. 140 ff.). This is a tall order. As for polemics, the character and career of Cicero was surely ancient history now, and irrelevant: in the contest against Antonius the agents of Octavian had live explosives and plenty of them. On the other hand, if Cicero's memory had been worth attacking at this date, a pamphleteer was not reduced to composing a mosaic from written sources. In style and substance the *Invective* is a superior piece of work. It is no gain to regard the *obtrectatores Ciceronis* as mere political hacks. Some of them at least were writing for the fun of the thing. The author of the *Invective* might be an Augustan stylist demonstrating what sort of reply Piso ought to have delivered to Cicero, *In Pisonem*.

The *Epistulae ad Caesarem senem* can hardly be dealt with in brief compass. It must suffice to say that Dr. Clift puts the second *Epistula* (in the manuscript order) in 49 B.C., the first in 46 B.C.—and holds them genuine both, for the style is Sallustian and Sallust was a partisan of Caesar. One might, however, add in passing that it is not at all certain that the real date of *Epistula II*—or even the dramatic date—is 49 B.C. At least Gelzer argued for 50, Carlsson for 51. Some might think that a discordance between adherents of authenticity debilitates their general thesis, but that would not follow on strict logic. Since it hardly seems possible to discredit utterly both *Epistulae*, there is a temptation to accept and utilize them. On the other hand, adequate attention has not always been paid (by others, or indeed by the reviewer) to the sharp distinction drawn by Mr. Last: the Camden Professor was not wholly unwilling to admit the first *Epistula*, but he damned the second (*CQ* xviii (1923), 42 ff., 151 ff.).

One point should be added that cuts all argumentation in root and principle. A common assumption is this: once the date of composition is established on grounds of historical accuracy or propriety, all is clear— at the given date nobody but Sallust could have written the tracts, for the style is Sallustian. Thus Dahlmann: 'sind aber die Briefe aktuell, dann sind sie von Sallust', *Hermes* lxix (1934), 389. The confidence was premature, the axiom a trap. As K. Latte pointed out when reviewing Gunnar Carlsson, *Eine Denkschrift an Caesar über den Staat* (Lund, 1936) in *JRS* xxvii (1937), 300 f., Sallust created his style according to a theory, by deliberate choice, and with the help, so Pollio alleged, of a technical adviser (Suetonius, *De gramm.* 10); and he did not create it until he renounced politics after the death of Caesar and elected history as fit occupation for a gentleman. Nobody is likely to have written Sallustian in 49 B.C., or in 46 B.C.— not even Sallust.

Arguing for the genuineness of a large batch of letters, speeches, and pamphlets, Dr. Clift defends her choice in these words: 'Much of the work that has here been accepted must have been firmly established in the libraries at the close of the Republican period to account for its transmission to a later age' (p. 122). There seems to be a *petitio principii*. Were these compositions approved by libraries, and by which libraries? And would it follow that they are authentic? The skill of the forger counts for something, likewise the ignorance, conceit, or cupidity of librarians. There were certainly some people with exact knowledge and high standards. One of them was Seneca the father, and Dr. Clift makes appeal to him: 'It would seem that there was little chance of fraudulent works escaping detection in the Augustan age, for Seneca was aware even of the false attribution of a declamation by Capito to Porcius Latro' (p. 149). The example (*Controv.* x, *praef.* 12) is self-destructive. Seneca was an expert on style, a fanatic about *declamationes*, a friend of Latro from the old school days in Spain. He wrote about the Augustan rhetors from his portentous memory many years after (certainly later than A.D. 34, perhaps towards 40). Others might well have been taken in meanwhile. Clearly they were.

With the passage of time error often became undetectable. Quintilian, we have seen, accepts the *Invective*; and Quintilian furnishes a quotation from a speech of C. Antonius against Cicero in the electoral campaign of 64 B.C. (*Inst. Or.* ix 3, 94). With emphasis on the merits of Quintilian, Dr. Clift takes this to prove the survival of a genuine speech (p. 92), and seeks support from Asconius. Now that scholar, in his commentary on Cicero, *In toga candida*, affirms that the only reply Antonius and Catilina were capable of making was personal abuse. He states that the speeches current under their names were forgeries—'feruntur quoque orationes nomine illorum editae, non ab ipsis scriptae sed ab Ciceronis obtrectatoribus: quas nescio an satius sit ignorare' (p. 94 Clark). Dr. Clift, however, maintains that Asconius, by damning the spurious, attests thereby the existence of genuine speeches by Antonius and Catilina. That is hardly a legitimate inference from the language of Asconius. Nor is the authority of Quintilian, deservedly high in many matters, here to be held decisive. Quintilian is not pronouncing on a document. He merely quotes from the work of P. Rutilius Lupus on figures of speech. If that carries the quotation back to the Augustan age it still cannot guarantee an authentic Antonius, *In Ciceronem*. Was Lupus a historical critic as well? Did he confine his choice of examples to rigorously verified material? The *schema* was too good to forgo—'sed neque accusatorem eum metuo, qui sum innocens, neque competitorem vereor, quod sum Antonius, neque consulem spero, quod est Cicero.' Asconius apologizes for even mentioning | the bogus elucubrations, 'quas nescio an satius sit ignorare'. It is not to be believed without demonstration that rhetoricians, librarians, or even scholars, had anticipated his flair and his accuracy. Augustus' chief librarian was Pompeius Macer, the son of Theophanes from Mytilene. The parent was an intriguer and a flatterer. Latin philology may not have been conspicuous among the arts and graces of the son.

Even a good scholar might go astray. The case of Fenestella is instructive. Asconius several times adverts upon opinions of that historian, whose prime aberration was to assert that Cicero had in fact defended Catilina before the *quaestio repetundarum* in 65 B.C. (p. 85 Clark). Asconius expresses his doubts, quietly and firmly, though without mention of any documents, genuine or forged. Fenestella was a reputable character, much addicted to facts, and Asconius, who eschews offensive superiority or elaborate refutations, elsewhere names him with respect. About the source of Fenestella's error he has not cared to inquire. It does not look like sheer invention or mere malice. The simplest solution is this—Fenestella had seen *Ad Att.* i 2 and had drawn a hasty inference from the words 'hoc tempore Catilinam competitorem nostrum defendere cogitamus'. That is quite possible, even if the collection of the letters to Atticus had not yet been published, as many believe. Or had he been dazzled by a *Pro Catilina*, some smooth parodist's exploit, some bibliophile's treasure?

The main thesis of this book, that the institution of public libraries at Rome encouraged a careful sifting of dubious literature, checked its propagation, and curtailed its survival, is in itself so reasonable as to appear self-evident. None the less, though the principle be sound enough, it cannot operate as cogent proof in any single instance. Human craft and human frailty subsist. And if the refined stylistic preoccupations of the ancients sharpened their critical taste, imitation and parody likewise became more accurate and sophisticated. Vulgar frauds of course might be quickly detected. Galen has an entertaining story about the Roman book market (xix 8 f. K). A man picked up a volume labelled Γαληνὸς ἰατρός. He read two lines and threw it down—the style was impossible. As Galen goes on to explain, literary standards had been steadily declining ever since the time when he received his own education.

Just as in the fine arts, with patronage and galleries as an incentive to profitable deception, to improvements of technique, so in literature. Another passage in Galen (xv 105 K) tells how the royal libraries of Alexandria and Pergamum provoked a torrent of pseudepigrapha. Touching Rome itself, the beneficent influence of the imperial establishments would be triumphantly confirmed if ancient scholars were in the habit of pointing to the absence or rejection of a book as sufficient proof of spuriousness. This does not appear to be so. Suetonius knew of elegiac verses and a prose epistle circulating under the name of Horace—and he spurned those objects, for stylistic reasons (*De poetis*, p. 121 Rostagni). On the other hand, genuine works might be deliberately excluded. Suetonius has curious details about the writings of Caesar the Dictator (*Divus Iulius* 55 f.). For example, the speech *Pro Q. Metello*, so Augustus thought, was not actually published by Caesar; and the Emperor had grave misgivings about *Apud milites in Hispania*, of which two versions existed. There is no indication that these texts were banned. That was, however, the fate of certain *juvenilia* of Caesar, which Suetonius records, without any opinion about authenticity from himself or from Augustus. The Emperor intervened with decision. He wrote a little letter to Pompeius Macer—'quos omnis libellos vetuit publicari in epistula quam brevem admodum ac simplicem ad Pompeium Macrum, cui ordinandas bibliothecas delegaverat, misit.' Yet, if official policy controlled the public libraries, it could not always impede circulation. Some shocking things were going about. 'Antoni scripta leguntur', says Ovid, and his own books fell under the interdict.

15

A Roman Post-Mortem
An Inquest on the Fall of the Roman Republic

MR. VICE-CHANCELLOR, LADIES AND GENTLEMEN:

Coming among you in response to an amicable and flattering invitation, namely to deliver the third of the Todd Memorial Lectures, I cannot feel myself wholly among strangers. Nor, I trust, will the theme selected for the discourse be altogether remote and unfamiliar. The series which opened so auspiciously with [R. E. Smith,] *The Aristocratic Epoch in Latin Literature* [(1947)] and went on to [H. Mattingly,] *The Emperor and his Clients* [(1948)] announces a high standard for emulation—and it also counsels the choice of a subject that shall deal not with books and texts and words only, but with the behaviour of men and governments.

When a war has been lost, a political system overthrown, or an empire shattered and dispersed, there is certain to be a post-mortem inquiry, and the discussion is seldom closed with the decease of the survivors: it may be perpetuated to distant ages, and, as strife is the father of all things, so is dispute and contention the soul of history. One of these great necrological argumentations is the fall of the Roman Empire in the West—a revolution, so the historian Gibbon pronounced, 'which will ever be remembered, and is still felt, by the nations of the earth'.

Another is the fall of the Roman Republic. Here the breach between the old and the new was not, it is true, so wide, and the damage was quickly repaired, with a stable order ensuing. The Republic had been far from Republican, and the new dispensation under the rule of Caesar Augustus was not wholly monarchical. Behind the political struggles in the last age of the Free State at Rome, and behind the story of wars and battles, can be discerned, as a steady process, the emergence of centralized government. |

The process is intelligible, but the causes of it and the stages are a perpetual theme for diagnosis and debate among scholars and historians. Perhaps the time has come to go back and discover what the Romans themselves thought about the catastrophe. Who was to blame? There were plenty of survivors, and the last convulsion was recent indeed to

Todd Memorial Lecture No. 3 (Sydney, 1950).

the contemporaries of Caesar Augustus. It opened in the year 49 B.C., when Julius Caesar, the proconsul of Gaul, invaded Italy, it went on through civil wars and the despotic government of the Triumvirate, and it closed in 31, when the last of the war-lords, Caesar's heir, was victorious at the battle of Actium. Already in 28 and 27 B.C. the shape of the new order, the Principate, was receiving public and legal definition.

Yet it is not at all easy to recapture the tone and arguments of the debate. No single and explicit statement exists anywhere. The written history of the time has vanished utterly, no political speech survives, no pamphlet, no memoirs. Compared with what went before and what came after, the Age of Augustus acquires the paradoxical dignity of an obscure and highly controversial period. Recourse must be had to official documents—with due caution; to the Augustan poets—again with due caution. And silence itself will be revealing. Important truths are often awkward truths, to be covered and disguised, from fear, from complicity, or for comfort.

The inquest may now begin. After a political catastrophe, why not turn round and inculpate the political system? A facile escape. It was denied to the Romans. The Republic was the very essence of Rome, it had endured through five centuries. Senate and People broke the Samnites, defied Hannibal and the Carthaginians, and brought down the successors of Alexander in the kingdoms of the East. Greeks might assert primacy in the arts and sciences, but not in the art of government. They might appeal to the wisdom of ancient legislators. In vain: their inferiority was registered by the turbulence of their civic history, and not least by the suspicious consolation of political utopias. The Romans could assert a | powerful counter-claim. Their constitution was created, not out of plan or theory, not by one man only, but by long generations and by the efforts of many statesmen.[1] Here in truth was the balanced and ideal commonwealth: to discern which was not beyond the power even of a Greek, if he travelled, learned practical wisdom—and discarded national conceit.

To indict the Republican system of government was not only painful but intolerable: at the most a Roman was prepared to recognize imperfections of detail, or the need for adjustments. Moreover, it argued a lack of courage and faith. Caesar Augustus had just restored the rule of Senate and People, taking for himself powers by delegation. Not King or Dictator, but Princeps.[2] For that act the First Citizen has been much praised, then and subsequently. The reasons that moved the master of the legions were not wholly sentimental or traditional. A legal definition of the supreme authority was attractive, indeed inevitable. It enabled

---

[1] Such was the opinion of Cato the Censor, reproduced in Cicero, *De re publica* ii 2.
[2] Tacitus, *Ann.* i 9: 'non regno tamen neque dictatura sed principis nomine constitutam rem publicam.'

Augustus to control and work the constitution more effectively, to check the ambitions of others, to canalize patronage, and to provide for the undisturbed transmission of the power.

The Republic being to the Romans both a necessary mechanism and a necessary way of thought, and therefore invulnerable, might not the recent calamities be put down to the fault of the governing class? What an opportunity for a rancorous democrat, what a theme for anger and invective! He might attack the aristocracy for their reckless ambition, careless of the commonwealth; he might arraign the shameless nepotism that protected and rewarded the feeblest members of their own order; he might denounce military incompetence, consigning thousands of Roman citizens to their deaths in the pursuit of glory and conquest; and he might round off the indictment with corruption, vice, and rapacity.

How the thing could be done, a retired politician had recently demonstrated. The historian Sallust in his narration of the Conspiracy of Catilina launched a general attack upon the oligarchy that governed Rome in the last age of the Republic. His technique, varying but concentrated to one | purpose, is instructive. Sulla, by victory in civil wars, by violence and by confiscation, brought the *nobilitas* back to power. Sulla is therefore regarded by Sallust as the author of all evil.[1] Catilina had been one of Sulla's men; the criminal ambitions of Catilina are made out to be a natural and inevitable product of the system that Sulla established.

But the historian has an even more damaging device. Cato was the firmest champion of that government, he waged a strong war in its defence against all subversive elements, and in the end he died for the Republic, achieving renown and consecration as a martyr in the cause of *Libertas*: Cato refused to submit to the victor in civil war, and preferred suicide to enslavement. Now Sallust in his monograph produces a speech by Cato in the Senate. It calls for the ultimate penalty against Catilina and his associates, and it carries a strong and bitter denunciation of sloth, greed, and iniquity against that party of which Cato was himself one of the leaders.

Cato reminded his audience how Rome had grown great in ancient days through valour, integrity, and justice; now, however, the State was poor and individuals were prosperous; the love of riches engendered the love of ease and luxury. Everything could be had for money or influence. Palaces and estates, wealth, possessions, and works of art, all were dearer to their owners than was the Commonwealth.[2] Not only that. The

---

[1] Sallust, *Bell. Cat.* 11, 4: 'sed postquam L. Sulla, armis recepta re publica, bonis initiis malos eventus habuit,' etc.

[2] Ibid. 52, 5: 'sed per deos immortalis! vos ego appello, qui semper domos villas signa tabulas vostras pluris quam rem publicam fecistis'; 52, 21 f.: 'sed alia fuere quae illos magnos fecere, quae nobis nulla sunt, domi industria, foris iustum imperium, animus in consulendo liber, neque delicto neque lubidini obnoxius. pro his nos habemus luxuriam

conspiracy, in Cato's words, had been engineered by men of birth and family—'coniuravere nobilissimi cives'.[1]

And finally, the supreme condemnation of the aristocracy; not luxury or crime, but mediocrity. Sallust composes a tribute to the contrasted excellences of Cato and of Caesar. What is his justification? Because, he says, Cato and Caesar were the only truly great men at Rome in their age.[2]

Whether the aristocracy deserved so savage a handling might be doubted. There was still virtue and capacity in the old families—and no monopoly of honesty (very far from it) in the commercial classes. What, on a narrow and partisan estimate, is construed as luxury or corruption may yet be a | manifestation of vitality; and the last age of the Republic, with much turbulence, enjoyed freedom of speech and produced a great flowering of oratory and poetry. It might have been more equitable to absolve the governing class as a whole, to turn the edge of censure against a venal plebs, rapacious businessmen, the intrigues of bankers, the political apathy of the middle class in the towns of Italy—and the exorbitant ambitions of the generals.

Irrelevant, however, is the incrimination or exculpation of the aristocracy as a class. Privilege had always existed; it belonged to the natural order of things. If privilege was asserted and exploited by those on top, it was accepted and admired by those beneath.[3] Rome had gone through a revolutionary process. But none of the leaders of parties most active therein fought to change the structure of society—only to augment their own rank, wealth, and power.

Nor could it have been expedient to attack or criticize the aristocracy under the new order of Caesar Augustus. The Revolution, now consolidated, was all for stability and conservation. Augustus for his ordering of the Roman State required not only the fabric of the Republic but the men and the families. They were to adorn the first ranks of the government, they were to act as leaders in society—and they were to be used in Augustus' own system of a monarchy that should be supported by an elaborate nexus of dynastic alliances in the aristocracy. In the civil wars he had fought against the *nobiles*. Victorious, and now a legitimate ruler, he became their friend and patron.

In the wars, the brave men and the loyal had perished, fighting in defence of the Republic against military despotism. Their names stand on record; but many of the most illustrious families in the Roman aristocracy

atque avaritiam, publice egestatem, privatim opulentiam; laudamus divitias, sequimur inertiam.'

[1] Sallust, *Bell. Cat.* 52, 24.

[2] Ibid. 53, 5: 'multis tempestatibus haud sane quisquam Romae virtute magnus fuit. sed memoria mea ingenti virtute, divorsis moribus fuere viri duo M. Cato et C. Caesar.'

[3] Cicero, *De re publica* i 43: 'tamen ipsa aequabilitas est iniqua, cum habet nullos gradus dignitatis.' Pliny, *Ep.* ix 5, 3: 'nihil est ipsa aequalitate inaequalius.'

are absent from the roll of honour of the Republic's dead. In fact, they survived the age of tribulation, and, for the most part, were ready to come to terms with the victor, for their mutual advantage.[1] What destroyed the *nobilitas* was not the wars of the Revolution but the murderous peace of the Caesars. |

To the heirs of the *nobilitas*, the Roman People were pledged (so it was widely held) to pay a tribute in return for the great services of their ancestors.[2] The Emperor now came to replace the People as the source of honours. Augustus by control of the elections abated the dangerous excesses of open political competition, and, by favour, accorded to the *nobiles* a preferential treatment. He also subsidized them with money grants; and by his bounty he rescued from obscurity ancient houses of the aristocracy which through misfortune or incompetence had long ago fallen out of the race for honours and glory. Names never heard of for centuries now return to adorn the roll of the Republic's magistrates, and with the passage of a few years the new monarchy which grew out of the Revolution exhibits a strongly aristocratic complexion, patrician houses like Claudii, Valerii, Fabii, and Cornelii being prominent in the consulate.[3]

The *nobiles* might regain prestige, but not such power as before. They had once behaved in war and peace with all the pride and independence of clan-chieftains or barons. It was now intended that they should be useful as well as decorative. Moreover, they were not allowed a monopoly: they had to share privilege and station with the new men emergent from the Revolution, the adherents of Augustus promoted and enriched for loyalty and service.

If the aristocracy had to surrender much of its real power, and abate its ambitions, all the greater was the temptation to insist upon the show and the trappings, to advertise the claims of birth and pedigree. More so, perhaps, than in the last epoch of the Republic. And in those aspirations of the nobility the new men might easily concur. They had every reason to support and magnify that station and rank to which they had recently been admitted; they cheerfully adopted its pretensions and its prejudices. Social mimicry is the constant accompaniment of political success. Dual though it is in origin, the new aristocracy of the Empire pays homage to the same ideals. |

Since the governing class as a whole, the past along with the present,

---

[1] Tacitus, *Ann.* i 2: 'cum ferocissimi per acies aut proscriptione cecidissent, ceteri nobilium, quanto quis servitio promptior, opibus et honoribus extollerentur.'

[2] Seneca, *De beneficiis* iv 30, 4: 'hic egregiis maioribus ortus est: qualiscumque est, sub umbra suorum lateat. ut loca sordida repercussu solis inlustrantur, ita inertes maiorum suorum luce resplendeant.'

[3] To say nothing of a Furius Camillus after three and a half centuries, or a Quinctilius Varus descended from the nobility of Alba Longa.

was thus protected from attack, it would be necessary to look for individual culprits. Might not some of the political leaders be incriminated, for pride and ambition, for blunders or incompetence, for the fatal refusal to make concessions and adjustments?

Cato in his own lifetime had incurred blame for that inflexible spirit (or noble obstinacy) which denied all compromise and sometimes appeared to harm the cause he was defending.[1] Moreover, Cato might deserve some share of responsibility for the clash of arms in which the Republic perished. Cato, it might have been said, was not merely a man of principle—he was a tenacious and astute politician. If he came in the end to support Pompeius the Great against Caesar, it was not from illusions about Pompeius. His preference was tactical—to break Caesar first, then Pompeius, if it could be done.[2]

Cato failed. But Cato through defeat and suicide became a force more potent than ever in his lifetime. There was hardly a Roman that could resist the spell.[3] Even his political enemies, such as Sallust, were quickly constrained to pay homage to his memory—and even Augustus could invoke Cato, in the interests of political stability and conservatism. Cato, it was said, preferred any government rather than none; and one of Cato's loyal followers proclaimed that even submitting to tyranny was better than civil war.[4] Now Augustus was of the opinion that it was better to have imperfect laws and abide by them than be always changing;[5] when asked his opinion of Cato, he had an answer: 'anybody who will not want the existing order to be altered is a good man and a good citizen';[6] and Augustus actually wrote a pamphlet on the subject of Cato.[7] The purpose and the argument do not lie beyond conjecture—a sermon on stable government.

Cato was dead and sanctified when Caesar's heir was making his début as a military adventurer. Not so Brutus and Cassius. They were his sworn enemies. Augustus, for all his tolerance, good sense, or duplicity, could hardly have | been expected to rehabilitate the memory of Brutus and Cassius. Those men had assassinated his adoptive parent, they had been duly condemned to death by a court of law. Nobody else, however,

---

[1] Cicero, *Ad Atticum* ii 1, 8: 'nocet interdum rei publicae; dicit enim tamquam in Platonis πολιτείᾳ, non tamquam in Romuli faece, sententiam.'
[2] Thus, when Pompeius was removed, Cato could prolong the struggle for *Libertas* against Caesar with a clear conscience. Cf. Lucan, *Pharsalia* ix 265 f.:

> unum Fortuna reliquit
> iam tribus e dominis.

[3] Compare the words of Velleius Paterculus, an ardent supporter of the Caesars (ii 35, 2): 'homo Virtuti simillimus et per omnia ingenio diis quam hominibus propior.'
[4] Plutarch, *Pompeius* 54; *Brutus* 12.   [5] Cassius Dio liii 10, 1.
[6] Macrobius ii 4, 8: 'quisquis praesentem statum civitatis commutari non volet, et civis et vir bonus est.'
[7] Suetonius, *Divus Aug.* 85.

was debarred from extolling Brutus and Cassius. It was generally recognized that the cause for which Brutus and Cassius fought at Philippi was the better cause. The best men were there also: they, or their sons, avowed it proudly under the rule of Augustus.[1] Devotion to the memory of the Liberators had not yet become a symptom or a proof of disaffection with the rule of the Caesars.

There remains Cicero, who was killed when standing in defence of the Republic, but who was not regarded by Republicans quite as one of themselves, either then or in his posthumous reputation. The political career of the great orator was open to damaging criticism on various counts. More often, it is true, for compliance than for obstinacy. Yet if Cicero might seem by his end amply to have redeemed himself from earlier weaknesses, there might well be two opinions about the wisdom of a policy that invoked civil war in the defence of the Commonwealth: to destroy Marcus Antonius, Cicero in the last year of his life raised up the young man, Caesar's heir, an adventurer with a private army.

That young man, a few months later, was one of the three who signed the death-warrant of Cicero. A shameful act, but one among many such acts. What, then, would be said or thought about Cicero when the era of the war was closed and Rome enjoyed concord and stability under the rule of Caesar Augustus? It was a delicate question then, and no single answer is now available.

Previously it had not been necessary to discredit the memory of Cicero (there was no Ciceronian party in Roman politics); the times changed quickly, and the contest for the supreme power with Marcus Antonius afforded (and required) more powerful weapons of propaganda. After the victory Cicero's memory was even less a political issue, and silence was the best remedy.[2] |

But the name of that Roman who so excelled in oratory as to be a worthy rival to Demosthenes could not always be avoided; and the historian of the civil wars would have to pronounce a verdict somewhere. A fragment survives, preserving the obituary notice as composed by Livy. It is sympathetic but balanced. Except in his death, Cicero did not bear adverse fortune as a man should; and as for his death, he suffered only what he would have inflicted on others had he been victorious in the struggle.[3]

An anecdote is instructive. Plutarch tells how Augustus one day came upon one of his grandsons reading a book of Cicero. The boy in dismay made fruitless attempts to conceal it. Augustus took the volume, stood

---

[1] Tacitus, *Ann.* iv 34: 'Messalla Corvinus imperatorem suum Cassium praedicabat.'
[2] Compare the opinion of Labienus, cited by the Elder Seneca (*Controv.* x 3, 6): 'optima civilis belli defensio oblivio est.'
[3] Cited by the Elder Seneca (*Suas.* vi 22): 'omnium adversorum nihil ut viro dignum erat tulit praeter mortem, quae vere aestimanti minus indigna videri potuit quod a victore inimico ⟨nil⟩ crudelius passurus erat quam quod eiusdem fortunae compos victo fecisset.'

there reading it for some time, and gave it back with the words: 'a great writer, and a great patriot'.[1]

The Princeps, it should seem, need not have confined his approbation within the walls of the palace. He could praise Cato if he chose, in the interests of ordered government: why not Cicero? Cicero was a champion of enlightened conservatism. There was much of value in his political thinking; and the ideal commonwealth which he depicted in the books *De re publica* drew its strength not from theory but from history, for it was nothing less than an exposition, with suitable embellishments (but no structural modification), of the Roman state in a past age of stability and felicity.[2]

That Caesar Augustus had recourse for guidance to the writings of Cicero, or to any writings, is not a convincing notion. That the phraseology employed by Cicero (and no doubt by many of Cicero's contemporaries) should recur in the Principate of Caesar Augustus can hardly prove anything more than the recurrence, in familiar and useful words, of political argumentation—and political deceit. The Augustan system took its origin from facts, not from books; its authors were politicians, diplomats, and generals, not theorists.

So much for the political leaders on the Republican side. For one reason or another it was impossible to make scapegoats of Cato, of Brutus, of Cicero. Flagrant by contrast | was the guilt of the military leaders who subverted the Commonwealth by their ambition and brought on the civil wars by their rivalries. In the opinion of Cato the trouble began, not when Caesar crossed the Rubicon but when, a dozen years earlier, Pompeius, Crassus, and Caesar formed a compact to control the State.[3] That opinion found favour and support: Asinius Pollio adopted the year 60 B.C. for the beginning of his history.[4]

Yet the three dynasts were not totally or unreservedly to be condemned. They were men of splendour and power, they exhibited *virtus* and they pursued *gloria*. If they augmented the dominions of the Roman People, they would have to be honoured at Rome—and Augustus paid suitable and especial honour to his predecessors in that role.[5]

Of the three, Crassus failed in his war beyond the Euphrates, and so

---

1 Plutarch, *Cicero* 49.
2 As surely emerges from statements in the tract itself, confirmed by *De legibus* iii 4, 12.
3 Plutarch, *Caesar* 13; *Pompeius* 47.
4 Horace, *Odes* ii 1, 1 ff.:

> Motum ex Metello consule civicum
> bellique causas et vitia et modos
> ludumque Fortunae gravisque
> principum amicitias et arma
> nondum expiatis uncta cruoribus.

5 Suetonius, *Divus Aug.* 31: 'proximum a dis immortalibus honorem memoriae ducum praestitit, qui imperium p. R. ex minimo maximum reddidissent.'

could properly be blamed for criminal aggression. But Pompeius and Caesar were resplendently successful in their conquests. Caesar was consecrated by the heir to his name, yet by paradox *Divi filius* when undisputed master of Rome seems to award the preference not to his parent but to Pompeius Magnus. The evidence is startling; it is consistent; and it comes from the three great writers of Augustan Rome that stand so close to the government—two poets and a historian.

In the *Odes* of Horace, Julius Caesar is not quite referred to as a person.[1] The *Aeneid* of Virgil is an epic poem devoted to the ultimate origins of Rome and the Julian House, highly symbolical and allegorical. Augustus is not only prefigured in Aeneas: he is revealed in three visions of the future. First, The Promise of Jupiter. To comfort Venus, the father of gods and men discloses the glory that is to be, its culmination in the young Caesar, conqueror of the nations to the world's end and a prince of peace.[2] Next, The Shield of Aeneas, with all Roman history portrayed as leading up to the victory of Rome and of Italy at Actium.[3] Thirdly, The Revelation of Anchises: the parent of Aeneas calls up before him in the lower world the muster-roll of Aeneas' line and of the heroes | of Rome, regal and Republican, down to 'Augustus Caesar divi genus', who will establish the Golden Age in Italy.[4]

Where is Julius Caesar? The list passes from Romulus to Augustus, but he is nowhere to be found in that vicinity. Caesar is segregated, being introduced later, along with Pompeius. Both stand outside of the chronological order of Roman history, and neither is referred to by name. That is not the most remarkable thing. Anchises with solemn adjuration exhorts them both to refrain from civil war. Which shall disarm first? Not Pompeius but Caesar.[5]

---

[1] The nearest he can go is the 'Iulium sidus' of *Odes* i 12, 47; the 'Caesaris ultor' of i 2, 44 is only a description of Augustus.

[2] *Aen.* i 286 ff.:
> nascetur pulchra Troianus origine Caesar
> imperium Oceano, famam qui terminet astris,
> Iulius, a magno demissum nomen Iulo.
> hunc tu olim caelo spoliis Orientis onustum
> accipies secura: vocabitur hic quoque votis.

[3] *Aen.* viii 678 f.:
> hinc Augustus agens Italos in proelia Caesar
> cum patribus populoque penatibus et magnis dis.

[4] *Aen.* vi 789 ff.:
> hic Caesar et omnis Iuli
> progenies magnum caeli ventura sub axem:
> hic vir, hic est, tibi quem promitti saepius audis,
> Augustus Caesar divi genus, aurea condet
> saecula qui rursus Latio.

[5] *Aen.* vi 832 ff.:
> ne, pueri, ne tanta animis adscuescite bella
> neu patriae validas in viscera vertite viris;
> tuque prior, tu parce, genus qui ducis Olympo,
> proice tela manu, sanguis meus!

The historian confirms the poet. For Livy it was a question whether the birth of Caesar were a greater blessing or a greater curse.[1] And Livy was so generous in his praise of Pompeius that Augustus called him a 'Pompeianus'. That did not, we are told, in any way impair the friendship between emperor and historian.[2] On the contrary, these men understood each other. Livy was quite sincere; and the exaltation of Pompeius, so far from offending Caesar Augustus, fitted admirably with his policy.

Whatever was known and remembered about the acts and ambitions of Pompeius the Great could be passed over: in the end he had fallen at Pharsalus commanding the armies of the Republic against Caesar. Whereas Caesar (whatever the rights and wrongs of the dispute) began an accursed war by his invasion of Italy; and Caesar the Dictator had been assassinated by honourable men.

It was expedient for Augustus to dissociate himself from Caesar: the one destroyed the Republic, the other restored it. How could that be done? Easily, and with the fairest pretext. Caesar had been deified, he was no longer a mortal man. When Caesar's heir himself died at the term of his long presidency of the Roman State, there were carried in the funeral procession the images of his ancestors, and also those of the great generals of the past. Pompeius Magnus was among them, but not Caesar.[3] The artifice of Augustus is patent. He exploited the divinity of his parent and paraded | the titulature of 'Divi filius'. For all else, Caesar the proconsul and Dictator was better forgotten.

An authentic scapegoat has been identified. And there were others. Upon Octavianus' partners in the triumviral powers, Aemilius Lepidus and Marcus Antonius, might be laid the responsibility for the proscriptions, and notably upon Antonius the guilt of the murder of Cicero. For the rest, Lepidus was a flimsy character, rapidly discarded, and by his very insignificance at the same time removed from blame and unworthy of rehabilitation. Not so the great Antonius, the true author of the Caesarian victory at Philippi and the rival of Caesar's heir in the supreme struggle for the dominion of the world.

The war of words began before the armed decision at Actium, and it was prosecuted afterwards, with no less intensity. Not only was it Antonius' fault, the renewed civil war—for his rival (it was claimed) wanted only peace, concord, and the restoration of Republican government. Not only criminal ambition, but criminal folly. Antonius had now become

---

[1] Seneca, *Nat. Quaest.* v 18, 4: 'nam quod de Caesare maiori volgo dictatum est et a Tito Livio positum, in incerto esse utrum illum nasci magis rei publicae profuerit an non nasci, dici etiam de ventis potest.'

[2] Tacitus, *Ann.* iv 34: 'Titus Livius, eloquentiae ac fidei praeclarus in primis, Cn. Pompeium tantis laudibus tulit ut Pompeianum eum Augustus appellaret; neque id amicitiae eorum offecit.'

[3] Cassius Dio lvi 34, 2 f.

an oriental monarch, aspiring to subjugate Rome and Italy to foreign rule. His habits were alien, his armies, his allies—and the Queen of Egypt his wife, 'sequiturque (nefas) Aegyptia coniunx'.[1]

The war as managed by Caesar's heir was a war solemnly and legally declared against Egypt. If Antonius stood by Cleopatra, he was stamped as a traitor and consigned to infamy. And so it turned out. The legend of Actium is a familiar theme, lavishly exploited by the Augustan poets.

After Caesar, Antonius is the second scapegoat, and much more satisfactory in the intensity of the emotion evoked, moral, patriotic, and xenophobic.

None the less, the account is not closed when Caesar and Antonius are indicted. Attractive though it might be to single out one man (or two) for execration, and an easy solution for the vulgar and the superficial, a scrupulous inquirer or a thoughtful patriot would have to confess that | the evil was deeper in its roots and more pervasive in its manifestations. Though it was hardly possible (as has been shown) to incriminate the whole governing class, they might share the guilt if it was nation-wide, and envisaged as moral and religious rather than political.

Through what sins and transgressions had the Roman People come so near to destruction? Various answers were available. An ancestral curse was working itself out: it originated in Troy, or at the founding of Rome when Romulus shed his brother's blood.[2] Or the national gods had been neglected, their sanctuaries crumbling in ruin.[3] Or the traditional ideals of morality and frugality had lapsed, generation after generation sinking deeper in luxury, crime, and corruption.[4]

The nation's guilt and the urgent need for a reformation are most eloquently declared in certain odes of Horace, which herald and support the social programme of Caesar Augustus. How far that programme succeeded is a large question. A historian a century later expresses his doubts; according to Cornelius Tacitus, luxury was unbridled from the War of Actium down to the fall of Nero.[5]

Nor, be it noted, was the moral outlawry of Caesar and of Antonius maintained in all its rigour. After a few years, it seems, the anger and the fervour about Actium abated in the consciousness of stability and prosperity. And the family of the renegade subsisted as an element in the Caesarian dynasty. The daughters of Antonius were at the same time

---

[1] *Aen.* viii 685 ff.:

> hinc ope barbarica variisque Antonius armis,
> victor ab Aurorae populis et litore rubro,
> Aegyptum virisque Orientis et ultima secum
> Bactra vehit, sequiturque (nefas) Aegyptia coniunx.

[2] e.g. Virgil, *Georgics* i 501 ff.; Horace, *Odes* iii 3, 21 ff.
[3] Horace, *Odes* iii 6, 1 ff. [4] Ibid. 46 ff.
[5] Tacitus, *Ann.* iii 55 (a digression following the speech in which Tiberius Caesar expressed a strong dislike for moral and sumptuary legislation).

nieces of Augustus, and from this line came three emperors of Rome—Caligula, Claudius, and Nero.

There were no personal and family causes of this nature to rehabilitate the memory of Caesar the Dictator. Justice was late in coming. As the years passed, however, the origins of the Empire could be seen in a proper perspective; and a historian might be inclined to replace Caesar in the series of the rulers of Rome, for various reasons, and especially if he were distrustful of Augustus and of Augustan valuations. | Tacitus frequently refers to Caesar, and never with disrespect; and he is hostile to the idealization of Pompeius the Great.[1]

Such is the termination of the post-mortem, and not wholly conclusive. It provokes a further question. Was the corpse wholly defunct? If a man looked about him he might be impelled to doubt it, for he could see the outer fabric of the Republic intact, the old families back in office, and the old phrases back in currency. Much had altered, it is true, but not everything for the worse. Though everybody made haste to bury and cover up the twenty years of tribulation, the period had not in fact been an orgy of continuous destruction. There were not battles every year; and many of the battles had been decided with little bloodshed, through the well-timed treason of political generals or the mass capitulations of citizen soldiers. Even the standing armies, the savage taxation, and the vast expropriations were not an unmixed evil: money circulated and energy was let loose.

Many of the profiteers of the wars became imperceptibly the profiteers of the peace. It is worth asking, which were the classes and regions to benefit from the centralized government that replaced the competitive anarchy of the Roman Republic? The answer can be briefly given.

The provincials gained protection from the master of Rome, and submitted to regular taxation in the place of arbitrary exactions. Caesar Augustus was also the patron of the urban poor, providing corn doles, and for some, allocations of land. The propertied class welcomed security and saw their estates rise in value. For businessmen the new régime held out new sources of investment, posts in the administration, and the prospect, if they wished it, of promotion into the senatorial order. As for the Senate itself, the lower members could now rise by merit or loyalty to the top, while the princes of the aristocracy, relieved from the expense and the dangers of competition for office, might qualify for the consulate by prerogative—through the patronage of Caesar Augustus. |

---

[1] Tacitus, *Hist.* ii 38: 'post quos Cn. Pompeius occultior non melior'; and, especially notable because of the context, which deals with the legislation of Augustus, *Ann.* iii 28: 'tum Cn. Pompeius tertium consul corrigendis moribus delectus, et gravior remediis quam delicta erant suarumque legum auctor idem ac subversor, quae armis tuebatur armis amisit.'

However, not all men are ready frankly to acknowledge benefits conferred upon them. The Empire could be acclaimed by the provinces, the lower orders, and by much of the middle class, commercial or landed. Not so easily by the aristocracy or by those who from tradition or snobbery were imbued by the same sentiments—or at least vocal in their expression.

The Empire needed no elaborate or sophistical justification to most classes and regions. Their feelings are known, or can be guessed. Imperial propaganda, as directed towards the inferior orders of society, might seem either superfluous or obvious and predictable. The upper classes needed a more subtle approach—or rather, it should be said, they gradually formulated the reasons and excuses for accepting the new order of things. How do men console themselves for the surrender of political freedom? With what arguments do they maintain that they have discovered the middle path, liberty without licence, discipline but not enslavement?[1] It would be an entertaining speculation, and not remote from the concern of the present age.

[1] The formula is well attested, e.g. in the funeral oration upon Augustus (Cassius Dio lvi 43, 4), and in the words of Galba when adopting Piso as his successor (Tacitus, *Hist.* i 16): 'neque enim hic, ut gentibus quae regnantur, certa dominorum domus et ceteri servi, sed imperaturus es hominibus qui nec totam servitutem pati possunt nec totam libertatem.'

16

Tacfarinas, the Musulamii, and Thubursicu

THE last foray of Tacfarinas in the seven years of his depredations, as recounted by Tacitus,[1] contains a pretty problem, textual and historical. Though defeated once more, the Numidian leader eluded capture. He rebuilt his bands and in A.D. 24 appeared before a town called Thubuscum, which he proceeded to invest.[2] Since in all the multitude of native towns in Tunisia and in Algeria with their *ineffabilia nomina* no such place is known, resort to emendation has been made. Lipsius proposed *Tupusuctu*; Nipperdey suggested *Thubursicum*. Which is preferable?

Mommsen in the *Corpus* supported *Tupusuctu* and the weight of his authority is still felt: recent editors of Tacitus, whether cautious or venturesome in their dealings with the text, have hesitated to adopt *Thubursicum* or even to commend it.[3] Worse than this: the very existence of the problem *Thubuscum oppidum* is totally ignored in a publication where the elementary facts at least should have been catalogued.[4] Yet the case for Tupusuctu had never been properly argued, still less proved. On the contrary, strong arguments were to hand in the narrative of Tacitus, in history and in geography, telling for Thubursicum against Tupusuctu.

First, Tupusuctu (Tiklat) or Tubusuctu. The spelling need not matter, but the character of the city and its site are | notable.[5] Tupusuctu is one of Augustus' colonies in Mauretania. The title is published in full on the earliest of its epigraphical documents, the bronze tablet recording the

---

[1] [For the story of the war, see P. Romanelli, *Storia delle Province romane dell'Africa* (1959), 227 ff. (accepting the conclusions of this article).]

[2] Tacitus, *Ann.* iv 24, 1: ' auget viris positisque castris Thubuscum oppidum circumsidet.'

[3] Mommsen in *CIL* viii, pp. 489 and 754. Of the latest editors of *Ann.* i–vi, who all keep *Thubuscum oppidum* in the text, Köstermann (Leipzig, 1934) mentions Nipperdey's *Thubursicum* in his *apparatus*, but in a misleading fashion, as though Mommsen supported it [corrected 2nd ed. (1965)]; M. Lenchantin de Gubernatis (Roma, 1940) correctly observes 'Thubursicum *Nipperdey: at cf. CIL viii, p. 754*'; while H. Fuchs (Zürich, 1946) has no comment.

[4] H. Treidler, 'Thubursicum', *RE* vi A, col. 621, ignores the problem and H. U. Instinsky, 'Tubusuctu', *RE* vii A, coll. 762 f., assumes without doubt or discussion that Tupusuctu was the place besieged by Tacfarinas.

[5] *AAA*, Feuille 7, 27. For the spelling *Tubusuctu* cf. the amphora stamps from Monte Testaccio, *CIL* xv 2634 f. To the evidence cited in 'Tubusuctu', *RE* vii A, col. 763, might have been added *AE* 1922, 136 (Alexandria): 'ex prov. Mauretan. Caes. Tub.', and *AE* 1934, 39, a dedication of the colony itself to the Emperor Vespasian.

Studies in Roman Economic and Social History in Honor of Allan Chester Johnson (1951), 113–30.

establishment of *hospitium* between a Roman official and 'colonia Iulia Aug. legionis VII Tupusuctu'.[1] It is situated about ten miles inland from the port of Saldae (Bougie), also a colony of the seventh legion. The region possesses considerable strategic importance, not only separating the mountain zones of Great Kabylia and Little Kabylia, but commanding one of the rare ways of access from the coast into the interior, namely the depression of the Wadi Sahel.[2]

It would be a remarkable fact, if a guerrilla leader had the effrontery—and the folly—to attack a Roman colony, with its strong walls and its military establishment: not only to attack it, but even to besiege it. Another Roman base, Saldae, was distant less than a dozen miles. What purpose did the military colonies serve? And no less remarkable, perhaps, that the consular historian, for all his aversion from technical terms, should insult and degrade a veteran colony, 'coloniam Romanam et partem exercitus', by applying the inferior and indistinctive appellation of *oppidum*.

There is no case for Tupusuctu. What of Thubursicum? Two places must be distinguished. The one is Thubursicum Bure (Teboursouk) or rather Thibursicum Bure, for the latter appears to be the better form.[3] Thibursicum may be eliminated at once—it lay well out of reach of the nomads and in the peaceful zone of the Roman province of Africa quite close to Thugga (Dougga) and only about thirty miles from Carthage. At this early date Thibursicum Bure cannot have been a place of any consequence and it did not acquire muni|cipal status before the Severan period. The other is Thubursicum Numidarum (Khamissa) or, to use the epigraphically attested form of the name, Thubursicu.[4] Of the subsequent prosperity of Thubursicu its ruins are a massive testimony. Its original importance, however, is guaranteed by the bare name *Numidarum*. Before its conversion into a *municipium* in Trajan's reign Thubursicu was nothing less than the capital of a large tribe. An altar, dedicated to the 'Genius gentis Numidiae', and two inscriptions, recording 'principes Numidarum', were found there.[5]

On a broad computation, Thubursicu lies about equidistant from Hippo Regius (Bône) and Cirta (Constantine) and Ammaedara (Haïdra); more narrowly, about halfway between Calama (Guelma) and Madauros

---

[1] *ILS* 6103.
[2] Cf. S. Gsell, *Histoire ancienne de l'Afrique du Nord* (Paris, 1927), v 280.
[3] *CIL* viii, p. 2577, cf. the inscriptions 1427 (= *ILS* 3926); 1439 (= *ILS* 1430); 25998.
[4] For the antiquities and history of Thubursicu see the exemplary work of S. Gsell and C. A. Joly, *Khamissa, Mdaourouch, Announa* (Alger and Paris, 1914–22), i, *Khamissa* (1914); also *ILA* i, p. 115. The place has yielded over 700 Latin inscriptions; also one Libyan inscription and one bilingual (Latin and neo-Punic) inscription.
[5] *ILA* i 1226 (= *ILS* 9391); 1297 (= *ILS* 9392); 1341 (= *ILS* 6800). Also *ILA* i 1424 probably mentions a princeps. On these chieftains and their *nomina* see below, p. 228, n. 1.

(Mdaourouch). The relevance of Thubursicu to the enterprises of Tac-farinas and its proximity to the central area of disturbance at once become evident. Tacfarinas, a Numidian deserter from the Roman auxiliary troops, began his insurgent career by organizing robber bands and soon became a leader of the Musulamii, who are described as a powerful people living near the empty lands ('propinqua solitudinibus Africae').[1] The Musulamii are one of the Gaetulian tribes. Though nomenclature is lax and though the pastoral tribes included in the general and convenient denomination of 'Gaetuli' are nomadic and elusive, the area over which the Musulamii ranged can be indicated in a tolerable fashion: the wide expanses of the Numidian plateau, plain and rolling country, south-eastward from the territory of Cirta and north-eastward from the Aurès Mountains, extending across the Algerian border into Tunisia.[2] |

When Augustus appointed Juba II king of Mauretania in 25 B.C., he assigned to him 'certain parts of Gaetulia'.[3] The policy of Augustus is evident. Africa was one of the provinces which he left to Senate and People and Augustus intended that the garrison should be kept very small. Perhaps there was a reduction about this time or soon afterward: troops were needed in Spain for the campaigns against the Cantabri and the Astures (26 and 25), and for the final subjugation, achieved by Agrippa (19). Thus Africa, though garrisoned by a legion and governed by a consular proconsul, was not of much military importance. To King Juba fell the duty of supervising the Musulamii on the west: on the north and on the east they marched with the Roman province of Africa. The Roman road from Carthage westward to Cirta by way of Sicca Veneria (El Kef) passed a little to the north of the Musulamian land, but the main route of military penetration, deviating a little short of Sicca and running south-west, entered their territory not far from Thala and cut across it at Ammaedara (Haïdra) and at Theveste (Tébessa). It was on this line that the legion advanced in the successive stages of the pacification of Numidia.

One episode, at least, in the story of Tacfarinas, namely the siege of Thubursicu, now becomes clear and intelligible. Thubursicu lies less than twenty miles north-west of Madauros (Mdaourouch), which town is on the fringe of the Musulamian area. Apuleius, who should have known, describes his city as half Gaetulian, half Numidian.[4] Though Tacfarinas

---

[1] Tacitus, *Ann.* ii 52, 2.
[2] On the territory of the Musulamii see especially J. Toutain, 'Le territoire des Musu-amii', *Mémoires de la société nationale des antiquaires de France* lvii (1896, publ. 1898) 271 ff.; *AAA*, Feuille 18, 519, and *ILA* i, p. 267. I have not seen L. Carton, *Les Musulamii* (Tunis, 1925). Among the peculiar features of the article 'Numidia' in *RE* will be noted the treat-ment of this tribe—a 'Bauernvolk' in the 'fruchtbare Ebene' north-west (*sic*) of the Aurès (xvii, col. 1360). The article 'Musulamii' (*RE* xvi, coll. 926 ff.) is also erroneous and defective.
[3] Cassius Dio liii 26, 2.   [4] Apuleius, *Apol.* 24.

in the seven years of his recorded career, operating against four Roman proconsuls, spread devastation far and wide along the edge of the settled lands from Mauretania to Tripolitania, getting help from Mauri, from Cinithii and | even from the remote Garamantes, most of his activities take their rise in the Musulamian country. Thubursicu was vulnerable, being a long way from the camp of the legion III Augusta, and there were not many Roman military posts along the frontier (if such it could be called) of the Roman province of Africa.

As has been said, Tacfarinas first emerges as a Musulamian leader in 17. There is, however, no indication to show where he met his first check, being defeated by the proconsul M. Furius Camillus.[1] Nor can the Roman fort, 'haud procul Pagyda flumine', be identified, the scene of an attack (and a heroic episode) in the proconsulate of L. Apronius;[2] but shortly afterwards Tacfarinas was repulsed and was defeated at Thala.[3] Thala is at one end of the Musulamian area. Then in 22, when Junius Blaesus took the field with an extra legion (IX Hispana) under his command, one of his columns had the special duty of protecting the villages of Cirta at the other extremity.[4] Finally, in 24, the siege of Thubursicu. The proconsul P. Dolabella came up and relieved the place: his first action was to establish military posts and to execute disloyal chieftains of the Musulamii.[5]

There hardly can be a doubt that the place besieged by Tacfarinas was Thubursicu Numidarum. Most students of Roman Africa will concur.[6] What should be the behaviour of | an editor of Tacitus? Palaeographically, the emendation is easy and seductive: Thubu⟨r⟩s⟨i⟩cum or Thubur⟨si⟩cum for Thubuscum. If hesitation be felt (and to emend presupposes a certainty, whereas there is no certainy that Tacitus himself did not make a slip about the orthography of an African town), an *apparatus* should mention Nipperdey's emendation and even mention it with approval.[7]

---

[1] Tacitus, *Ann.* ii 52, 4.   [2] Ibid. iii 20, 1.   [3] Ibid. iii 21, 2.   [4] Ibid. iii 74, 2.
[5] Ibid. iv 24, 2. Tacfarinas escaped and met his end at Auzea (ibid. iv 25, 1). This is presumably, though some have doubted, the fort Auzia (Aumale) in Mauretania, over 200 miles to the west of Thubursicu (*AAA*, Feuille 14, 105).
[6] Not long after R. Cagnat (*L'Armée romaine d'Afrique et l'occupation militaire de l'Afrique sous les empereurs* (Paris, 1892), 21) and A. Pallu de Lessert (*Fastes des provinces africaines* (Paris, 1896–1902), i 110) had assumed without question that the place was Tupusuctu, J. Toutain produced the arguments for Thubursicu (op. cit. 281). Cagnat in his second edition ((Paris, 1913), 22 f.) mentioned Thubursicu, with strong approval of the emendation in Tacitus, but did not commit himself wholly: 'la question ne saurait être résolue d'une façon certaine.' Nor were Gsell's remarks as decisive as one might have expected: 'on a supposé avec assez de vraisemblance' (*Khamissa* (1914), 12); 'peut-être l'*oppidum* Thubuscum' (*ILA* i, p. 115). T. R. S. Broughton (*The Romanization of Africa Proconsularis* (Baltimore, 1929), 91 and 105) saw no difficulty in accepting Thubursicu. Cf. also A. N. Sherwin-White, 'Geographical Factors in Roman Africa', *JRS* xxxiv (1944), 10, 'accepting Nipperdey's emendation'. On the other hand, by retaining Tupusuctu, L. A. Cantarelli's essay has lost some of its value ('Tacfarinate', *Atene e Roma* iv (1901), 3 ff., reprinted in his *Studi romani e bizantini* (Roma, 1915), 199 ff.).
[7] This has not been done by recent editors (cf. above, p. 218, n. 3). Palaeographically, the

If the present inquiry serves to elucidate a detail in the narrative of Tacitus and support an emendation, that is something, but it is not the end of the matter. The truth about Thubursicu renders the whole story of Tacfarinas more coherent and enables it to be seen, not as a fragmentary series of raids or recurrent exercises in desert warfare, but as part and parcel of a long process—Rome's dealings with the nomads in Numidia from the time of Augustus to the time of Trajan. The Musulamii are the main problem, the central area of disaffection.

About Augustan military operations in this region, next to nothing can be ascertained. Though the prime exploit of a proconsul was Cornelius Balbus' march to the far Garamantes in Fezzan, which earned him a triumph in 19 B.C., his predecessor, L. Sempronius Atratinus, had also triumphed from Africa, presumably for actions nearer home, on the borders of the province itself.[1] The next detail discoverable is the *ornamenta triumphalia* of L. Passienus Rufus (*cos.* 4 B.C., *procos.* towards A.D. 3).[2] By A.D. 6, however, a regular Bellum Gaetulicum has acquired shape and proportion. According to | Cassius Dio the Gaetuli were angered with King Juba of Mauretania and were unwilling to submit to Roman rule: they broke loose, rose against Juba, spread devastation over neighbouring territories, inflicted defeats on Roman troops. Cossus Cornelius Lentulus (*cos.* A.D. 1) put an end to the war.[3] Florus and Orosius describe the adversaries of Lentulus as 'Gaetuli et Musulamii'.[4] The added detail is valuable. The Musulamii are not to be regarded as a people distinct from the Gaetuli, they are in fact Gaetuli; and Lentulus chose the wider term (and the more honorific) for the *cognomen* which he might not assume for himself but could transmit to his son, 'Gaetulicus'. Similarly the younger Junius Blaesus, commemorating in a verse inscription his service under his father in the war against Tacfarinas, speaks of his exploits against 'Gaetulas gentes'.[5]

By every analogy of African warfare the disturbances quelled by Lentulus must have been raging for some years; and his victory will have been preceded by the operations, of varying utility, conducted by several proconsuls, beginning perhaps with Passienus Rufus. In the time of this governor a Roman citizen and his wife at a place in the Plaine du Sers near the Roman colony of Assuras express gratitude for their preservation.[6] The occasion may have been a raid of the nomads northward into

case for reading *Thubur⟨si⟩cum* is very strong. The Codex Mediceus frequently confuses the letters *r* and *s* and *Thubussicum* could easily give *Thubuscum*: for the dropping of an *s* cf. the *se lustrabo* of the Codex (*Ann.* i 7, 2), restored as *Seiu⟨s⟩ Strabo*. [*Thubu⟨r⟩s⟨i⟩cum* is accepted by Köstermann[2] (1965).]

[1] *CIL* i², p. 77 (= *Inscr. It.* xiii 1, 86). Cf. for these wars Cagnat, op. cit.[2] 1 ff.
[2] Velleius Paterculus ii 116, 2; *ILS* 120.
[3] Dio lv 28, 3 f. Cf. the inscription from Lepcis (Magna) in *AE* 1940, 68 [= *IRT* 301].
[4] Florus ii 31; Orosius, *Hist. adv. Pag.* vi 21, 18.
[5] *ILS* 939, 12 (Mt. Eryx).   [6] *ILS* 120.

the province. There would be no inconvenience in dating Passienus'
command as far back as A.D. 1 or even 1 B.C., for the five years' interval
between consulate and proconsulate was liable to be abbreviated by
favour or by necessity. Moreover, it is likely enough that a second
legion was brought to Africa to reinforce III Augusta: the people of
Thugga set up a dedication in honour of the younger Passienus Rufus,
military tribune of XII Fulminata, 'pro [ami]citia quae eis [cum]
patre est'.[1] |

In these and in other matters the story of Tacfarinas provides a corro-
borative parallel. The prominence and the space which it receives at the
hands of Tacitus may well seem disproportionate. Dio and Suetonius
omit him altogether and only one of the epitomators, Aurelius Victor,
has a bare reference: 'Gaetulorum latrocinia quae Tacfarinate duce passim
proruperant.'[2] Where is the explanation? Not merely in the fact that one
of Tacitus' sources was the acta senatus, which gave due prominence to
the actions of proconsuls. Nor yet in the deliberate amplification of a
theme reminiscent of Sallustius, the archetypal Roman historian, and his
Bellum Iugurthinum. The contrast with Cassius Dio reveals the personal
prepossessions and the artistic devices of an author who composed the
Annales of the Empire in the form and in the spirit of the Republic. Since
there were no more great foreign wars and because domestic affairs were
dull or deplorable, the historian was sharply aware that he needed relief
and variety, wherever it might be found. Tacfarinas was welcome, to
recall also (and in a melancholy tone) the wars of earlier days: M. Furius
Camillus bringing back imperatoria laus to his family after an intermission
of nearly four centuries and Junius Blaesus the last proconsul to win and
bear the title of imperator. That is a sufficient reason. It might be added,
but it would perhaps be a supererogation, that, while Tacitus was writing
the Annales, the career of a leader of irregular cavalry in Trajan's wars
commanded some attention. Lusius Quietus, the Moorish chieftain, after
conspicuous services in the eastern lands, was suddenly elevated to the
consulate by Trajan and was suddenly suppressed in Hadrian's first year,
when for conspiracy against the new ruler the Roman Senate voted the
condemnation or ratified the execution of the Four Consulars.

Tacfarinas is also welcome to any who seek to understand the Bellum
Gaetulicum of Lentulus—indeed, it is all one subject. Though the Gaetulian rising may have spread far and wide, for example, like that of Tacfarinas, south-eastward to the tribe of the Cinithii beside the Lesser Syrtis,
and though | the city of Lepcis (Magna) in Tripolitania records with
gratitude the termination of the Bellum Gaetulicum,[3] it began as a revolt

---

[1] ILS 8966; cf. R. Syme, 'Some Notes on the Legions under Augustus', JRS xxiii (1933),
25 ff.
[2] Victor, De Caesaribus 2, 3.   [3] AE 1940, 68.

against Juba and its centre was no doubt among the Musulamii. Whether Roman encroachments on the pasture lands of the nomads were in any way responsible, it cannot be said;[1] but the duration and the gravity of the disturbances will have been an incentive to impose stricter methods of control. The earliest verifiable camp of the legion III Augusta is at Ammaedara (Haïdra).[2] It may have been established as a result of Lentulus' war. In A.D. 14/15 under the proconsulate of L. Nonius Asprenas the legion was building a military road from the camp by way of Capsa (Gafsa) to Tacape (Gabès) on the shore of the Little Syrtis.[3] Ammaedara is in the south-east of the Musulamian country. A legion stationed here not only menaced the Musulamii and cut them off from the Cinithii and other peoples—it represented a loss of land as well. Two years only and two proconsulates (those of L. Aelius Lamia and A. Vibius Habitus) after Asprenas—and the insurrection is rekindled among the Musulamii.[4]

The defeat of Tacfarinas in 24 was not followed by a lasting peace. In 44 a proconsul was specially appointed: Ser. Sulpicius Galba, holding office for two years.[5] The disturbances in Mauretania consequent on the Roman annexation no doubt involved the nomads between that kingdom and the province of Africa. Galba for his actions earned the *ornamenta triumphalia*—which would not have been expected, for | Caligula in 39 had removed the legion from the control of the proconsul, making the legate independent. A casual phrase in the epitomator Aurelius Victor reveals the source of the trouble: the Musulamii again.[6] Dolabella in 24 had executed the chieftains of the Musulamii. It may have been then or it may have been now that a Roman military official was given supervision over this recalcitrant people. One of these Roman *praefecti* happens to be known, L. Calpurnius Fabatus of Comum, grandfather of the wife of Pliny the Younger: he is styled '[pr]aef. cohortis VII Lusitan. [et] nation. Gaetulicar. sex quae sunt in Numidia'.[7]

Decisive steps affecting the Musulamii were taken by the Flavian emperors. From Ammaedara the legion moved forward to Theveste, about twenty-five miles to the south-west. The change had been made certainly

---

[1] It is not very likely. Rostovtzeff assumed that the engrossment of land for colonists from Italy provoked a later insurrection, that of Tacfarinas ([*SEHRE*², 319; 683, n. 74]). But observe the arguments of Broughton, op. cit. (p. 221, n. 6), 91.

[2] As demonstrated by F. de Pachtère, 'Les camps de la troisième légion en Afrique au premier siècle de l'empire', *CRAI* 1916, 273 ff. Cf. *ILA* i, p. 286.

[3] *ILS* 151. An inscription from Lepcis ([*IRT* 346]) shows that Asprenas' tenure was of three years, i.e. A.D. 12–15. [Cf. *JRS* xlv (1955), 30 = *Ten Studies in Tacitus* (1970), 43.]

[4] The inscription in *AE* 1940, 69 [= *IRT* 930] proves that Lamia was proconsul under Tiberius (i.e. 15/16) and not, as some scholars have supposed, in 13/14. The proconsulate of A. Vibius Habitus (*AE* 1913, 40) therefore occupies the year 16/17, preceding M. Furius Camillus. [Cf. Syme, l.c. (above, n. 3).]

[5] Suetonius, *Galba* 7 f.   [6] Victor, op. cit. 4, 2: 'caesaque Musulamiorum manus.'
[7] *ILS* 2721.

by 83, when Iavolenus Priscus was legate of the army of Africa.[1] More-over, Roman military posts were established at or near Mascula (Khen-chela), about fifty miles beyond Theveste and halfway to Lambaesis (Lambise, near Batna).[2] Ammaedara became a veteran colony.[3] So much for the southern flank of the Musulamii. On the north at Madauros they were now to be watched by another Flavian colony.[4] The final pacifica-tion and organization of Numidia followed early in the reign of Trajan. A comprehensive process, both military and civil, it is discoverable only from inscriptions.

In 100 the legion III Augusta under the legate L. Munatius Gallus is found at work, constructing the colony of Thamugadi (Timgad).[5] Thamugadi is about 100 miles west of Theveste. Now Theveste became a Roman colony, being enrolled in the tribe Papiria.[6] The inference is clear. Though | the legion is not unequivocally attested at Lambaesis until the time of Hadrian,[7] Lambaesis is barely a dozen miles from Thamugadi: the transference of the legion must belong to the beginning, not to the end, of Trajan's reign.[8] And that transference is linked with other operations. Though it was still premature to penetrate and to pacify the Aurès Moun-tains, the isolation of the *massif* was a practicable measure. Roads encircle it: from Lambaesis south-westward by the Pass of Calceus Herculis (El Kantara) to the station of Ad Piscinam (near Biskra) and from Ad Piscinam eastward to Ad Maiores (Besseriani) in the zone between the Aurès and the Shotts. The latter road was built in 105, as was the fort at Ad Maiores.[9]

That is not all. The legion now established far to the west at Lambaesis outflanks the Musulamii, while the road leading from Theveste to the new camp along the northern skirts of the Aurès by way of Mascula and Thamugadi cuts them off from the south. The Musulamii are now hemmed in and constricted. The best of their land has been confiscated for Roman colonies or imperial domains or private estates. With what remains they must make shift and indeed, no longer able to raid the

---

[1] *ILA* i 3122 (= *ILS* 9089). The inscription in *CIL* viii 23165 (Thiges), erected under Iavolenus' command, is dated to A.D. 83.

[2] There is no evidence that Mascula itself was a military station. But observe an inscrip-tion of A.D. 76 at Aquae Flavianae, five miles to the west (*CIL* viii 17725), and a dedication to Domitian at Vazaivi, a dozen miles south-east (*CIL* viii 17637).

[3] *CIL* viii 302, 308. [4] *ILA* i 2152.

[5] *ILS* 6841.

[6] *AAA*, Feuille 29, 101; *ILA* i, p. 286.

[7] [But see now *Libyca* i (1953), 189 f.: 'L. Tettius Iulianus leg. Aug. pr. pr. [leg. III] Aug. muros et castra a solo fecit' (A.D. 82—but originally set up 81).]

[8] Cf. R. Syme, 'Notes sur la légion III^a Augusta', *REA* xxxviii (1936), 182 ff. and *CAH* xi 147. The late Trajanic or early Hadrianic dating was widely held, e.g. Cagnat, op. cit.² 433; Dessau, 'Lambaesis', *RE* xii, col. 539; Ritterling, 'Legio', *RE* xii, col. 1497.

[9] *CIL* viii 22348 f. (milestones); 2478, 2479 = 17971 (the fort).

Numidian farmers, they must turn themselves to agriculture for susten-
ance. Various boundary stones attest the operations of Roman governors
delimiting the Musulamian territory.[1] One, between Ammaedara and
Theveste, belongs to the governorship of L. Munatius Gallus, late in 102
or in 103.[2] Others were erected by his successor, L. Minicius Natalis (cos.
suff. 106). They proclaim the bounds which separate the Musulamii from
the colony of Madauros, from a small native community near Theveste,
from an imperial property, and from the private estate of Valeria Atticilla.[3] |

The Musulamii are thus confined in a pocket of land, for the most part
not highly productive, between the two highways leading westward
from proconsular Africa, namely the road to Cirta and the road to Lambaesis. Previously controlled by a Roman officer, they can soon be put
under civilian management. An inscription reveals the remarkable career
of a Numidian of Calama (Guelma), east from Cirta and north-west from
Thubursicu. After acquiring the Roman citizenship and the name T.
Flavius Macer and residing at the Flavian colony of Ammaedara, where
he held the offices of *duumvir* and *flamen perpetuus*, he was given charge of
the Musulamii with the title *praefectus gentis Musulamiorum*.[4]

The reduction and the pacification of the nomads enabled the Roman
government to proceed with the organization of the Numidian territory
to the north and to transfer it from the sphere of the legate to that of the
proconsul. Calama, with the tribe Papiria, is presumably a Trajanic
municipium and Thubursicu Numidarum is certainly so.[5] The approximate
date at which Thubursicu was constituted is not beyond conjecture. In
100 it is still described as a *civitas*.[6] Dedications were made, however, at
the Capitolium of Thubursicu in 113 by the proconsul, C. Pomponius
Rufus (cos. suff. 98).[7] It is likely enough that previously, while still tribal,
the Numidian territory around Thubursicu had been under the legate
(though no inscriptions of legates in fact have been found there); and it is
a fair inference that Thubursicu did | not come under the proconsul until
it had been converted into a *municipium*.

[1] For a full account of the process see Broughton, op. cit. (p. 221, n. 6) 96 ff., 121 ff.
[2] ILA i 2939 (= ILS 5959). Trajan's titulature has 'Dacicus'.
[3] ILA i 2828 (= ILS 5958a); 2978; 2988; AE 1923, 26 (= ILT 1653). There was also an enclave of Musulamii farther to the south-east, in the regio Beguensis between Thala and Sufetula (CIL viii 270).
[4] ILA i 285 (= ILS 1435): 'T. Flavio T.f. Quir. Macro / IIvir., flamini perpe/tuo Ammaedarensium, / praef. gentis Musulamio/rum, curatori frumenti / comparandi in annona[m] / urbis facto a divo Nerva Tra/iano, proc. Aug. praediorum / saltum [Hip-]poniensis et Thevestini, / proc. Aug. provinciae Siciliae, / munici[pes] municipi.'
[5] For Calama cf. ILA i, p. 20. The inscription quoted in the preceding footnote gives an approximate indication of date; and the dedication to M. Cornelius Fronto (ILA i 280 (= ILS 2928)) belongs c. A.D. 135. For Thubursicu: ILA i, p. 115 and Gsell's fuller discussion in Khamissa (1914), 14 ff. The inscription ILA i 1240 gives the title, viz. municipium Ulpium Traianum Aug. Thubursicu. The first duumvir is Trajanic, ILA i 1300.
[6] ILA i 1244.   [7] ILA i 1230-2, cf. 1282.

An additional piece of evidence, a single name at Thubursicu, seems to hold hopes of precision. Numidia, in large or in small items, illustrates the way in which Roman names spread and become popular. A cardinal instance is the prevalence of the names 'Sittius' and 'Sallustius', recalling earlier history: the adventurer from Nuceria in Campania, who captured Cirta for Caesar and received a whole principality for his reward, and the Sabine senator, whom Caesar appointed as the first governor of Africa Nova. Now at Thubursicu the civic council pays honour to Larcia Laeta, wife of A. Larcius Macrinus, 'princeps gentis Numidarum'.[1] The *gentili-cium* 'Larcius' is not at all common in the African provinces: all told, there are only six other Larcii.[2] In this instance the source of it can be ascertained beyond doubt: the Numidian chieftain (and his wife) must have received the Roman citizenship from A. Larcius Priscus, legate of the army of Africa in the reign of Trajan.[3] As Larcius Priscus became consul suffect on 1 September 110, his tenure falls within the period 106–10: he was probably the immediate successor of L. Minicius Natalis (*cos. suff.* in the summer of 106), last attested as legate in 105, though it is just possible that another governor intervened.[4] |

It might seem plausible that Thubursicu was constituted a *municipium* under the governorship of A. Larcius Priscus. Reflection suggests a doubt. One must allow for previous individual grants of the franchise. If so, who more eligible than a chieftain of the Numidae? That being so, since Thubursicu was presumably a *municipium* by 113, it might have been constituted by the next legate, succeeding Priscus in 110. His identity has not been recorded, but he was surely one of the consuls of 112 or 113 or 114. The consuls of the first two years are all known (from the *Fasti Ostienses*), but not those of 114.[5]

[1] *ILA* i 1297 (= *ILS* 9392): 'Larciae / Laetae A. Larci Macrini / principis gentis Numi/darum et flaminis perpetui / uxori cui ordo statuam publi/ce ponendam cum decre-visset, / ipsa contenta honore sua pecun. / posuit. D.d.'

[2] *ILA* i 1735 (Thubursicu, two brothers); *CIL* viii 3260 (Lambaesis, a soldier's sister); 15667 (Ucubi, a magistrate); 20978 (= xvi 56) (a witness on a diploma of the army of Africa in A.D. 107); *ILT* 1611 (Sicca, a woman called Larcia Lallosa).

[3] Two inscriptions from Thamugadi give his *cursus*: *ILS* 1055 and *AE* 1908, 237; cf. also the milestone *CIL* viii 10324 (= 22382). The inference was drawn by Cagnat, 'Inscrip-tion inédite de Khamissa', *CRAI* 1904, 478 ff., but the date of Larcius Priscus' command at that time could not be ascertained. (His consulate in A.D. 110 was revealed by a fragment of the *Fasti Ostienses* (*Inscr. It.* xiii 1, 5, XXII), first published in 1932.)

[4] For L. Minicius Natalis, who succeeded L. Munatius Gallus in A.D. 103 (or perhaps late in 102) cf. E. Groag, *RE* xv, coll. 1828 ff. If Minicius left in 105 and if Larcius' tenure were 107–10, a gap could be provided. [This now seems unlikely; see W. Eck, *Senatoren von Vespasian bis Hadrian* (1970), 164 f.]

[5] *Inscr. It.* xiii 1, 202 f., XXII. The *gentilicia* of two *suffecti* in 113 are not preserved, only the *cognomina* Noricus and Urbicus. The next legate attested in Numidia after A. Larcius Priscus is L. Acilius Strabo Clodius Nummus in 116 (*ILA* i 2829 (= *ILS* 5958b); 2939 *bis*). [See Syme, *JRS* xlviii (1958), 5 = below, pp. 385 f. For the consuls of 114 (including a Clodius Nummus), known from a new fragment of the *Fasti Potentini*, see now Degrassi, *FCIR* 34, and Syme, *JRS* xliii (1953), 150 f. = below, pp. 234 ff.]

There is another *princeps* at Thubursicu, called L. Avillius Celer.[1] His
name might prompt the search for a member of the senatorial Avillii
Celeres who might have been legate at some time before 113 or proconsul of Africa subsequent to that date.[2] But there are many traps and
uncertainties in these matters, many puzzles in the nomenclature of the
African provinces. Thus one cannot help being struck by the dispropor-
tionate number of Vettidii (*al.* Vetidii) at Thubur|sicu. No fewer than
thirteen inscriptions name them, as against five from the rest of North
Africa.[3] Another noteworthy phenomenon is the prevalence of Laberii:
fourteen inscriptions.[4] The student of imperial prosopography might be
tempted to look for a link with illustrious Laberii, namely L. Laberius
Maximus, prefect of Egypt in 83, and probably prefect of the guard, and
his consular son, M'. Laberius Maximus.[5] These Laberii came from the
small town of Lanuvium in Latium.[6] The son conceivably might have
been commander of the army of Africa.[7]

[1] *ILA* i 1424: 'L. Avillius / Celer / pr.' The only other Avillii at Thubursicu are his
family (ibid. 1425–7).
[2] A Cn. Avilius Celer might be discoverable, lurking under the name of Cn. Avidius
Celer Fiscillinus Firmus, viz. *TAM* ii 701 (Araxa): Γναίου Αὐιδ[ίου] Κέλερος Φ[ι]σκιλλε[ίνου];
ii 1188 (Phaselis): Γναίου Αὐιδίου Κέλερος / [Φισκιλλεί]ͅνου Φίρμ[ο]υ, πρεσβευτοῦ ἰδίου / [καὶ
ἀν]ͅτιστρατήγου. Now there was a Cn. Avilius Firmus, legate of Lycia–Pamphylia under
Vespasian (*TAM* ii 132 (Lydae); *IGRR* iii 725 (Myra)), cf. *PIR*², A 1413: probably the same
person as the owner of the acephalous inscription at Arretium (*CIL* xi 1834 (= *ILS* 1000)).
If it were supposed that in the two inscriptions cited above a *Δ* in the *gentilicium* has been
misread as a *Δ*, Cn. Avilius Celer Fiscillinus Firmus would emerge, identical with the
Vespasianic Cn. Avillius Firmus or at least a member of the same family. In any case the
person 'Cn. Avidius Celer' (*PIR*², A 1403) must be regarded as under suspicion. [W. Eck,
ZPE vi (1970) 74, n. 41, reports that the *Δ* is clear in *TAM* ii 701 and 1188 and could
be read (dotted) ibid. 132. If so, the identification cannot be maintained.] The name
'Fiscillinus' suits an origin from Arretium very well. Compare the rare *gentilicium* 'Fiscilius',
attested for a senator in 28 B.C. (*CIL* xi 7412 (near Viterbo)), and otherwise, apart from a
freedman at Rome (*CIL* vi 17941), apparently found only on the Etruscan border of
Umbria (*CIL* xi 4668 (Todi); 5191 (Vettona); 5228 (Fulginium)).
[3] At Thubursicu, *ILA* i 1236, 1355–66. They are pretty clearly of native origin—observe,
e.g., the significant nomenclature of M. Vetidius Mustiolus Musti f. (*ILA* i 1355 (= *ILS*
6832)). The other African inscriptions of Vetidii are *ILA* i 2712 *bis* and 2713 (Madauros);
CIL viii 4122 and 3625 (Lambaesis); 20934 (Tipasa of Mauretania). No senatorial Vettidius
exists; but if Q. Vettidius Bassus, procurator of Thrace in A.D. 88 (*IGRR* i 781), had a son,
he no doubt would have been eligible for the Senate.
[4] *ILA* i 1346–8, 1722–32.
[5] *RE* xii, coll. 249 f. (Stein), 250 ff. (Groag). For the plausible conjecture that L. Laberius
Maximus passed from the prefecture of Egypt to the command of the praetorian guard in
84, cf. A. Piganiol, 'Le codicille impérial du papyrus de Berlin 8334' in *CRAI* 1947, 376 ff.
[6] Since Borghesi (or earlier) it has been assumed that L. Laberius Maximus, aedile of
Lanuvium in A.D. 42 (*ILS* ii 6194), belongs to this family. Add Κόιντος Λαβέριος Λευκίου
Μαικία in the *consilium* of a Roman magistrate (? 129 B.C.): text as published by A. Passerini,
'Le iscrizioni della agorà di Smirne concernenti la lite tra i publicani e i Pergameni',
Athenaeum xxv (1937), 252 ff. [= Sherk, *RDGE*, no. 12]. The tribe Maecia is the tribe of
Lanuvium.
[7] But it is most unlikely. The year of his consulate is now recorded by the *fasti* from
Potentia as 89 (cf. *Athenaeum* xxvi (1948), 116). [He was *cos.* II with Trajan in 103 (see
Degrassi, *FCIR* 31).]

An examination of the evidence about Laberii at Thubursicu debilitates that seductive hypothesis. Three of them are of magisterial rank, they all come from the colony of Sicca Veneria, they all bear its tribe, the Quirina.[1] For the rest, all the freeborn males with a tribe also have the Quirina.[2] (Obviously an immigrant family from Sicca.[3]) There are only seven other inscriptions of Laberii in all Africa: two at Madauros, two at Sicca, one at Cirta, one at Sigus in the | territory of Cirta, one about a soldier at Lambaesis.[4] What is their ultimate origin? There is some reason for regarding the Laberii as an Italian commercial family; for example, they occur at Delos.[5] Now Sicca is an Augustan colony. From Sicca the Laberii percolate westward (and so does their name, being assumed as well by natives). A close parallel are the Avianii, coming from Sicca and from Hippo Regius.[6] The name 'Avianius' also harks back to an Italian commercial family in the last age of the Republic, notably represented by Cicero's friend, C. Avianius Flaccus, a grain-dealer at the Campanian port of Puteoli (Pozzuoli).[7]

If the date for the organization of the *municipium* at Thubursicu baffles precision, probability puts it under A. Larcius Priscus or his successor. And though dates are not always to be had (and not always needed) in a slow operation like the advance of a Roman frontier or the spread of municipal institutions, the evidence, by unusual good fortune, not only reveals imperial policy at work in the Musulamian land and in the regions adjacent to the north and to the south, but also explains the stages as well as the nature of the comprehensive process which concluded in a few years the pacification of Numidia.

The stages appear to be three in number: (1) the colony | at Thamugadi in 100: this implies, if it does not presuppose, the transference of the legion from Theveste to Lambaesis; (2) in 103–5 two processes, the one military, the other civil, namely the encirclement of the Aurès Mountains and the

---

[1] *ILA* i 1346–8.   [2] *ILA* i 1725–9.

[3] Cf. Gsell, *Khamissa* (1914), 33.

[4] *ILA* i 2573 f. (Madauros); *CIL* viii 16099 and 27649a (Sicca); 7540 (Cirta); 19160 (Sigus); 18068, b 42 (Lambaesis, a soldier from Tipasa).

[5] Cf. F. Münzer, *RE* xxiii, col. 248, citing *BCH* xxxvi (1912), 45 (Delos) and *Inschriften von Priene* (Berlin, 1906), 114.

[6] Cf. Gsell (*Khamissa* (1914), 33), adducing Avianius Marcellus Pescennianus, magistrate both at Thubursicu and at Sicca (*ILA* i 1294), and Avianius Marcellus described as *Hipponiensis* (*ILA* i 1378). Other Avianii also have the tribe Quirina (*ILA* i 1421, 1422). Avianii (with 35 items in the index of *CIL* viii) are fairly widely distributed over the African provinces. More significant are the figures quoted above about the Vetidii and the Laberii (see p. 228): there is a strong concentration of them at Thubursicu and the rest are attested for the most part in adjacent districts of Numidia. None is found in the tracts of the proconsular province east of Sicca. These data of nomenclature reveal something about early colonists from Italy and about the subsequent stream of commerce and settlement.

[7] Cicero, *Acad.* ii 80; *Fam.* xiii 35, 1; 75, 1 f. For freedmen of this family cf. *RE* ii, coll. 2372 f., and the important observations of W. Schulze, *Zur Geschichte lateinischer Eigennamen* (Berlin, 1904), 584.

delimitation of the Musulamian territory; (3) the establishment of *municipia* at Calama and at Thubursicu.

As a result of these operations Numidia acquires a frontier to the south and its defences are linked with the forts in the east of Mauretania. Furthermore, the *provincia* of the legate acquires a clearer outline, even though it be not officially designated a province until the time of Septimius Severus—it is the zone of the military frontier, with the Cirtan territory attached, but surrendering a tract of Numidian land to proconsular Africa. The *municipia* of Calama and Thubursicu complete and round off a region of settled conditions and civilized life, stretching eastward from the boundaries of Cirta towards Sicca, and they are now placed under the authority of the proconsul of Africa.[1]

The Numidian contribution to the Roman Empire is impressive, coming first from colonists, then from natives. The earliest consul from Africa appears in 80 or shortly before that date. He is a Pactumeius from Cirta, of Italian colonial stock, deriving from a commercial family in Campania which may have emigrated with P. Sittius in Caesarian days.[2] Thubursicu, the capital of a native tribe, first enters recorded history in A.D. 24, when it is beleaguered by a horde of wild Musulamii: the first senator from Thubursicu is a certain P. Postumius Romulus, perhaps only two or three generations | after it became a *municipium*.[3] In the days of Tacfarinas there were no cities in that vicinity. The phrase employed by Tacitus is noteworthy—'nullo etiam tum urbium cultu'.[4] It is the only hint in all recorded literature, and faint enough it is, of the process begun and completed in the historian's own age.

---

[1] For the boundary of the proconsular province see *ILA* i, pp. x f. The dates at which other places in this zone (Tipasa, Thagaste, Naragarra, Thagura, and Zattara) acquired municipal status are by no means easy to determine, even approximately, cf. Gsell, *Khamissa* (1914), 21.

[2] *ILS* 101, either Pactumeius Clemens (*CIL* viii 7057) or Pactumeius Fronto (*cos. suff.* A.D. 80). Both Clemens (*CIL* viii 7057) and Fronto (*AE* 1914, 247) were adlected *inter praetorios* by Vespasian. Such magnates from Cirta are surely colonial aristocrats, not, as sometimes assumed (e.g. *CAH* xi 490), 'romanized Africans'. For the abundant evidence for Pactumeii in Campania and in the eastern lands see F. Münzer, *RE* xviii, coll. 2153 f.

[3] *ILA* i 1290. For the prosperity of Thubursicu and the attention there paid to the higher education, as exemplified by certain of the Vetidii and by the grammarian Nonius Marcellus, see the precise and eloquent account of Gsell, *Khamissa* (1914), 35 f.

[4] *Ann.* ii 52, 2.

17

REVIEW

A. Degrassi, *I fasti consolari dell'Impero Romano dal 30 avanti Cristo al 613 dopo Cristo*[1]

THE register of the Roman consuls can serve sundry purposes. At the simplest and lowest, it will fix a date or establish a man's identity. In the absence of written history, however, it becomes history itself, as can be demonstrated for divergent epochs, Republican and Imperial; and, even where historians exist, they will often have to be supplemented by exploiting this evidence, or subverted.

'Libertatem et consulatum'. Nobody could restore the one without the other. The Republic of Caesar Augustus duly brought back the system of annual consulates and regular elections. How the thing was managed is here irrelevant: the names of the chosen are a document. Then the structure of the *Fasti* becomes revealing, for *suffecti* soon emerge, and multiply in the course of time. Certain lengthy or anomalous lists tell their own story. Thus the fatal year 69. Or again, 90: the Emperor Domitian and M. Cocceius Nerva (*cos. II*) lead off, followed by no fewer than eleven *suffecti*. The civil war of January 89 explains the plethora—these are the loyal men. Similarly, Domitian having been removed, 97 must have been lavish—and heterogeneous; and no sooner has a successor been discovered by (or for) Nerva than the results stand out on the peculiar *Fasti* of 98.

In normal seasons the choice of consuls reveals the policy of emperors —or rather, perhaps, the forces an autocrat is seldom able to resist. The men who serve Caesar and the Empire impose their claims and promote their own adherents; nor can birth and wealth easily be debarred from honour. Where the record is abundant, it illuminates the whole upper · order at Rome, and categories of merit or success can be divined. With the intrusion of more and more suffect consuls, the eponymous consulate retains (and sometimes reinforces) its prestige. Few achieve it, save the sons of consuls. In the developed system the exceptions command attention. Thus the first *ordinarii* to be appointed | by Trajan, namely Cornelius Palma and Sosius Senecio, opening the year 99. Conversely, the existence of an *ordinarius* will often encourage one to suppose that his parent had

[1] Rome, 1952.

been a *suffectus* one generation earlier. Epigraphic discoveries sometimes confirm in a welcome fashion.

The supreme distinction is to hold the *fasces* more than once. A third tenure is rare and remarkable. It puts a man close to the supreme power. After Vipsanius Agrippa the first is L. Vitellius, colleague of Claudius Caesar in the censorship; then Licinius Mucianus, who, not wanting empire for himself, had put up Vespasian; seven more names follow in half a century, and the series closes with Julius Servianus, who attained that high pinnacle in extreme old age (134).

Second consulates are much more frequent. The record is significant, by the entries and also by the omissions, and certain contrasts strike the eye. For example, the *consul iterum* is hardly ever eponymous under the Flavian dynasty, but regularly so after the year 103. Again, instances are frequent in the early years of Domitian's reign and of Trajan's, but in each case fall off well before the end (two only after 85, one after 109). Hadrian is sparing with the honour altogether, and Antoninus Pius awards it only twice. About Hadrian the *Historia Augusta* makes a firm assertion —'tertio consules, cum ipse ter fuisset, plurimos fecit, infinitos autem secundi consulatus honore cumulavit' (*Hadr.* 8, 4). That is false. The facts are there. Another allegation in the same source is less vulnerable to scrutiny (and sometimes finds credence), viz. that Hadrian's successor left good governors in office for periods of seven or nine years (*Pius* 5, 3). This is contrary to all that is known or surmised about the steady routine of administration under that ruler, and several of the imperial provinces of praetorian rank (such as Numidia or Lycia–Pamphylia), with the roll of legates almost complete, might be enough to justify a denial.

Iterated consulates proclaim the higher public servants or friends of the dynasty; and there can seldom be any doubt about the social quality of the *ordinarii*. Much more, however, can be got from the *Fasti*. The name of a consul, ancient or recent, Latin, Italian, or provincial, will indicate the trend of history. Under Augustus a Lollius and a Tarius continue the Revolution. The *nobiles* come back, it is true, with effulgence of historic names, and some that had been for long ages in eclipse, but new *gentes* are rising. A change is manifest after A.D. 4—the next five years show no fewer than six consuls with *gentilicia* never seen before on the Roman *Fasti*. It will be assigned in large measure to Ti. Claudius Nero—who has now become 'Ti. Caesar Augusti f.' His principate exhibits the first consul from Narbonensis, Valerius Asiaticus, in 35. The fact came to light not long ago, on a fragment of the *Fasti Ostienses*. It is a surprise—but not a paradox, given other things about Tiberius Caesar, and certain influences to be detected as potent in the last years of his reign.

No history surviving from antiquity has traced the progressive enlargement of the Roman governing class, age by age and region by region—

the best statement available is brief and impressionistic, namely Tacitus
on the *principes* of Gallia Comata (*Ann.* xi 24), adapting and improving
the speech of Claudius Caesar (*ILS* 212). Casual and fragmentary evidence
has to be invoked, for example inscriptions revealing two consuls from
Asia towards the end of Domitian's reign, or that man from Pergamum,
C. Julius Quadratus Bassus (*cos. suff.* 105), who led a Roman army in the
conquest of Dacia and governed three provinces of consular rank (Cappadocia, Syria, and Dacia). When a senator's origin is not obvious or specified, the study of nomenclature and the pursuit of local dynastic families
can yield striking results. From bare names in periods of history apparently
void or vague the whole process of social change emerges. At the top,
the consulate. Republic or Monarchy, it helps to answer the principal
questions in political life.

I. All the calendars of consuls engraved on stone were collected and
edited recently by Attilio Degrassi. They fill a massive and sumptuous
volume, *Inscriptiones Italiae* xiii 1 (1947). While the evidence for the
Republican period is now complete, digested, and accessible, something
additional was needed for the Empire. The material is heterogeneous and
scattered. Not to say often inferential. Literature contributes, in a wide
range, from Martial and Pliny to Aelius Aristides or the record of some
Christian martyrdom; there are certain written calendars with lists of
eponymous consuls composed in late antiquity; and, apart from actual
Fasti like those at Ostia, names of consuls used as dates accrue from a
variety of objects—gravestones, military diplomata, commercial contracts from Pompeii and Herculaneum, birth registers in Egypt, brick
stamps, and the vintage labels of wine jars.

Liebenam's handy list in the series of *Kleine Texte* (1909) was long out
of date. It had been known for some time that Degrassi had a volume
ready for the press. It is now to hand, and it offers much more than
Liebenam ever did. The *Fasti consolari* are set forth in the following
order. First, the 'elenchus consulum' from 30 B.C. to A.D. 613. This registers
the consuls year by year; their full nomenclature is given; and, helped by
the resources of typography, Degrassi is able to provide some information
about variants and about the sources. Further, at the bottom of each page
are noted and briefly discussed a number of those consuls whose year,
though not ascertained, admits | a fairly close approximation. The second
half is an alphabetical list, cataloguing the 'consoli di età meno certa'. To
be useful for ready reference, a book of this type would require several
indices. Degrassi provides one of *nomina* and one of *cognomina*. There are
also three brief supplementary lists: consulates indicated in a peculiar
manner (e.g. 'Duo Gemini' for the year 29), consulates of rulers or heirs
apparent, and *designati* who did not actually enter upon office. Only one
thing seems to be lacking. It would have been convenient to have a register

in one place of the hitherto unidentified pairs of consuls, like Severus and Flavus on the Colchester diploma (*CIL* xvi 130).

About the quality of this volume, no words need be wasted, and it would be pointless to compliment a pupil of Bormann upon his vigilance and sagacity. The mere industry required is enormous. A small detail anywhere can elude the most careful of editors, and there is always the chance that he may be taken unawares by new discoveries. Even without much fresh material, prosopographical studies, by refining the technique, hasten their own obsolescence. Various lists of senators or of provincial governors, long useful, are now out of date. Books as recent as that of Lambrechts on the Senate from A.D. 117 to 193, published in 1936, or, a narrower theme, Hüttl's *Fasti* for one reign (*Antoninus Pius* ii (1933)), call for a thorough revision. It is even possible to suggest several modifications in Stein, *Die Legaten von Moesien* (1940). Work goes on apace. One need only allude to two welcome accessions recently—the list of senators in Garzetti's *Nerva* (1950), and the huge repertorium of Barbieri, *L'albo senatorio da Settimio Severo a Carino* (1952).

There are many hazards in this form of study. Homonyms and polyonyms infest the forest of senatorial nomenclature. They are often very difficult to label and identify. And, in the great mass of detail, nobody can hope to be immune from slips about names, figures, and references. They can occur anywhere. A portion of the *Acta Fratrum Arvalium* (*CIL* vi 2086) carries a consul suffect of 155, 'M. Gavius ['. The first edition of *PIR* knows him not, nor the second, nor the encyclopaedia of Pauly-Wissowa.

Degrassi marks by an asterisk the years now complete with their consuls. The sign has been inadvertently attached to 149. Another useful device is the *lemma* 'non ci furono altre coppie di consoli'. It can be appended to 154, and perhaps also to 114 and 115; on the other hand, it is not beyond doubt for 84. Two consuls figure in the index who cannot elsewhere be traced, a Caninius under Vespasian and a L. Coelius Festus, marked '119?'. M. Plancius Varus was not governor of Britain (p. 19), nor was C. Bruttius Praesens proconsul of Asia (p. 35). Apart from mere errata, there cannot help being some mistakes of date, identity, or attribution. Moreover, exigencies of space debar the editor from arguing properly certain points in dispute: the student will have to do some work for himself, and that is all to the good.

Nobody who pays any attention to the study of Latin inscriptions can have failed to benefit from Degrassi's learning—and from his generosity; and it is his way to make a handsome acknowledgment for the smallest of contributions in return. His modesty and candour come out in the preface—'io mi auguro sinceramente che, ritornata una vera pace tra i popoli, documenti usciti numerosi da scavi intensificati in tutto il mondo romano rendano in breve volger di anni necessario un aggiornamento di questo mio lavoro. Intanto, sarò grato ai colleghi che vorranno segnalarmi manchevolezze ed errori.' Echoing that hope, the reader will be happy to congratulate the good fortune that has enabled the editor to include in his *Addenda* (p. 288) a small but precious fragment from Ostia:

> [L. NERATIVS PRISCVS, M.] ANNIVS VERVS
> [. . . . ., L. DOM]ITIVS APOLLINARIS
> [. . . . .], Q. ATILIV[S AGRICOLA]

This fragment belongs to the year 97. It makes several things clearer. Most important, Annius Verus and Neratius Priscus, already known as a consular pair (*Dig.* xlviii 8, 6), but difficult to place: the former is the grandfather of the Emperor Marcus, the latter is the famous jurist. Domitius Apollinaris occurs as 'consul designatus' in a letter of Pliny that casts some light (but not enough) upon the political vicissitudes of Nerva's reign (*Ep.* ix 13, 13). It seemed that his *praenomen* should be 'Lucius' (cf. *PIR*², D 133), but the piece of the *Fasti Ostienses* discovered in 1939 (*FO* xiv) revealed a *suffectus* in January of the year 98, 'Cn. Domitius [. . . . . .]', and provoked a temporary revision (cf. *PIR*², D, *Addenda et Corrigenda*, p. xii). Domitius Apollinaris being now, however, certified for 97, Cn. Domitius awaits identification. Perhaps an unknown person —perhaps rather a second consulate for Cn. Domitius Tullus (*PIR*², D 167), succeeding Nerva as colleague of Trajan, and preceding 'Sex. Julius Frontinus II'. As for Q. (Glitius) Atilius Agricola, it was known that he passed from the governorship of Gallia Belgica to his consulship precisely in 97 (*ILS* 1021 and 1021a). Let us hope that another piece of luck may disclose some more of the *suffecti*, such as | Cornelius Tacitus (whether the *praenomen* be Publius, or, as Sidonius thought, Gaius)— or better still, L. Licinius Sura (if, as seems most likely, this was his year).

The notable supplements from inscribed stones accruing recently belong to the Flavio-Antonine age. Some are very valuable—not only whole years, but long runs of years. Thanks to two discoveries, the list for 85–96 is all but complete. New fragments of the *Fasti Ostienses* came to light in 1939. One tablet (*FO* xiii *s* and *d*, reproduced in *Inscr. It.* xiii 1, pp. 192 and 194) carries in parallel columns the *Fasti* of two series of years, namely 84–6 (beginning about half-way through 84) and 94–6: of the former, on the left side of the block, only the last letter or letters of each line is preserved, but the latter, though broken at the right edge, is complete enough for certitude. The gap was all but bridged in 1948, when a large slab from Potentia, in Picenum, was published (N. Alfieri, *Athenaeum* xxvi, 110 ff., whence *AE* 1949, 23). On its left side it has the consuls from mid-86 down to a point early in 93: the bottom right side of this series is truncated at 92 and 93, but other evidence (*FO* xii *d*) supplements

the year 92. Combining the *Ostienses* and the *Potentini*, Degrassi produces the register of 85–96 with only three gaps, viz. (1) a *suffectus* in
★ May 85, the colleague of 'Po]llio filius', (2) in 86 the colleague of Q. Vibius
Secundus, and (3) the rest of the year 93 after its first *suffectus*, T. Avidius
Quietus. It may be added that this reconstruction involves a certain perplexity about 85 (see below, pp. 243 f., on the second consulate of T. Aurelius
Fulvus).

As for 97, there is now the new Ostian fragment cited above; and the
following year, with FO xiv (first published in 1939), though carrying
problems of identification, is complete, except for a consular pair in the
nundinum November–December (which one would be entitled to assume).
★ Next, heterogeneous information fills out 100, so it appears, except for
★ one *suffectus*, the colleague of Q. Acutius Nerva (Pliny, *Ep.* ii 12, 2).
Then Ostia furnishes 105 entire (FO xix), and a fragment (FO xx) makes
it possible to reconstruct 107. Soon after comes the long run, from 109
to 113 (FO xxii), and here the right-hand portion of the *Fasti Potentini*
supervenes providentially; it supplements two of the names for 113 that
are imperfect on the *Ostienses*; and, although truncated on the right, it
furnishes the structure of 114 and 115 (three pairs in each year), and,
combined with other evidence, leaves only one *suffectus* a blank in each
year. That is to say, providing this copy has omitted no consuls; and, if
this is so, Degrassi could have appended to 114 and to 115 his note 'non
★ ci furono altre coppie di consoli'. Ostia supplies 116. Hence the eight
years 109–16 form a complete series, with only two places missing. It
becomes easy to pin down within narrow limits a number of unattached
consuls.

Hadrian's reign provides a contrast. It is very thin—only two entire
years, 127 and 128 (FO xxiv–xxvi), and in 128 two of the *suffecti* are
represented only by their *praenomina*. Under Antoninus Pius, however,
there are two agreeable stretches. The years 146–8 are entire, save for the
mere *praenomina* of two men (FO xxvii and xxviii); and 152–4 form a
structure (FO xxix and xxx), though several names are very fragmentary
and one has left no trace at all. Finally, but also defective, the year 160
(*Inscr. It.* xiii 1, 572), and a small but valuable piece (FO xxxvii), which
the editor plausibly assigns to 165.

II. There may be some profit in essaying a rapid survey of the period
from Vespasian to Pius inclusive. First of all, the ordered sequence of
consuls both certain and certainly dated, where conjecture should have
no place, even though the method be precise and the results agreeable.
The editor prints 'Sex. Iulius Fr?]on[tinus?]' as a *suffectus* in the summer
of 74. Another person, though not known in fame and achievement, has
★ parity of rights, M. Hirrius Fronto, consular legate of Cappadocia.
Moreover, there is a genuine difficulty (cf. Anderson's note on *Agricola*

17, 3). Taking time and travel into account, the military province of Britain where Frontinus succeeds Cerialis would be left unduly long without a governor in spring and summer: Petillius Cerialis had come back to hold a second consulate, which is attested on 21 May (*CIL* xvi 20). For the year 99 Degrassi registers an 'ignoto console per la terza volta', referring to Pliny, *Pan.* 58, 1. That rests upon a misconception: 'erat in senatu ter consul cum tu tertium consulatum recusabas.' The reference is surely to the year 98 (cf. *Pan.* 60, 1), and the person in no doubt—Fabricius Veiento. The latest testimony, in fact, to that old rogue's survival. Next, the ']etiliu[s]' suffect in 103 is filled out as '[P. M]etiliu[s Sabinus? Nepos II?]', following the suggestion of A. Garzetti, *Nerva* (1950), 141. Which is in a way attractive, but might be premature. Briefly stated, it involves the fusion of two characters who might be distinct, (1) the Domitianic consular, (Metilius) Nepos, the governor of Britain, who is replaced by Avidius Quietus in 97/8 (cf. *CIL* xvi 43), and (2) the Nepos who in 105 is addressed by Pliny as 'maximae provinciae praefuturus' (*Ep.* iv 26, 2). The province there referred to was boldly elucidated by Groag—Pannonia (*RE* xv, col. 1401). Some hesitation will subsist. Among the *suffecti* of 116 is 'Q. Co[rnelius Senecio Annianus?]'. The supplementation reproduces the nomenclature of a senator and consul whose *cursus* (*CIL* ii 1929) probably belongs to the time of Antoninus Pius (cf. E. Groag, *Phil. Woch.* 1933, 1382), indeed, almost certainly. | Furthermore, if he were consul in 116, one of his posts, the proconsulate of Bithynia, would bring him into collision with the governor Cornutus Tertullus (*ILS* 1024), the presumed successor of Pliny. The consul of 116 must be content with 'Q. Co[', eschewing speculation. Nor, under 128, can one accept 'Q. [Planius Sardus Varius Ambibulus]'. As legate of Numidia there is attested 'Q. Planius Sardus [......] Ambibulus', described as 'cos.' (*AE* 1911, 111 = *ILS* 9486), now certified as L. Varius Ambibulus in 132 (*AE* 1950, 59), to be presumed as consul for 132 or 133; and a L. Varius Ambibulus was in fact consul (*CIL* x 3864). Therefore the *suffectus* in 128 is only a *praenomen*, 'Q.', like a certain 'M.' in the previous *nundinum* (colleague of L. Valerius Flaccus). Similarly in 153 '[C. Iulius Max?]imus' should be reduced to virtual anonymity. There was an Arval Brother of that name in 155— but there is also a Sex. Caecilius Maximus (*AE* 1947, 59) whose nomenclature fits the spacing on the stone much better (*FO* xxix), and who can be identified with the recipient of a rescript from Antoninus Pius (*Dig.* xlix 14, 2, 5): for the present there is no compulsion to evoke various persons with the *cognomina* 'Primus' and 'Maximus'. Again, as a suffect in 154 '[Cn. Iulius Ve]rus' appears both attractive and certain. There would be time for Julius Verus to hold Germania Inferior and pass rapidly thence to Britain, where he is first attested in 158 (*Eph. Ep.* ix 1230).

Yet it might not be so. He could have been consul *c.* 151, and thus immediate successor in Germania Inferior of Salvius Julianus (*ord.* 148).

III. Next, the consuls not directly attested and nailed down to a year. In this book they are put separately under two rubrics, according to the closeness of the approximate dates: page by page, below the line for the one class, while the others form the list of 'consoli di età meno certa'. Let them here be taken together, for the method is the same. The limits within which a man's consulate should fall depend upon a variety of clues and combinations. Briefly, his presumed age, the quality of his family, the type of his official career, and the dates of known posts held before or after the consulate. The 'suus annus' in the last epoch of the Republic is the forty-third. It appears to hold under the Principate, and not all achieve it. But some can get there earlier. The reign of Augustus, continuing the Triumvirate, exhibits youthful consuls. Birth now qualifies, in its own right and regularly: a man of consular family can become consul at thirty-two. Not that they all do—but it is clear that there has supervened a lowering of the prescribed age in the *leges annales*, not registered by any of the ancient historians, and seldom noted by the moderns. At the same time, the service of the Caesars brings an acceleration, with *novi homines* able to reach the consulate after a praetorian province at thirty-seven or thirty-eight. The first clear case is Q. Veranius, quaestor in A.D. 37 (as the neglected inscription from Cyaneae, in Lycia, showed, *IGR* iii 703), praetor probably in 42, and, going out to be the first legate of Lycia–Pamphylia, consul for his reward, in 49. That is to say, quite a young man (not yet fifty) when he died as legate of the military province of Britain (Tacitus, *Ann.* xiv 29: for Veranius, see E. Birley, *DUJ* 1952, 88 ff. = *Roman Britain and the Roman Army* (1953), 1 ff.; also the new inscription from Rome, published with full commentary by A. E. Gordon, *University of California Publications in Classical Archaeology* ii 5 (1952), 231 ff.). As it develops, this type of career normally shows, between praetorship and consulate, two posts only, the command of a legion and one of the imperial praetorian provinces. They occupy a man for half-a-dozen years. Observe the case of P. Metilius Secundus (*suff.* 123 or 124), as elucidated by Groag (*RE* xv, coll. 1402 ff.). Metilius is with the Arval Brethren in January 118, but not subsequently in that year, and not in 119: he has gone to command a legion, thence to Numidia (*ILS* 1053, cf. *CIL* viii 17844 (of 121) and 22173 (of 123)). The praetorian province is vital in his career, practically designating a man to the consulate: compare what Tacitus says about the governorship of
★ Aquitania (*Agr.* 9, 1). Under the Flavian and Antonine emperors this type of advancement acquires remarkable regularity. Not only is the formula 'cos. des.' attached to governors before they leave their pro-
★ vinces—after a time they sometimes hold the *fasces* in absence. Where

there are gaps in the *Fasti*, the praetorian legates of Caesar's provinces have a strong claim. The provinces they govern, eight in number under the Flavian emperors, rise with Trajan to twelve—Arabia is added, Pannonia Inferior, Thrace, and Galatia (severed from Cappadocia towards the end of the reign). And, since Hadrian reduced Dacia to praetorian rank, but made Judaea consular, the same total holds under Antoninus Pius. Fairly full evidence is available for several provinces. Five of them (Numidia, Dacia, Lycia–Pamphylia, Pannonia Inferior, and Thrace) can show as many as six to nine legates each in the period 138–61. The normal tenure being triennial, on an average four consuls each year will derive from this type of promotion, and, where dated consulates are frequent, the pattern can clearly be discerned. Elsewhere these praetorian legates should be held in reserve, on the flank, as it were, of the *Fasti*. Not but what death or mischance might intervene. Thus Suellius Flaccus, the general who annihilated the Nasamones, now attested as legate of Numidia in 87 (*IRT* 854), seems to have missed the consulate: the years 87–92 are preserved entire. And one will note that governor of Arabia whose tomb is at Petra (*CIL* iii 14148[10]). It is Degrassi's | principle to adduce only those governors for whom the title 'cos. des.' is attested. One or two are in fact omitted, like Ammius F[?laccus], legate of Arabia (*PIR*[2], A 561), whose date is not certain, or Q. Tullius Maximus, early in the reign of Marcus Aurelius (cf. A. Stein, *Röm. Reichsbeamte der Provinz Thracia* (1920), 29). And it would be only pedantry to point out, on the other hand, that P. Cassius Dexter (*ILS* 1050, cf. *PIR*[2], C 490) may not have left Cilicia alive. It is his medical man who vows and versifies: καὶ κλεινὴν ὕπατον πέμψον ἐς Εἰταλίην.

From all such hazards a properly attested consular province is exempt. Instead, a wide range of dating, at least for the imperial provinces. Here merit, accident, or a political emergency can interrupt the tendency towards routine. Thus a rapid advancement to military commands will invite speculation. It would be expected when a dynasty changes, and new groups surge forward: it also occurs late in the reigns of Vespasian, Domitian, Hadrian, and Pius. While, by contrast, at almost any time an elderly legate may be found governing a military province—from the vicissitudes of patronage, or for an emperor's security.

For calculation backwards, the proconsulates of Asia and Africa are especially valuable, offering as they do so many precise dates and sequences. Two hazards have to be watched. The first concerns the nature of the evidence. Name, date, and identity may all be uncertain. Thus three proconsuls of Asia under Trajan are attested only by coins, and their *gentilicia* are missing, viz. Secundus, Hadrianus, and M. Scapula. The second is the interval of years. It begins with five—note a clear case recently emerging, M. Licinius Crassus Frugi (*cos.* 14 B.C.), proconsul of Africa in 9/8 B.C.

(*IRT* 319). Various perturbations soon ensue, the system recovers and seems to be settling down to a ten-year interval when it is wrecked by
★ Tiberius. It recovers again, exhibits regularity, but tends to a lengthening, especially noticeable in the late years of Trajan (sixteen or even seventeen
★ years being attested). Otherwise, under Trajan, Hadrian, and Pius fourteen or fifteen years can be taken as the standard; and no instance of less than thirteen years can so far be established between 103/4 (a dated
★ consulate) and 161. Both the wider fluctuations, according to the period, and the small variations at any time (caused by accident or the preference given to social rank and the number of a man's children) have to be taken into careful account. For Asia the most recent catalogue is that drawn up by Magie, *Roman Rule in Asia Minor* ii (1950), 1580 ff. It can be revised in several particulars.

Important in themselves, the consular proconsuls impinge on a variety of problems in history or literature, to mention only the date and order of Pliny's letters or the movements and maladies of the sophist Aelius Aristides. Argument for dating from consulate to proconsulate or vice versa can be a very tricky business, even when one of the two points is secure, but it is sometimes well worth the attempt. Thus, even negatively, to support Plinian chronology. When A. v. Premerstein wanted to prove that Julius Bassus, praetorian proconsul of Bithynia, was consul in 105 and identical with a Trajanic general partly homonymous, namely C. Julius Quadratus Bassus, he found that he had to put the prosecution of Julius Bassus not in 103 or 104 (as Mommsen), but in 100, and in consequence another prosecution, that of Varenus Rufus, in 102 (*SBAW* 1934, 72 ff.). This device involved indirectly the dating of several consulates and proconsulates, with unhappy results (cf. R. Syme, *JRS* xxxvi (1946), 163), and could have been rejected even if Ostia had not disclosed a vital fact, '[L. Acilius] Rufu[s]', suffect consul in March 107 (*FO* xx): Acilius Rufus was consul designate when the attack on Varenus Rufus began (Pliny, *Ep.* v 20, 6). Mommsen's dates for both prosecutions can stand: it was unfortunate that Magie allowed himself to be influenced by Premerstein's arguments, or to reach similar conclusions (op. cit. 1456 and 1458).

With these hazards and conditions in mind, some of the unattached consuls can now be put to the test. Here and there a closer dating could be essayed without effort or discomfort, on various criteria. To take half a dozen instances. Civica Cerialis is assigned 'prima dell'82' (the date when his governorship of Moesia is attested (*CIL* xvi 26)). It would do no harm to say '*c.* 76'. Civica was killed while proconsul of Asia, presumably 88/9 (cf. Tacitus, *Agr.* 42, 1): the proconsulate for which Julius Agricola (*suff.* 77) was eligible should be that of 90/1. The alternatives 93 or 97 are suggested for the consulate of C. Cornelius Rarus Sextius Na[?so], proconsul of Africa before Q. Pomponius Rufus (*suff.* 95); see the note in

IRT 523: surely 93, to confirm which, note the *gentilicium* of a *suffectus* of that year on the *Fasti Potentini*, read by the editor as 'Çoṛi['; see *Athenaeum* xxvi (1948), 131. Intricate yet compelling arguments can be brought to bear upon M. Scapula, the proconsul of Asia (who, by the way, ought to be provided with a *gentilicium* and identified as a son of M. Ostorius Scapula, the consul of 59). A coin of Cotiaeum reveals him, *BMC*, *Greek Coins*, *Phrygia* 166—yet not a solitary coin, as stated by Fluss in *RE* ii A, col. 354. There is a second specimen, recorded by Macdonald (*Hunterian Coll.* ii 483), which certifies the reading and dispels the doubts made public in *PIR*[1], S 189. The imperial titulature shows ἄριστος but not Παρθικός, therefore the proconsul's tenure cannot be earlier than 114/5. On the other hand, Q. Fulvius Gillo Bittius Proculus claims 115/6 (*IGR* iv 172, with the eleventh acclamation of Trajan), and Ferox should go | in 116/7 (cf. the coins cited in *RE* x, col. 587). Therefore M. (Ostorius) Scapula will have been consul either in 97 or in the last *nundinum* (November–December) of 98. Degrassi has '97/100'. His dating of Q. Fulvius Gillo, namely '99 c. o poco dopo' should also be modified. This man was *praefectus aerarii Saturni* in 97, when Pliny launched his attack upon his colleague, Publicius Certus, as a result of which 'obtinui tandem quod intenderam; nam collega Certi consulatum, successorem Certus accepit' (*Ep.* ix 13, 23). There is no reason to postpone unduly the consulship then assured to Fulvius Gillo: let him be consul either at the end of 97 or in the final *nundinum* of 98: either date could accord with his proconsulate of Asia. Chance, and the barely credible, can here be invoked. A condemned inscription, one of the *Ligorianae*, ends with a consular date: 'votum susceptum | iii non. Decemb. | Vettio Proclo | Iullo Lupo cos.' (*CIL* vi 616*). Like other products from the same source, the inscription might have embodied genuine details (others are certainly based on documents that have survived). The *nomen* 'Bittius' in Pliny (*Ep.* ix 13, 13) puzzled some copyists, and most editors until modern times: 'Vettius' was easy and familiar. As for the consular partner, there ought to be a consular Julius Lupus in this period, the stepfather of the son of T. Aurelius Fulvus (*ord.* 89, cf. *HA Pius* 1, 6). This man is certified as a consul, with the *praenomen* 'Publius' (*ILS* 8430a). Doubts must therefore be felt about Mommsen's total rejection of the *Ligoriana* (*Ges. Schr.* iv 373, cf. *PIR*[1], I 262): the inscription was not noticed in *RE* x, col. 664, or in *PIR*[2], A 509 f. It now becomes difficult to dismiss outright a welcome adjunct to the *Fasti* of 97 or 98.

Next, an oriental (and regal) consul. Julius Alexander is not merely Trajanic in date: he can be assigned earlier than 109: observe his place among his consular kinsmen on the inscription from Ancyra (*OGIS* 544). If the *Fasti Potentini* were correct, and did not omit the suffect of 115, T. Statilius Maximus Severus Hadrianus (*AE* 1911, 95), there are only

★ two places vacant in the series 109–16. For the one, in 114, there is a certain candidate, P. Valerius Priscus, proconsul of Africa in 127/8 (*IRT* 361): cf. Degrassi's note in his *Addenda* (p. 288), 'probabilmente nel 114'. Nor should the other, in 115, be baffling: P. Juventius Celsus, praetor in 106 (cf. Pliny, *Ep.* vi 5, 4), proconsul of Asia before Lamia Aelianus, the
★ *ordinarius* of 116 (cf. the inscription from Claros, *JŒAI* viii (1905), 167). Finally, the proved or presumed character of a man's official career can sometimes be invoked. For example, the *novus homo* and promoted *eques* T. Flavius Longinus Marcius Turbo, legate of Moesia Inferior in 155: he can hardly have been consul as early as *c.* 145 (as Degrassi, following Stein in *PIR²*, F 305). This man was quaestor of Aelius Caesar (*IGR* i 622), that is to say, 136 or 137. Now T. Statilius Maximus (*ILS* 1062), who was praetorian *iuridicus* of the combined Pannonian provinces under Aelius
★ Caesar, is *consul ordinarius* in 144. Marcius Turbo has to rise to the praetorship, and after that half-a-dozen years are needed for his legionary command and governorship of Lugdunensis. His consulate should there-
★ fore be put in 149 or 150 (for 146–8 are full).

IV. These instances are fairly straightforward, and, apart from providing hints about method, might not be assigned any great value for history. Elsewhere the problems are more complex (or elusive), with cause and scope for many differences of opinion. For example, various members of that nexus (provincial in preponderance) which, forming under the Flavian emperors, seizes the power with Trajan as its representative and furnishes Rome with the dynasty of the Antonines, the dominant strains being the descendants of Aurelius Fulvus and Annius Verus. Casual items have recently accrued, but the subject has never been dealt with as a whole, and manifold obscurities subsist. The theme is important—and
★ I should not wish to neglect it.

Meanwhile, a few details can be touched upon, if only to show up some of the gaps and the perplexities. M. Ulpius Traianus, commanding the legion X Fretensis under Vespasian in the Jewish War, was clearly destined to be one of the 'principes viri' when Vespasian acquired the imperial power. When was he consul? Degrassi gives the date 68/9. The latter year is excluded (its consuls being known), the former may be too early: Traianus was still in Palestine, at Jericho, when last heard of towards the
★ end of April 68 (Josephus, *BJ* iv 450). Surely 70 is preferable. Coeval with the Emperor Trajan's father was T. Aurelius Fulvus, legate of III Gallica, first in the Orient and then in Moesia, from 64 to 69 (*ILS* 232; Tacitus, *Hist.* i 79), and comparable in importance, even without a recent find that reveals him consular legate of Hispania Tarraconensis (the
★ *tabellae defixionum* from Emporiae, *AE* 1952, 122). Fulvus, like Traianus, ought to be among the earliest of Vespasian's consuls, in 70. That is not all. According to the *Historia Augusta*, 'per honores diversos ad secundum

consulatum et praefecturam urbis pervenit' (*Pius* 1, 2). When was he consul for the second time? Or was he ever? Degrassi is inclined to deny it, supposing that his *ornamenta consularia* (acquired when he was legionary legate in 69) may have been regarded by the *HA* as the equivalent of a consulate—'forse dall'autore della *Vita* è considerato, secondo l'uso del suo tempo, come primo consolato la concessione degli *ornamenta*. Non sembra che sia stato console ordinario nell'85' (p. 19). So desperate a remedy seems a counsel of despair. It can be recalled that there are | other *consules iterum* to be inserted somewhere, such as C. Rutilius Gallicus and M. Arrecinus Clemens, presumably in 82–5—not to mention the third consulates of Vibius Crispus and Fabricius Veiento, which must surely be either in 82 or 83, years opened by the Emperor Domitian with T. Flavius Sabinus and Q. Petillius Rufus II respectively as colleagues. Now there are two distinct (and hazardous) arguments that could be invoked to support a second consulate for Fulvus in 85. First, certain written calendars produce as Domitian's colleague in 85 a 'Fulvus' or 'Rufus': cf. Mommsen, *Chron. Min.* i 57, 222, 284, 416; ii 139. This was accepted in *PIR*[1], A 1255 (and elsewhere) as a consulate of T. Aurelius Fulvus—his first, which, given his career and rank, is scarcely to be conceived. Groag in *PIR*[2], A 1510, was agnostic—'*num idem fuerit* Fulvus consul ordinarius a. 85 cum imp. Domitiano XI, *plane incertum*'. Next, a piece of the *Fasti Ostienses* that appeared to carry a negative certitude (*FO* xiii s, cf. Degrassi's comments, *Inscr. It.* xiii 1, 221): the *ordinarius* of 85 with Domitian was ']r. Mess. II', that is to say L. Valerius Catullus Messallinus (*ord.* 73). It might seem safest to leave it at that, consigning Fulvus to the unascertainable. None the less there is a conjecture that should be raised (if only to be rebutted soon or late). The two lines on the *Ostienses* preceding ']r. Mess. II' end with ']Celsus' and ']vos II' respectively. Degrassi assumes them both to be Ostian *duoviri*. Now those magistrates occupy a line each on the record of 85, but not (apparently) in 86 (*FO* xiii s); a line each in 91, the next clear evidence (*FO* xii d), but not in 94, though in 95 (*FO* xiii d); and again, when next attested, 102 and 105, *duoviri* occur side by side on one line (*FO* xvi–xvii and xix). That is to say, on the analogy of the years 86, 94, 102, and 105 (against 85, 91 and 95) there is a case for regarding ']vos II' not as a *duovir* of 84 but as the *consul ordinarius* of 85. Hence a chance that T. Aurelius Fulvus was in fact consul in 85, opening the year with Domitian. If this were so, consequences would follow, none unwelcome. There would be room for two more consuls than Degrassi's pattern admits, viz. a colleague (presumably a '*cos. II*') for Valerius Messallinus, and a colleague for the *suffectus* in the next line, ']atus'. Now consuls with that ending of a *cognomen* are not common; and there is a pair attested, namely M. Arrecinus Clemens II with L. Baebius Honoratus (*CIL* xii 3637). This might seem too good to be true. Caution is requisite. One will bear in mind the rarity under the Flavians of *consules iterum* in the eponymate. There are only two cases in the reign of Domitian, Q. Petillius Rufus (82) and M. Cocceius Nerva (90): Petillius was connected with the dynasty, and the *nobilitas* of the Cocceii went back to the age of the Triumvirs. None the less, it is perhaps too soon to deny Aurelius Fulvus (especial services to the Flavians might be surmised) and proclaim Valerius Messallinus as Domitian's colleague in 85; and if, on this hypothesis (more it cannot be), the consular pattern of 85 appears abnormal (what Degrassi prints is in itself easy and unobjectionable), it will be recalled that some of the years 82–5 must have looked very peculiar, given the iterations to be fitted in.

The son of Fulvus became consul (*HA Pius* 1, 3), as *ordinarius* in 89, see various calendars (referred to in *PIR*², A 1509), confirmed by *ILS* 7864, 'Fulvo et Atratino': the *Fasti Potentini* now give the full nomenclature. He did not live for long thereafter, but predeceased his parent, as may be inferred from what is said of his son (born in 86): 'pueritiam egit cum avo paterno, mox cum materno' (*HA Pius* 1, 9). That boy adopted the nomenclature of his maternal grandparents, being styled 'T. Aurelius Fulvus Boionius Arrius Antoninus'—and is known to posterity as the
★ Emperor Antoninus Pius. The maternal grandfather, Arrius Antoninus, was consul in 69—and again consul (*HA Pius* 1, 4, cf. Pliny, *Ep.* iv 3, 1). The second consulate is a problem. Groag in *PIR*², A 1086, says 'fortasse imperante Nerva', citing the not firmly attested calendar date 'Sabinus et Antoninus', which Mommsen rejected (*Chron. Min.* i 255, cf. *Ges. Schr.* iv 381). Arrius, a cultivated fellow and a versifier, was a friend of the Emperor Nerva, and 97 was a propitious year for elderly survivals. It would hardly be an act of violence to remove him from Degrassi's list of 'consoli di età meno certa'. (On the other hand, T. Aurelius Fulvus may have been dead by now, and his public distinction authorizes an earlier
★ date for his second consulate: not but what it *could* have been 97.)

Under injunction from Hadrian, the third Aurelius Fulvus adopted as his son the grandson of M. Annius Verus (and nephew of his own wife). The first consulate of M. Annius Verus is now certified in 97 (cf. above), but some of his family connections remain obscure. No epigraphic docu-
★ ment has yet revealed the consulate of his wife's father, Rupilius Bonus, or, for that matter, even his name. Rupilius remains enigmatic—and invites conjecture. Between the Annii and Hadrian's family there existed a tie of kinship, according to Cassius Dio (lxix 21, 2). It cannot be ascertained. An attempt has recently been made by Carcopino in his seductive study 'L'hérédité dynastique chez les Antonins', *REA* lxxi (1949), 262 ff. He asks (not unreasonably) whether Trajan's niece Matidia may not have been married more than once—not only to L. Vibius Sabinus but to

Rupilius Bonus. If that were so, Vibia Sabina, Hadrian's wife, and Rupilia Faustina, who married M. Annius Verus, would be half-sisters (op. cit. 317). However, ages and generations might cause trouble here, | since Annius Verus (*suff*. 97) was probably only half-a-dozen years younger than Trajan (born in 53), whose grand-niece he is deemed to marry; and a link (not of blood, be it noted) that owed its existence to Vibia Sabina would not have counted much or well with Hadrian, who detested his wife.

Various other families should be kept in mind, notably the Dasumii from Corduba, represented by the man of the monstrous testament (*CIL* vi 10229), whose adopted son is manifestly P. Dasumius Rusticus, *ordinarius* with Hadrian in 119. The date of his consulate has not been recorded. However, he is clearly the L. Dasumius who was proconsul of Asia under Trajan (*CIG* 2876). There is a chance here for a close dating (Degrassi suggests 93 or 97). Coins of Thyatira show a man called Hadrianus 'proconsul' (*BMC, Greek Coins, Lydia* cxxii, referring to a coin in Munich, and to Waddington, *Fastes*, 179; Waddington listed three coins, but perhaps they boil down to only one; however, since the coin at Munich was verified by R. Heberdey, *JŒAI* viii (1905), 232, it does not matter, and the doubts expressed in *PIR*[1], H 2a can be dispelled). Groag suggests that Hadrianus and L. Dasumius may be identical (*PIR*[2], D 14, cf. *Addenda*, p. 14). This conjecture is duly noted by Degrassi—and is highly attractive. Were it accepted, one might go further. With L. Dasumius Hadrianus as consul suffect in 93, a proconsulate of Asia in 106–7 would fill a gap and will enable one to construct the series from 103/4 (a firm date, that of C. Aquillius Proculus, suffect in 90) to 112/3 (almost certainly the year of Cornelius Tacitus, suffect in 97).

Dasumius the testator was a friend of L. Julius Ursus Servianus (*cos. II ord.* 102, *III ord.* 134), who is to superintend the funeral (*CIL* vi 10229, l. 110). The first consulate of this great personage (married to a daughter of Trajan's cousin, namely Domitia Paulina the sister of Hadrian) is a problem. Degrassi suggests that he was consul either before 87 or in 93. It is impossible to discuss briefly the difficulties about the persons called Julius Ursus—one can only mention L. Julius Ursus, suffect in 98 (*FO* xiv), whom Groag assumed to be a *cos. II* (*RE*, Supp. vii, col. 1624), which is attractive. Hadrian's brother-in-law bears, from his second consulate onwards (102), the nomenclature 'L. Julius Ursus Servianus'. May he not originally have been Ser. Julius Servianus? That is the name of a *suffectus* of 90. The age of the man would fit. When compelled to end his life by Hadrian in 136 or 137 Servianus was in his ninetieth year (*HA Hadr.* 15, 7; Dio lxix 17, 1).

Several other members of this group may be briefly indicated, on the score of consulates. As has been shown above, P. Julius Lupus, the stepfather of the boy who was to become the Emperor Antoninus Pius, might be put at the end of 97 or of 98. L. Vibius Sabinus, the husband of Trajan's niece Matidia, is variously problematical. Though his full nomenclature was divined long ago by Borghesi, he was not admitted to *PIR*. He might be the senator '|bio C.f./[S]abino' of a fragmentary inscription at Asisium (*CIL* xi 8020), who is a *septemvir epulonum*, as is also a nameless consul on another fragment from the same city (ibid. 5383). The consulate of L. Vibius Sabinus, it is true, stands nowhere unequivocally attested—though there is the pair 'Sabinus et Antoninus' of certain late imperial calendars, which suits 97 very well (cf. *PIR*[2], A 1086), the colleague then being Arrius Antoninus (consul for the second time, surely in 97). However, if Matidia's husband lived long enough to reach the *fasces* in 97, he cannot have survived for many months: compare what Hadrian said about that lady in the funeral oration (*CIL* xiv 3579). On Mommsen's supplement, it can be taken to imply that she joined Trajan's household in or soon after 98—'[venit ad avunculum brevi post adeptum pri]ncipatum, ac deinceps', etc.

P. Calvisius Tullus (*ord.* 109) is an important member of the group, husband of Domitia Cn. f. Lucilla (the daughter of Cn. Domitius Tullus) and father of Domitia P. f. Lucilla (the mother of Marcus). The *Historia Augusta* credits him with a second consulate (*Marcus* 1, 3), not yet established, and not in itself to be impugned: it could fall in 120 or 121, if he was still alive. None the less, it is strange that Calvisius Tullus was not an *ordinarius*. A fresh possibility is opened by the *Fasti Ostienses* of 98 (*FO* xiv): if the 'Cn. Domitius[' there disclosed is in fact Cn. Domitius Tullus for the second time (and members of this group were then very influential indeed), it might be that the maternal ancestor of Marcus designated by the *HA* as twice consul ought to be, not the maternal grandfather, but the great-grandfather. The passage (*Marcus* 1, 3) already contains one error of fact or spelling, viz. 'Domitia Calvilla' for 'Domitia Lucilla'. It might be defective in other ways. Suppose a *homoeoteleuton* to have caused some words to fall out: a conjecture could, by supplying the second consulate of Domitius Tullus, abolish that of Calvisius Tullus. One could then read 'mater Domitia Lucilla Calvisii Tulli ⟨filia, avia materna Lucilla Domiti Tulli⟩ bis consulis filia'. There would be an additional advantage in this— it would allow the *HA* to supply the 'avia materna' of Marcus, for it goes on to name the 'avia paterna', that is, Rupilia Faustina, daughter of Rupilius Bonus. Let it be recalled, however, that this is a conjecture sup-

* porting a conjecture.

Something, but not very much, can be said about L. Pedanius Fuscus Salinator, consul *c.* 84, his proconsulate of Asia falling fairly early in the reign of Trajan (*ILS* 8822 and coins cited in *RE* xvii, coll. 20 f.). His son married Julia, daughter of Servianus, about the year 107 (Pliny, *Ep.* vi

26, 1), | became the *ordinarius* of 118—and is otherwise a name and a cipher. That is all there is to be known about the next in the succession to Hadrian when Hadrian came to the power. Named by Pliny as a young man of promise, a peer of Pedanius, is a certain Ummidius Quadratus (*Ep.* vi 11, 1). He was *suffectus* in 118, and subsequently incurred the dislike of Hadrian (*HA Hadr.* 15, 7). If the Ummidii were not already linked in some way to the dynasty, they soon became closely attached, for the son of this man made a splendid marriage in 136 or 137, acquiring for bride Annia Cornificia, sister of Marcus Aurelius (*HA Marcus* 4, 7; 7, 4)—and no doubt an early consulate, not long after the accession of Antoninus Pius. An Ummidius Quadratus, legate of Moesia Inferior, is revealed by the inscription of a *beneficiarius* at the fort of Charax, near Yalta (*AA* 1911, 236, cf. A. Stein, *Die Legaten von Moesien* (1940), 70). Degrassi, following Stein, suggests 'prima del 155'. Why not *c.* 140? Persons of the social élite in the new imperial aristocracy come young to the consulship, even without a dynastic attachment; take for example the Sosius Priscus *ordinarius* in 149, having been born in 117 (*ILS* 1106). The son of this Ummidius is the *ordinarius* of 167.

V. Not only are many dates in doubt, of great persons as of small, in the period here under review. There are consulates that may never have occurred. Not everybody will feel happy about Peregrinus ('81 c. o poco dopo') proconsul of Asia when St Timothy suffered martyrdom at Ephesus on 22 January A.D. 97—as is stated in a hagiographical source from the second half of the fourth century (*Acta S. Timothei*, ed. H. Usener, Prog. Bonn (1877), 13). One objection, it is true, could be dispelled. The proconsul of Asia in 96/7 (summer to summer) listed by Degrassi and by Groag (*PIR*[2], C 436) is Carminius Vetus, on the basis of *AE* 1899, 71. This man can (and perhaps should) be transferred to 97/8.

Several iterated consulates of the second century, culled from the literary evidence, need to be carefully scrutinized. They must be suffect consulates, if authentic; yet none such have yet been certified by inscriptions subsequent to 103 under Trajan, Hadrian, Pius, Marcus, or Commodus. Accident can of course be invoked. For example, it would be presumptuous to deny that P. Calvisius Tullus (*ord.* 109) could have held the *fasces* a second time: the *Historia Augusta* gives him a second consulate (*Marcus* 1, 3; cf., however, above). Other details in later and inferior sections of that compilation can be justly suspected—hopeless confusion or sheer invention. The jurist P. Salvius Julianus (*ord.* 148) was certainly related to the Emperor Didius Julianus (born in 133 and consul suffect in 175): cf. *PIR*[2], D 77. The *HA* produces an absurdity (and perhaps two errors)—'proavus fuit Salvius Iulianus, bis consul, praefectus urbi' (*Didius Iulianus* 1, 1). Degrassi omits this second consulate of the jurist (perhaps

rightly), though the thing is not impossible. Likewise a certain Septimius Severus. The *HA* registers two consular relatives of the future emperor, Aper and Severus (*Severus* 1, 2), presumably paternal uncles. The former will be P. Septimius Aper, suffect in 153. The latter remains enigmatic, despite recent information about the family accruing from Lepcis. He appears to be the same as the Septimius Severus 'bis iam consularis' (*Severus* 1, 5) who secured from Marcus the *latus clavus* for his young kinsman (born in 146), and is duly attached to the stemma of the family in *IRT*, p. 19. None of the more radical critics of the *HA* seem to impugn him; he stands unassailed in *PIR* as in *RE*; and there is no reason why a Septimius Severus should not lurk among the numerous unidentified Severi on the *Fasti*, e.g. one in 155 and one in 160, also '[Ve]rus' or
★ '[Seve]rus' in 154. However that be, a second consulate by the early years of Marcus ought to have aroused disquiet. There are no iterations under Pius after 146, and only three under Marcus before 173—all three for members of well-established senatorial families. Who was this knight's son from Lepcis that he should deserve so signal an honour? It would be premature in this place to go further and question his existence, yet it will be noted that dubious characters can occur in this *Vita*, namely Aetius and Probus, allegedly sons-in-law of the Emperor (*Severus* 8, 1 f.), about whom Mommsen, though conservative in his approach to the *HA*, could not feel quite happy (*Ges. Schriften* vii 346). Bersanetti, in his recent article on the Severan family circle, seemed amiably disposed towards these creatures (*Athenaeum* xxiv (1946), 37). He said nothing about the 'bis iam consularis'.

So far the *HA*. Philostratus (*Vit. Soph.* ii 1, 1) and Suidas assert that the parent of Herodes Atticus was twice consul. Herodes himself was *ordinarius* in 143, but, although he lived till about 176, was probably not consul again (cf. Groag in *PIR²*, C 802, discussing *Vit. Soph.* ii 1, 8). One ought not to suppress a doubt about his father's second consulate. It is accepted by Stein, *PIR²*, C 801. Degrassi (p. 117) refers to two inscriptions (*IG* vii 88; *SIG³*, 859 A), which, however, throw no light on the point.

Next, certain identities that can be called into question, or possible doublets. The consular orator and poet Silius Italicus had two sons. The elder became consul, the younger was confidently expected to accede to the *fasces* soon after, but died (Martial viii 66, cf. ix 86; Pliny, *Ep.* iii 7, 2). Degrassi prints a Silius Italicus, consul *c.* 93. Perhaps a supererogation. L. Silius Decianus might | be the man, *suffectus* in September 94. Again, as argued above, the first consulate of the illustrious L. Julius Ursus Servianus is probably represented by Ser. Julius Servianus, consul suffect in 90. A Valerius Paulinus is mentioned during the prosecution of Julius Bassus in 103 or 104 (Pliny, *Ep.* iv 9, 20 f.): it is not necessary to assume him different from Pliny's friend C. Valerius Paulinus, consul suffect in 107. Sallustius Lucullus, the mysterious legate of Britain (Suetonius, *Dom.* 10, 3), might be the same person as P. Sallustius Blaesus (*suff.* 89), assuming him polyonymous, but one cannot tell.

Two consuls of manifest importance are alluded to by Fronto (p. 217 N = Haines ii 20): 'Traiani proavi vestri ductu auspicioque nonne in Dacia captus vir consularis? nonne a Parthis consularis aeque vir in Mesopotamia trucidatus?' The former is often identified with the hero of a narration in Dio (lxviii 12): Λογγῖνον δέ τινα στρατοπέδου ʽΡωμαϊκοῦ ἐξηγούμενον. If this Longinus is in fact a consular, in command of an army (and not a legionary legate), there is a faint chance that he was Cn. Pompeius Longinus (*suff.* 90), legate of Moesia Superior in 93, of Pannonia in 98 (*CIL* xvi 39; 42). The second is certified by Dio (lxviii 30, 2) as Maximus. E. Hauler, deciphering another passage in Fronto (p. 209 N = Haines ii 214), recovered his name as 'Appius Santra' (*WS* xxxviii (1916), 166 f.). Hence we have the consul Appius Maximus Santra, *PIR*[2], A 950; Degrassi, p. 112. It should be recalled that Hauler reported 'ziemlich schattenhafte Buchstaben', and gave his reading as 'Appius Santra'. Now a Lappius Maximus is possible: he could be a son of A. Lappius Maximus (*suff.* 86, legate of Germania Inferior in January 89). At the same time, there is a person highly eligible, T. Julius Maximus (*suff.* 112), as was suggested by the reviewer when discussing his *cursus* (*ILS* 1016: Nemausus) in *Laureae Aquincenses* i (1938), 218 ff. A recently discovered diploma gives him an additional military post, showing him legate of Pannonia Inferior in July 110 (*AErt* lxxviii (1951), 78; *AArchHung* i (1951), 192 f.). This, by the way, dispels the possibility that Julius Maximus might have gone straight from a legionary command to the consulate, as did D. Terentius Gentianus (*ILS* 1046: Sarmizegethusa).

The eloquent Fronto had an eloquent friend called Postumius Festus. The 'traditional' date of his consulate is *c.* 143. That need not worry one unduly, and when a ']mius Festus' emerges as *suffectus* in 160, it is tempting to identify them—the more so because Fronto's friend was great-grandfather of a man who was *praefectus urbi* in 271. Very tempting. Yet Degrassi could be defended for keeping them apart. Postumius Festus is mentioned along with two other senators in a letter of Fronto that ought to belong a year or two earlier than 160 (p. 200 N = Haines i 295). On the order of the names, it could be argued that Festus is junior to Servilius Silanus (*suff.* 152): yet, on the other hand, fragmentary phrases towards the end of the letter seem to imply that all three men are of consular rank.

So far the dubious consulates or suspected doublets. They should stay on sufferance until certainty comes, otherwise there is a risk of destroying evidence. Several entries, however, must be expunged. Thus a Publicius (or Publilius) Tullus, consul in the period 93–100, proconsul of Asia between 103 and 114 (p. 28): this is in reality L. Baebius Tullus, *suffectus* in 95, proconsul of Asia presumably in 110/1 (see *PIR²*, B 29). Similarly, M. Junius, governor of Cappadocia in 114 (Dio lxviii 19, 1), cannot stand as a consul of unattested date. He must be M. Junius Homullus (*suff.* 102), for coins reveal a Homullus legate in the sixteenth year of Trajan (E. A. Sydenham, *The Coinage of Caesarea in Cappadocia* (1933), 73).

   Again, Degrassi has a consular pair, 'Lucius' with 'Se[', assigned to the early years of Domitian (p. 128, with citation of *NSA* 1891, 167). These men are L. Junius Caesennius Paetus and P. Calvisius Ruso Julius Frontinus, the year is 79, and the inscription is the same as *OGIS* 594 = *IGR* i 420 = *AE* 1950, 31 B (from Puteoli). Another pair, 'Praesens et Torquatus' (p. 134) will also have to go. The inscription cited in support (*CIL* vii 422: Piercebridge) registers the *ordinarii* of 217, as Haverfield showed with an improved reading (*Eph. Ep.* ix 1131). Some scholars have recently been tempted to allocate this phantom pair to the year 124, there discovering the consulate of C. Bruttius Praesens (cf. for example the notes on the inscription from Mactar, *AE* 1950, 66). That was not helpful: Bruttius, the friend of Hadrian and legate of Cilicia when Trajan died there, must have been speedily promoted by the new emperor, whose position was precarious, acceding to the consulate in 118, or in 119 at the
★ latest (Degrassi has '*c.* 121'). Finally, A. Larcius (p. 46), stated to be governor of Syria in 162 on the basis of *CIL* iii 6715: the later reading (ibid. 14177) produced a different person as legate, namely P. Julius Geminius Marcianus (of Arabia, not Syria). The Larcius who in fact governed Syria came there in a season of emergency (97 or 97/8), an ex-quaestor bearing the title 'legatus Augusti leg. III Scythicae, pro legato
★ consulare provinc. Syriae' (*AE* 1908, 237, cf. *ILS* 1055).

   VI. Impugning or even expelling some consuls, can one evoke other
★ names to compensate? By mischance Aufidius Umber has slipped out, consular legate of Cappadocia in 101/2 (*PIR²*, | A 1395). There is also a Secundus, governor of that province in the fourteenth year of Trajan (i.e. 111), whom a coin in the British Museum certifies; cf. E. A. Syden-
★ ham, *The Coinage of Caesarea in Cappadocia* (1933), 73. A sad fate dogs this man—Sydenham omitted him from the prefatory remarks where legates are discussed (ibid. 12 f.), and he has no place in Magie's list (*Roman Rule in Asia Minor* ii (1950), 1597). Secundus is clearly the predecessor of M. Junius Homullus (attested in 113 and in 114). As for his identity, observe the Trajanic proconsul of Asia, Secundus, whom a coin of Attaea in Mysia discloses, apparently unique (Mionnet, *Recueil* iv 240, n. 275). This proconsul could be Q. Vibius Secundus (*suff.* 86). Perhaps, but not necessarily the same person as the governor of Cappadocia. Mere age would not be a bar: P. Calvisius Ruso, consul in 79, is attested for Cappa-

docia precisely in 106/7 (*PIR²*, C 350), and Cn. Pedanius Fuscus Salinator, consul *c.* 84, held some military province or other round about 109 (Pliny, *Ep.* x 87, 3).

More important, there is one more L. Neratius Priscus than Degrassi allows for. The *Fasti Potentini* recently showed one person of that name consul in 87. Before then a certain perplexity existed, enhanced by A. Berger's treatment (*RE* xvi, col. 2549), and there could still be confusion and error, as in the remarks of A. Garzetti, *Nerva* (1950), 146 f. The unpublished fragment of the *Fasti Ostienses* cited in Degrassi's *Addenda* (p. 288) brings clarity. Fixing the consulate of M. Annius Verus to 97, it enables a Neratius Priscus to be supplied as his colleague, for this consular pair gave their names to a *senatus consultum* that penalized castration (*Dig.* xlviii 8, 6). That measure was not Domitian's—he proceeded authoritatively by edict (Martial ii 60; vi 12; Statius, *Silvae* iv 3, 13). It belongs clearly to Nerva's reign (Dio lxviii 2, 4). The consul of 97 can now be identified as the famous jurist, the brother of L. Neratius Marcellus (*suff.* 95). He was governor of Pannonia (*ILS* 1033, cf. 1034): presumably in 102–5, succeeding Glitius Agricola (*suff.* 97), to be followed by (Metilius) Nepos (compare what Pliny says to that person, *Ep.* iv 26, 2, with E. Groag, *RE* xv, col. 1401). However, even without the recent epigraphic discoveries that concern consuls in 87 and in 97, a plain fact was available— a younger Neratius Priscus, governor of Pannonia Inferior (as praetorian legate), and later of Pannonia Superior, hence consul, it will be presumed, early in the reign of Hadrian. He is named along with his parent on *ILS* 1034—and, for convenience of record, let it be noted that he was *septemvir epulonum.*

Another consul who must be added is a Pollio, to impinge upon the vicissitudes of the sophist Aelius Aristides in the early fifties as proconsul of Asia (*Or.* l 94 and 96). That Pollio was generally identified as T. Pomponius Proculus Vitrasius Pollio, who married a cousin of the Emperor Marcus and was *cos. II ord.* in 176: see, for example, W. Hüttl, *Antoninus Pius* ii (1933), 50. Since, however, a dated inscription puts his governorship of Moesia Inferior in 157 (*AE* 1937, 247), his first consulate should fall in the period 150–5, cf. A. Stein, *Die Legaten von Moesien* (1940), 73. Stein drew the moral and indicated the existence of an earlier Vitrasius Pollio. He can in fact be nailed down fairly precisely. First, he was legate of VII Gemina at a time when a Junius Homullus was governor of Tarraconensis (*ILS* 2404, cf. *CIL* ii 3415); and this Homullus, whether or no the military tribune serving under his father in Cappadocia in 114 (Dio lxviii 19, 2), could have been consul *c.* 130. Secondly, a Vitrasius Pollio when legate of Lugdunensis received a rescript from Hadrian (*Dig.* xxvii i 15, 77). His consulate ensuing from that post could therefore be put about 137, with a proconsulate in Asia about fifteen years later to fit the

Pollio of Aelius Aristides. Not that there is certitude—there could have
been an earlier Fufidius Pollio, the unattested parent of the *ordinarius* of
166. The chronology of Aelius Aristides still proves vexatious, despite the
★ detailed investigation of Hüttl (*Antoninus Pius* ii (1933), 33 ff.) Three
proconsuls Pollio, Severus, and Quadratus follow in that order of time,
but it cannot quite be taken for certain that they occupy three successive
years. Severus, though that *cognomen* is so common, is patently the famous
C. Julius Severus from Ancyra, of royal stock (*ILS* 8826; *OGIS* 544, etc.),
consul probably in 138. For the third man, the standard identification is
L. Statius Quadratus (*ord.* 142), who superintended the martyrdom of the
★ octogenarian Polycarp, and it can hold, in spite of a new (but exiguous)
possibility, Ummidius Quadratus, husband of Annia Cornificia and
consul *c.* 140 (cf. above, p. 247). These problems all deserve looking into
again—and the only new evidence is what can be established about the
sequence of proconsuls.

So far, three unattested consuls emerge in the period—Aufidius Umber,
a Lucius Neratius Priscus, and a Pollio: Secundus may be identical with a
known consul. One will add Marcellus the proconsul of Africa (*ILAfr*
591: Aunobaris), presumably of the time of Hadrian or Pius; cf. Groag
in *RE* xiv, col. 1490, who suggests C. Publicius Marcellus (*suff.* 120) or
★ Q. Pomponius Marcellus (*suff.* 121). The same inscription refers to
'Cornuti decretum, clarissimi viri', and Groag on second thoughts was
inclined to regard this Cornutus as a proconsul (earlier than Marcellus),
not a proconsul's legate (*PIR²*, C 1508). A supplement to this problem
now comes from Lepcis, 'ex decr. Marcelli procos.' (*IRT* 304). It would
be premature to regard this Marcellus as a known consul—or to ask
whether Cornutus might not be Pliny's friend, consul in 100 and proconsul
★ of Africa, or of Asia | (*ILS* 1024). Then there is a Septimius Severus
(*HA Severus* 1, 2, and 5), who may well have been consul, though not
consul twice (discussed above). And the chances of certain authentic
characters will have to be kept in mind. To take one example. There is
the provincial governor Julius Candidus to whom Antoninus Pius sent a
rescript (*Dig.* xlviii 2, 7, 3), if he be the same person as the praetorian
proconsul of Achaia under Hadrian *c.* 136 (*IG* vii 70).

There is no point in multiplying conjectures, and one should be content
if they are few and modest in a standard work of reference. None the less,
an inspection of obscurities concerning persons called Vibius will disclose
at least one of the hidden consuls. Degrassi published a small fragment
(*FO* xxxi, *Inscr. It.* xiii 1, 208). It contains the name 'Vibius'. According
to Degrassi, a municipal magistrate at Ostia. Yet it could (or perhaps
should) be a consul of the last *nundinum* of the year, for the next lines
belong to the short annual chronicle of events, which normally follows
the list of consuls. The notice is truncated, but not hopeless:

K · NOV · NOC[TV
K ·]IAN · VMM[IDIVS
CONSVLAT

Degrassi plausibly assumes the notice to refer to a *suffectus*, an Ummidius, who resigned office in the second half of December. Better perhaps one who died 'in consulatu'. However, the point is irrelevant. What is the date? 'Litterarum formae ad Flaviorum aetatem ducere videntur' (*Inscr. It.* xiii 1, 239). That being so, one might be tempted to suggest the year 93 (and it was not a healthy year). Another Ummidius Quadratus is anyhow most welcome, as parent of C. Ummidius Quadratus (*suff.* 118). But, if the above suggestion is conceded, there is also a consul Vibius now to be reckoned with. Perhaps a Vibius Varus, in the ancestry of the *ordinarius* of 134 (who was clearly a person of some note, colleague of 'Servianus tertio'). There is a case for such a person quite apart from *FO* xxxi. The diploma fragment from Stockstadt on the Main (*CIL* xiii 11796a) was unfortunately omitted from *CIL* xvi; E. Birley drew attention to it, in his review of that volume (*JRS* xxviii (1938), 225), reading the consul's name as 'V]ibio Va[ro' instead of ']abio Va[lente]'. Now this consul belongs to a November; he cannot be identical with the *ordinarius* of 134; and the editor in *CIL* xiii observes that the diploma is 'fortasse aetatis Domitiani, vix recentior prioribus annis Traiani'. The diploma and *FO* xxxi might belong to the same year. Not necessarily, however. And, without these two documents, there was still a Vibius to be watched, L. Vibius Sabinus, the husband of Trajan's niece Matidia and father of Vibia Sabina (cf. above, p. 246). To sum up, therefore, these hazards and complications about Vibii: if hesitations subsist about L. Vibius Sabinus, at the very least a Vibius Varus ought to be conceded.

Degrassi admits a number of fragmentary names to his list of 'consoli di età meno certa', such as ']anus Lon[', governor of Britain on the diploma dated by that elusive pair of consuls whose *cognomina* are Severus and Flavus (*CIL* xvi 130). Two or three more could go in, though there is often the risk that they are identical with known consuls. To the Flavian period belongs [C]aesidius (*PIR*², C 184), or possibly [P]aesidius, whose fragmentary inscription at Carthage bears the word 'cos.', or perhaps '[pro]cos.' (*CIL* viii 12539). A governor of Dacia and consul is honoured by a dedication at Sarmizegethusa (*CIL* iii 1465). The stone is split vertically, and the right-hand half surviving shows that the man's name ended in '-dius', his *cognomen* in '-o'. Speculation might seem pointless about his identity, so Stein, *Die Reichsbeamten von Dazien* (1944), 27. None the less, this person must be kept on the books. Possibly a known consul, and if so surely P. Orfidius Senecio (*suff.* 148). That name suits the spacing—and there is room for a new legate of Dacia in the triennium

145-8. But it might have been an unknown Fufidius Pollio, or even perhaps Claudius Pollio, the new Arval Brother recently revealed (*AE* 1947,
59). Next, a truncated *curator operum publicorum* called ']us C.f. Papiria
Sabinus', in function (so it appears) on 12 September 152 (*AE* 1917/18,
111). Degrassi omits him—no doubt because he tacitly identifies him
with L. Petronius Sabinus (*suff.* 145). Various reasons would here counsel
a suspension of judgement. Finally, a new consular pair ']mus' and
'C. La[', holding office in May: see the fragment from the *Acta Fratrum
Arvalium* published and discussed by A. Ferrua in *Epigraphica* vii (1945),
27 ff., whence *AE* 1947, 59. This piece, which contains the names of
nine Brethren, is assigned by Ferrua to the period 120-40. Careful comparison with the lists of 145 and 155 (*CIL* vi 2084, 2086) might support
the belief that it belongs *c.* 150. As for the consular pair, nothing can be
done with the one, a Maximus, Postumus, or Primus. The other could be
an *ignotus*—yet he might be C. Etrilius Regillus Laberius Priscus, legate of
Cilicia and consul under Pius (*ILS* 8827). One can note for help and
guidance that 146-8 are complete, and there is no place for any such pair
in the period 152-5. |

The familiar literary evidence might have something to offer. Valerius
Marinus is registered under 69 among the *designati* who never held office.
That is not so sure. Observe the language of Tacitus (*Hist.* ii 71): 'et
Valerium Marinum destinatum a Galba consulem distulit, nulla offensa,
sed mitem et iniuriam segniter laturum.' Marinus was only postponed.
Another man was dropped—'Pedanius Costa omittitur, ingratus principi
ut adversus Neronem ausus et Verginii exstimulator'. He has also failed
to achieve an entry in Pauly–Wissowa. Next, from Suetonius' catalogue
of the victims of Domitian. The list opens with the words 'complures
senatores, in iis aliquot consulares, interemit: ex quibus Civicam Cerealem
in ipso Asiae proconsulatu', etc. (*Dom.* 10). There are ten names. Nine are
certainly of consular rank. The one remaining, Salvius Cocceianus, should
not be excluded, Otho's nephew and related (it may be presumed) to a
man whom the Flavian emperors liked and honoured, M. Cocceius Nerva.
A mark of interrogation beside the name of Salvius Cocceianus would
save the proprieties.

By paradox, it stands nowhere on record that one of the most eminent
senators of that age ever held the *fasces*, M. Aquillius Regulus. A strong
hint may be discovered in Tacitus, who suitably introduces invective and
a prophecy early in the year 70—'retinete, patres conscripti, et reservate
hominem tam expediti consilii ut omnis aetas instructa sit, et quo modo
senes nostri Marcellum, Crispum, iuvenes Regulum imitentur. invenit
aemulos etiam infelix nequitia: quid si floreat vigeatque? et quem adhuc
quaestorium offendere non audemus, praetorium et consularem ausuri
sumus?' (*Hist.* iv 42). Regulus possessed an oratorical gift that amounted

to genius, with great wealth and influence. As Pliny observes (*Ep.* i 5, 15), 'est enim locuples, factiosus, curatur a multis, timetur a pluribus.' How could they have kept him out?

APPENDIX

These additional notes are intended to correct and supplement items treated in the original review. They do not attempt to provide all new consuls of the period 70–161. [The reader should now consult the numerous and well-informed entries by Werner Eck in *RE*, Suppl. xiv (1974).]

The consular list for 84. More consuls should be assigned to the period 82–5 than Degrassi allowed for. W. Eck suggests at least nine (*Senatoren von Vespasian bis Hadrian* (1970), 60).

¹ This fragment was not the right side of a block, as assumed by Degrassi, but the left. See the publication by G. Barbieri, *Studi romani* i (1953), 367, Pl. 1, whence *AE* 1954, 220. Further, R. Syme, *JRS* xliv (1954), 81 f. where the 'Se[', colleague of Atilius Agricola, is identified as Sex. Hermetidius Campanus.

² A second consulship for Cn. Domitius Tullus in 98. See below, on P. Calvisius Tullus and, more explicit, *Tacitus* (1958), 793.

³ For the problem of Sura's consulate, *Tacitus*, 35, 73, 641 (with a preference for the year 97). It is still not possible to make a decision between 93 and 97. The problem is complicated by the acephalous inscription *ILS* 1022, generally assigned to this man. C. P. Jones argues for Sosius Senecio (*cos.* 99, *cos. II* 107), in *JRS* lx (1970), 98 ff. See, however and further, the long note by Eck (op. cit. 144). As Eck points out, it is not safe any longer to adduce *AE* 1923, 33 as evidence for a governorship of Germania Inferior by Sura *c.* 98–100.
There is now much more to be said about the consuls of 97. The Ostian fragment *AE* 1954, 222, which Barbieri wished to assign to 100, was discussed, along with other pieces recent or unpublished, by F. Zevi at the Epigraphic Congress at Munich in September 1972 (see further next note): he has courteously permitted his manuscript to be used in the annotation to this paper. The fragment shows an ']ius Piso' as *suffectus* below a *cos. III*. That will fit the year 97. Therefore Piso was the colleague of Arrius Antoninus (*cos. II suff.* in this year, cf. above, p. 244). That entails, so he argues, the expulsion of L. Vibius Sabinus, the colleague previously conjectured (see below, note on p. 253).
On Zevi's reconstruction, the year 97 had five pairs of *suffecti*. Licinius Sura, he suggests, took office with Atilius Agricola on 1 Sept., with the last two months left for Cornelius Tacitus and M. Ostorius Scapula. On this showing it was as consul, and not as legate of Belgica (praetorian, after Glitius Agricola) or as legate of Germania Inferior, that Sura was signally active in the elevation of Trajan (cf. *Epit. de Caes.* 13, 6). [Cf. also Zevi in *LF* xcvi (1973), 125 ff.]

⁴ The *Fasti Ostienses*. See now the careful edition of L. Vidman, in the publications of the Czechoslovak Academy (*Rozpravy Československé Akademie Věd*) lxvii 6 (1957). For the Flavio-Trajanic period the most important accessions since Degrassi's book are as follows:

A. E. Equini, *Epigraphica* xxix (1967), 2. As consul for the second time on 15 March, 74, is disclosed L. Junius Vibius Crispus. See further below, n. 1 on p. 243.
B. The four fragments published by Barbieri, *Studi romani* i (1953) (= *AE* 1954, 220 ff.), 365 ff., viz., (*a*) *AE* (cit.) 220, of 97 (discussed in the last note); (*b*) 221, belonging to the end of 98 and proving the existence of a consular pair for November–December; (*c*) 222, assigned by him to 100: rather 97; cf. last note; (*d*) 223, the *suffecti* of 103.
C. Three unpublished fragments reported by F. Zevi in Sept. 1972 (see last note).

(a) 'Frugi', a *suffectus* of 88 whom the *Fasti Potentini* omitted. That is, Libo Rupilius Frugi (on whom cf. below, n. 3 on p. 244).

(b) A piece from the right-hand column of a year, giving the terminal letters of five *suffecti*, viz.

]ICVS
]CVS
]NVS
]LVS
]LIS (or possibly]RIS)

Assigned by Zevi to 93 for a good reason: the figures at the bottom; LX]XV, indicate the sum of Domitian's *congiarium* after the campaign of 92.

(c) A considerable fragment of the year 100, beginning with '] Iulius Ur[sus' (a line to himself), and ending with the two known pairs covering the last four months of the year. After Ursus, patently *cos. III* (for he had a second consulate in 98 (cf. *Tacitus*, 636; 642)), the next line shows ']cius Macer' and 'C. Cilnius Proculus' both new, and the latter item is important because of occupations hitherto assigned to his elder homonym, *suffectus* in 87. The other novelty is in the third line, L. Fabius Tuscus as the colleague of Acutius Nerva, i.e. on 1 July. (He is perhaps from Baetica: cf. *CIL* ii 1537, a magistrate of that name at Ulia.)

At this point it may be convenient to register Flavio-Trajanic consuls accruing from other documents:

(1) The new Moesian diploma from Gradac shows L. Pasidienus Firmus as colleague of Domitian (his third consulship) on 28 April, 75. See M. Mirković, *Epigraphische Studien* v (1968), 177 (= *AE* 1968, 446); S. Dušanić, *Epigraphica* xxx (1968), 59 ff. (= *AE* 1968, 7).

(2) *AE* 1969, 6 (Pflaum) reveals the pair C. Fisius Sabinus and M. Annius Messalla. Early Domitianic. For the latter person cf. *IRT* 516.

(3) 'Pollio f.' and his colleague in 85. See next note.

(4) L. Caesennius Sospes in 114. See n. 4 on p. 236.

p. 236   1 The colleague of 'Pollio f.' in 85. The consular pair is now disclosed as 'P. Herenio [*sic*] Pollione, M. Herenio Pollione f. çọṣ.' on an inscription published by S. Panciera in *RSA* iii (1973), 96.

2 The surprise for the year 100 is now a third consulate established for L. Julius Ursus succeeding Julius Frontinus (*cos. III*), Trajan's colleague (see above, n. 4 on p. 235). It had previously been conjectured by G. Barbieri (op. cit. 371 = *AE* 1954, 222). (Cf. *Tacitus* (1958), 636; 643.) The corollary of this new discovery is to expel T. Vestricius Spurinna (the previous and general assumption). According to Pliny, two senators (not named) received second consulships from Nerva, third consulships from Trajan (*Pan.* 60, 5; 61, 7).

3 Observe that the *suffecti* of 103 are now complete (G. Barbieri, op. cit. 573 = *AE* 1954, 223).

4 The years 114 and 115. For 114, the Thracian diploma in the Sofia Museum (still unpublished) discloses L. Caesennius Sospes as the missing *suffectus*, cf. *Hermes* lxxxv (1957), 493 [= pp. 351 f. below]. For the problems of 115, R. Syme, *Historia* xiv (1965), 347 ff. = *Danubian Papers* (1971), 230 ff.; *Historia* xviii (1969), 355 f. [= pp. 777 ff. below]; G. Barbieri, *MEFR* lxxxii (1970), 263 ff. The latter scholar reconfirms M. Pompeius Macrinus (Neos Theophanes), and argues that Q. Asinius Marcellus is not a *suffectus* but a deceased *praefectus urbi*, replaced in that function by Q. Baebius Macer (*suff.* 103). Furthermore, P. Valerius Priscus should not go in either year; see also remarks in *REA* lxvii (1965), 347 f. [= pp. 633 ff. below], where *IRT* 361 is emended. Instead, c. 120, with the African proconsulate about the year 135 (cf. now Eck, op. cit. 212).

5 The consulate of Julius Frontinus. Cf. *PIR*², I 322: '73 ut videtur'. As for M. Hirrius Fronto Neratius Pansa, see the inscription of his *cursus* published by M. Torelli, *JRS* lviii (1968), 170 ff. His consulate should go best in 76. If so, there may be reason to follow Degrassi and restore [SEX. IVLIVS FR]ON[TINVS] in the *F. fer. Lat.* for 74, cf. *FC*, p. 21. The old obstacle to this was that Frontinus was proconsul of Asia in 82/3 (still in *PIR*², I 322), i.e. too soon for a consul of 74. But the new inscriptions from Phrygian

Hierapolis have now revealed him proconsul in 86/7 (Eck, op. cit. 77–93) or 84/5 or 85/6 (thus C. P. Jones, reviewing Eck, *Gnomon* xlv (1973), 689 f.

¹ For identity problems concerning the Metilii, see *JRS* lviii (1968), 138 [= pp. 699 f. below]. A puzzling novelty there registered is a P. Metilius Nepos consul (*ordinarius*) for the second time in 128, revealed by two papyri from the 'Cave of the Letters' near En-Gedi (*IEJ* xii (1962), 259).

² For the province to which Metilius Nepos (identified with the consul suffect in 103) was appointed in 105 (Pliny, *Ep.* iv 26, 2), see *Gnomon* xxix (1957), 522 = *Danubian Papers* (1971), 185 f. He may have held some other consular province before Pannonia.

³ 'Q. Co[', suffect in 116. Eck (op. cit. 231) is in agreement, against G. Alföldy, *Fasti Hispanienses* (1969), 119.

⁴ L. Varius Ambibulus (*suff.* 132 or 133). This item serves to date the 'Propinquus', colleague of an 'Ambibulus' (*CIL* xv 127), and permits the new conjecture that 'Propinquus' belonged to the nomenclature of the important consular at Tarraco (*CIL* ii 6084): adopted by Eck, op. cit. 45.

⁵ The consulate of Cn. Julius Verus: *PIR²*, I 618 has 'potius ca. a. 151 quam a. 154'.

¹ For the cardinal role of the praetorian provinces, see *Tacitus* (1958), 648 f.; 655 f.; *Historia* xiv (1965), 342 ff. = *Danubian Papers* (1971), 225 ff.; Eck, op. cit. 2 ff.

² For consulates in absence, *JRS* xlviii (1958), 1 ff. [= pp. 378 ff. below].

This governor, L. Aninius Sextius Florentinus, is now attested for 127 by a papyrus, *IEJ* xii (1962), 259; cf. *Historia* xiv (1965), 355 f., n. 60 = *Danubian Papers* (1971), 239, n. 60.

¹ For the interval under Tiberius, *JRS* xlv (1955), 29 f. = *Ten Studies in Tacitus* (1970), 43 f.

² For the proconsuls of Asia and Africa, A.D. 69–96, Eck, op. cit. 83 f.; 89 (lists 234, 236). For Asia, 103/4 to 120/1, *Tacitus* (1958), 665—with an essential rectification: Cornutus Tertullus (*suff.* 100) was there registered as 'Asia *or* Africa'; he is expelled from Asia by the proconsulate of Q. Servaeus Innocens (*suff.* 101), now emerging on an inscription of Ephesus (*JŒAI* xliv (1959), Beiblatt 266). Cf. remarks in *REA* lxvii (1965), 343; *JRS* lviii (1968), 146 [= pp. 630 ff., 713 ff. below]. The early Hadrianic proconsuls of Asia are fixed as far as 126/7, for Q. Pompeius Falco (*suff.* 108) is attested for 123/4 (*AE* 1957, 17). For Africa under Hadrian, *REA* lxvii (1965), 342 ff. [= pp. 629 ff. below]. For Africa under Pius, ibid. lxi (1959), 310 ff. [= pp. 461 ff. below].

³ There may be an illustrious exception. The jurist P. Juventius Celsus (*suff.* ? 117, *cos. II* 129) was assigned to 130/1 in *Historia* xiv (1965), 349 f. = *Danubian Papers* (1971), 232 f. Chr. Habicht, however, has strong arguments for 129/30 (*Altertümer von Pergamon* viii 3 (1969), 56 ff.). Cf. below, n. 2 on p. 242.

¹ M. Ostorius Scapula. To go in 97, cf. *Tacitus* (1958), 641, 665. And 99 should be the year of Ti. Julius Ferox (ib. 665). Eck admits 100 as possible (op. cit. 183).

² The pair Bittius Proculus and Julius Lupus: to go in the last two months of 98, cf. *Tacitus* (1958), 642. *PIR²*, I 389 is inconclusive, however.

³ Julius Alexander in 108: accepted in *PIR²*, I 136.

¹ For the *suffecti* of 114, above, n. 4 on p. 236. In any event P. Valerius Priscus must be rejected.

² As for P. Juventius Celsus, the year 115 is excluded, for in 114 he took the place of T. Statilius Maximus Hadrianus as governor of Thrace, as the diploma attests, cf. *Hermes* lxxxv (1957), 493 [= below, pp. 351 ff.]. Therefore *suff.* ? 117. For his proconsulate of Asia, cf. above, n. 3 on p. 240.

³ The argument from T. Statilius Maximus (*cos.* 144). He was generally identified with the ']Maximus' of *ILS* 1092. But that consular might be Claudius Maximus: observe the arguments of J. Fitz, *AAntHung* xi (1963), 258 ff., reinforced by Syme, *Historia* xiv (1965), 352 f. = *Danubian Papers* (1971), 236 f. But observe T. Atilius Maximus, whose consulate may fall *c.* 142; cf. an argument later adduced: *Danubian Papers*, 190.

⁴ For this Marcius Turbo see further *JRS* liii (1962), 87 ff. [= pp. 541 ff. below].

⁵ See now *Tacitus* (1958), 603 f., 791 ff.

⁶ For M. Ulpius Traianus as suffect in 70, see J. Morris, *JRS* xliii (1953), 79 f.

⁷ T. Aurelius Fulvus as legate of Tarraconensis. He might have gone there in 70 as a

258   *Review of A. Degrassi*

praetorian and held the fasces in absence, cf. *JRS* xlviii (1958), 7 [= pp. 388 f. below];
HSCPh lxxiii (1969), 216 [= p. 755 below]. A date subsequent to his consulship is preferred by G. Alföldy, *Fasti Hispanienses* (1969), 19 ff.

p. 243   1 Rutilius Gallicus' second consulate is registered as ? 85 in *Tacitus* (1958), 643 (i.e. as
colleague of Valerius Messallinus). Similarly ? 83 for the third consulates of Vibius Crispus
and Fabricius Veiento: accepted by Eck, op. cit. 61. Vibius Crispus now emerges on the
Fasti Ostienses as L. Junius Vibius Crispus, *suff. II* on 15 March, 74; see above, n. 4 on p. 235,
A; and Eck (*ZPE* ix (1972), 259 ff.) has recently argued that *AE* 1952, 168 (Arelate)
shows M. Pompeius Silvanus (*suff.* 45) as *cos. d*[*esignat. III*] for ? 83, presumably deceased
before taking office.
    2 For Aurelius Fulvus as the *cos. II* of 85, see also H. Nesselhauf, *Gnomon* xxvi (1954),
270: accepted by Eck, op. cit. 57.

p. 244   1 For the nomenclatures used by the third Aurelius Fulvus, see *Emperors and Biography*
(1971), 78.
    2 This notion about the second consulship of Aurelius Fulvus may now be ruled out.
But nothing precludes Arrius Antoninus in 97, cf. above, n. 3 on p. 235.
    3 The consular 'Rupilius Bonus' was long an enigma: cf., for the facts and conjectures,
Tacitus (1958), 795. The convincing emendation 'Rupili ⟨Li⟩boni⟨s⟩' in *HA Pius* 1, 4 was
produced by A. R. Birley, *Historia* xv (1966), 249 ff. Libo Rupilius Frugi was consul suffect
in 88: see above, n. 4 on p. 235, C(*a*).

p. 245   1 L. Julius Ursus, to be admitted without doubt as *suff. II* in 98. Furthermore, *suff. III* in
100, cf. above, n. 4 on p. 235, C(*c*), and n. 2 on p. 236.
    2 The identity of Ser. Julius Servianus (*suff.* 90) and the great *cos. ter.* L. Julius Ursus
Servianus is not to be doubted. Cf. *PIR*², I 569 = 631. He was son by adoption of L. Julius
Ursus (*suff. III* 100).

p. 246   This conjecture does not seem to have been impugned. On 'Rupilius Bonus', see
above, n. 3 on p. 244.

p. 247   1 For the history of the Ummidii, *Historia* xvii (1968), 72 ff. [= pp. 659 ff. below].
It can be argued that the *suffectus* of 118 is the legate of Moesia Inferior attested by the
inscription at Charax, in office *c*. 121–4 (ibid. 88 f. [= pp. 675 ff. below]; *Dacia* xii (1968),
335 = *Danubian Papers* (1971), 218). For the problem of his son's presumed consulship,
Historia xvii 98. The grandson is the *ordinarius* of 167.
    2 Carminius Vetus. Eck prefers 96/7 for his proconsulate of Asia (op. cit. 148). His
colleague as suffect in ?83 is almost certainly M. Co[rnelius Nigrinus], see *Dacia*, N.S. xii
(1968), 332 (= *Danubian Papers*, 214 f.). But an article by G. Alföldy and H. Halfmann,
Chiron iii (1973), 331 ff. invalidates the suggestion there put forward that M. Cornelius Nigrinus Curiatius Maternus is Hadrianic and identifies him with the Domitianic
consul.
    3 The sentence may be regarded as an addition made by the author of the *HA* to his
basic source. The jurist is to be presumed uncle of the emperor. For this family see T. D.
Barnes, *Bonner Historia-Augusta-Colloquium* 1968/9 (1970), 45–58.

p. 248   The necessary uncle has been disclosed as C. Septimius Severus: see the inscription
AE 1967, 536, and the *Tabula Banasitana, CRAI* 1971, 468 ff.; also J. H. Oliver, *AJP*
xciii (1972), 336 ff. For the Emperor's family and relations, A. R. Birley, *Septimius Severus*
(1971), 293 ff.

p. 249   1 This possibility would evaporate if P. Sallustius Blaesus were identical with 'Velleius
Blaesus, ille locuples consularis', whose decease is recorded by Pliny (*Ep.* ii 20, 7).
    2 On T. Julius Maximus see further *Historia* xiv (1965), 345 ff. = *Danubian Papers* (1971),
228 ff.

p. 250   1 Bruttius Praesens. For his consulate and the order of his provincial governorships
(Cappadocia, then Moesia Inferior), see *Historia* ix (1960), 374 f.; ibid. xviii (1969), 352 ff.
[= pp. 489 ff. below]; *Dacia* xii (1968), 335 = *Danubian Papers* (1971), 218 f.
    2 A. Larcius Priscus in Syria in 97/8: see *Tacitus* (1958), 631.

3 Aufidius Umber. An inscription from Pisidian Neapolis, now at Antioch, seen by G. W. Bowersock and C. P. Jones, adds the nomen 'Orfitasius'. (See C. P. Jones, *Gnomon* xlv (1973), 689.)

4 Secundus the governor of Cappadocia. Inspection of the coin (and of another in Paris) by T. B. Mitford reveals the date as 127/8; further, L. (?) Statorius Secundus as a governor on *IGR* iii 110. For these welcome discoveries see his paper in *Byzantion* xxxvi (1966), 474. Also Eck, op. cit. 200. Hence a new consul (? *c.* 123) and a new governor in the interval between Bruttius Praesens (? 121–4) and Flavius Arrianus (? 130–6). The *nomen* 'Statorius' is indistinctive but uncommon.

1 For the three Neratii Prisci, *Hermes* lxxxv (1957), 480 ff. [= pp. 339 ff. below]; *Historia* xiv (1965), 350 f. = *Danubian Papers* (1971), 233 f. Also the *addendum* to Ch. xii of that volume (p. 189), which adduces the new inscription from Saepinum proving that the third Neratius Priscus was a plebeian. However, Neratius Marcellus (*suff.* 95), his father's brother, was a patrician, having been adopted by M. Hirrius Fronto Neratius Pansa (*suff. c.* 75); cf. *Hermes* lxxxv (1957), 491 f. [= pp. 349 ff. below].

2 Junius Homullus, *suff. c.* 130: accepted in *PIR²*, I 759.

1 Proconsuls in Aelius Aristides: see (with caution) C. A. Behr, *Aelius Aristides and the Sacred Tales* (1968), 133 ff. Cf. G. W. Bowersock, *Greek Sophists in the Roman Empire* (1969), 36 f., 84 f. (Quadratus); *HSCP* lxxii (1967), 289 ff. (Albus); and cf. T. D. Barnes (see next note). On L. Antonius Albus, see now W. Eck, *Epigraphische Studien* ix (1972), 17 ff., developing the suggestion of J. H. Oliver and D. J. Geagan that he is the honorand of an acephalous inscription from Corinth (*AJA* lxxii (1968), 156 ff.). But that suggestion may be epigraphically doubtful.

2 For the date of the martyrdom of Polycarp see, however, T. D. Barnes, *JThS* xviii (1967), 433 ff.

3 Marcellus the proconsul of Africa. Clearly not Publicius Marcellus (*suff.* 120). Rather Q. Pomponius Marcellus (*suff.* 121), cf. *REA* lxvii (1965), 343 [= p. 630 below]; W. Eck, op. cit. 213.

4 Cornutus Tertullus was certainly proconsul of Africa; cf. above, n. 2 on p. 240.

FO xxxi and the consulate of an Ummidius (Quadratus) in 93. The thesis developed in this paragraph appeared coherent—and turns out to be highly vulnerable. That was briefly indicated by F. Zevi at the Epigraphic Congress: he published the full exposition in *DA* vii (1973), 52 ff. *FO* xxxi, he argues, belongs to 115, as do xxxv (which registers something about a Vestal Virgin and an earthquake) and also, on Barbieri's showing, xxiii (which reveals 'M. Pompeius Mac]rinu[s'): see now Barbieri, *MEFR* lxxxii (1970), 263ff.

Various consequences follow. The 'VM[' of *FO* xxxi is not a consul but a newly appointed Vestal Virgin, i.e. a young daughter of C. Ummidius Quadratus (*suff.* 118), whose marriage took place *c.* 106 (Pliny, *Ep.* vii 23, 3). The parents of this man, the grandson of old Ummidia Quadratilla, therefore remain an enigma.

Further, the 'Vibius' on the first line of the fragment. For various reasons 93 seemed too early for the Stockstadt Diploma (*CIL* xiii 11796a = xvi, *Suppl.* (1955), 172), which probably reveals a Vibius Varus as consul suffect. Let it therefore go in 115. As for L. Vibius Sabinus, conjectured *suffectus* in 97, observe Zevi's reason for expelling him in favour of an ']ius Piso' as colleague of Arrius Antoninus (above, n. 3 on p. 235).

M. Regulus. The inference is approved by Eck, op. cit. 76. A fragment of the *Fasti Ostienses* assigned to 93 by F. Zevi (above, n. 4 on p. 235, C(*b*)) has a name ending in ']lus' conjectured to be that of Regulus. Other names might occur, such as 'Proculus' or 'Homullus' —and one would expect Regulus' consulate to fall a dozen years earlier. Another consulate to be gleaned from literary evidence might be that of (M.) Flavius Aper: from Pliny, *Ep.* v 13,5, cf. *JRS* lviii (1968), 139 f. [= pp. 701 f. below].

18

A. E. Gordon, *Potitus Valerius Messalla*
Consul Suffect 29 B.C.[1]

DIUTURNITY or eclipse, the patrician houses exhibit the extreme vicissitudes. Some went out quickly, others endured for long ages, and, even if
intermittent on the *Fasti*, might return and shine with new splendour
before the end. After 164 the *gens Manlia* shows no consul again until 65.
By coincidence an equal gap interrupts the line of the Valerii Messallae:
161 to 61. The Manlii cannot produce any more consuls, but a second
Valerius holds the *fasces* in 53. Then, in the generation thereafter, three
consuls occur in close vicinity to the War of Actium (32, 31, and 29),
and three more embellish the Republic of Caesar Augustus (12, 3, and
A.D. 5).

By what arts or resources did the Valerii Messallae manage to come
back? Sulla the Dictator was ensnared by a Valeria, that alert young
divorcée who captured his attention at the games (Plutarch, *Sulla* 35). A
happy accident. Sulla's fifth choice of a wife could easily have fallen on
some other lady. Deliberate policy induced the Dictator, who stood champion of the *causa nobilitatis*, and whose victory was the *victoria nobilium*,
to rehabilitate the most ancient houses as necessary substance and adorn-
ment of the traditional order. Sulla himself was a decayed patrician
—no consul in the family for two centuries. Caesar the Dictator (it is no
paradox) extended his favour to patricians; and Caesar's heir, the man
of the proscriptions, carried forward by plebs and army, would be no less
eager to enlist partisans of birth and pedigree. It was some time before
he could hope for notable support from that quarter. However, the
narrative of the *Bellum Siculum* discloses three young patricians on his
side—Ap. Claudius Pulcher, Paullus Aemilius Lepidus, and M. Valerius
Messalla Corvinus. After fighting for the Republic at Philippi, Corvinus
had thrown in his fortunes with M. Antonius; and it was Corvinus who
in a later day coined a phrase to hit off a renegade of no social pretensions,
the agile Dellius, 'desultor bellorum civilium' (Seneca, *Suas.* i 7).

Of Corvinus, consul for 31 in the place of Antonius, there is abundant

[1] Berkeley and Los Angeles 1954.

Journal of Roman Studies xlv (1955), 155–60.

knowledge, and sundry problems adhere to his life and actions. The coeval Valerii are not much more than names. M. Messalla, *suffectus* in 32, is a date on the *Fasti*, and, perhaps, the recipient of a dedication at Pergamum (*IGR* iv 431), whereas Potitus has been treated very shabbily, through obstinacy or subservience among scholars of the modern age. In the narration of Cassius Dio (li 21, 2) a certain Messalla Potitus, suffect consul, offers public sacrifice when the victor of Actium made his entrance into Rome, that is, August of 29. Now the *Fasti Venusini* attest no consuls suffect for that year. Following the lead of Borghesi, Mommsen affirmed that Dio had made a mistake: there was no such person as Potitus, distinct from the epigraphically certified M. Messalla (*suff.* 32). Various inscriptions cropped up, notably that of Magnesia ad Sipylum (*OGIS* 460 = *IGR* iv 1338), which showed a Messalla | Potitus proconsul of Asia, but confusion and uncertainy prevailed. Observe, for example, *PIR*[1], V 94, or Dessau's comment on the 'Potitus Messalla' of the *Acta Ludorum Saecularium* (*ILS* 5050, line 150). It is a dismal story. Even the discovery of the epitaph (in 1908) did not help. Editing that inscription (*ILS* 8964), Dessau stated 'consul fuit aut a. 722 aut a. 725'. At length the *Fasti* of the *Magistri Vicorum*, published for the first time in 1935, demonstrated that both 32 and 29 had a Valerius for suffect consul, the latter styled 'Potit(us) Valeri(us)'. Some scholars, however, incautiously retain a vestigial remnant of the old error. Thus Broughton adduces 'M. Valerius Messalla Potitus' (*MRR* ii 418). That is incorrect. [Corrected *Supplement* (1960), 66.] 'Potitus' is a *cognomen* used as *praenomen*. Compare the 'Paullus' of Paullus Aemilius Lepidus (*suff.* 34)—or, for that matter, 'Magnus' in the nomenclature of Pompeius' second son, Magnus Pompeius Pius (*ILS* 8891 [= *ILLRP* 426]), or indeed, surpassing 'Magnus', the *praenomen* 'Imperator' used instead of 'Gaius' by the heir of Caesar.

Professor A. E. Gordon has undertaken to edit the epitaph of Potitus, which will figure in the album of dated Latin inscriptions on which he has long been at work. [A. E. and J. S. Gordon, *An Album of Dated Latin Inscriptions*, 4 parts in 7 volumes, Berkeley / Los Angeles, 1958-65.] He registers the *testimonia* for Potitus, and notes the evidence for other Valerii in Asia. There is, however, a new document for the dossier about which something must first be said.

In the *Actes* of the Second Epigraphic Congress of 1952 (published in 1953), Professor Louis Robert in a footnote (p. 224) reported the names of several Roman dignitaries on the inscriptions he found at Claros, among them Manius Valerius Messalla Potitus. In response to inquiry, M. Robert has generously sent me the text, with an amicable encouragement to cite or publish it (and, he adds, some time must elapse before the abundant yield from Claros can be published as a collection). The text, from a statue basis in the exedra on the Sacred Way near the Temple, appears to present no epigraphical peculiarities. It runs as follows: ʿΟ δῆμος | Μάνιον Οὐαλέριον | Μεσσάλαν Ποτῖτον | ταμίαν ἀρετῆς ἕνεκεν καὶ πάτρωνα ὄντα τῆς | πόλεως.

The only problems are identity and date. The person could be no other than Potitus, the consul of 29. One assumption is required—that he was originally 'Manius' until, yielding to the contemporary fashion of historical or exorbitant *praenomina*, he decided to transfer his second *cognomen* and use it in place of 'Manius'. Changes of this kind are not merely deduced—they happen to have a clear literary authentication. The Sabine 'Nero', borne by the elder of the two Claudii as a *cognomen*, was taken by his younger brother in place of another *praenomen*; cf. Suetonius, *Divus Claudius* 1, 1: 'patrem Claudi Caesaris Drusum, olim Decimum mox Neronem praenomine.'

If that be so, when was Potitus quaestor of Asia? His age being uncertain (see further below), a wide margin would offer, from about 48 to 35. The earlier years are less likely—notable events, a full historical record, and a number of quaestors attested. Potitus could be assigned to the period 38–35: one more of the many aristocratic adherents of Marcus Antonius.

Caution is prescribed. Perhaps another, an unknown Messalla. Potitus certainly had one son, L. Valerius Messalla Volesus (*cos.* A.D. 5). He might have had two. Volesus held the office of *monetalis* towards 6 B.C., styled on the coins 'Volusus Valerius Messalla' (*BMC, R. Emp.* i 46). Now there is also an unidentified 'Messalla' on the coinage of the same period, one in a college of four along with Apronius (i.e. L. Apronius, *suff.* A.D. 8), Galus and Sisenna (ibid. 46 ff.). This Messalla could have been a 'Manius', brother of the consul of A.D. 5: that *praenomen*, it will be noted, is ancestral in the family, whereas none of the Messallae hitherto had been called 'Lucius'. The exact chronology of the Augustan *monetales* is controversial, and is here irrelevant. It must suffice briefly to have indicated the possibilities emerging from the Claros inscription of Mʼ.Valerius Messalla Potitus.

Professor Gordon's commentary on *ILS* 8964 is clear, sensible—and exhaustive (as this meticulous editor teaches one to expect). Many questions come into the discussion—relationships, nomenclature, the senatorial career, the precise titulature of certain offices, and the abbreviations current in the Augustan epoch. The study is most welcome. Münzer's Berlin dissertation *De gente Valeria* (1891) is not easy to come by, and *RE* has not quite reached the Messallae. [They are now in vol. viii A, treated mostly by Münzer and Hanslik.] The same reasons may furnish pretext and excuse if the present review goes into the detailed history of that family.

First, ancestry. Who was the parent of Potitus? The consuls of 61 and 53 are homonymous, each a M. Valerius Messalla, and presumably first cousins (p. 45). Modern writers know them as 'Niger' and 'Rufus' respectively. What is the validity of those appellatives? Gordon makes a firm statement—'there is not the slightest evidence that I can find that the consul of 53 had a second cognomen Rufus' (p. 35). He observes that the only references to a Messalla Rufus occur in Pliny the Elder (viz., among the authors used in Books vii and xxxiv, and as vouching for a story in vii 173). | However, the consul of 53 was certainly a writer, and there can hardly be any doubt that 'Rufus' is identical with that consul. Why would one of the patrician Messallae need to be so designated—if there were not a contemporary homonym? 'Rufus' and 'Niger' are not *cognomina* but nicknames. The consul of 61 is hardly in a better case than he of 53, though the authentication is at first sight superior. He is termed 'Niger' by Asconius (18), and by Dio in the list of consuls prefixed to Book xxxvii: note also a late calendar (Mommsen, *Chron. Min.* i 215 [*Fasti Hydatiani*]). But it is not to be supposed that 'Niger' would figure on any document of the Roman People or on any family record.

Homonyms often cause trouble. There was a '⟨M.⟩ Messalla' among the young *nobiles* present in court during a famous trial in the year 80 (*Pro Sex. Roscio Amerino* 149). Which of the two? Carcopino opted for the consul of 53, arguing his extreme youth from the date of his consulate (*Sylla* (1931), 162). The argument does not hold; for Rufus is close coeval to Niger, since he was standing for the praetorship in 63 (*Pro Sulla* 42). The relationship of Rufus to Sulla's Valeria could (and should) have been adduced as very important for more reasons than one (see further below).

To distinguish homonyms, the Romans could employ various devices. Thus 'pater' or 'filius' if father and son had identical names. For example 'C. Cestium patrem' (*Ann.* vi 7, 2), where H. Fuchs, a recent editor, revives Lipsius' conjecture 'praetorem': but observe the consul of A.D. 35 and the *suffectus* of 42, each styled 'C. Cestius Gallus'. Again, the possession of a priesthood, as in the case of the two L. Pisones, consuls in 15 and in 1: the former *pontifex*, the latter *augur*. Now Niger was a *pontifex* (*ILS* 46). That label could have been useful, for the consul of 53 is 'M. Messalla augur' (Gellius xiii 15, 3). And, of course, filiation. Niger is 'M. f. M'. n.' (*ILS* 46). That style is uniformly employed on the *cippi* he set up along the Tiber when censor in 55 (*CIL* i² 766—nineteen specimens, almost all complete: three of them in *ILS* 5922 [see *ILLRP* 496]), whereas his colleague P. Servilius Vatia is only 'C. f.'. Unfortunately, the filiation of Rufus is nowhere preserved. He was presumably 'M'. f. M'. n.' (see below).

Niger, it should seem, is the parent of Corvinus, who is styled 'M. f. M. n.' on the *Fasti Triumphales* [*Inscr. It.* xiii 1, 87]. Further, there is an indication on the inscription of Niger (*ILS* 46), which probably came from a family monument on the Velia: the same block has a fragmentary name to the left, ']M. n / .... inus'; compare Dessau's note and Gordon's photograph (plate 9A). Therefore, though it cannot quite be proved that Potitus was not Corvinus' brother, that would be most unlikely, and it is a fair assumption that Potitus is the son of Rufus. Furthermore, the mysterious M. Valerius Messalla, consul suffect in 32, will also be a son of Rufus. There is a *denarius* with 'Messal. f.' on the obverse, 'patre cos.' and 's. c.' on the reverse [Sydenham, *CRR* 934]. It is scarcely possible not to attribute the coin to the year 53. If the person is the *suffectus* of 32, that is most important for ages and stages in careers. Corvinus, consul in 31, has 59 for the year of his birth in the *Chronicle* of Jerome. That cannot be right, as was demonstrated by H. Schulz (*De M. Valerii Messallae aetate*, Prog. Stettin 1886). Most scholars would now accept 64 (not all, however, have drawn the consequence for the age of Livy, who is bracketed with Corvinus by Jerome [see p. 414 below]). As for Potitus, Gordon, when reconstructing his career, assumes him to have been a youthful consul, born *c.* 62 (p. 45). That might not be so. There were also middle-aged opportunists, who had been left behind in the fierce competition of the revolutionary years. His brother Marcus, if correctly identified with the *monetalis* of 53, must have been nearly fifty when he slipped into a suffect consulship in 32. Not but what, again, there could be wide divergences in the age of brothers. The parent, it will be noted, cannot have been born later than 102. His vicissitudes are worth recapitulating— not consul until 53, condemned in 51 for bribery despite an acquittal which the eloquence of Hortensius had extorted from the jury, restored to senatorial rank by Caesar the Dictator and living on into the Principate of Augustus (he was augur for fifty-five years: Macrobius i 9, 14), having suitably occupied his leisure with the study of sacerdotal law and Roman antiquities (a notable authority on the *pomerium* and on *imperium*: Gellius xiii 14 f.).

The illustrious Corvinus had two consular sons, Messallinus in 3 B.C. and M. Aurelius Cotta Maximus Messallinus in A.D. 20 (*PIR²*, A 1488, to be amalgamated, despite Groag, with 1487). There are various problems concerning the marriages of Corvinus, which need not be discussed here. The son of Potitus is patently L. Valerius Messalla Volesus, consul in A.D. 5 with Cinna Magnus—and a murderous proconsul of Asia (*Ann.* iii 68, 1; Seneca, *De ira* ii 5, 5). There was another consul of the Messallae in the Principate of Augustus, viz. M. Valerius Messalla (Barbatus) Appianus (*PIR²*, V 89), who died in office early in 12 B.C. By birth a Claudius Pulcher, presumably son of Ap. Pulcher (*cos.* 38). For the adopting parent, Borghesi proposed Rufus, the old augur. Somebody a generation later is preferable. Possibly Corvinus (as tentatively suggested in *Roman Revolution* (1939), 423), but the *suffectus* of 32 would be a better idea (cf. Gordon, p. 52). The alliance between Valerii and Claudii is worth a comment—perhaps the first attested since those Sabine families had come to Rome. |

The epilogue on the Valerii can be brief. Of the descendants of Rufus, no consular son for Messalla Volesus, and none for Messalla Appianus. There was, it is true, Messalla Barbatus, described as a 'consobrinus' of the Emperor Claudius (Suetonius, *Divus Claudius* 26), who died, it might be surmised, before he reached consular age: he cannot have been born later than 12 B.C. His widow, Domitia Lepida (*PIR*², D 180), was transferred in matrimony to Faustus Sulla (*cos.* 31), and they had a son who was consul in 52. (These data are relevant to the age of Barbatus' daughter, the notorious Valeria Messallina, whom some, extenuating, assume very young (only fifteen according to *CAH* x 672) when she married Claudius, probably in 39.) As for the descendants of Niger, M. Valerius Messalla (*PIR*¹, V 92), a grandson of Corvinus, was consul in 20 along with his uncle Cotta Messallinus, but is otherwise totally unknown; and the next generation saw his son consul in 58 as colleague of the Emperor Nero, a fact which recalled the consulship of his great-grandfather in 31 B.C., as 'pauci iam senum meminerant' (*Ann.* xiii 34, 1). This man, the last consul of the Valerii Messallae, took a subsidy from Nero. Such was the end of a patrician house. Their blood, however, was conveyed (through the female line) by persons known to the historian Tacitus—the excellent Vipstanus Messalla, military tribune in 69, and that evil man, L. Valerius Catullus Messallinus, twice consul under the Flavian dynasty.

Discussing Potitus, Gordon was under no obligation either to pursue the Valerii to the end or to go back beyond the consuls of 61 and 53. Yet it might have been worth while to scrutinize ancestors. The inscription of Magnesia ad Sipylum (*OGIS* 460) describes Potitus as patron and benefactor διὰ προγόνων. No known Messalla previously can be brought into connection with the province Asia. Is the phrase to be taken literally? G. suggests that a governorship held by a Valerius of another branch might serve as sufficient explanation, and he points to L. Valerius Flaccus (*suff.* 86), probably in Asia *c.* 92 (cf. *MRR* ii 18 f.)—the son's governorship in 62/1 being excluded (he decides), because he was prosecuted for extortion. This expedient is not very helpful. The common ancestors of Messallae and Flacci lie centuries back, in the earliest years of the Roman Republic. Might there not have been a suitable Messalla in the two generations after the consul of 161? Now, there was a Valerius Messalla prosecuted by Metellus Numidicus (*cos.* 109) for offences against *socii* (Gellius xv 14, 1). Is he identical with the Valerius Messalla who was a *legatus* in 90 in the *Bellum Italicum* (Appian, *BC* i 40, 179)? Münzer left the question open (*De gente Valeria* (1891), 52), but the two men are amalgamated in *MRR* ii 32. [Corrected *Supplement*, 65 f.; cf. now *RE*, s.v. 'Valerius', nos.

248 and 249.] Yet it might seem that the action of Metellus belongs to earlier years in his life, not to the time when he was a senior statesman. A Messalla praetor *c.* 120 and governor of Asia would be the missing grandfather of Niger and Rufus (always assuming them cousins), and he would have Manius for *praenomen*, since the style of Niger is 'M. f., M'. n.' As for the next generation, the Valerius Messalla *legatus* in 90, probably praetor 92 or 91, will be either Marcus, the father of Niger, or Manius, (presumably) the father of Rufus.

It can be deduced that Rufus' father married a Hortensia—Rufus himself was a nephew of the great orator (Valerius Maximus v 9, 2). Furthermore, Sulla's Valeria was a relative of Hortensius (*cos.* 69). Plutarch calls her ἀδελφή (*Sulla* 35). An error (cf. Münzer, op. cit. 52), but not all have noticed it—Carcopino describes her as a 'demi-sœur' of Hortensius (*Histoire romaine* (1935), 487). How and when the error arose is not certain. There could be a remedy. Somebody may have conjectured ἀδελφιδῆ in Plutarch, but there is no trace of this in the *apparatus* of Lindskog–Ziegler (1926). However it be, Sulla's new wife as the niece of Hortensius and the sister of young Rufus is a fact not irrelevant to the setting of the defence of Roscius in 80.

To come at last to the inscription (*ILS* 8964). For guidance a photograph is supplied (plate 7), a squeeze (plate 8), and a drawing with the supplements proposed (plate 9b). The epitaph of Potitus thus emerges as follows, the supplements being in italics to the right of the irregular line:

POTIT VS·VA*LERIVS·M·F·MESSALLA*
XV·VIR·SAC·FA*C·III·VIR·MON·TRIB·MIL*ᶜ
Q·PR·VRB·*COS·PRO·COS·PROV*
ASIA E·BIS·LE*G·AVG·PR·PR·PROV·SYRIAE*

On this basis, Gordon investigates the life and career of Potitus (Summary, p. 53). He assumes that Potitus was born in 62, or not long before (p. 45). However, as indicated above, the man might have been older than that, especially if his brother Marcus was *monetalis* in 53. The datings proposed for the earlier posts of Potitus therefore become vulnerable—but defensible, if Potitus is the quaestor of Asia honoured at Claros (cf. above). Not that it can matter much. Attention should go to the posts subsequent to his consulship. The words 'Asiae bis' show that Potitus governed Asia for two years | in succession. Dessau was less than himself when he observed 'mirum eum dici proconsulem bis, non proconsulem per biennium'. There is no anomaly: cf. Gordon's comments, with examples of the style by which tenures longer than annual are described (p. 39). One could further add that in this instance 'bis', and not 'iterum', would be the proper equivalent of 'pro cos. II'. As for the date, Gordon puts the proconsulate in the period 25–20 B.C., as is reasonable at first sight—and indeed attractive, supposing his *biennium* astride the critical year 23. An earlier date would not in itself be excluded. Compare M. Tullius Cicero (*suff.* 30). He is attested as proconsul (Seneca, *Suas.* vii 13), and his name and head occur on a coin of Magnesia ad Sipylum. Hence Grant puts him before 27. Grant proposes 29/8 (*FITA* (1946), 385), but 28/7 is not absolutely ruled out. Proconsuls in the decade after Actium are a topic of no small interest. The latest list is that of D. Magie, *Roman Rule in Asia Minor* ii (1950), 1580. It will have to be supplemented as fresh evidence accrues, or different attributions impose themselves. For example, Magie assigns C. Norbanus Flaccus (*cos.* 38) to the Triumviral period. That cannot be—the man was not a partisan of Antonius. Inspection of the two edicts cited by Josephus (*AJ* xvi 166 and 171) discloses the name Καῖσαρ. Not, however, ὁ Σεβαστός, therefore Norbanus is probably to be dated before 27 (despite Grant, op. cit. 383). Again, L. Volcacius Tullus (*cos.* 33) had to be reckoned with, even without the new fragment from Apamea which certifies [ἀνθυ]πάτου before his name: it is incorporated in Ehrenberg and Jones, *Select Documents* (second edition, 1955), no. 98. (Previously [ἀρχιερέως] had been conjectured, which was not plausible.) And there is another welcome addition to knowledge. A stone that had been lurking for many years at Leiden carries an edict or letter of the consuls of 27 (i.e., Augustus and Agrippa) in Greek, and a Latin letter consequent thereon, addressed to the magistrates of Cyme in Aeolis by the proconsul Vinicius (the *praenomen* is missing), and containing the phrase 'iussu Aug[usti] Caesaris' (I owe this information to the courtesy of Dr. H. W. Pleket).[1] Clearly L. Vinicius M. f., suffect consul in 33, his proconsulate being therefore 28/7, or, better, allowing for due delays in official transactions, 27/6. It therefore becomes more likely that the *biennium* of Potitus is close to 23.

Much more elusive is the other post. Gordon supplements 'leg. [Aug. pr. pr. prov. Syriae]'. In the Commentary he suggests the period 18–13. He also weighs the claims of various other provinces, including Illyricum (cf. the Summary, p. 53). Let it at once be said that Illyricum is not at all plausible. According to Dio (liv 34, 4) that province, which he styles ἡ Δελματία, was transferred to Augustus in 11. Not to be neglected, but surely a year or two too late. The last proconsul of Illyricum might have been M. Vinicius (*suff.* 19) who in 13 began the *Bellum Pannonicum* under the superintendence of M. Agrippa (Velleius ii 96, 2)—though, indeed, Vinicius could be an imperial legate.

Syria looks more promising, but there are hazards and complications—and the whole period 27–13 ought to come into the reckoning. First, the

---

[1] [First published by Pleket in *The Greek Inscriptions in the 'Rijksmuseum van Oudheden at Leyden'* (1958), no. 57; frequently discussed since.]

position of Agrippa. It is not easy to accept a consular legate in Syria when Agrippa was in the eastern lands, either in 23–21 or in 17–13 (the problems are too complex to be discussed in this place). Secondly, other known *legati*. M. Tullus Cicero is said to have become governor of Syria —no title specified (Appian, *BC* iv 51, 221). The precise dating is a problem, cf. *Rom. Rev.* 303, where 29–27 or 27–25 were suggested: the year of his proconsulate of Asia, could it be fixed, is here relevant. Then there is the mysterious Varro in 24 or 23 (Josephus, *BJ* i 398; *AJ* xv 345). Nor will one omit the arguments of L. R. Taylor for a governorship of M. Titius (*suff.* 31) in 20 (*JRS* xxvi (1936), 161 ff.), while rejecting that scholar's attribution of the *titulus Tiburtinus* (*ILS* 918).

It is best to suspend judgement. The significant fact is a consular *nobilis* as legate of Caesar Augustus in the first epoch of the new dispensation. Very few *nobiles* were thus employed: cf. *Rom. Rev.* 329 f. (which omitted to notice Potitus). The ruler preferred *novi homines* of praetorian rank. The older Potitus is, and the less a soldier, the more plausible becomes his role as administrator of one of the military regions in the *provincia* of Caesar Augustus.

Surmise about the precise region depends on the supplementation of the epigraphic text. What is presented is acceptable so far as balance goes and length of lines. But a doubt arises about each line. The first might be longer by two letters, and two spaces, if the grandfather's name had been added, 'M'. n.', to comfort the genealogist and instruct an ignorant posterity. Potitus' coeval in consular standing, Messalla Corvinus, was 'M. n.'

Next, line 2. For the priesthood the form 'xv vir sac. fa[c.]' does not happen to be registered among the variants in Dessau's selection. That is no bar—but 'fa[ciund.]' or 'fa[ciundis]' is not ruled out either. Further, there might have been a second priesthood of this successful patrician. Not, to be sure, one of the 'quattuor amplissima'. But Potitus could have been, for example, a *fetialis*. Those experts, who guaranteed that a war was a just war, had not been heard of for a century or more until Caesar's heir employed them to declare hostilities against the Queen of Egypt, nothing being said about Marcus Antonius (Dio l 4, 5). That is not all. The post 'iii vir mon.' is proposed | in this line. A difficulty arises. The traditional and standard designation is 'iii vir a. a. a. f. f.' Variations occur—but not at an early date—such as 'iii viro ad monetam' (*ILS* 1028: late Flavian) or 'iii vir monetalis a. a. a. f. f.' (*ILS* 1029: Hadrianic). But, so far as I can see, going by the inscriptions in Dessau, the bare 'iii vir monetalis' cannot be paralleled before the third century (*ILS* 1175; 1185). Nor is 'trib. mil.' attractive. Surely 'tr. mil.'

The third line clearly carries on after 'pr. urb.' to 'c[os.]' and to the proconsulate of Asia. How was the proconsulate formulated in words?

Gordon proposes '[pro cos. prov.] / Asiae'. The abbreviation 'prov.' arouses disquiet. Reverting again to Dessau, one discovers that only one of the senatorial inscriptions of the first century shows 'prov.', viz. 969 (Claudio-Neronian). If 'provincia' is abbreviated, the form 'provinc.' dominates (*ILS* 913, 928, 937, 963, 969, 972, 983, 987, 996, etc.). Hence a longer line, with 'provinc.' or 'provinciae'—or indeed, a shorter, omitting the word altogether.

And now, the fourth line—'Asiae bis, leg. [Aug. pr. pr. prov. Syriae].' Where every syllable may count, observe that 'pr. pr.' for 'pro pr.' is hardly to be expected on an elegant document of Augustan Rome. In Dessau's selection it seems not to arise until *ILS* 996 (Flavian). That is a trifle compared with the general problem of the proper titulature for Caesar's legate. The Augustan parallels are not numerous enough for certitude, since various categories have to be eliminated. For example, those *legati* of the early Empire, quaestorian or praetorian, whose inscriptions carry the bare 'leg. Aug.' and imply that the men lacked the *imperium pro praetore*: presumably the persons who come in time to be styled legates of legions (the first epigraphic instance is *ILS* 940, of the reign of Tiberius). Again, though there is no essential difference between a praetorian *legatus pro praetore* and a consular, for each has five *fasces*, it will be convenient to regard only the latter. And there is a criterion of diverse nature—a provincial dedication is not the same thing as an epitaph or an *elogium*. Several variants occur. Thus the 'pro pr.' is omitted from one inscription of L. Volusius Saturninus (*cos.* A.D. 3) at Aenona (*ILS* 923), but is present on another, presumably deriving from some other Dalmatian town (*ILS* 923a), while P. Silius Nerva (*cos.* 20 B.C.) is 'leg. pro pr.' only, lacking the 'Aug.' at Carthago Nova (*CIL* ii 3414). And the case of Paullus Fabius Maximus (*cos.* 11 B.C.) is instructive. 'Legatus Caesaris' at Lucus Augusti (*CIL* ii 2581), he is 'leg. pro pr.' at Bracara (*ILS* 8895).

How then would Caesar's legate be designated on a funeral monument at Rome, gravestone or *elogium*? The system of the imperial provinces took time to develop. In the beginning was the *provincia* of Caesar Augustus, in brief the military and predominant regions Spain, Gaul, and Syria, where he abolished proconsuls and took the supreme authority himself, governing through *legati pro praetore* either consular or praetorian in rank (cf. *Rom. Rev.* 329; 393). Hence not governors of the imperial provinces, but *legati* in different regions of Caesar's *provincia*. The true and original situation is reflected in titulature. Thus the acephalous *elogium* from Tusculum (*ILS* 8965), which can hardly belong to anybody but M. Vinicius (*suff.* 19 B.C.) has '[legatus pro] pr. Augusti Caesaris in [Illyrico]'. The style shows a significant survival. The gravestone of Ummidius Quadratus (Neronian in date) describes him as 'leg. divi

Claudi in Illyrico, eiusd. et / Neronis Caesaris Aug. in Syria' (*ILS* 972: Casinum).

That being so, 'leg. Aug. pro pr. prov. Syriae' becomes difficult to credit. The possible variants being numerous, e.g., omission or not of 'pro pr.' and abbreviation or not of Augustus' name, speculation becomes hazardous. Observe, however, that the letters of the first line are larger than those of the fourth, that the spacing in the third line is generous. If 'M'. n.' were added to the first, the third could tolerate 'provinc.', and there would be room in the fourth for 'leg. [Caesaris Augusti in Syria]'.

Be that as it may, the formulation is important. And now (after omitting many things), to terminate. Discussing Potitus, one cannot help being put in mind of M. Tullius Cicero, his consular senior by a year, who governed both Asia and Syria. There are a number of forged inscriptions of the Cicero family, allegedly discovered at Rocca d'Arce, between Arpinum and Aquinum. Some are grotesque, but one (*CIL* x 704*) is not bad at all. Mommsen accepted it at first in the *Inscriptiones Regni Neapolitani* (1852), 4320. Orelli (572) printed it, eschewing responsibility, but Wilmanns (1114) betrayed no suspicions. The dedication, honouring the orator's son as 'patronus', describes him as 'cos., pro cos. prov. Asiae, leg. imp. / Caes. Aug. in Syria'. Forgers exhibit a wide variation both in purpose and in talents. Was this man perhaps exploiting some genuine inscription? If not, his erudition deserves all honour: he knew what only the elder Seneca and Appian among the literary authorities have revealed, the provincial governorships of M. Cicero. The formulation 'prov. Asiae' is not attractive, but the style for 'governor of Syria' shows rare insight.

19

Missing Senators[1]

THE study of persons carries with it many hazards, even when it operates by selection. An attempt to establish any kind of complete catalogue incurs the added risk of omissions. For the Roman Empire, the material is vast and forbidding: an editor can hardly fail to miss some names and facts, even within restricted categories, whatever his sagacity and industry. Though the Republic is at first sight more manageable, its closing epoch begins to anticipate the Empire by the plethora of names and heterogeneity of sources. A repertorium was sorely needed. It has recently been produced: *The Magistrates of the Roman Republic*.[2] This noble achievement compiles the register of the Roman State from the first consuls to the year of Actium. The author, T. R. S. Broughton, has cast his net wide. *MRR* takes in even equestrian officers, all the priests, and the Virgins of Vesta; and some categories, like that of legates, embrace a great variety of people and activities. Moreover, among the appendices is a Supplementary List of Senators (*MRR* ii 487–98).

Whom to admit or exclude, it cannot have been easy to draw the line. As for senators, unequivocal attestation of status has clearly been demanded. Otherwise there might be no end. The literary texts reveal certain persons who can hardly not have been senators. Thus the Roman Stoic Q. Lucilius Balbus, or (a brother or cousin) L. Lucilius Balbus, that eminent lawyer who had instruction from Mucius Scaevola and passed it on to Ser. Sulpicius Rufus.[3] Again, the stories about the vicissitudes of the proscribed as retailed by Appian must contain the names of some unattested senators: for example, Haterius,[4] perhaps none other than the parent of the orator Q. Haterius (*cos. suff.* 5), whose family is designated senatorial by the careful Tacitus.[5]

---

[1] [The senators here listed were entered by Broughton in his *Supplement* (1960). However, that work (of course) could not fully include the onomastic and prosopographical material here presented.]

[2] Vol. i: 509–100 B.C.; Vol. ii: 99–31 B.C. (Philological Monographs no. xv, New York, 1951, 1952).

[3] For these people see below under LUCILIUS.

[4] Appian, *BC* iv 29.

[5] *Ann.* iv 61. *PIR*[1], H 17, however, suggests that the proscribed Haterius is the orator's brother. Also F. Münzer, *RE* vii, col. 2513. [But cf. *PIR*[2], H 24.]

Historia iv (1955), 52–71.

On a rigorous canon it was right to bar these men. Apart from them, *MRR* will be found to have left out a number of indubitable senators. Some have to be tracked down in obscure recesses of literature, some extricated from premature amalgamation with other persons. Familiar writings can yield an unexpected harvest, and there is often profit to be gleaned from close scrutiny of the context in which a man is named. Previous works of reference had their deficiencies (the encyclopedia of Pauly–Wissowa shows some startling omissions), and | detriment can accrue along with all bounty of *MRR*—its precise and ready answers may encourage young and old to neglect the reading of Latin authors.

Hence the list of senators here presented.[1] It amounts to forty-five names, ranging in order of the alphabet from an Aemilius Lepidus to the parent of C. Verres. A minority fall within the purview of *MRR* i; the rest belong to the period 99–31. Obscure men, for the most part. There were many such in the generation after Sulla, when the Senate comprised about six hundred members. And necessarily so. Of the total, not more than two thirds can be identified at any time. Many of them must bear the stigma of 'homo novus parvusque senator'.[2] They could not be denied the *dignitas* of a *senator populi Romani*, however little they might show to deserve it:[3] socially (that is, by count of wealth and education) they were no better than the higher knights, some indeed calamitously inferior. It is often sheer hazard that such persons get mentioned at all. Thus the flagrant scandal of a bribed jury-court in the year 74 produces the names of nineteen: ten corrupt, nine virtuous.[4] Good and bad together, they make up a splendid collection of nonentities. Here and elsewhere nomenclature often helps as a guide—and it is clear that there was a mass of municipal senators.[5]

For convenience the list will admit one or two men hanging on the margin of authentication: otherwise they may be wholly lost to view. For example, the senatorial rank of P. Calpurnius Lanarius and of Domitius Apulus happens not to be directly attested, that of Q. Aemilius Lepidus might be called into question. Again, others might (if the facts were known) be identical with known senators: the mysterious Publius belongs to this class, likewise the man whose *cognomen* is Balbus. And it is open to anybody to argue (or rather guess) that Asconius, reporting the senator P. Cornificius, made a mistake for Q. Cornificius.

There is another margin, that of time and period. *MRR* takes in, with

---

[1] In supplementation of the long review in *CP* 1 (1955), 127–38.
[2] *Bell. Afr.* 57, 4.
[3] Cicero, *Pro Caecina* 28: 'senator populi Romani, splendor ordinis, decus atque ornamentum iudiciorum, exemplar antiquae religionis, Fidiculanius Falcula.' An obscure *nomen* —and a disreputable character.
[4] To be culled from the *Pro Cluentio*, along with *In Verrem* i 38 f.
[5] Cf. R. Syme, *PBSR* xiv (1938); 4 ff.; 23 f. [= above, pp. 91 ff., 110 ff.].

due warning, seven senators, known only from inscriptions that do not permit an exact date.[1] They might well be Augustan—and six of them are also registered | by S. J. de Laet in his lists of the Senate under the early Caesars.[2] So far so good. There are others, however, that have been passed over in both works. One is Q. Ovinius, who was with Antonius at Alexandria in 30 (strictly speaking a year too late for *MRR*, and therefore no doubt omitted). He is perhaps hardly worth bothering about. But six senators, revealed by inscriptions, ought to find a home somewhere. Various criteria, such as the absence of *cognomen* or the style and formulation of the document, suggest an approximate dating—that is, from late Republican to early Imperial. For clarity, the six are marked with asterisks.[3]

By way of supplement to *MRR* a bare catalogue of the forty-five names might have seemed enough, equipped with the relevant *testimonia*, with the six asterisks and with several marks of interrogation. However, some of the people on the list are men of consequence, like the great political manager P. Cornelius Cethegus; there is a neglected proconsul of the last age of the Republic, L. Quinctius Rufus; and one or two members of notable families like the Aemilii and the Sulpicii come in. And, although the majority matter little for themselves, corrupt jurors or proscribed senators have their uses. They can throw light upon incidents in history or exemplify layers of the social structure. Attention has therefore been given to problems of nomenclature and local origins.[4]

Q. AEMILIUS LEPIDUS. Named in a list of sudden deaths taken from Verrius Flaccus. Among them are 'Q. Fabius Maximus in consulatu suo . . ., item C. Volcalcius Gurges senator, omnes adeo sani atque tempestivi ut de progrediendo cogitarent, Q. Aemilius Lepidus iam egrediens incusso pollice limini cubiculi, C. Aufustius egressus, cum in senatum iret, offenso pede in comitio' (Pliny, *NH* vii 181). *MRR* admits Volcalcius, but not the next two names. However, Q. Aemilius Lepidus is registered as a senator by Groag (*PIR*², A 374), with the remark 'incertum cuius aetatis', implicitly (and rightly) rejecting an identification with the consular Q. Aemilius M'. f. Lepidus (*cos*. 21, son of the consul of 66). Perhaps the

---

[1] Viz. M. Ampudius (*CIL* i² 812: Formiae); C. Appuleius Tappo (i² 814 = *ILS* 906: Aquileia); L. Caecina (i² 2515: Volsinii); M. Fruticius (i² 826 = v 3339: Verona); Q. Sanquinius (i² 837 = *ILS* 905: Lorium?). Also C. Cestius Epulo (vi 1374 = *ILS* 917: Rome) and]cius Balbus (*AE* 1934, 85: Cos). For the last of these (noted as B 40a in *PIR*² iii, Addenda p. xix) see below under C. PACCIUS C. F. BALBUS. All seven (except, naturally, Sanquinius) have entries in *PIR*², A–F.

[2] *De Samenstelling van den Romeinschen Senaat* (1941), nos. 24, 441, 447, 179, 321, 453. He missed]cius Balbus.

[3] Viz. Fonteius Q. f.; C. Nunnuleius C. f. Nudus; Pacceius L. f.; C. Paccius C. f.; C. Paccius C. f. Balbus; T. Resius T. f.

[4] It is pleasant to acknowledge help or advice on certain items from Professor Fraenkel, Professor Broughton, Mr. P. M. Fraser, and Mr. E. Badian.

missing father, known only from the filiation, of M. Aemilius Q. f. M. n. Lepidus (*cos.* 78); perhaps, however, a son of M. Lepidus the Triumvir (*cos.* 46)—he had several children (Cicero, *Phil.* xiii 8; *Ad M. Brutum* i 18, 6), the eldest of whom was Marcus, husband | of a Servilia. Marcus was put to death in 30 for alleged conspiracy (*PIR*², A 368). Quintus can be deduced from the filiation of M'. Lepidus (*cos.* A.D. 11), who is 'Q. f. M. n.'; and Quintus (one will assume) married a daughter of Faustus Sulla and Pompeia Magni f., for his daughter was descended from Sulla and Pompeius (Tacitus, *Ann.* iii 22, 1, discussing Aemilia Lepida, the sister of M'. Lepidus, *cos.* A.D. 11).

SEX. ALBESIUS. Senator in 43 (Cicero, *Phil.* xiii 28). Named after 'Asinius quidam senator voluntarius, lectus ipse a se', as a parallel phenomenon— 'non novi Sex. Albesium, sed tamen neminem tam maledicum offendi, qui illum negaret dignum Antonii senatu'. The *nomen* happens not to be attested; but it would be premature to substitute the 'Albidius' of three MSS., or 'Albedius' (Klebs, *RE* i, col. 1312; *TLL* i, s.v. 'Albius', 1495 f.). 'Albisius' is very close, of which Schulze (*LE* 119) cites half a dozen instances, among them one from Gallia Narbonensis (*CIL* xii 3394: Nemausus): 'Albisiae Cn. f. Secundae ex testamento'. The stone is described as 'cippus magnus litteris bonis saeculi primi'. In this instance 'Albisius' is presumably a native name, latinized. The only Albidius known to history is the man about whom Cato the Censor made a joke, 'Albidium quendam qui bona sua comedisset et novissime domum quae ei reliqua erat incendio perdidisset' (Macrobius ii 2, 4: not in *RE*). Cato said 'quod comesse non potuerit, id combussisse'.

L. ANNIUS. Senator in 307, expelled by the censors 'quod quam virginem in matrimonium duxerat repudiasset, nullo amicorum consilio adhibito' (Val. Max. ii 9, 2). Not elsewhere attested, and not in *RE*. Roman historians and moralists, eager to demonstrate how late it was before divorce emerged at Rome, preferred to single out the conduct of Sp. Carvilius Maximus in the year 227 (for the evidence, see *RE* iii, col. 1631). Valerius Maximus was himself unaware that he had asserted the traditional view a few pages earlier—'repudium inter uxorem et virum a condita urbe usque ad quingentesimum annum nullum intercessit, primus autem Sp. Carvilius uxorem sterilitatis causa dimisit' (ii 1, 4).

P. ANNIUS ASELLUS. Senator, who died in 75 (Cicero, *In Verrem* ii 1, 104, where the manuscripts give the *praenomen* as 'C.': emended from § 107, § 113, and 2, 21). Klebs in *RE* i, col. 2264 registered him as 'C. Annius Asellus'. Note 'P. Ann.' and 'P. An.' on Sicilian *aes*, presumably struck by quaestors, *CIL* i², p. 764, nos. 384, b–c (from M. Bahrfeldt, *RSN* xii (1904), 408): listed in *MRR* ii 478.

Cn. Aufidius T. f. Entitled ὁ στραταγὸς τῶν 'Ρωμαίων (*SIG*³ 715: Rhegium). Not in *RE*. The lettering, as Dittenberger points out, must be earlier than the beginning of the first century B.C., and the formulation of the title is also an indication. The propraetor Cn. Aufidius who governed Asia *c*. 106 | (cf. *MRR*) was 'Cn. f.' (*IG* xii 5, 722: Adramyttium). There is, however, a 'Cn. Auf[idius]' on the *SC de agro Pergameno* (presumably of 129)—no. 51 on the list of A. Passerini, *Athenaeum* xxv (1937), 271 [also of R. K. Sherk, *Roman Documents from the Greek East*, no. 12]. The *nomen* is common (in both senses of the term), and first emerges in Roman annals with a Cn. Aufidius, tribune of the plebs in 170 (Livy xliii 8, 2). The senatorial Aufidii down to Cn. Aufidius Cn. f. Orestes (*cos*. 71) and T. Aufidius (*pr*.? 67) may all belong to one family.

C. Aufustius. Senator who died suddenly (Pliny, *NH* vii 181, quoted above under Q. Aemilius Lepidus). There was a writer on grammar called Aufustius, generally assigned to the Ciceronian period (so Klebs, *RE* ii, col. 2299; Schanz–Hosius, *Gesch. der röm. Lit.* i⁴ (1927), 603). Since, however, he dedicated a volume to Asinius Pollio (*GL* vii 35, 1), the Triumviral or early Augustan period might be a better place (cf. Funaioli, *GRF* i (1907), 491 f.), and he could have figured in *PIR*. The name is uncommon. Schulze (*LE* 211) cites ten inscriptions from Rome and various parts of Italy. Add nine from the provinces (from *TLL* ii, under 'Aufius'), among them three from Africa (notably *CIL* viii 69—a knight at Gurza in A.D. 65). That region, it will be recalled, is remarkable in furnishing specimens that are rare enough in Italy, e.g. 'Farsuleius', 'Fidiculanius', 'Furfanius'. The local distribution of names ending in '-ustius' has never been investigated. The first of them to appear on the consular *fasti* is L. Apustius Fullo (226)—also the last for two and a half centuries until a Sallustius (A.D. 27). See also below, M. Fidustius.

M. Baebius. Senator in 74 and close friend of A. Cluentius Habitus (Cicero, *Pro Cluentio* 47; 53). The name, which Schulze claims as Etruscan (*LE* 133), is widespread throughout Italy, and indistinctive.

] L. f. Ouf. Balbus. Senator on the *SC de Aphrodisiensibus* of 35 (P. Viereck, *Sermo Graecus* (1888), xix, p. 40, cf. p. vii). The editor supplemented [Μᾶρκος ᾿Αττιος Λε]υκίου υἱὸς ᾿Ωφεντεῖνα Βάλβος, which is not helpful—and not confirmed by the later emergence of P. Attius P. f. Ouf. on the bronze tablet of Asculum (*CIL* i² 709 = vi 37045 = *ILS* 8888 (incomplete) [= *ILLRP* 515]).[1] There is no warrant for invoking M. Atius Balbus, the maternal grandfather of Caesar Augustus, or any other conjectural member of that family: they are Atii, not Attii (cf. inscriptions of their freedmen, *CIL* xiv 2179 f.), and Aricia, their home-town, was enrolled in the Horatia. The *cognomen* 'Balbus' is so common as to deter

---

[1] [See now Sherk, *RDGE*, no. 29, accepting Syme's views as passed on by Broughton.]

speculation. One might, however, mention in passing that the *praenomen* 'L.' was used by the Lucilii Balbi (see below, under LUCILIUS) and by the Octavii Balbi: for the latter family observe L. Octavius Balbus, probably a senator, like his contemporary P. Octavius Balbus (*Pro Cluentio* 107), but not expressly designated as such by Cicero (*In Verrem* ii 2, 31). Of neither family is the tribe known. |

Further, L. Saenius L. f., suffect consul for the last two months of 30, should be kept in mind[1]—he had the misfortune to be omitted from Degrassi's *Fasti Consolari* (1952), but is registered in the Index as 'L. Saenius (Balbinus)'. The documents assign no *cognomen* (*Inscr. It.* xiii 1, 170; 254; 283; *CIL* viii 22640[1]), but a passage in Appian is relevant (*BC* iv 50). Appian, mentioning one of the proscribed called Balbinus who returned when peace was made with Sex. Pompeius and became consul not long after, goes on to speak of Balbinus' attitude at the time of the conspiracy of the young M. Lepidus (i.e. in 30). There is also a Balbinus, unexplained, in Cicero, *Ad Att.* xiii 21, 3: 'de Metello et Balbino'. Despite the agnosticism of Nagl (*RE* i A, col. 1722), the 'Balbinus' of Appian can hardly be dissociated from the consul L. Saenius; and the Balbus senator in 35 might be identical, or a member of the same family. Nobody, however, has doubted that the parent of the consul is to be discovered in that L. Saenius who in 63 read out an important letter he had received from Faesulae (Sallust, *Cat.* 30, 1). The *gentilicium* is patently Etruscan (for examples of 'Saena' and 'Saenius' see *LE* 93), and it occurs also as the name of a city Saena Julia (the modern Siena: not in *RE*), a Caesarian or Triumviral colony (earlier at least than 27). Saena, it appears, was constituted from previously Volaterran territory. Its tribe is the Oufentina (Kubitschek, *Imp. Rom. Trib. Discr.* (1889), 87 f.). See also below, under C. PACCIUS C. F. and C. PACCIUS C. F. BALBUS.

M. BARBATIUS POLLIO. Partisan of Antonius. Cicero speaks of 'illa naufragia Caesaris amicorum, Barbas Cassios, Barbatios Polliones' (*Phil.* xiii 3, where Clark in the Oxford text (1916) inserts a comma between the last two words, likewise Schoell (Teubner, 1918)). Clearly Barbatius, quaestor of Antonius in 41 (Appian, *BC* v 31), certified as M. Barbatius (*BMC, R. Rep.* ii 98 ff. = Sydenham, *CRR* (1952), 1180 ff.). Perhaps 'M. Barbatius Pollio aed. cur.' (*ILS* 9261); cf. *PIR²*, B 50. In any case, Antonius' quaestor is to be kept apart from Barbarius Philippus, the runaway slave who became praetor (*Dig.* i 14, 3, cf. the Βάρβιος Φιλιππικός of Suidas); cf. *PIR²*, followed in *Rom. Rev.* (1939), 196: Dio (xlviii 34, 5) has the incident, but not the name, under the year 39. *MRR* (ii 372, cf. Index) amalgamates, wrongly, offering M. Barbatius Philippus as quaestor of Antonius and no entry for M. Barbatius Pollio. For examples of the

---

[1] [On this man see E. Wistrand, *Horace's Ninth Epode* (1958), 42 ff.]

name 'Barbatius' see *LE* 349; *TLL* ii 1728. 'Barbarius' just exists—*CIL* x 1199 (Abella); xii 1756 (Valentia).

CALPURNIUS. Senator *c.* 90. Pliny, after recording how Caepio and Drusus quarrelled about a gold ring, 'unde origo socialis belli et exitia rerum', proceeds 'ne tunc quidem omnes senatores habuere, utpote cum memoria avorum multi praetura quoque functi in ferreo consenuerint, sicut Calpurnium et Manilium, qui legatus C. Marii fuerit Iugurthino bello, Fenestella tradit' (*NH* xxxiii 21). For the interpretation of the passage see Münzer, *Beiträge zur Quellen/kritik der Naturgeschichte des Plinius* (1897), 345 f. The identifications present various problems. For Manilius, or rather Manlius, see Münzer, *RE* xiv, col. 1155. As for Calpurnius, the same scholar suggested L. Calpurnius Piso Frugi (*pr. c.* 112), while recognizing that 'consenuisse' did not fit (*Beiträge* 346, but without that reservation in *RE* iii, col. 1365). Indeed, this Piso was killed in Spain when praetor or propraetor (Cicero, *In Verrem* ii 4, 56; Appian, *Ib.* 99).

There is, it is true, an unattached L. Piso in this period, στρατηγός in Asia (mentioned along with C. Labeo and M. Hypsaeus on *Inschr. v. Priene* 121). *MRR* registers him as governor of Asia earlier than 90, perhaps earlier than 100. But there are reasons for believing that Piso (and the other two στρατηγοί) were active in Asia shortly before 83, not necessarily as governors of the province; cf. Münzer, *RE* xxi, coll. 15 f. Who is this L. Piso? He may be relevant to another problem. The standard opinion (which *MRR* reproduces) has a L. Calpurnius Piso tribune of the plebs in 89, identified with L. Piso Frugi, praetor in 74. Not plausible: the two should be dissociated. The 'Lucius Calpurnius Piso' of Sisenna fr. 17, author of a law adding two new tribes (cf. another *Lex Calpurnia* in fr. 120), must go in 90, not in 91, for he occurs in the third book of Sisenna's *Historiae*. Further, he can (and perhaps should) be praetor, not tribune. Therefore presumably L. Calpurnius Piso Caesoninus (attested at the time of the *Bellum Italicum* by Cicero, *In Pisonem* 87), the son of the consul of 112. Therefore perhaps the στρατηγός.

However that may be, Calpurnii Pisones are best kept apart from the reckoning. The Pisones, like other *nobiles*, tend to eschew the *gentilicium*; compare the nomenclature 'L. Sulla', 'C. Caesar', 'M. Metellus'; whether referred to by one name or by two, they will seldom be called 'Calpurnii'. Thus Pliny, a little further on, alluding to the consul of 133 and his son (i.e., precisely the L. Piso praetor *c.* 112) says 'Piso Frugi filium ex privata pecunia donavit' (*NH* xxxiii 38). The odds are that the ex-praetor Calpurnius who wore the iron ring to the day of his death was not a Piso or a Piso Frugi. Rome may have known other Calpurnii Bestiae than the consul of 111 and his grandson, tribune of the plebs in 62; and the parent of M. Calpurnius C. f. Bibulus (*cos.* 59) remains only an item or cipher in his son's nomenclature. Frugality and conservatism would not be out of place in the family of Calpurnius Bibulus.

P. CALPURNIUS LANARIUS. Legate of the proconsul C. Annius in 81. Sallust (*Hist.* i 95M) has the phrase 'Calpurnius cognomento Lanarius'; and Plutarch, patently deriving from Sallust, describes how Lanarius, by killing Julius Salinator (i.e. Livius Salinator, as established by C. Cichorius, *Römische Studien* (1922), 256), enabled Annius to make the passage of the Pyrenees: Καλπουρνίου δέ τινος ἐπίκλησιν Λαναρίου δολοφονήσαντος τὸν Ἰούλιον καὶ τῶν στρατιωτῶν τὰ ἄκρα τῆς Πυρήνης ἐκλιπόντων, ὑπερβαλὼν ὁ Ἄννιος | ἐπῄει χειρὶ μεγάλῃ τοὺς ἐμποδὼν ἀναστάς (*Sertorius* 7). Lanarius is commonly described as a traitor and an assassin (A. Schulten, *Sertorius* (1926), 45; J. Carcopino, *Histoire romaine* ii (1936), 502; R. Gardner (in a vague allusion), *CAH* ix (1932), 320). *MRR* refuses him an entry, but happens to mention him incidentally as an officer of Annius (ii 78). Indeed, it is clear that Lanarius is not a disloyal Sertorian but a responsible commander under Annius; not author of a murder but of a military stratagem, of some Thermopylean flank movement. Compare Sallust, *Hist.* i 97M: 'paucos saltum insidentis'. The word δολοφονήσαντος in Plutarch has proved deceptive. The Latin original may have had 'fraus' or 'astus'; compare Tacitus, *Ann.* xii 33: 'astu locorum fraude prior' (whatever remedy be adopted in this passage: Fuchs adds 'et' after 'astu'). Plutarch's account is very compressed. The Sertorian general perished in the course of operations, perhaps during the retreat; cf. Sallust, *Hist.* i 36M: 'Salinator in agmine occiditur'.

Touching the age and status of Lanarius, observe that a P. Calpurnius Lanarius figures in a dispute about house-property at Rome before 91 (Cicero, *De officiis* iii 66). The incident can be dated by the reference to M. Cato, the parent of Uticensis, who died when a candidate for the praetorship (Gellius xiii 20, 40), about 93 (Plutarch, *Cato* 1). The moneyer P. Calpurnius (not precisely to be dated) could perhaps have been the parent of Lanarius (*BMC, R. Rep.* i 968 = Sydenham, *CRR* 468). None of the Pisones owns to the *praenomen* 'P.'

CASSIUS SABACO. Expelled from the Senate in 115 (Plutarch, *Marius* 5). This friend of Marius is clearly not a person of class or consequence. 'Sabaco' should be regarded as a nickname rather than as a *cognomen* (and might therefore be added to Hug's list of 'Spitznamen' in *RE* iii A, coll. 1837 ff.). Its connotation may be unsavoury. Observe the adjective σαβακός, applied to hetaerae (*Anth. Pal.* vii 222, 2: Philodemus of Gadara). The name of the hetaera Σαλαβακχώ might be relevant (Aristophanes, *Eq.* 765; *Thesm.* 805). Derisory nicknames sometimes stuck .That was the fate of Scipio Nasica (*cos.* 138), called 'Serapio' from his striking resemblance to the slave of a pork-dealer (Pliny, *NH* vii 54). Cassius Sabaco is mentioned incidentally in *MRR*, under the events of 115 (with the *cognomen* wrongly spelt), but is absent from the Index and from the Supplementary List of Senators.

CILLO. Proscribed senator, discovering his fate as he issued from the Curia (Appian, *BC* iv 27). As Münzer pointed out (*RE* vi, col. 2503), hardly to be identified with the moneyer L. Flaminius Chilo, for whom Münzer accepted Mommsen's date of 45: he probably belongs either to 43 or to 42 (*BMC, R. Rep.* i 4198; 4201 = Sydenham, *CRR* 1088 f.).[1] The *cognomen* 'Chilo' or 'Cilo' is not as uncommon as it might seem. It is borne in this period by the following persons: P. Vettius Chilo, 'homo equestris | ordinis honestissimus atque ornatissimus', the brother of Verres' quaestor and of Verres' wife (*In Verrem* ii 3, 166 ff.); the Catilinarian senator Q. Annius (Sallust, *Cat.* 17, 3; 50, 4), who is identical with Q. Annius Chilo (Cicero, *In Cat.* iii 14, accepting Halm's 'Annium' for the 'Manlium' of the MSS.: not registered by Klebs in *RE* i, col. 2263); Cilo, the unidentified friend of the Pompeian (C.) Toranius (*Ad. fam.* vi 22, 1: July, 45); P. Magius Cilo, the man who inexplicably assassinated his friend and patron, the consular M. Marcellus, at the Piraeus on 23 May 45 (*Ad fam.* iv 12, 2, etc.; cf. Münzer, *RE* xiv, coll. 441 f.).

However, since Appian calls the senator Κίλλων, 'Cillo' or 'Gillo' ought also to find mention, however rare they may be. There was a slave called Cillo, an expert on drainage, who was delayed by the collapse of a tunnel at Aesernia when Cicero had need of his services (*Ad Q. fratrem* iii 1, 3: not in *RE*); otherwise only a single fortuitous instance (*CIL* viii 11243: Capsa). 'Gillo', however, occurs in senatorial nomenclature with Q. Fulvius Gillo (*pr.* 200), to return after nearly three centuries with M. Fulvius Gillo (*cos. suff.* A.D. 76), the parent (probably adoptive) of Q. Fulvius Gillo Bittius Proculus (*suff.* ?98). Juvenal employs the name (i 40), not in an honourable context.

P. CORNELIUS CETHEGUS. Important senator in the time of Marius and Sulla. *MRR* lists only the moneyer (P. Cornelius?) Cethegus (Index, cf. p. 437 without the mark of interrogation), who cannot be closely dated (*BMC, R. Rep.* ii, p. 271 (not numbered) = Sydenham, *CRR* 553). He might, or might not, be identical with the famous P. Cethegus, who in any event deserves a separate entry. According to Cicero, Cethegus knew the *res publica* inside out—'totam enim tenebat eam penitusque cognoverat; itaque in senatu consularium auctoritatem adsequebatur' (*Brutus* 178). What is known about his career furnishes a commentary—a partisan of Marius and a public enemy, he passed over to Sulla and exerted much influence under the restored oligarchy as a master of intrigue and corruption (*RE* iv, col. 1281). He was the author of (or was subsequently

[1] [43 according to M. H. Crawford, *Roman Republican Coin Hoards*.]

credited with) various pieces of jobbery in the year 74. He died not long after (cf. Cicero, *Pro Cluentio* 84): coeval with men already prominent before the *Bellum Italicum*, e.g. C. Julius Caesar Strabo Vopiscus, curule aedile in 90, as is stated explicitly (*Brutus* 178).

P. CORNIFICIUS. Senator in 52, from Asconius 32: 'dein proximo senatu P. Cornificius ferrum Milonem intra tunicam habere ad femur alligatum dixerat'. Cf. *Pro Milone* 66. Omitted from the index of Clark's edition. There is no reason to hold him identical with the L. Cornificius who was among the fairly numerous (and heterogeneous) prosecutors of Milo (ibid. 34; 48). That person may well be the L. Cornificius who prosecutes M. Brutus in absence under the *Lex Pedia* in 43, serves Octavian as an admiral in the Sicilian War, and rises to the consulate in 35 (*PIR*², C 1503). The respectable Cornificii are Q. Cornificius, candidate for the consulate of 63 (a good man, but not to be | rated very high: *Ad Att.* i 1, 1; Asconius 73), not heard of after 62, and his homonymous son, quaestor 48, praetor probably 45, who fell in battle (42) after a long struggle to hold Africa for the Republic.

That Cornificii should exhibit an interest in Annius Milo is no surprise, for they too came from Lanuvium, as may be deduced from the Juno Sospita on the coins struck in Africa by the younger Q. Cornificius (*BMC, R. Rep.* ii, p. 578, nos. 26 ff. = Sydenham, *CRR* 1352). It was a mishap that the deduction was not made and exploited by Münzer in *RE* iv, coll. 1605 ff.

C. CURTIUS. Adlected into the Senate by Caesar (Cicero, *Ad fam.* xiii 5, 2). A victim of Sulla's proscription, which engulfed his fortune, he had been able to retrieve, 'tamquam e naufragio', enough to purchase an estate at Volaterrae. The title of this being dubious, Cicero intercedes with the land-commissioner Q. Valerius Orca, arguing that this unfortunate man is in danger of forfeiting rank and station—'quem ordinem ille ista possessione amissa tueri vix potest'.

DOMITIUS APULUS. Partisan of M. Antonius (Cicero, *Phil.* xi 13). Like the other eleven persons in the company here derided, Domitius may well be senatorial (cf. *Rom. Rev.* (1939), 132). The things said about him (bankruptcy and poison) are no bar. He is not, however, to be found among the nineteen names later catalogued of the Antonian Senate (*Phil.* xiii 26 ff.). There is another non-aristocratic Domitius with an ethnic *cognomen*, the poet Marsus (*PIR*², D 153).

CN. EGNATIUS CN. F. Senator in 74, disinherited by his father for having taken bribes (Cicero, *Pro Cluentio* 135). The father (also a senator) is styled 'Cn. Egnatius pater', which proves that their *praenomina* were identical: compare Tacitus, *Ann.* vi 7, 2: 'C. Cestium patrem', which a recent editor (H. Fuchs) alters to 'praetorem'. Therefore the son cannot be the same person as the moneyer C. Egnatius Cn. f. Cn. n. Maximus (*BMC, R. Rep.* i, 3274 = Sydenham, *CRR* 786), though that was believed possible by Münzer (*RE* v, col. 1997) and assumed without question in *MRR*. Moreover, the context shows that Cn. Egnatius the father had another son: the moneyer can therefore be dated, if so desired, later than 74. These are not people of any distinction (and the parent was expelled from the Senate in 70). The name 'Egnatius' is claimed by Schulze as Etruscan, with examples in support (*LE* 187 f.)—but with no indication that it is borne by indigenous Samnites in various historical periods, for example Gellius Egnatius (Livy x 18, 1, etc.), and Marius Egnatius, the insurgent-leader in 90 (Livy, *Per.* lxxv; Velleius ii 16, 1; Appian, *BC* i 40 f.).

M. FIDUSTIUS. The twice-proscribed senator. Pliny (*NH* vii 134) gives the reason and the (predictable) author of the second calamity—'superstes | Sullae vixit, sed usque ad Antonium, constatque nulla alia de causa ab eo proscriptum quam quia proscriptus fuisset'. The name is exceedingly rare (*LE* 404). At Rome only freedmen (*CIL* vi 17925; 3524 f.), six in number, apart from 'L. Fidusti / M. f. / Voltinia' (17926 = i² 1305). Outside Rome only at Nepet, an old Latin colony not far away (*CIL* xi 3200 = *ILS* 89; 3205 = *ILS* 4948; 3233): the second of these inscriptions is of some interest, revealing Fidustia L. f., the mother of Q. Veturius Q. f. Pom. Pexus, an equestrian officer of fairly early date, who was a 'lupercus Fabianus ex collegio Virtutis'. The tribe of Nepet is not certain. Kubitschek printed 'Stellatina' with a query and with diffidence (*Imp. Rom. Trib. Discr.* (1889), 86).

*FONTEIUS Q. F. Attested as quaestor (presumably of Africa) by *CIL* vi 31713 = *ILS* 901: '] Fonteio Q. f. / q. / mancup. stipend. ex Africa'. Groag (*PIR²*, F 462) estimates 'sub finem liberae rei publicae vel temporibus Augusti'. Clearly a member of that Tusculan family which, with its first praetor in 178, reaches the consulate in 33 with C. Fonteius Capito, the friend of Antonius, and lasts until the consul of A.D. 67. The *praenomen* 'Q.' is elsewhere found only in the filiation of a Fonteius senator in 143 (*SIG³* 679, ii [= Sherk, *RDGE* 7], l. 39), or perhaps rather 161 (cf. *MRR* i 444).

FULVIUS SEPINUS. Senator refused permission to fight as a gladiator in 46 (Dio xliii 23, 5, where Boissevain restores Σεπῖνος: R. Stephanus' correction Σετῖνος had held the field for a long time, and is presupposed by Münzer, *RE* vii 279). For examples of the well-attested 'Sepius' and 'Seppius' (Etruscan), see *LE* 277. Further, curiosity might be excited by the person and *cognomen* of Q. Fulvius Lippinus, who established game-parks on his estates near Tarquinii and was a pioneer in cultivating snails (Varro, *Res Rusticae* iii 12, 1; Pliny, *NH* viii 211; ix 173): that *cognomen* is independently attested for P. Sextius Lippinus Tarquitianus, quaestor of Macedonia in A.D. 14 (*CIL* iii 717 = *ILS* 4055: Samothrace). That is not all. Suetonius has a relevant notice about the spectacles of 46—'munere in foro depugnavit Furius Leptinus stirpe praetoria et Q. Calpenus, senator quondam actorque causarum' (*Divus Julius* 39, 1). Has there been confusion somewhere between a Fulvius and a Furius? Münzer (*RE* vii, col. 279) refuses to pronounce—and 'Leptinus' is legitimate, cf. Q. Lepta, Cicero's *praefectus fabrum* in Cilicia (*Ad fam.* iii 7, 4, etc.). *MRR* omits both persons. Which is justifiable for Furius Leptinus, since Suetonius' words, taken strictly, mean that no actual senators fought as gladiators; but Fulvius Sepinus ought to remain on record.

C. GEMINIUS. Senator in 39: from an unpublished inscription of Cos, noted in *RE*, Supp. iii, col. 542, cf. 528 (under 'Fonteius'). Perhaps that Geminius whom friends of M. Antonius dispatched to him in 32, urging him to make peace with Octavianus and give up Cleopatra (Plutarch, *Antonius* 59). His | tribe is the Camilia, the tribe of Tibur. Since Anto, a son of Hercules, is the eponymous ancestor of the Antonii (Plutarch, *Antonius* 4), the Tiburtine cult of that god might make one wonder about their origin and look (not in vain) for Tiburtine links and partisans.

Geminii seem indigenous in Latium; compare old inscriptions at Praeneste (*CIL* i² 169–71; 62 = *ILS* 3419 [= *ILLRP* 132]); and it was a Geminius who, with another man, was charged with building the temple of Castor and Pollux at Cora (*CIL* i² 1502 = *ILS* 3386 [= *ILLRP* 60]). No Geminius secured entry to *MRR*, but a friend of Pompeius must have come very near it, being of the officer class at least: he was allowed to take over the beautiful Flora, and he saw active service against M. Brutus in the Cisalpina in 77 (Plutarch, *Pompeius* 2; 16).

C. HERENNIUS. Senator in 74 (Cicero, *In Verrem* i 39). Münzer (*RE* viii, col. 663) assumes that he was condemned for taking bribes shortly after 80, and amalgamates him with the homonymous tribune in Sallust (*Hist.* ii 21M) and with the Sertorian general who was killed at Valentia in 76 (ibid. ii 98, 6; Livy, xci fr.; Plutarch, *Pompeius* 18). *MRR* apparently concurs. The Ciceronian context, however, naming C. Herennius along with C. Popilius and M. Atilius (Bulbus), and stigmatizing the conduct of all three in the year when C. Verres was *praetor urbanus*, reveals him as one of the corrupt jurymen of 74.

JUVENTIUS. Senator *c.* 80, deduced from Cicero's address to his son, M. Juventius Laterensis (*pr.* 51): 'quaeris etiam, Laterensis, quid imaginibus tuis, quid ornatissimo atque optimo viro, patri tuo, respondeas mortuo'

(*Pro Plancio* 51). There was a M. Juventius Pedo, juryman in 74 (*Pro Cluentio* 107); also a T. Juventius, an orator and lawyer (*Brutus* 178), probably the same person as the C. Juventius of *Dig.* i 2, 2, 42. For a new Juventius Laterensis see the next item.

The Juventii derive from Tusculum (*Pro Plancio* 19). Rising to curule office in the same generation as the Fonteii, they quickly outdistance them with a consul (M'. Juventius Thalna in 163), but could never again recover that dignity, despite efforts and pretentiousness. Their last known member is the praetor of 51, who, legate of M. Lepidus in 43, committed suicide when that person abandoned the Republic and joined Antonius (*RE* x, coll. 1366 ff.).

M'. (JUVENTIUS) L. F. LATERENSIS. Senator of praetorian rank. *AE* 1940, 129 reported (but did not reproduce) a number of statue bases from Calymna (published by M. Segre in *Memorie . . . della R. Deputazione di Storia Patria per Rodi* iii (1938), 43), with inscriptions recording restorations by Πόπλιος Σερουίλιος Ποπλίου υἱὸς ἀνθύπατος and by Μάνιος Λατερήνσιος Λευκίου υἱὸς στρατηγός. They are now to be found in *ASAA* xxii/xxiii (1952), 158 ff., with plates lxxvii–lxxix. The Laterensis inscriptions are n. 130 A, Cb, Da, and E: Segre also (ibid. 160) claims a parallel instance of Laterensis' operations from another city (*Milet* i 2, n. 14). |

Segre assumes that the person is M. Juventius Laterensis, praetor in 51. Similarly *AE* 1940, 129. But he is a Manius, not a Marcus—and a new character. What is his date and function? P. Servilius Isauricus (*cos.* 48) was proconsul of Asia from 46 to 44, but Laterensis does not have to belong to the same time. On one of the bases (n. 130 D) both officials occur: the records of their restorations have been inscribed respectively above (Laterensis—name supplemented) and below (Isauricus) an earlier Hellenistic epigram. For present purposes it will be enough to point out that M'. Laterensis might be several years, or a whole generation, earlier: conceivably a governor of Asia *c.* 77.

LUCILIUS. Senator of the mid-second century, cited by his son Q. Lucilius Balbus for a session in 162 and for a celestial phenomenon of 129 (Cicero, *De natura deorum* ii 11; 14). Münzer (*RE* xiii, coll. 1639 f.) is agnostic, *MRR* omits. The artifice is transparent. But Cicero could not invent a senator, nor would he exhibit ignorance about the family of a man he claims to know. Even when the scene of a dialogue was remote, he took pains about identity and status; compare his demands upon Atticus (*Ad Att.* xiii 30, 2, etc.). As for the *De natura deorum*, he was present himself. The dramatic date is surely 76, a year permitting easy recognition and definition, as Cicero had so recently pointed out; cf. *Brutus* 318: 'unum igitur annum, cum redissemus ex Asia, causas nobilis egimus, cum quaesturam nos, consulatum Cotta, aedilitatem peteret Hortensius'. The interlocutors were C. Aurelius Cotta (*cos.* 75), Q. Lucilius Balbus, and C. Velleius (*De natura deorum* i 15). Only Velleius is expressly designated a senator: that was advisable, as he was the least well known, and an Epicurean. One will observe the link with the *De oratore*, where Cotta is a character, and where, as being also friends of L. Licinius Crassus (*cos.* 95), Velleius and the 'duo Balbi' (i.e. Quintus and his brother, or cousin, Lucius) all appear in one paragraph (iii 78). Lucius (*Brutus* 154) is presumably identical with L. Lucilius L. f., governor of Asia about the year 90 (*Inschr. von Priene* iii 111, ll. 136 and 147; cf. Münzer, *RE* xiii, col. 1637). Quintus was probably a senator, like his father before him. No Lucilii Balbi figure in *MRR*, and none is attested after the 'duo Balbi'. One might perhaps wonder about the L. Lucilius who was with Ap. Claudius Pulcher in Cilicia (*Ad fam.* iii 5, 1); but there is little profit in evoking unattached Balbi, for the *cognomen* is too common.

M. (Minucius) Basilus. Senator in 74 (Cicero, *Pro Cluentio* 107). Clearly related to, and perhaps a brother of, that L. Minucius Basilus who adopted his sister's son M. Satrius (*De off.* iii 74). On these people, cf. C. Cichorius, (*Römische Studien* (1922), 175 f.), who drew attention to L. Minucius L. f. Vel. on the tablet of Asculum (*ILS* 8888 [= *ILLRP* 515]), followed by Münzer, *RE* xv, coll. 1947 ff. They come from Picenum.

*C. Nunnuleius C. f. Nudus. Described as 'leg. pro praet.' (*CIL* xiv 3546 = *ILS* 3414: Tibur). The inscription is a dedication to Hercules Victor, set up | in memory of Nunnuleius by his wife, Pomponia L. f. He is listed as *PIR*[1], N 196, and is late Republican or early Imperial (E. Groag, *RE* xvii, col. 1474). For *nomina* in '-uleius' and '-oleius', see Schulze, *LE* 457 ff., who cites no instance of 'Nunnuleius'. It is exceedingly rare—not even in *CIL* vi. Add *CIL* x 1318 (Nola). There is a Numoleius on the Capuan inscription *CIL* i[2] 678 = *ILS* 3397 [= *ILLRP* 715] (of the year 106). Comparable rarities deserve study, such as 'Burbuleius', 'Eppuleius', 'Farsuleius', 'Justuleius', 'Pantuleius', 'Rabuleius', 'Septumuleius'.

Q. Ovinius. Partisan of Antonius, put to death at Alexandria by Octavian 'ob eam maxime notam quod obscenissime lanificio textrinoque reginae senator populi Romani praeesse non erubuerat' (Orosius vi 19, 20, from Livy, or rather an epitome of Livy). Varro has 'Ovinius' among the names derived from animals (*Res Rusticae* ii 10); compare the Oscan 'Ovius' (Münzer, *RE* xviii, coll. 1996 f.); also 'Ovidius', suitably authenticated among the Paeligni by P. Ovidius Naso and by the equestrian magnate L. Ovidius Ventrio (*CIL* ix 3082: Sulmo). The *nomen* 'Ovinius' is very uncommon, with no place in Roman annals between the *Lex Ovinia* shortly before 312 (Festus 290L) and C. Ovinius Tertullus *cos.*

suff. c. A.D. 194 (*PIR*¹, O 127), except for this appropriately named senator, whom Livy commemorated for discredit, himself a son of Patavium—which was the leading town in the manufacture of woollen goods.

*PACCEIUS L. F. Recorded by an inscription at Tibur: 'Pacceio L. f. / q. pro pr. / Ostienses / navicularei' (*CIL* xiv 3603 = *ILS* 6171); *PIR*¹, P 5; Dessau in *CIL* xiv estimated it as 'aetatis ut pote circiter Augusti'. Now lost, cf. *Inscr. It.* i 1, 119. The (verbose) article of M. Hofmann (*RE* xviii, coll. 2060 f.) contributes nothing.

*C. PACCIUS C. F. Recorded on an inscription at Tarracina: 'C. Paccius C. f. . . . / Xvir ad hastam, [quaestor?] / ludos Honoris e[t Virtutis fecit],' etc. (*CIL* x 8260 = *ILS* 5051); *PIR*¹, P 7. The unparalleled designation for the 'Xvir stlitibus iudicandis' should indicate an early date. The article of M. Hofmann (*RE* xviii, coll. 2063 f.) adds nothing. The *nomen* 'Paccius' (which is the Latin form of the Oscan 'Pakis') is common and vulgar. The nearest it can be said to approach distinction is with the successful prosecutor C. Paccius Africanus, *cos. suff. c.* A.D. 67 (Tacitus, *Hist.* iv 41; *IRT* 342, cf. *AE* 1949, 76) and with Paccia Marciana, the first wife of Septimius Severus (*HA Severus* 3, 2; *CIL* viii 19494 = *ILS* 440; *IRT* 410 f.).

*C. PACCIUS C. F. BALBUS. Recorded on an inscription of Teanum Sidicinum which fades out after the third line (*Eph. Ep.* ix, p. 217, n. 883): 'C. Paccius C.f. / Balbus pr. / pro cos.' *PIR*¹, P 8; the article of M. Hofmann (*RE* xviii, col. 2065) divagates into loose speculation about *iuridici* in Italy.

For convenience of reference the legate ']cius Balbus' may here be mentioned (*AE* 1934, 85: Cos), who is listed in *MRR* (ii, p. 483), from D. Magie, | *Roman Rule in Asia Minor* ii (1950), 1587. The inscription can as well be early Imperial as late Republican. It runs . . . . ἐτί]μασε / . . . . . . κιον Βάλ/βον [πρεσ]βευτὴν καὶ ἀν/τιστράτηγον τὸν ἑατο[ῦ] /πάτρωνα [ἀ]ρετᾶς ἕνεκα / καὶ εὐνοί[α]ς [τ]ᾶς ἐς αὐτόν. Recourse to the original publication (G. Patriarca, *Bull. Mus. Imp. Rom.* iii (1932), 3) shows further that the *praenomen* must have been 'Aulus', 'Lucius', or 'Marcus': for *praenomen* and *nomen* together there is space for about eight letters before the]κιον at the end of the *nomen*. Speculation would not be fruitful, despite the *cognomen* 'Balbus', the item L. F. OUF. BALBUS discussed above, or the foregoing PACCIUS at Tarracina, the tribe of which town is the Oufentina.

L. PETTIUS. A Roman embedded in a Pergamene decree, Josephus *AJ* xiv 251: τῆς τε βουλῆς ἡμῶν Λούκιος Πέττιος ἀνὴρ καλὸς καὶ ἀγαθὸς προσέταξεν ἵνα φροντίσωμεν ταῦτα οὕτως γενέσθαι καθὼς ἡ σύγκλητος ἐδογμάτισε, προνοῆσαί τε τῆς ἀσφαλοῦς εἰς οἶκον τῶν πρεσβευτῶν ἀνακομιδῆς. The document is held to belong *c.* 132, and Pettius must be a Roman senator, not a member of the council of Pergamon; cf. Münzer, *RE* xix, col. 1381, followed by R. Marcus (in his Loeb edition, Vol. vii (1943), ad loc.), who favours Reinach's reading of τῇ τε βουλῇ in the opening phrase. For the Oscan *nomen* 'Pettius' see Münzer, op. cit., who registers along with significant local instances the only Pettii known to name or fame, viz. Herius Pettius of Nola (Livy xxii 43, 9 ff.) and the friend of Horace (the dedicatee of *Epodes* xi).

] FAL. PLAUTUS. Senator on the *SC de Aphrodisiensibus* of 35 (P. Viereck, *Sermo Graecus* (1888), xix, p. 40, cf. p. vii [Sherk, *RDGE* 29]). Unidentifiable. Observe similarly, a generation later, the *praetor peregrinus* of A.D. 2 with the *cognomen* 'Plaut(us)' (on the *Fasti Arvalium, Inscr. It.* xiii 1, 297): he is wrongly taken for a Plautius by *PIR*[1], P 341 and by S. J. de Laet, *De Samenstelling van den Romeinschen Senaat* (1941), 71. The Rubellii Plauti (of Tibur, tribe Camilia) were not yet senatorial in the Triumviral period; and (apart from the tribe) the date is presumably too early for L. Sergius Regis f. Arn. Plautus (*CIL* ii 1406 = *ILS* 2922), the young patrician who is sometimes identified with the man who wrote on Stoic philosophy (see *PIR*[1], S 378 and A. Klotz, *RE* ii A, col. 1719, who suspends judgement).

On the *cognomen* 'Plautus', presumably Etruscan, see the comments of Münzer, *RE* xxi 53. There was a corrupt juryman in 61 called Plautus, named along with Spongia and Thalna (Cicero, *Ad Att.* i 16, 6). He voted in the interest of P. Clodius Pulcher, but could not safely be amalgamated with 'L. Sergius, armiger Catilinae', one of Clodius' instruments in violence (*De domo* 13 f.; 21; 87).

PUBLIUS. Legate in the period 78–67: from Sallust, *Hist.* fr. 6 *incert.* M: 'pactione amisso Publio legato' (cited by Donatus to illustrate Terence, | *Phormio* 141 'nunc amitte quaeso hunc'). Now P. Clodius Pulcher (*q.* 61) was certainly in the East in 68 and 67, first with L. Lucullus and then with Q. Marcius Rex (Plutarch, *Lucullus* 34; Dio xxxiv 17, 2 f., etc.), but one should heed the warning uttered by Maurenbrecher ad loc.—'Publii legati nomine neminem nisi P. Clodium, Luculli legatum, significari potuisse iusto audacius editores statuerunt'. Certain peculiar *praenomina* such as 'Appius', 'Mamercus', and 'Servius' can stand alone, without the *gentilicium* or *cognomen*, in historical prose; also others, in the vicinity of a family-name, cf. Sallust, *Jug.* 36, 4: 'Albinus Aulo fratre . . . relicto', which justifies 'Aulus' in 37, 3; Tacitus, *Hist.* iv 40, 3: 'ipsi Publio' (because P. (Egnatius) Celer has been mentioned a few lines earlier). At the same time, a possible corruption of the *nomen* 'Publilius' could be kept in mind. It happens frequently, e.g. in Cicero, *Ad Att.* xii 24, 1; 28, 3 (for Publilius, the brother of Cicero's second wife). Further, one might well feel suspicious about 'Publius Gallus eques Romanus', an unexplained character in Tacitus, *Ann.* xvi 12, 1 (*PIR*[2], G 66).

To illustrate a possible Publilius in Sallust, there is no Publilius known of the period, except perhaps the parent (unattested) of Cicero's Publilia, and the man in Val. Max. viii 7, 5: 'Publilius vero senator et Lupus Pontius eques Romanus, suis temporibus celebres causarum actores, luminibus capti eadem industria forensia stipendia executi sunt'. That passage, by the way, ought to have been adduced (as relevant but not conclusive) in *RE* xvii, col. 866, touching *Dig.* iii 1, 1, 5: 'refert etiam Labeo Publilium caecum Asprenatis Noni patrem aversa sella a Bruto destitutum cum vellet postulare.' It is there suggested that 'Publilium' is a mistake for the *praenomen* 'Publium', that the man is the father of the *rhetor* P. Nonius Asprenas known only from the pages of the Elder Seneca (*PIR*[1], N 96).

L. QUINCTIUS L. F. RUFUS. Proconsul, attested by *IG* xii 5, 924 (Tenos): ὁ δῆ[μος] | Λεύκιον Κοΐν[τιον Λευ]|κίου υἱὸν Ροῦφον ἀνθύ|πατον τὸν ἑαυτοῦ | σωτῆρα καὶ εὐεργέτην |, etc. The lettering is said to indicate the middle of the first century. The man should be proconsul of Macedonia, possibly of Asia. As for identity, observe L. Quinctius, the tribune of 74, 'homo maxime popularis' (*Pro Cluentio* 77, etc.). When praetor he agitated to have Lucullus superseded in his provinces (Plutarch, *Lucullus* 33, cf. Sallust, *Hist.* iv 71M). This appears to be in 68 (and that date is adopted in *MRR*), though 69 is not impossible. A governor was sent out to Asia for 68/7, P. Cornelius Dolabella (see *MRR* ii 142); Cilicia was allotted to one of the consuls of the year, Q. Marcius Rex. If praetor in 68, L. Quinctius could have been proconsul of Macedonia in 67/6: that would involve shifting the Rubrius under whom Cato served as a military tribune (Plutarch, *Cato* 9) one year back, to be praetor in 69 (*MRR* has 68). However, it must be noted that L. Quinctius, like certain other persons to whom Cicero in the *Pro Cluentio* alludes not | amiably, seems to be dead by 66, when that speech was delivered; cf. § 110: 'atque idem quanto in odio postea fuit illis ipsis per quos in altiorem locum ascenderat! neque iniuria. facite enim ut non solum mores et adrogantiam eius sed etiam voltum atque amictum atque etiam illam usque ad talos demissam purpuram recordemini.' The proconsul Rufus can be a different person, a quarter of a century later: there is a place available in 53/2, Macedonia or Asia (the suggestion in *MRR* ii 233 to have C. Cosconius praetor in 54 and proconsul of Macedonia in 53/2 is attractive, but not a proof). Indeed, later still, for the lettering does not exclude an Augustan date (so Mr. Fraser informs me). Hence perhaps a proconsul of Achaia.

Curiosity is baffled (and must remain so) about the identity of L. Quinctius, whose daughter Asinius Pollio married: he was proscribed, and perished at sea (Appian, *BC* iv 12; 27). Nothing else is known: hardly perhaps 'L. Quinctius familiaris meus' who was assaulted and robbed of a letter (*Ad Att.* vii 9, 1). An inscription reveals various members of a Lanuvine family, among them Quinctia L. f. Rufa, wife of a scribe; her husband's grandmother was Thoria A. f., a known local name. As for the patrician Quinctii, except for a pair of moneyers, and for the quaestor T. Crispinus (*Pro Fonteio* 1), they can show no member between the consul of 123 and the consul of 9.

*T. RESIUS T. F. *Legatus pro praetore* (*PIR*[1], R 36). The inscription (*CIL* xi 5029: Mevania) runs: 'T. Resio T. f. Aim. / leg. pr. pr. / locus sepulturae ipsi / posterisq. eius ob plurima / erga suos municipes / merita publice datus.' This rare *nomen* is Etruscan; cf. Schulze, *LE* 220: add *CIL* xi 7941, also from Mevania. The only other instance from Umbria or Etruria is the *primus pilus* A. Resius A. f. Sab. Maximus (xi 1741: Volaterrae), who had previously been a centurion of Legio XI in Dalmatia (iii 2883 = *ILS* 5953: boundary stones between the territories of Corinium and Nedinum). Elsewhere in Italy (outside Rome) only in the North (v 3141 f.: magistrates at Vicetia; 6782: Eporedia). Note also 'Rhesius', which occurs in the nomenclature of the polyonymous Umbrian senator C. Aufidius Victorinus (*cos. suff.* A.D. 155), cf. *AE* 1934, 155. The man of Mevania may have earned the gratitude of his fellow citizens for things done (or not done) when a land-commissioner in the period between Caesar and Caesar Augustus; compare Q. Valerius Orca, who had that function, with the title of *legatus pro praetore*, in the year 45, active (or feared active) at Volaterrae (Cicero, *Ad fam.* xiii 4 f.; cf. above on C. CURTIUS). [Perhaps add 'Fertor Resius, rex Aequiculus' (see *ILLRP* 447, with comments).]

SERGIUS. One of the proscribed, later the only senator to vote against the motion declaring M. Antonius a public enemy (Appian, *BC* iv 45)—or rather, stripping him of his powers (cf. Dio l 4, 3; 6, 1). Unidentifiable. A Πούπλιος Σέρριος is attested as a senator early in 44 (Josephus, *AJ* xiv 220), whom some assume to be a Sergius (e.g. Münzer in *RE* ii A, col. 1392). For the *nomen* | 'Serius', cf. W. Schulze, *LE* 229 f., who cites no instance of 'Serrius'. Note further 'Sertius', with the Roman knight Cn. Sertius (Cicero, *In Verrem* ii 2, 119) and T. Sertius Gallus, 'honestus et ornatus adulescens' (*Pro Milone* 86). For Sergii, above under PLAUT(US). [For a M. Serrius M. f., see *RDGE* 12, line 41.]

Q. SERGIUS. Senator in 90 (Cicero, *Pro Cluentio* 21). He held in his *ergastulum* in the Ager Gallicus the young M. Aurius of Larinum, who had been captured in the *Bellum Italicum*. None of the patrician Sergii of the Republic has the *praenomen* 'Q.': *CIL* i[2] 1715 [= *ILLRP* 543] offers a local Q. Sergius, quaestor at Aquilonia in Samnium.

SERVIUS CORDUS. The man who buried Pompeius Magnus on the shore of Egypt (*Auct. de vir. ill.* 77, 12, where the *cognomen* appears as 'Codrus').

Lucan furnishes his rank (*De bello civili* viii 715 ff.): 'e latebris pavidus decurrit ad aequora Cordus / quaestor ab Idalio Cinyraeae litore Cypri. / infaustus Magni fuerat comes.' It is idle to impugn this incident. Lucan states that Cordus belongs to history (782), 'te fama loquax omnis accepit in annos', and promises him rapid pardon from Caesar (784 ff.). The author of an epic poem on recent and remembered history might take the liberty of inventing a common soldier, like the Marsian Nasidius, who with others perished horribly from snake-bite (ix 70); hardly, however, a Roman knight, and certainly not a person of senatorial rank. A Cordus issued coins together with Kalenus (presumably Q. Fufius Calenus, *tr. pl.* 61, *pr.* 59); cf. *BMC, R. Rep.* i 3358 = E. Sydenham, *CRR* 797: date uncertain, but recent estimates tend towards the early sixties, which would be far too early for a quaestor of 48.[1]

The moneyer L. Servius Rufus belongs in 43 or 42 (*BMC, R. Rep.* i 4204 f. = Sydenham, *CRR* 1081 f. [41 in Crawford, *Coin Hoards*, Table xv]): the reverses of his two types plainly assert an origin from Tusculum. To preclude confusions, it may be as well to state that another *monetalis* of the period, M'. Cordius Rufus (*BMC, R. Rep.* i 4037 ff. = Sydenham, *CRR* 976 ff.), also comes from Tusculum, as is indicated by some of his types and confirmed by *CIL* i² 782 = *ILS* 902 [= *ILLRP* 414].

SULPICIUS RUFUS. Grandfather of Ser. Sulpicius Q. f. Rufus (*cos.* 51). As Cicero states, the *nobilitas* of his coeval, the patrician jurist, was a fact more familiar to scholars and researchers than to the Roman voter (*Pro Murena* 16). Cicero proceeds 'pater enim fuit equestri loco, avus nulla inlustri laude celebratus'. The phraseology shows that the grandfather was a senator.

SER. SULPICIUS SER. F. RUFUS. Son of the patrician jurist (*cos.* 51). He was absent from the session of the Senate in February 43 which commemorated his dead parent—'adflictus luctu non adest' (Cicero, *Phil.* ix 12). Otherwise there is no proof that he was a senator, no trace of any office or post held during the Civil War, though he was Caesarian in sentiment at the outset. Supposing him born *c.* 80, he can easily be identified with the young Ser. | Sulpicius who helped the jurist at a prosecution in 63 (*Pro Murena* 56, etc., cf. Münzer, *RE* iv A, col. 861). The *monetalis* Ser. Sulpicius (*BMC, R. Rep.* i 3907 = Sydenham, *CRR* 931) is almost certainly a Galba (cf. Münzer, *RE* iv A 737), perhaps identical with the senator Ser. Sulpicius who was in Africa with Juba in 49 (Caesar, *BC* ii 44, 3): in any case distinct from Ser. Sulpicius Galba, praetor in 54 and a Caesarian. The survival of Ser. Sulpicius Rufus subsequent to 43 presents a problem. He is last heard of for certain in June of that year (*Ad fam.* xi 24, 2), and

---

[1] [In Crawford, *Roman Republican Coin Hoards*, these moneyers appear in Table xiii, *c.* 70. Cordus is indexed under 'Mucius', without explanation.]

might, as Münzer suggests, have perished in the proscriptions (*RE* iv A, 862).
But Münzer also points to Horace, *Sat.* i 10, 85 f.: 'Pollio, te, Messalla,
tuo cum fratre simulque / vos, Bibule et Servi, simul his te, candide
Furni'. The Servius included in this group of cultivated and literary
personages ought to be the jurist's son: he married a sister of Messalla
Corvinus (Jerome, *Adv. Iovinianum* i 46, from Seneca, *De matrimonio*).
Moreover, men of birth tend to evade or survive proscription (cf. *Rom.
Rev.* (1939), 192). It might seem obvious and inevitable to amalgamate the
Servius of Horace with the Ser. Sulpicius in the younger Pliny's catalogue
of the eminent senators who wrote light verse (*Ep.* v 3, 5) and with the
erotic poet in Ovid, *Tristia* ii 441: so Münzer, *RE* iv A, col. 862; Schanz–
Hosius, *Gesch. der röm. Lit.* ii⁴ (1935), 273, and others. That may be premature. Ovid's phraseology needs close attention—'nec minus Hortensi, nec
sunt minus improba Servi / carmina. quis dubitet nomina tanta sequi?'
Hortensius, also in Pliny's catalogue, is the consular orator: for the *testimonia* about his verse see *RE* viii, col. 2484; Schanz–Hosius, op. cit. i⁴
(1927), 287. Therefore the Servius named beside him as representing
'magna nomina' could perhaps be the consular jurist. The son, who may
(or may not) have written poems is clearly the parent of the poetess
Sulpicia. This is denied (pointlessly) in Schanz–Hosius (op. cit. ii⁴ (1935),
273), where an (unverifiable) son is evoked instead.

TITIUS. Senator from Spain. The *Bellum Africum* records how Metellus
Scipio put to death the 'duo Titii Hispani adulescentes, tribuni legionis V,
quorum patrem Caesar in senatum legerat' (28, 2). Cf. Münzer, *RE* vi A,
coll. 1556 f., arguing, against Cichorius (*Röm. Stud.* (1922), 252), that
'Hispanus' is an 'ethnic' designation, on the way to becoming a *cognomen*;
also R. Syme, *Rom. Rev.* (1939), 80. The *nomen* permits no deductions.

VALERIUS MESSALLA. Praetor c. 120. He was prosecuted by Metellus
Numidicus (*cos.* 109) for extortion practised on *socii* (Gellius xv 14, 1 f.).
Münzer leaves it open whether or no he be identical with the Valerius
Messalla attested as *legatus* in 90 in the *Bellum Italicum* (Appian, *BC* i 40);
cf. *De gente Valeria* (Diss. Berlin 1891), 52. *MRR*, however, amalgamates.
The entries ought to be kept separate. A prosecution would fit the earlier
career of Metellus, not the later. As for identity, this Messalla will repre-
sent the missing | generation after the consul of 161: the *praenomen*
'Manius' could plausibly be supplied from the nomenclature of the consul
of 61, M. Valerius M. f. M'. n. Messalla (registered on the *cippi* he set up
when censor in 55, *CIL* i² 766: three of them in *ILS* 5922 [one in *ILLRP*
496]). The homonymous Messallae, the consuls of 61 and 53 (conveniently known as 'Niger' and 'Rufus' respectively), look like first cousins:
the common grandfather is therefore a M'. Messalla.

Magnesia ad Sipylum honours Potitus Valerius Messalla (*suff.* 29) as patron and benefactor διὰ προγόνων (*OGIS* 460). No Messalla, so far as known, had governed the province Asia. Hence a slight perplexity: cf. A. E. Gordon, *Univ. of California Pub. in Class. Arch.* iii 2 (1954), 43 f. That scholar adduces the Valerii Flacci. Are they close enough to count? Now the evidence of Gellius (xv 14, 1 f.) discloses a Valerius Messalla governing a province *c.* 120. If M'. Messalla, then a direct ancestor of Potitus. In fact, his great-grandfather, for Potitus is the son of Messalla (Rufus), consul in 53.[1]

VERRES. Senator in 71, parent of C. Verres *praetor urbanus* in 74 and governor of Sicily (Cicero, *In Verrem* ii 2, 95, cf. 102). 'Verres' is a *nomen*, as stated long ago by Mommsen (*Röm. Forsch.* i² (1864), 51), and proved (*Ges. Schr.* viii (1913), 13 f.). There is nothing in Pais's notion that Verres might have been a Cornelius (*Ricerche sulla storia e sul diritto pubblico di Roma* ii (1916), 320 ff.). Mommsen cited two inscriptions with the *nomen* (*CIL* vi 8846; 39031). He might also have noted *In Verrem* i 23: 'inventum tamen esse fortem amicum ex eadem familia, Q. Verrem Romilia, ex optima divisorum disciplina, patris istius discipulum atque amicum'. For this device of nomenclature (used to avoid possible confusions), cf. 'T. Annius Velina' (*Brutus* 178). The Romilia is the tribe of Sora, a Latin colony (Kubitschek, *Imp. Rom. Trib. Discr.* (1889), 31). It does not necessarily follow that this is the home-town of the senator. The termination of the name indicates Etruria, or regions subject to the Etruscan civilization (cf. *LE* 286). The only known senator with such a *gentilicium* is the aedile P. Menates (*CIL* i² 829 = *ILS* 5802 [= *ILLRP* 463], cf. Münzer, *RE* xiv, col. 776).

The connections of the Verres family are not at all distinguished. The praetor's mother was probably a Tadia (*In Verrem* ii 1, 128); and he married a Vettia, sister of the knight P. Vettius Chilo and of his quaestor T. Vettius (ibid. 3, 166). The latter is presumably the same person as the moneyer T. Vettius Sabinus (*BMC, R. Rep.* i 3370 = Sydenham, *CRR* 905) and T. Vettius, praetor in 59 (*Pro Flacco* 85). [But cf. *Verr.* ii 2, 64 and 138: a *cognatio* with the Metelli?]

---

[1] [On these Valerii, cf. pp. 265 f. above.]

20

Some Friends of the Caesars

WHEN the last of the dynasts won sole power in the world, he had no choice but to enlist his adherents in the management of it. They were already there—senators, knights, and freedmen. The personal friends of Caesar Augustus take in a wide range, from the men of consular rank, the *principes civitatis*, to common soldiers—and foreigners will not be excluded, the kings and tetrarchs. It was expedient for a Princeps to be *civilis*; an *imperator* took pride in knowing his *commilitones* by name and exploit; and the Caesars from the beginning showed themselves wondrously accessible to the claims of clients and petitioners. Various anecdotes exemplify. Augustus defended Scutarius, one of his *evocati*, in a court of law; and he intervened to rescue Castricius, who had given him information about the conspiracy of Varro Murena.[1] Again, when Augustus was present at a *hospitalis cena* at Bononia and the talk fell on loot and sacrilege, his host, an Antonian veteran, speaking as one who knew, told him that the golden dish from which he was eating was the leg of the goddess Anaitis;[2] and as *hospes* the Princeps learned from the centenarian Romilius Pollio the famous recipe for health and a long life—'intus mulsum, foris oleum'.[3]

The monarch has a court from the outset. Not so much the ceremonial (which both Augustus and Tiberius eschewed) as the habits, and the appendages—doctors and magicians, philosophers and buffoons. There would be no point, for example, in cataloguing the *convictores Graeculi* of Tiberius Caesar,[4] but his entourage on the island in the last days mattered very much. Tiberius was a convinced believer in the science of the stars. Other ages and the recent time (despotisms or constitutional monarchies) exhibit the secret power wielded by the astrologer, by the court physician, or by some casual but devious confidant.

The term *amicus* is nothing if not comprehensive. It | quickly becomes definite, and can be employed like a title. Categories develop among the friends of Caesar. Thus Seneca can mention the *cohors primae admissionis*.[5]

---

1 Suetonius, *Divus Aug.* 56, 4.   2 Pliny, *NH* xxxiii 83.   3 Ibid. xxii 114.
4 Cf. Suetonius, *Tib.* 56 f.
5 *De Clem.* i 10, 1. [Cf. *De Ben.* vi 34 for the general principle and Republican precedents.]

American Journal of Philology lxxvii (1956), 264–73. © Johns Hopkins University Press.

Moreover, provincial governors are designated as *amici* of the ruler. The first instance is the letter of Caesar Augustus to the city of Cnidus, thus styling Asinius Gallus (*cos.* 8 B.C.), proconsul of Asia in 6/5 B.C.[1] Further-more, Gallus is one of a group who have their names and portraits on coins in Asia and in Africa. Some of those proconsuls, but not all, are related in various ways to the ruling house. It is therefore not unreasonable to describe them as *amici principis*.[2] The date and period at which the honour of coin portraits was permitted would be worth knowing, for its political relevance. The limits are fairly narrow. Six of the seven pro-consuls in question cannot be proved earlier than 10 B.C. or later than 4 B.C.[3] The seventh, however, L. Passienus Rufus (*cos.* 4 B.C.), seems eccentric, and no stretch of argument could bring him into relationship with the dynasty.[4] Usage seems sporadic, as well as the evidence.[5] Several eminent personages of the period lack the honour, notably Iullus An-tonius (*cos.* 10 B.C.), proconsul of Asia and husband of the elder Marcella.[6]

There are also *comites*. By its nature, that is an exact term. A certain Cn. Pullius Pollio may have been a *comes* of Augustus in Gaul (i.e. in 16–13 B.C.)—it depends on the supplement believed best for a mutilated inscription.[7] The first | clear epigraphic instance of the word itself comes a little later—that L. Licinius who was 'comes da[tus . . . a divo A]ug. C. [Caesari]'.[8] Then, beyond cavil, Sex. Palpellius Hister, 'comiti / Ti. Caesaris Aug. dato ab divo Aug.'[9]

Not all the large and motley company that benefit from the friendship and favours of an emperor can be deemed to carry weight in counsel and policy. Contrariwise, the men who exercise a genuine and pervasive influence must often be guessed or postulated—rank and honours, office or employments. Thus iterated consulates or the post of *praefectus urbi*. It is therefore difficult to register the friends and counsellors of the Caesar in a manner that shall satisfy all criteria, and all critics. Better, perhaps, to include too many than too few.

---

[1] *SIG*³ 780 [= Sherk, *RDGE* 67, line 11].

[2] M. Grant, *From Imperium to Auctoritas* (1946), 228 ff., cf. 387 ff.; *Aspects of the Principate of Tiberius* (1950), 52.

[3] Not all of the individual datings suggested by Grant are plausible, e.g. 5/4 B.C. for Paullus Fabius Maximus, consul in 11 B.C. (*FITA* 387). The whole question deserves to be looked into again.

[4] For the coin, struck when he was proconsul of Africa, M. Grant, ibid. 139 f. His governorship falls sensibly later than those of the other six proconsuls.

[5] Cf. the early and isolated phrase ἀνὴρ ἐπιφανέστατος used in the time of Augustus of a proconsul (*SIG*³ 785 [= *RDGE* 70, line 4]: Chios). Presumably a Greek equivalent for 'vir clarissimus'. For the history of the latter title see M. Bang in Friendländer's *Sittenge-schichte Roms*⁹, iv (1921), 77 ff.

[6] *PIR*², A 800.   [7] *ILS* 916 = *CIL* xi 7553 (Forum Clodii).

[8] *CIL* vi 1442. Cf. also 1515 (a lost inscription and a bad copy): '[comiti] / L. Caes Augusti [f.].' The person is a Ti. Sempronius Ti. f. Gracchus.

[9] *ILS* 946.

The latest list to be produced adds up to nearly four hundred names.[1]
It suggests certain observations by the way, and brief addenda.
First of all, personal friends of some rulers. A number of nonentities
have to be admitted, such as the knights Baebius Longus and Calenus,
said to be friends of M. Aurelius.[2] Also the poet Voconius, whoever he
be, who enjoyed the amity of Hadrian.[3] Therefore, if Voconius, why not
Florus, commemorated by a famous and familiar interchange of verses
with the same emperor?[4] Or indeed, Q. Horatius Flaccus? Augustus
offered him a secretarial post, and letters are cited.[5]

Next, *comites*. Horace in the *Epistulae* furnishes useful evidences about
the *cohors* of Tiberius in the eastern lands in 20 B.C.—and the word *cohors*
is twice employed.[6] Notable among its members are Julius Florus and
Albinovanus | Celsus, the latter designated as *comes* and *scriba*.[7] One or
other of them might have survived into the principate of Tiberius Caesar.
That ruler, though distrustful in his nature, and capricious, exhibited an
attachment to old friends, as witness that Lucilius Longus (*suff.* A.D. 7) who
had been with him on Rhodes.[8] By contrast, the treatment of Palpellius
Hister, whom Augustus had planted on the retinue of Tiberius on one
occasion.[9] A chill seems to have supervened.[10] Palpellius received no marks
of esteem. He came to the consulate late in life, under another emperor,
in the year 43.

Time and season have to be watched. The list claims Barea Soranus
(*suff.* 52) and Thrasea Paetus (*suff.* 56) as friends of Vespasian. Those items
derive from a speech of Helvidius Priscus in Tacitus.[11] Whatever be the
validity of the statement, both men were dead before Vespasian came to
the power. They should be left out—as in fact is the Batavian Julius Civilis,
who, taking up arms in 69, appealed to the *amicitia* that bound him to
Vespasian.[12]

Then there is another category: personages whose rank as *amici* or
comites happens to lack precise attestation. The list appears to take in
almost all the known holders of iterated consulates in the first two

---

[1] In J. Crook, *Consilium Principis* (1955), 148–90.   [2] *HA Marcus*, 3, 8.
[3] Apuleius, *Apol.* 11. Crook (op. cit. 190) suggests that he may be Pliny's literary friend
Voconius Romanus (*PIR²*, L 210)—who, however, is not attested as a poet. Perhaps the
Voconius Victor in Martial (*PIR¹*, V 613). [For a literary *comes* of Tiberius, see now *AE*
1960, 26, and Panciera, *Epigraphica* xxxi (1969), 112 ff.: perhaps the son of the great
Zoilus of Aphrodisias (misunderstood *AE* 1969–70, 22), though this is disbelieved by
Robert (*REG* lxxxiv (1971), 499).]
[4] *HA Hadr.* 16, 3 f. Cf. *PIR²*, A 650.   [5] Suetonius, ed. Roth, p. 297.
[6] *Ep.* i 3, 6; 8, 14.
[7] Julius Florus receives *Ep.* i 3, also ii 2, which addresses him as *bono claroque fidelis amice
Neroni*. Celsus is the dedicatee of i 8 (and mentioned in 3, 15). Note also Septimius (i 19).
[8] Tacitus, *Ann.* iv 15, 1.   [9] *ILS* 946.
[10] Like Julius Montanus, *tolerabilis poeta et amicitia Tiberii notus et frigore* (Seneca, *Ep.*
122, 11).
[11] Tacitus, *Hist.* iv 7, 2.   [12] Ibid. 13, 2.

centuries of the Empire. Four are missing, viz. Q. Sanquinius Maximus, C. Antistius Vetus, M. Pompeius Silvanus, and A. Lappius Maximus (with second tenures respectively in 39, 50, 75, and 95).

Similarly, the Prefects of the City. One looks for three of the four attested holders of the post between 32 and the early years of Claudius: L. Aelius Lamia, L. Piso, and Q. Sanquinius Maximus.[1] If other *praefecti* are admitted, for example Q. Baebius Macer (*suff.* 103), who was in office in 117 (no | precise evidence states that he was an *amicus* of Trajan),[2] these three ought not to be denied an entry. L. Aelius Lamia (*cos.* 3), consular legate long ago *in Germania Illyricoque*,[3] surely falls within the ambit of Tiberius' close friends: dying after a brief tenure (32/3), he was accorded the honour of a public funeral.[4] L. Piso (*cos.* 27) is none other than the elder son (he changed his *praenomen*) of Cn. Piso, the ill-starred governor of Syria, the friend whom Tiberius had been compelled to disown. As for Q. Sanquinius Maximus, that mysterious character (consul in an unattested year under Tiberius), one fact speaks volumes—a second consulate in 39, with no precedent since T. Statilius Taurus in 26 B.C.

And finally, persons of consequence among the agents and helpers of the Caesars who do not happen to be certified by the label of an iterated consulate. If the chief credit for Vespasian's policy in the East is to be assigned to Licinius Mucianus and Eprius Marcellus, men of craft and experience,[5] others should not be lost to view. Vespasian early in his reign sent L. Caesennius Paetus (*cos.* 61) to be governor of Syria.[6] He had been in the East before (not to his credit). He was married to a Flavia Sabina.[7] Then there is M. Ulpius Traianus (*suff.* ? 70), who had commanded a legion under Vespasian in Judaea, and was to hold Syria from 74 to 79.[8] The son of that Traianus (*cos.* 91) was presumably an *amicus* of Domitian—as is not stated in the *Panegyricus* of Pliny. Also Cn. Julius Agricola (*suff.* 77): Tacitus cannot suppress the fact that the Emperor was named in Agricola's will.[9]

Two entries among the consular governors might be called into question. D. Terentius Scaurianus (*suff. c.* 104), Trajan's first legate of the newly conquered Dacia, is clearly an impor|tant person.[10] He is not expressly attested as an *amicus* of that emperor. Nor has the younger

---

[1] Viz., in the interval between L. Piso (*cos.* 15 B.C.) and L. Volusius Saturninus (*cos.* A.D. 3).
[2] *HA Hadr.* 5, 5. [Perhaps appointed 116: see Barbieri, *MEFR* lxxxii (1970), 263 ff.]
[3] Velleius, ii 116, 3.   [4] *Ann.* vi 27, 2.   [5] J. Crook, op. cit. 122.
[6] For the evidence, *PIR*², C 173.   [7] *ILS* 995.
[8] *PIR*¹, V 574, cf. *ILS* 8970 (Miletus). An inscription from Antioch reported by L. Robert (*CRAI* 1951, 255) puts him in Syria already in 74.
[9] *Agr.* 43, 4.
[10] Cf. E. Groag, *RE* v A, coll. 669 ff.; A. Stein, *Die Reichsbeamten von Dazien* (1944), 9 f. [Much more so—and perhaps strengthening his claim—in the light of M. Speidel, *JRS* lx (1970), 142, 151 ff. (see especially 153).]

L. Minicius Natalis a strong claim.[1] If he enjoyed the favour of Hadrian at early stages in his career, he could not keep it, or profit by it. Quaestor in 121 (and legate, in the same year, of his parent the proconsul of Africa), he was kept out of the consulate, which he did not reach until Hadrian was dead, in 139.[2] There would have been better warrant for admitting his father (*suff.* 106), who held Pannonia in the critical year of Trajan's death, or Q. Pompeius Falco (*suff.* 108), whom Hadrian transferred from Lower Moesia to Britain.[3] Several of Hadrian's allies were already ensconced in the great commands by 117.

The foregoing examples will suffice to demonstrate how difficult it is to draw the line.[4] At the same time, apart from those examples, twenty names might be adduced in the period from Augustus to Hadrian, heterogeneous and on various criteria, both attested personal friends of the rulers and men of weight whose claims can be urged without scandal or sophistry.[5]

ALEXANDER THE ALABARCH (*PIR*[2], A 510). Said by Josephus to have been a friend of Claudius Caesar before his accession (*AJ* xix 276). Worth noting in view of the resplendent career of his son, Ti. Julius Alexander, who, procurator of Judaea under Claudius, became Prefect of Egypt towards the end of Nero's reign, and rose yet higher: see now E. G. Turner, *JRS* xliv (1954), 54 ff., discussing, among other things, *P. Hibeh* 215.

ASCONIUS LABEO. Voted the *ornamenta consularia* at the same time as Nero's father was honoured with a posthumous statue (*Ann.* xiii 10, 1). Labeo had been Nero's legal guardian after the death of Passienus Crispus (*cos. II* 44), his stepfather, which (it can be inferred) occurred at some time between 44 and the early months of 47. The Asconii come from Patavium, as is patent: '] Asconius Q. f. Labeo', a local priest | (*CIL* v 2848), could have been cited under *PIR*[2], A 1205. Observe the great scholar Asconius Pedianus; and 'Asconius' figures in the full nomenclature of Silius Italicus (*cos.* 68), as is revealed by his edict at Aphrodisias in Caria (*CR* xlix (1935), 216 f.).

C. ATEIUS CAPITO (*suff.* 5). The great lawyer, *humani divinique iuris sciens* (*Ann.* iii 70, 3). Of no small value as a sacerdotal expert—he interpreted the Sibylline Oracle on which were based the *Ludi Saeculares* of 17 B.C. (Zosimus ii 4). The obituary notice (*Ann.* iii 75) is notable on several counts. Augustus, so the historian asserts, speeded Capito's career to the

---

1 *ILS* 1061; cf. 1029.
2 His consulate is disclosed by a new diploma, *CIL* xvi (Suppl.), 175.
3 *ILS* 1029 (Natalis); 1035 f. (Falco).
4 Cf. Mr. Crook's own remarks (op. cit. 25).
5 Not included among the twenty are certain *comites* referred to above, p. 294.

consulate in order to give him primacy before his rival Antistius Labeo, who was Republican by family and sentiment, whereas *Capitonis obsequium dominantibus magis probabatur.*

C. CAECINA TUSCUS. The son of Nero's foster-mother (Suetonius, *Nero,* 35). There are no grounds for calling him 'Graeco-Oriental' (as A. Momigliano in *CAH* x 727). In a sudden but transient crisis of 55 Nero wished to remove Afranius Burrus from his command of the Guard, and, according to the historian Fabius Rusticus, had actually sent *codicilli* to Tuscus, giving him the appointment (*Ann.* xiii 20, 2). Tuscus was later Prefect of Egypt, from 64 to 66, preceding Tiberius Alexander (cf. A. Stein, *Die Präfekten von Ägypten* (1950), 35 ff.).

C. CILNIUS PROCULUS (*suff.* 87). In the fragmentary inscription from Arretium (*CIL* xi 1833, cf. *NSA* 1925, 224), E. Groag (*PIR*[2], C 732) plausibly restores one of his posts as '[comiti Imp. Caes. Traiani] Hadriani A[ug.]'.

TI. CLAUDIUS ATTICUS HERODES (*cos.* 143). The Athenian sophist and millionaire. A Latin inscription in Sweden (provenance unknown), cited in the notes to *SIG*[3] 863, describes him as 'q. imp. Caesaris / Hadriani Aug. inter ami/cos, trib. pleb., praetorem'.

EPICTETUS. The ex-slave. Cf. *HA Hadr.* 16, 10: 'in summa familiaritate Epictetum et Heliodorum philosophos . . . habuit'. Not unimportant, for Hadrian detested pomposity and class distinctions.

CN. HOSIDIUS GETA (*suff.* ? 45). An acephalous inscription (*ILS* 971), at Histonium, the home-town of this family, could be supplemented to yield '[comiti divi] / Claudi in Britannia'. Cn. Hosidius Geta had been active in Mauretania in 42 (Dio lx 9, 1), and is generally identified with the (praetorian) legate in Britain Γάϊος Ὁσίδιος Γέτας (ibid. 20, 4, where Reimarus' emendation to Γναῖος is standard). Groag, however, suggests that the latter might be a distinct person, hence possibly the subject of *ILS* 971 (*RE* viii, col. 2490). |

C. LITERNIUS FRONTO. According to Josephus a certain Fronto, one of the friends of Titus, was empowered to decide the fate of the captives after the fall of Jerusalem (*BJ* vi 416, cf. 419). Clearly Liternius Fronto (ibid. 233). The reference, missed by Stein in *RE* xiii, col. 746, was duly cited in *Die Präfekten von Ägypten* (1950), 39. Note that his governorship of Egypt belongs, not in 69/70, but in 78 or 79, cf. the revision of *AE* 1937, 236 produced by H. G. Pflaum, *Latomus* x (1951), 473.

M. MAENIUS AGRIPPA L. TUSIDIUS CAMPESTER. Roman knight with military service (including an *expeditio Britannica*), described as 'hospiti divi

Hadriani, patri senatoris' (*ILS* 2735: Camerinum). His son is clearly the
']s Campester', suffect consul under Pius or Marcus (*AE* 1945, 37 =
Inscr. It. xiii 1, 210), perhaps in 165; cf. A. Degrassi, *I Fasti Consolari*
(1952), 46.

P. Memmius Regulus (*suff.* 31). The consul who helped to suppress
Seianus. Not attested among the counsellors of Claudius or Nero. But
observe the testimony rendered by Nero. If Nero died, 'habere subsidium
rem publicam', and in elucidation Nero mentioned the name of Regulus
(*Ann.* xiv 47, 1).

P. Petronius Turpilianus (*cos.* 61). Honoured by Nero for loyal services
(of what nature it is not specified) after the conspiracy of C. Piso was
detected and crushed: his reward, the *ornamenta triumphalia*, likewise conferred on the praetor-designate M. Cocceius Nerva and on Ofonius
Tigellinus, the Prefect of the Guard (Tacitus, *Ann.* xv 72, 1). Three years
later Petronius was Nero's general in Italy in the last days, faithful perhaps
to the end. (*Hist.* i 6, 1, cf. 37, 3; Plutarch, *Galba* 15 and 17; Dio lxiii
27, 1a.)

P. Pomponius Secundus (*suff.* 44). The tragic poet. According to Pliny,
who wrote his biography, Pomponius entertained Caligula to a banquet,
with costly and historic wine (*NH* xiv 56). He was half-brother of the
ruler's consort Milonia Caesonia, as were also Cn. Domitius Corbulo, the
great general, and P. Suillius Rufus (*suff. c.* 44). For these, some of
the children of the much-married Vistilia (*NH* vii 39), see C. Cichorius,
Römische Studien (1922), 429 ff. [and pp. 805 ff., below].

Septimius. A mutual friend of Augustus and of Horace, cf. 'ex Septimio
quoque nostro' (Suetonius, ed. Roth, p. 227). Clearly (cf. *PIR*[1], S 306)
the person to whom *Odes* ii 6 is dedicated, and who is commended to
Tiberius in *Ep.* i 19.

C. Stertinius Xenophon. Claudius' chief doctor, with him in the invasion of Britain, and the recipient of military decorations (*SIG*[3] 804:
Cos). It was in response to his entreaty | that the Emperor, so he affirmed
in an oration to the Senate, proposed *immunitas* for Cos (*Ann.* xii 61).
The court physician presumably commanded great influence with
Claudius. M. Artorius Asclepiades (*PIR*[2], A 1183) cannot have played a
comparable role with Augustus: he was lost at sea not long after the Battle
of Actium (Jerome, *Chron.* 187 H).

P. Sulpicius Quirinius (*cos.* 12 b.c.). The obituary, from Tiberius' speech
in the Senate requesting a public funeral (*Ann.* iii 48), recapitulates his
services, among them the post of guide and mentor to C. Caesar in the
East. Quirinius had been careful to cultivate Tiberius in the period of

his reclusion at Rhodes; and later, as an ex-governor of both Galatia–Pamphylia and of Syria, he must have had a place in the councils of both rulers.

THRASYLLUS. The great astrologer (*PIR*[1], T 137). He passed the ordeal at Rhodes contrived by Tiberius who 'incolumem fore gratatur, quaeque dixerat oracli vice accipiens inter intimos amicorum tenet' (*Ann.* vi 21, 3). Perhaps the parent of Ti. Claudius Balbillus (*PIR*[2], C 813 and B 38); cf. C. Cichorius, *Römische Studien* (1922), 370 ff. In any case, highly influential on Capreae: Cichorius further suggested that Ennia Thrasylla, wife of Sutorius Macro, the Prefect of the Guard, was the granddaughter of Thrasyllus.

VALERIUS LIGUR. The Augustan precedent invoked by Claudius Caesar when he asked that his Prefect of the Guard, Rufrius Pollio, should be allowed a seat in the Senate whenever he was present himself (Dio lx 23, 3). Perhaps an Augustan *praefectus praetorio*; cf. *PIR*[1], V 68, where it is suggested that he may be identical with Varius Ligur (V 189).

VALERIUS PAULINUS. Procurator of Narbonensis in 69. Himself a citizen of Forum Iulium, he caused the region to revolt from Vitellius, 'strenuus militiae et Vespasiano ante fortunam amicus' (Tacitus, *Hist.* iii 43, 1). Hence the prospect of a brilliant career, and it was reasonable to identify him with Paulinus, Prefect of Egypt early in the reign of Vespasian (Josephus, *BJ* vii 434). So *PIR*[1], V 105. However, *P. Oxy.* 1266, line 25 (of 72/3), discloses a different *gentilicium*, probably 'Caunius'; cf. R. Syme, *JRS* xliv (1954) 116, adducing the reading of C. H. Roberts.

Q. VERANIUS (*cos.* 49). Legate of Britain in 58, 'supremis testamenti verbis ambitionis manifestus: quippe multa in Neronem adulatione addidit subiecturum ei provinciam fuisse, si triennio proximo vixisset' (*Ann.* xiv 29, 1). His advancement had been rapid—quaestor in 37 (*IGR* iii 703: Cyaneae in Lycia), and tribune of the plebs in 41, when he carried | negotiations for Claudius between the Guard and the Senate (Josephus, *AJ* xix 229 ff.), to become (after the governorship of the new province of Lycia–Pamphylia) *ordinarius* in 49 at about thirty-seven. A loyal friend of the dynasty—the father, who had served under Germanicus Caesar in the East, was active in the prosecution of Cn. Piso (*Ann.* iii 10, 1, etc.). For further particulars, see the new inscription, edited by A. E. Gordon, *Univ. of Cal. Publ. in Class. Arch.* ii (1952), p. 234, whence *AE* 1953, 251.

21

Piso and Veranius in Catullus

Two friends of Catullus had the good fortune to go abroad in the retinue of a proconsul, alert no doubt for gain or adventure, but getting no profit in the end:

Pisonis comites, cohors inanis (28, 1).

They were Veranius and Fabullus. One of the reasons for their disappointment crops up in another poem (47). Piso (so Catullus alleges) bestowed his favours, with long and copious banquets, on other familiars:

Porci et Socration, duae sinistrae
Pisonis, scabies famesque mundi
Vos Veraniolo meo et Fabullo
Verpus praeposuit Priapus ille?

The time and date of this sojourn in foreign parts seems to be adequately documented by Catullus. The first of the two poems implies that Veranius and Fabullus are still with Piso. Catullus asks how they are faring, and whether they have had enough. He alludes to his own miscalculation with Memmius, goes on to draw the moral ('pete nobiles amicos'), and ends by calling down curses on both Piso and Memmius. Now C. Memmius, praetor in 58, went out to govern Bithynia in 57, for the tenure 57/6. The poem should be set in the period 57–55. Who was Piso? Who but L. Calpurnius Piso Caesoninus, consul in 58 with A. Gabinius, and assigned Macedonia as his consular province, *extra sortem* by a *lex Clodia*. He held the province until the summer of 55, succeeded by Q. Ancharius. Taste and refinement signalize this Piso, Greek companions, and an undis|guised addiction to the precepts of Epicurus. The parallel with Memmius (the patron of Lucretius) happens to be closer than it needs to be.

Piso Caesoninus has two claims upon posterity, diverse and contrasted. The one reputable, but obscured and neglected—Piso stood for concord and good sense when others (whom a later age condones or exalts) were for extreme measures against Marcus Antonius in 44 and 43.[1] The other

[1] Cf. *Rom. Rev.* (1939), 135 f.; 170; 172, etc.

Classica et Mediaevalia, xvii (1956), 129–34.

claim is notorious and detrimental: Piso, returning from Macedonia, was pilloried and traduced by the master of Roman eloquence, by the dominant wit and humorist of the age.[1]

Cicero's renown and Piso's infamy have all but eclipsed another consular Piso, namely Marcus. As the learned Asconius found it necessary to observe when expounding the text *In Pisonem* 62 to his sons, 'quis hic M. Piso fuerit, credo vos ignorare'. About this man, by birth a Piso Frugi and adopted by a Pupius, a number of details can be pieced together. For present purposes let it suffice to state that after his praetorship he governed one of the Spains, whence he returned to hold a triumph in 69; that, after having been a legate of Pompeius Magnus in the campaigns against the Pirates and against Mithridates, he was elected consul for 61 as colleague of M. Messalla (Niger).

A devotee of Greek studies, deeper and more scholarly (it could be affirmed) than Caesoninus, he had embraced the Peripatetic persuasion, with Staseas of Neapolis as his instructor and domestic chaplain from the years of his early youth.[2]

Not that M. Pupius Piso, his brand of philosophy, or any provincial governorship can plausibly be brought into relation with Catullus and the friends of Catullus. Piso was looking forward, it is true, to a consular province, as a casual item reveals. It was Cicero who blocked and baffled him in the summer of 61. Cicero leapt into the arena, kept Piso on the run, and took Syria from him.[3] What happened in the sequel, no man can tell, whether the consul was, or was not, allocated | some other province. Several could be thought of. Possibly Cilicia—no proconsul is known after Pompeius Magnus, and nothing at all about the province until it was proposed for Gabinius in the first draft of the *lex Clodia*.[4] Possibly, Hispania Citerior—though no consular as governor is attested in either of the Spains since 70 until Q. Metellus Nepos (*cos.* 57), who held the province for two years (56–54).[5] Speculation is idle, and noxious. Piso (who was some eight years senior to Cicero) fades out and dies, with never a word to demonstrate his survival subsequent to the year of his consulate.[6]

Failing any fact to the contrary, it is best to stick to Piso Caesoninus. The proconsul and his 'comites', Veranius and Fabullus, have a chrono-

---

[1] 'We feel no temptation to whitewash Piso'—so Butler and Cary in their edition of *De prov. cons.* (Oxford, 1924), 88. Why not?
[2] *De oratore* i 104 f.; *De finibus* v 75 (Staseas); *Brutus* 235 f.; 210 (Piso's Greek training, and eloquence).
[3] *Ad Att.* i 16, 8: 'Pisonem consulem nulla in re consistere umquam sum passus, desponsam homini iam Syriam ademi.'
[4] *Pro Sestio* 55; *De domo sua* 23. Perhaps the intention had been to augment Cilicia by transferring from the province Asia the three dioeceses of Phrygia; cf. *CP* 1 (1955), 130.
[5] Dio xxxix 54, 1 f. (under 55).
[6] The tribute in the *Schol. Bob.* (on the *Pro Flacco* (fr. 10) of 59) might be posthumous.

logical bearing on the life and writings of Catullus, that imbroglio of problems where dogma and ingenuity have their habitation, where argument moves in circles, and no new passage in or out.[1] At the most, some modest profit might accrue if the peregrinations of Veranius and Fabullus could be clarified. The attempt is worth making, for more reasons than one.[2]

Piso's province was Macedonia, of which no hint in Catullus (28 and 47). On the other hand, two other poems earlier in the collection show that Veranius (and the inseparable Fabullus), had visited Spain, and precisely the province Hispania Citerior. In the first the poet acclaims the return of Veranius:

> Venisti. O mihi nuntii beati!
> Visam te incolumem audiamque Hiberum
> narrantem loca facta nationes (9, 5 ff.). |

The second alludes to napkins of linen, the product of Saetabis— 'sudaria Saetaba ex Hiberis' (12, 14)—sent as a present by Veranius and Fabullus.

What shall be the solution? Two voyages abroad or only one? If one, a Piso will have to be conjured up, a proconsul governing Hispania Citerior in 57/6, about the time when Catullus himself was in Bithynia with Memmius (and L. Piso in Macedonia).[3] Which can hardly be done. Therefore, two voyages, the earlier to Spain.

It might have been a private tour. Nothing connects Veranius with Spain. Catullus knew his family (9, 4), and there is a chance, a faint chance, that Verona is their home.[4] But, for all that is known, Fabullus could have been a 'Hispaniensis' like that Egnatius whom the poet derides as a 'son of Celtiberia' (37, 18 f.)—and who may be identical with the Egnatius

---

[1] See P. Maas, *CQ* xxxvi (1942), 79 ff.; R. J. M. Lindsay, *CP* xliii (1948), 42 ff.; R. G. C. Levens, *Fifty years of Classical Scholarship* (1954), 288 ff. (critical, negative, and astringent); C. L. Neudling, *A Prosopography to Catullus. Iowa Studies in Class. Phil.* xii (Oxford, 1955). [See now K. Quinn, *Catullus. The Poems* (1970), pp. xii ff., and Commentary (*passim*).]

[2] [Veranius is listed in *RE* viii A, col. 2414.]

[3] Thus Lenchantin de Gubernatis in his commentary on 28 (2nd ed., 1933), suggests that M. Pupius Piso went to Hispania Citerior in 57; cf. also P. Maas, *CQ* xxxvi (1942), 80. Against, and in favour of two journeys of Veranius and Fabullus, R. J. M. Lindsay, *CP* xliii (1948), 42 ff. W. Kroll on 9, 1 (2nd ed., 1929) referred all four poems to one journey; and, on 28, he made light of the arguments in favour of L. Piso the proconsul of Macedonia. See now, for L. Piso and for two journeys of Veranius and Fabullus, C. L. Neudling, op. cit. 42 ff., 65 f., 182 f.

[4] A Verania Vera was detected at Verona by B. Schmidt, cf. his *Prolegomena* (1887), xlix. Also emphasized by R. J. M. Lindsay, *CP* xliii (1948), 44—but of no class, somebody's 'contubernalis' (*CIL* v 3787), and she looks 'native'; cf. for that *cognomen CIL* xiii 652; 12027. Nor is Valeria C. f. Fabulla (3441) enough to clinch the argument. It is worth noting (but not quite a proof against Verona for the origin of Catullus' friend) that the senatorial Veranii of the early Empire have the tribe Clustumina (*RE* viii A, col. 940).

who wrote a poem *De rerum natura*.[1] It is worth recalling how frequently the name-form 'Fabius Fabullus' occurs in Spain—no fewer than eight instances on the inscriptions of the peninsula.[2]

Otherwise the hopeful pair went to Hispania Citerior with a proconsul. The praetorship of L. Piso Caesoninus should fall in 61, hence the tenure 50/59 is not excluded. P. Lentulus Spinther, praetor in 60, had Hispania Citerior in 59/8. No little interest attaches to the identification of provincial governors in this season, many of them adherents | already acquired of the dynasts Pompeius, Crassus, and Caesar, or willing to be won.[3] Spinther later affirmed that he got his province by patronage of Caesar;[4] and Piso, whom the combine decided to put into the consulate of 58 along with Gabinius, became Caesar's father-in-law in the course of 59.

It was sometimes necessary to rescue a political ally. An anecdote relates the humiliation that a Lucius Piso incurred when on trial for offences in a province—'L. Piso a L. Claudio Pulchro accusatus quod graves et intolerabiles iniurias sociis intulisset'.[5] The name of the prosecutor cannot be right as it stands in the text, for the patrician Claudii eschewed the *praenomen* 'Lucius'.[6] Some suppose P. Clodius Pulcher to be meant, hence a prosecution in the summer of 59.[7] That might be correct. Cicero says nothing about this item of discredit in the speech *In Pisonem*. His silence could be variously interpreted—and the beginning of the oration is defective. It had something to report, for example, about the delinquencies of Piso's grandfather, the consul of 112, whom a fragment styles 'homo furacissimus'.[8]

Indeed, the anecdote might refer to the prosecution of the grandfather, a transaction of some importance that has tended to slip out of history. Piso was charged with extortion, a Gaul being among the witnesses. The defence enlisted two advocates of note and weight, M. Scaurus and L. Crassus.[9] The name of the prosecutor is not registered. The case may belong (it could be conjectured) to the political début of that great man C. Claudius Pulcher (*cos.* 92), of whom | so little survives in history, but fortunately one testimony of the most potent.[10]

---

[1] Macrobius vi 5, 2; 12.   [2] Cf. E. Groag, *RE* v, col. 1770.
[3] Cf. *Rom. Rev.* (1939), 35 f.   [4] Caesar, *BC* i 24, 4.
[5] Valerius Maximus viii i, 6.   [6] [Suet. *Tib.* I.]
[7] L. Lange, *Röm. Alterthümer* iii (1876), 288; F. Münzer, *RE* iii, col. 1387; Drumann–Groebe, *Gesch. Roms* ii[2] (1902), 52. Not registered by T. R. S. Broughton in *MRR* ii (1952). W. Kroll on Catullus 9, 1 referred to this possibility, citing Münzer's article.
[8] *In Pisonem*, fr. 11.
[9] *De oratore* 265; 285. Omitted by Münzer, *RE* iii, col. 1387, but exploited in xiv, col. 438 (on Magius, a *praefectus* under Piso). Not in *MRR*; cf. *CP* l (1955), 136 f.—where there ought to have been a reference to P. Fraccaro, 'Scauriana', *RAL* xx (1911), 186. Cf. now H. Malcovati, *ORF*[3] (1967), 163; 258. [But 'Gallus' may be the witness's name.]
[10] *Brutus* 166: 'eodem tempore C. Claudius, etsi propter summam nobilitatem et singularem potentiam magnus erat, tamen etiam eloquentiae quandam mediocritatem adferebat.' [For

It cannot, therefore, quite be proved that Piso governed a province in 60/59, or that the province was Hispania Citerior. But this much can stand: two journeys of Veranius and Fabullus, and the identity of the proconsul they hoped to exploit in 57.

his career, as far as known, see *MRR* ii 547; add now L. Gasperini, *QAL* v (1971), 53 f.; hence *AE* 1967, 532, with a partly imaginary *cursus*; see *Phoenix* xxv (1967), 134 ff.]

22

Seianus on the Aventine

A T some time in the first half of 23 B.C. the consul Varro Murena fell foul of Caesar Augustus. He had to be suppressed. The *Fasti Capitolini* register this man as colleague of the Princeps, with words of annotation after the name. All that happens to survive is]*est*.[1] Enough to show that no pretence was made of his having resigned. A colourless and inoffensive formula covered up the fate of Murena, presumably [*in mag. mortuus*] *est*. None of the other inscribed calendars (so far as extant) carries the name of this consul. They all have the *suffectus* who was appointed to take his place, namely Cn. Calpurnius Piso, masked as an *ordinarius*, and standing as colleague of the ruler.

Varro Murena was close to the inner circle of government: the great Maecenas had married his sister. Fifty-three years later a grand-nephew of Murena held the *fasces* as colleague of Tiberius Caesar—none other than L. Aelius Seianus, Prefect of the Guard.[2] Betrothed to a princess of the dynasty (Julia, the daughter of Drusus Caesar), Seianus was in possession of *imperium proconsulare*, and expected more. The two consuls resigned early in May. On 18 October arrived the 'verbosa et grandis epistula' from Capreae, signifying the doom of Seianus.

No official list ever afterwards would disclose the fact that Aelius Seianus had been *consul ordinarius* in 31. Fortunately there were historians, and a mutilated inscription found at Rome alludes to the manner of his election.[3] |

---

[1] *CIL* i² 70. Degrassi suggests '*damn(atus)*' in *Inscr. It.* xiii 1, 59. Not necessary—and too revealing. [There has been a great deal of discussion on this inscription, on the date of the trials, the consul's identity and related matters. See Shelagh Jameson, *Historia* xviii (1969), 204 ff., with recent bibliography.]

[2] The relationship was deduced from *ILS* 8996 (Volsinii), which reveals a Terentia as the mother of Seius Strabo, by C. Cichorius, *Hermes* xxxix (1904), 161 ff. His *stemma* is adopted in *Rom. Rev.* (1939), table VI. [But see G. V. Sumner, *Phoenix* xix (1965), 134 ff.]

[3] *CIL* vi 10213 = *ILS* 6044. For drawings, *IRN* (1852) 6807: Hübner, *Exempla* (1885), 1038. A thick marble slab, 'litteris bonis et accuratis', according to Mommsen in *IRN*. Line 8 is in larger letters than the rest. Mommsen was enthusiastic about the *comitia* on the Aventine—'deutet das nicht auf eine republikanische Verschwörung, deren Haupt Seian gewesen?' (*Die römischen Tribus* (1844), 208). More guarded in *Röm. Staatsrecht* iii (1887), 348—where, however, he wrongly assumed that Seianus was consul when he fell. Not many historians have exploited this curious document. Dessau suggested that the Aventine

---

It runs as follows:

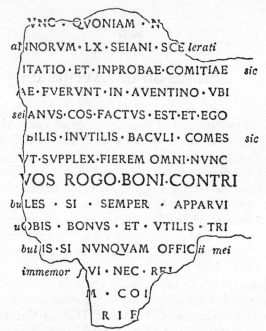

```
 ̣ṾṆC̣ · QVONIAM · Ṇ
aᶥ NNORVM · LX · SEIANI · SCE lerati
   ITATIO · ET · INPROBAE·COMITIAE    sic
   ΛE · FVERVNT · IN · AVENTINO · VBI
sei ANVS·COS·FACTVS · EST·ET·EGO
   ᴅILIS · INVTILIS · BACVLI · COMES    sic
   VT·SVPPLEX·FIEREM OMNI·NVNC
   VOS ROGO·BONI·CONTRI
bu LES  ·  SI  ·  SEMPER  ·  APPARVI
uᴐBIS · BONVS · ET · VTILIS · TRI
bul IS·SI NVNQVAM OFFIC ii mei
immemor  VI · NEC · REL
          M · COI
          R I F
```

The document is more than peculiar. What is its type, and how did the thing come to survive? No clear answer can be given—and, at the same time, authenticity has never been called in question. An old man is speaking, [de]bilis inutilis baculi comes.[1] He alleges a claim on the indulgence of his fellow-tribesmen for something done (or not done) when Seianus was elected consul. Seianus' methods are stigmatized. For]itatio one might suggest [efflag]itatio, attaching to that word (and not to 'Seiani') the adjective sce[lerata], or sce[lesta]. A strong word, and a rare word. Tacitus suitably puts it into the mouth of the angry Tiberius, denouncing the grandson of Hortensius for his importunacy—'non enim sunt preces istud sed efflagitatio'.[2] Before this, efflagitatio is attested only three times, all in the correspondence of Cicero.[3] One instance has a singular felicity. Munatius Plancus adverts upon the manœuvres of Caesar's heir in the

had to be used because the Campus Martius was cramped (*Gesch. der röm. Kaiserzeit i* (1926), 70). A. Rosenberg took Tacitus to task for neglecting the incident (*Einleitung u. Quellenk. zur röm. Gesch.* (1921), 257). No allusion in F. B. Marsh, *The Reign of Tiberius* (1931).

¹ By a strange aberration Hirschfeld (in the note on *CIL* vi 10213) assumed that some (Sextius) Baculus was meant, appealing for the name to the Caesarian centurion P. Sextius Baculus (*BG* ii 25, 1). Whence *TLL.*

² *Ann.* ii 38, 2.

³ *Ad fam.* v 19, 2; x 24, 6; *Ad M. Brutum* i 16, 11. Not again until Ausonius and Symmachus, cf. *TLL.*

summer of 43 B.C., upon his 'cogitationem consulatus bimestris summo cum terrore hominum et insulsa cum efflagitatione'.¹ However, | there might not be room on the inscription for *efflagitatio*, and *flagitatio* would do, likewise a vigorous and uncommon word.²

The election of Seianus, it is here stated, took place on the Aventine— 'inprobae comitiae / [qu]ae fuerunt in Aventino ubi / [Sei]anus cos. factus est'. How could this be? The Comitia Centuriata met in the Campus Martius; and, even after elections had been transferred from Campus to Senate by Tiberius in A.D. 14, there still remained vestigial ceremonies of the ritual to be gone through on the Campus before a consul was well and truly created. Indeed, a whole incantation—'longum illud carmen comitiorum'.³

Tiberius was disliked, and his memory execrated. His successor, so it is recorded, went back on the ordinances of Tiberius and restored elections to the People.⁴ It mattered not at all, and he soon dropped the silly notion. The intent is clear—not only a reaction from Tiberius but an advertisement of the old Republic. Caligula was a son of Germanicus—and Germanicus (it was fondly alleged) could have brought back *libertas*.⁵ Election by the Sovereign People was the palladium of the Free State, both aristocratic and democratic: 'libertatem et consulatum L. Brutus instituit'.⁶

The show and pretence of direct election by the Populus Romanus could have been put up again at any time after 14. Various devices offered. One is known. The *Lex Valeria Cornelia* of A.D. 5 had brought into operation a kind of pre-election, which was conducted by the specially created *centuriae*, restricted in their composition to senators and knights.⁷ It is not clear, however, that this electoral body can have retained any important role after 14. . . .⁸

Seeking popular support, Seianus might have tried to revive the full and ostensibly sovereign Comitia Centuriata. He did something else. If the testimony of the inscription is to be accepted, it indicates that a part

---

¹ *Ad fam.* x 24, 6.
² Also in Tacitus (*Ann.* xiii 50, 1); previously only Terence, *Phormio* 352; Cicero, *Topica* 5. [It is doubtful whether there is room even for *flagitatio*.]
³ Pliny, *Pan.* 63, 2. Cf. Dio lviii 20, 1 ff.   ⁴ Dio lix 9, 6, 20; Suetonius, *Cal.* 16, 2.
⁵ *Ann.* i 33, 2. Cf. Suetonius, *Tib.* 50, 1 (on the father of Germanicus).
⁶ *Ann.* i 1, 1.
⁷ As revealed by the *Tabula Hebana*, first published in 1947. For the text see now J. H. Oliver and R. E. Palmer, *AJP* lxxv (1954), 225 ff.; Ehrenberg and Jones, *Select Documents Illustrating the Reigns of Augustus and Tiberius* (2nd ed., 1955), 94a.
⁸ Tacitus is plain and explicit—'tum primum e campo comitia ad patres translata sunt' (*Ann.* i 15, 1). The testimony of the consular historian should never have been doubted, and cannot be infringed: it is clear that from now on the main and central act in elections was performed in and by the Senate. It was no help to suppose that Tacitus made a mistake —'patres' instead of a mixed electoral assembly that included knights as well as senators. Thus G. Tibiletti, *Principe e magistrati repubblicani* (1953), 169. Cf. A. H. M. Jones, *JRS* xlv (1955), 18.

of the electoral ceremonies was staged this time on the Aventine—or at the very least, some preliminaries.

Now the Aventine signifies not the Populus Romanus but the plebs. It was the place of extraneous cults, and of secessions; Diana of the Latins had | her temple there, built by injunction of Servius Tullius, and the Aventine was the stronghold of C. Gracchus. The hill remained outside the Roman *pomerium* down to the time of Claudius Caesar.

Caesar Augustus was the *patronus* of the Roman plebs, and the claim to protect the populace was embodied in the *tribunicia potestas* of the emperors. Tiberius, however, made little effort to win the affection of the masses, and he hated games and spectacles. Seianus might make amends. If he hoped to slide gently into the power through the help and agency of the old emperor, he needed in the first place support from men of family and repute in the Senate, and from the army commanders.[1] He had allies there. But it was also worth the effort to draw to himself the urban *clientela* of the dynasty, to solicit the 'plebs sordida et circo ac theatris adsueta'.[2]

The Roman plebs was not just a mass and a mob. It had a corporate existence. In 29 or 30 separate embassies went to Tiberius and Seianus, from Senate, from Knights, from the plebs (with their tribunes and aediles); and they instituted prayers and sacrifices separately.[3]

Seianus was a *novus homo*. He might reflect upon the resplendent fortune of Vipsanius Agrippa, whose family and origin could not stand comparison with his own, he might exploit in his own favour the past history of Rome. There were old legends to be read in a recent and classic writer. Indeed, the best and most beneficent among the kings of Rome had been *novi homines*.[4] Above all, Servius Tullius, who was the son of the captive woman, Ocrisia from Corniculum, a small town in old Latium.[5]

As was suitable, temples and altars of Fortune tend to have Servius assigned as their founder.[6] The most illustrious was the shrine in the Forum Boarium.[7] That temple had an ancient and mysterious shrouded

---

[1] For his relatives and partisans, Z. Stewart, *AJP* lxxiv (1953), 70 ff.; F. Adams, ibid. lxxvi (1955), 70 ff. [Sumner, op. cit.]

[2] As Tacitus calls them (*Hist.* iv 4, 3).

[3] Dio lviii 2, 8.

[4] Livy iv 3, 17: 'optimis regum, novis hominibus'.

[5] Livy iv 39, 5; iv 3, 12. For the variants, and her name (Ocrisia), E. Marbach, *RE* xvii, coll. 1781 ff.

[6] For the evidence, G. Wissowa, *Religion und Kultus der Römer*² (1912), 256 ff.; Platner-Ashby, *A Topographical Dictionary of Ancient Rome* (1929), 212 ff.; W. Hoffmann, *RE* vii A, coll. 814 ff.

[7] Adjacent to Fortuna in the Forum Boarium was Mater Matuta, likewise assigned to Servius Tullius, and with the same foundation-day (June 11). For the sites in the area, H. Lyngby, *Beiträge zur Topographie des Forum-Boarium-Gebietes in Rom* (1954), esp. 37. For the excavations under S. Omobono, G. Lugli, *Roma Antica. Il centro monumentale* (1946).

image, of the goddess, or, as some thought, of the monarch himself.[1]
Ovid is positive: |

> sed superiniectis quis latet iste togis?
> Servius est, et constat enim.[2]

However that may be, the sacred vestment was nothing less than the *toga regia undulata* which Servius had worn, woven by the hand of Tanaquil, so the learned Varro bore witness.[3]

According to Dionysius of Halicarnassus, the original temple had been consumed by fire, and everything perished except the statue, which, though of wood, was gilded over; and, he adds, only the statue is old, the rest being patently due to restoration.[4] It happens to be recorded that there was a fire in 213, a rebuilding the year after.[5]

Dionysius says nothing about any vestments. Faith or scepticism can draw comfort from what is reported about other relics at Rome. When a conflagration destroyed the Chapel of the Salii on the Palatine, the augural staff of Romulus was found intact.[6] Even better, the linen corslet dedicated in the Temple of Juppiter Feretrius by Cornelius Cossus (only a century later than Servius Tullius). Augustus had gone into the temple. He had read the inscription, which proved that Cossus was consul (not military tribune) when he won the *spolia opima*, so Augustus told Livy.[7]

Like the linen corslet, the statue of Fortuna has a certain interest for history as well as legend, for fact as well as fraud. It concerns the aspirations of Aelius Seianus, and his fate. Seianus had in his house an image of Fortuna that had belonged to Servius Tullius. It was his habit to worship that image, and he was terrified when it turned its back to him.[8] Clearly the famous statue from the Temple of Fortuna in the Forum Boarium.[9] The elder Pliny adds confirmation, and a date. He says that the vestments of Servius Tullius survived intact, defying moth and decay, for 560 years, down to the death of Seianus.[10] Hence a new fact in history. It can be

---

542 ff.; *JRS* xxxvii (1946), 3 f. Foundations of two temples were found, side by side, of the third to second century B.C. Also, however, a rubbish dump, which yielded, along with the terracotta head of a warrior (*JRS* xxxvi, pl. VII), other fragments, bucchero ware and Corinthian pottery, indicating the existence of a temple in the sixth century.

[1] Pliny, *NH* viii 194, cf. 197; Festus, p. 282 L.; Nonius, p. 278 L.; Valerius Maximus i 8, 11.

[2] *Fasti* vi 570 f. [3] Cited by Pliny, *NH* viii 194. [4] *Ant. Rom.* iv 40.

[5] Livy xxiv 47, 15; xxv 7, 6. For the fire, cf. also Ovid, *Fasti* vi 625; Valerius Maximus i 8, 11.

[6] Cicero, *De div.* i 30.

[7] Livy iv 20, 7. The item occasions varied speculation [see pp. 417 ff. below].

[8] Dio lviii 7, 2.

[9] The identity of the two statues has sometimes been overlooked, e.g. by W. W. Fowler, *The Roman Festivals* (1899), 156 f.

[10] Pliny, *NH* viii 197: 'Servi Tulli praetextae quibus signum Fortunae ab eo dicatae coopertum erat duravere ad Seiani exitum, mirumque fuit neque diffluxisse eas neque teredinum iniurias sensisse annis quingentis sexaginta.'

taken that the mob assailed and looted the mansion of Seianus on that October day in 31. The vestments perished then, but not perhaps the statue.[1] Seianus and the Fortuna of Servius Tullius, that is enough to make it credible that the previous year witnessed some kind of electoral pageantry, | staged by the great *novus homo* on the plebeian hill. Another clue leads from the goddess to Seianus, but devious and abstruse.

The loyal and obsequious Velleius Paterculus, introducing his panegyric of the indispensable minister with the theme 'magna negotia magnis adiutoribus egent', goes on to a general laudation of new men and imported merit. He begins his list with Coruncanius, after whom and before Cato he names Sp. Carvilius Maximus—'equestri loco natum Sp. Carvilium et mox M. Catonem, novum etiam Tusculo urbis inquilinum'.[2] This man held the consulate twice (293 and 272), each time as colleague of the eminent patrician L. Papirius Cursor. He was also censor, a fact which only Velleius has transmitted.

Coruncanius we knew, consul in 280, and *pontifex maximus* many years later (in 254), the first plebeian to hold that office. In the company of Coruncanius one expects to discover those inescapable worthies M'. Curius Dentatus (*cos.* 290, 275, 274) and C. Fabricius Luscinus (282, 278). These three are the canonical and consecrated *novi homines* of the epoch of the war against Pyrrhus. A band of brothers, according to Cicero, steady, frugal and unimpeachable.[3]

Why Carvilius? Cicero nowhere invokes him as a paragon of civic virtue, nor is his name registered in the edificatory collection of Valerius Maximus. Carvilius has no bed or niche in the *hortus siccus* of the Roman heroes preserved through the ages down to the last days of the Empire. A modern catalogue, erudite and exhaustive, accords him no entry.[4]

Carvilius must have mattered very much. His censorship presumably falls between 290 and 286, in which period a *lustrum* happens to be attested.[5] Great wars had terminated, with a wide extension in the dominion of the Roman People. The next item on historical record in this dark and momentous interval is the secession of the plebs, composed by the dictator Hortensius, that enigmatic figure—no parent is known, no son, no other office, and he died while dictator, so it is recorded.[6] It was not easy for a *novus homo* to establish his fame and family. No consular sons continued the newly earned *nobilitas* of Coruncanius, of

[1] So at least it has been inferred from what Pliny says about Nero: 'construxerat aedem Fortunae quam Seiani appellant a Servio rege sacratam' (*NH* xxxvi 163).
[2] Velleius ii 128, 1.   [3] *Laelius* 39; *Cato maior* 43.
[4] H. W. Litchfield, *HSCPh* xxv (1914), 1 ff. The Sp. Carvilius of an anecdote in Cicero (*De oratore* ii 249), a man lamed by a wound in war, is an isolated item, beyond date and identity.
[5] Livy, *Per.* xi [see *MRR* i 184 f.].   [6] Ibid.: 'isque in ipso magistratu decessit.'

Curius, of Fabricius. Carvilius was more fortunate. Sp. Carvilius Sp. f. C. n. Maximus Ruga was consul in 234 and in 228, perhaps the son, perhaps a grand-nephew. The memory of the second Carvilius survives, documented by the double opprobrium of moral delinquency and political folly. Carvilius is pilloried in the standard tradition as the first Roman to divorce his wife. The charge | happens to be false—at least, if records such as these can safely admit the canons of true and false.[1]

The other thing is even more abominable. After the carnage at Cannae, Carvilius came out with a proposal that the Roman Senate should be supplemented by an adlection of new members from the Latin towns. Whence horror and indignation, with an authoritative pronouncement from the venerable Fabius Maximus. The bare notion, he exclaimed, would have to be blotted out for ever—'id omnium maxime tegendum occulendum obliviscendum'. Therefore, so Livy adds (with no misgivings about the authenticity of what he relates), the Senate concurred: 'eius rei oppressa mentio est.'[2]

No other Carvilius got as far as the consulate. They fade out, the last senator of the name being casually attested in 129.[3] Some ancient families, absent from the *Fasti* for centuries, were discovered and brought to renewed lustre through the patronage of Caesar Augustus. Patrician, however, rather than plebeian. No Carvilius or Carvilia is known worth flattering by mention of the ancestor.[4]

The Carvilii left no good memory behind them. Velleius, who is desperately anxious to conform to safe and received opinions about Roman history, passes over the inevitable Curius and Fabricius, evoking instead Sp. Carvilius Maximus. The reason might be worth looking for.

Consul in 293 and victorious in the field, Carvilius built a shrine to Fors Fortuna, 'prope aedem eius deae ab rege Servio Tullio dedicatam'.[5] Servius' temple was on the right bank of the Tiber, near the first milestone out of Rome. Now Fors Fortuna was celebrated by the Roman plebs in one of its principal festivals (and slaves were not excluded). It occurred on 24 June, hilarious and bibulous, on land and on the water. Ovid testifies,

> ferte coronatae iuvenum convivia lintres
> multaque per medias vina bibantur aquas.

---

[1] For the abundant and repetitive *testimonia*, *RE* iii, col. 1631. Valerius Maximus, after duly producing Carvilius (ii 1, 4), goes on blissfully to record an earlier transgressor, L. Annius (ii 9, 2). Cf. *Historia* iv (1955), 55 [= p. 274 above].   [2] Livy xxiii 22, 9.

[3] Sp. Carvilius, the 22nd name on the *SC de agro Pergameno* [Sherk, *RDGE*, no. 12]. He has the Sabatina, one of the four tribes formed from the territory of Veii.

[4] There had been a Roman knight, Carvilius Pollio, with a taste for novel and expensive furniture shortly before the *bellum civile Sullanum* (Pliny, *NH* xxxiii 144; cf. ix 39). Note also 'ab atriis Sapalas et Carvilios' (Q. Cicero, *Comm. Pet.* 10—not in *RE*). The only entry the Empire can show is Carvilius Pictor (*PIR*², C 454), the author of *Aeneidomastix* (Donatus, *Vita* xliv 1, 180).   [5] Livy x 46, 14.

plebs colit hanc quia qui posuit de plebe fuisse
fertur et ex humili sceptra tulisse loco.¹ |

There is a vexed problem, but hardly relevant to the principal inquiry:
how many temples were there of Fors Fortuna across the river?² The
Augustan calendars know two, the one near the first milestone (in
the gardens of Caesar the Dictator), the other near the sixth, close by the
grove of the Arval Brethren.³ The latter has a claim to be Carvilius'
temple—at least an inscription of late Republican date reveals two freedmen of the name Carvilius in a confraternity worshipping Fors Fortuna
at that site.⁴ Livy may be in error about the location of the temple dedicated by Carvilius.

It is suitable that the *novus homo* Carvilius should follow and emulate
Servius Tullius in the cult of Fors Fortuna. He might have contributed
something to the memory or legend of his predecessor. The mother of
Servius Tullius is said to have come from Corniculum, somewhere in the
territory north-east from Rome in the direction of Nomentum and the
Sabine border. The grandfather of another king, Tullus Hostilius, was an
immigrant from Medullia in the same region.⁵ According to an erudite
and perhaps perverse authority, namely Claudius Caesar, Cameria was
the home of Coruncanius.⁶ Corniculum, Cameria, and Medullia were
among the Latin towns captured by Tarquinius Priscus.⁷ The *nomen*
'Carvilius' is rare (apart from low-class people on inscriptions at Rome),
and might seem promising, but it cannot be tied to any locality.⁸ A Latin
origin for the family, known and remembered, is rendered attractive (but

---

¹ Ovid, *Fasti* vi 779 ff. For the plebeian and popular character of other festivals associated
with Servius Tullius, such as the *Compitalia* and the *Nundinae*, cf. *RE* vii 816.
² For the problem, Platner-Ashby, op. cit. 212 ff.; S. M. Savage, *MAAR* xvii (1940),
26 ff.
³ [*Inscr. It.* xiii 2, 88f., 92, 187 (texts); 473 (commentary).]
⁴ *CIL* i² 977 = *ILS* 9253. There is a freedman Carvilius, member of some collegium or
other, on i² 1005 (Insula Tiberina). For low-class Carvilii as political agents, Q. Cicero,
Comm. Pet. 10.
⁵ Dionysius, *Ant. Rom.* iv 1.
⁶ Tacitus, *Ann.* xi 24, 2. It can be conjectured that this instructive item, though not in
the *Oratio Claudi Caesaris* as extant (*ILS* 212: Lugdunum), was lifted by the historian from
some other learned disquisition. The standard (or at least the only other) attribution is
Tusculum (*Pro Plancio* 20). There is no point in 'combining' the two notices (as some do),
with Cameria put in the territory of Tusculum. As for M'. Curius, Cicero says he was
municipal, that is all (*Pro Sulla* 23); and there is nothing on record about the *origo* of
Fabricius.
⁷ Livy i 38, 4; cf. Dionysius, *Ant. Rom.* iii 49 f. For the early towns in the region, Nissen,
It. Landeskunde ii (1902), 563; A. N. Sherwin-White, *The Roman Citizenship* (1939), 9.
⁸ *TLL*, *Onom.* ii 219f. However, the early instance from Praeneste is useful—L .
CARVILIO · L · F (*CIL* i² 110). Otherwise only freedmen in *CIL* i² (977; 1005). The
place Carventum (Dionysius, *Ant. Rom.* v 61; cf. Livy iv 53, 9 etc.) eludes identification. For
Carve[, cognomen of the consul of 458, see Degrassi, *Inscr. It.* xiii 1, 92. The root *Carv-* is well
attested in the Celtic lands (cf. Holder, *Alt-celtischer Sprachschatz*); and the British chieftain
Carvilius will not be forgotten (*BG* v 22, 1).

is not proved) by the fact that a Roman annalist attributed the proposal made after Cannae to a Carvilius.

Fors Fortuna emerges early in the reign of Tiberius. That emperor earned no fame for magnificence of constructions. Posterity credits him with two new works only, the temple of Divus Augustus and the *scaena* of the Theatre of | Pompeius, which had been destroyed by fire.[1] Tiberius in fact went in for a lot of repairing.[2] Otherwise, any initiative of this parsimonious ruler was (and is) worth noting. The historian Tacitus records several items at the end of the year 16. Not only a triumphal arch to commemorate the recovery of standards lost in Germany, but 'aedes Fortis Fortunae Tiberim iuxta in hortis, quos Caesar dictator populo Romano legaverat, sacrarium genti Iuliae effigiesque divo Augusto apud Bovillas dicantur'.[3]

Fors Fortuna is among the most patently plebeian of the Roman deities. The patrician Claudii were arrogant and oppressive, haters of the plebs, according to the Roman legend as transmitted by Livy and others. There is another side—a family conscious of its alien origin long ago out of the Sabine country, promoting *novi homines*, and alert to extend its *clientela* among the urban populace.[4]

The senator Velleius Paterculus will not have been wholly oblivious when the Senate in 16 voted a temple to Fors Fortuna (whether a new construction or a remodelling of Servius' shrine, it is here irrelevant). That goddess evoked the name of Sp. Carvilius. And Velleius (like everybody else) will have known what it signified when Seianus took Fortuna from the Forum Boarium to be his peculiar and domestic protector.

Velleius and Seianus were acquaintances of long date. They had both been on the staff of the prince C. Caesar in the eastern lands.[5] When Velleius wrote (in 29 or 30), the fortune of the great *novus homo* seemed beyond doubt or hazard. Velleius ends his work with a solemn prayer to the gods of Rome: when Tiberius is called to a higher station (let it be as late as possible) may he consign the burden of empire to shoulders strong enough to bear it.[6] Velleius advertised his hopes and his allegiance. It is a fair conjecture that Velleius shared the fate of Aelius Seianus.[7]

Fortuna was an immigrant goddess, perhaps deriving from Etruria. Seianus came from Etruscan Volsinii, and the poet Juvenal, registering the

---

[1] *Ann.* vi 45, 1; cf. Suetonius, *Tib.* 47; *Cal.* 21.

[2] Dio lvii 10, 1 f.; cf. Tacitus, *Ann.* ii 41, 1. 49 (a respectable total). Velleius is naturally exuberant—'quanta suo suorumque nomine exstruxit opera!' (ii 130, 1).

[3] *Ann.* ii 41, 1.

[4] Mommsen, *Röm. Forsch.*[2] (1864), 287 ff. Also, with especial emphasis on the urban plebs, G. C. Fiske, *HSCPh* xiii (1902), 1 ff.

[5] *Ann.* iv 1, 1; Velleius ii 101, 2 f. [6] Velleius ii 131.

[7] As did one historian at least, viz. Bruttedius (*PIR*[2], B 158), cf. *Ann.* iii 66, 4, with Juvenal x 83. [*Contra* G. V. Sumner, *HSCPh* lxxiv (1968), 296 f.]

hopes and prayers of Seianus, duly refers to the goddess of fate worshipped at Volsinii:

si Nortia Tusco
favisset, si oppressa foret secura senectus
principis.[1] |

It may not perhaps be safe and expedient to go further and adduce the view that Servius Tullius himself was really an Etruscan. That doctrine was proclaimed to the Senate in 48 by Claudius, with appeal to Etruscan authorities: he was identical with the Etruscan Mastarna, a companion of Caeles Vibenna.[2] Claudius had written, in Greek, twenty books of *Tyrrhenica*.[3] Seianus might (or might not) have been familiar with this striking (and perhaps wilful) departure from the standard tradition of the Romans. . . .[4]

If Seianus chose the Mons Aventinus as the scene for parading his ambitions, he showed veneration for good King Servius, and a wanton defiance of history and legend, of *auspicia* and of *omina*. A man did not have to consult the writings of Messalla the augur to know that the place lay under a curse—'quasi avibus obscenis ominosum'.[5]

Remus had chosen the Aventine, there watching the skies for an omen, and Remus had been killed by Romulus. 'Remo cum fratre Quirinus', thus did Virgil hail the prospect of concord at Rome after fratricidal strife. In the course of time, ignorance applied the reference to the partnership between Augustus and Agrippa.[6]

Seianus was coming close to parity in the power with Tiberius Caesar. The emperor cherished him; their statues stood side by side in places of public honour. But Tiberius came to conceive doubt, suspicion, and fear. He discarded his friend and associate, compassing his doom most craftily. Fortuna forsook her worshipper, his allies among the consulars drew back, and the Roman plebs was not going to help him now:

sed quid
turba Remi? sequitur fortunam, ut semper, et odit
damnatos.[7]

[1] Juvenal x, 74 ff. For Nortia, L. R. Taylor, *Local Cults in Etruria* (1923), 154 ff.; E. Bernert, *RE* xvii, coll. 1048 ff.

[2] *ILS* 212: 'si nostros sequimur, captiva natus Ocresia, si Tuscos, Caeli quondam Vivennae sodalis fidelissimus' etc. He then proceeds: 'mutatoque nomine (nam Tusce Mastarna ei nomen erat).' This is no place to pursue the attractive topic of Mastarna, and the many problems.

[3] Suetonius, *Divus Claudius* 42, 2. That he wrote in Greek is not wholly reassuring. For the Etruscological studies of the Emperor see J. Heurgon, *CRAI* 1953, 92 ff.; *Latomus* xii (1953), 402 ff.

[4] Seianus and Claudius were acquainted, and all but related. For the (abortive) betrothal of their children, foreshadowed as early as 20, see *Ann.* iii 29, 4; iv 7, 3; Suetonius, *Divus Claudius* 27, 1. Further, Aelia Paetina, the second wife of Claudius, may belong to Seianus' family: see the new stemma produced by F. Adams, *AJP* lxxvi (1955), 75 [and the stemma in G. V. Sumner, *Phoenix* xix (1965), 137]. [5] Quoted in Gellius xiii 14, 6.

[6] Servius on *Aen.* i 292, cf. *Rom. Rev.* (1939), 345. [7] Juvenal x 72 ff.

23

Missing Persons[1]

CATALOGUE or single item, it is easy to fall into errors of detail about names and persons. Nobody can hope to be immune. That does not need to be said (or confessed) once again.[2] But something will have to be said about the latest instalment of Pauly–Wissowa, which departs further than ever from the standards that guided the inception and the middle years of that noble enterprise.[3] Articles continue to swell in a manner out of proportion to the 'growth of knowledge', and the facts tend to be obscured, lost in lengthy disquisitions or swallowed up by the 'literature of the subject'. And there are far too many items. An attempt seems to have been made to rope in all sorts of people from the inscriptions, persons of low degree as well as those Roman knights with only local honours or military service which the *Prosopographia Imperii Romani* eschews.

Modesty and accuracy would have been enough. Without those virtues, anything can happen to an encyclopedia. Orthography is not a strong point of this volume. Neither is nomenclature. The senator L. Ligus, brother of M. Octavius Ligus, parades with a new and unexplained *gentilicium* as 'L. Vecilius Ligur';[4] and an argument is based on the allegation that Cn. Pompeius (*cos. suff.* 31 B.C.) had the filiation 'L.f.'[5] There are also confusions and doublets. Hence some more characters that never existed.[6] At the same time, valuable pieces of evidence have been overlooked. The reader is not allowed to learn that the eloquent Varius Geminus was the first senator from among the Paeligni;[7] and those who

---

[1] [Several of these entries, concerning the Roman Republic, had in fact been written by Münzer and appeared in viii A 2 (1958). They are marked ★.]

[2] Cf. observations on *MRR* in *CP* l (1955), 127 ff.; *Historia* iv (1955), 52 ff.

[3] Viz., the first *Halbband* of Vol. viii A, published at the end of 1955: *Valerius Fabrianus bis P. Vergilius Maro*. 'Fabrianus' (also in the text) is a mistake for 'Fabianus'.

[4] L. Ligus (*In Verrem* ii 2, 23). For these Octavii, F. Münzer, *RE* xvii, col. 1851.

[5] Referred to in the article on Messalla Corvinus (col. 154). He is 'Q. f.' In xxi, col. 2265, he is presented with a son, Sex. Pompeius Q. f. (*suff.* 5 B.C.). Non-existent.

[6] Thus 'C. Valerius L. f. Flacianus' (*sic*) is really 'C. Valerius L. f. Flacc(us) Tanur'. (*CIL* xiv 4704); and there is no justification for the 'Valerius' in 'C. (Valerius) Flavius', legate in Africa (Pliny, *NH* xix 4). The strange item '[Vale]r(ius) Mess(alla) (Flavius?)' betrays no awareness of the fact that the person alluded to (on the *Fasti Ostienses*) is none other than L. Valerius Catullus Messallinus, consul for the second time in 85.

[7] *ILS* 932 (Superaequum).

are curious about the marriages of the Messallae will look in vain for the brick-stamp with the mark 'Calpurniae Corvini'.[1]

About the Roman imperial administration, certain queer notions are disclosed. C. Valerius Maximus, 'leg. [Aug.] prop[r.]', is assigned senatorial | Narbonensis as his province, while C. Valerius Severus (*suff.* 124) governs Lycia–Pamphylia (imperial) subsequent to his consulate, as a proconsul, and the consular Valerius Urbicus is presented with the title 'procurator operum publicorum'. Again, the Roman army: casual consultation of *diplomata* has enlisted several native cavalrymen in the belief that they are *equites Romani*.[2]

That being so, it might seem too late or too little to complain of mere omissions. None the less, a short and succinct list might serve sundry purposes. Hence the forty-one names that follow. No fewer than thirteen of them stand on record in *PIR*[1]. For principle of selection that work has been taken as a guide, to the exclusion, for example, of military knights, even though there be some useful specimens to hand.[3] Furthermore, for convenience, five items have been registered that may not, or could not, have become accessible to the editors and collaborators.

Brevity and the facts have the first claim, avoiding as far as possible bibliography, controversy, and the attractive by-paths.[4] Attention has been given to nomenclature—some *nomina* are patent rarities and can be assigned to a town or a region, while others, unobtrusive on first inspection, turn out to be singularly uncommon.[5]

L. VALERIUS FIRMUS. Equestrian officer and procurator of Arabia not long after the annexation: C. H. Kraeling, *Gerasa* (1938), nos. 173 (*AE* 1930, 92) and 174. His tribe is the Poblilia, indicating Verona, where there happen to be Valerii Firmi (*CIL* v 3311; 3680; 3809).

[? VALE]RIUS FRONTO. Governor of Thrace in 135. Revealed by the inscription on the basilica at Pautalia, which is cited by J. and L. Robert, *Bull. ép.*, *REG* lxvii (1954), under no. 172. 'Valerius Fronto' happens to occur in the nomenclature of a *clarissimus iuvenis*, L. Servilius Domitius Valerius Fronto Lucianus (*CIL* v 3902: territory of Verona), but is not distinctive enough for guidance. Moreover, several other *gentilicia* are not

---

[1] *NSA* 1889, 186 = no. 249 in the list of H. Bloch, *HSCPh* lviii–ix (1948). Two specimens of the stamp, found together.

[2] Thus L. Valerius Pudens, L. Valerius Cainenis f. Tarvinus, and Valerius Valeri f. Valens (from *CIL* xvi 28; 102; 120). Similarly Valerius Longus (*SEG* ii 850): only a ἱππεύς.

[3] Observe, e.g., L. Valerius Priscus of Vienna, honoured with a public funeral at Patavium (*CIL* v 2841).

[4] One or two of the missing persons are so important (and so well documented) that the best remedy is to cite the most recent modern treatment. For example, the consular Q. Venidius Rufus, and Cn. Vergilius Capito (Prefect of Egypt).

[5] Cf. *JRS* xxxix (1949), 6 ff. [= *Ten Studies in Tacitus* (1970), 58 ff.] (on some names in *Ann.* i–vi); *Historia* iv (1955), 52 ff. [= pp. 271 ff. above] (senators missing from *MRR*).

ruled out, e.g. 'Papirius'. The jurist Papirius Fronto (*PIR*¹, P 86) cannot be closely dated.

(VALERIUS) MESSALLA. *Monetalis*, one in a college of four towards 6 B.C., along with Apronius (i.e. L. Apronius, *cos. suff.* A.D. 8), Galus, and Sisenna (not | otherwise known), cf. *BMC*, *R. Emp.* i 46 ff. Presumably distinct from 'Volusus Valer. Messal.' (ibid. 46), who is the consul of A.D. 5 and perhaps his brother.

M'. VALERIUS MESSALLA POTITUS. Quaestor in Asia, revealed by the inscription found at Claros by L. Robert and first published in *JRS* xlv (1955), 156 [pp. 261 f. above]. Two alternatives were there proposed. He could be either Potitus Valerius Messalla (*suff.* 29 B.C.), supposing that person to have been originally a Manius who dropped his *praenomen* and used 'Potitus' in its place, or an unknown son, hence brother of L. Valerius Messalla Volesus (*cos.* A.D. 5), and perhaps identical with the *monetalis* Messalla of the preceding item.

[? VALE]RIUS SEVERUS.¹ Legate of Lycia–Pamphylia, consul, legate of one of the two Germanies, proconsul of Africa (*Inscr. lat. de l'Algérie* 1283: Thubursicu Numidarum). He clearly belongs to the period from Hadrian to Marcus inclusive. A priesthood, that of *sodalis Hadrianalis*, standing in the praetorian posts of his *cursus* along with *XV vir s. f.*, seems to offer a clue; it might, however, be out of chronological order, so Groag suggests, in Ritterling–Stein, *Fasti des röm. Deutschland unter dem Prinzipat* (1932), 88. Hence identity is not wholly excluded with a known governor of Lycia–Pamphylia, viz. C. Valerius Severus (*PIR*¹, V 134), consul suffect in 124. The article devoted to that person (*RE* viii A, coll. 223 f.) omits to register the inscription from Thubursicu—and contains several patent errors. It will naturally be observed that, while '[Vale]rius' is easy and attractive on the inscription at Thubursicu, the man might have had some other *nomen*. There was, for example, a L. Elufrius Severus, proconsul of Crete in 100 (*PIR*², E 57)—an item also present in the nomenclature of the polyonymous *ordinarius* of 114, P. Manilius Vopiscus Vicinillianus L. Elufrius Severus Julius Quadratus Bassus (*ILS* 1044). No need to add that there are a number of unattached Severi among the *suffecti* of the Antonine age.

VALERIUS VALENS. Commander of the fleet at Misenum (*CIL* x 3336 = *ILS* 3756); *praefectus vigilum* between 241 and 244, 'v(ices) a(gens) praef(ectorum) praet(orio)' (*CIL* xiv 4398 = *ILS* 2159). *PIR*¹, V 147. [A homonym as 'praef. coh. [I? M]aced.' at Cyrene, *PBSR* xxx (1962), 37 = *AE* 1969–70, no. 638.]

¹ [This man is now known to be the proconsul of Africa C. Septimius Severus (*MEFR* lxxv (1960), 389 ff. = *AE* 1967, 536), hence not identical with C. Valerius Severus.]

C. VALERIUS VIBIANUS. 'V(ir) p(erfectissimus), praeses' of the *provincia Tripolitana* (*IRT* 577: Lepcis, cf. *CIL* viii 22763 = *ILS* 9352).

Q. VALGIUS M. F. The sixth name on the *SC de agro Pergameno* [Sherk, *RDGE*, no. 12]. The *nomen*, which acquired fame with the poet C. Valgius Rufus (*suff.* 12 B.C.), was unfortunately omitted by Wilhelm Schulze from his massive compilation. For guidance observe C. Valgius Hippianus, who purchased an estate 'in agro Fregellano' (Cicero, *Ad fam.* xiii 76, 2): the name 'Hippius' is Oscan. Also 'P. Valgius P. f. P. n. Tro. Barba', a local magistrate and military tribune (*CIL* x 5582: Fabrateria Nova). There are half a dozen Valgii in Africa, including the next item.

L. VALGIUS MAURICUS. 'V(ir) e(gregius)', dedicant of *ILS* 9016 (Sufetula).

VALLIUS. There was a *Lex Vallia* (Gaius iv 25): earlier than *leges Juliae*, cf. *MRR* ii 474. The *nomen* does not permit close localization (Schulze, *LE* 376). |

VALLIUS SYRIACUS. A *rhetor* mentioned several times by the elder Seneca; put to death by Tiberius, guilty only of the friendship of Asinius Gallus (Dio lviii 3, 7): *PIR*[1], V 171.

L. VALLIUS TRANQUILLUS. Procurator governing Mauretania Tingitana, attested on January 9, 88 (*CRAI* 1952, 192 = *AE* 1953, 74 = *CIL* xvi 159). A certain L. Vallius Tranquillianus is commemorated by his parents (of no class) on an 'ara marmorea litteris optimis' at Ficulea (*CIL* xiv 4040).

VARENA Q. F. MAIOR. Wife of M. Lartidius Sex. f., as appears from the dedication set up at Tibur by M. Varenus Diphilus, their joint freedman, to '[M. Lart]idio Sex. [f.] / . . . . pr.', and to 'Varenai Q. f. / Maiori' (*Inscr. It.* iv 1, 224 f.). The lady occurs there again (226), the freedman more than once (221 f. = *ILS* 6240 f.); and he makes a dedication 'pro salute et reditu Caesaris' (74 = *AE* 1922, 78). Another freedman of the pair, M. Varenus Clarus, is attested at Nola in A.D. 21 (*CIL* x 1333). The husband, M. Lartidius, is patently the son of Sex. Lartidius, legate in Asia under the proconsul Asinius Gallus in 6/5 B.C. (*ILS* 97: Ephesus), and the letters surviving of the inscription that refers to him could be supplemented to show a magistracy or a promagistracy. The *nomen* 'Varenus' deserves attention. Not only do the epigraphical instances point to Umbria e.g. L. Varenus L. f. Lucullus, equestrian officer and magistrate at Fulginiae (*CIL* xi 5220). The speech of Cicero *Pro L. Vareno* dealt with local feuds and murders in the vicinity of Fulginiae (cf. the fragments 3, 4, and 8), and Silius Italicus, who knew his Cicero, has a 'Mevanas Varenus' (iv 544). Schulze duly produced those facts. *RE* ignores the clue in Silius; it also omits Pompulenus (*Pro Vareno*, fr. 5).

*Vargula. A friend of C. Caesar Strabo Vopiscus and a wit, comparable to Granius the auctioneer (Cicero, *De or.* ii 244). Otherwise known only for the joke about certain Sempronii—'puer, abige muscas' (ibid. 247). For the root, cf. 'Vargunteius'; for the termination, 'Barbula', 'Decula', 'Nucula', 'Tegula'.

*M. Varisidius. Roman knight, friend of L. Munatius Plancus, conveying dispatches to Cicero in 43 (*Ad fam.* x 7, 1; 12, 2). A rare *nomen*, cf. Schulze, *LE* 249. The evidence points to the North. Add Varisidius Nepos, nephew of Pliny's friend Calvisius Rufus of Comum (*Ep.* iv 4, 1); and observe a Varisidius at the native settlement at Ig near Emona (*CIL* iii 10740).

*T. Varius T. f. Sabinus. Honoured at Delphi for services rendered when he was there μετὰ τοῦ στρατηγοῦ Πλαιτωρίου (*SEG* i 165). Broughton in *MRR* identifies the governor as M. Plaetorius Cestianus, putting his praetorship in 64, his proconsulate of Macedonia in 63/2, after L. Manlius Torquatus (*cos.* 65).

Varro. Poet and friend of Martial (v 30, presumably of December 89). *PIR*[1], V 196. The senator P. Tullius Varro is not excluded. Though his career did not proceed further than the command of a legion, under Vespasian, and the proconsulate of Macedonia (*ILS* 1002), one does not have to assume an early | death (as E. Groag, *RE* vii A, col. 1326). His sons are P. Dasumius Rusticus (*PIR*[2], D 15), *consul ordinarius* in 119 (whom Dasumius the testator had adopted), and P. Tullius Varro (*ILS* 1047), *cos. suff.* 127. Their births should fall in the period 84–90.

*Varus. Proscribed senator (Appian, *BC* iv 28): not registered in *MRR*. [Added *Suppl.* (1960), 67.] Captured when lurking in the marshes near Minturnae, he first tried to pass himself off for a brigand, but, on the prospect of torture, protested against the outrage to a man of his station —ὕπατόν με γεγενημένον. No such consul is known. What is the solution? Perhaps one of the ten ex-praetors granted the *consularia ornamenta* by the Dictator (Suetonius, *Divus Iulius* 76, 3, cf. (not so precise) Dio xliii 47, 3). Thus Holzapfel, *Phil. Woch.* (1900), 811 f. Perhaps there is another explanation. The Latin original might have had some such phrase as 'summo me populi Romani imperio usum'. The term could be applied to the *imperium* of a praetor (Cicero, *De lege agraria* ii 34, cf. 32).

*L. Varus. Left by Cassius in charge of the garrison at Rhodes in 42 (Appian, *BC* iv 74). Styled 'L. (Quinctilius) Varus' and amalgamated in *MRR* ii 368 and 465 with the 'Varus Quinctilius' who committed suicide after the Battle of Philippi (Velleius ii 71, 2). That person, however, who is named in a short list of distinguished men, is patently Sex. Quinctilius Varus (*q.* 49), parent of the consul of 13, cf. *CP* l (1955), 135. [Accepted

Suppl. (1960), 52.] The *cognomen* of L. Varus being common, there is no point in here speculating about his *nomen*.

VASSONIUS. Husband of Nitionia Avitiana, 'clar. fem.', deduced from the name of her son, Vassonius Gellianus: on the sarcophagus found at St. Maurice in the Valais, cf. Howald–Meyer, *Die röm. Schweiz* (1940), 211, no. 66. The *gentilicia* are patently native ('Nitionius', ibid. nos. 67 f.; 'Vassonius', no. 68). For 'Vassus', 'Vassius', 'Vassiacus', 'Vassorix', etc. see Holder, *Alt-celtischer Sprachschatz*. It might be noted in passing that 'Vassius' (recorded, but without examples, in *LE* 425, cf. 450) is attested in central Italy, e.g. eight specimens in *CIL* ix. [See *ILLRP* 104a: a Vassius as a magistrate at Praeneste.] Further, 'Vassellius', 'Vassidenus', 'Vassidius' (*LE* 428; 449; 452).

★VATIENA. Addressed and solicited by Laevius—'mea Vatiena, amabo' (Morel, *FPL* fr. 28). Compare Catullus 32, 1: 'amabo, mea dulcis Ipsitilla.'

★VATIENUS. Husband of a Cornelia, revealed by *CIL* i² 821 [= *ILLRP* 384]: '[Corn]elia L. Scipion[is f.] / Vatieni.' The stone is described as 'fragmentum tituli litteris maximis et satis antiquis sepulcri cuiusdam ad viam Salariam siti.' Mommsen (cited in *CIL*) suggested that the lady might be a daughter of L. Scipio Asiagenus (*cos.* 83). The question of identity and the relationship between the names 'Vatienus' and 'Vatinius' had better be reserved for fuller treatment somewhere else. The only other epigraphic instances of 'Vatienus' seem to be a 'P. Vatienus P. l.' (*CIL* vi 39023) and the 'P. Vatienus P. f. Quireina' of the Roman inscription now at Prague (*BCAR* lv (1928), 293). Sabine, as is P. Vatinius (*cos.* 47).

VATRONIUS. Writer of *palliatae* in *Corp. Gloss. Lat.* v 80: 'Burrae Vatroniae, | fatuae ac stupidae, a fabula quadam Vatroni auctoris quam *Burra* inscripsit, vel a meretrice Burra'. Detected by Buecheler, *RhM* xxxiii (1878), 309 f., who pointed to the name at Praeneste—there are now six if not seven early instances (*CIL* i² 171; 332–6; 1400, cf. 1450 [*ILLRP* 106, 264, 872]). For 'Vatronius' (and 'Vaternius'), *LE* 250. It got to Africa: *CIL* viii 4130; 8972; 22988.

VEDIUS AQUILA. Legate of XIII Gemina in 69 (Tacitus, *Hist.* ii 44, 1; iii 7, 1). *PIR*¹, V 212.

L. VEHILIUS. Entitled 'q. pro pr.' on a fragmentary inscription at Hippo Regius (*Libyca* ii (1954), 386 = *AE* 1955, 148).

M. VEHILIUS. *Pontifex* and proconsul of Cyprus. The first word of a dedication at Paphos was read as M. VPHILIO (*BCH* li (1947), 143, whence *AE* 1928, 17), and the person, identified as an 'Ofilius' or 'Ofillius', passed into works of reference, e.g. *RE* xvii, col. 2041. The patent emendation is M. VEHILIO, which I passed on to several persons, some time ago, among them Mr. Grant (cf. *FITA* (1946), 152) and Mr. Mitford. For the history of this document and a revised text (the first three letters are now missing), see T. B. Mitford, *Report of the Department of Antiquities, Cyprus, 1940–1948* (1954), 8 f. M. Vehilius (*RE* viii A, col. 581), one of the praetors of 44 B.C., refused a province from M. Antonius' allocation (Cicero, *Phil.* iii 25): not elsewhere attested. It is not altogether easy to fit him in subsequently as a proconsul of Cyprus. There might have been a homonym in the next generation—and one will not forget the fragment 'M. Vehilio' at Pisidian Antioch (*CIL* iii 6860, reproduced as though unpublished in *JRS* xiv (1924), 199). The *nomen* (absent from *LE*) is Praenestine, cf. 'Vehilia M. f.' (*CIL* i² 338 f.), cited in *Rom. Rev.* (1939), 91; and 'Vehia' (4281).

L. JULIUS VEHILIUS GRATUS JULIANUS. Prefect of the Guard, probably from 189 to 191. *PIR*¹, I 402. [See *RE*, Suppl. xii, coll. 509 f. (Hanslik).] For his prefecture, A. Passerini, *Le coorti pretorie* (1939), 308 f. His long career is registered on *ILS* 1327 (Rome). He is the Julius Julianus of an inscription set up at Palmyra (his origin) in 167/8 (*ILS* 8869, improved in *AE* 1933, 208 = *SEG* vii 145): omitted by Passerini, as was also *CIL* v 4343 (Brixia). The latter document reveals him under the name of T. Julius Julianus, commander of *coh. I Pannoniorum* (cf. *ILS* 1327), making a dedication (not long before 167) in honour of M. Nonius Macrinus (*suff.* 154), legate of Pannonia Superior.

M. VEHILIUS PRIMUS. Styled '*cur. r.p. Cosilinatium*' (*ILS* 9359: near Salernum).

VEIANIUS. Two brothers of that name, bee-keepers of genius on a *iugerum* of land, known to Varro—'duo milites se habuisse in Hispania fratres Veianios ex agro Falisco locupletis' (*RR* iii 16, 10). For the *nomen*, Schulze, *LE* 251—which does not, however, register all the instances: there are no fewer than ten in *CIL* xi.

*Q. VELANIUS. Equestrian officer (Caesar, *BG* iii 7, 4; 8, 2). One might wonder whether or not to read 'Veianius': observe the notorious perplexity, | 'Falanius' or 'Faianius' in Tacitus, *Ann.* i 73, 1 f., on which cf. *JRS* xxxix (1949), 12 [= *Ten Studies in Tacitus* 68 f.]. Hübner impugned 'Velanius' as 'nomen nullum' (*Eph. Ep.* ii 73). But Schulze (*LE* 377) adduced 'velanial' (*CIE* 130: Volaterrae) and other Etruscan instances; also 'Q. Vela[' (*NSA* 1893, 380: near Nursia in the Sabine country)— who might, however, be a 'Velatius'. For that *nomen* (not in *LE*), cf. *CIL* vi 1970; 32314 f. 'Velanius' so far has not come to light even in Africa, which produces specimens of the rarest Italian *gentilicia*, cf. on 'Aufustius', *Historia* iv (1955), 56 [= p. 275 above]. [See entry in *RE* viii A 2 (1958), coll. 2398 f., by Gundel.]

P. VELLAEUS. Praetorian legate in charge of the army of Moesia under Poppaeus Sabinus (Tacitus, *Ann.* iii 39, 1). *PIR*[1], V 231.

VELLAEUS TUTOR. The consul of the *Lex Junia Vellaea* and the *SC Vellaeanum*. *PIR*[1], V 232. Now L. Junius Silanus and C. Vellaeus Tutor were *suffecti* in 28 (cf. the next item), whereas Ulpian puts the *SC* under Claudius with 'M. Silanus et Vell[a]eus Tutor' as the consular pair (*Dig.* xvi 2, 1). Hence, apparently, a double error. Moreover, M. Junius Silanus, the *ordinarius* of 46, is ruled out—his colleague is known, and all the *suffecti* of the year. Another M. Silanus has been produced from *CIL* xiv 3471 (Sublaqueum), where Hülsen's improved reading gives 'M. Iunio Silano, A [. . . . .] cos.' as a pair (presumed *suffecti*), previous to 56, the *ordinarii* of which year are mentioned on the document. Cf. Bruns, *Fontes*[7], no. 156; *PIR*[2], I 834; Degrassi, *I Fasti Consolari* (1952), 15. The colleague of this Silanus might be A. Ducenius Geminus (*PIR*[2], D 201). Still no Vellaeus Tutor, however; and the present observations are restricted to stating the problem and the evidence.

C. VELLAEUS TUTOR. *Suffectus* with L. Junius Silanus, attested in December, A.D. 28: *ILS* 6099; 6099a. *PIR*[1], V 233. The *gentilicium* is preternaturally rare. Not at Rome, or anywhere in the provinces of the West. As for Italy, apart from *CIL* v 8297 (Aquileia), only in Apulia and Samnium: *CIL* ix 351; 405 (= *ILS* 8263); 406 (Canusium); 968 (Aquilonia). Canusium, which further yields a 'C. Vell[' (404), is clearly their home.

VENIDIUS QUIETUS. *Praetor tutelarius* early in the reign of Severus (*Dig.* iv 4, 11, 2). *PIR*[1], V 244, cf. *PIR*[2], A 435.

Q. VENIDIUS RUFUS MARIUS MAXIMUS L. CALVINIANUS. Important personage, *cos. suff. c.* 200. *PIR*[1], V 244. For his career and provincial commands see Ritterling–Stein, *Fasti des röm. Deutschland unter dem Prinzipat* (1932), 79 f.; G. Barbieri, *L'Albo senatorio da Settimio Severo a Carino* (1952), no. 519. As for the *gentilicium*, 'Venidius' is, like 'Venius', very rare indeed. Schulze (*LE* 379) cites ']Venidius Q. f. Arn. Kalenus', a magistrate at Clusium (*CIL* xi 2124), and a Venidius at Cumae (*Eph. Ep.* viii 118, no. 452); and observe further that all the inscriptions of Rome can show only one Venidius, on a fragment (*CIL* vi 30518[15]). Barbieri (op. cit.) adds a Venidius Rufus on an unpublished inscription from Ephesus, and a Venidius in Africa, viz. Q. Venidius Gallio (*CIL* viii 60: Hadrumetum). Add M. Venidius Vitul(us), quaestor at Teanum Sidicinum in | A.D. 45 (*AE* 1909, 78 = *Inscr. It.* xiii 1, 264), and Venidia Quartilla (*I. l. Afr.* 284: Thuburbo Maius). The only Venidius in *RE* viii A, viz. M. Venidius Rogatianus, 'e. v. a ducenaris' (*CIL* xiv 2939: Praeneste), can claim a certain relevance. The *cognomina* 'Rogatus' and 'Rogatianus' cry aloud for an origin from Africa (see the index of *CIL* viii). As for the 'Marius

Maximus' in the nomenclature of the consular, observe L. Marius Maximus Perpetuus Aurelianus (*PIR*[1], M 233), *cos. suff. c.* 199.

VERANIUS. Friend of Catullus, abroad in Hispania Citerior (9, 5 ff.; 12, 14 ff.); also among the *comites* of a Piso (28; 47), presumably L. Calpurnius Piso Caesoninus (*cos.* 58), proconsul of Macedonia. See further *C & M* xvii (1956), 129 ff. [= above pp. 300 ff.]. The *tribus* of the senatorial Veranii of the early Empire is the Clustumina—which is appended to the nomenclature of local notables who received the franchise from Q. Veranius (*cos.* A.D. 49), the first governor of the new province of Lycia–Pamphylia (cf. A. E. Gordon in *RE* viii A, col. 940). That tribe points to Umbria in the first instance; but it is compatible with the old Sabine country. [See entry in *RE* viii A 2 (1958), coll. 2414 f., by Schuster.]

L. VERATIUS. Objectionable person who went about committing assaults and paying compensation in cash. From the jurist Antistius Labeo, quoted by Gellius xx 1, 13: 'L. Veratius fuit egregie homo improbus atque inmani vecordia. is pro delectamento habebat os hominis liberi manus suae palma verberare', etc. The only Veratius of any consequence is the *frater Arvalis* of the Flavian period, L. Veratius Quadratus, *PIR*[1], V 269; *RE* viii A, col. 968—where perhaps should be added a reference to ']tius Quadratus leg. Aug. pr. pr.' (*CIL* ii 189: Olisipo). The *nomen*, which is not very common, is attested before the Republic ends on Delos (*CIL* i[2] 2249 f.) and at Carthago Nova (2270 = ii 3433 [= *ILLRP* 777]): no other instances in *CIL* i[2]. Noteworthy is the frequency in Gallia Narbonensis (thirty-six in *CIL* xii, which is nearly as many as in all the Italian volumes of *CIL*). A number of these specimens will really be 'native' in origin, like some other names in 'Ver-'. Observe that *CIL* xiii (Gaul and the Germanies) can show eleven Veranii, some of whom look very suspicious (registered in *RE* viii A, col. 967). [See now L. Veratius L. f. at Caere: *AE* 1969–70, no. 192.]

VERCONIUS TURINUS. Fraudulent friend of an emperor (*HA Alexander Severus* 35 f.; 67, 2), put to death in an appropriate manner: 'fumo punitur qui fumum vendidit' (36, 2). *PIR*[1], V 271. Fictitious, like Verconius Herennianus, the alleged *praefectus praetorio* of Aurelian (*Aurel.* 44, 2). For the *nomen*, presumably Celtic, Schulze (*LE* 100) cites *CIL* xi 884 (Mutina), but also draws attention to 'Vercius' (ix 3252: Corfinium).

VERENIA. With Gegania, the first of the Vestal Virgins, the next pair being Canuleia and Tarpeia (Plutarch, *Numa* 10). Münzer in his thorough discussion hesitated to assume that a Verania is meant, because the earliest Veranius on record anywhere is the friend of Catullus (*Philologus* xcii (1937), 53). The *nomen* 'Verenius' seems not to exist. On the other hand, a Veranius wrote on | sacerdotal antiquities (*PIR*[1], V 264), late Republican or early Augustan since he is cited by Verrius Flaccus. A revealing fact.

M. VERG[?ILIUS]. Proconsul of Cyprus, on a coin in the possession of Borghesi (*Œuvres* ii 22). *PIR*[1], V 273. The type, according to Borghesi, was the same as that of a coin of A. Plautius—Salaminian Zeus and the name on the reverse. For which, see *BMC Cyprus*, 73, n. 4 (2 and 3 have the temple of Aphrodite at Paphos). The coinage of A. Plautius commemorates the return of Cyprus to government by proconsuls in 22 B.C., so M. Grant suggests (*FITA* (1946), 143). If that were certain, the proconsul (*PIR*[1], P 343, to be distinguished from P 341, who is a Plautus) could hardly be identical with A. Plautius, suffect consul in 1 B.C. (as the *Fasti* of the *Vicorum Magistri* revealed in 1935 [*Inscr. It.* xiii 2, 95]: ignored in *RE* xxi, coll. 26 f.). However that may be, Borghesi's coin, though not reported since, must be kept on record somewhere. There is a P. Vergilius M. f. Pontianus among the *curatores* of the Tiber under Tiberius, subsequent to A.D. 23 (*CIL* xiv 4704).

CN. VERGILIUS CAPITO. Prefect of Egypt from 47 to 52. *PIR*[1], V 276. For the evidence for his prefecture, A. Stein, *Die Präfekten von Aegypten in röm. Zeit* (1950), 30 f.; for his activity in Miletus (where his family is domiciled), L. Robert, *Hellenica* vii (1949), 206 ff. [See entry in *RE* viii A 2 (1958), coll. 2419 ff., by R. Stiglitz.]

24

Antonine Relatives: Ceionii and Vettuleni

S P A N I S H with Trajan and Hadrian, the dynasty of the Antonines comes out as Narbonensian with Antoninus Pius, and the strains are blended in Marcus Aurelius. So far the rulers. They emerge as the product of an intricate nexus of family alliances, some reaching a long way back. Italian components belong to the amalgam, most important the Ceionii. When Hadrian at the age of sixty began to think about the succession, his choice fell upon L. Ceionius Commodus, consul in 136, whom he adopted as L. Aelius Caesar, in the last weeks of that year. Death quickly brought the design to naught, imposing other contrivances, as a result of which the son of Aelius Caesar (adopted along with Marcus by Pius) came to be the partner of M. Aurelius in the imperial power, namely L. Verus.

There are three homonymous consuls of the Ceionii in three successive generations.[1] The first is the first known senator in that family, and he is already a personage: *consul ordinarius* in 78 and almost at once governor of Syria (that was by no means normal), after which he slips out of historical record. The name of his wife happens to be known—she was Appia Sex. f. Severa, from some town of Gallia Narbonensis.[2] Perhaps not his first, or only, wife.

The second is only a name and date. He shared the *fasces* in 106 with Sex. Vettulenus Civica Cerialis. It can be | inferred that he married a lady called Plautia—and Plautia, whose name stands nowhere attested, has to be divined and evoked from the nomenclature of her descendants. On the decease (or divorce) of her husband, she was transferred to C. Avidius Nigrinus (*suff.* 110).[3]

The third, born about 100 and praetor in 130, was *consul ordinarius* in 136 with Sex. Vettulenus Civica Pompeianus for colleague. Having been the stepson of Avidius Nigrinus, he married the daughter of Nigrinus (by a former match).[4] This is the L. Ceionius Commodus who by act and favour of Hadrian became L. Aelius Caesar.

---

[1] *PIR²*, C 603–5.
[2] *ILS* 1003 f. (near Rome). Her father has the tribe Voltinia.
[3] As is deduced from 'Avidia Plautia Nigrini fil.', described as *amita* of L. Verus (*ILS* 8217). Cf. E. Groag in *PIR²*, A 1408, with stemma on p. 287.
[4] *HA Hadr.* 23, 10.

Athenaeum xxxv (1957), 306–15.

About pedigrees and connections in the dynasty of the Antonines, many facts are missing. Odd collaterals are sometimes instructive. There was a certain M. Civica Barbarus, the consul of 157.[1] He is described as uncle of L. Verus: he brought his bride Lucilla to him during the Parthian War.[2] Therefore he must have been a brother of L. Aelius Caesar (*cos.* 136), a much younger brother, and perhaps not by the same mother. Furthermore, given the observed fact that persons of this eminence reach the consulate in their thirty-third year, or not much later, his father, L. Ceionius Commodus (the *ordinarius* of 106), will have lived on to about the year 123. The sources did not happen to attest the *gentilicium* of the consul of 157. None the less, it seemed safe to call him M. (Ceionius) Civica Barbarus.

That was the standard view. Many relationships depend upon casual details, sporadic discoveries, or plausible constructions. A single fact can easily overturn them. Such has now happened for the consul of 157. A Greek dedication in his honour at Argos reveals the public offices of his career—*triumvir monetalis*, quaestor of Antoninus Pius, praetor, consul. Also, it confirms his relation to the dynasty—brother of | L. Caesar and uncle of the Augusti (i.e. Marcus and Verus) and describes him as *comes* of L. Verus. Also, and more important, it discloses his correct nomenclature. He is styled 'M. Vettulenus Sex. f. Quir. Civica Barbarus'.[3]

Hence not a Ceionius but a Vettulenus. His parent is either the consul of 106 or the consul of 136 (each colleague of a Ceionius). Which shall it be? The scholar who published the inscription, with full and exhaustive commentary, opts for the latter.[4] Sex. Vettulenus Civica Pompeianus (*cos.* 136) would therefore be the third husband of Plautia. He married her after the execution of Avidius Nigrinus in 118. Therefore L. Caesar (*cos.* 136) and M. Vettulenus Civica Barbarus (*cos.* 157) are in fact halfbrothers. And a new stemma can be built up.[5]

Ages and generations counsel a doubt. Plautia is the mother of L. Aelius Caesar, who was born in or about the year 100. Now Sex. Vettulenus Civica Pompeianus, the *ordinarius* of 136, is the close coeval of L. Caesar, his colleague in the consulship. It would have to be assumed that Vettulenus had married his colleague's mother—a woman old enough to be his own mother: this was a match which produced the consul of 157, hence not contracted much later than 123 (when he will have been about twenty-three years old).

---

[1] *PIR*[2], C 602. Add *AE* 1939, 109 (Athens), a dedication by his friend Herodes Atticus. [See now *Hesperia* xxvi (1957), 220.]

[2] *HA Marcus* 9, 4.

[3] P. Charneux, 'M. Vettulenus Civica Barbarus', *BCH* lxxxi (1957), 121 ff., with photograph on p. 123. This enables the editor to reconstruct (136 ff.) a fragmentary dedication elsewhere (*Inschr. v. Olympia* 541).

[4] Ibid. 125.   [5] Ibid. 130.

Not impossible, but barely credible. It is preferable to assume that the third husband of Plautia was the Vettulenus consul in 106, who belongs to the same generation as her first and second. His sons are therefore Pompeianus, the consul of 136 (by a former wife, conjecturally a Pompeia), and Civica Barbarus (by Plautia), the consul of 157.

Plautia exemplifies a common phenomenon in the history of imperial Rome: a fragment of knowledge rescued from the waters of oblivion, but a figure of consequence in the social and political history of the time. What was the ancestry of | this lady? The only contemporaneous Plautii in the senatorial order are illustrious indeed, the descendants of M. Plautius Silvanus (*cos.* 2 B.C.). Plautia, it can be supposed, was a daughter of L. Aelius Lamia Plautius Aelianus (*cos.* 80), sister of L. Lamia Aelianus (*cos.* 116).[1] That family shows another link. In the reign of Hadrian a young man called Lamia Silvanus was betrothed to Aurelia Fadilla, the elder daughter of T. Aurelius Fulvus (*cos.* 120), the later Emperor Antoninus Pius.[2] Presumably a son of the consul of 116, hence a nephew of Plautia.

The three marriages of Plautia can now be summed up, discussed, and exploited. She was long enough the wife of L. Ceionius Commodus (*cos.* 106) to produce a son born precisely (it may well be) in 100, the future L. Aelius Caesar. At this point ingenious conjecture has intervened. As follows. The Ceionius Commodus whom Hadrian adopted was in reality his own son, the product of adultery with Plautia. That is why Hadrian chose him for successor. And, a further step, Plautia was divorced by the injured husband: Avidius Nigrinus then (or subsequently) took her over.[3]

It would be entertaining to speculate about the conduct of young Hadrian in the first years after his kinsman acquired the imperial power (Hadrian married Vibia Sabina, the grand-niece of Trajan, about the year 100); it would be refreshing to discover aspects of social life not revealed in the correspondence of Pliny (divorce has no place in his decorous pages); and it would be profitable to give some attention to a number of persons who happen to receive no missives from Pliny, such as Hadrian, Ceionius Commodus, and Avidius Nigrinus. For all that, it does not have to be assumed that Hadrian, freshly married to Vibia Sabina, chose to seduce the wife of Ceionius Commodus. Various reasons tell against the new discovery of an ancient scandal.

The Ceionii, though perpetuated from the consul of 78 to the colleague of Marcus Aurelius, were not long-lived as indi|viduals. Let it be taken that death, not divorce, made Plautia, wife of the consul of 106, available to C. Avidius Nigrinus (*suff.* 110).[4]

---

[1] *PIR*[2], A 205; 204.   [2] *PIR*[2], A 206.   [3] J. Carcopino, *REA* li (1949), 262 ff.
[4] Cf. P. Charneux, op. cit. 127. That does not, in itself, demolish the notion that the consul of 136 might have been an illegitimate son of Hadrian. Adultery could still be opined—with the further refinement of an ignorant or complaisant husband.

About Avidius Nigrinus, many things remain enigmatic.[1] If he is to be identified with the Nigrinus tribune of the plebs in 105, active and eloquent, he must have benefited by unusual favour to reach the consulate in 110.[2] He governed Dacia (in the last years of Trajan, it could be conjectured, when various friends of Hadrian were coming to the fore). The first year of Hadrian's rule witnessed his destruction. Along with three other consulars he was put to death.[3] The charge was conspiracy, the evidence fails to carry conviction. Perhaps Hadrian's agents, notably the Guard Prefect Acilius Attianus, acted with undue precipitance. Some or other of the four may previously have been hostile to Hadrian. Hardly Nigrinus. The *Historia Augusta* asserts that Hadrian intended to nominate Nigrinus as his heir and successor:[4] presumably a notice deriving from the Emperor's *Autobiography* (which conveyed other items of defence and apologia).

Hadrian in 136 adopted L. Ceionius Commodus, the husband of Nigrinus' daughter. Perhaps the tardy reparation of a grievous and regretted error.

Nigrinus destroyed in 118, Plautia took a third husband. He was coeval with the others and belonged to the same group—for the conjoint consulates of Ceionii and Vettuleni in 106 and 136 are a clear sign of alliance or propinquity. Neither Plautia nor Sex. Vettulenus Civica Cerialis (*cos.* 106) had passed the age for procreation; and their son (it appears) was M. Vettulenus Civica Barbarus, born about 123 and consul in 157.

A new and satisfactory stemma can therefore be produced. Valuable items, it is true, are lacking, which might show an | even closer interlocking of families in the friendship and alliance of Hadrian. For example, the first wife of Avidius Nigrinus, or the husband of Avidia Plautia, his daughter by his second marriage (with Plautia).

There is excuse for a variety of conjectures in the family tree of the Antonines. One person with the *nomen* 'Ceionius' can find plausible attachment, viz. M. Ceionius Silvanus (*cos.* 156).[5] His *cognomen* suggests descent from the Plautii. The easiest assumption is that his parent was a son of L. Ceionius Commodus (*cos.* 106) and of Plautia, who died before the consular age (otherwise he would surely have been *consul ordinarius*). Hence an unattested and short-lived brother of L. Caesar—and his son, M. Ceionius Silvanus, was therefore a first cousin of L. Verus.

Further, for completeness, another strain can be detected in the pedigree. The two sisters of L. Verus, granddaughters of Plautia, bear the names

[1] *PIR*[2], A 1408.
[2] Pliny, *Ep.* v 13, 6; 20, 6; vii 6, 2; 4.
[3] *HA Hadr.* 7, 1 f.; Dio lxix 1, 5.
[4] *HA Hadr.* 7, 1.
[5] *PIR*[2], C 610, cf. Groag's note: 'pertinere videtur ad domum consularem et mox Augustam.'

Ceionia Plautia and Ceionia Fabia.[1] Whence derives the 'Fabia'? Now one of the sons of Plautia, namely M. Vettulenus Civica Barbarus (*cos.* 157), has the cognomen 'Barbarus'. A Fabius Barbarus is indicated somewhere in the ascendance. It should seem that Plautia's parent (the consul of 80, cf. above) married the daughter of a Fabius Barbarus. A person of that name can be produced.[2]

More important, the strengthening of old links through new alliances. Ceionia Fabia married a certain Plautius Quintillus (*cos.* 159).[3] Like his presumed brother, Plautius Aquilinus (*cos.* 162), he is only a name—or rather part of a name, for he may well be polyonymous, the 'Plautius' in his no|menclature coming from the maternal line.[4] Once again a Plautia is to be surmised, the mother of these two *ordinarii*. Hardly the lady of the three husbands, assigning her a fourth, and five more years of fecundity after the birth of Civica Barbarus, the consul of 157. Conceivably Avidia Plautia, the daughter of Nigrinus. Further speculation would not be profitable, but one fact can be added. The marriage of Plautius Quintillus produces a son, consul in 177: he takes for wife one of the daughters of Marcus Aurelius.[5]

Such was the fortune attending upon two families that first reach the consulate as adherents of Vespasian. They deserve a brief annotation.

For the first Ceionius a post stands on record shortly before his consulship. It is revealed by the inscription on the North-west Gate at Gerasa, certified to the year 75/6.[6] Enough survives of the title of Ceionius to prove that he was not legate of a legion but *legatus Augusti pro praetore*.[7] An important consequence may be deduced: he was legate of Judaea, and the cities of the Decapolis must at this time have been in the *provincia* of

---

[1] *PIR*[2], C 614; 612.

[2] Viz. Q. Fabius Barbarus Antonius Macer, *cos. suff.* with C. Licinius Mucianus *c.* 64 (*PP* iii (1946), 381). Observe also Q. Fabius Barbarus Valerius Magnus Julianus (*suff.* 99). The nomenclature suggests provincial extraction.

[3] The consul of 177, M. Peducaeus Plautius Quintillus, is described as a son of Ceionia Fabia on the Ephesian inscription published by J. Keil, *Klio* xxxi (1938), 296, whence *AE* 1939, 127. Keil suggests that he derives the 'Peducaeus' from adoption by the consul of 141, M. Peducaeus Stloga Priscinus.

[4] The two Plautii may be sons of the mysterious L. Epidius Titius Aquilinus (*cos.* 125).

[5] Cf. *AE* 1939, 127. Presumably Fadilla (*PIR*[2], F 96).

[6] *IGR* iii 1356. The revised text of C. B. Welles (*Gerasa*, 398, no. 50) disposes of Groag's doubts about the reading of the date. [W. Eck, *Senatoren von Vespasian bis Hadrian* (1970), 101, n. 41, refuses to accept this, as Ceionius reached the consulship (78) before L. Flavius Silva Nonius Bassus, attested there in 74 (on his calculation) and *cos.* 81. This is certainly irregular, but Eck's suggestion that Ceionius is attested merely as legionary legate shows that he did not read either Syme or Welles (both of whom he cites) with proper care: Welles (quoted by Syme) demonstrated that the remains of the inscription *necessitate* the restoration πρεσβευτοῦ Σεβαστοῦ ἀντιστρατήγου. He perhaps assumes excessive regularity in career patterns at this date: see Syme, *JRS* xlviii (1958), 1 ff. = 378 ff. below. On this inscription see now Bowersock, *JRS* lxiii (1973), 138 f.]

[7] Viz. πρε[σβευτοῦ Σεβαστ]οῦ ἀντ[ιστρατήγου].

that governor.[1] Ceionius might previously have commanded a legion in the Eastern lands, perhaps even as quaestorian, when (or even after) Vespasian was proclaimed in 69.

Two Vettuleni got the consulate from Vespasian. Sex. Vettulenus Cerialis is on record as legate of V Macedonica in Palestine in 67 and in 70; he was honoured with a double set of military decorations; and, after the departure of Titus, | he was left in charge of the army.[2] His consulate should fall about 73 or 74. He had a brother, C. Vettulenus Civica Cerialis, consul suffect about 76. The two Vettuleni went on to govern in succession the great military province of Moesia, attested there respectively in 78 and in 82.[3] Thereafter there is no news of the elder. The younger, when proconsul of Asia [perhaps] in 88/9, was put to death by order of Domitian—and by act (it can be inferred) of the procurator.[4]

The inscription of the last Vettulenus, namely Civica Barbarus (*cos.* 157), showing no magistracy between quaestorship and praetorship, proves that he was a patrician. Vettuleni and Ceionii may be among the families adlected into that order by Vespasian and Titus when censors. It cannot be affirmed, for later rulers are known to have exercised the prerogative.

To conclude, local origins. The tribe of Civica Barbarus is disclosed as the Quirina. That is no surprise. A stray Vettulenus of the early Principate, namely the senator T. Vettulenus P. f. Quadratus, also has it.[5] That fact, taken with the distribution of their uncommon *nomen*, ties them down to the Sabine region.[6] No surprise either that Vespasian had friends and allies in his own country. The Petillii, who were related to the Flavii, may likewise be Sabine.[7] When the | Flavian generals after crossing the Apennines halted at Mevania in Umbria, they were met there by Petillius

---

[1] There was trouble (but not a war) with the Parthians *c.* 75, cf. Pliny, *Pan.* 14; Victor, *Epit.* 9, 12; *Caes.* 9, 10. It might be desirable for the legate of Syria to have his attention free for regions further north.

[2] *PIR*[1], V 351. The Sex. Vettulenus Cerialis of *ILS* 2690 (Venafrum), husband of Lusia Galla, might not be this man but his father. The inscription (acephalous) recording the military decorations was found at Carthage (*ILS* 988). Vettulenus may have gone on to be proconsul of Africa (*c.* 85).

[3] *CIL* vi 22, 28. [Sex. Vettulenus is now attested as early as April 75 (see Eck, op. cit. 121). For the possibility that the acephalous *AE* 1955, 123 belongs to him (thus E. Birley), see the discussion by Eck, op. cit. 92 f.]

[4] Tacitus, *Agr.* 42, 1, cf. *ILS* 1374. [On the date, see Eck, op. cit. 86 f.]

[5] *CIL* vi 31773: 'T. Vettulenus P. f. Quir. Quadratus / pr. pro cos. tr. pl. / Vettulena T. [f.] Polla filia'. The style and offices indicate an early date. Another member of this family is the quaestor Vettulenus Quadratus (*CIL* x 7245: Lilybaeum).

[6] In *CIL* ix all the instances (apart from 3406: Aufinum) are Sabine, viz. 4742 (Reate); 4553 and 5605 (Nursia). Further, two from Cascia in the territory of Nursia (*NSA* 1893, 376, nos. 23 f.), the latter of whom, Sex. Vettulenus Sedatus, is an *octovir*, but has the tribe Palatina, indicating libertine extraction. The others are of no social consequence.

[7] Tacitus speaks of 'propinqua adfinitas cum Vespasiano' (*Hist.* iii 59, 2). E. Swoboda suggests Aquileia as a possible origin (*RE* xix, col. 1149). The evidence (*CIL* v 1330; *NSA* 1925, 24, no. 5) is not strong enough.

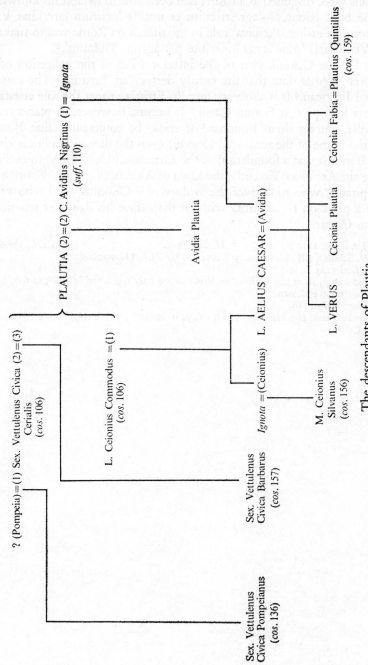

The descendants of Plautia

Cerialis who, disguised as a rustic, had been able to exploit his knowledge of the back country—'agresti cultu et notitia locorum custodias Vitelli elapsum'.[1] Further, Petillius' role in the march on Rome was to make for the Via Salaria 'transversis itineribus per agrum Sabinum'.[2]

As for the Ceionii, two of the inferior *Vitae* in the collection of the *Historia Augusta* state that the family derives 'ex Etruria'.[3] The *nomen* is indeed Etruscan.[4] It is also very rare. In Etruria proper the sole attestation is on a lead pipe at Forum Cassii.[5] It occurs, however, in places on the Aemilia, among them Bononia.[6] It could be conjectured that Bononia was the home of the senatorial Ceionii: even the literary tradition knows that Bononia was a foundation of the Etruscans.[7] Only forty miles distant along the Aemilia is Faventia, the town of Avidius Nigrinus, the ostensible conspirator, who took over the widow of a Ceionius—and who would have a place on the stemma without that, since his daughter married L. Aelius Caesar.[8]

[1] *Hist.* iii 59, 2.   [2] *Hist.* iii 78, 3.   [3] *Aelius* 2, 8; *Verus* 1, 9.
[4] W. Schulze, *LE* 186. Its rarity is revealed by *TLL, Onomasticon.*
[5] *CIL* xi 3324.
[6] Tile-stamps from the territory of Bononia are duly registered in *PIR*², C 603, but no firm conclusion is drawn.
[7] Pliny, *NH* iii 119.
[8] For Faventia, *HA Hadr.* 7, 2; *Verus* 1, 9. In *Aelius* 2, 9 that *origo* is wrongly assigned to the Ceionii.

25

The Origin of the Veranii

'Veranius' is an uncommon *gentilicium*, with brief and transient notice in Roman annals.[1] The earliest Veranius on record is the friend of Catullus. According to Catullus (28; 47), he was abroad on the staff of a governor while, or just after, the poet was with Memmius (*pr.* 58) in Bithynia. The governor was a Piso, clearly L. Piso (*cos.* 58), proconsul of Macedonia till the summer of 55.[2] Veranius, it emerges elsewhere (9, 5 ff.; 12, 14 ff.), had also been in Hispania Citerior, accompanied here too by his insepar-able Fabullus. Veranius may, or may not, have been an author, identical with the Veranius who wrote on religious antiquities—who again might be the Veranius Flaccus whom Caesar Augustus derided for his affected and archaic style.[3]

Two senators of the name are discovered under the rule of Julii and Claudii. Q. Veranius, *comes* of Germanicus Caesar in the eastern lands, was among those who insisted that the prince be avenged, took a share in the prosecution of Cn. Piso, and got a priesthood for his reward. Tacitus gives him prominence by naming him no fewer than five times in the company and context of P. Vitellius.[4] As for his son, likewise Q. Veranius, *pietas* towards the dynasty, a signal service rendered to Claudius Caesar, and (it is a fair conjecture) some help from the great master of patronage L. Vitellius, carried him much further—the first governor of the new

[1] All the Veranii are registered by A. E. Gordon in *RE* viii A, and all instances of the *nomen* (967 f.). [The friend of Catullus, ibid. coll. 2414 f., by M. Schuster.] A suspicious feature should be noted—'Veranius' no fewer than eleven times in *CIL* xiii. Many of these will be native in origin, and 'pseudo-Latin'; cf. 'Veracius', and (sometimes) 'Veratius'. For such fabricated *nomina* see W. Schulze, *LE* 48 ff.; E. Birley, *Roman Britain and the Roman Army* (1953), 165 ff.

[2] As has generally been assumed, although some vaguely invoke M. Pupius Piso (*cos.* 61), who may not have been extant in 57/6. See now *C & M* xvii (1956), 129 ff. [= above pp. 300 ff.]

[3] Veranius the antiquarian: *PIR*[1], V 264; *RE* viii A, col. 937; Veranius Flaccus: Suetonius, *Divus Aug.* 86, 3. It is a clue to the date of the former that he was cited by Verrius Flaccus. A trace of his operations might be surmised in the notice of the first pair of Vestal Virgins, Verenia and Gegania (Plutarch, *Numa* 10). The *nomen* 'Verenius' does not appear to exist. Münzer was puzzled and hesitated to assume that a Verania must be meant (*Philologus* xcii (1937), 53).

[4] Tacitus, *Ann.* ii 74, 2; iii 10, 1; 13, 2; 17, 2; 19, 1. Cf. further *JRS* xlvi (1956), 20. [= *Ten Studies in Tacitus* (1970), 55 f.].

Classical Quarterly, N.S. vii (1957), 123–5. Reprinted by permission of the Classical Journals Board.

province of Lycia–Pamphylia, *consul ordinarius* in 49, legate of Britain in 57 or 58 (succeeding old Didius Gallus), where he died before a year had elapsed, ambitious and still in the prime of life.[1]

It would be useful to have the provenance of the Veranii. Catullus knew his friend's family, at least he refers to 'fratresque unanimos anumque matrem' (9, 4). It has been supposed that Verona was their home.[2] If that were so, they cannot be the ancestors of the senatorial Veranii, whose tribe is the Clustumina—as is proved by the fact that the Clustumina, attached to their *nomen*, is found in families of Lycian notables which patently derive name and citizenship from grants made by Q. Veranius when Lycia was annexed.[3] |

At first sight, the Clustumina points powerfully to Umbria. A large number of communities have it, enrolled at the time of the *Bellum Italicum*. Elsewhere, two towns only, Larinum in Samnium—and Forum Novum in the Sabine country.[4]

Now all Umbria can produce nothing closer to a specimen of the name 'Veranius' than a woman called Messia Veranilla.[5] That being so, it is legitimate to cast a glance at the Sabine country, or rather that part of it which had been in close relations with Rome and Latium from early times. Whereas the tribe Quirina covers the rest of Sabinum, this tract, the south-west, is eccentric: the Sergia at ancient Cures and at Trebula Mutuesca, the Clustumina at Forum Novum. Moreover, a Roman historian, producing a Sabine centurion to harangue the citizen body, makes him state his tribe—'Sp. Ligustinus tribu Crustumina ex Sabinis sum oriundus, Quirites.'[6] The family of Q. Veranius had property in the old Sabinum. There is no evidence for Forum Novum, it is true; but there is a tile with 'Q. Verani' at Trebula Mutuesca, and at Cures two *seviri*, descendants of freedmen of a Q. Veranius, namely Q. Veranius Sabinus

[1] *Ann.* xiv 29, 1 (not omitting his last will and testament). For his career see now *AE* 1953, 251, with the exhaustive commentary of A. E. Gordon, *Univ. of Cal. Pub. in Class. Arch.* ii 5 (1952), 231 ff.

[2] B. Schmidt in his *Prolegomena* (1887), xlix; R. J. N. Lindsay, *CP* xliii (1948), 44. Only one, a lady of no class, Verania Vera (*CIL* v 3787). Observe, for that style of 'native' nomenclature, *CIL* xiii 652; 12027.

[3] Cf. A. E. Gordon, *RE* viii A, col. 940. The best and earliest instance is *IGR* iv 914 f.—from Cibyra, perhaps temporarily in his *provincia*. A close parallel are Ummidii in Cyprus (e.g. *IGR* iii 950), showing the Teretina, which is the *tribus* of the proconsul C. Ummidius Quadratus, of Casinum (*PIR*[1], V 600).

[4] W. Kubitschek, *Imp. Rom. Trib. Discr.* (1889), 41, 55. He prints 'Clustumina' with a query. *CIL* ix, citing two inscriptions (4789, 4808), omits the query. The Claudia is also found there (4790). A new inscription brings no certainty—'L. Clarius L. f. C[..] / M. Atius M. f. Cla./p.p.' (published by C. Pietrangeli, *Epigr.* ii (1940), 287, no. 5). But observe the fragment '] Clu. V[' (ibid. 289, no. 12). [L. R. Taylor, *Voting Districts of the Rom. Rep.* (1960), 271, accepts it as certain.]   [5] *CIL* xi 4491 (Ameria).

[6] Livy xlii 34, 2. For Crustumerium and the tribe Clustumina see W. Kubitschek, *De Romanarum Tribuum Origine ac Propagatione* (1882), 15; K. J. Beloch, *Röm. Gesch.* (1926), 159, 174 ff., 270, etc. [Taylor, op. cit., Index, p. 333.]

and Q. Veranius Asclepiades, offered the town a public banquet in A.D. 147.[1]

For rarity, and for other reasons, the name 'Servaeus' suggests a parallel. Like 'Veranius', it is attested for the first time in the last age of the Republic—a *publicanus* in Gaul *c.* 74, and a man elected tribune of the plebs in 51, but condemned for bribery.[2] Then Q. Servaeus, one of the *comites* of Germanicus, and one of the prosecutors of Cn. Piso.[3] Finally, and the last of this family, '[Servaeus In]noc(ens)' whom the *Fasti Ostienses* disclose as consul suffect in 82, and Q. Servaeus Innocens (*suff.* 101). The *gentilicium* cannot be attached to any town or region of Italy as *origo* of these Servaei.[4] The next senatorial Servaei belong to a later age, coming from Africa (from Sufetula and from Gigthi): hence the surmise that a Servaeus had once been proconsul of that province.[5] But they should rather belong to old immigrant stock. Africa furnishes notable instances of rare Italian *gentilicia*.[6]

'Veranius' is a *nomen* so uncommon that it encourages one to link the first | Veranius and the last, illustrating the vicissitudes of men and families, of society and government. The first Veranius emerges as client of a Piso, of that active and excellent proconsul of Macedonia whom Cicero traduced. The last, the successful *novus homo*, rose high as a client of the Caesars and gave his daughter in marriage to one of the Pisones, Piso Licinianus, who derived his lineage from the dynasts Pompeius and Crassus—and who was selected by Galba to be his son and partner in the power. Thereafter the name lingers sporadically among persons of low degree, save in Lycia, where it is perpetuated in families of the local aristocracy.

---

[1] *CIL* ix 6078[71] (Trebula); 4957 (Cures): the solitary instances in the volume. Note that Trebula can show a Verana P. f. Polla (4938). The *nomen* 'Veranus' is exceedingly rare. Schulze cites one other instance (*LE* 379, *add.*), viz. vi 31723.

[2] *Pro Fonteio* 19; *Ad fam.* viii 4, 2.   [3] *PIR*[1], S 398.

[4] Very rare. Not in *CIL* i[2], v, ix, x, xi, xiv, and only eight instances at Rome (vi). A notable instance abroad is the *primipilaris* T. Servaeus Sabinus and his centurion son (*CIL* iii 14398; *JRS* xviii (1928), 189 = *AE* 1930, 109: near Iconium).

[5] E. Groag, *RE* ii A, col. 1755 (on the *suffectus* of 101). The African senatorial Servaei, unfortunately omitted from *RE*, are *PIR*[1], S 399, 400 (cf. *ILS* 8978), 402, 403. [Now in *RE*, Suppl. xiv, coll. 663 f. (Eck).]

[6] Cf. *Historia* iv (1955), 56 [= p. 275 above], discussing 'Aufustius', with a reference to 'Farsuleius', 'Fidiculanius', 'Furfanius'.

26

A Fragment of Sallust?

WHEN Sertorius, passing through the Straits, touched land a little way beyond the mouth of the river Baetis, he encountered certain seafaring men newly returned from a voyage to the Fortunate Isles. They told him about the delectable site, whereupon he conceived a strong desire to sail thither and establish a colony, remote from tyranny and the interminable wars. The prospect held no appeal for the crude Cilician pirates who had been conveying Sertorius, and he went to Mauretania instead.

Plutarch reports the story.[1] It is supported by fragments (all too few) from the *Historiae* of Sallust.[2] Plutarch's biography (or Plutarch's source) draws in large measure on Sallust. That is manifest and admitted.[3] The language sometimes betrays traces of a Latin original, and defective translation or unskilful compression can be surmised.[4] In the present context a small item perhaps suggests Latin usage rather than Greek. A Greek writer | might have referred to the Pillars of Hercules: Plutarch has the 'Strait of Gades'.[5]

In Latin, *fretum* is the normal word to designate a strait. In the first place, the channel between Italy and Sicily. Then, as conquest and the horizon widened, the Hellespont or the Bosporus, and the *fretum Gaditanum* that led to the outer Ocean. Prose or verse, the narrow seas that sunder lands and continents could not fail to challenge any stylist to an effort of vigorous or poetical diction.[6] The ambitious Sallust (it is a fair conjecture) would evoke the Strait of Gades in some brief and memorable phrase, not to be undervalued by writers in the aftermath—historians, geographers,

---

[1] *Sertorius* 8 f.   [2] *Hist.* i 100–3 (ed. B. Maurenbrecher, 1893).
[3] H. Peter, *Die Quellen Plutarchs in den Biographien der Römer* (1865), 61 ff.; B. Maurenbrecher (in his *Prolegomena* (1890), 27 ff.); A. Schulten, *Sertorius* (1926), 5 ff.
[4] The verb δολοφονεῖν in *Sertorius* 7 is responsible for the belief that a certain Calpurnius Lanarius was a traitor who murdered the Sertorian partisan Livius Salinator; but Lanarius is really an officer on the other side, the author of a crafty stratagem that forced the passage of the Pyrenees; and, according to Sallust, 'Salinator in agmine occiditur' (*Hist.* i 36). Cf. R. Syme, *Historia* iv (1955), 58 f. [= p. 278 above].
[5] *Sertorius* 8: διεκβαλὼν τὸν Γαδειραῖον πορθμόν. Not that this is wholly conclusive, cf. Pliny, *NH* iii 74: 'Porthmos a Graecis [sc. nuncupatus], a nobis Gaditanum fretum.'
[6] Thus Lucretius i 720 (the Sicilian Strait) or Ammianus xxxi 16, 7: 'fretum quod Pontum disterminat et Aegaeum'. The verb 'distermino' first appears in prose with Mela and Seneca: once in Tacitus (*Ann.* xi 10, 2).

Eranos lv (1957), 171–4.

grammarians. Where should it be sought? The scholiast on Juvenal, commenting on the first line of the *Tenth Satire*, produces the following definition: '⟨Gades⟩ sunt in Atlantico mari[s] Hispaniae proxim⟨a⟩e, ubi se angustissimo divortio inter columnas Herculis in medi[o]terraneos sinus Oceanus infundit.'[1]

The language is choice, and the expression 'angustissimo divortio' turns out to be precious and recondite. The word 'divortium' belongs to the geographical vocabulary, it is true, but it happens to be portentously rare as a synonym for 'fretum'.[2] There is only one other example of its use with an adjective in the superlative. That example is significant. Tacitus introduces his digression on the situation of Byzantium with the words 'namque artissimo inter Europam Asiamque divortio Byzantium in extrema Europa posuere Graeci' (*Ann.* xii 63, 1).

Explaining Byzantium, Tacitus knew his duty—he must | allude to the historian who wrote the famous excursus 'De situ Ponti'. He registers in appropriate language the abundance of fish—'quippe Byzantium fertili solo fecundo mari, quia vis piscium immensa Pontum erumpens et obliquis subter undas saxis exterrita omisso alterius litoris flexu hos ad portus defertur' (63, 2). No commentator has missed the fragment from Sallust's *Historiae*—'qua tempestate vis piscium Ponto erupit' (iii 66). And indeed, Tacitus here surpasses his model with a poetical turn, making the verb 'erumpo' take the accusative. Further, 'subter' occurs nowhere else in his writings. There may be some more Sallust in this chapter. Conceivably the adjective 'fecundus', which happens not to be attested for Sallust, but which is favoured by Tacitus in geographical contexts (six other instances).[3] Then, a little further on, the prosperous Byzantines are styled 'quaestuosi et opulenti' (63, 3): the adjective 'quaestuosus' is elsewhere admitted only once by Tacitus, to describe and deride the appearance of the Roman soldiers in Syria, 'nitidi et quaestuosi' (xiii 35, 1).

The preceding chapter (on the history of Byzantium) also deserves scrutiny. It suitably exhibits 'qua tempestate', the fifth instance of that phrase in the *Annals*—and the last (the subsequent books reveal, along with sundry other features, a less frequent recourse to the Sallustian manner). Further, the concluding sentence: 'quando ea loca insiderent quae transmeantibus terra marique ducibus exercitibusque simul vehendo commeatu opportuna forent.' The verb 'transmeo' is unique in Tacitus; and one might invoke from Sallust 'civitatem com⟨meati⟩bus Italicis oportu⟨nam⟩' (*Hist.* iii 6).

That Tacitus should exploit Sallust on the Strait of Gades, modifying

---

[1] Ed. Wessner (Teubner, 1931).

[2] Apart from the scholion on Juvenal and Tacitus, *Ann.* xii 63, 1, the only clear instance of its application to a strait of the sea appears to be Silius, *Punica* xiv 18 (cf. *TLL*).

[3] viz. *Agr.* 12, 5; *Germ.* 5, 1; *Hist.* i 11, 1; iv 50, 4; *Ann.* iv 65; xiii 57, 1. Note also *Germ.* 45, 7; *Hist.* i 2, 2; iv 73, 3; *Ann.* i 79, 2.

the phrase a little and transferring it to the Bosporus, nothing more natural and easy. His devices are patent in other passages. Earlier in Book xii he had occasion to speak of a recalcitrant vassal, Mithridates the ruler of the Bosporan king|dom. The hazards of warfare in the distant steppe are set forth vividly: 'suscipi bellum avio itinere importuoso mari: ad hoc reges ferocis, vagos populos, solum frugum egenum: taedium ex mora, pericula ex properantia' (xii 20, 1). This description of the empty lands of the nomads is taken from Africa. Compare Sallust, *Jug.* 54, 9 'aviis itineribus'; 17, 5 'mare saevom importuosum'. The archaic and poetical 'egenus' might be Sallustian.[1] Tacitus has one other example of 'importuosus', in the brief and stylized digression on Capreae (iv 67, 2). But it is 'properantia' that sets the seal. Before Tacitus only in *Jug.* 36, 3, and afterwards only twice, in late authors.[2]

It should not be premature or fanciful to reclaim 'angustissimo divortio' from a scholiast and assign it to the predecessor and model of Cornelius Tacitus.

[1] Not in Tacitus before the enhanced style of the *Annals*—and then seven times. *TLL* is instructive—Virgil (four times), Livy (once), and frequently in late writers.

[2] Furneaux in his commentary registers 'properantia' but misses the Sallustian colouring of the passage as a whole. As for 'properantia', only in Julius Valerius i 43; Martianus Capella vi 607 (information supplied by the Direction of *TLL*).

27

The Jurist Neratius Priscus

FAMILIES in their rise and duration are a theme that cannot fail to charm and detain. The Neratii, indigenous at Saepinum in the heart of Samnium, show a local magistrate in the last age of the Republic. Then a gap, and, when next heard of, the Neratii acquire the consulate under the rule of the Flavian emperors; and the name persists in the senatorial order, though lineage and relationships are obscure, to a late epoch.[1]

Their most illustrious member is the master of Roman jurisprudence, L. Neratius Priscus, who flourished in the time of Trajan. As with so many of his peers among the consular worthies, rank and offices may stand on record, but the personality is elusive. Nor can the language of his legal pronouncements | yield any guidance.[2] Apart from that, various problems subsist—the age of the jurist, the year of his consulate, the detail of his career and public occupations.

An inscription at Saepinum exhibits two consulars of the name, patently father and son:[3]

> L. Neratius L. f. [Vol. Priscus]
> praef. aer. Sat., cos., l[eg. pr. pr. prov.]
> Pannonia.
> L. Neratius L. f. Vol. Pr[iscus f., cos.]
> VII vir. epul., leg. Aug. pr. pr. P[annonia]
> inferiore et Pannonia [superiore.]

Two other stones have the name and titles of the elder Neratius Priscus, with the same formulation: the one set up by the *scribae quaestorii*, the other in accordance with the testament of a freedman.[4] It seemed clear enough that the elder was the jurist. Also the same person as the colleague of M. Annius Verus in the consular pair that gave its name to a *senatus*

---

[1] E. Groag, *RE* xvi, coll. 2540 ff. The article on the jurist (2549 ff.) is by A. Berger: not quite adequate on points of history.

[2] A. Berger (ibid. 2549), citing with disbelief several attempts.

[3] *CIL* ix 2455 = *ILS* 1034. Lines 1 and 4 are in larger letters than the rest.

[4] *CIL* ix 2454 = *ILS* 1033; *AE* 1927, 17. Both documents have 'leg. pr. pr. in prov. Pannonia', which should perhaps be restored on the other inscription.

Hermes lxxxv (1957), 480–93.

consultum registered in the *Digest*: 'Neratio Prisco et Annio Vero consulibus'.[1] The first consulate of Annius Verus (*II ord.* 121, *III ord.* 126) lacked attestation. Dates ranged from 83 to 98.[2] Hence uncertainty about the period at which Neratius Priscus was governor of Pannonia. But, in any event, it could not be later than the year 107, the province having been divided after Trajan's first war against the Dacians or (at the latest) during the second.[3]

As for the younger, who held a priesthood (he was *septemvir epulonum*), he governed Pannonia Inferior as a legate of praetorian rank. His consulate, in close sequence on that post, was presumed to fall in the late years of Trajan or early under Hadrian (see further below). For various reasons it can safely be taken that he was not governor of Pannonia Superior before the reign of Hadrian.[4]

So far so good. Not enough facts, but no clash of facts. On any theory or reconstruction, a clear distinction holds between the two consular homonyms of the Saepinum inscription and the approximate dating. New epigraphic data have recently supervened. One discovery imported perplexity (or premature certitudes), but a second, coming soon after, appears to permit a clarification. |

The consular *Fasti* of Potentia in Picenum, published for the first time in 1948, revealed a L. Neratius Priscus, consul suffect in 87 with C. Cilnius Proculus.[5] It was tempting to identify this man with the jurist and with the legate of undivided Pannonia.[6] Not all scholars, however, kept clear of misconceptions. And not all faced the problem, who then could be the consular colleague of M. Annius Verus, how should that consular pair be explained (or explained away).[7]

Ostia brought salvation. There emerged, first noted in print in 1952, a piece of the *Fasti Ostienses*: three lines showing three successive *suffecti* of the year 97, Annius Verus the first of them.[8] It was assumed that the fragment represented the right-hand column of a list of consular pairs. However, when duly published in the next year by the discoverer, the fragment was seen to belong to the left column, with the beginning of

---

[1] *Dig.* xlviii 8, 6; cf. *PIR*[1], N 46.

[2] Cf. *PIR*[2], A 695, where is noted the inscription on a lead tessera 'Vero Pri[...] cos.' (*CIL* xv 8008).

[3] E. Ritterling in his catalogue of legates of Pannonia, *Arch.-ep. Mitt. aus Oesterreich-Ungarn* xx (1897), 16 f.

[4] E. Ritterling, op. cit. 18; *AErt* xli (1927), 283; E. Groag, *RE* xvi, coll. 2547 f.

[5] N. Alfieri, *Athenaeum* xxvi (1948), 116 f., whence *AE* 1949, 23.

[6] W. Kunkel, *Herkunft u. soziale Stellung der röm. Juristen* (1952), 144 f.; J. Crook, *Consilium Principis* (1955), 232; R. Hanslik, *RE* xxiii (1957), col. 6.

[7] The exposition of A. Garzetti was confused and confusing (*Nerva* (1950), 145 f.); and A. Degrassi identified the consular colleague of Annius Verus with the *septemvir epulonum* of *ILS* 1034 (*I fasti consolari* (1952), 130).

[8] Registered by Degrassi in the *Aggiunte* to his *Fasti consolari* (1952), whence R. Syme, *JRS* xliii (1953), 150 [= p. 235 above].

the *praenomen* of another consul visible in the second line.[1] Hence the pair

[M.] Annius Verus [L. Neratius Priscus].

That supplement can stand as correct. Indeed, on the available evidence, 97 ought to have been confidently postulated as the year in which this pair held the *fasces*. They sponsored a *senatus consultum* against castration.[2] Just such an action is reported by the historian Cassius Dio in his account of Nerva's reign.[3] There was also a measure of Domitian, it is true, belonging to his early years. But Domitian proceeded authoritatively, by edict.[4] Also a measure of Hadrian, likewise an edict.[5] And no device can impose a Neratius Priscus as colleague of Annius Verus in his second consulate (121), or in his third (126).[6]

An important consequence followed. There must be three consular homonyms of the Neratii, not two. That is, the *suffectus* of 87; the *suffectus* of 97; | and the *septemvir epulonum*, legate of Pannonia Inferior, consul, legate of Pannonia Superior.[7] There is no way out. It is not admissible to identify the *suffecti* of 87 and 97, on the hypothesis of a second consulate. Even without the negative (and convincing) testimony of the inscription at Saepinum, there is an irrefragable argument: in the collegiate pair of 97, M. Annius Verus could not stand in front of a *cos. iterum*.

Even so, it was not at once apparent which of the two attested *suffecti* is the jurist, and whether the jurist is the same person as the legate governing Pannonia before it was divided.[8]

First, the first of the three consulars, the *suffectus* of 87. He is best left

---

[1] G. Barbieri, *Studi Romani* ii (1953), 367, whence *AE* 1954, 220. Cf. also R. Syme, *JRS* xliv (1954), 81.

[2] *Dig.* xlviii 8, 6.   [3] Dio lxviii 2, 4.

[4] Martial ii 60; vi 12; Statius, *Silvae* iv 3, 13; *Chron. Paschale*, p. 465 Bonn.

[5] *Dig.* xlviii 4, 2 (with a reference to *edictum meum*).

[6] The *ordinarius iterum* or *tertio* normally resigns very soon, his colleague stepping into his place as the first name in a second pair. Thus in 121 the second pair is Cn. Arrius Augur with another (*AE* 1959, 78 = *CIL* xvi 168). Annius' colleague in 126 was C. Eggius Ambibulus. Brick stamps register the pair *Propinquus et Ambibulus* (*CIL* xv 127; 375; 1228b); cf. H. Bloch, *Bull. Comm.* lvi (1938), 195 f. Perhaps, however, collegiate *suffecti* of a later year: observe L. Varius Ambibulus (*suff.* 132 or 133), on whom *JRS* xliii (1953), 152 [= p. 237 above (with n. 4 on p. 257)].

[7] G. Barbieri, op. cit. 369; R. Syme (reviewing Degrassi), *JRS* xliii (1953), 159 [= p. 251 above (with n. 1 on p. 259)]; A. Garzetti, *Aevum* xxvii (1953), 549 ff.; H. Nesselhauf (reviewing Degrassi), *Gnomon* xxvi (1954), 267.

[8] The *suffectus* of 97 is admitted as the legate of Pannonia by M. Pavan, 'La provincia Romana della Pannonia Superior', *MAL*[8] vi (1955), fasc. 5, 410 f. But W. Reidinger assumes the *suffectus* of 87, and puts him in 94–7, *Die Statthalter des ungeteilten Pannonien und Oberpannoniens, Antiquitas*, Reihe 1, Band 2 (1956), 58 f. His statement about the *suffectus* of 97 (p. 169) is confused and erroneous. [See *Danubian Papers* (1971), 184 f., 189.] Further, R. Hanslik, in an addendum to Berger's article on the jurist, betrays no knowledge of the new Ostian fragment and is not accurate about the structure of the *Fasti Potentini* for 87 (*RE* xxiii col. 6).

by himself, to stand only as a name and a date. No post or function can with any plausibility be assigned. The interval before the next consulate of a Neratius Priscus is short, but no occasion for disquiet. In imperial Rome the first consul of a family often arrived late, the son, however, benefiting from birth and status as a member of the new nobility. Thus C. Visellius Varro (*suff.* 12), quickly followed by his son Lucius (*cos.* 24). Or better, C. Cestius Gallus (*cos.* 35), with a homonym consul suffect in 42: clearly father and son.[1] Moreover, and apart from that, it may turn out that the *suffectus* of 87 is only an adoptive parent (see below).

Next, L. Neratius Priscus, consul suffect with M. Annius Verus in 97. The jurist (it is recorded) was the brother of L. Neratius Marcellus;[2] this man was consul suffect in 95 and legate of Britain (? 101–4), born (it might be supposed) about 59, if not in that very year.[3] To establish the approximate age of the jurist, the data furnished by the *Digest* about the schools of jurisprudence are relevant, and ought to be exploited (though not without careful inspection).[4]|

The Proculian School was held to derive ultimately from Antistius Labeo (the rival of Ateius Capito). After Labeo its leader was the elder Nerva (*suff.* 22 or 23). Then Proculus (who cannot be identified). Then Pegasus, consul suffect under Vespasian and attested in 83 as Prefect of the City. After Pegasus came the elder Juventius Celsus. His rank and status are not known. The only clue is the fact that he was present in the *consilium* of the consul P. Ducenius Verus (*suff.* 95).[5] The succession then passed to the younger Celsus, along with Neratius Priscus. Now Celsus was praetor in 106, consul in the last years of Trajan.[6] It is strange that the *Digest* should name the younger Celsus in front of Neratius Priscus (on any count his senior in years), but not perhaps alarming: Celsus' parent preceded on the list, the one name attracted the other, and he may have had a longer survival as well as higher public honours than Neratius Priscus, for he was consul for the second time in 129. However that may be, the collocation tells against the notion that the Neratius Priscus who was leader of the Proculian School had been consul as long ago as 87.

---

[1] Cf. Tacitus, *Ann.* vi 7, 2 (under 31): 'C. Cestium patrem.' Some editors accept and print Lipsius' 'praetorem'.

[2] *Dig.* xxxiii 7, 12, 43.

[3] *CIL* ix 2456 = *ILS* 1032 (acephalous). Cf. *PIR*[1], N 43; E. Groag, *RE* xvi, coll. 2542 ff. For the dating of his governorship of Britain, Pliny, *Ep.* iii 8, 1; *CIL* xvi 48 (of 19 January, 103). His consulship was revealed by *FO* xiiid, first published in 1939 [= *Inscr. It.* xiii 1, 194–5; see A. R. Birley, *Epigr. Stud.* iv (1967), 68].

[4] *Dig.* i 2, 2, 47. For the nature of the two schools, F. Schulz, *History of Roman Legal Science* (1946), 119 ff.; W. Kunkel, *Herkunft u. soziale Stellung der röm. Juristen* (1952), 340 ff.

[5] *Dig.* xxxi 29, *praef.*

[6] For his praetorship, Pliny, *Ep.* vi 5, 4; for his consulship, 115 has been suggested (*JRS* xliii (1953), 154 [= p. 242 above]), because he was proconsul of Asia before Lamia Aelianus, the *ordinarius* of 116 (cf. the inscription from Claros, *JŒAI* viii (1905), 166). See, however, below, p. 351, n. 8 [abandoning 115 and suggesting 117].

It is assumed that the *Digest* is correct. But what if there is a mistake latent in the phrase 'Celso patri Celsus filius et Neratius Priscus'?[1] Were Neratius Priscus and the younger Celsus perhaps not joint leaders in the Proculian School, but in fact successive? That supposition could fit an identification of the jurist with the *suffectus* of 87 no less than with the *suffectus* of 97. It would be an easy and attractive assumption that the jurist rose to the consulate by civil arts, producing a son (*suff.* 97) who was legate of Pannonia. Except for *viri militares*, the first consul in a family would not be likely to attain the *fasces* before the age of forty. The jurist lasted into the reign of Hadrian (see below). That a lawyer should still be active thirty years after his consulship is no strain on credence.

Hence a faint doubt ought to be uttered, and allowed to subsist. On the existing evidence, however, it seems safest to identify the jurist with the legate of Pannonia.

As for the *suffectus* of 87, it is likely enough that he was proficient (or more than that) in the science of the law, as heir of a tradition. Let it be recalled that Antistius Labeo married a Neratia.[2] Further, there may have been some earlier legal Neratius: who was Proculus?[3] The *suffectus* of 87 himself may | have been eclipsed by Pegasus, obscured by the subsequent fame of his son. Not all of the great lawyers are registered in the pages of the *Digest*. Were it not for Tacitus, C. Caninius Rebilus (*suff.* 37) would not be known.[4]

The emperor Trajan invoked the help of Neratius Priscus and of Titius Aristo on a point of jurisprudence.[5] Both men are therefore commonly described as members of that Emperor's *consilium*.[6] Aristo was known to Pliny as a teacher of law: he receives two missives and is the subject of a third.[7] Neratius in the *Digest* cites Aristo frequently, and is himself mentioned by Celsus. Apart from the *Digest*, the only written source to name Neratius Priscus clearly and unequivocally is the *Historia Augusta*, in two passages.[8] The one is the famous and peculiar anecdote of Trajan's views about the succession (of which more later). The other states that he was one of the jurists in Hadrian's *consilium*.

The career of this eminent senator is all but a blank. The inscriptions at Saepinum register his public distinctions in the most summary fashion: the rubric cannot be called a senatorial *cursus*. There is only 'praef. aer.

---

[1] *Dig.* i 2, 2, 47.   [2] *Dig.* xxxiv 2, 32, 6.

[3] A vexed problem. W. Kunkel, after an exhaustive discussion (op. cit. 123 ff.), opts for Cn. Acerronius Proculus (*cos.* 37). He assumed that Proculus must have been a consul. That is not necessary. It would have been worth noting that the *cognomen* 'Proculus' recurs among the consular Neratii, viz. L. Neratius C. f. Proculus (*ILS* 1076), suffect consul in the early years of Pius.

[4] *Ann.* xiii 30, 2: 'ex primoribus peritia legum et pecuniae magnitudine.'

[5] *Dig.* xxxvii 12, 5.   [6] Cf., however, the doubts of W. Kunkel, op. cit. 141.

[7] *Ep.* v 3; viii 14; i 22.   [8] *HA Hadr.* 4, 8; 18, 1.

Sat., cos., leg. pr. pr. in prov. Pannonia'. The prefecture of the *Aerarium Saturni* is comparable to the praetorian provinces in the portion of Caesar, and indeed equipollent. To hold one of those provinces seems to carry a promise of the consulate.[1] Further, the length of tenure seems about the same—normally some three years, sometimes a little less. In 97 the two prefects in office were Bittius Proculus and Publicius Certus. When Pliny launched his attack on Certus, it was objected by one of the orator's consular friends 'lacessis hominem iam praefectum aerarii et brevi consulem'.[2] In the upshot of that incident, Certus was passed over, while Proculus secured designation.[3] This collegiate pair had been appointed by Domitian.[4] Perhaps not long before his death. Accelerated promotions and a quick turnover can be easily explained after a change of ruler. Neratius Priscus will have been one of their immediate predecessors, from about 93 to 95 or even 96.

The Neratii benefited from the favour of Domitian. Marcellus held the *fasces* in 95, taking the place of the Emperor on the Ides of January: a high distinction, and close to being *consul ordinarius*. His brother may already have been designated (after vacating the treasury post) before Domitian was assassinated. As with certain other *suffecti* of 97 (among them the orator | Cornelius Tacitus), it does not have to be assumed that he owed the honour to Nerva or the friends of Nerva.[5] Everything indicates that the list of 97 was long—and heterogeneous.[6] Not, indeed, that there could be any reason to deny that Neratius Priscus was well in with Nerva before and after his accession. Nerva, though not himself among the legal luminaries (far from it), had a tradition in his family (father and grandfather); and, consul for the second time in 90 as colleague of Domitian, this prudent adept of the diplomatic arts no doubt exercised a gentle and effective influence on patronage.

It would be natural to assume that Neratius, like most senators ambitious for the consulate, had commanded a legion at some time after his praetorship. But it is not quite certain. Not all of the men whom favour or chance brought to the consular military provinces had been legionary legates. Personal reasons counted, or civil accomplishments; thus Trajan's friend Julius Quadratus of Pergamum, legate of Syria from 100 or 101 to 104.[7] Speculation about Neratius' earlier career has nothing to go on—

[1] Tacitus, *Agr.* 9, 1. For this type of province, cf. observations in *JRS* xliii (1953), 152 f. [= pp. 238 f. above].   [2] *Ep.* ix 13, 11.

[3] Ibid. 23. Proculus is Q. Fulvius Gillo Bittius Proculus (*PIR*[2], F 544), probably *suffectus* in the last two months of 98 (*JRS* xliii (1953), 154 [= p. 241 above (with n. 2 on p. 257)]; xliv (1954), 82).

[4] *Ep.* ix 23.

[5] Observe that some of the *suffecti* of 69 were *ex destinatione Neronis* (Tacitus, *Hist.* i 77, 2).

[6] Compare 69. Barbieri assumed that three pairs of *suffecti* would be enough to account for the months March–December 97 (op. cit. 367 ff.). Against, *JRS* xliv (1954), 82.

[7] *ILS* 8819.

and one hypothesis can be brushed aside. A fragment from Tlos shows that a Neratius was legate of Lycia–Pamphylia, one of those praetorian provinces which normally foreshadow a consulship.[1] Who might he be? Not the *suffectus* of 87.[2] Other governors stand in the way, viz. T. Aurelius Quietus (*suff.* 82), succeeded in 81 by C. Caristanius Fronto (*suff.* 90), then P. Baebius Italicus (*suff.* 90), who, a legionary legate in 83, is attested there in 85.[3] Not the *suffectus* of 97—he was prefect of the *Aerarium Saturni*, itself the qualifying post.[4] Again, not the third Neratius Priscus, the *septemvir epulonum*, for his province of that rank was Pannonia Inferior: it is highly anomalous for one man to hold two such posts.[5] Conceivably therefore L. Neratius Marcellus (*suff.* 95), supposing that he had a brief occupancy (? 92–4), that he succeeded Julius Quadratus (*suff.* 94), whose tenure could be put in 89–92.[6] If so, the next legate, L. Domitius Apollinaris (*suff.* 97), will also have had only two years, for he was back in Rome by December, 96.[7] | But it is preferable to resign the Lycian inscription to some other and unverifiable Neratius.[8]

Priscus governed Pannonia before it was divided. The date is now clear, triumphantly vindicating the conjecture of a scholar who long ago divined the consular year of Priscus and put his governorship in the period 102–6.[9] Priscus is thus closely parallel to Marcellus, consul suffect in 95, legate of Britain *c.* 101–4. Q. Glitius Agricola (*suff.* 97), governor of Pannonia and decorated in the First Dacian War, left to assume his second consulate in January 103, taking over the *fasces* from Trajan.[10] The tenure of Priscus might run to 105. Who was his successor? Perhaps (it has been conjectured) P. Metilius Sabinus Nepos (*suff.* 103), addressed by Pliny as *maximae provinciae praefuturus*.[11] For Pannonia speaks the fact that his son (or nephew) served as military tribune in X Gemina, one of the

[1] *IGR* iii 1511 = *TAM* ii 2, 568. The inscription in fact honours the son of a governor.
[2] Thus W. Reidinger, op. cit. 58.
[3] For the evidence, *PIR*[2], A 1592; C 423; B 17.
[4] E. Groag, discussing the *septemvir epulonum*, suggested that his parent the jurist might have been governor of Lycia–Pamphylia (*RE* xvi, col. 2547).
[5] Exceptional circumstances no doubt explain the transference of Q. Pompeius Falco (*suff.* 108) from Lycia–Pamphylia to Judaea *c.* 106 (*ILS* 1035 f.). [See p. 383 below.]
[6] *ILS* 8819. Hence parallel to Ti. Julius Celsus Polemaeanus (*suff.* 92) in Cilicia (*ILS* 8971): the appointment in 89 of these two men, the first consuls from oriental families, would not lack significance for Domitian's imperial policy.
[7] Martial xi 15. The governorship of Apollinaris (*PIR*[2], D 133) is attested by *IGR* iii 559 = *TAM* ii 2, 570 (Tlos).
[8] [See now *Danubian Papers*, 189: an inscription cited by J. and L. Robert, *REG* lxxi (1958), *Bull. ép.* no. 294, makes the governor M. Hirrius Fronto Neratius Pansa. For date and position, see Eck, *ZPE* vi (1970), 74 f.]
[9] E. Ritterling, *Arch.-ep. Mitt. aus Oesterreich-Ungarn* xx (1897), 14 ff. Most now see that to be inescapable. The notable and explicit exception is W. Reidinger—the *suffectus* of 87 as legate in 94–7 (op. cit. 58 f.).
[10] *ILS* 1021a. The diploma *CIL* xvi 47 bears the date 19 Nov. 102, but does not prove that he had not already departed from Pannonia.
[11] *Ep.* iv 26, 2. Cf. the army commander Sabinus (ix 2).

legions of that province.[1] Nepos was still at Rome in May 105.[2] Perhaps, however, Pannonia was his second consular province, not his first.[3]

The date of Neratius Priscus' governorship has a further relevance. In one of his earlier letters Pliny forwarded an amiable petition to an army commander called Priscus, requesting some kind of post for one of his equestrian friends, Voconius Romanus.[4] Hence three connected problems —identity, province, and date. A single solution is demanded—and such could be propounded. The language of Pliny is worth inspecting: 'regis exercitum amplissimum: hinc tibi beneficiorum larga materia, longum praeterea tempus quo amicos tuos exornare potuisti.'[5] Observe the last phrase, and the word 'potuisti' (not 'possis'). It implies that Priscus had already been in office for some time.[6] Now the tenure of Pannonia by Neratius Priscus did not begin until 102 (probably quite late in the year). The position of the missive in the collection suggests an earlier date, in or about the year 100 (the two letters preceding refer to the prosecution of Marius Priscus, which terminated in January 100). Therefore not Neratius Priscus. The alternative is the leader of the rival school of jurisprudence (the | Sabinian), namely Javolenus Priscus (*suff.* 86). Javolenus was legate of Syria at some time between 90 and 101.[7] Some have supposed that he might be the legate in 97, whose ambiguous attitude provoked rumours at Rome about the time when Pliny attacked Publicius Certus.[8] That legate (it is clear) departed, died, or was executed, for a certain A. Larcius Priscus, ex-quaestor of Asia, in command of the legion IV Scythica, is discovered as acting governor of Syria.[9] Javolenus became proconsul of Africa (perhaps from 100 to 101).[10] He could have been Trajan's first consular legate in Syria, from 98 to 100, the predecessor of Julius Quadratus. That would fit the letter of Pliny.

Two points can be added. First, Syria seems a more congenial destination than Pannonia for Voconius Romanus, a man of quiet habits and literary tastes, who is discovered some years later at his home town,

---

[1] *ILS* 1053, cf. E. Groag, *RE* xv, col. 401.

[2] *CIL* vi 2075 (*Acta Fratrum Arvalium*).

[3] Inspection of the cursus of the younger Metilius (*ILS* 1053) reveals the possibility that he had been tribune in another legion before X Gemina, probably therefore in another province. If his consular kinsman governed Pannonia, it might not have been before 107 or 108. His governorship of Pannonia, discounted by W. Reidinger (op. cit. 67), is silently omitted by M. Pavan.

[4] *Ep.* ii 13.   [5] Ibid. 2.

[6] Cf. H. Dessau in *PIR*[1], N 46: 'cum exercitum amplissimum iam per aliquot annos regeret.'

[7] *ILS* 1015, cf. *CIL* xvi 36 (Germania Superior, in 90).

[8] *Ep.* ix 13, 11. Cf. St. Gsell, *Essai sur le règne de l'Empereur Domitien* (1894), 332. Also, dubitatively, R. Syme, *Philologus* xci (1936), 243 f.

[9] *ILS* 1055; *AE* 1908, 237 (Thamugadi).

[10] *ILS* 1015. [B. Thomasson, *Die Statthalter der röm. Provinzen Nordafrikas von Augustus bis Diocletianus* (1960) ii 55, gives no date, but puts him between Marius Priscus and Q. Pomponius Rufus.]

Saguntum by the sea, superintending the vintage, Pliny's efforts to get him into the Senate having apparently (or rather patently) proved a failure.[1] Secondly, it is precisely to his friend Voconius that Pliny about the year 106 reports a ludicrous item concerning the behaviour of Javolenus Priscus at a recitation party.[2] Previous discussions of the problem (which Priscus and which province) have neglected to exploit the letter to Voconius or invoke as relevant the life and habits of that person.

Given a *cognomen* as common and indistinctive as 'Priscus', further investigation among the correspondents of Pliny is hardly likely to be remunerative. One item, however, seems to have been overlooked. Two letters go to the address of a certain Priscus who appears to be exercising jurisdiction in the Transpadane zone of Italy.[3] One of Pliny's friends was on his staff, Saturninus by name.[4] It is therefore permissible to see in Priscus a special commissioner operating in this region about 106. Observe that C. Julius Proculus (*suff.* 109), between his legionary command and his consulate, held the post of 'leg. Aug. p. p. region. Transpadanae'.[5] The Priscus of the Plinian letters | defies identification. Perhaps Neratius the consular jurist—on the face of things a suitable occupation, but no great honour for one who had been legate of Pannonia. Perhaps rather (and Julius Proculus comes in for support) a man of praetorian rank such as M. Trebatius Priscus (suffect consul in 108, but otherwise unknown).

The consular jurist remains not a little enigmatic. No proconsulate of Asia or Africa, that peak of the senator's career, to which Neratius Priscus would have acceded about fifteen years after his consulship: compare Cornelius Tacitus (*suff.* 97), whose governorship of Asia should be put in 112/3. The proconsulate could not have been omitted from the inscription, however brief the *titulus*. Worse, no priesthood. That office likewise (if one of the four *amplissima sacerdotia*, or, next in rank thereafter, the honour of *sodalis Augustalis*) could not fail. The inscription registers the fact that his son was *septemvir epulonum*. Again, no second consulate from

---

[1] *Ep.* ix 28, 2. For his town and full nomenclature, cf. [*PIR*², L 210. See further pp. 480 ff. below.] [2] *Ep.* vi 15. [3] *Ep.* vi 8; vii 8; cf. vii 7, 1; 15, 3.
[4] *Ep.* vii 7 f.; 15. Presumably the recipient of ix 38. But distinct from the Pompeius Saturninus who received i 8 and v 21, whose literary pursuits are recorded in i 16—and who will be the Saturninus whose death is reported in v 7. A distinction is drawn between Pompeius Saturninus and Saturninus in *PIR*¹, P 491. They are amalgamated in the index of M. Schuster's edition (Teubner, 1933), whereas *RE* chooses to omit Pompeius Saturninus. For the existence of homonymous persons called Pompeius Saturninus cf. i 16, 1: 'amabam Pompeium Saturninum (hunc dico nostrum) laudabamque eius ingenium.' [See, however, p. 707 below.]
[5] *ILS* 1040. The main function of that official might be the levying of recruits for the legions: cf. Mommsen, *Staatsrecht* ii³ (1887), 850; *Ges. Schr.* v (1908), 279 f.; G. E. F. Chilver, *Cisalpine Gaul* (1941), 229 f. But he holds the *imperium pro praetore*, therefore cannot be denied civil jurisdiction. In Proculus' *cursus* the post is the exact equivalent of a praetorian province.

Trajan. Neratius Priscus survived that ruler. Perhaps not for long—at least not for any public honour like the prefecture of the City or a second tenure of the *fasces*. His brother Marcellus at last achieved a second consulate in 129, with the jurist P. Juventius Celsus for colleague. Annius Verus, however, quickly rose to the second and to the third (121 and 126); and he was *praefectus urbi*.

All the more disconcerting therefore (if taken seriously) is the anecdote in the *Historia Augusta*, conveying the testimony of Trajan's high esteem. A strong persuasion held (so that work affirms) that Trajan wished the succession to go, not to Hadrian, but to Neratius Priscus. Many of the Emperor's friends were in accord, and Trajan once said to Neratius Priscus: 'commendo tibi provincias si quid mihi fatale contigerit.'[1]

When an emperor announces who is *capax imperii*, the matter claims attention. In surviving literature the topic first emerges with the account of speculation by Augustus when close to his end, an account inserted by Tacitus from a subsidiary source, interrupting the report of a debate in the Senate: it is instructive on more counts than one.[2] As for the anecdote about Trajan, some take it for a true report going back to that time, and use it as valuable evidence.[3] And some are further impelled to wonder which Neratius Priscus was meant: since the jurist was coeval with the Emperor (or conceivably older), | might it not be his son, the *septemvir epulonum*?[4] That refinement can promptly be discarded. The person deemed competent to bear the burden of empire does not have to be a man in his youthful prime. He can be an elderly consular. Thus (another story) Trajan at a banquet, when asked if he could name ten men capable of empire, exclaimed that there was one, Julius Servianus.[5] Or, better perhaps, what Tacitus reports about Nero.[6] When he fell ill, loyal courtiers voiced their apprehensions—'finem imperio adesse'. Nero reassured them—'habere subsidium rem publicam'—and he named Memmius Regulus. Now Regulus had been consul long ago, in 31. Anecdotes of this type and model imply that the man who has thus been singled out by an emperor will incur peril of his life. Compare Tacitus, 'vixit tamen post haec Regulus quiete defensus.' And the consulars whom Augustus

---

[1] *HA Hadr.* 4, 8. [See further *Emperors and Biography* (1971), 126 f.]

[2] *Ann.* i 13, 2 ff. Compare, for the detail, *JRS* lv (1955), 22 ff. [= *Ten Studies in Tacitus* (1970), 30 ff.]. Not irrelevant (it can be argued) to the destruction of four men of consular rank (a plot being alleged) in the first year of Hadrian's rule.

[3] W. Weber, *Untersuchungen zur Gesch. des Kaisers Hadrianus* (1907), 30; W. Hartke, *Römische Kinderkaiser* (1951), 115.

[4] E. Groag, *RE* xvi, col. 2548.

[5] Dio lxix 17, 3. Zonaras has Ἀδριανός, which Boissevain prefers and prints. But there is nothing against the Τραιανός of Xiphilinus; cf. E. Groag, *RE* x, col. 885. Indeed, everything for. Servianus, husband of Hadrian's sister Domitia Paulina, is clearly to be identified with the Ser. Julius Servianus revealed as *suffectus* in 90 by the *Fasti Potentini*. He was born c. 47 (Dio lxix 17, 1; *HA Hadr.* 15, 8).

[6] *Ann.* xiv 47.

on his death-bed designated as *capaces imperii* were with one exception brought to destruction through the contriving of Tiberius, so the historian alleges.[1] The *Historia Augusta* registers sundry persons whom Hadrian disliked or destroyed. Neratius Priscus happens not to be among them. But a Marcellus is on the list, driven to commit suicide by Hadrian.[2]

Neratius Priscus belongs to the school of jurisprudence that originated with Antistius Labeo (and Labeo married a Neratia). Labeo was Republican in sentiment, hence (according to Tacitus) not in favour with Augustus. The government had more use for his rival, Ateius Capito.[3] Labeo was also old-fashioned in doctrine, refusing to admit anything that had not been sanctioned by tradition and the ancient books, so Capito petulantly complained.[4] The inscriptions at Saepinum exhibit an archaic simplicity of formulation. They suppress the word 'Aug.' from the titulature of an imperial legate, and the style 'in prov.' was surely long out of date. Tradition commanded a sentimental veneration at Rome, sometimes excessive or purely formal. Nothing discoverable in the legal doctrine of Neratius Priscus shows him unduly or detrimentally | conservative. Nor, despite the derivation from Antistius Labeo, can the Proculian School be contrasted on this point with the Sabinian. C. Cassius Longinus (*suff.* 30), one of the leaders of the latter school, is brought on by Tacitus as an avowed champion of the *vetus mos*—and perhaps over-harsh in his emulation of antiquity.[5] It would therefore be premature to suppose that Neratius Priscus was in any way either honoured or slighted by Trajan for reasons of doctrine. No rival or preferred master of Roman jurisprudence got a second consulate from that emperor.

To conclude, status and relationships. The acephalous *cursus* of a legate of Britain at Saepinum is convincingly assigned to L. Neratius Marcellus.[6] He was made a patrician by the emperor Vespasian. Annius Verus (*suff.* 97) was adlected into that order by Vespasian and Titus when they held the censorship (73/4).[7] Clearly when young, about the time when he

[1] *Ann.* i 13, 3: 'omnesque praeter Lepidum variis mox criminibus struente Tiberio circumventi sunt.'
[2] *HA Hadr.* 15, 4. Perhaps not L. Neratius Marcellus (*II ord.* 129), but, so some have supposed, C. Quinctius Certus Publicius Marcellus (*suff.* 120). But this man, legate of Germania Superior and of Syria, appears to have outlived Hadrian, cf. *AE* 1934, 231.
[3] *Ann.* iii 75, 2: 'sed Labeo incorrupta libertate et ob id fama celebratior, Capitonis obsequium dominantibus magis probabatur.' It was a tradition that Labeo had refused the consulship (*Dig.* i 2, 2, 47). But there is nothing in the allegation reported by Tacitus that Augustus accelerated the consulate of Ateius Capito (*suff.* A.D. 5) to put him ahead of Labeo.
[4] Cited in Gellius xiii 12, 2.
[5] Compare his oration after the murder of the *praefectus urbi* by his slaves (*Ann.* xiv 43 f.). The discordant citizens of Puteoli did not appreciate his efforts to impose social harmony—'severitatem eius non tolerabant' (xiii 48).
[6] *CIL* ix 2456 = *ILS* 1032 [Birley, l.c. (above p. 342, n. 3)].   [7] *HA Marcus* 1, 2.

assumed the *toga virilis*. The same will hold for the anonymous (and un-identifiable) senator who was a *comes* of Trajan in 98/9.[1] Also for the two Neratii, Marcellus and Priscus. The honour may have been withheld from their parent, whoever he was.[2]

And who was he? Testamentary adoptions and the licences of sena-torial nomenclature come into the reckoning. Marcellus and Priscus were brothers. Possibly only through adoption, but presumably by blood Priscus (it could be suggested) was adopted by L. Neratius Priscus (*suff.* 87). If so, who then was the real and original father of the two brothers?

Attention must go to M. Hirrius Fronto Neratius Pansa (*suff. c.* 74), attested as legate of Cappadocia–Galatia in 78/9.[3] He is clearly of close kin to Marcellus and Priscus. Now Marcellus served as military tribune of a legion in that province, namely XII Fulminata.[4] That would suit the assumption that his birth falls in 59, or very close to that year. His second consulate in 129 may have been designed as a commemorative honour.

There is something more—a relationship with the family of Corellius Rufus (*suff.* ?78). Two facts have been adduced that seem to converge First, the *consul ordinarius* of 122, Corellius Pansa, whose *cognomen* (not common) recalls the nomenclature of M. Hirrius Fronto Neratius Pansa.[5] Second, the daughter of Corellius Rufus, viz. Hispulla. Pliny mentions her young son and suggests a teacher for him. The letter should belong *c.* 101, the notice can fit the consul of 122. Pliny does not furnish the name of Corellia's husband, but he refers | allusively to the boy's grandfather, to his father, and to his father's brother: 'quamquam illi paternus etiam clarus spectatusque contigerit, pater quoque et patruus illustri laude con-spicui.'[6] It thence appears that Corellia had married a person of fame and consequence, one of two brothers, their parent being *clarus spectatusque* (that is to say, a consular). This man, the boy's grandfather, may be Neratius Pansa the legate of Cappadocia.[7] A further step can be taken. Either Priscus or Marcellus was the husband of Corellia. Presumably the latter. It is no objection that Marcellus' inscription at Saepinum was set up by his wife Vettilla: she need not have been his first wife, or only wife. Corellius Pansa (*cos.* 122) can therefore be the son of Neratius Marcellus, coeval with the third Neratius Priscus—and indeed his first cousin. He

---

[1] *ILS* 1019.

[2] [Another inscription from Saepinum now shows the *septemuir* to have been tribune of the plebs, hence a plebeian: see *Danubian Papers*, 189, where it is suggested that his father (*suff.* 97) and Neratius Marcellus may still be brothers.]

[3] *PIR*[1], H 129; E. Groag, *RE* xvi, coll. 2545 f. [See p. 345, n. 8 above, and M. Torelli, *IRS* lviii (1968), 70–5.]

[4] *ILS* 1032.

[5] *PIR*[2], C 1293. Groag also drew attention to a Neratius Corellius, land-holder among the Ligures Baebiani (*ILS* 6509, col. ii, 1, 14). [See now p. 714 below, on *AE* 1969–70 106.]

[6] *Ep.* iii 3, 1.   [7] As Groag suggested, *PIR*[2], C 1293; *RE* xvi, col. 2546.

was entitled to display a fuller nomenclature than 'Corellius Pansa'.¹ So were other Neratii, it can be presumed. But there are enough problems in the Neratii as it is.²

A summary statement can be put forward. Neratius Pansa, the legate of Cappadocia, had two sons, who were adlected into the patriciate. The elder, Marcellus, became consul suffect in 95, the younger was adopted by L. Neratius Priscus (*suff.* 87), his kinsman and probably his uncle. Marcellus (according to the *Digest*) was the brother of the jurist. That person is therefore L. Neratius Priscus, consul suffect in 97, hence legate of Pannonia in 102–5. No other combination seems to work.

It will be expedient to subjoin a word about the last of the three homonymous consulars, the *septemvir epulonum*. Various dates have been proposed for his governorship of Pannonia Inferior and ensuing consulate.³ If the limits for Pannonia Inferior could be narrowed, that would supply a clue. The first known legate of the new province was P. Aelius Hadrianus, suffect consul in 108.⁴ The second, as a military diploma of 110 reveals, was T. Julius Maximus Manlianus (*suff.* 112).⁵ The next on record is P. Afranius Flavianus, attested by a diploma of September 114:⁶ perhaps the successor of Julius Maximus, perhaps not. | When was this man consul? If the *Fasti Potentini* correctly reproduce the structure of both 114 and 115 as three pairs of consuls, there would be room for only one additional *suffectus* in each year.⁷ There are claimants available. But the *Fasti Potentini* may not be correct, hence conceivably a place for P. Afranius Flavianus in 115.⁸ But it would be safer to lodge him in 117 (116 is

---

¹ Compare, for the preference for a *gentilicium* deriving from the female line, C. Ummidius Quadratus (*suff.* 118), grandson of Ummidia Quadratilla (*Ep.* vii 24).
² Groag notes the polyonymous 'L. Neratius L. [f. . . . . . .] Iunius Macer' (*CIL* ix, 2513: Saepinum), admitting the possibility that he is identical with L. Neratius Marcellus or with L. Neratius Priscus, the *septemvir epulonum* (*RE* xvi 2541 f.).
³ Thus E. Ritterling suggested that he was appointed legate of Pannonia Inferior *c.* 119 (*AErt* xli (1927), 284), but Groag was prepared to admit a tenure *c.* 114–7 (*RE* xvi, col. 2547). W. Reidinger proposes to put his consulate *c.* 115 (op. cit. 70), M. Pavan says 'certamente negli ultimi anni di Traiano' (op. cit. 412).   ⁴ *HA Hadr.* 3, 9; *ILS* 308.
⁵ *CIL* xvi 164. His *cursus* previous to that post is supplied by *ILS* 1016 (Nemausus). The diploma shows that he cannot have acceded direct to the consulate after his legionary commands, a possibility envisaged by R. Syme, *Laureae Aquincenses* i (1938), 282 [= *Danubian Papers*, 99, with addenda 107 f.: it also follows that, if he did serve as legionary legate under D. Terentius Scaurianus, he must have left long before the governor, still attested in Dacia in 110].   ⁶ *CIL* xvi 61.
⁷ With this proviso about the *Fasti Potentini* it was suggested (*JRS* xliii (1953), 154 [= p. 242 above]) that P. Valerius Priscus, proconsul of Africa in 127/8 (*IRT* 361), should be put in 114 (i.e. as the missing colleague of C. Clodius Nummus), P. Juventius Celsus in 115, because he was proconsul of Asia before Lamia Aelianus, the *ordinarius* of 116 (as shown by the inscription at Claros, *JŒAI* vii (1905), 166). [But see next note.]
⁸ Indeed, new evidence accrues to subvert previous argument and conjecture. A Thracian diploma (knowledge of which I owe to the courtesy of H. Nesselhauf and K. Schubring) reveals L. Caesennius Sospes as colleague of C. Clodius Nummus on 19 July 114. P. Valerius

complete, revealed by the *Fasti Ostienses*). Therefore, taking Flavianus'
term to end about 117, Neratius Priscus could be his successor, hence
consul in 119 or 120.[1]

It is better to suspend judgement. A later date is not excluded. This
consul is the son of a man who will have acceded to the *fasces* well before
the standard age. Nor was Hadrian, that capricious ruler, always eager to
promote rapidly the sons of eminent consulars. L. Minicius Natalis (*suff.*
106) was holding Pannonia Superior when Trajan died, a post of no small
consequence.[2] His son, quaestor about the year 121, did not reach the
consulate until after the decease of Hadrian, being *suffectus* in 139.[3]

Data are lacking. In all the twenty-one years' reign of Hadrian, only
one legate of Pannonia Inferior is on record, viz. L. Attius Macro (*suff.*
134).[4] Similarly, the governorship of Pannonia Superior. Between Minicius Natalis (appointed by Trajan) and the sending of Aelius Caesar in
137, only one legate, a certain Cornelius Proculus (*suff.* ? 124), attested
in 133.[5]

Priscus will have to be expelled from that year—and, given the date of his proconsulate
(127/8), his consulship should not be subsequent to 115 (which year in any case means an
unexpectedly short interval before the proconsulate). The diploma was issued for soldiers
who had served under Statilius Maximus and were dismissed by the next legate of Thrace,
Juventius Celsus. The former is attested as *suffectus* in 115 (*AE* 1911, 95): the consulate
of the latter will now presumably have to go in 117. Still no room, however, for P. Afranius
Flavianus in 115. [For the date of P. Valerius Priscus' consulate and proconsulate see now
p. 256 (n. 4 on p. 236) above, and cf. *Danubian Papers*, 232.]

    [1] [*Historia* xiv (1965), 350 f. = *Danubian Papers*, 233 f. inclines to a later date as prefer-
able, though not later than 126.]
    [2] *ILS* 1029, cf. *CIL* xvi 64 (of 116).
    [3] *ILS* 1061. His consulate, hitherto presumed to fall in 133 or 134, is now revealed in
139 (*AE* 1955, 17 = *CIL* xvi 175).
    [4] *AE* 1937, 213. [Cf. *Danubian Papers*, 225 ff.]   [5] *CIL* xvi 76 f.

28

C. Vibius Maximus, Prefect of Egypt

DIGNITY and public station separate the two orders at Rome. Everything else can bring them together. Not only do many knights derive from the same families as members of the Senate—they may surpass the average senator in wealth or in polite accomplishments. It is no surprise to discover erudition and letters among the high equestrian officials in the service of the Caesars. Enough to register that phenomenon, the elder Pliny; or Titinius Capito, secretary *ab epistulis* and *praefectus vigilum*, an author and one of the patrons of literature in the reign of Trajan;[1] or Pompeius Planta, the Prefect of Egypt, who wrote a narrative of the battle of Bedriacum.[2]

C. Vibius Maximus belongs to this class and type. When Statius in the year 92 gave his *Thebais* to the world, the edition was accompanied by a dedicatory epistle to the address of Vibius Maximus, conveying amity and gratitude (*Silvae* iv, *praef.*). Further, an ode published in 95 acknowledges what the epic owed to a friend's exacting taste (iv 7, 25 ff.),

> quippe te fido monitore nostra
> Thebais multa cruciata lima
> temptat audaci fide Mantuanae
> gaudia famae.

What more can be known about this man? Not all of the coeval persons designated by the name 'Maximus' in the poems of Martial or the correspondence of Pliny can be sorted out and labelled. Too much to hope. But Martial has a Vibius Maximus on clear and undisputed record (xi 106), and so has Pliny (iii 2). Surely C. Vibius Maximus, who rose to the prefecture of Egypt, attested between August 103 and March 107.[3] A noteworthy character, were there not a further and double cause for curiosity. On three inscriptions in Egypt his name has been deliberately erased;[4] and a document registers precise allegations of moral delinquency against an official called Maximus.[5]

---

[1] An author and patron of letters: Pliny, *Ep.* i 17; v 8; viii 12. His career *ILS* 1448 (Rome).
[2] *Schol.* on Juvenal ii 99.
[3] A. Stein, *Die Präfekten von Ägypten in römischer Zeit* (1950), 50 ff.
[4] *IGR* i 1148; 1175; 1357. On the last of these only the *gentilicium* is erased.
[5] *P. Oxy.* 471. Also a small fragment now lost (*Gr. lit. Pap.* 42).

Vibius Maximus could not fail to excite attention.[1] Certain perplexities subsist. Not all of them have been noticed or appraised. Moreover, there is | room for conjecture. Questions ought to be put. Which were the administrative posts he held before he became Prefect of Egypt, and where is his town and origin to be sought?

The honorific ode of Statius shows Vibius Maximus in Dalmatia in 95, salutes the birth of a son, and evinces impatience for his return to Italy. A valuable fact emerges. At some time previously, Vibius had been commander of a regiment of auxiliary cavalry in Syria (iv 7, 45 ff.):

> tu tuos parvo memorabis ensis
> quos ad Eoum tuleris Oronten
> signa frenatae moderatus alae
> Castore dextro.

It must be asked, what was he doing in Dalmatia? Since the post of *praefectus alae* is the summit of the *militia equestris*, it would be a fair surmise that Vibius had gone on to be procurator of Dalmatia, a surmise that could be supported by the poet's reference to the Dalmatian mountains and the pallid workers in the mines underground (iv 7, 13 ff.):

> quando te dulci Latio remittent
> Dalmatae montes ubi Dite viso
> pallidus fossor redit erutoque
> concolor auro?

So far so good. There is a surprise, and a complication. A military diploma of the year 93 reveals a C. Vibius Maximus as prefect of the Cohors III Alpinorum stationed in Dalmatia.[2] What is the solution? Identity has generally been assumed.[3] There is a difficulty. Not everything was normal at this time in Dalmatia, it is true. The diploma names the governor of the province, Q. Pomponius Rufus. This man was consul suffect in 95—hence a praetorian governing a province that was normally consular.[4] None the less, it lacks parallel or explanation that a knight who has been *praefectus alae* should descend to be *praefectus cohortis*. Doubt can be conceived about the identity of the two persons, and doubt is legitimate.[5] The *nomen* 'Vibius' being so common throughout Italy, and the nomenclature 'C. Vibius Maximus' indistinctive, a homonym is not quite

---

[1] For a full discussion and bibliography see now H. A. Musurillo, *The Acts of the Pagan Martyrs* (1954), 150 ff.

[2] *CIL* xvi 38. The imperial titulature is that of 93 but the suffect consuls (indicating the date of issue) belong to 94, as the *Fasti Ostienses* have revealed (*Inscr. It.* xiii 1, 914).

[3] *PIR*[1], V 389 (now largely obsolete); A. Stein, op. cit. 53; H. A. Musurillo, op. cit. 152. [*RE* viii A, s.v. 'Vibius', col. 40.]

[4] Cf. A. Stein, *Die Legaten von Moesien* (1940), 59 f. Various reasons for the anomaly (no other praetorian governors are attested) might be canvassed. For the *cursus* of Pomponius Rufus, *IRT* 537 (Lepcis). [See *Danubian Papers* (1971), 193 f., 202.]

[5] H. G. Pflaum, cited in J. Schwartz, *CE* xxvii (1952), 256. Also E. Birley (by letter).

excluded, however unplausible might appear the coincidence of time |
and place that would have to be postulated. Perhaps a relative of the
procurator: compare *tribuni laticlavii* given posts in legions when a parent
or kinsman is consular commander of the army.[1]

Whatever his employment in Dalmatia, Vibius Maximus soon turns
up at Rome. The eleventh Book of Martial commemorates the Saturnalia
of December 96—and invokes the licence of that festival to cover a mass
and sequence of indecencies (xi 2). Towards the end comes a short and
unobjectionable item (106),

> Vibi Maxime, si vacas havere,
> hoc tantum lege: namque et occupatus
> et non es nimium laboriosus.
> transis hos quoque quattuor? sapisti.

The poet's language, if pressed, may supply a clue of some value.
Vibius Maximus is 'occupatus' but he is not 'nimium laboriosus'. That
suits the position and comportment of a government official during the
holiday season. The word 'occupatus' accords well with the functions
of some regular employment.[2] Similarly, 'occupationes'. When Pliny,
writing to a certain Minicius, uses 'istas occupationes' (vii 12, 5), the
consulship can perhaps be divined of C. Minicius Fundanus (*suff.* 107);[3]
and the 'occupationes' of a Justus and a Sabinus (vii 2; ix 2) point to the
consular command of armies.[4] A conjecture can therefore be put forward:
Vibius held an office in December 96, he was perhaps *praefectus vigilum*.
He might have benefited alertly from the change of government (Domitian assassinated in September)—or, no less alert, have retained under
Nerva the post he got from Domitian. Titinius Capito was secretary *ab
epistulis*, continuous under Domitian, Nerva, and Trajan.[5]

Next, the time and manner of his accession to the prefecture of Egypt.
Pliny, writing to Vibius Maximus, draws attention to the merits of
Arrianus | Maturus, the leading citizen of Altinum, a quiet decent man
who preferred to remain in the equestrian order though he could easily

---

[1] It might be worth pointing out that his command of Coh. III Alpinorum equitata could
have had a temporary and abnormal importance if it was the regiment now stationed at or
near Salonae, the principal city in Dalmatia and seat of the governor. Something like a half
of the inscriptions mentioning this cohort come from Salonae; for the details, G. M.
Bersanetti, *Bull. del Museo dell'Imp. Rom.* xii (1941), 50 (*App.* to *Bull. Comm.* lxix).

[2] Thus Pliny to Julius Servianus (iii 17, 1). The language of the letter suggests that he
was with Trajan in the Dacian campaigns.

[3] The possibility (or more than that) that the epistle is addressed to Fundanus is not
noticed by Groag in his article on that person (*RE* xv, coll. 1820 ff.).

[4] The former (it can be conjectured) is L. Fabius Justus (*suff.* 102), legate of Syria in
109 (*AE* 1940, 210), holding a military command *c.* 106. The latter is patently P. Metilius
Sabinus Nepos (*suff.* 103), that is, the Metilius Nepos whom Pliny *c.* 105 addresses as 'super
haec occupatissimus, maximae provinciae praefuturus' (iv 26, 2): on whom cf. E. Groag,
RE xv, coll. 1400 ff. Pliny's own 'occupationes' (i 10, 10; ii 8, 3) are presumably official.

[5] *ILS* 1448.

have become a senator. Pliny suggests that his correspondent may be able and willing to produce a job for Maturus: something 'quod sit splendidum nec molestum' (iii 2, 5). It is natural and easy to suppose that Pliny is soliciting the newly appointed Prefect of Egypt. Vibius was in Egypt by August of 103, succeeding C. Minicius Italus, who is last attested in May of that year.[1]

Before the thing is taken for sure and certified, an alternative ought to be brought into the reckoning. The letters of Pliny keep to a more or less chronological order (at least where they can be tested by reference to public transactions, consular dates, and the like), running from 97 to 108. There are discrepancies, to be sure. The author was not always careful enough in his arrangement. For example, at a very early place comes Pliny's intention to visit Comum (iii 6, 6), which probably eventuates in 104, but is over (iv 13, 3; 30, 1) before it is described (v 14). Again, among letters apparently belonging to the year 105 occurs one that carries a premature allusion to the expected consulate of Minicius Fundanus (iv 15, 5). But Fundanus does not become consul until May 107 (and the 'occupationes' of his consulship are alluded to subsequently, in vii 12, 5). The letter to Vibius Maximus comes as the second in Book iii. Except for iii 6, none of the letters included in that book can be proved to belong as late as 103. The last of them may be placed by the author to suggest that it is also the latest in date: namely the report of the decease of Martial, which cites the poet's praise of his eloquent patron and which terminates with Pliny's tribute to the single-minded devotion of a literary artist: 'at non erunt aeterna quae scripsit: non erunt fortasse, ille tamen scripsit tamquam essent futura' (iii 21, 6).[2]

It can be argued that Pliny's solicitation of Vibius Maximus belongs, not to 103, but rather to 101. That is to say, he was not Prefect of Egypt at the time, but holding some other office with resources of patronage. What could it be? Vibius might well be *praefectus annonae*, coming after C. Minicius Italus—whom he was to succeed in the governorship of Egypt in 103.[3] The employment appropriate to the unambitious man of Altinum could be the post of 'adiutor', suitably vague, but decorative, and even useful (if one wished). It now existed in Rome, with the *Annona*, as well as in Egypt. Compare Sex. Attius Suburanus, described as 'adiut. Iuli Ursi praef. annonae, eiusdem in praefect. Aegypti'.[4]

That a Prefect of Egypt should rise by way of the *Vigiles* and the

---

[1] A. Stein, op. cit. 49 f. [G. Bastianini, *ZPE* xvii (1975), 279 f.]

[2] A suitable conclusion (be it noted) and also self-testimony to the author himself, if *Ep.* i–iii were published as a group.

[3] Minicius' tenure of the *Annona* is registered on his cursus (*ILS* 1374: Aquileia).

[4] *AE* 1939, 60 (Heliopolis). [A. N. Sherwin-White, *The Letters of Pliny* (1966), 211 (cf. 286), rejects this hypothesis. He thinks that iv 12, 7 (*laudis suae . . . peregrinatione*) shows that Arrianus was overseas, hence presumably with Vibius Maximus in Egypt.]

Annona, nothing more natural. Though always liable to be disturbed by favour, personal | antagonisms, and court politics, the system of promotion develops a strong tendency to regularity in the period from Vespasian to Hadrian. The evidence is not complete, it is true. Between 71 and 120 only four *praefecti vigilum* stand on record.[1] Also, only seven *praefecti annonae*.[2] But the names are known of seventeen Prefects of Egypt.[3] Further, thirteen persons are attested as having commanded the Praetorian Guard.[4] To illustrate the paths of promotion, the following statistics can be adduced. Three of the four *praefecti vigilum* end as Prefects of Egypt (one by way of the *Annona*). All seven *praefecti annonae* go on to govern Egypt, and four of them subsequently command the Guard.[5]

There are gaps in the previous occupations of several Prefects of Egypt, among them Vibius Maximus. It would be worth knowing what he was doing between 95 and 103. If the above conjectures are admitted, he held the *Vigiles* (perhaps preceding Titinius Capito) and the *Annona* (after Minicius Italus).

Vibius Maximus left Egypt in spring or summer of 107, to be followed by a man of lesser pretensions, Ser. Sulpicius Similis, who began as a centurion.[6] Similis, who had also been *praefectus annonae*, is first attested in Egypt in August 107.[7]

It was about now (or not long after) that Pliny wrote a letter to a certain Maximus. Maximus had composed a polemical treatise against his enemy Planta. That person having died, the time had come to publish, frankly and nobly, so Pliny affirms (ix 1, 1). Planta is surely none other than the knight C. Pompeius Planta, attested as Prefect of Egypt between 98 and 100.[8] Also a writer. This Maximus can therefore be identified without discomfort as Vibius Maximus.

The ex-Prefect was soon confronted by graver preoccupations, arising from his conduct in Egypt. A papyrus discloses part of the indictment against an official called Maximus—various charges, notably and lavishly

---

[1] P. K. Baillie Reynolds, *The Vigiles of Imperial Rome* (1926), 123.

[2] Viz. Julius Ursus (*AE* 1939, 60); C. Tettius Africanus (*CIL* xi 5382); L. Laberius Maximus (*ILS* 5049); M. Mettius Rufus (*CIL* xii 671, with the new fragment reported by H. G. Pflaum (*Latomus* x (1951), 475), from E. Benoît, *Mém. de l'Inst. hist. de Provence* ix (1932), 141); C. Minicius Italus (*ILS* 1374); Ser. Sulpicius Similis (*Frag. Vat.* 233); M. Rutilius Lupus (*AE* 1940, 38).

[3] A. Stein, op. cit. 191 f.—omitting Q. Marcius Turbo as not definitely certified as Prefect of Egypt, but inserting in 78 or 79 C. Liternius Fronto (*AE* 1937, 236, revised by H. G. Pflaum, *Latomus* x (1951), 473). [See D. W. Reinmuth, *BASP* iv (1967), 83–96.]

[4] A. Passerini, *Le coorti pretorie* (1939)—omitting the Emperor Titus, Crispinus (inferred from Juvenal iv 1 ff.) and Parthenius; but adding Julius Ursus and Laberius Maximus on the basis of *P. Berol.* 8334, as interpreted by A. Piganiol, *CRAI* 1947, 376 ff., followed by R. Syme, *JRS* xliv (1954), 117.

[5] Viz. as *praefecti praetorio*, not only Mettius Rufus and Sulpicius Similis, but also Julius Ursus and Laberius Maximus (*P. Berol.* 8334; cf. the preceding note).

[6] Dio lxix 19, 1.   [7] A. Stein, op. cit. 53.   [8] Ibid. 48 f.

the scandal of a 'puer delicatus'.¹ The transgressor, it appears, is none other than a Prefect | of Egypt: precisely C. Vibius Maximus, as is confirmed by the erasure of his name on three inscriptions. One of them is on a temple which he began to construct, but which was terminated in May 109, after his departure.² His condemnation (it can be argued) is subsequent to that date. So much for the prefecture of C. Vibius Maximus.³

To conclude, origin and family. Two pieces of evidence can be adduced. First, Martial, when referring to a poem about a dove written by Arruntius Stella (of Patavium), thus addresses a Maximus (i 7),

> Stellae delicium mei columba,
> Verona licet audiente dicam,
> vicit, Maxime, passerem Catulli.
> tanto Stella meus tuo Catullo
> quanto passere maior est columba.

The phrase 'tuus Catullus' suggests Verona. Compare the hendecasyllabic effort of Sentius Augurinus cited by Pliny (iv 27, 4),

> canto carmina versibus minutis,
> his olim quibus et meus Catullus
> et Calvus veteresque, etc.

Surely this poet is a citizen of Verona.⁴

Secondly, Pliny to a Maximus (vi 34, 1)—'recte fecisti quod gladiatorium munus Veronensibus nostris promisisti, a quibus olim amaris suspiceris ornaris.' The phrase 'Veronenses nostri' might be taken to imply that one of the persons comes from Verona.⁵ Pliny goes on to add a further reason to commend Maxi|mus' benefaction to that city. It was also the city of Maximus' (deceased) wife—'inde etiam uxorem carissimam tibi et probatissimam habuisti.'

¹ *P. Oxy.* 471; cf. above [p. 353, n. 5].
² *IGR* i 1148, cf. A. Stein, op. cit. 52.
³ For a further complication, see J. Schwartz, *CE* xxvii (1952), 254 ff. That scholar reports an inscription of 126 on which the Prefect's name has been erased; he argues that this was the son of C. Vibius Maximus, takes him for the guilty man of *P. Oxy.* 471, and suggests that his condemnation caused the parent's name to be obliterated on the three inscriptions. H. G. Pflaum (cited on p. 256) accepts the notion of two homonymous Prefects of Egypt, but prefers to identify the second (in 126) with the C. Vibius Maximus attested as 'praef. coh. III Alpinorum' in Dalmatia in 93 (*CIL* xvi 38). Neither hypothesis seems cogent or helpful. On the one, a Prefect aged thirty; on the other, aged about sixty-five. Preferably an *Ignotus* in 126.
⁴ By full nomenclature Q. Gellius Sentius Augurinus (*PIR*², G 135), proconsul of Achaia under Hadrian (*ILS* 5947a).
⁵ Cf. Pliny to Junius Mauricus—'ex illa nostra Italia' (i 14, 4). Not perhaps quite enough to prove that Mauricus was, like Pliny, a son of the North.

Vibius Maximus, if correctly to be identified as the Maximus of the above passages, is not the only Maximus of Transpadane origin among the correspondents of Pliny. Two missives (iii 20; iv 25) go to a Messius Maximus—or rather Maesius Maximus.[1] Bergomum can show a Maesius Maximus of some local consequence and standing.[2] Observe as relevant (but no proof) a Maximus who inherited from a Valerius Varus, the latter being in debt to Atilius Crescens (whose town must be either Bergomum or Mediolanium).[3]

Vibius is known as a friend and patron of letters well before the end of Domitian's reign. Statius testifies.[4] The ode to Maximus reveals a valuable detail about his family and rank in society. The poet prays that the son of Vibius will in due course emulate his father and his grandfather. Vibius will tell the boy about his service in Syria when he commanded a regiment of cavalry. As for the grandparent (iv 7, 49 ff.),

> ille ut invicti rapidum secutus
> Caesaris fulmen refugis amaram
> Sarmatis legem dederit, sub uno
> vivere caelo.

A problem arises. This man appears to be a senator, present with Domitian on his campaign against the Sarmatae Jazyges in 92. Perhaps on the Emperor's staff as *comes*; possibly even the consular legate of Pannonia?[5] But further, is he the father of Vibius Maximus? That is assumed by commentators on Statius.[6] Perhaps, however, the parent of Vibius' wife —and here brought in without being named because he is a known and conspicuous personage.[7] Knights of | superior quality easily acquire brides from the best senatorial families. In either event, whether the son of a senator or son-in-law, Vibius Maximus claimed a high estimation in

---

[1] M. Schuster (Teubner, 1933) prefers and prints 'Maesius'.

[2] *CIL* v 5138.

[3] *Ep.* vi 8, 4, cf. 2: 'oppida nostra unius diei itinere dirimuntur.'

[4] *Silvae* iv, *praef.*: 'Maximum Vibium et dignitatis et eloquentiae nomine a nobis diligi satis eram testatus epistula quam ad illum de editione Thebaidos meae publicavi.'

[5] The identity of the governor of Pannonia at this time is not certain. Perhaps (it has been suggested) A. Lappius Maximus (*suff.* 86), who as legate of Germania Inferior at the beginning of 89 crushed the revolt of Antonius Saturninus. Two reasons could be adduced. First, his second consulate in 95, second, identity with the Norbanus of Martial ix 84, who had been absent from Rome for six years. Cf. now W. Reidinger, *Die Statthalter des ungeteilten Pannonien und Oberpannoniens von Augustus bis Diokletian* (1956), 54 ff. There is, however, a chance that the Norbanus of Martial is equestrian (? procurator of Raetia), and to be identified with the Norbanus who was Prefect of the Guard with T. Petronius Secundus in 96 (Dio lxvii 15, 2). [Cf. *Danubian Papers* (1971), 184, 189.]

[6] F. Vollmer (1898); H. Frère (Budé, 1944), mainly deriving from Vollmer, in his note on *Silvae* iv, *praef.*

[7] Observe Dessau in *PIR*[1], V 389: 'gener (potius quam filius) viri qui Domitiani bello Sarmatico comes fuerat.'

Roman society long before he came anywhere near the prefecture of Egypt.[1]

[1] Cf. Statius, *Silvae* iv, *praef.* And it could perhaps be regarded as irrelevant whether or no he is the Veronese Maximus of Martial (i 7), and of Pliny (vi 34), as suggested above: that *cognomen* is so common.

An additional item deserves to be registered somewhere, a gravestone in the Vatican Museum (*CIL* vi 1538): 'd. m. s. / C. Vibio C. fil. / Maximo / Egriliano / laticlavio / pius vixit /annorum XXVIII / mens. XI / o. t. b. q.'. Clearly a young man who for one reason or another had not gone on to senatorial magistracies—possibly because of his parent's disgrace. But it would not be permissible here to discover a son (? an elder son) of the Prefect of Egypt. The formulation is against so early a date, especially the 'pius vixit'. The Egrilii are an Ostian family (*PIR*[2], E 46 ff.), their first consul probably Trajanic. [Peter White, *Historia* xxii (1973), 275 ff., denies the identification of Statius' friend with the Prefect of Egypt and questions his identification with the friend of Martial.]

29

Imperator Caesar: A Study in Nomenclature

EACH and every Roman citizen must possess at the very least a *praenomen* and a *nomen*, to constitute, along with the filiation and the tribe, his official designation; and the *praenomen*, duly abbreviated, continues to figure in any formulation that requires a man's *état civil*, from public documents down to funerary inscriptions. Otherwise, apart from its use in domestic or familiar intercourse, the *praenomen* tends to be suppressed in the last age of the Roman Republic. Various fashions can be detected as they grow and spread. A well-known person may be referred to by one of his other names only, *nomen* or *cognomen*, thus 'Pompeius' and 'Caesar'. Especially notable and destined finally to prevail in serious prose is the practice of designating a man by two names, the *nomen gentilicium* and the *cognomen*, as in 'Asinius Pollio'. Significant variations, almost categories, can be registered, according to the type of literature or the social status of the individual. The same holds for a further innovation, that inversion which places the *cognomen* before the *gentilicium*, as in 'Balbus Cornelius'. It begins with persons of low degree, and gradually ascends the social scale. Cicero never permits himself to refer to contemporary members of the *nobilitas* in this manner.

Not but what the *praenomen*, ostensibly a trivial item of nomenclature, exhibits powers of resistance, precisely among the *nobiles*. The proper and choice fashion of designating those exalted personages, in formal or honorific address, seems to be by *praenomen* (abbreviated) and *cognomen*. Thus 'L. Sulla', 'P. Scipio', 'C. Caesar', 'M. Metellus'. The name of the *gens* being omitted in this formulation, that of the family or branch takes its place and is elevated into the rank and status of a *nomen*. So much so that the filiation, which normally follows the *nomen* and precedes the *cognomen*, will conform to the change of function, with M. Caecilius Q. f. Metellus being styled on his coins 'M. Metellus Q. f.'[1] Here 'Metellus' is patently doing duty as a *nomen*. An instructive extension of this procedure is furnished by the name 'M. Piso M. f. Frugi'.[2] This man's father, the consul M. Pupius Piso, was a Calpurnius Piso by birth, adopted by a

[1] E. A. Sydenham, *The Coinage of the Roman Republic* (1952), 719.
[2] Sydenham, 824 ff.

Historia vii (1958), 172–88.

certain M. Pupius. The son, it appears, was eager to suppress the un-decorative *nomen* 'Pupius', and emphasize his noble lineage. Technically not a member of the gens *Calpurnia*, he could not call himself 'Calpur-nius', but he took the ancestral cognomen 'Piso' and converted it into a *nomen*.[1]

Predilection for the aristocratic *cognomen* is in no way enigmatic. The *gentilicia* of the *nobiles* forfeit much of their distinctiveness through being transmitted to clients and freedmen and consequently vulgarized. There came to be myriads of Cornelii, most notorious the freedmen of L. Sulla the Dictator. The address by *praenomen* and *cognomen* is therefore proper to the *nobilitas*. Cicero never applies the form 'L. Balbus' to L. Cornelius Balbus, an alien who derived his name 'Cornelius' from his patron, one of the Cornelii Lentuli.

Moreover, certain *praenomina*, restricted almost wholly to the aristo-cracy, or rather to its primordial nucleus, the patriciate, are quite anoma-lous. 'Servius' belongs all but exclusively to the Sulpicii, 'Appius' to the one branch of the Claudii, the Claudii Pulchri. Such peculiar *praenomina* make mock of all rules. So closely is 'Servius' associated with the *gens Sulpicia* that, to take an extreme example, Tacitus can employ it as though it were a *gentilicium* and write 'post Iulios Claudios Servios'.[2] And 'Appius' instead of 'Claudius' was attached to a road or an aqueduct: 'via Appia' and 'aqua Appia'. Cicero refers to the consul of 54 B.C. as 'Appius' with-out the marked and perhaps excessive familiarity which the use of a *praenomen* would normally imply.[3] This, it is true, is in letters, not in public pronouncements or in serious prose. Livy, however, writing history, will name an historic Claudius simply as 'Appius'.[4] Finally, not only does 'Appius' oppose a certain resistance to abbreviation or stand by itself: unlike the normal *praenomen*, it is not transmitted to freedmen.[5]

Paradoxically but not inexplicably, the revolutionary age enhances the pride and the ambition of the *nobiles*, and the first dynasty to rule at Rome is patrician, the line of the Julii and Claudii. Sulla, Caesar, and Augustus all made conspicuous efforts to bring back the patriciate to a rank of leadership in the *nobilitas*. One sign of exorbitant personal claims is the choice of abnormal *praenomina*. As is fitting, Sulla the Dictator opens the roll. Taking 'Felix' as his own *cognomen*, he transmutes it and gives it to his son as a *praenomen* in the shape of 'Faustus'; and Faustus Sulla with appropriate bravado inscribes the 'Faustus', standing alone, on his coins.[6] Then after an interval L. Aemilius Paullus, the second son of that Aemilius

---

[1] Though this man (*pr.* 44 B.C.) may have taken that further step, for he (not his parent) may be the 'M. Calpurnius M. f. Piso Frugi [pr.]' of *CIL* i² 745. [But see E. Badian, *Acta of the Fifth International Congress of Greek and Latin Epigraphy* (1971), 209–14.]

[2] *Hist.* ii 48, 2.   [3] e.g. *Ad fam.* i 9, 4: 'me cum Caesare et cum Appio esse in gratia.'
[4] iii 36, 1.   [5] Hence 'P. Clodius Ap. l. Eros' (*CIL* i² 1282).
[6] Sydenham, 879 ff.

who raised civil war to overthrow the Dictator's ordinances, transfers his *cognomen* to his own son, who is called Paullus Aemilius Lepidus (*cos. suff.* 34 B.C.). A Valerius (*suff.* 29 B.C.) brings back the ancient name 'Potitus'; and before long two Fabii publicize an ancestry that is both Aemilian and Scipionic by the *praenomina* 'Paullus' and 'Africanus' (the consuls of 11 and 10 B.C. respectively). To the same generation as the Fabii belongs a plebeian *nobilis*, but of dynastic family, Iullus Antonius (*cos.* 10 B.C.), the younger son of the Triumvir. The choice of the name 'Iullus', which belonged in old time to the Julii, shows how Marcus Antonius advertised | *pietas* towards his dead friend and leader, Caesar the Dictator: Iullus Antonius was born about 43 B.C. Contemporary to within a few years are the two heirs of the Claudii Nerones, the stepsons of Augustus. Both bear a name ancient in their family, 'Nero', which, like 'Appius', is of Sabine origin. But whereas the elder conforms to established practice and is simply Ti. Claudius Nero, the younger has the name as a *praenomen* and is called Nero Claudius Drusus.[1]

That a *cognomen* should be taken and exploited as a *praenomen* is not so outrageous an operation as it might on the surface appear. Denoting originally a person as a person, the *cognomen* is by nature akin to the *praenomen*. Reference has already been made to the frequent practice of dropping the *praenomen* and inverting the other two names. In the order *cognomen* and *gentilicium*, as in 'Balbus Cornelius', it may not be altogether fanciful to suppose that the displaced *cognomen* has something of the force and function of a *praenomen*: the inversion is not at all arbitrary. Cicero, it has been observed, does not apply this licence to the names of persons of consequence. It is, however, only fair to mention that the two young *nobiles* who completed the monumental gate which Ap. Claudius Pulcher (*cos.* 54 B.C.) dedicated at Eleusis, do not disdain to call themselves 'Pulcher Claudius' and 'Rex Marcius'.[2]

Two significant fashions in the nomenclature of the *nobiles* have now been adverted upon, viz. a predilection for the type 'C. Caesar', with consequent neglect of the *gentilicium*, and a taste for fancy *praenomina*. Both are illustrated by the sons of Cn. Pompeius Magnus. The elder, who fell at Munda, uses the form 'Cn. Magnus'.[3] The younger maintains the family cause for a decade against the heirs to Caesar's power; and, having likewise adopted the paternal *cognomen*, goes on to exhibit startling combinations and permutations. It is not always easy to date them, but one case happens to be authenticated with welcome precision. In a speech delivered before the Roman Senate on the first day of January 43 B.C., Cicero refers to him as 'Sextus Pompeius Gnaei filius Magnus';[4] before the end of March he occurs in the draft of a *senatus consultum* as 'Magnus

---

[1] His original *praenomen* had been 'Decimus' (Suetonius, *Divus Claudius* 1, 1).
[2] *ILS* 4041.   [3] Sydenham, 1035 ff.   [4] *Phil.* v 41.

364 Imperator Caesar: A Study in Nomenclature [174

Pompeius Gnaei filius'.[1] Therefore 'Magnus' has moved into the place of a *praenomen*.

Other and further devices were already, it seems, being played upon. 'Pietas' was familiar as the badge of the Metelli: it was plagiarized by their allies and adopted as the battle cry of the Pompeian loyalists at Munda.[2] Sextus, the surviving brother, affected 'Pius' as a *cognomen*. Fleeing at first to Lacetania in Hispania Citerior, he returned before long to Ulterior and raised war against the Caesarian generals, engaging first C. Carrinas, then Asinius Pollio.[3] The signal defeat of Pollio may without discomfort be assigned to the spring | or early summer of 44 B.C. Hence presumably Sextus' imperatorial acclamation. Certain of his Spanish coins can therefore be assigned to the interval between this event and his assumption of the title of 'praefectus classis et orae maritimae', which office was voted to him in the next year by the Senate after the Battle of Mutina (April 43 B.C.).[4] Bronze coins struck by Eppius, one of his legates in Spain, represent his name as 'Magnus Pius'—that is, *praenomen* and *cognomen*.[5] But there are also certain mysterious denarii, struck, it appears, at the town of Salacia, on which he figures as 'Sextus Magnus Pius'.[6] In terms of strict nomenclature, these words can be interpreted as *praenomen*, *gentilicium*, and *cognomen*. That is to say, in this instance, 'Magnus' has been promoted to the rank of a family name. It may seem far-fetched as an explanation—but there was soon to be a Caesarian parallel.

His position legalized with the rank of a commander of the seas, the young adventurer moved closer to Italy, and by the end of the year 43 B.C. he had established himself in Sicily, which island he occupied and held until his defeat in 36 B.C. The coins which Sextus struck as 'praef. clas. et orae marit.' uniformly show his name as 'Magnus Pius'.[7] The onomatological function of those two words is demonstrated and confirmed by a dedication set up by one of his legates at Lilybaeum—'Mag. Pompeio Mag. f. Pio'.[8] The process thus becomes clear. The young Pompeius has discarded the *praenomen* 'Sextus' long ago; and the experiment with 'Magnus' as a *gentilicium*, as exemplified in the Spanish denarii showing 'Sextus Magnus Pius', has not been repeated. Though the old

[1] *Phil.* xiii 50, cf. 8: 'Magnum Pompeium, clarissimum adulescentem'.
[2] Appian, *BC* ii 104.   [3] Appian, *BC* iv 83 f.; Dio xlv 10.
[4] Dio xlvi 40, 3; Velleius ii 73, 2.
[5] Sydenham, 1045. [Doubts are raised by T. V. Buttrey, *NC* xx (1960), 93.]
[6] Sydenham, 1041 ff. Six types (two of them without 'Pius'). Grueber, *BMC, R. Rep.* ii 370 f., registered three. On these coins see further H. Bahrfeldt, *NZ* xxix (1897), 50 f.; L. Laffranchi, *RIN* xxv (1912), 511 ff.; M. Grant, *From Imperium to Auctoritas* (1946), 22 f.; 409. It should be noted that the town is 'Salacia cognominata urbs imperatoria' (Pliny, *NH* iv 116). Its coins have 'Imp. Sal.' and 'Imp. Salac.' on the reverse (Vives y Escudero, *La moneda hispánica* iii (1924), 26). [Buttrey, op. cit. 95 f., unconvincingly argues against any connection with Salacia.]
[7] Sydenham, 1344 ff.   [8] *ILS* 8891 (Lilybaeum).

family name has not been altogether lost sight of, as witness the inscription from Lilybaeum, the nomenclature 'Magnus Pius' is preferred, in the style of *praenomen*+*cognomen*. As 'Cn. Magnus', the elder of the sons of Magnus is unexceptionable: the younger, 'Magnus Pius', is revolutionary and foretells the monarchy.

There was another pretender, Caesar's heir, whose ambition outstripped Pompeius and the sons of Pompeius. C. Julius Caesar (for so he chose to be known, spurning the 'Octavianus' that would have perpetuated the memory of his real parentage) was able to parade as 'Divi filius' as soon as the Senate and People consecrated his adoptive father early in 42 B.C.[1] A few years later | he discards the *gentilicium* of the Julii and the *praenomen* as well, and bursts into official nomenclature with a portentous and flamboyant *praenomen* as 'Imp. Caesar'.

Aristocratic preference for the *cognomen* has already been observed; and a *cognomen* could be given the function of a *gentilicium*. In one case, indeed, the transmutation was thorough and official. In 59 B.C., if not earlier, M. Junius Brutus, adopting the name of a maternal kinsman, became a Servilius Caepio in the strange style of 'Q. Caepio Brutus'.[2] Closely parallel is the case, already quoted, of M. Piso Frugi. Like 'Piso' and 'Caepio', 'Caesar' is henceforth converted into a *gentilicium*. The more striking phenomenon, however, is the use of 'Imperator' as a man's first and individual name.

For this style the earliest unequivocal and contemporary evidence is provided by coins struck by Agrippa, consul designate, when commanding in Gaul: that is to say, in 38 B.C.[3] Is this a new and sudden thing, is there a discernible line of development, a precedent even?

If there were an exact precedent, the problem would be simple. And such a precedent is alleged. Cassius Dio states that in 45 B.C. the Senate voted to Caesar the Dictator the title of 'imperator' as a proper name.[4] Dio is explicit. It was, he says, something distinct alike from the traditional imperatorial salutation and from the designation of a commander in possession of *imperium*: it was precisely the title of imperial power borne by the Emperor in his own day. Further, the title was to pass to the sons and to the descendants of Caesar. Dio also reverts to this grant under the year 29 B.C., after he has spread himself at some length on the speeches of Agrippa and Maecenas: he affirms that Octavianus now adopted the hereditary title that had been conferred upon Caesar.[5] Moreover,

---

[1] Dio xlvii 18, 3. It is notable and important, however, that 'Divi f.' cannot be attested on his coins before 38 B.C.; cf. K. Kraft, *JNG* iii–iv (1952–3), 69.

[2] The 'Q. Caepio hic Brutus' of *Ad Att.* ii 24, 2 finds confirmation later in Cicero's draft of the *senatus consultum* in February of 43, 'Q. Caepio Brutus pro consule' (*Phil.* x 26). Cf. Sydenham, 1287 ff.

[3] Sydenham, 1329; 1331.   [4] Dio xliii 44, 2 ff.   [5] Dio lii 41, 3.

Suetonius also records the bestowal of the *praenomen imperatoris* on the Dictator.[1] These passages in Dio and in Suetonius have been the occasion of perpetual argumentation. It may be said at once that no other author, contemporary or subsequent, is aware of this momentous innovation; that no coin exists, or inscription, attesting 'Imperator Caesar' as the nomenclature of Caesar the Dictator.[2]

Such are the facts. There is anachronism in Dio's view of the original function of the *praenomen* 'Imp.' There are other anachronisms and anticipations | in his account of the prerogatives of the Dictator. The hereditary *praenomen* is matched by hereditary transmission of the office of *pontifex maximus*.[3] There is also the permission accorded to Caesar to offer the *spolia opima*, even though he had not killed an enemy leader with his own hands.[4] That is grotesque—the *spolia opima*, forgotten for centuries, did not emerge into Roman politics until 29 or 28 B.C. when the inopportune claim of an ambitious proconsul caused Octavianus no little embarrassment.[5]

There is no Caesarian precedent for the *praenomen* of Caesar's heir. Nor is there a Pompeian precedent: there is nothing abnormal in Sextus Pompeius' use of the imperatorial acclamation after his name. It has been suggested, it is true, that on one of the surviving specimens of his Spanish denarii (belonging to 44/3 B.C.), the legend 'Imp. Sex. Magnus' both could and should be read.[6] If this were conceded, 'Imp.' still does not function as substitute for a *praenomen*, as in 'Imp. Caesar', but is merely prefixed to the *praenomen*. At the most, admitting the suggestion, a sporadic deviation has been detected, patently of no subsequent influence on the nomenclature of Sextus Pompeius, or of anybody else.[7]

A different approach to the problem is indicated. The retention of 'imp.' after a general's name might appear to give it something of the function of a *cognomen*; and a *cognomen* can be transferred and used as a *praenomen*.

The Republican general, acclaimed after victory by his troops, has the

---

[1] *Divus Julius* 76, 1. It is difficult to argue that Suetonius and Dio do not mean the same thing. Dio's phrase ὥσπερ τι κύριον must not be neglected.

[2] Cf. D. McFayden, *The History of the Title Imperator under the Roman Empire* (Chicago, 1920), 11 ff. Scholars are naturally reluctant to throw over the evidence of Dio, and various attempts are made to utilize it. See, for example, A. v. Premerstein, *ABAW*, N.F. xv (1937), 245 ff.; A. Alföldi, *Studien über Caesars Monarchie* (Lund, 1953), 28 ff.; K. Kraft, *JNG* iii/iv (1952–3), 64 ff. [See R. Combès, *Imperator* (1966), 123 ff.]

[3] Dio xliv 3, 3.   [4] Dio xliv 4, 3.

[5] Dio li 24, 4, cf. H. Dessau, *Hermes* xli (1906), 142 ff.; E. Groag, *RE* xiii, coll. 283 ff.

[6] M. Grant, op. cit. 22 f.; 409. Accepted by Alföldi, op. cit. 30.

[7] Indeed, 'Imp.' may not belong at all before the 'Sex. Magnus'; cf. K. Kraft, op. cit. 68. The coin in question is Sydenham, 1043 (reproduced on pl. 27) = *BMC*, *R. Rep.* ii 371, 94 (pl. CI, 12).

right to carry 'imp.' with him until he enters the City again, to keep the title for the day of his triumph only, if the celebration be approved by the Senate, otherwise to forfeit it at once. It might happen that an *imperator*, thwarted by the 'calumnia inimicorum' and condemned to wait for a long time and perhaps in vain, would linger for months or for years outside the sacred precinct, tenacious of his imperatorial acclamation and the laurelled *fasces*. The advent of the civil war surprised a retiring proconsul of Cilicia, M. Tullius M. f. Cicero imp., still in possession of the *imperium* and all the paraphernalia, and thus technically available for high command. The experience of other wars and other ages shows military men not eager to relinquish the titles and aura of authority when the office has lapsed. Pompeius Magnus had earned three acclamations and three triumphs; hence three periods in his career amounting to a fair sum of years, in which he had borne the title as of right until a triumph supervened and abolished it. Victory and the prestige of victory had abode with | Magnus from his earliest enterprises. For Magnus, or for others, there must have been a temptation to overstep the proprieties and assume that the appellation still adhered to his name, befitting Rome's greatest soldier. Furthermore, in this age a second or a third salutation is not necessarily indicated by a numerical symbol. A dedication set up at Auximum in 52 B.C., nine years from his last triumph, styles him 'Cn. Pompeius Cn. f. Magnus imp.'[1] The dedication is an official act of the colony of Auximum, in the region Picenum which the Pompeii dominated. This being so, it is not inconceivable that other documents showing Pompeius as 'imp.' also belong to periods in his career when he had no legal right to the appellation. Nor, to take a later instance, is it surprising to find that a *vir triumphalis* of the Triumviral period, Ap. Claudius Pulcher (*cos.* 38 B.C.), keeps 'imp.' after his triumph—and after his death. It has remained a part of his title and honours, like 'cos.'[2]

The behaviour of Caesar might have been expected to furnish useful guidance—Caesar's aspirations to tyrannical power as well as to military glory are commonly detected at a quite early stage in his career, and transgressions against the spirit and the letter of the Roman constitution are taken as a matter of course. Yet Caesar the proconsul of Gaul seems wholly indifferent to the imperatorial salutation, not bothering to assume one until quite late in his conquest of Gaul—at least none is recorded in his *Commentaries*.[3] The honour had indeed been sadly debased of recent years, if the last three proconsuls of Cilicia were worth it, L. Lentulus, Ap. Pulcher, and M. Tullius Cicero; and Caesar himself in the narrative

[1] *ILS* 877.   [2] *ILS* 890.

[3] The inscription at Issa in Dalmatia, recording a deputation sent to Aquileia, has ἐπὶ Γαίου Ἰουλί[ου] Καί[σαρος] / αὐτοκράτορος [Sherk, *RDGE*, no. 24, ll. 10 f.]. But this is perhaps irrelevant because of the common use of αὐτοκράτωρ to describe a Roman holder of *imperium* (cf. below).

of the Civil Wars makes an ironical comment about the cheap and paltry distinction arrogated to himself by Metellus Scipio.[1] Caesar bears his Gallic acclamation till his triumph in 46 B.C., though he has entered the city in the meantime—and then before long there is another acclamation and a triumph celebrated from Spain (October 45 B.C.). In strict propriety he should now have given it up. Precisely what happened is not clear: Cassius Dio, as has been stated, records a decree of the Senate after the triumph to the effect that Caesar should be permitted to retain the title 'imp.' But, as Dio understands and expounds the matter, this is the *praenomen imperatoris*, and Dio is manifestly in error. It is not certain that all the honours voted to the Dictator in the last months of his life were in fact adopted by him. If the right to retain 'imp.' was both offered and accepted, and that could be argued, it comes to very little. The legend 'Caesar imp.' occurs on the coins of three out of the four masters of the Roman mint in 44 B.C. Alternatives are 'Caesar dict. | quart.', changing to 'Caesar dict. perpetuo', and 'Caesar parens patriae' (posthumous).[2] The title thus has no exclusive significance. It is absent from the Dictator's official nomenclature on the *Fasti Consulares*.

To return to Caesar's heir. His first acclamation had been registered in the War of Mutina, in April 43 B.C. The date and occasion of the second has not been established, while the third is recorded for the first time on Agrippa's coins of 38 B.C. The evidence does not permit any significant deductions about his employment of 'imp.' after his name between the first salutation and the third. Now, however, the *praenomen* 'imp.' emerges. The denarius carries the legend 'Imp. Caesar Divi Iuli f.', but on the aureus the formula is peculiar—'Imp. Divi Iuli f. ter'.[3] That is to say, the 'imp.' in the notation of the third acclamation is thrown into the position of the *praenomen*. On the face of things this style might seem to demonstrate beyond doubt that the *praenomen* 'Imp.' derives from the imperatorial salutation.

At the same time, it must be admitted that this explanation may not carry the whole truth. Even if the line of derivation seems clear, the full force and validity of the *praenomen* in the titulature 'Imp. Caesar' may be of another kind. Prepossession with the imperatorial salutation should not

---

[1] *BC* iii 31, 1: 'detrimentis quibusdam circa montem Amanum acceptis imperatorem se appellaverat.'

[2] These coins have naturally excited much interest—and controversy. Cf. A. Alföldi, op. cit. 1 ff.; K. Kraft, op. cit. 7 ff.; C. M. Kraay, *NC*[6] xiv (1955), 18 ff. (criticizing Alföldi's chronological arrangement). Kraay presents the attractive view that coins with 'Caesar imp.' are contemporaneous with the others, but from a different mint—and to be explained by the imminent campaigns of the Dictator.

[3] Sydenham, 1331 and 1329 respectively. [Combès, *Imperator*, 134 ff., following Degrassi, *Inscr. It.* xiii 1, 345, accepts the *Fasti Barberiniani* for 40 B.C. (*Im[p. Caesar] / ouans . . .*) as contemporary evidence for the use of the *praenomen* as early as 40. But there is no evidence for incision precisely in that year.]

be allowed to obscure a wider use, or uses, of the word 'imperator'. It can denote the magistrate or promagistrate holding *imperium*; and further, in normal or traditional prose usage, a general or commander. Laxity, impropriety, or confusion is only to be expected in the revolutionary age—'non mos, non ius'. And there was respectable precedent for 'imperator' as a convenient and attractive title.

When a magistrate or promagistrate had been hailed as 'imperator', a certain incompatibility seems to have been felt between that name and the titles of his authority, consul or proconsul, praetor or propraetor. They tend not to occur in conjunction, and the more splendid name prevails. Thus as early as 189 a proconsul in Spain in an edict describes himself as 'L. Aimilius L. f. inpeirator'.[1] The title cannot fail to have appealed to the Roman general, expressing as it did the prestige of victory and the claim to victory's crown, the triumph at Rome; and to the provincial, in the western lands and even more in the eastern, it conveyed the fact of a power that was regal and military in a clearer and simpler fashion than did 'consul' and 'proconsul'. Translated into Greek, 'imperator' is αὐτοκράτωρ; and αὐτοκράτωρ, by extension, can render | the Roman titles of magistracy or promagistracy.[2] The historian Josephus quotes an edict pronounced by the proconsul P. Dolabella at Ephesus early in 43 B.C. He is styled Δολοβέλλας αὐτοκράτωρ.[3] Now it might even be doubted whether P. Dolabella had by this time recorded an imperatorial salutation. In his journey from Rome Dolabella, it is true, had had a brush with insurgent Republicans in Macedonia, and he had dispossessed Trebonius, the proconsul of Asia. But those incipient stages of civil war should have provided no occasion or excuse for him to be acclaimed as 'imperator'.

In the Civil Wars, Caesarian and Triumviral, generals of all parties freely added 'imp.' to their names: a notable exception is the constitutionalist M. Porcius Cato.[4] Not all of them could properly assert a right to legal authority; and it is fair to suppose that 'imp.' could derive not so much from a victory as from an act of usurpation, that it could represent not merely a claim to a triumph one day but a title of authority and command. Thus, for all that one can tell, Sex. Pompeius might have taken the title 'imp.' when he raised the Pompeian standard in Hispania Citerior (45/4 B.C.), and not when he defeated a Caesarian general subsequently in Hispania Ulterior (spring or early summer of 44 B.C.).

There was no limit to usurpations of title or prerogative. The dynasts set men of equestrian rank in command of armies of Roman legions and conceded them the appropriate honours. Thus Octavianus' marshal, the

---

[1] *ILS* 15. For subsequent instances, A. Rosenberg, *RE* ix, coll. 1141 f. A good instance is the milestone from Pont-de-Treilles (in the Aude): 'Cn. Domitius Cn. f. / Ahenobarbus / imperator / XX' (*AE* 1952, 38).
[2] Cf. A. Rosenberg, *RE* ix, col. 1142; E. J. Bickermann, *CP* xlii (1947), 138 f.
[3] *AJ* xiv 225.   [4] Sydenham, 1052 ff., where he is 'pro pr.'

notorious Salvidienus Rufus, is 'imp.' as early as 40 B.C.[1] After a time, when the Triumvirs felt their authority was stronger, or desired to advertise a return to settled government, restrictions might be imposed. In 36 B.C. Octavianus forbade the wearing of the purple cloak by commanders not of senatorial status;[2] and Cornelius Gallus, the Roman knight, bold and ostentatious though he be, does not dare to usurp the title 'imp.' for his exploits in the invasion of Egypt, when he commanded a whole army coming from Cyrenaica and captured Paraetonium (30 B.C.).

Finally, the plain and simple meaning of 'leader' or 'commander'. That sense is old in the Latin language, being in no way an innovation created by the revolutionary epoch of the great *imperatores*, the extensive *imperia*, and the monarchic dynasts. It will be enough to cite Plautus in support, 'deinde utrique imperatores in medium exeunt';[3] Lucretius has 'induperatorem classis';[4] and Sallust is not irrelevant, describing the institution of the consulate in language that is deliberately archaic and non-technical— 'annua imperia binosque imperatores sibi fecere.'[5] Official titulature may exercise only a slight influence on linguistic developments. A notable parallel can be discovered in the ways in | which the Greek East came to employ αὐτοκράτωρ, Καῖσαρ, βασιλεύς as designations for the Roman Emperor.[6] Similarly ἡγεμών possessed its own independent validity as a descriptive term, and would have retained it, even if ἡγεμών had not been adopted by Augustus as an official rendering of 'princeps'. When Strabo uses the word he is not just translating a Latin title into Greek.[7]

The wider connotations of 'imperator' being admitted, it will appear plausible that the *praenomen* 'Imperator' embodies and advertises the peculiar claim of Octavianus to be the military leader *par excellence*. The poet Catullus had acclaimed C. Caesar the proconsul of Gaul as 'imperator unice'.[8] What was irony in Catullus now became with Caesar's heir an item of official nomenclature—'Imp. Caesar Divi f.'

If the year was 38 B.C., the date is singularly felicitous. Octavianus made an elaborate attempt to invade the island of Sicily: he was easily defeated by Pompeius, and a tempest destroyed the remnants of his fleet. The contrast between official propaganda and known facts is not seldom to be observed in the career of Octavianus.

The young Caesar stood in sore need of prestige, comfort, and advertisement. The Caesarian leaders made much of their loyalty to the Dictator, emulating in passionate resolve to avenge him. Devotion to the virtue of *pietas* was precluded from full flower and recognition, for

---

[1] Sydenham, 1326.   [2] Dio xlix 16, 1.   [3] *Amphitruo* 223.
[4] v 1227.   [5] *Cat.* 6, 7.
[6] Cf. A. Wifstrand, *ΔΡΑΓΜΑ Martino P. Nilsson . . . dedicatum* (1939), 529 ff.
[7] Strabo vi 288; vii 314; xvii 840.
[8] Catullus 29, 11; cf. 54, 7. Compare later Cicero, *Pro Ligario* 3: 'cum ipse imperator in toto imperio populi Romani unus esset.'

the young Pompeius had annexed 'Pius' long ago as part of his name. Nor was there any distinction left in the mere retention of an imperatorial salutation. Salvidienus had had it, though not a senator, the upstart admiral Laronius was to take it twice.[1] Agrippa, the modest and faithful marshal, victorious in Gaul this year, not only declined the triumph that would have emphasized his leader's discomfiture but also singled himself out from lesser men by refusing ever after to bear the vulgar distinction of 'imp.' after his name.[2] What was good enough for Laronius or for a mere aristocrat like Appius Claudius Pulcher, was not good enough for Marcus Agrippa.

It has been conjectured that no other than Agrippa first hit upon the device of publicizing the young Caesar as the unique *imperator*; and it may have been his own salutation in Gaul that was surrendered to the leader's titulature, there to figure as 'imp. III'. Agrippa had been playing tricks with his own name. In 38 B.C., if not earlier, he is 'M. Agrippa', having dropped the *gentilicium* 'Vipsanius'. |

If the new Caesarian *praenomen* is in effect something more than a transferred imperatorial salutation, Sextus Pompeius turns out to be strikingly relevant. Caesar's heir needed every weapon for the contest, and propaganda not least when his generalship proved defective. From 44 or 43 B.C. onwards the young Pompeius had been asserting 'Magnus' as his *praenomen*. 'Imperator' looks like a Caesarian counterblast and overbid against the Pompeian emblem.[3] No longer 'C. Iulius Caesar' or 'C. Caesar', the Caesarian leader is now 'Imp. Caesar'. That style represents precisely *praenomen* and *nomen*. Similarly, the 'Divus' in 'Divus Iulius' might be interpreted as a *praenomen*, designating that individual Julius who happens to have become a god. And there will be no reason to quarrel with Tacitus for his practice of emphasizing the personality of Caesar the Dictator by means of the form 'Dictator Caesar'.

The reason for giving importance to these terms is not to assert to the utmost a pedantry of onomatological study. Doctrines of the gravest moment in Roman public law are concerned. Should 'Imp.' as a part of Octavianus' name be regarded as possessing any legal force? Now it has been seen that 'imp.' not only commemorates a salutation but can be retained after a general's name as a kind of title; it may also have been understood as a claim to exercise authority, especially when borne by commanders whose status was dubious or usurped, like the sons of Pompeius, or the Republican admiral Cn. Domitius Ahenobarbus.[4] One

---

[1] *CIL* x 8041[18] (Vibo, on a tile).
[2] It occurs, however, on *ILS* 8897 (Ephesus) and on the original dedication of the Maison Carrée at Nemausus (*CRAI* 1919, 332).
[3] Given 'Magnus Pompeius' in 43 (*Phil.* xiii 50), the facts are clear. The notion that Sex. Pompeius imitated Octavian (M. Grant, op. cit. 23; 415 f.) is erroneous.
[4] Sydenham, 1176 ff.

might cite as an extreme instance Labienus, styling himself 'Parthicus imp.'[1]

Even if this be conceded, it does not follow that, as some believe, the *praenomen* 'Imperator' in Octavianus' nomenclature is actually a title of competence, signifying the possession of *imperium*, even of an *imperium maius*.[2] Nobody can prove that opinion. The facts exhibit 'Imp. Caesar' as a name constructed on the model of 'Faustus Sulla' or 'Magnus Pius'. The events of the year 38 B.C. provide a strong presumption that 'Imperator' is a retort to 'Magnus'. Regarded as a personal name, 'Imp.' is exorbitant, far outdistancing any predecessor or competitor. So is Caesar's heir. 'Imp.' is a name of power, precise yet mystical, a monopolization of the glory of the *triumphator*, but it is not a title of authority.

The next modification of the Caesarian name comes neither after the victory of Actium nor after the fall of Alexandria: it commemorates the return of normal government, as proclaimed in the month of January 27 B.C. A grateful Senate duly votes to Caesar a *cognomen* of more than mortal amplitude. He now has three names: 'Imperator Caesar Augustus' is his complete and | official designation. It occurs on the consular *Fasti*, on dedications which the ruler makes or receives, on edicts he pronounces. And in this fashion does the historian Livy entitle him in a reference to the closing of the Temple of Janus, solemn and almost epigraphical in its conception—'post bellum Actiacum ab Imperatore Caesare Augusto pace terra marique parta'.[3]

But it was not customary save in official documents to refer to a Roman by the sum total of his *tria nomina*; and the new *cognomen* at once adds to the permissible variations in the formula with two names. The following brief observations may be made about prose usage, conjectural because of the scantiness of contemporary prose evidence. 'Imperator Caesar' is used in his dedication by Vitruvius, writing, or completing, his work on architecture soon after 27 B.C.:[4] Vitruvius was an old officer. 'Imperator Augustus' seems not to be found. The form is parallel to 'Magnus Pius'. Perhaps the collocation of two such highly individual and peculiar names as the *praenomen* 'Imperator' and the personal *cognomen* 'Augustus' was not aesthetically satisfying.[5] 'Caesar Augustus' on the other hand, *nomen* and *cognomen*, would conform to the fashion that had been growing up in the previous generation. 'Caesar Augustus' may be described as normal prose order. Inversion had also been becoming more respectable in the nomen-

---

[1] Sydenham, 1356.   [2] As has been urged by M. Grant, op. cit. 415 ff.
[3] i 19, 3.
[4] Vitruvius i 1, 1: 'cum divina tua mens et numen, Imperator Caesar, imperio potiretur orbis terrarum', etc. Otherwise he is 'Caesar' (seven times), but 'aedes Augusti' occurs (v 1, 7).
[5] Observe, however, some coin issues, *BMC, R. Emp.* i 17 ff., 51 ff., etc.

clature of *nobiles*, as witness 'Rex Marcius'. The inverted form 'Augustus Caesar' throws the word 'Augustus' into sharp relief. It occurs in the other two references of Livy.[1] *Cognomina*, it has been shown, are in origin and nature akin to *praenomina*. The name 'Augustus' is peculiar to 'Imp. Caesar', it can be taken very much as a *praenomen*. That order, 'Augustus Caesar', even occurs sporadically on inscriptions where an especial emphasis seemed fitting or desirable.[2]

Imperfect though it is, the evidence appears to indicate a certain recession of 'Imperator'. That was only to be expected. 'Imp.' is in fact a *praenomen*, and the remarkable new *cognomen* introduces the forms 'Caesar Augustus' and 'Augustus Caesar', in conformity with the observed tendency of Roman usage to affect two names. Moreover, the *praenomen* 'Imp.', assumed in civil war during the contest against Magnus Pompeius Pius, is redolent of the age of the despots. Emphasis now falling upon peace and 'normal conditions', the military propaganda of the government abates. The glory of Romulus, much advertised after Actium, is allowed to fade into the background. Actium itself is transcended by the achievements of the new régime of constitutional government, 'libertas et principatus'. |

As published on coins after 27 B.C., the ruler's titulature eschews the *praenomen* for the most part. That avoidance can tell something about official propaganda, nothing about public law.[3] Not only are 'Caesar' and 'Augustus' in use, alone or together, but new titles, 'trib. pot.', 'pontifex maximus', and 'pater patriae' in turn become available and permit many variations.

From the inception of the Triumvirate to the last day of December 33 B.C., the official competence of Octavianus reposed upon the title 'III vir r. p. c.'[4] Throughout the year 32 B.C. he holds no office. During the years 31–28 B.C. his only link with the *res publica* is the consulate, which gives legal cover, in so far as it can be given, to a paramount *imperium* not different from that of the Triumvir;[5] and from the first constitutional settlement to the second, from 27 B.C. to 23 B.C., the consulate is likewise the sole title of authority that appears in the titulature of Caesar Augustus, although his *imperium* embraces the better part of the Empire.

Since 'Imp.' is not even a title, still less a title of competence, but precisely a part of the ruler's name, its presence or absence cannot be taken

---

[1] iv 20, 7; xxviii 12, 12.

[2] e.g. *ILS* 110 (Pola); 139, l. 11 (Pisae); 915 (Histonium).

[3] Grant (op. cit. 417 ff.) argues that the recession of 'Imp.' is to be explained by the abandonment of government by *imperium maius*.

[4] That is, assuming that (whatever the legal term of the *Lex Titia* as renewed in 37) Octavian resigned triumviral powers at the beginning of 32 B.C.

[5] As Tacitus firmly and neatly indicates, 'posito triumviri nomine consulem se ferens' (*Ann.* i 2, 1).

as evidence about changes in the character of Augustus' *imperium*, in 27 B.C. or at any other time. It had not in fact been uniformly employed before 27 B.C. To some scholars it has been a distressing fact that the *imperium* should not be indicated either in the name or in the titulature of Caesar Augustus. Yet it is a fact. Similarly, the *Res Gestae Divi Augusti* do not reveal the vast *provincia* voted in 27 B.C. and carrying with it command over almost all the armed forces of the Republic, or the modification of the *imperium* in 23 B.C. which extended it to cover the public provinces in the form of *imperium maius*. After that date the ruler could (and, be it said, should) have borne 'pro cos.' on his titulature.

One cannot but suspect that preoccupation with the law and the constitution has led to a certain neglect of patent facts about nomenclature. The praenomen 'Imp.' has more weight and splendour than an ordinary name, as Pinarius Scarpus, Antonius' general in the Cyrenaica, showed when he commemorated his surrender by the legend 'Imp. Caesari Scarpus imp.'[1] None the less, and even though it may embody a claim to power as well as prestige, it has no legal force, no constitutional significance: it is a *praenomen* in rank and function. So closely does it adhere to Caesar Augustus that it is not transmitted to his son by adoption and successor, Ti. Caesar.[2] Many years were to pass before the | *praenomen imperatoris* became what Cassius Dio fancied it was from the beginning, the title of the imperial office.[3]

'Augustus' goes even further than 'Imp.' as a name: it is almost superhuman; yet 'Augustus' is not a title of competence but precisely a *cognomen*, and as such subject to inversion in the emphatic form 'Augustus Caesar'. Indeed 'Augustus' was felt to be so peculiar to Caesar Augustus that Ti. Caesar, so it is recorded, did not employ it more often than he could help.[4]

In short, Caesar Augustus, the ruler of Rome, exalts himself above all rivals or forerunners in the choice of names as of titles. By contrast, Caesar the Dictator is modest and sober, Marcus Antonius the Triumvir an arrant traditionalist, without even the advertisement of a *cognomen*. Yet Caesar Augustus, in nomenclature as in his dealings with the *res publica*, exhibits ostensible obedience to the rules, and thereby discloses his essential enormity. The thing is monstrous. He even has *tria nomina*, precisely 'Imperator Caesar Augustus'.

As has been demonstrated, in certain branches of the Roman *nobilitas* the *cognomina* tend to pass into *nomina*. 'Caesar' goes the whole way, and the 'Iulius' is discarded, not merely in current use but in official record.

---

[1] Sydenham, 1282 ff.

[2] It occurs sporadically, e.g. *ILS* 151; *IRT* 329.

[3] For the stages and variations, cf. A. Rosenberg, *RE* ix, coll. 1149 f. The first ruler to bear 'Imp. Caes.' as a regular title is Vespasian.

[4] Suetonius, *Tib.* 26, 2 (exaggerated).

'Caesar' is a *gentilicium* in the form 'Imp. Caesar', and so it continues in the names of Augustus' adopted sons, first, from 17 B.C., C. Caesar and L. Caesar, then, from A.D. 4, Ti. Caesar. At the same time, however, the old name of the Julii is not entirely obscured. It is transmitted to freedmen and to persons granted the Roman citizenship; it is retained by the princesses of the Julian line; and, as the dynastic names reveal on the arch at Ticinum (erected in A.D. 7/8),[1] it emerges in the next male generation of the 'domus regnatrix': the sons of Ti. Caesar, the one of his body, the other adopted, are styled 'Drusus Iulius Caesar' and 'Germanicus Iulius Caesar' respectively, and the two sons of Germanicus are also 'Iulii'. Another prince, Agrippa's posthumous son, also belonged now to the *gens Iulia*; but Agrippa Julius Caesar, having been relegated, is not allowed a place on the Ticinum arch.

What Marcus Agrippa himself did with his name is highly instructive. According to the elder Seneca, he deliberately discarded the *gentilicium* 'Vipsanius' because it patently revealed his humble origin.[2] Of the flavour of the name 'Vipsanius' there is no doubt. It had never been known before. There was no Vipsanius even among the municipal adherents of C. Marius or among the Roman knights and financiers of the generation following, let alone in the Senate. The motive assigned by Seneca is sometimes called into question. Needlessly. Octavianus' other marshal of the early days, Salvidienus, seems to have felt a little unhappy about a non-Latin *gentilicium*, and even to have modi|fied its form—at least his coins of 40 B.C. style him 'Q. Salvius imp. cos. desig.'[3] Therefore M. Vipsanius Agrippa is exalted to M. Agrippa. The proud plebeian not only emulates the nobles by employing his *cognomen* as a *gentilicium*, he imposes it, exclusively. 'M. Agrippa' is parallel to 'Imp. Caesar'.

The *gentilicium* of a noble house, being transferable to freedmen and aliens, might approximate by its very vulgarization to the ignobility of a patently plebeian name like 'Vipsanius'. And so, with the rise of the Julii, 'Iulius' goes the way of 'Cornelius'. The Roman knight L. Julius Vestinus, the friend of Claudius Caesar, had a senatorial son, the consul of 65: he drops the 'Julius' and calls himself 'M. Vestinus Atticus'. A common and indistinctive *gentilicium* will elsewhere be inferred where the sources omit it. Thus the enigmatic M. Primus, proconsul of Macedonia in 23 B.C., if his name has been correctly transmitted, is certainly not a *nobilis*, with such a *cognomen*.[4] Conjecture is safer with A. Atticus, an equestrian officer who fell at the Battle of the Mons Graupius: he was probably a Julius Atticus.[5] Finally, M. Aper, the low-born orator from Gaul, from a

[1] *ILS* 107.   [2] Seneca, *Controv.* ii 4, 13. It emerges with females and freedmen.
[3] Sydenham, 1326.   [4] Dio liv 3, 2.
[5] Tacitus, *Agr.* 37, 6. Observe the procurator M. Julius Atticus (*CIL* xii 1854: Vienna), or Julius Atticus, the writer on viticulture, of whom Agricola's father was 'velut discipulus' (Columella i 1, 14).

'civitas minime favorabilis', who plays a leading part in the *Dialogus* of Tacitus, is surely a Julius or a Flavius.[1]

Those examples illustrate and support Seneca's comment on 'Vipsanius'. Agrippa usually got his way. No surviving coins or inscriptions transgress his interdict. The nomenclature of his youngest son (commonly known as Agrippa Postumus) will demonstrate to the full that 'Agrippa' has become a *nomen*; and a further permutation emerges, precisely parallel to the changes enforced upon 'Magnus' by the son of Pompeius Magnus. The infant, before receiving a *praenomen*, carries 'Agrippa' as a *gentilicium*, being 'Pup. Agrippa M. f.';[2] and the boy similarly is 'M. Agrippa M. f.' in 5 B.C.[3] Then, in A.D. 4, he passes into the Julian House, being adopted by Augustus, and the appropriate form of nomenclature ensues, 'Agrippa Iulius Caesar'.[4] The stages are clearly discernible by which 'Agrippa' moves from *cognomen* to *gentilicium*, but reverts to a *praenomen*: such indeed it had been in ancient days.

The tendency of the Roman *praenomen* to lose importance in the last age of the Republic is contradicted only among the *nobiles*; and the practices of the *nobiles* foreshadow the triumphant anomalies of the Caesarian dynasty.

An eccentric *praenomen* like 'Appius' or 'Faustus' can stand by itself. It is therefore not surprising to find that Tacitus employs 'Appius' and 'Mamercus' | in this fashion.[5] The *praenomina* of princes suitably usurp this distinction. The milder form of the licence is when the context, by an indication of relationship, allows the family name to be understood, or when the name 'Caesar' has previously been mentioned. Thus a prose writer like Velleius Paterculus proceeds to speak of 'Gaius' barely; and in Tacitus 'Tiberius' is almost without exception the sole appellation for the emperor Ti. Caesar.

There is a further consequence touching orthography. Peculiar *praenomina* tend to resist abbreviation. In the early Empire as in the late Republic, 'Gaius', 'Lucius', and 'Marcus' are the commonest of all *praenomina*. If they belong, however, to members of the ruling house, they acquire distinction and relief, and so may be written out in full. Thus on the *Res Gestae*: 'filios meos, quos iuvenes mihi eripuit fortuna, Gaium et Lucium Caesares'.[6] Moreover, the common practice of referring to a man by two names only (whether he has two, three, or more) may sometimes, in serious prose, have permitted the writing out in full of the *praenomen*,

---

[1] His *civitas*, *Dial.* 7, 1. The item 'Iulius Aper' occurs in the nomenclature of the polyonymous consul of 169 (*ILS* 1104), grandson of Q. Pompeius Falco (*suff.* 108). But observe the senator Flavius Aper (Pliny, *Ep.* v 13, 5), who looks like an ex-consul, and who is presumably the parent of M. Flavius Aper (*cos.* 130). [Cf. pp. 701 f., below.]

[2] *ILS* 141.   [3] *ILS* 142.   [4] *CIL* x 405.

[5] *Dial.* 21, 7: 'inter Menenios et Appios'; *Ann.* iii 66, 1: 'Mamercus antiqua exempla iaciens'.   [6] *RG* 14.

for emphasis or for variety. This is another, and a larger question. An examination of Tacitus' practice might reveal, not just the whims of transcribers, but devices of orthography expressing stylistic preferences.[1]

To conclude. In spite of the tricks and permutations, the house of the Caesars submits after all to rules of nomenclature. The man of destiny himself, the 'Divi Filius', though portentous and unexampled, is not unexplained: as 'Imp. Caesar Augustus' he owns to 'tria nomina'. The founder of the monarchy at Rome proclaimed that he had restored the 'res publica'. And, truly enough, the fabric is there, 'senatus leges magistratus', and the names, 'eadem magistratuum vocabula'. The genuine and unbroken continuity belongs elsewhere; it is exhibited in the development of dynastic politics, and even in the small matter of nomenclature. The Julii, the dominant faction of the *nobilitas*, are now known as the 'Caesares'. Caesar the Dictator disdained to emulate Sulla Felix and Pompeius Magnus by adopting an ostentatious *cognomen*. Caesar's restraint is impressive. His heir goes far beyond 'Felix' and 'Magnus'. He refurbishes the whole name, in every single member, transmuting 'C. Julius C. f. Caesar' into 'Imp. Caesar Divi f. Augustus'.

The fortune of Caesar and of Caesar's heir was miraculous. Other claimants there were in the *nobilitas*, of ancient fame and pretension, and Fate might have ordained it otherwise. The last Scipio of any consequence in Roman history is that P. Scipio who was adopted by Metellus Pius and who contributed the | double prestige of Scipiones and Metelli to the Pompeian alliance when he gave his daughter Cornelia to Pompeius Magnus in 52 B.C. Metellus Scipio raised proud assertion of family tradition and of military glory, not always adequate, but commemorated for all time by his dying utterance on the stricken field in Africa, 'imperator se bene habet'.[2] On coins he so disposes his titulature as to throw 'Scipio imp.' into relief and emphasis.[3] If the power had gone in the end to one of his line, Rome might have known as her ruler not 'Imp. Caesar Augustus', but 'Imp. Scipio Pius'.[4]

---

[1] Cf. R. Syme, *JRS* xxxviii (1948), 124 f. Some editors have insisted on abbreviating *praenomina* (both normal and abnormal) which the Codex Mediceus gives in full.

[2] Livy, *Per.* cxiv. [3] Sydenham, 1046 ff.

[4] The above is the text of a lecture delivered in the University of Heidelberg in 1952. Annotation has deliberately been kept to a minimum. [On the whole of this subject, cf. now J. Deininger, 'Von der Republik zur Monarchie', *Aufstieg und Niedergang der röm. Welt* i 1 (1972), 982–97.]

30

Consulates in Absence

WHATEVER the devices that operated or the forms and pageantry on public show, access to the consulate was carefully regulated by the Caesars from the beginning. History discloses no sign of any senator reaching the *fasces* against the will and wish of Caesar Augustus. If later writers speak of the ruler as having 'given the consulate', it is an abbreviation rather than a misconception.[1]

Tacitus puts on brief record the principles followed by Tiberius Caesar in the award of honours. He looked to birth, to military excellence, and to distinction in the civilian arts.[2] The formulation will excite no surprise. It corresponded to the tradition of the Republic, when the paramount claim was pedigree, though not always frankly avowed by the *nobiles* or ungrudgingly conceded by outsiders. In comment on Cato, Livy, eschewing pedigree, adduces three types of merit: law, eloquence, and military renown.[3]

The Caesars duly confer the consulate for birth, in its own right; and they promote adherents for loyal service. There is a further development. What had begun as the *provincia* of Caesar Augustus, managed for him by his *legati*, praetorian or consular according to circumstances (and the former predominate at first), evolves into the system and hierarchy of the imperial provinces. By the middle years of Augustus' reign, five consular commands can be discerned, rising at its end to seven. More ex-consuls being needed, *consules suffecti* become a regular feature.

For the senator the consulate retains its inherent value: the goal of a man's career and the entrance of his family into the new nobility of the Empire. For the Emperor, apart from patronage, it serves as a source of consular governors. The urban and magisterial functions decline in importance.

---

[1] Seneca, *De clem.* i 9, 12 (Cinna Magnus); Tacitus, *Ann.* ii 43, 2 (Cn. Piso). Compare, in general terms, *De ira* iii 31, 2: 'dedit mihi praeturam: sed consulatum sperabam. dedit duodecim fasces: sed non fecit ordinarium consulem.'

[2] *Ann.* iv 6, 2: 'mandabatque honores nobilitatem maiorum, claritudinem militiae, inlustres domi artes spectando.'

[3] xxxix 40, 5: 'ad summos honores alios scientia iuris, alios eloquentia, alios gloria militaris provexit.'

Cassius Dio, discussing the Augustan arrangements for the administration of the imperial provinces, comes out with a startling allegation. Consuls and praetors (he affirms) frequently governed provinces during their year of office, and the practice recurred sporadically even in his own day.[1] Dio is not merely guilty of anachronism, as elsewhere in these matters. He is wrong. The new dispensation gave rise to the phenomenon of absent consulates, it is true, but not until a long time elapsed. The process, which touches politics as well as administration, is worth investigating as a whole.

One line leads through the praetorian provinces in the portion of Caesar. They were five in number under Tiberius: the three Gauls, Lusitania, Galatia. Next, with Caligula, the command of the legion III Augusta in Africa, which, though not strictly a province, can for brevity be styled 'Numidia'. Claudius adds Lycia–Pamphylia, an arrangement which after a short intermission (the Lycians liberated by Nero, or better, by Galba) is perpetuated by Vespasian. The Flavian total is eight, Judaea and Cilicia accruing, but Galatia removed to join Cappadocia as a new consular province. Trajan brings the decisive augmentation. They are twelve by the end of his reign, with Arabia, Pannonia Inferior, and Thrace, also Galatia severed from Cappadocia when Armenia was annexed. The total subsists under Hadrian: Dacia, consular in the first epoch after Trajan's conquests, became praetorian, but Judaea was soon elevated to consular status.[2]

The next reign suitably exhibits the system in its regular working. The normal tenure is one of three years, hence on an average four men can hope to reach the *fasces* each year by this avenue of promotion.

The evidence is pretty full. In the period 138–61 five of the praetorian provinces | can show from six to nine governors (Numidia, Dacia, Pannonia Inferior, Thrace, Lycia–Pamphylia).[3] The *Historia Augusta* alleges that Antoninus Pius kept good governors in office for stretches of seven or nine years.[4] That is false. Further, the presupposition is highly vulnerable. Undiscriminating praise for rulers who make a habit of protracting provincial governorships neglects the detrimental consequence which disturbs a routine system of promotion and annoys legitimate aspirations.

[1] liii 14, 2: καὶ πολλοὶ καὶ στρατηγοῦντες καὶ ὑπατεύοντες ἡγεμονίας ἐθνῶν ἔσχον, ὃ καὶ νῦν ἔστιν ὅτε γίγνεται.

[2] Dacia by 120, cf. *CIL* xvi 68; Judaea under Q. Tineius Rufus, the governor when the rebellion broke out in 132 (E. Groag, *RE* vi A, coll. 1376 ff.), for Tineius' consulship is now certified in 127 (*FO* xxvi [= *Inscr. It.* xiii 1, 204–5].)

[3] For the details, see W. Hüttl, *Antoninus Pius* ii (1933). Several items have since accrued

[4] *HA Pius* 5, 3. The notion has been uncritically supported by W. Hüttl, op. cit. i (1936), 329.

The system, brought to perfection under the Antonines, was inaugurated (it appears) by the Flavian rulers. Not abruptly, and not without precedent.

Evidence about the praetorian legates under the Julii and Claudii is scanty, but casual items disclose rapid or direct access to the *fasces*. The eloquent L. Fulcinius Trio, active in the prosecution of Cn. Piso, the governor of Syria, received an admonishment from Tiberius: he must not be too precipitate, Caesar would take care of his advancement.[1] The Emperor kept his word. Fulcinius Trio entered on his consulship on 1 July 31. An inscription shows that he had been governing Lusitania in the month of January.[2] Again, Ser. Sulpicius Galba, who held Aquitania, for about a year only.[3] That post will fall not long before his consulship of 33. Galba's career benefited all through from birth and high favour with the dynasty. The *novus homo* from Patavium, Sex. Papinius Allenius (with no especial services on record), praetor in 27, became *consul ordinarius* in 36 after a praetorian province.[4] That is a prompt advancement.[5] Nor will one omit Q. Veranius who, praetor in 42 or 43, was selected by Claudius Caesar to organize the new province of Lycia–Pamphylia: after a *quinquennium* there, he came back to hold the *fasces* on 1 January 49.[6] Veranius, *quaestor Caesaris* when Tiberius died in 37 and exploiting another change of ruler in 41, when as tribune of the Plebs he managed delicate negotiations between Claudius and the Senate, was likely to prosper in any event from an inherited loyalty to the house of Germanicus: his father had been a legate of Germanicus and was prominent in the prosecution of Cn. Piso.

Few could hope to come near Veranius; but the alert T. Eprius Marcellus seemed to be shaping well. Praetor in 48, he proceeded to Lycia–Pamphylia after no long interval (?53–6).[7] The ensuing prosecution in 57, though abortive, may have held him back, and he did not obtain his consulship until 62, perhaps refurbished in the meantime by a tolerable proconsulate in Cyprus.[8] That province duly paid Eprius homage at the peak of his power and influence when a second change of air (three years in the proconsulate of Asia) brought him to a second consulate in 74.[9]

Not all praetorian governors in this period could be confident of acceding to the *fasces* quickly, or at all. The Flavian dynasty brings a change, and the approach to a more systematic regulation of the *cursus* of

---

[1] *Ann.* iii 19, 1.   [2] *AE* 1953, 88.   [3] Suetonius, *Galba* 6.
[4] *ILS* 945.
[5] Denied in *RE* xviii 2, col. 983. That article exhibits other peculiarities.
[6] Cf. the new inscription (*AE* 1953, 251), published and discussed by A. E. Gordon, *Univ. of Cal. Pub. in Class. Arch.* ii 5 (1952), 231 ff. On his career cf. also E. Birley, *Roman Britain and the Roman Army* (1953), 1 ff.; *PBA* xxxix (1953), 203. It is possible that Veranius left Rome for the East when still praetor.
[7] *Ann.* xiii 33, 3.   [8] *AE* 1956, 186 (Paphos).   [9] *ILS* 992 (Capua).

senators in imperial employ. It has something to do with the evolution of
the legionary command. Under Julii and Claudii a number of legates
continued to be quaestorian. Thus Papinius Allenius and Eprius Marcellus.[1] It is not easy to discover an example once the new system got
going. A type of preferential *cursus* for predestined *viri militares* now
emerges: only two posts after the praetorship, namely the legion and the
province, hence an employment abroad (usually perhaps continuous) of
five or six years.[2] An early consulate may follow, about the age of thirty-
eight. The primordial example is Cn. Julius Agricola (*suff.* 77), who had
been legate of XX Valeria Victrix and governor of Aquitania. Notable
parallels occur in the course of the next thirty years. Others will be surmised, such as L. Fabius Justus (*suff.* 102), the friend of the historian
Cornelius Tacitus.[3] |

If Caesar (or one of the masters of patronage) selects a man for a
praetorian province, it looks like a firm prospect of the consulate, and can
so be described, as when Vespasian appoints Agricola to the governorship of Aquitania.[4] Further, and consequentially, a governor might
become *consul designatus* before he left his province. The earliest instance
on explicit record is L. Octavius Memor, legate of Cilicia in 77 or 78.[5]
The next is A. Larcius Priscus in Numidia, consul suffect in 110.[6]

The system did not yet work smoothly, with a triennial sequence of
governors each uniformly holding the *fasces* about three years later. Certain facts about Lycia–Pamphylia are instructive.[7] As follows:

> – ? 78. Sex. Marcius Priscus (*suff.* ? 79)[8]
> – 80. M. Petronius Umbrinus (81)
> 80 and 81. T. Aurelius Quietus (82 or 83)
> 81. C. Caristanius Fronto (90)
> 85. P. Baebius Italicus (90)

Even later, in the reign of Hadrian, this province fails to show the
desirable and desiderated uniformity. The monument of Opramoas at

---

[1] *ILS* 945; *AE* 1956, 186. [On career patterns from 69 to 138 see now W. Eck,
Aufstieg u. Niedergang ii 1 (1974), 158 ff.]

[2] Cf. *JRS* xliii (1953), 152 f. [= p. 238 above]; xlvii (1957), 133 f. [= *Ten Studies in
Tacitus* (1970), 115 ff.]. Also E. Birley, *JRS* xl (1950), 67.

[3] Cf. *JRS* xlvii (1957), 134 [= *Ten Studies in Tacitus*, 112, 116 f.].

[4] *Agr.* 9, 1: 'provinciae Aquitaniae praeposuit, splendidae imprimis dignitatis administra-
tione ac spe consulatus cui destinarat.'

[5] *IGR* iii 840 (Seleuceia).   [6] *ILS* 1055 (Thamugadi).

[7] For the names and *testimonia* see the latest list, in D. Magie, *Roman Rule in Asia Minor*
(1950), 1598, unfortunately without the consular dates. That scholar missed M. Petronius
Q. f. Umbrinus, who is revealed by an inscription of Attaleia (*Türk Tarih Kurumu Beleten*
xi (1947), 95, no. 12).

[8] [W. Eck, *ZPE* vi (1970), 65 ff., argues that Sex. Marcius Priscus was governor of Lycia
before Vespasian's accession, quite probably under Nero, and left early in Vespasian's reign.
He would put the consulship in 71 or 72.]

Rhodiapolis certifies the order in time of three legates, C. Trebius Maximus, T. Pomponius Antistianus, and C. Valerius Severus:[1] *suffecti* in 122, 121, and 124 respectively. Some scholars even insert into this sequence, after Trebius Maximus, the name of a Calestrius Tiro, attested by an inscription of Cyaneae.[2] For what reason? They are no doubt influenced by the emergence of a T. Calestrius Tiro, consul suffect in 122.[3] The conclusion is not imperative. The governor could perhaps be dissociated from the consul and assigned to a later date.

There is a strong temptation to conjure up praetorian legates to fill gaps in the lists of consuls or permit guesswork about future advancement to consular commands. Various hazards and uncertainties subsist. Though there is a presumption that the governor will proceed to his consulship, mishap, loss of favour, or a natural decease must be allowed for. Domitian's legate of Numidia who destroyed the desert tribe of the Nasamones, Cn. Suellius Flaccus, appears to have missed that honour. He was legate in 87:[4] the consular *Fasti* are complete from 87 to 92. And a splendid mausoleum at Petra was reared for a governor of Arabia who died in office.[5]

Nor were all of the praetorian governorships in equal esteem. Under Hadrian and Pius four of the twelve carried the command of a legion, namely Numidia, Pannonia Inferior, Dacia, and Arabia. Their governors stand in surest prospect of a consular command (of which there were eleven). By contrast, Lycia–Pamphylia. Of thirty-two legates discoverable between 43 and 161, only six are known to have held consular provinces later on.[6]

The value and function of these posts is clear. It is no surprise that in course of time legates should be permitted to continue in office and hold the *fasces* in absence. Several instances can be detected in the reign of Antoninus Pius. The earliest on plain record happens to be explicitly registered by an inscription. The *cursus* of P. Pactumeius Clemens registers him in Cilicia, governor under Hadrian, consul, governor under Pius.[7] Confirmation (where none is needed) shows him consul in June 138, just before the decease of Hadrian.[8]

The procedure, which proclaims the decadence of the supreme magistracy, seems natural and harmless enough. Nothing suggests a sudden

[1] *IGR* iii 739 = *TAM* ii 905.

[2] *IGR* iii 704. Thus E. Kalinka, in *TAM* ii 3 (1944), 349 f.; D. Magie, op. cit. 1599.

[3] *AE* 1942–3, 84 = *CIL* xvi 169. [See now pp. 779 ff. below.]

[4] *AE* 1940, 70 = *IRT* 854.   [5] *CIL* iii 14148[10].

[6] For the names, Magie, op. cit. 1598. Add M. Calpurnius M. f. Rufus under Claudius (*Türk Tarih Kurumu Beleten* xi (1947), 94, no. 10), and M. Petronius Q. f. Umbrinus *c.* 80 (ibid. 95, no. 12).

[7] *ILS* 1067: 'legato eiusdem in Cilicia, / consuli, legato in Cilicia Imp. Antonini Aug.'

[8] *CIL* xvi 84.

innovation, and it will be expedient to look for earlier traces or premonitions. |

After commanding a legion in the First Dacian War, Q. Pompeius Falco (*suff.* 108) proceeded to Lycia–Pamphylia.[1] Presumably in 103, to take the place of Trebonius Mettius Modestus, consul suffect in that year.[2] Then he passed on to Judaea. That is anomalous, and noteworthy.[3] No second tenure of such provinces can be certified earlier than 161. The first plausible instance after Falco may belong to that year or soon after—an anonymous legate governed Cilicia and Galatia.[4]

An emergency in the East may be the reason for Falco's transfer, calling for the employment of an experienced *vir militaris*. In 105–6, Arabia was annexed by the legate of Syria, A. Cornelius Palma. Disturbances may have arisen in Judaea about this time, or a threat from Parthia. However that may be, Falco will have been transferred to Judaea in 105: his predecessor had been C. Julius Quadratus Bassus, also a military man, who assumed the *fasces* on 1 May of that year.[5]

One of the two inscriptions chronicling the *cursus* of Falco exhibits, after his governorship of Judaea, the word 'consularis'.[6] Hence some have supposed that Falco held the province as a consular. That would not pass belief, neither would an absent consulate.[7] Strict proof is needed. It will be safer to assume that the word is only a provincial stonecutter's erroneous expansion of the title 'cos.', which otherwise would be missing.[8] The other inscription betrays no sign that Falco's governorship of Judaea was consular.[9] Further, a letter of Pliny, which might be assigned to the summer or autumn of 108, shows him at Rome.[10] An entry in the *Fasti Ostienses* indicates that Falco [presumably] became consul on 1 September.[11]

Two other praetorian legates under Trajan demand attention, neither exempt from perplexities. After Arabia was annexed, it was garrisoned

[1] *ILS* 1035 (Tarracina); 1036 (Hierapolis–Castabala).
[2] That governor (*IGR* iii 523 = *TAM* ii 134) was consul in 103, cf. the new Ostian fragment, *AE* 1954, 223.
[3] Not noted in *RE* xxi, col. 2270. That article is otherwise defective: for example, it fails to register *CIL* xvi 69, the diploma that shows Platorius Nepos succeeding Pompeius Falco in Britain in 122.
[4] *CIL* iii 254 (Ancyra): 'leg. Augustorum pr. pr. prov. Galat. item prov. Ciliciae'. In this instance, however, the two provinces might have been temporarily joined in a season of crisis.
[5] Cf. the inscription from Pergamum as interpreted by A. v. Premerstein, *SBAW* 1934, Heft 3 [see *PIR*², I 507]. [On Arabia, see G. W. Bowersock, *ZPE* v (1970), 39.]
[6] *ILS* 1036: 'leg. Aug. leg. X Fret. et leg. pr. pr. / [p]rovinciae Iudaeae consularis.'
[7] Cf. E. Groag in *RE* xiii, col. 1883 (when discussing Lusius Quietus). A possible consular governor of Judaea under Trajan is the Atticus of Hegesippus quoted by Eusebius, *Hist. eccl.* iii 32; cf. Groag in *PIR*², A 1338.
[8] Cf. Dessau ad loc.   [9] *ILS* 1035. Nor does *AE* 1957, 336 (Tomi).
[10] *Ep.* ix 15.   [11] [*Inscr. It.* xiii 1, 198–9.]

by a legion, drawn no doubt from the army of Syria.[1] And, as in Judaea, the commander and the governor are one person. The earliest known governor, often presumed the first, is C. Claudius Severus who, as numerous milestones attest, constructed the road 'a finibus Syriae usque ad mare Rubrum'.[2] The stones are dated to the years 111, 112, and 114. Furthermore, the inscription of the north gate at Gerasa, of 115, describes Severus' rank as consular.[3] It therefore seemed safe to identify him with the ']dius Severus' whom the *Fasti Ostienses* produced among the *suffecti* of 112.[4]

So far so good. A new document casts interesting sidelights upon conditions in Arabia after the occupation—and presents certain problems. It is a letter sent by Julius Apollinarius, an Egyptian who had been drafted into the legion at Bostra (*P. Mich.* 466).[5] The writer describes the hardships of military life, among them breaking stones; and he goes on to say that he petitioned Claudius Severus to be appointed his personal secretary, but could only get the position of *librarius* in the legion. He styles the governor as Κλαύδιον Σε[ουῆ]ρ[ο]ν τὸν ὑπατικόν (ll. 25 f.). Further, the same person is alluded to in the phrase ἀπὸ τοῦ ὑπατικοῦ τῆς / λεγεῶνος (ll. 31 f.). These two designations for Claudius Severus are peculiar items that scholars have failed to notice, let alone confront and explain. What can ὁ ὑπατικὸς τῆς λεγεῶνος be assumed to mean? It is duly rendered, to be sure, as 'Latin *consularis*, the commander of the legion';[6] or, for that matter, 'le consulaire | de la légion'.[7] No parallel is adduced from the terminology of the imperial administration, whether Latin or Greek.

That is not the end of the matter. The terminology would be comprehensible after 112, Claudius Severus, legate of a legion and at the same time governor of Arabia, having acquired consular rank in that year. Therefore the document would not belong to the early season of the occupation of Arabia. But the document carries a precise date (corresponding to 26 March) in the tenth year of Trajan: that is to say, in 107.[8] Hence a difficulty. The first impulse might be to question the papyrus reading of the date. But the reading of Trajan's regnal year (it is affirmed) is not in doubt.[9] If then C. Claudius Severus can properly be styled ὑπατικός as early as the year 107, where is the explanation?

It would be no remedy to assume an earlier consulate for Claudius

---

[1] Possibly VI Ferrata, which was there later. For a detailed study of the occupation, C. Préaux, *Phoibos* v (1950–1), 123 ff. [Revised Bowersock, *ZPE* v (1970), 37 ff.]

[2] e.g. *ILS* 5834. They are listed in *PIR*², C 1023.

[3] *AE* 1927, 147 = *SEG* vii 844 = *Gerasa* (1938), 401, nos. 56 f.

[4] *FO* XXII [*Inscr. It.* xiii 1, 200–1], cf. Groag in *PIR*², C 1023; Degrassi, *I Fasti consolari* (1952), 33.

[5] Published by H. C. Youtie and J. G. Winter in *Michigan Papyri* viii (1951).

[6] Thus the editors.   [7] Thus C. Préaux, op. cit. 126.

[8] l. 47: ἔτους ι Τραιανοῦ τοῦ κυρίου Φαμενὼθ λ.

[9] As Professor H. C. Youtie courteously informs me.

Severus, dissociating him from the ']dius Severus' of 112, and conjuring up, for example, an Annidius Severus to fill that place.[1] The rank and seniority of Claudius Severus is conveyed by his position among the consular kinsmen whom Julius Severus of Ancyra parades on his inscription: he comes last, after Julius Quadratus (*suff.* 105), King Alexander (? 107 or 108) and Julius Aquila Polemaeanus (110).[2]

Taking the tenth year of Trajan as a secure and certified date on the papyrus, it would have to be supposed that the Egyptian soldier Julius Apollinarius, though literate and presentable, fell into grave improprieties of title and terminology. Unfamiliar hitherto with either legionary legates or praetorian governors of the senatorial order, he innocently applied the term ὑπατικός to Claudius Severus, the governor of Arabia, who combined both functions. More likely, perhaps, that he dropped a symbol when writing the date.[3]

Without the papyrus (and whatever be the interpretation of its language), Claudius Severus seems adequately confirmed as a praetorian legate who went on after his consulship (as witness the milestones of 114 and the Gerasa inscription of 115).

Next there is L. Acilius Strabo Clodius Nummus, legate of Numidia, attested by three inscriptions.[4] Trajan's entitlement (not yet 'Parthicus'), would point to the early months of 116, but the acclamation, 'imp. XIII', belongs a little later.[5] This governor has been identified with the polyonymous L. Stertinius Quintilianus Acilius Strabo C. Curiatius Maternus Clodius Nummus of an Ephesian inscription: he set it up in honour of his parent, C. Clodius Nummus, who had been quaestor of Asia.[6] The son is presumed to have been adopted by an Acilius Strabo: hence the 'L. Acilius Strabo Clodius Nummus' of the African inscriptions.

Now comes the problem. The *Fasti Potentini* reveal a C. Clodius Nummus, consul suffect in 114;[7] and a later document shows him holding the *fasces* on 19 July of that year.[8]

If the legate of Numidia and the consul are one and the same person, a clear case is established: a praetorian legate consul in absence and going

---

[1] i.e. the consular Annidius Severus (*ILS* 7378), who might be identical with the Adsidius (?) Severus to whom Trajan sent a rescript (*Dig.* xlviii 19, 5); cf. Groag in *PIR²*, A 107 and 625.　　　　　　　　　　　　　　　　　　　　　　　　　　　[2] *OGIS* 544.

[3] [On ὑπατικός as simply = 'governor' (an early instance of this usage to be presumed here), see Bowersock, *ZPE* v (1970), 42. The usage was clearly at first colloquial, as the phrase ὑπατικὸς τῆς λεγεῶνος must in any case be.]

[4] *Inscr. lat. de l'Algérie* 2829 (correcting *ILS* 5958b); 2939b (with the erroneous 'imp. XIIII' for 'imp. XIII'); 2989. Cf. *PIR²*, A 83.

[5] For the vexed chronology of the salutations in 116, see F. A. Lepper, *Trajan's Parthian War* (1948), 44 f.

[6] *CIL* iii 429; cf. Groag in *PIR²*, A 83; C 1175.

[7] *AE* 1949, 23.

[8] For an indication about this unpublished document (a Thracian diploma) I am deeply grateful to H. Nesselhauf and K. Schubring.

on for two full years thereafter.[1] Trajan, when he began the war in the East with the annexation of Armenia in 114, was 'imp. VI'; and 'imp. XIII' is the latest salutation to be registered. An error occurs on one of these African inscriptions, 'imp. XIIII', which is impossible.[2] But even if (as is wholly illegitimate) an error were supposed on all three of the African inscriptions, that is to say 'imp. VIII' being the real date (and the absence of 'Parthicus' tells against 'imp. XIII'), none the less the consulship of L. Acilius Strabo Clodius Nummus would still be an absent one, for the two imperatorial salutations (VII and VIII) cannot have been registered before the summer of 114, still less reported in Africa before Clodius Nummus would have departed to assume his consulship. |

The alternative would be to suppose C. Clodius Nummus (*suff.* 114) a different person from L. Acilius Strabo Clodius Nummus, legate of Numidia in 116. If so, the latter is a potential consul suffect in 117.

However that may be, the next legate on record under Trajan is T. Sabinius Barbarus, in 117.[3] He is attested as consul suffect on 9 July 118.[4] Then a gap, it appears, before P. Metilius Secundus, whom a milestone of 123 certifies as *cos. des.* (i.e. *suffectus* either in 123 or 124).[5] He was present with the *fratres Arvales* in May of 118, but lapses from their proceedings.[6] His legionary command (XI Claudia) and the governorship of Numidia can be confined without discomfort to the ensuing quinquennium.[7]

Given Claudius Severus in Arabia, the prolongation of a legate of Numidia subsequent to his consulship cannot be a strain on belief. Those provinces, along with Judaea and Pannonia Inferior, are in a way exceptional because of their military importance. It is unfortunate that no other evidence of anomalies is to hand. But the war in the East was to produce various irregularities and disturbances.

So far examples have been adduced of a natural development in the praetorian provinces, leading to absent consulates. The practice need not denote any grave emergency. There is another phenomenon, arising in abnormal seasons when an emperor is himself absent from Rome for some time, or, better, has been proclaimed abroad and needs to promote his adherents rapidly, sending them without delay to the consular commands.

The first instance that can be detected is instructive for guidance. It occurs in the early months of 70, when Licinius Mucianus was managing

---

1 As assumed without argument in *Tacitus* (1958), 649. [Thomasson, *Die Statthalter der röm. Provinzen Nordafrikas* (1970) ii 165 f., puts the governorship in 115/6, after the consulate: this has to assume a special mission for a consular.]

2 *Inscr. lat. de l'Algérie* 2939b.   3 *ILS* 9380 f.

4 *CIL* vi 2078.   5 *ILS* 5835. For his *cursus*, *ILS* 1053.   6 *CIL* vi 32374.

7 Cf. Groag in *RE* xv, col. 1404.

Rome and the government for the absent emperor. He sent Q. Petillius
Cerialis to deal with the insurrection in Lower Germany.¹ That task
completed, Cerialis proceeded to the governorship of Britain. He was
now a consular.² From Britain he came back to hold a second consulate
in May 74. No time is available for Cerialis to hold the *fasces* before
going to the Rhine. Epigraphic evidence, a pair of military diplomas,
registers Vespasian and Titus as still the *consules ordinarii* on 7 March 70.³
Cerialis may, or may not, already have been *consul designatus* when he
set forth.⁴

It is a question how long the names of Vespasian and Titus continued
to occupy the consular *Fasti* of this year. An inscription from Rome (not
governmental) employs this dating on 24 May.⁵ Other documents can
be added, though not perhaps cogent: there are tablets of contracts from
Herculaneum of June and also of July.⁶ Both Trajan and Hadrian signalized their first year by eponymates of six months (in 98 and 118). It will
further be observed that no consul is present when the Capitol was dedicated on 21 June. The praetor Helvidius Priscus presided at the ceremony.⁷
Mucianus' second consulate in 70 came next after the eponymous pair.⁸
Now Mucianus, as appears from the narrative of Tacitus, had not yet
gone away to Gaul.⁹

The case of Petillius Cerialis encourages the search for parallels. Vespasian had no compunction about creating new senators after his proclamation by the eastern armies; and quick promotion would beckon to
legionary legates if they happened to be senior *praetorii*. In Judaea Vespasian had three legions with him:¹⁰ V Macedonica under Sex. Vettulenus
Cerialis, X Fretensis under M. Ulpius Traianus, and XV Apollinaris under
Titus (quaestorian). Proceeding to Egypt in the winter of 69–70, he left
Titus to finish the war. Of the legates, Vettulenus stayed on with Titus
and took part in the siege of Jerusalem, Titus' post was occupied by M.
Tittius Frugi, while Traianus had departed: | A. Larcius Lepidus now
commanded X Fretensis, having been brought from the quaestorship of
Crete.¹¹

---

¹ *Hist.* iv 68, 1; 71, 1. Josephus (*BJ* vii 82) is confused, but supports an absent consulate.
² *Agr.* 8, 2.   ³ *CIL* xvi 10 f.
⁴ Cf. the lengthy discussion of Ph. Fabia, *RPh* xxxiv (1910), 5 ff. He thinks that Cerialis
could have been 'adlectus inter consulares' (op. cit. 41). [This is certainly the prima facie
implication of Josephus. But the fact that at some time he held a consulate is shown by the
specification 'consul iterum' in 74 (*CIL* iii, p. 852).]
⁵ *AE* 1915, 100 (Rome), cf. A. E. Gordon, *CP* l (1950), 194 f.
⁶ *AE* 1955, 198.   ⁷ *Hist.* iv 53, 2.
⁸ *FO* xi, as interpreted by J. Morris, *JRS* xliii (1953), 79 [correcting *Inscr. It.* xiii 1, 190–1].
⁹ Cf. *Hist.* iv 68.
¹⁰ For the evidence, which is nowhere in dispute, see E. Ritterling in *RE* xii, under the
different legions.
¹¹ Josephus names the three legionary legates at the fall of Jerusalem (*BJ* vi 237). For
Larcius Lepidus cf. also *ILS* 987.

Where had Traianus gone? His name can be supplied on the *Fasti* as consul immediately after that of Mucianus.[1] But there is no need to suppose that he had to be present in Rome only and precisely for the ceremonial of that office. Traianus might have accompanied Mucianus to Rome, it is true; rather may he be conjectured with Vespasian in Egypt. Perhaps he was not to see the City for many years. There is a chance that Traianus remained in the East to become Vespasian's first legate of Cappadocia–Galatia before acceding to Syria in 73–4.[2]

The Syrian garrison under Mucianus numbered three legions. He took one with him to Europe, VI Ferrata (no legate is named). The second, XII Fulminata, was withdrawn at the beginning of 70 to reinforce Titus' army. From Jerusalem it was sent to Melitene in Cappadocia,[3] where it stayed as part of the garrison of the new province. It had probably departed before the fall of the city—at least no legate is reported at Titus' council on Mount Scopus.[4] The third, IV Scythica, was the legion encamped nearest to Antioch. It happened more than once that the legate took charge of the province when a governor died or departed.[5] Late in 70 Cn. Pompeius Collega suppressed a riot at Antioch: the consular legate, L. Caesennius Paetus (*cos.* 61), had not yet turned up.[6] Collega later became legate of Cappadocia–Galatia, where he is attested in 76:[7] no need, however, to fancy that he was either the first governor or an absent consul.

Another legionary legate will repay scrutiny. T. Aurelius Fulvus had been commander of III Gallica as long ago as 64 under Corbulo.[8] Shortly before the end of Nero's reign he conducted the legion to Moesia; and, repelling a Sarmatian incursion in the winter of 69–70, he was awarded the *ornamenta consularia*, as were the other two legates.[9] This legion took the lead in bringing over the Moesian army to the side of Vespasian.[10] The consular M. Aponius Saturninus being inert or wavering, somebody must have operated with skill and resolution. To the legate Fulvus, the author of the *Historiae* attributes no action (or lack of it) at this juncture. Not that he will have lacked adequate information. It is his way (and an element in his strength) to save up significant details for use at a later point—and T. Aurelius Fulvus, who had a second consulate and the Prefecture of the City, was no doubt to recur in the *Historiae*.[11]

When the Danubian armies invade Italy, another legate is discovered in charge of III Gallica, namely Dillius Aponianus.[12] Various clues lead

---

[1] Cf. J. Morris, *JRS* xliii (1953), 79.   [2] For this conjecture, cf. *Tacitus* (1958), 31.
[3] Josephus, *BJ* vii 18.   [4] Josephus, *BJ* vi 237.
[5] *ILS* 1055 (in 97/8); 8826 (in 132).   [6] Josephus, *BJ* vii 58 f.   [7] *ILS* 8904.
[8] *ILS* 232.   [9] *Hist.* i 79, 5.   [10] *Hist.* ii 85, 1; 96, 1.
[11] *HA Pius* 1, 4. For his second consulate, the eponymate of 85 has been urged by R. Syme, *JRS* xliii (1953), 155 [= p. 243 above]; H. Nesselhauf, *Gnomon* 1954, 270. Against, A. Degrassi, *Athenaeum* xxxiii (1955), 112 ff.   [12] *Hist.* iii 10 f.

from Corbulo's men to Mucianus, Vespasian, and the proclamation: both Mucianus and Ti. Julius Alexander, the Prefect of Egypt, had been with Corbulo in Armenia.[1] Where was Fulvus lurking in the late autumn of 69? He may have gone to join the new ruler, and reinforce his merits.[2] Seniority and presumed services would mark him out for an early consulate, perhaps away from Rome.

No consular governorship of this experienced *vir militaris* stood on record. A recent discovery comes in most welcome. Fragments of *tabellae defixionum* were found in funerary urns unearthed at Emporiae: they carry, among other details, the names of 'Titus Aurelius Fulvus legatus Augusti', of 'Rufus legatus Augusti', and of 'Maturus procurator Augusti.'[3] The quality of the two *legati* seems clear: the governor of Tarraconensis and a praetorian legate.[4] |

It must be asked, how and when did Fulvus come to govern this province? Perhaps for a brief tenure in 70, before his consulate. Tarraconensis lay vacant at this time, after the departure of Cluvius Rufus. Mucianus, among other devices to undermine the influence of Antonius Primus and delude his ambitions, artfully held out the prospect of Tarraconensis.[5] He succeeded—and this consular province may in fact have gone to another ex-legate of a legion, Aurelius Fulvus. The first Vespasianic governor previously attested is Ti. Plautius Silvanus Aelianus (*suff.* 45), who was not there for long, returning in 73 to open the next year as *ordinarius*. He is still in Rome at the dedication of the Capitol in June 70.[6]

A later occasion is not excluded. Fulvus might have governed Tarraconensis *c.* 75–8. That is, between C. Vibius Crispus and Valerius Festus. The former was there at the time of the census in 73–4;[7] the latter had arrived by 79.[8]

Various engaging possibilities ensuing on the proclamation of Vespasian have been indicated. The next crisis to disturb routine and hierarchy is not a little like a proclamation—Nerva's adoption of M. Ulpius Traianus, the legate of Upper Germany, in October 97. Evidence is scanty, but one fact stands out. In 97 or 98 A. Larcius Priscus, quaestor of Asia, arrived in

[1] Pliny, *NH* v 83; Tacitus, *Ann.* xv 28, 3.
[2] Cf. the journey of Tettius Julianus, the quaestorian legate of VII Claudia (*Hist.* ii 85, 2; iv 39, 1; 40, 2).
[3] *AE* 1952, 122.
[4] H. G. Pflaum, cited under *AE* 1952, 122, adduces as a parallel *CIL* ii 2477 = *ILS* 254 (Aquae Flaviae in Callaecia). In that instance the *legatus* named after the governor is the commander of VII Gemina. Now Spain was quickly stripped of its legions by Mucianus (*Hist.* iv 68, 4); and VII Gemina probably did not go there till 74 (*ILS* 2729, cf. 9052; *CIL* xiii 11542). The legate Rufus might be a *iuridicus*: if so, perhaps the earliest discoverable. [But see G. Alföldy, *Fasti Hispanienses* (1969), 14 f., 67 ff., for earlier instances.]
[5] *Hist.* iv 39, 4. [6] *Hist.* iv 53, 2.
[7] *AE* 1939, 60 (the *cursus* of Sex. Attius Suburanus, his *adiutor*).
[8] *ILS* 254. [This view is accepted by G. Alföldy, *Fasti Hispanienses* 20.]

Syria, there to command IV Scythica and act as governor of the province.[1] In the spring of 97 disturbing rumours were current about the attitude and ambitions of the consular legate (a person unfortunately anonymous).[2]

Trajan himself stayed abroad until the latter part of 99. It was a situation likely to exhibit anomalous promotions and even absent consulates. Some of his adherents may have been kept in his company instead of going to Rome for consulships. The retiring governor of Belgica was Glitius Agricola, prominent not long after as legate of Pannonia and consul for the second time.[3] His consulship falls in 97, presumably in the summer.[4] The chance that he remained in Belgica might perhaps be canvassed.

Intricate problems beset the great Licinius Sura, to whom a late epitomator assigns a notable role in the elevation of Trajan.[5] If he was consul in 97, not in 93 (the only two years available), an absent consulship becomes possible.[6] His could have been a brief tenure in the last two months, even the last month, of the year. Nothing can yet be advanced with any confidence about his whereabouts and occupations in this year. However that may be, an abbreviation of the normal intervals can reasonably be postulated for some of the legionary legates and praetorian governors in the period 97–100.[7]

Trajan not only increased the number of the praetorian provinces from eight to twelve. He permitted an exceptional tenure for the first governor of Arabia (several years as praetorian, three as consular). Further, a legate of Numidia appears to have been prolonged for two years. The Emperor's absence (from the autumn of 113) and the Parthian campaigns might be expected to produce anomalies of various kinds.

Among those who perished in the great earthquake at Antioch was Πέδων ὁ ὕπατος, according to Dio.[8] That is, M. Pedo Vergilianus, *ordinarius* in 115. This item naturally comes into the long disputations about the date of the catastrophe. Not to any conclusion. Some scholars argue that Pedo met his death within the strict limits of his consulship, i.e. in January or February of 115. That argument depends on an over-literal (and at the same time superficial) interpretation of the phrase used by Dio. A *consul*

---

[1] Cf. his *cursus*, ILS 1055; AE 1908, 237 (Thamugadi). To the same occasion may belong C. Julius Proculus, anomalously *tr. mil.* of IV Scythica after his quaestorship (ILS 1040): i.e. the deputy of Larcius Priscus; cf. a presumed parallel in 70 (ILS 1000).

[2] Pliny, *Ep.* ix 13, 10 f. [G. Alföldy and H. Halfmann (*Chiron* iii (1973), 361 ff.) argue that it was M. Cornelius Nigrinus Curiatius Maternus.]   [3] ILS 1021; 1021a.

[4] Cf. the new fragment of the *Fasti Ostienses*, AE 1954, 220.

[5] Ps.-Victor, *Epit.* 13, 6.

[6] Groag, adducing for Sura the acephalous *elogium*, ILS 1022, suggested that he might have been the successor of Glitius Agricola in Belgica—and consul in absence (RE xiii, coll. 475 f.). [Against this, see C. P. Jones, JRS lx (1970), 98 ff., arguing that the *elogium* is that of Sosius Senecio.]

[7] Cf. JRS xlvii (1957), 134 [= *Ten Studies in Tacitus* (1970), 116 f.].

[8] lxviii 25, 1.

ordinarius is the consul of the year, distinctive and eponymous. Dio's title implies nothing more. Hence no argument against December of 115 as the date of the earthquake.[1] |

Rome could have spared without loss or repining a consul to convey the eager homage of a loyal Senate, but it might not suit the Emperor to send back for obsolete ceremonial a praetorian legate with signal exploits in the field. D. Terentius Gentianus (the son of Scaurianus, Trajan's first governor of Dacia) reached the consulate before he was thirty.[2] After his praetorship he had held one post only, that of *legatus Augusti*: that is, not a provincial governor but legate of a legion or commander of an army corps. The narrative of the campaigns (partial perhaps as well as fragmentary) nowhere discloses his name. The *Fasti Ostienses* show him consul suffect in the summer of 116.[3] Did the Imperator allow this man to slip away and go back to Italy?

Energetic generals were sorely needed in the course of this year. Mesopotamia rebelled in the rear of the Imperator, the Parthians came back, and a consular commander, a certain Maximus, fell in battle. Seleuceia, the great city, was recaptured by two legates, Erucius Clarus and Julius Alexander.[4] They can be identified as the consular pair 'Clarus et Alexander' of the next year.[5] Either or both might have remained with Trajan.

Lusius Quietus the Moor played a notable part in quelling the insurrection. According to Dio, Trajan enrolled him among the *praetorii*, gave him the consulate, and appointed him to govern Judaea.[6] Trajan's successor promptly dismissed Lusius from that command.[7] The consulate of Lusius has to be assigned to 117 (the *Fasti Ostienses* have the list complete for 116). Urbs Roma was spared the spectacle of a native chieftain flaunting the *insignia* of the supreme magistracy.[8]

Not all of Trajan's generals, young or old, enjoyed the friendship of Hadrian or were able to win his confidence. It stands on record that he later conceived a dislike for Terentius Gentianus.[9] Nothing indicates that Gentianus, or Erucius Clarus or Julius Alexander, for all their military excellence, obtained military provinces from Hadrian.

The sudden death of Trajan put Hadrian in a difficult position. His own friends had already been coming to the front, but he now had to find the

[1] Cf. F. A. Lepper, op. cit. 87. It may be noted that that scholar is extremely reluctant to concede absentee consuls (op. cit. 85 f.).

[2] *ILS* 1046a (inscribed by his sister on a pyramid in Egypt); 1046 (Sarmizegetusa), his *cursus*.

[3] [*Inscr. It.* xiii 1, 202–3.]   [4] Dio lxviii 30, 2.

[5] Mommsen, *Chron. min.* i 255.

[6] Dio lxviii 32, 5. Cf. Groag, *RE* xiii, coll. 1881 ff. Lusius may have been in Judaea before his elevation to the consulate. It hardly matters.

[7] *HA Hadr.* 5, 8.   [8] [Accepted *PIR²*, L 439.]   [9] *HA Hadr.* 23, 5.

men to govern eleven consular provinces. Quick transfers and promotions can be surmised—and once again, perhaps, men whom the new ruler wished to have in his company or send to the various armies without passing through the capital.

A brief word might go to Bruttius Praesens, whose life and career exhibits so many paradoxes.[1] He was governor of Cilicia when Trajan died at Selinus in the early days of August, 117. Bruttius will not have had to wait long for the *fasces*. He governed Cappadocia and Moesia Inferior, but there is no sign that those posts fall at the very beginning of Hadrian's reign.[2] It may be presumed, however, that Platorius Nepos went quickly to Germania Inferior. He had been governing Thrace.[3] His consulate falls early in 119—possibly in absence.

When Hadrian reached Rome in July of 118, his position was awkward and hazardous. Four of his enemies (real or fancied) among the marshals of Trajan had been destroyed for treason, the Senate ratifying their execution. Further, it was not any emergency of frontier warfare or the decease of a consular legate in Dacia (Julius Quadratus Bassus), but high politics and a ruler's insecurity that produced a great Danubian command for a Roman knight, Marcius Turbo. The full record of governors from 115 to 120 would be variously instructive.[4]

[1] His *cursus* has been revealed by *AE* 1950, 66 (Mactar) and *IRT* 545 (Lepcis), the latter acephalous. For commentary, G. Ch. Picard, *Revue africaine* xciv (1950), 25 ff.; G. Ch. Picard and H. G. Pflaum, *Karthago* ii (1951), 91 ff. [See pp. 489 ff. below.]

[2] Precisely when, it is a question. However, since *AE* 1950, 66 has Cappadocia before Moesia Inferior and links it to Moesia Inferior by the word 'item', the sequence in time ought to be clear. The reverse order is postulated in *Karthago* ii (1951), 97. [See *Dacia* xii (1968), 335 = *Danubian Papers* (1972), 218 f. for suggested dates.]

[3] *ILS* 1052.

[4] Cf. *Tacitus* (1958), 243 ff. One purpose of the present paper is to explain and support the brief allusions to absent consulates in that book (op. cit. 252, 641, 649). Reasons of space (and the author's perplexity about *P. Michigan* 466) forbade a discussion of Claudius Severus, the legate of Arabia (above, pp. 384 f.). [On Marcius Turbo see pp. 541 ff. below.]

For advice and help I am much indebted to Mr. E. W. Gray and Mr. F. A. Lepper.

3 1

Sabinus the Muleteer

THE tenth poem of the collection of Virgilian *Catalepton* parodies Catullus' 'Phaselus ille'. It describes the career of a muleteer active on the roads of the Cisalpina, especially in the parts beyond the Po:

> Sabinus ille, quem videtis, hospites,
> ait fuisse mulio celerrimus (1 f.).

The man has changed his *cognomen*:

> iste post Sabinus ante Quinctio (8).

He has also changed his condition:

> sed haec prius fuere: nunc eburnea
> sedetque sede seque dedicat tibi,
> gemelle Castor et gemelle Castoris (24 ff.).

The interpretation of the last three lines is difficult. The simplest view is the following. Sabinus the ex-muleteer has become a magistrate, he sits upon an ivory chair. What kind of magistrate, municipal or Roman? Hardly the former: most scholars understand the latter, taking 'eburnea sede' to refer, very precisely, to the *sella curulis* of a magistrate of the Roman People, namely curule aedile, praetor, or consul. Further, he had dedicated to Castor and Pollux a sculptured relief showing himself arrayed in the *insignia* of his office, which image the strangers are invited to contemplate.

That is not all. A historical problem is involved. In the sixteenth century the scholar Victorius identified the muleteer Sabinus with P. Ventidius (praetor and consul in 43 B.C.), the proverbial upstart of the revolutionary period. At first sight the theory is seductive. Most scholars and historians have accepted it.[1] And it is suitably | consecrated in manuals

---

[1] Thus T. Frank, 'Virgil's Apprenticeship II', *CP* xv (1920), 107 ff., esp. 116 f.; E. Fraenkel, 'Vergil und Cicero', *Mem. r. Acc. Virg. di Mantova*, N.S. xix–xx (1926/7), 219; F. Münzer, *RE* i A, coll. 1592 ff.; K. Büchner, ibid. viii A, col. 1082. Observe, however, that H. Gundel in the article on Ventidius does not go further than 'vielleicht' (ibid. col. 798).

---

of Latin literature. Ventidius was called a muleteer by Cicero and by Plancus.[1] Also, popular verses are preserved, acclaiming his consulate:

> concurrite omnes augures, haruspices!
> portentum inusitatum conflatum est recens.
> nam mulas qui fricabat, consul factus est.[2]

Surely there could not have been a pair of such portents.

Further, a connecting link was discovered between Sabinus, the muleteer of the poem, and the notorious P. Ventidius. Cicero, writing to the Caesarian C. Trebonius, says that he has given a copy of his *Orator* to Trebonius' friend Sabinus, who appears to be an honest man, judging by his *cognomen*—but one never knows, for he may have assumed it, in the fashion of candidates for office. The passage must be quoted: 'Oratorem meum—sic enim inscripsi—Sabino tuo commendavi: natio me hominis impulit ut ei recte putarem: nisi forte candidatorum licentia hic quoque usus hoc subito cognomen arripuit; etsi modestus eius vultus sermoque constans habere quiddam a Curibus videbatur. Sed de Sabino satis'.[3]

In the first place, the dating of the letter. Some placed it in 44 B.C. But Mommsen and Sternkopf independently established the true date beyond dispute, in 46 B.C. or early in 45.[4] Sternkopf did not concern himself with Sabinus. Mommsen, however, following Bücheler, identified him with Sabinus the muleteer of *Catalepton* x.[5] Given the date of the letter, said Mommsen, he must be regarded as a candidate for the quaestorship in 46 B.C. The poem, however, interpreted precisely, refers to a *sella curulis*. A quaestor had no right to it. Therefore the poem should attest praetorship or consulate. P. Ventidius the muleteer, identified with Sabinus | of like profession, was presumably a candidate in 44 B.C. for the praetorship of the next year. It follows that the poem was written in 44 or 43 B.C.

So far the construction, strained and artificial. It has not escaped criticism. Birt, Merrill, and Rostagni all dissented;[6] and Zimmermann dismissed the attribution of *Catalepton* x to P. Ventidius as 'ganz unmöglich': he deprecated conjecture in this matter.[7]

Now the link which connects the Sabinus of the poem with the his-

---

[1] Cicero, quoted by Pliny, *NH* vii 135: 'mulionem castrensis furnariae'; *Ad fam.* x 18, 3 (Plancus): 'Ventidiique mulionis castra despicio'.
[2] Gellius, *NA* xv 4, 3.   [3] *Ad fam.* xv 20, 1.
[4] Mommsen, 'Zur Gesch. der Caesarischen Zeit. II. Ciceros erster Brief an Trebonius', *Ges. Schriften* iv 174 ff.; W. Sternkopf, 'Über zwei Briefe Ciceros an C. Trebonius', *Jahrbücher für cl. Philologie* cxlvii (1893), 424 ff. Tyrrell and Purser, while admitting the justice of their arguments, none the less retain the letter at the beginning of 44 B.C.
[5] Mommsen, op. cit. 174 ff.; F. Bücheler, 'Catalepton', *RhM* xxxviii (1883), 507 ff., esp. 518 f.
[6] Th. Birt, *Jugendverse u. Heimatpoesie Vergils*, 114 ff.; E. T. Merrill, 'On Cic. *Fam.* xv. 20', *CP* viii (1913), 389 ff.; 'Ventidius and Sabinus', *CP* xv (1920), 298 ff.; A. Rostagni, *Virgilio minore* (1933), 39.
[7] F. Zimmermann, 'Vergil u. Catull', *Phil. Woch.* 1932, 119 ff.

torical 'muleteer' P. Ventidius is really very fragile. In the poem, the muleteer Quinctio changes his *cognomen* to Sabinus. But Cicero does not accuse Trebonius' friend precisely and literally of changing his *cognomen*. Cicero is writing in a frivolous vein, playing with the supposition that Trebonius' friend may not be a genuine 'Sabinus'. His words have been taken to prove that Sabinus was a candidate for office—'nisi forte candidatorum licentia hic quoque usus hoc subito cognomen arripuit'. But the words could suggest the contrary—'hic quoque'. In fact, Cicero's joke depends on the pretence that Sabinus is a complete stranger to him, that his credentials might be dubious. What is the 'candidatorum licentia' to which Cicero refers? Perhaps a general practice of candidates.[1] Yet it may be rather something very definite indeed, the assumption precisely of the *cognomen* 'Sabinus' to lend respectability to some dubious character—'hoc cognomen'. The Sabines were proverbial for virtue and antique gravity.

The link snaps. No valid reason subsists for discovering in Trebonius' friend either the muleteer 'Sabinus ante Quinctio' or P. | Ventidius. As for Ventidius, most works of history or literature, by a modern convention, describe him as 'Ventidius Bassus'. It may be observed that no contemporary or official source gives him any *cognomen* at all, not Cicero in his *Letters*, not the *Fasti* or the *Acta Triumphalia*. If he had a *cognomen* at all, which could be doubted, it was 'Bassus'. But only three writers, Gellius, Eutropius, and Rufius Festus, mention 'Bassus'.[2] The latter two probably derive from Suetonius, who was a careful scholar; and Gellius refers to Suetonius in his account of Ventidius.[3] So 'Bassus' may be right. If so, then on the accepted theory Ventidius is truly remarkable, being Quinctio, Sabinus, and Bassus in turn. He usurps the name 'Sabinus', redolent of ancient virtue, only to discard it.

Ventidius was Picentine by origin. Two reputable authorities say so.[4] The muleteer of *Catalepton* x appears to be Cisalpine,

> Cremona frigida et lutosa Gallia
> tibi haec fuisse et esse cognitissima
> ait Sabinus: ultima ex origine
> tua stetisse dicit in voragine. (12 ff.)

[1] So Tyrrell and Purser, but the examples they provide are merely L. Antonius Pietas and L. Trebellius Fides (if we believe Cicero, *Phil.* vi 11). These are special cases. Münzer, *RE* i A, col. 1593, discusses the matter more fully, referring to 'Thurinus' as a famous instance of a *cognomen* which was taken for a time and then dropped (Suetonius, *Divus Aug.* 7, 1). On the change of *cognomen*, compare Dessau, 'Der Name des Apostels Paulus', *Hermes* xlv (1910), 347 ff., esp. 356 ff. He adduces the case of the freedman L. Crassicius, who altered his *cognomen* from Pasicles to Pansa (Suetonius, *De gramm.* 18).

[2] Gellius, *NA* xv 4, 2; Eutropius vii 5, 1; Rufius Festus, *Brev.* xviii 2. Eutropius calls him 'L. Ventidius Bassus'.

[3] Gellius, *NA* xv 4, 4.

[4] Gellius, *NA* xv 4, 2: 'eum Picentem fuisse genere et loco humili'; Dio xliii 51, 4: οὗτος γὰρ τὸ μὲν ἀρχαῖον ἐκ τοῦ Πικήνου ὥσπερ εἴρηταί μοι ἦν.

But that point perhaps need not be pressed. The words 'ultima ex origine' are taken over unchanged from the original of the parody.[1]

Everybody knows that P. Ventidius had been a muleteer. In antiquity he was the prime example of the *novus homo* who had risen fast and gone furthest. But his prominence is not due solely to the contrast between the profession he had followed and the curule office to which he attained. Ventidius embodies a more startling paradox—a captive led in a Roman triumph by his enemies, yet surviving to celebrate a triumph himself, the first from Parthia—and the last for two whole centuries. 'Infra Ventidium deiectus Oriens.'[2] |

The fame of Ventidius has eclipsed all other muleteers. In the formidable company of low-born praetors and consuls of the revolutionary age, Picentine, Umbrian, Lucanian, or of no known origin at all, was Ventidius the solitary recipient of that opprobrious label? It remains to investigate the meaning of the word 'mulio'.

As Gellius records, Ventidius made his living by supplying under contract animals and vehicles for provincial governors.[3] Caesar got to know him, took him to the Gallic provinces and used his services; and Ventidius entered the Senate by holding the tribunate of the plebs. That is to say, Ventidius had been a *publicanus*. Not a reputable profession—but not a bad beginning. P. Rupilius (*cos.* 132 B.C.) is said to have been a *publicanus* in Sicily: he owed his rise to the patronage of Scipio Aemilianus.[4] That the term 'mulio' does not have to be taken literally is shown by a casual and precious item from a later age. When T. Flavius Vespasianus, a senator of consular rank, went in for transport operations, men called him in derision a 'mulio'.[5]

So much for the sordid occupation of P. Ventidius. His town of origin is not certified. Perhaps the rebel Picentine city of Asculum, where he was captured as an infant. Auximum, it is true, a town in the same region, owned to Ventidii of some local repute in this period.[6] But they are best left out of account, for Auximum was a Roman colony. As for his parentage, there is a chance that a P. Ventidius was among the insurgent

---

[1] Cf. Münzer, *RE* i A, col. 1594. The champions of Ventidius are compelled to make this concession—unless they just ignore the difficulty altogether.   [2] Tacitus, *Germ.* 37, 4.

[3] Gellius, *NA* xv 4, 3: 'post, cum adolevisset, victum sibi aegre quaesisse eumque sordide invenisse comparandis mulis et vehiculis, quae magistratibus, qui sortiti provincias forent, praebenda publice conduxisset, in isto quaestu notum esse coepisse C. Caesari et cum eo profectum esse in Gallias.' If these words are strictly interpreted, it might be argued that Ventidius' earliest activities as a muleteer were somewhere else than in the Gallic provinces. Picenum, or on the Flaminia?   [4] Valerius Maximus vi 9, 8; Cicero, *Laelius* 73.

[5] Suetonius, *Divus Vesp.* 4, 3: 'rediit certe nihilo opulentior, ut qui prope labefactata iam fide omnia praedia fratri obligarit necessarioque ad mangonicos quaestus sustinendae dignitatis causa descenderit; propter quod vulgo *mulio* vocabatur.'

[6] Plutarch, *Pompeius* 6. Noted in *Rom. Rev.* (1939), 92. The manuscripts, however, give better support for another name. Therefore perhaps Vettidii rather than Ventidii; cf. K. Ziegler in his edition; H. Gundel, *RE* viii A, col. 793.

generals in the *Bellum Ita|licum*: it depends upon the reading adopted in the text of Appian.[1] Various defeated causes turned for succour and revenge to the *clientela* of Caesar.[2] Italia is there represented as well as the municipal adherents of Marius and Cinna. Ventidius, like other persons whom the social terminology of Roman politics brands as disgusting upstarts, may well come of an office-holding family in his own place. In short, of the class of 'domi nobiles'. When Ventidius marched against the Parthians he had with him as quaestor or legate a certain Poppaedius Silo.[3] Surely a descendant of the great Marsian of that name, the consul of federal Italia.[4]

The noble houses that fought for Italia against Rome suffered heavily from their defeat. Some individuals may have deserted the lost cause, like Statius the Samnite;[5] and some families may have retained estates and social standing—Pollio, the grandson of the Marrucine general Herius Asinius, acquired the best education that Rome could give. But others were despoiled and degraded, driven beyond the seas to Spain.[6] Others again forced to the ultimate indignity of mercantile pursuits. Vettius Scato was a Marsian leader who fell in battle. Thirty years later there may be discovered among the adherents of P. Clodius an impoverished Marsian who bore the historic name of Vettius Scato: he seems to have adopted the profession of house-agent.[7]

The greater part of warfare is movement and supply. Caesar discovered and promoted the army-contractor Ventidius, who became a general of splendid talent. By a swift march after the campaign of Mutina he saved Antonius from destruction; and he was more than a match for the mobile Parthians. Ventidius is not the only example of business capacity applied to warfare. In 46 B.C. a cer|tain Rabirius Postumus is found organizing supply for the army that invaded Africa.[8] Rabirius, newly elevated to senatorial rank, had been a prince of the *publicani*, controlling for a time the finances of the kingdom of Egypt and equipping fleets on his own account.

Nor should the equestrian officers of the Roman army be neglected, *praefecti* in command of cavalry and, above all, the *praefectus fabrum*, who was a kind of chief of staff to the provincial governor. *Praefecti* were often

---

[1] Appian, *BC* i 47, 204. Viereck reads Πόπλιος Οὐέττιος, that is, P. Vettius Scato, the Marsian leader. But there is a case for Πόπλιος Οὐεντίδιος; cf. H. Gundel, *RE* viii A, col. 795.

[2] *PBSR* xiv (1938), 18 ff. [= pp. 105 ff. above]; *Rom. Rev.* (1939), 86 ff.

[3] Dio xlviii 41, 1. Not in *MRR*.   [4] As suggested in *PBSR* xiv (1938), 21.

[5] Appian, *BC* iv 25, 102.

[6] L. Decidius Saxa (*tr. pl.* 44 B.C.), the alleged 'Celtiberian', may belong to such a family. Cf. *JRS* xxvii (1937), 127 ff. [= pp. 31 ff. above.]. Observe Cn. Dec(id)ius the proscribed Samnite (*Pro Cluentio* 161, cf. Tacitus, *Dial.* 21, 6).

[7] Cicero, *De domo sua* 116. Presumably the same person as the 'Vettius manceps' of *Ad Att.* vi 1, 15; cf. iv 5, 2.

[8] *Bell. Afr.* 8, 1; 26, 3.

men of great ability and long service.¹ The Civil Wars set a high standard in warfare: a natural result is the emergence of knights. Salvidienus, of obscure origin and alien *gentilicium*, won the *Bellum Perusinum* for Caesar's heir; it might be conjectured that he had been an equestrian officer in the armies of Caesar. Cornelius Gallus' first known military command is of high rank and high renown—he led an army of Roman legions to the invasion of Egypt in 30 B.C. Gallus was a Roman knight from the province of Narbonensis, of native dynastic stock, not an immigrant.²

Now there was a certain C. Calvisius Sabinus, of no small notoriety.³ He first turns up commanding a mobile column under Caesar in 48 B.C. He may easily have begun as a contractor of supplies or an equestrian officer. His earliest known magistracy is the praetorship (presumably in 46 B.C.).⁴ Calvisius rose high, consul in 39, a *vir triumphalis*, and standing not far behind Statilius Taurus among the marshals of Caesar's heir. Taurus in fact first emerges on record in the company of Calvisius in 43 B.C. (perhaps one of his legates). According to Cicero, they form a single and composite monster, a Minotaurus.⁵

Calvisius' origin is nowhere stated. It can be conjectured that he came from the Latin colony of Spoletium. An inscription found there commemorates the *pietas* of one of the consular Calvisii.⁶ Clearly | this man's —and a reference to the Ides of March, when Calvisius along with one other senator (L. Marcius Censorinus) made a vain attempt to protect the Dictator.⁷

The class and type of C. Calvisius Sabinus is clear—a Caesarian *novus homo* of municipal stock who becomes praetor. Calvisius, it appears, was praetor in 46 B.C. Cicero, writing in that year, playfully admits the possibility that Trebonius' friend Sabinus may bear an assumed *cognomen*, that he may have imitated a practice of candidates at elections.⁸ Now Trebonius' friend himself need not here be regarded as such a candidate. The language of Cicero is perhaps against that interpretation. Nor is there any call to identify him with C. Calvisius Sabinus, though it might be so; the *cognomen* is of the commonest. But it will be relevant to observe that a *novus homo* called Sabinus did become praetor in that year. Not that this

¹ *Rom. Rev.* (1939), 70 f.; 355 f.
² Cf. the arguments adduced in *CQ* xxxii (1938), 39 ff. [= pp. 47 ff. above].
³ *PIR²*, C 352.   ⁴ *MRR* ii 295.
⁵ *Ad fam.* xii 25, 1: 'magna senatus approbatio consecuta est cum summo gaudio et offensione Minotauri, id est Calvisi et Tauri.' The term can have seemed appropriate. To a Roman, the word 'Sabinus' connoted implacable severity; and Minos was the grim judge of the dead.
⁶ *CIL* xi 4772 = *ILS* 925.
⁷ Nicolaus, *Vita Caesaris* 26, 96; cf. *Rom. Rev.* (1939), 221. That disproved the general assumption that the Spoletine inscription belongs to the consul of 4 B.C. (*PIR²*, C 353). In any case the lettering tells for an earlier date (autopsy, briefly reported in *CP* l (1955), 134, reviewing *MRR*).
⁸ *Ad fam.* xv 20, 1; cf. above.

is necessary, either for the interpretation of the letter—or for any other purpose.

Nobody, it is true, calls Calvisius Sabinus a 'mulio'. Yet Ventidius may not have been the only Caesarian military man whose activities incurred that appellation. Nor, indeed, could one ever hope to prove that Calvisius is the muleteer Sabinus of *Catalepton* x. There were long roads in Cisalpina, many muleteers, and frequent calls for transport when Caesar governed the Gallic provinces. But Ventidius is in a worse case than Calvisius. The muleteer of the poem is precisely denominated as 'Sabinus ille': there is no evidence that P. Ventidius bore the *cognomen* 'Sabinus'.[1]

[1] It would be a tricky expedient to argue that the author of *Catalepton* x, wishing to make a mock of P. Ventidius, called him 'Sabinus' in order to escape reprisals: the poet might fall foul of a *novus homo* no less formidable than Ventidius, namely C. Calvisius Sabinus.

32

Livy and Augustus

THE historian Livy led a quiet and regular existence. Not much material for a biographer, and no temptation for research or invention. Though Livy was a classic in his own lifetime, he escaped the fate of Virgil, whose writings became a prey to scholarly exegesis and were diligently scrutinized in the search for clues and allusions. That is all to the good. None the less, various questions have to be asked if an attempt is made to approach the author as a person, not merely as a classical text, to appraise his design and purpose without being content to exploit what survives of his writings as a repertory of fact or fable, as an excuse for erudite investigation into historical sources and lost historians. The questions concern Livy's origin and time of life, his education, character, and pursuits.

An estimate of the historical qualities of Livy is impaired by the hazard that has transmitted only a quarter of his great work. What has survived is singularly vulnerable to criticism. In the first Decade the author takes leave of legend only to plunge into fiction. Aware of his plight, he has no principle or method to guide him—and none was available. Later, arriving at a period which offered a reliable and contemporary record, he must submit to confrontation, for accuracy and insight, with the formidable Polybius.

Livy has been doubly unfortunate in what chance preserves. The Roman found consolation in ancient annals, and repose from the recent era of tribulation. But, as he says in his *Praefatio*, he was intending to go on and narrate the history of his own time. Livy enjoyed length of days, and was able to complete an enormous task in one hundred and forty-two books. He went on after the war of Actium and the triumph of Caesar's heir, terminating the work at 9 B.C. A friendly view of what lies within the scope and power of a historian might suppose the later books to be Livy's prime achievement. He cannot be judged by it. Tacitus was more lucky. Apart from his annals of Rome under Julii and Claudii, the arbiters of praise and blame may appeal, if they so wish, to | the *Historiae* in which Tacitus narrated events within his own time and knowledge.

Born in 59 B.C. and living until A.D. 17 (on the standard and conven-

Harvard Studies in Classical Philology lxiv (1959), 27–87. Reprinted by permission of the President and Fellows of Harvard College. Copyright Harvard University Press 1959.

tional assumption), Livy was closely coeval with Caesar Augustus. The historian is the shining glory of Augustan prose, and its solitary survivor (if one omits a technical writer like Vitruvius, or the declaimers of whose performance the elder Seneca transmits a number of samples). Style or sentiment, how far can Livy be regarded as typical, and a safe guide to anything? Livy's picture of the Roman past is patently schematic and wildly anachronistic, not to say fraudulent. Some take it to reflect the Augustan colour and atmosphere, with Livy as a perfect embodiment of the ideals prevalent or advertised in that epoch, comparable to what Virgil and Horace disclose. Hesitations might be felt. The beliefs about religion, patriotism, and morality discoverable or subsumed in the writings of Livy may have an earlier origin. Livy was a grown man long before the new dispensation came into force. And indeed, what is meant by 'Augustan'?

That is a large problem, and important. The present inquiry is restricted in scope. It will put three questions. First, Livy's plan, with consequent remarks about the chronology of his life and the rhythm of his operations. Secondly, how early did Livy make a beginning? (That touches 'Augustan' influences or tendencies.) Thirdly, how did he manage the history of his own time, and especially the reign of Caesar Augustus?

I. *The Plan and Structure*

Livy dominated subsequent historians—at least for the period of the Republic. Hence something can be discovered. For the last generation of the Republic and the time of Caesar, the use of Livy by Cassius Dio can be presumed—and proved. But the indications of such use grow slighter and slighter, to vanish after the Battle of Actium.[1] For the rest, various scraps and vestiges in late compilers.

The investigation of the stages by which such Livian material was transmitted to those writers is an intricate and controversial pursuit.[2] At one time it was the fashion to refer almost everything to a single *Epitome* of Livy, composed as early as the reign of Tiberius. Some recent studies have attempted to invalidate that theory. Klotz argued that certain items supposed to be Livian really come from collections of *Exempla*, deriving from sources employed by Livy; and, instead of invoking an original *Epitome*, he suggested that from time to time | different lists of contents, separated from the parent work, passed into independent circulation.[3] In his latest formulation, Klotz spoke of such summaries enlarged to form

---

[1] E. Schwartz, *RE* iii, col. 1698; M. A. Levi, *Il tempo di Augusto* (1951), 415 ff.
[2] See, e.g., O. Rossbach in his edition of the *Periochae* (Teubner, 1910); A. Klotz, *RE* iii, coll. 823 ff.; M. Galdi, *L'epitome nella letteratura latina* (1920).
[3] *Hermes* xliv (1909), 198 ff.; xlviii (1913), 542 ff.; *RE* xiii, coll. 823 ff.

an elementary manual of Roman history.¹ However that may be, the
existence of a genuine *Epitome* can be established beyond doubt. It was
used, for example, by Florus and by Orosius in their detailed and more or
less concordant accounts of Augustus' Cantabrian campaign of 26 B.C.²

One list of contents in fact survives, the *Periochae*, as they are called.
A production of limited utility, based on an *Epitome*. The editor had his
idiosyncrasies in the choice and arrangement of his material. The summaries can vary in length from three lines to over thirty. Nor does he
always keep to the strict order of events in individual books, but often
appends a brief comment on the contents of a book, as though by an
afterthought, using the phrase 'praeterea . . . continet'. The triumph of
Pompeius Magnus (September 61 B.C.) is put after Caesar's first campaign in Gaul, at the end of Book ciii. Livy cannot have postdated such a
striking event by three years. Again, at the end of Book cxxxiii, after
Octavianus' triumph (29 B.C.), comes the conspiracy of the young Lepidus, which occurred in the previous year. The *Periocha* of Book cxli
(10 B.C.) mentions the restoration of military standards by the Parthians
—which certainly belongs to 20 B.C. The editor in a cursory glance at an
epitome of cxli had probably seen a reference to Parthian submissiveness
—but it was the surrender of the four sons of Phraates as hostages in 10 B.C.,
an event later than and quite distinct from the *signa*.³

Moreover, the editor's industry flagged and failed. The summaries of
the latest books become very meagre. The *Periochae* of Books cxxxviii–
cxlii inclusive take up less space than is allotted to single books at earlier
stages; certain names and events mentioned there, out of all historical
importance, seem to reflect personal interests of the writer, for example,
the identity of the first Gallic high priest of the Altar of Rome and
Augustus at Lugdunum and the names of two noble Nervii who fought on
Drusus' side in the invasion of Germany.⁴ When he made his summaries,
two books (cxxxvi and cxxxvii), covering (it appears) the years 24–17 B.C.
inclusive, had been lost from the manuscript he worked on.⁵ Hence the
Periochae give a miserable idea of the last section of Livy, the nine books
(cxxxiv–cxlii) covering the Principate of Caesar Augustus from 28 to 9 B.C.

Brief and defective, the *Periochae* still provide information—and pro-
voke speculation—about the plan and structure of Livy's work. | Artistic
design should certainly be looked for; but the more elaborate reconstruc-
tions, such as that of Nissen, based on rigid divisions and subdivisions, on
intricate correspondences between groups of books and totals of years,

---

¹ *Philologus* xci (1936), 67 ff.   ² Below, p. 442.
³ Strabo xvi 1, 28, p. 748. M. Titius, the legate of Syria, received the hostages. His tenure
probably falls in 13–10 B.C.
⁴ *Per.* cxxxix: 'sacerdote creato C. Iulio Vercondaridubno Aeduo'; cxli: 'Chumstinctus
et Avectius, tribuni ex civitate Nerviorum.'   ⁵ Cf. O. Rossbach, ad loc.

will be rightly suspected;[1] and the variety of schemes that can be proposed is a deterrent.

A division of the work by decades is attested in late antiquity by the letter of Pope Gelasius.[2] Furthermore, the historian appears originally to have contemplated the division by fives and tens—at least the first five books are a definite unit, marked by the occurrence of a new preface with Book vi. But the end of Book x in 294 B.C. seems devoid of any significance. The historical break surely came a little later, in 290, with the two triumphs of M'. Curius. Indeed, Books vi to xv form a decade and have a unitary subject—Rome resurgent after the Gallic catastrophe and achieving the conquest of Italy. Book xvi, with an excursus on the origins of Carthage, introduces the First Punic War; the decade of the Second Punic War (xxi–xxx) is a unit; and perhaps the next ten books also, though the death of a foreign king, Philip V of Macedon, and the accession of Perseus, recounted at the end of Book xl, is not necessarily a significant date for the writer of Roman annals.

From the end of the Second Punic War to the tribunate of Livius Drusus in 91 B.C., decades appear undiscoverable. The events permit different subdivisions; and those most plausible to a modern critic might not have commended themselves to a historian in antiquity.[3] Perhaps there is an end with Book xlviii, a new beginning at Book xlix, namely the outbreak of the Third Punic War, with a new preface.[4]

Yet surely it is Book lii that is the end of an epoch. It contains the triumphs of Aemilianus, Metellus, and Mummius, the winding up of the Roman wars in Africa, in Macedonia, and in Hellas (145 B.C.). Internal dissensions were soon to usurp the central interest hitherto belonging to the foreign wars against Rome's rivals for the empire of the Mediterranean. Here Polybius made an end—and left the point where later historians might take up the story, Posidonius and Strabo. A patriotic repudiation of Greek influences or an abnormal passion for originality might have tempted a writer to demolish the established categories and construct the history according to a new design. He would not find it easy or remunerative. The view that the fall of Carthage introduced a change in the development of Roman politics and a decline in Roman morals had become an established truth.

The *Periocha* of Book lii ends with the triumph of Mummius. From

---

[1] H. Nissen, *RhM* xxvii (1872), 539 ff. Klotz enjoins caution (*RE* xiii, col. 820). [P. A. Stadter (*Historia* xxi (1972), 287 ff.) has tried to revive the view that Livy's arrangement was strictly by pentads and decades, at least down to cxx.]

[2] *CSE* xxxv 456.

[3] The latest attempt is that of J. Bayet in his edition of Book i (Budé, 1940), xii ff. He suggests four groups for the period in question, viz. xxxi–xl; xli–xlvii; xlviii–lii; liii–lxx.

[4] Book xlix seems a better beginning than xlviii (which Bayet favours). The *Periocha* opens with 'tertii Punici belli initium' etc.

this point to Livius Drusus and the *Bellum Italicum* in 91 B.C.—the | latter the beginning of the age of civil wars—there is no clear indication of plan. A modern writer would probably work up the Gracchan seditions into a recognizable historical unit. There is no sign that Livy did. Nor do the disturbances in the sixth consulate of Marius justify a break at the year 100 B.C. (Book lxix).

The following general plan may have suggested itself to Livy. The period from the end of the Second Punic War to the *Bellum Italicum* (Books xxxi to lxx or lxxi) divides into two large halves, the break coming before or after the Third Punic War (i.e. at the end of Book xlviii, or the end of Book lii). The second half presents no obvious point of subdivision. Perhaps, in the author's scheme, the year that witnessed the death of Scipio Aemilianus (129 B.C., Book lix) was a convenient halfway house.

If Livy began his work with decades in mind, they cracked and broke under pressure of the matter. And, in the revolutionary age, the surge of history grew ever more swift and turbulent, bursting the barriers of the annalistic design. The historian could no longer make the end of a book coincide with the end of a year. This is evident from the *Bellum Italicum* onwards.

That event is the turning point in Roman history between the Battles of Zama and Actium. The war against the Italici was a kind of civil war.[1] As such Livy can hardly have failed to narrate it, himself a citizen of that extended *Italia* of the North, only recently incorporated in the Roman Commonwealth, but a vital element in the new Italo-Roman patriotism of the unified nation.[2]

Modern historians, following the precedent of Appian, commonly lead off the history of the revolutionary age with the actions of the tribune Ti. Gracchus, which sowed the seeds of dissension—and first caused blood to flow in the streets of Rome. Yet it was the tribunate of Livius Drusus that quickly and sharply provoked the series of wars which ended only with Actium. Their termination brought not only peace to Rome but the union of Italy.

Livy appears to be hurrying forward to Drusus and the *Bellum Italicum*: he compresses the events of seven years (98–92 B.C. inclusive) into one Book (lxx). It is not at once clear whether Book lxxi or Book lxxii should mark the beginning of his history of the Revolution. Book lxx, ending with the year 92 B.C., contains the origin of Drusus' proposals in the desire of the Senate to regain control of the law-courts, and a first indication of the programme of the aristocratic demagogue—'perniciosa spe largi-

[1] Cf. Florus ii 6, 1: 'si verum tamen volumus, illud civile bellum fuit.'
[2] A different conception invokes in contrast to Livy the wider and Italian sympathies of Asinius Pollio. Thus E. Gabba, *Appiano e la storia delle guerre civili* (1956), 82 ff.

tionum plebem concitavit'. Book lxxi proceeds with the details, *leges agrariae frumentariaeque*, the *lex* | *iudiciaria*, and the offer of citizenship to the Italians; further, the meetings and plots of the Italian leaders and the assassination of Drusus. Book lxxii plunges into the action: 'Italici populi defecere: Picentes Vestini Marsi Paeligni Marrucini Samnites Lucani. initio belli a Picentibus moto', etc.

Harmony of numbers would indicate Book lxxi as the beginning of a new series, Book lxx as an end—forty books from the Second Punic War.[1] Decades may have been a convenience for publication; but, as has been shown, the material could no longer be properly disposed according to decades. There is no break between Books lxx and lxxi. Drusus' programme lies athwart them; and in Drusus are summed up and united the political contentions of the preceding forty years. The proper and dramatic beginning of the revolutionary wars might therefore seem to be the actual revolt of the peoples of Italia, narrated by Livy at the beginning of Book lxxii. Yet the annalistic principle of arrangement was probably dominant after all. The first act of the *Bellum Italicum*, the rising at Asculum, took place before the end of the year 91 B.C. For this reason it is perhaps preferable to suppose that the new section of Livy's work began not with the actual outbreak of hostilities but with the calendar year 91 B.C., that is, with Book lxxi. This theory is confirmed by the evidence of Eutropius and of Orosius, in which the year of the consuls Sex. Caesar and L. Philippus is given emphasis as the beginning of a new series of events.[2]

If the narrative from this point onwards were not to reproduce all too faithfully the chaos of events, it was desirable for the author to adopt some plan or other for arranging and subdividing his matter. It will be presumed that Livy was not content to be carried on—and carried away—by the stream of events; and one indication of his design survives. Books cix–cxvi, taking the story from the outbreak of the war between Pompeius and Caesar down to the assassination of the dictator, form a unit: they are described in the *Periochae*, one by one, as Books i–viii of the *bellum civile*.

It is by no means easy to establish other subdivisions. Yet it is expedient to investigate in more detail the structure of the rest of Livy's work, for the better understanding of the last portion, the contemporary history down to 9 B.C. The most recent theory, that of Bayet, disposes it into nine groups, varying in length from five to seventeen books.[3] This arrangement is open to criticism on several counts. Instead, an easy, organic, and harmonious grouping can be proposed.

[1] Thus Bayet, op. cit. xiii.   [2] Eutropius v 3, 1; Orosius v 17, 1.
[3] Viz. lxxi–lxxvi, the Italian War; lxxvii–xc, to the death of Sulla; xci–xcvi, Pompeius' reconquest of Spain; xcvii–ciii, from Crassus' victory over the Slaves to the triumph of Pompeius; civ–cviii, Caesar's conquest of Gaul; cix–cxvi, from the outbreak of the Civil War to the death of Caesar; cxvii–cxxxiii, from the advent of Octavianus to the end of the Civil Wars; cxxxiv–cxlii, from the salutation of Octavianus as *Augustus* down to 9 B.C.

The story of the Revolution from the outbreak of the *Bellum Italicum* to the triumph of Octavianus in 29 B.C. falls itself into three large | divisions, sharp and inevitable: the Ten Years' War, the generation of precarious or fraudulent peace, the Twenty Years' War.

First of all, the *Bellum Italicum* and the wars of Marius and Sulla. The latter blended inextricably with the former. The amnesty accorded to the insurgents was of limited effect; large parts of Italy remained beyond the control of the Roman government; even Sulla's victory at the Colline Gate (82 B.C.) did not mean the end, for Volaterrae and Nola still held out, until 80 B.C. The subject forms a unit, and it had already commended itself for such treatment. The *Historiae* of L. Cornelius Sisenna began with the *Bellum Italicum* and went as far as 82 B.C., perhaps a little further.[1] Also, one section of the historical works of L. Lucceius, the friend of Pompeius and of Cicero, embraced the two wars, as Cicero clearly states: 'Italici belli et civilis historia.'[2] The propriety of treating the first epoch of civil strife as a single whole is evident. The only question is, where was it to end? with Sulla's ordering of the constitution, with his abdication, or with his death? Or would the annalistic principle pass over each of these dates and begin with the consuls of 78 B.C., M. Lepidus and Q. Catulus?

It is a remarkable fact that no ancient source registers the precise date of Sulla's abdication. Some scholars would put it in 79 B.C., even as late as the summer.[3] That is not likely. Perhaps Sulla divested himself of dictatorial powers when he laid down his second consulship on the last day of December 80 B.C.[4] That would be a highly appropriate ending for a book, a new period to open with the consuls of the restored Republic, Ap. Claudius Pulcher and P. Servilius.

Two compilators are here of value, Orosius and Eutropius. Orosius begins a new section with the words 'creatis itaque P. Servilio et Appio Claudio consulibus visus est tandem Sulla privatus. hoc fine conclusa sunt duo bella funestissima, sociale Italicum et Sullanum civile. haec per annos decem tracta', etc.[5] Thus a war of ten years ends with 80 B.C. Orosius proceeds to narrate the four great foreign wars that from 78 B.C. confronted the restored oligarchy. As for Eutropius, his fifth book ends with the Ten Years' War, designated as such; and the sixth opens with the series of foreign wars (under the consuls of 78 B.C.).[6]

This may be the conception of Livy—and it is highly acceptable. The

---

[1] Cf. H. Peter, *HRR* i² (1914), cccxl.   [2] *Ad fam.* v 12, 2.

[3] To support a venturesome and vulnerable thesis, Carcopino put the abdication after the consular elections in the summer of 79 B.C., *Sylla ou la monarchie manquée* (1931), 265 ff.

[4] As suggested by E. Gabba, commenting on Appian, *Bella civilia* i 103, 480 (in his edition of that book, 1958). [For the end of 81 B.C., see E. Badian, *Athenaeum*, N.S. xlviii (1970), 8–14.]

[5] Orosius v 22, 2, cf. 23, 1 (four great wars under the consular date of 78 B.C.).

[6] Eutropius v 9, 2; vi 1, 1.

last events in the *Periocha* of Book lxxxix are the reduction of Nola and Volaterrae (and Mytilene): no mention, however, of the abdication of Sulla. The *Periocha* of Book xc opens with the death and funeral of Sulla (spring 78 B.C.). The first section of the age of the Revolution may therefore be described as the 'First Civil War' or the 'Ten Years' War'; it was told in nineteen books, lxxi–lxxxix. |

On this hypothesis the second section begins with the year 78 B.C. That was in fact the point where Sallust began—'res populi Romani M. Lepido Q. Catulo consulibus ac deinde militiae et domi gestas composui.'[1] The style and the sentiments of Sallust were repugnant to Livy. But history was a highly conservative art; and the historian regarded it as a convenience, if not as a duty, to follow the grouping of events—and even the proportion and emphasis—of his predecessors. This important consideration is ignored by those who make Book xc the end, not the beginning, of a group of books.[2]

This, the next portion of Livy, fills nineteen books (xc–cviii). The beginning was recommended by convenience as well as by the example of Sallust. The end was determined by the artistic propriety—not to say necessity—of making a new start in 49 B.C. with the recurrence of an epoch of civil wars. Book cix is entitled *civilis belli primus*; it may well have had a separate preface; and it begins with 'causae civilium armorum'. The influence of this introduction can clearly be discerned in later writers, especially in Florus and in the *Pharsalia* of the poet Lucan.[3]

Books cix–cxvi form a separate unit. But the end of Caesar did not mean the end of the civil wars—that period terminates only with the victory of Caesar's heir, consecrated by the triple triumph of 29 B.C. (Book cxxxiii). That, not 31 or 30, is the date. The period had lasted for twenty years, as the *Periocha* of Book cxxxiii states: 'imposito fine bellis civilibus altero et vicesimo anno.'[4] The third section is therefore made up by Books cix–cxxxiii (49–29 B.C.).

Such are the three large sections dictated by the history of the years 91–29 B.C., namely the Ten Years' War, the Restored Republic, and the Civil Wars. Groups of twenty, nineteen, and twenty-five books respectively. They carry sixty-three years of history, which, by a close coincidence, are narrated in sixty-three books (lxxi–cxxxiii).

[1] Sallust, *Hist.* i 1 M.
[2] As Nissen, *RhM* xxvii (1872), 546; Bayet, op. cit. xiv. The fact that Book xc contained Sulla's death has presumably misled them. But Sulla's abdication would have been a better date for terminating a period of history.
[3] Cf. M. Pohlenz in 'Επιτύμβιον *Swoboda* (1927), 201 ff.
[4] Compare the *senatus consultum* of 8 B.C. concerning the month of August, notable for victories, but especially because 'finisque hoc mense bellis civilibus impositus' (Macrobius i 12, 35). Also Velleius ii 89, 3: 'finita vicesimo anno bella civilia', and Tacitus, *Ann.* iii 28, 1: 'exim continua per viginti annos discordia'. For definitions of *bella civilia* in relation to Lucan's plan, cf. R. T. Bruère, *CP* xlv (1950), 217 ff.

These are large groups. Each of them, however, admits further sub-division, so as to produce, without Procrustean methods, shorter and more convenient sections, like the Caesarian unit (eight books) mentioned above, of from eight to ten books in length.

The military history of the Ten Years' War baffles bisection.[1] But the end of C. Marius provides a break. The *Periocha* of Book lxxx records his decease and his character: 'vir cuius si examinentur cum virtutibus vitia, haud facile sit dictu utrum bello melior an pace perniciosior fuerit. adeo quam rem p. armatus servavit, eam primo togatus omni genere fraudis, postremo armis hostiliter evertit.' Marius died on 13 January 86 B.C. The events of those weeks made it impossible to terminate a book with the last day of December. The Ten Years' War therefore falls into | two manageable units, one of ten books, the other of nine (lxxi–lxxx and lxxxi–lxxxix).

There seems no obvious and inevitable point of division in the next group, the Restored Republic. It can be argued that in Livy's conception the figure of Pompeius Magnus dominated these books; and it has been proposed to divide them at Book xcvi, with the reconquest of Spain, and at Book ciii, with the triumph of Pompeius.[2] The history of these years and the order of events in the *Periochae* yield little support to this theory. An easier break can be found. Nor does Livy follow Pollio and make the consulate of Metellus and Afranius the beginning of a historical period. He cannot help, however, reflecting Pollio's conception of the conspiracy of the three *principes*, Pompeius, Crassus, and Caesar.[3]

The *Historiae* of Sallust ended in 67 B.C. The date appears accidental, the historian having died before his work was completed. None the less, the year 67 was a cardinal date in the decline and fall of the Sullan oligarchy.[4] That was certainly the subject of Sallust's history, whatever the limit he had set himself. Not Caesar, he could argue, but Pompeius was the destroyer of the Republic. The *Lex Gabinia* granted military power described as 'monarchic'.[5] If Livy follows Sallust in opening a new period at 78 B.C., a suitable ending for it was indicated at 67 B.C. Livy would now have to turn to other sources. The next proposal in favour of Pompeius was the *Lex Manilia*, brought forward in January 66 B.C. Book c opens

[1] Bayet's division (op. cit. xiv) of the history of 91–79 B.C. into two groups, six books and fourteen (lxxi–lxxvi and lxxvii–cx), is not attractive.

[2] Thus Bayet (op. cit. xiv). Klotz (*RE* xiii, col. 819) also assumes a break at the end of Book ciii and a new section beginning with civ—'prima pars libri situm Germaniae moresque continet.' Both scholars follow the *Periocha* of ciii, which terminates with the triumph of Magnus. But it cannot be believed that Livy neglected to narrate the triumph of Pompeius (61 B.C.) until he had recounted Caesar's campaign against the Helvetii (58 B.C.). The editor of the *Periochae* does not deserve such confidence.

[3] *Per.* ciii: 'conspiratio inter tres civitatis principes facta est.' Cf. Florus ii 13, 8 ff. (valuable here). Orosius neglects the notion entirely.

[4] H. M. Last, *CAH* ix (1932), 349.   [5] Plutarch, *Pompeius* 25.

with the *Lex Manilia*. The last generation of the Republic therefore forms two units of ten and nine books respectively, namely the twelve years covered by Sallust (Books xc–xcix) and the *libri a fine Sallusti Crispi* (Books c–cviii)—not that Livy would have wanted to call them by that name.

Thirdly, the Civil Wars, in twenty-five books (cix–cxxxiii). The subject can be divided into three units, approximately equal in length. The first comprises eight books (cix–cxvi: see above), narrating the Caesarian wars and the Dictatorship. The second unit opens inevitably with the coming of Caesar's heir to Rome—and concludes, just as inevitably, with the Battle of Philippi (Books cxvii–cxxiv). Both Appian and Cassius Dio put Philippi at the end of a book.[1] They could hardly do otherwise. That battle signed the death-warrant of the Republic; and it was honoured in the traditions of the Roman aristocracy as Pharsalus was not. Livy had an amiable propensity for narrating the deaths of famous men.[2] Such obituaries often came in handy to conclude a book or a series of books (for example, Livius Drusus, Marius, and Caesar). Philippi meant the extinction of a party as well as | a cause. The Battle of Pharsalus had been comparatively merciful to the Roman aristocracy. At Philippi there fell not Brutus and Cassius only, but a host of illustrious men. Many a noble family was cut off. As Velleius observes, no other war was so murderous—'non aliud bellum cruentius caede clarissimorum virorum fuit.'[3] No doubt but that Livy recounted their names and their lineage. After a gap in the text the *Periocha* of Book cxxiv ends with 'inter quos Q. Hortensius occisus est'.

Eight books for Julius Caesar, eight more till Philippi, and nine from Philippi to the triumph of Octavianus fill the tale of the Civil Wars in twenty-five books. Finally, as the appendix, nine books on Augustus, or rather on *res publica restituta*. The latest event mentioned in Book cxxxiii is the triumph of 29 B.C. The brief summary of Book cxxxiv opens with the words 'C. Caesar rebus compositis et omnibus provinciis in certam formam redactis Augustus quoque cognominatus est'. It may be presumed that those words cover Augustus' restoration of 'normal' government, which was proclaimed as complete at the session of the Senate on 13 January 27 B.C. It was not, however, a single act but a series of measures carried out, as Augustus himself says, in the course of his sixth and seventh consulates (28 and 27 B.C.).[4] The process was initiated (it can be affirmed) early in 28 B.C. The citizens of Rome then saw the consular *fasces* handed over, after the proper and Republican fashion of monthly alternation,

---

[1] Appian's conclusion is notable (*Bella Civilia* iv 137, 577 ff.).
[2] Seneca, *Suas.* vi 21: 'hoc semel aut iterum a Thucydide factum, item in paucissimis personis usurpatum a Sallustio, T. Livius benignius omnibus magnis viris praestitit.'
[3] Velleius ii 71, 2.   [4] *Res Gestae* 34.

from one consul to his colleague, from Caesar's heir to Marcus Agrippa.[1]
That is to say, presumably on the first day of February 28 B.C.[2]

Book cxxxiii closed with the climax of the triumph. Roman domestic
transactions of 28 B.C. belong therefore to the beginning of the next book,
to the new section. That book (cxxxiv) has plenty of room for the constitutional settlement of 28–27 B.C., for, apart from that, it appears to have
contained only Augustus' sojourn at Narbo on the way to Spain and the
campaigns of M. Licinius Crassus, the proconsul of Macedonia (29 and
28 B.C.), postdated; and those campaigns even overflow into Book cxxxv.[3]

From the outbreak of the *Bellum Italicum* a series of seven sections
varying from eight to ten books in length and arranged in three large
groups emerges, supplemented by a final nine books on Augustus. Smaller
subdivisions may from time to time have been made, according as the
nature of the material and the convenience of the author demanded. For
example, the second section of the Civil Wars admits a division after the
Proscriptions (Book cxx); and the third can be approximately halved
with the suppression of Sex. Pompeius, 36 B.C. (Book cxxix), a date which
Octavianus at the time professed to | regard as the end of the Civil Wars.[4]
Thus the two units covering the period 44–29 B.C., Books cxvii–cxxiv and
Books cxxv–cxxxiii, fall easily enough into the subdivisions cxvii–cxx,
cxxi–cxxiv, cxxv–cxxix, cxxx–cxxxiii, each ending at a point where the
history provides a break. But it is not desirable in such matters to postulate
systems of undue harmony—or complexity. It is enough to demonstrate
the existence of three large groups, namely the Ten Years' War, the post-
Sullan order, and the Civil Wars, comprising seven units approximately
equal in length, with an appendix of nine books. The scheme is as follows:

lxxi–lxxx	The *Bellum Italicum* to the death of Marius
lxxxi–lxxxix	To the end of the war in Italy
xc–xcix	The years 78–67 B.C.
c–cviii	The years 66–50 B.C.
cix–cxvi	The Civil Wars to Caesar's death
cxvii–cxxiv	To Philippi
cxxv–cxxxiii	To the triumph of Octavianus
cxxxiv–cxlii	The Republic of Caesar Augustus

Further questions now arise. When did Livy draw up his plan; what
term and limit did he set; and when did he complete the latest portion of
his history?

---

[1] Dio liii 1, 1. The passage has generally been misunderstood by constitutional precisians,
e.g. in *CAH* x (1934), 123. Or, by others, passed over, e.g. *Rom. Rev.* (1939), 306.
[2] For this notion, cf. *Tacitus* (1958), 365; 408.
[3] Since Crassus was not allowed to celebrate his triumph until July of 27 B.C. (cf. below,
pp. 418 ff., for these transactions), there was perhaps an excuse for narrating his campaigns
under 27 (i.e. in cxxxiv). But not under 26.
[4] Appian, *Bella civilia* v 130, 541 f.

Livy, it can be argued, wrote his *Praefatio* about 27 B.C., probably after the completion of Books i–v, as an introduction to the first instalment of the work.[1] He announces an intention of carrying the narrative down to his own time, to the Civil Wars, *haec nova*. The preface of Book xxxi confirms the plan as 'the whole of Roman history'.[2]

When and where did he intend to stop? It has been assumed by Nissen, and by most scholars since, that Livy intended to go on to the death of Caesar Augustus; that the year 9 B.C., which he reached, is in fact an unsuitable or inexplicable termination; that the author left his work unfinished when he died in A.D. 17.[3]

It will be observed on the contrary that Livy did not estimate in advance the duration of Augustus' life—or his own chances of survival. A high expectation of life might, it is true, be conceded to a studious citizen of Patavium, an exemplar of the regular habits which conferred so wide a notoriety upon that virtuous *municipium*; and no | contemporary in his wildest hopes or fears could fancy that the heir of Caesar (born in 63 B.C.), fragile and often ill, would live on and on, enduring until the year we call A.D. 14. But that would be a frivolous argumentation. It misses the point. Livy, despite all his predilection for the great and the good, all a patriot's gratitude towards the author of the present happy dispensation, was not writing a biography of the First Citizen. He was writing *res Romanae*.

In Livy's original plan the goal was evident: Actium, the end of the Civil Wars, and the triumph of the young Caesar:

> at Caesar, triplici invectus Romana triumpho
> moenia, dis Italis votum immortale sacrabat.[4]

Reaching that limit in the composition of his histories, he decided to go further (one may conjecture). He added the supplement of nine books (cxxxiv–cxlii). In the preface to one of his late books Livy said that though he had earned glory enough, the spirit drove him on.[5] Perhaps he was referring to those books, the last section of his work.

It remains to discuss briefly the grounds for the prevalent opinion about

[1] Below, pp. 416 ff.
[2] xxxi 1, 2: 'profiteri ausum perscripturum res omnis Romanas.'
[3] Nissen went so far as to affirm that six more books would be required (*RhM* xxvii (1872), 558). Compare also A. Klotz, *RE* xiii, col. 818; Schanz–Hosius, *Gesch. der. röm. Literatur* ii⁴ (1935), 300; A. Rosenberg, *Einleitung u. Quellenkunde zur röm. Geschichte* (1921), 146. Bayet (op. cit. xi) hints at 'une date plus caractéristique, peut-être la mort d'Auguste'. Also M. L. W. Laistner, *The Greater Roman Historians* (1947), 80: 'Livy's original plan may have been to carry his *History* down to the death of Augustus, an event which he himself only survived by three years.'
[4] *Aen.* viii 714 f.
[5] Quoted in Pliny, *NH, praef.* 16: 'satis iam sibi gloriae quaesitum, et potuisse se desidere, ni animus inquies pasceretur opere.'

the conditions in which Livy ended his life and his work. It has been suggested by Klotz, in all gravity, that Book cxlii is unfinished.[1] He argues from the brevity of the _Periocha_. But that is a characteristic which it shares with other books of this group; and it is not nearly the shortest. Books cxxxix–cxlii recount the events of 12–9 B.C., one book a year. It was the triumphant culmination of the great wars of conquest in Illyricum and beyond the Rhine. The military operations of 9 B.C., the death of Drusus in Germany, and all the fuss about his obsequies gave matter and scope enough.

One problem remains. Not only did Livy die, so it is held, with the pen in his hand (for that is the consecrated phrase).[2] In three years or less (A.D. 14–17) he had written no fewer than twenty-two books (cxxi–cxlii). The manuscripts of the _Periocha_ of Book cxxi bear the superscription 'qui editus post excessum Augusti dicitur'. What does this statement mean?

Klotz argues that Livy himself, in the _exordium_ of that book, affirmed that he was now writing after the death of Augustus. Klotz interprets 'dicitur' as 'dicitur a Livio'.[3] That is not the only explanation available. The redactor of the _Periochae_, as is known, did not refrain from making additions or comments of his own. The superscription may be merely an inference. It has been suggested that the redactor found in Book cxxi some statement or other that could hardly have been made public in the lifetime of Augustus.[4] That notion is plausible only at | first sight, and at short sight. Book cxxi seems mainly devoted to the operations of Cassius against Dolabella. Where is the matter for offence? Octavianus had revoked the decree of the Senate outlawing Dolabella. A trifle in those times. The preceding book told of the Proscriptions: for a historian the most delicate episode in all the versatile and unedifying career of the young Caesar.

It will be observed that the superscription does not say 'scriptus' but 'editus'. Hence no warrant for the hasty assumption that Book cxxi (and the twenty-one books following thereupon) were indited after A.D. 14. An easier hypothesis would be preferable: Books cxxi–cxlii, composed towards the end of the reign of Augustus, were held back for some reason or other and not given to the world till later.

---

[1] _RE_ xiii, col. 818; cf. Bayet, op. cit. xv.

[2] A. Klotz, _RE_ xiii, col. 818: 'offenbar hat ihm der Tod die Feder aus der Hand genommen'; Schanz-Hosius, _Gesch. der röm. Literatur_ ii[4] (1935), 300: 'wenn ihm nicht der Tod die Feder aus der Hand nahm'; A. Rosenberg, op. cit. 146: 'der Tod entriss ihm die Feder'; A. H. McDonald, _OCD_ (1949), 509: 'he probably died pen in hand' [deleted in the second edition (1970)].

[3] _RE_ xiii, col. 819. Cf. Bayet (op. cit. xvi): 'la tradition manuscrite des _Periochae_ nous atteste bien que le livre CXXI fut composé après la mort d'Auguste.' Also A. Rostagni, _La letteratura di Roma repubblicana ed augustea_ (1939), 389, cf. 456. Like other scholars, Rostagni suggests that Livy referred to the death of Caesar Augustus in cxxi—and referred to his own continuance in writing (attested by Pliny, _NH, praef._ 16).

[4] Thus O. Rossbach in his edition (Teubner, 1910), xxiii.

It has been shown that the large group of books comprising the twenty-one years of the Civil Wars (cix–cxxxiii, from 49 to 29 B.C.) falls naturally into three units. They end with Caesar's death, with the Battle of Philippi, and with the triumph of Octavianus. These three units were followed by the nine books of the *res publica restituta*, all four units being of equivalent length and bulk. This grouping was imposed by the history itself. It does not follow, however, that the instalments published by the author corresponded exactly with the units into which he disposed his material for convenience of composition—and for necessities of structure. Livy began with exact decades, but could not keep it up. Yet decades perhaps suited scribes or publishers; and the division of the whole work into decades is attested in late antiquity.[1]

If the superscription of Book cxxi is to be accepted and utilized (and that is a large question), it could be conjectured that Livy had stopped publication for a time: Book cxx, containing the proscriptions, in fact provides a break.

In any event, the assumption that Livy took only three years (or less) to write the last twenty-two books is bold—and fragile. Many theories about the composition of Livy's work suppose a fairly equable rate of production, on an average something like three books a year.[2] In itself nothing would forbid the assumption that the old man was writing steadily to the end. Varro set about his *Res Rusticae* at the age of eighty.

But there is nothing to explain the swift acceleration at the end, enabling him to polish off the crowded epoch from the Proscriptions to the death of Drusus (43–9 B.C.) in three years—or less. Livy had acquired greater facility, we are told.[3] Perhaps. His task had now become easier.[4] Not at all. The contemporary period was both more arduous and more dangerous. Livy was a pioneer. |

It is a fanciful picture, and nothing more—the veteran devotee of Clio, tired but insatiable, lashing himself into a feverish activity that only death can arrest. The reality may be more sober—and more instructive. Livy (there is nothing against it) may have quietly laid aside his pen several years before death supervened. Nor is it likely that he ever hoped or aspired to anticipate the decease of Caesar Augustus. Furthermore, the year 9 B.C., so far from being unsuitable for termination, was unavoidable —and in fact felicitous.[5]

---

[1] Above, p. 403.

[2] Schanz–Hosius, op. cit. 299. U. Kahrstedt arrived at an average of 100 to 108 days per book (*Gesch. der Karthager* iii (1913), 143).

[3] Bayet, op. cit. xxv: 'la rapidité croissante du travail de l'historien, attestée pour les derniers livres.'

[4] Bayet, op. cit. xvi: 'la rapidité de composition des derniers livres, où l'historien avait moins de questions à développer.' Wight Duff assumed the fact but essayed no explanation (*A Literary History of Rome to the Close of the Golden Age* (1909), 642).

[5] Below, pp. 447 f.

It is time to look at the ostensible data about the duration of Livy's life. According to the *Chronicle* of Jerome, the historian was born in 59 B.C.[1] That is the canonical date. It is registered in most of the handbooks of Latin literature, large or small, with never a sign of doubt or word of warning. It happens to be insecure.

Scholars dutifully intent on one author at a time and reluctant to abandon a fixed point of reference have neglected to question the general validity of those items concerning Latin authors which Jerome took from Suetonius, *De viris illustribus*, to provide supplementary annotation in his translation of Eusebius. Jerome, it is clear, operated in a casual and careless fashion. Where there are facts to check him, he can be convicted of gross errors: thus Catullus dying in 58 B.C., or Asinius Gallus in A.D. 14.[2]

Now Jerome brackets Livy with the orator Messalla Corvinus under 59 B.C. Messalla, to judge by his role at the Battle of Philippi and the date of his consulship (31 B.C.), can hardly have come into the world as late as 59 B.C. It is reasonable to postulate 64 B.C. or thereabouts. Thus Borghesi long ago, and most scholars concur. Jerome is wrong. How and why did he go wrong? Perhaps (it has been suggested) he found a consular date in his authority, 'Caesare et Figulo', and misread it, hastily assuming the notorious 'Caesare et Bibulo'. That is to say, 59 B.C. instead of 64 B.C.[3]

So far, and satisfactorily, Messalla Corvinus. It is surely illegitimate to accept the change of date for Messalla and not to admit it for Livy. Yet few have drawn the inference and ventured to posit 64 for Livy.[4] Synchronisms of this type were a device that appealed to the researchers of antiquity, often facile or fraudulent. Thus the birth of Cornelius Gallus was conveniently assigned to Virgil's year, 70: Jerome puts his death in 27 B.C., 'XLIII aetatis anno'.[5] Gallus, however, may have been a few years older than Virgil. As for Livy, let the year 64 be taken as approximately correct —if only for the reason that there is nothing else to go by. And there can be advantage in that date. |

That is not all. Jerome also furnishes the date of Livy's death, which he puts in A.D. 17: 'Livius historiographus Patavi moritur.'[6] Is this any good? Again, Messalla Corvinus is relevant. Jerome indicates A.D. 12 or 13 as

---

[1] *Chron.* p. 164 H (under the Year of Abraham 1958): 'Messalla Corvinus orator nascitur et Titus Livius Patavinus scriptor historicus.'

[2] For these and other items consult the full and careful study of R. Helm, 'Hieronymus' Zusätze in Eusebius' Chronik und ihr Wert für die Literaturgeschichte', *Philologus*, Supp. xxi 2 (1929).

[3] H. Schulz, *De M. Valerii Messallae aetate* (Prog. Stettin, 1886), 6.

[4] Conspicuous and all but solitary is G. M. Hirst, *CW* xix (1926), 138 f. = *Collected Classical Papers* (1938), 12 ff.

[5] *Chron.* p. 164 H. Dio, however, narrates the death of Gallus under 26 B.C. (liii 23, 5 ff.). It is illicit to combine that date with Jerome's statement of the poet's age and put his birth in 69 or 68, as Schanz–Hosius, op. cit. 170. Cf. observations in *CQ* xxxii (1938), 40 [= pp. 48 f. above].

[6] *Chron.* p. 171 H.

the year of his decease (A.D. 12 in the best manuscript).[1] Some therefore, for various reasons, have been disposed to accept A.D. 13.[2] But there is a strong reason against. Jerome gives the age of Messalla as seventy-two. If one reckons from 64, not 59, that points to A.D. 8 as the year of his death. Which is welcome. It accords with evidence in Ovid which implies that Messalla died before the poet's departure into exile.[3] Therefore A.D. 8 ought to be accepted.[4] Not but what there are some recalcitrants.[5]

It has become evident that no reliance can be put on Jerome's date for the decease of Livy. The historian might have prolonged his life beyond A.D. 17. Hence consolation and support for those who wish to believe that Livy wrote no fewer than twenty-two books subsequent to 19 August A.D. 14. But that does not have to be taken seriously.

There is another line of argument. If Messalla's death is to be placed four or five years earlier than the calculation based on 59 B.C., why not Livy's death also? The solitary and ultimate datum about Livy's time of life, found by Suetonius and transmitted by Suetonius, might have been his decease at the age of seventy-five. An assumption (or a mistake) putting the date of his birth in 59 B.C. would give A.D. 17 for his extinction. But if in fact 64 B.C. was the true (or approximate and estimated) date of his birth, his death would then fall in or about A.D. 12.

If that be so, namely a span of life from 64 B.C. to A.D. 12, the period of Livy's writing takes on a different aspect, and various assumptions will have to be challenged.

Postulating a continuous period of regular labour for nearly forty-five years (from about 27 B.C. down to A.D. 17), some scholars have deduced an average output of about three books a year. But the author's rhythm may not in fact have been steady or unbroken. Nor is there anywhere a sign to show that he spent as much as four months on any single book. To take an example. His sources can be divined, and his methods of work, in the period from the aftermath of Hannibal's War to the final defeat of Macedon (Books xxxi–xlv). It would be a bold man who argued that Livy needed more than two or three weeks to produce Book xxxi.

Nothing therefore forbids the notion that Livy, going to work about

[1] For the evidence, R. Helm, op. cit. 46 ff.

[2] Thus *PIR*[1], V 90; F. Marx, *WS* xix (1897), 150 ff. The fact that Frontinus (*De aq.* ii 102) records under A.D. 13 the appointment of another *curator aquarum* after Messalla [and, we are told, as successor to him] was clearly allowed predominant weight—and it is not easy to explain away.

[3] *Ex Ponto* i 7, 29 f.; cf. *Tristia* iv 4, 25 ff. [Marx, l.c., shows that, on the contrary, the lines preceding *Ex Ponto* i 7, 29 clearly imply that Messalla was alive when Ovid fell into disgrace.]

[4] Thus J. A. Hammer, *Prolegomena to an Edition of the Panegyricus Messallae* (1925), 10; Schanz–Hosius, op. cit. 23.

[5] The recent article on Messalla Corvinus (*RE* viii A, col. 136) asserts that the evidence points 'eindeutig' to A.D. 13. R. Helm, discounting the data in Jerome, came to the conclusion that the orator was apparently dead before A.D. 1 (op. cit. 51).

29 B.C., had reached Book cxxxiii and with it the end of the Civil Wars by A.D. 1—if not some years earlier. A pause may have ensued. After which, the turn of events in A.D. 4 (Augustus' adoption of | Tiberius) may have encouraged him to go on and produce his epilogue, covering the years 28 to 9 B.C. Those nine books could have been terminated by A.D. 10 or 12—whether or no the historian be deemed to have lived on and survived Augustus.

A new date for Livy's birth having been proposed and rendered plausible (64 B.C. instead of 59), the question must be faced: how soon is the historian likely to have discovered his vocation and begun his vast enterprise?

II. *When Did Livy Begin?*

Livy's first book provides a clear date. In his reference to the closing of the Temple of Janus in 29 B.C., after the War of Actium, he describes the victor by the solemn appellation which the Senate conferred on 16 January 27 B.C.—'quod nostrae aetati di dederunt ut videremus, post bellum Actiacum ab Imperatore Caesare Augusto pace terra marique parta.'[1] But Livy does not mention the second closing of Janus, after the Spanish campaigns of 26 and 25 B.C. The passage was therefore written between 27 and 25 B.C.

There is also the *Preface*, its grave and gloomy tone implying that the salvation of Rome is not yet assured. And perhaps a definite indication to justify pessimism—'haec tempora quibus nec vitia nostra nec remedia pati possumus.'[2] What does this refer to? It has been argued that as early as 28 B.C. a beginning had been made with legislation for moral reform, but it came to nothing. Propertius in an early poem alludes to the abrogation of a law which had menaced his extra-marital felicity:

certe gavisa es sublatam, Cynthia, legem.[3]

Perhaps the law had never been passed, only proposed. However, Propertius can be used to date the *Preface*.[4]

Caution is in place. It is far from clear that Livy conveys a reference to any legislative enactment of any year. What the author has in mind is the general condition of the Roman People over a tract of years. His words might apply to a time before the War of Actium.[5] Or a time subsequent. Or even both. Livy speaks of *vitia nostra*, interpreting a political crisis in

---

[1] i 19, 3.   [2] *Praef.* 9.   [3] Propertius ii 7, 1.
[4] This was first suggested by H. Dessau, *Festschrift O. Hirschfeld* (1903), 461 ff. His view is generally registered with respect (e.g. Schanz–Hosius, op. cit. 300), or firmly accepted (A. Rosenberg, op. cit. 147). [Cf. G. Williams, *JRS* lii (1962) 29 ff., with further development.]
[5] I owe this point to Mason Hammond.

terms of morality. What then are the *remedia* that are so hard to accept? Presumably order and concord. That is to say, in political terms, the acceptance of centralized government as the only guarantee of Rome's salvation. Compare the formulation adduced by men of understanding at the obsequies of Caesar Augustus—'non aliud discordantis patriae remedium quam ut ab uno regeretur'.[1] If such is the | *remedium*, it cannot be expected that an imperial people with the tradition of the Republic can feel eager or happy in acquiescence.

It follows that Livy's words ought not to be tied and restricted to a precise date. His remarks would fit the aftermath of Actium when Caesar's heir stood supreme, *potentiae securus*; but they do not (it can be claimed) preclude a date subsequent to the settlement of 28 and 27 B.C. Disquiet lurked beneath the surface, stability was precarious.[2]

The common assumption is that Livy began to compose his history between 27 and 25 B.C.[3] It is a little premature. The *Preface*, by reason of its character and amplitude, is not merely the preface of Book i, but the author's general introduction, published at the head of a large section of the work (Books i–v at least). Similarly, the invocation of Octavianus at the beginning of the first book of the *Georgics* is the proem of the completed work, all four books. Such prefaces are commonly the latest portions to be composed. Moreover, there is no warrant that the name 'Augustus', perhaps even the whole sentence about the closing of Janus in 29 B.C., is not a later insertion, added at some time subsequent to the original composition of the narrative.[4]

Nor, another point, does the historian's use of 'augustus' as an epithet furnish a clue. The word occurs, in the comparative form 'augustior', in relation to Hercules and to Romulus.[5] Hence the notion that Livy was writing Book i subsequent to January 27 B.C.[6] Like other archaic and venerable words, 'augustus' may now have been in fashion, otherwise it would not have been annexed for Caesar's heir on the proposal of the senior consular, the alert Munatius Plancus.[7]

So far guess and argument, much of it negative or inconclusive. Nothing forbids the conjecture that several books, say the first five, had been written before 27 B.C. Strong confirmation is furnished by an episode in

---

[1] Tacitus, *Ann.* i 9, 4. Cf. *Hist.* i 1, 1: 'omnem potentiam ad unum conferri pacis interfuit.'
[2] Below, pp. 424 f.
[3] e.g. A. Klotz, *RE* xiii, col. 818; Schanz–Hosius, op. cit. 300; A. Rosenberg, op. cit. 147.
[4] W. Soltau, *Hermes* xxix (1894), 611 ff., J. Bayet, op. cit. xvii. Hammond supports this opinion strongly. [See now the arguments of T. J. Luce, *TAPA* xcvi (1965), 209 ff.]
[5] i 7, 9; 8, 2. Observe also *Praef.* 7: 'ut . . . primordia urbium augustiora faciant.'
[6] L. R. Taylor, *CR* xxxii (1918), 158; G. M. Hirst, *AJP* xlvii (1926), 347 ff. = *Collected Classical Papers* (1938), 1 ff.
[7] Velleius ii 91, 1 etc.

Book iv. Livy narrates in vivid language the famous exploit of A. Cornelius Cossus, the *tribunus militum* who killed with his own hand Lars
Tolumnius, the King of Veii, and consequently dedicated the *spolia opima*
in the Temple of Juppiter Feretrius. Then comes a digression.[1] The author
states that he had followed the consensus of the annalists, who described
Cossus as a military tribune. But there was documentary evidence, the
titulus ipsis spoliis impositus, which proved that the dedication was made
by Cossus as consul.

Livy was apprised of the facts by Caesar Augustus himself, who had
gone into the temple and read the inscription of Cossus, on a linen
corselet. Livy bows to this authoritative pronouncement. As he says, it
would be almost sacrilege not to.[2] He then proceeds to register a | diffi-
culty: not only the annalists in concert but also the *libri lintei* cited by
Licinius Macer put the consulship of Cossus a decade later. But that year
(428 B.C.) could not be suitable for an exploit of war—there was indeed
a whole *triennium* of inactivity because of plague. Finally, referring to
commands held by Cossus still later, he deprecates speculation—'vana
versare in omnes opiniones licet'—and ends on a firm and ironical note
of confidence: Cossus cannot have perjured himself with a mendacious
inscription in the sight of Juppiter and Romulus.[3]

The historian did not go and look for himself; and in the course of his
narrative, when he reaches the consulate of Cornelius Cossus, he makes
no modification.[4] The antiquarian digression is probably a later insertion
by the author.[5]

The question of the *spolia opima* was irrelevant to Livy. Not so to
Caesar Augustus. Nor was the master of Rome moved by a generous
impulse to rescue from error a deserving but uncritical historian: high
politics were involved.[6]

In 29 B.C. M. Licinius Crassus, proconsul of Macedonia, defeated the
Bastarnae in battle and slew their chieftain, Deldo. Crassus claimed the
spolia opima.[7] That honour had been earned by no Roman general for

---

[1] iv 20, 5–11.

[2] iv 20, 7: 'prope sacrilegium ratus sum Cosso spoliorum suorum Caesarem, ipsius templi
auctorem, subtrahere testem.'

[3] iv 20, 11: 'Iovem prope ipsum, cui vota erant, Romulumque intuens, haud spernendos
falsi tituli testes.'

[4] iv 32, 4 (428 B.C.): 'qui priore bello tribunus militum . . . spolia opima Iovis Feretrii
templo intulerit.'

[5] As suggested by W. Soltau, *Hermes* xxix (1894), 611 ff.; *Livius' Geschichtswerk, seine
Komposition und seine Quellen* (1897), 18. Bayet claims other insertions in Book iv (Budé,
1946, 125). On Livy's methods of composition in this book see R. M. Ogilvie, *JRS* xlviii
(1958), 40 ff. [The passage continues to be discussed, with the most varied theories and
interpretations put forward. See, *inter alia*, P. G. Walsh, *PACA* iv (1961), 30 f.; Luce, op.
cit. (above, p. 417, n. 4), 211–18.]

[6] First divined by Dessau, *Hermes* xli (1906), 142 ff.

[7] Dio li 24, 4.

two centuries and was all but forgotten, save by antiquarians.[1] The spirit of the times and the policy of the government encouraged the revival of ancient practices. This manifestation, however, was most distasteful to the young Caesar, who monopolized for himself all military glory and who, precisely in these years, aspired to the renown—and even to the name—of Romulus. A way was found.

According to Cassius Dio, Crassus could have dedicated *spolia opima*— if he had been the holder of full and paramount *imperium*.[2] That is to say, consul not proconsul. Dio (it is true) attests no claim presented, no debate, no disallowance. But what he registers is instructive. The passage in Livy permits a step further: dispute and the mooting of historical precedents. The inscription of Cornelius Cossus is sharply relevant. It demonstrated that only a consul qualified for the *spolia opima*.

It is not clear that the official argument against Crassus was above reproach, let alone the *pièce justificative*. Was the inscription authentic? On a document of the fifth century B.C. the holder of the supreme *imperium* would surely have been designated as *praetor* rather than as *consul*. Hence a suspicion of forgery somewhere.[3]

Or was Octavianus the victim of an honest mistake? Most modern accounts postulate his good faith, an assumption that would have startled most contemporaries of that young man, whatever their political | allegiance. One scholar has in fact devised an explanation. The *cognomen*, 'Coso', he suggests, was barely legible: Octavianus read it as 'cos'. But here too a question arises. Would *cognomina* have occurred on early documents?[4]

Despite these objections, scholars have been found to accept the inscription as 'certainly contemporary' and as 'conclusive evidence'.[5] Hence large assumptions, not only about the veracity of Octavianus, but about the preservation of fragile documents through long centuries.[6]

All manner of venerable objects were kept in temples. They tend to survive, whatever the fate of the edifice—conflagration or ruin and collapse. For example, the augural staff of Romulus was found undamaged when the Chapel of the Salii was destroyed by fire.[7] Or again (and most significant), the statue of Fortuna and its vestments in the shrine in the Forum Boarium. The vestments were nothing less than the toga woven by

---

[1] Dio reports a vote of the Senate that Caesar should have the right to dedicate *spolia opima*, even if he had killed no enemy general (xliv 4, 2). That is a patent anachronism— and instructive for the estimate of certain other honours allegedly voted.

[2] Dio li 24, 4.   [3] Thus Dessau, op. cit. 142 ff.

[4] O. Hirschfeld, *Kl. Schriften* (1913), 398 f. [For good faith, see also F. Càssola, *RSI* lxxxii (1970), 5–31, suggesting that the inscription was in an *adyton*.]

[5] *CAH* vii 507 f.; x 125.

[6] The difficulty could be got around by supposing that the family restored the inscription in a more recent age. Thus J. H. Bishop, *Latomus* vii (1948), 187 ff.

[7] Cicero, *De div.* i 30.

Tanaquil for Servius Tullius (the learned Varro vouched for it), and they
survived intact, defying worm and decay, for five hundred and sixty
years down to the catastrophe of Sejanus. So far the elder Pliny.[1] Another
authority (Dionysius of Halicarnassus) affirms that the original Temple
of Fortuna had burned down; the statue itself escaped (being gilded), but
everything else was the product of restoration.[2] The fire happens to stand
on record. It occurred in 213 B.C.[3]

The sixth King of Rome is only a century earlier than Cornelius Cossus.
Garment for garment, there is not much to choose. But motive intervenes.
The opportune discovery of important documents in sacred edifices tends
to happen when political morality—and palaeographic science—are at a
low level. Caesar's heir was no novice—suspicion must attach to the
extracts from the last will and testament of Marcus Antonius, produced
at the proper time and recited with the proper effect, before the Roman
Senate, a few years earlier.[4]

The restoration of the temple of Juppiter Feretrius was undertaken at
the suggestion of Atticus—so his friend and biographer, Cornelius Nepos,
records.[5] Atticus, a sound scholar, was the most learned student of prosopography in that age. The objects preserved in the temple may have
excited his personal curiosity. Atticus died on 31 March 32 B.C.,[6] therefore
a certain time had elapsed since operations began. Not only the fabric
but perhaps the dedications required and received the attentions of the
restorer. Such works were not always carried out in any spirit of super-
stitious reverence for ancient materials. The shrine itself was in a sorry
condition—roofless and falling down, according to Cornelius Nepos.[7]
Indeed, Augustus in the *Res Gestae* | does not name it on the list of
buildings repaired but reckons it among his own new constructions;[8] and
Livy describes Augustus as 'ipsius templi auctor'.[9]

When did Augustus visit the temple? Perhaps in the company of
Atticus, before the rebuilding. That is to say, four or five years before
the revelation made to Livy. The original inscription may no longer
have been in existence when its tenor became a matter surpassing antiquarianism.

Crassus was voted a triumph in 29 B.C., but this is not necessarily the
date of his uncomfortable demand and its official rejection. The proconsul

---

[1] Pliny, *NH* viii 197. With this goes the remarkable fact reported by Dio (lviii 7, 2) that
Sejanus had a statue of Fortuna in his house—i.e. taken from the Forum Boarium. The
vestments perished, it can be assumed, on 18 Oct. A.D. 31. For a reconstruction, cf. *Hermes*
lxxxiv (1956), 257 ff. [= pp. 308 ff. above].

[2] Dion. Hal. *Ant. Rom.* iv 40.   [3] Livy xxiv 47, 15; cf. xxv 7, 6.

[4] For the problems concerning this document, see now J. Crook, *JRS* xlvii (1957), 36 ff.

[5] Nepos, *Atticus* 20, 3.   [6] Ibid. 22, 3.

[7] Ibid. 20, 3: 'cum . . . vetustate atque incuria detecta prolaberetur.'

[8] *Res Gestae* 19.   [9] iv 20, 7.

of Macedonia fought another campaign, in the next year. It was perhaps not until late in 28 B.C., on Crassus' return to Italy, that the manner in which he proposed to stage his triumph became a political issue, namely not merely the procession to the Capitol, but the dedication of the spoils stripped from Deldo the Bastarnian. Crassus was a *nobilis*, grandson of a great political dynast, rival in military glory and coeval with Caesar's heir. The armed proconsuls were the greatest menace to his primacy.[1]

The unseasonable ambitions of Crassus (it has been suggested) were one of the things that constrained the heir of Caesar to publish his Restoration of the Republic on 13 January 27 B.C.[2] An attractive notion, recalling history from doctrine or propaganda to facts and personalities. On the other hand, it was easy for the new Romulus to discern, without that incident or incentive, the utility of a *res publica* (not sentimental but practical); and the process of advertising a return to normal government had begun quite early in 28. No sooner was the process deemed and proclaimed complete than the ruler took special powers, namely a vast *provincia* for ten years, abolishing proconsuls in the territories of main military importance and danger. That solution could have been devised without M. Licinius Crassus.

Livy (it can be divined) benefited from a helpful admonition of Augustus after 28 B.C., after he had recited (or even published) Book iv. The inception of the work therefore lies a few years back. How far? A recent theory, that of Bayet, dates the completion of Books i–v before the years 31–29 B.C.[3] Bayet suggests that Book i was first of all published separately; then Books ii–v; then, in 27–25 B.C., a second edition of Books i–v, along with Books vi–x. Further, by 19 B.C., Livy had finished Books xi–xxx.

That is an earlier dating than any hitherto advocated. In some ways it is attractive. To be in a position to issue Books i–v in the period | 31–29 B.C., Livy must surely have made a beginning in 34 or 33 B.C. He needed time and practice to find his method and his style.

The arguments, it must be admitted, are not altogether cogent. Livy, giving in Book i a solemn account of the dedication of the shrine of Feretrius by Romulus, makes no mention of Augustus' rebuilding—or of the rebuttal of Crassus' claim.[4] Hence Bayet argues that this book, and

---

[1] The triumph had been voted jointly to Octavianus and to Crassus; and, according to some accounts, says Dio (li 25, 2), it was only the former that took the salutation of *imperator*. It is in fact the seventh, registered in 29 B.C. (*ILS* 81). Crassus, however, was allowed to celebrate a triumph, but not until July 27 B.C. [Crassus may not have returned until 27: Dio is vague on the time taken by his campaigns.]

[2] E. Groag, *RE* xiii, coll. 283 ff. This opinion is viewed with favour in *Rom. Rev.* (1939), 308 f.

[3] Bayet, op. cit. xvii ff. [On all this see Luce, op. cit. (above, p. 417, n. 4).]

[4] i 10, 6 f.

probably the following books as well, down to Book iv at least, were written before 31–29 B.C.[1]

That is logical but not convincing. Juppiter Feretrius was only one among the numerous constructions of Augustus—'templorum omnium conditor aut restitutor'.[2] Still less was the historian of regal Rome bound to mention the failed pretensions of Crassus. Livy was not really interested in the precise qualifications for the *spolia opima*; he only inserted a note in Book iv after being admonished by Augustus; and he probably regarded the whole business as a vexatious perturbation in a smooth and satisfactory narrative, which had been guaranteed by the consensus of the written sources. It was nuisance enough when annalists were discrepant. Observe his remark three chapters further on: 'Licinio libros haud dubie sequi linteos placet; Tubero incertus veri est. sit inter cetera vetustate cooperta hoc quoque in incerto positum.'[3]

Nor should the general question of artistic propriety be omitted from any discussion of what an ancient writer ought, or ought not, to say.

In Book i the historian paid an adequate tribute to the unique quality of the *spolia opima*. His observations were not rendered obsolescent by an abortive incident in his own day (the claim of Crassus). He says: 'bina postea inter tot annos, tot bella opima parta sunt spolia; adeo rara eius fortuna decoris fuit.'[4]

Livy did not want to disfigure the annals of early Rome, poetic and legendary, by the continual obtrusion of modern names and modern incidents. The closing of Janus he could hardly avoid; and the antiquarian note in Book iv was forced upon him. Livy's technique in reflecting or suggesting the present is careful and subtle. Observe, for example, the speech of the tribune Canuleius in Book iv.[5] The orator expounds doctrines of some political moment. Not only the claim of merit against pedigree, adducing Kings of Rome who were *novi homines*. He argues that, since the City is destined to endure for ever, and will grow all the time, new forms of authority, *nova imperia*, can be expected to emerge. That formulation suits the avowed monarchy of Caesar's heir—it does not have to be assigned to the primacy of Caesar Augustus in the restored Republic.

Again, the firm stand of Camillus against a proposal to take the seat | of government from Rome to Veii.[6] It has a certain relevance to history, propaganda, or fiction about the time of the War of Actium. Scholars have not been slow to fix on the rumour reported by Suetonius that Caesar the Dictator intended to transfer the capital to the eastern lands.[7]

---

[1] Bayet, op. cit. xviii. The lower date depends on his assumption that Crassus' claim and its rebuttal occurred in 29 B.C.   [2] iv 20, 7.
[3] iv 23, 3. For Macer and the *libri lintei* see R. M. Ogilvie, *JRS* xlviii (1958), 40 ff.
[4] i 10, 7.   [5] iv 3 f.   [6] v 51 ff.
[7] *Divus Julius* 79, 4: 'migraturum Alexandream vel Ilium.'

Some take the notion very seriously and exploit it with conviction.[1] Too much has been made of this item. But it will be recalled as relevant that Antonius for long years had been ruling from Alexandria the eastern dominions of Rome.[2]

It was not left for Livy to be the first to produce an oration by Camillus. The legend had a long past. It had taken tone and episode from various epochs and individuals, including the Scipiones and Sulla.[3] Livy may owe much of his colour and emphasis to a writer thirty or forty years earlier.[4] Camillus, the Second Founder of Rome, is a link between Romulus and Augustus, to be sure.[5] But it does not follow that Livy, extolling Camillus, had his eye on the present all the time—or even very much.

In further support of an early dating, Livy's attitude towards the traditions of the *gens Iulia* is invoked—scepticism about Ascanius, an unfriendly portrayal of certain Julii. So much so that the pair of fulsome references to Augustus looks like a palinode or palliative.[6]

Mentioning Aeneas' son by Lavinia (Ascanius, the founder of Alba Longa), Livy states that it is uncertain whether this Ascanius is the same person as the Ascanius son of Aeneas and Creusa, also known as Iulus, whom the Julii claim as their ancestor.[7] What else could he say? The discrepancy existed. Once the Julii had identified Ascanius, son of Aeneas and Creusa, as Iulus, it was hardly possible for them to have the advantage both ways, to claim descent from the Kings of Alba Longa as well, but they did their best. One form of the legend, presumably that current in the time of Julius Caesar, is preserved by Dionysius of Halicarnassus.[8] It is highly instructive: Ascanius-Iulus founds Alba Longa, it is true, but not the dynasty, for that had to come from the union of Trojan and native blood. The next King is Silvius, son of Aeneas by Lavinia. Ascanius-Iulus takes a priesthood instead, so the Julii were able to assert a sacerdotal legitimation, not unwelcome to Caesar the *pontifex maximus*.

For Livy, a full discussion of such traditions, combinations, or fictions would be tedious and inconclusive. As he sensibly remarks, 'quis enim

---

[1] e.g. E. Meyer, *Caesars Monarchie und das Principat des Pompejus*[3] (1922), 521: 'zweifellos durchaus zutreffend.'
[2] Cf. *Rom. Rev.* (1939), 305 f.
[3] F. Münzer, *RE* vii, col. 324 ff.; O. Hirschfeld, *Kl. Schriften* (1913), 273 ff.; E. Täubler, *Klio* xii (1912), 219 ff.; A. Momigliano, *CQ* xxxvi (1942), 111 ff.; J. Bayet in his edition of Book v (Budé (1954), 155).
[4] Cf. F. Klingner, *Gnomon* xi (1935), 577 ff., reviewing E. Burck, *Die Erzählungskunst des T. Livius* (1934). Klingner even points to Valerius Antias as perhaps 'der Camillus-Historiker' (op. cit. 587).
[5] Below, p. 431.
[6] Bayet, op. cit. xix: 'si bien que les passages ampoulés où Caesar Augustus est loué finissent par faire figure de palinodie, ou, au moins, de palliatif.'
[7] i 10, 7.
[8] Dion. Hal. *Ant. Rom.* i 70 f. On which see the valuable observations of E. Norden, *Neue Jahrbücher* vii (1901), 259; 279 ff.

rem tam veterem pro certo adfirmet?'[1] If, however, Livy be held lacking in respect towards the traditions of the Julian House, what shall be said of the conduct of the irreproachable Virgil? In the first book of the *Aeneid* he regards Ascanius-Iulus as the founder of Alba | Longa and ancestor of a line of kings.[2] In the sixth, however, not a word of Ascanius-Iulus; it is Silvius, son of Aeneas and Lavinia, who heads the regal pedigree.[3]

Livy's observations about certain Julii turn out to be harmless enough. Cn. Julius Mentho (*cos.* 431 B.C.) dedicated a temple of Apollo without waiting for the lot to decide between him and his colleague.[4] Both consuls, though otherwise on bad terms, had previously opposed the Senate's insistence that a dictator be appointed—Livy speaks of their *pravitas*.[5] In 408 B.C. two military tribunes with consular powers, C. Julius Iulus and P. Cornelius Cossus, were likewise recalcitrant.[6] It was not the habit of Livy to suppress or distort the accounts transmitted by the annalists; and there is no evidence that Augustus (or anybody else) bothered about the Julii of the fifth century B.C. Nor was his wife, Livia Drusilla, likely to take offence at Livy's account of the behaviour of her ancestor Salinator in his censorship, especially his *foedum certamen* with his colleague.[7]

Ascanius and the Julii can be dismissed. No unequivocal evidence demands the completion of Books i–v as early as the period 31–29 B.C. Their publication in 27–25 B.C., however, remains a reasonable assumption. Was it a second edition, supplemented by a further instalment, Books vi–x? Bayet appeals to certain indications in these books which appear contemporaneous in tone and feeling with the *Preface*. They are general references to the pernicious effects of wealth and luxury and to the Civil Wars.[8] They prove nothing. Official optimism is misleading. The memory of the Civil Wars did not fade all at once—nor did the dangers of their recrudescence. Peace had been proclaimed, but insecurity subsisted; and the moral regeneration of the Roman People had not become in any way manifest. Stability was guaranteed only by the leader of the Caesarian party. The health of Augustus was precarious. In fact, he nearly died, more than once. The tone and sentiments of the *Preface* might even have been in harmony with the contemporary situation, had it been composed as late as 23 B.C., the critical year that witnessed the conspiracy of Varro Murena and a rift in the Caesarian party.[9] The age was still 'haec tempora quibus nec vitia nostra nec remedia pati possumus'. Similarly the second ode of Horace's first book, though probably written in 28 B.C.,

---

[1] i 3, 2.   [2] *Aen.* i 267 ff.   [3] *Aen.* vi 763 ff.
[4] iv 29, 7.   [5] iv 26.   [6] iv 56 f.   [7] xxix 37.
[8] vii 25, 9: 'adeo in quae laboramus sola crevimus, divitias luxuriamque'; 40, 2: 'nondum erant tam fortes ad sanguinem civilem'; ix 19, 15: 'absit invidia verbo et civilia bella sileant.'
[9] Cf. *Rom. Rev.* (1939), 335 f., where *Praef.* 9 is cited. [On the conspiracy and the problems involved see S. Jameson, *Historia* xviii (1969) 204 ff.]

is not out of date in 23 B.C., but highly relevant and worth quoting to illustrate the political situation.

There is no indication about the second Decade. A passage in the third, however, has arrested the attention of scholars. In Book xxviii | Livy refers to the pacification of Spain, 'ductu auspicioque Augusti Caesaris'.[1] That was not finally and properly achieved until Agrippa's campaign in 19 B.C. Hence it is often argued that the publication of Books xxi–xxx falls after that year.[2] Not necessarily. In the official conception, Spain was conquered by Augustus in 26–25 B.C. A loyal writer reflects it. Thus Velleius Paterculus, who suppresses all mention of the subsequent campaigns.[3] Augustus' ostensible conquest of Spain was the justification for the second closing of Janus in 25 B.C. Subsequent operations are irrelevant. The phrase of Livy, 'ductu auspicioque Augusti Caesaris', admits a precise interpretation—the Bellum Cantabricum conducted by Augustus in person (26 B.C.), and the campaigns of his legates in the next year while the *imperator* lay ill at Tarraco.[4] It is perfectly open for anyone to assert that the third Decade was written before 19 B.C.—and to deny it, if reason be shown.

It cannot be said that Bayet's case has been proved. Perhaps the strongest plea is the tone of the *Preface*, encouraging an early date, before the years of peace. For the rest, most of the positive arguments are singularly fragile. But something is gained. At the very least it can be taken that the years 27–25 mark, not the beginning of Livy's work, but the actual publication of a substantial portion, Books i–v. Perhaps some of those books had been completed two years earlier. When Octavianus returned to Italy, Virgil recited before him in Campania the four books of the *Georgics*.[5] The victor of Actium may also have been gratified in the year of his triumph by a first acquaintance with the newest historical compositions. But that notion is over-hazardous.

If Livy began his work about the time of the War of Actium—or, rather, shortly after it—certain conclusions emerge, of great moment for the history of Latin literature. It is a matter that far transcends the mere biography of Livy or the rhythm of his production.

According to the *Chronicle* of Jerome, both Livy and Messalla Corvinus were born in 59 B.C. Too late for the one, that date should also be too late for the other.[6] Even if born in 64, not 59, Livy by Roman standards was still youthful for a historian—history had normally been written

---

[1] xxviii 12, 12. [2] e.g. A. Klotz, *RE* xiii, col. 818; Schanz–Hosius, op. cit. 300.
[3] Velleius ii 90, 4. He is refuted by Dio in 24, 22, and 19 B.C. (lii 29, 1 ff.; liv 5, 1 ff.; 11, 2 ff.).
[4] For the Spanish wars see further below, p. 442. [5] Donatus, *Vita* 27.
[6] Above, pp. 414 ff.

by senior statesmen, as pastime or consolation. On the other hand, his character and tastes were already formed.

What preparation did Livy bring to his task? Some may toy with the notion that he discovered his vocation in youth and spent the years from twenty to thirty in historical studies.[1] Nothing in his writings lends any support. On the contrary.[2]

What then was his training and equipment? The Transpadane zone | of Italy could furnish a good education, as witness Catullus and Virgil; and Livy belonged (it is tempting to assume) to the 'better sort' at Patavium.[3] Livy may have come late to Rome. Whatever be thought of the reproach of *Patavinitas*, there might be good cause for reckoning him provincial, not metropolitan, in his outlook.

Athens he perhaps knew not at all. A young man's visit would have fallen in the troubled period that interrupted the studies of Messalla, of Cicero's son—and of Q. Horatius Flaccus. Perhaps he went there in later life, in the season of his established fame.[4] But no clear sign can be discovered of travel anywhere else.[5]

Livy studied in the schools of rhetoric—and may have taught there. A professor, a certain L. Magius, married his daughter.[6] Further, Livy compiled for the use of his own son a treatise on style in the form of a letter.[7] This work was probably written after the beginning of his *Histories*. But that question defies certainty—and matters little. Livy came to history not from a career of politics, not from antiquarian pursuits, but from rhetoric.

Of the prose authors of Augustan Rome, Livy is the sole survivor. He is not altogether easy to estimate. The writing of history had its own requirements, also certain traditions and characteristics.[8] But the theory and practice of oratory can be invoked, on a sane and temperate view of Cicero's pronouncement that history is 'opus . . . unum oratorium maxime'.[9]

---

[1] M. L. W. Laistner, *The Greater Roman Historians* (1947), 77.

[2] K. Witte, *RhM* lxv (1910), 419; H. Dessau, *Gesch. der röm. Kaiserzeit* i (1926), 540: 'ohne ernstliche Vorstudien'.

[3] The affirmation of A. Rosenberg that he obviously did not belong to the 'Adelsgeschlechter' of Padua (op. cit. 144) is not supported by evidence or argument. His presumed gravestone, 'T. Livius C. f. sibi et suis', etc., with two sons and a wife, Cassia Sex. f. Prima (*ILS* 2919), registers no local magistracy. Laistner (op. cit. 67) betrays strange misconceptions about citizenship and nomenclature. [It is doubtful whether that stone, using *cognomina* to distinguish sons with the same *praenomen*, can be early enough to be Livy's tombstone.]

[4] There is the inscription *IG* iii 594 = ii² 4141: ἡ βουλὴ | Λίβιον (near the Propylaea). It is adduced by P. Graindor, *Musée belge* xxviii (1923), 135; *Athènes sous Auguste* (1927), 96.

[5] It is perhaps a little hopeful to say that 'his work reflects knowledge of the Empire, presumably gathered in travel' (A. H. McDonald, *OCD* (1949), 509) [deleted in the second edition (1970)].   [6] Seneca, *Controv.* x, *praef.* 2.

[7] Quintilian x 1, 39. For other writings of Livy, see Seneca, *Ep.* 100, 9.

[8] The subject is too large to be dealt with in this place. For an acute appraisal of Livy in relation to his predecessors see A. H. McDonald, *JRS* xlvii (1947), 155 ff.

[9] *De legibus* i 2.

The oratorical style in vogue in that age is well known from the specimens of declamations preserved by the elder Seneca, by his own comments—and his own practice. The new style was a development of the Asianic tendency; it aimed at swiftness, splendour, and point; it employed poetical and elevated vocabulary; and it often degenerated into bombast and preciosity.[1] Yet it had attractive qualities, such as that *vigor* which Seneca praised in T. Labienus, the orator and historian.[2]

Fashions changed rapidly in the revolutionary age, and the tyranny of the Triumvirs, by banishing oratory from the Comitia and the Senate, drove it into the schools. The prevalence of the declamation dates from this period.[3] The restoration of the Republic was powerless to check the trend (how could it?); and the growth of despotism confirmed its sway. Declamation and the new style are inextricably bound together.

Livy stood by Cicero. He urged his son to read Demosthenes and Cicero, to esteem other writers by their approximation to the classic pair.[4] The eloquence of Cicero had quickly lost favour. Something | of it, however, was inherited by Messalla, to judge by descriptions of his oratory—elegant and ornate, but somehow lacking in force.[5] Of the orators after Cicero, Messalla should have been most to the liking of the young Livy; but Messalla was much at the wars; and no evidence reveals what friends, guides, and patrons the man from Patavium found in Rome of the Triumvirs.

There were various patrons of literature. Asinius Pollio had been the friend of poets, both of Catullus from Verona and of Helvius Cinna from Brixia (*tr. pl.* 44 B.C.).[6] He was also the first patron of Virgil.[7] If his interest in the rising talent of the towns of Transpadana directed his attention to Livy, their relations were not likely to be close or cordial. The elderly Cornelius Nepos, himself a Transpadane, was no doubt more accessible. He had been a friend of Cicero—and he was writing history (of a kind). The book *De viris illustribus* appeared about 35 B.C. Further, Nepos was on intimate terms with Atticus, who still survived, his vitality unimpaired.[8]

Now as later, Livy's life flows in a hidden stream. Nothing connects him with any of the great senatorial patrons of letters in Augustan Rome. The circle of Maecenas knows him not. His only attachment appears to

---

[1] E. Norden, *Die antike Kunstprosa* i (1898), 270 ff.
[2] Seneca, *Controv.* x, *praef.* 5: 'color orationis antiquae, vigor novae.'
[3] Ibid. i, *praef.* 12.   [4] Quintilian x 1, 39.
[5] Ibid. x 1, 113; cf. Tacitus, *Dial.* 18, 2.   [6] Catullus 12; Charisius, *GL* 124 K.
[7] As can be argued from *Ecl.* viii 11: 'a te principium, tibi desinet.' This looks like the original dedication—before the poet was impelled to praise the heir of Caesar (*Ecl.* i). Cf. *Rom. Rev.* (1939), 253. [G. W. Bowersock, *HSCP* (1971), 76 ff., would regard Octavian as the patron addressed in *Ecl.* viii.]
[8] According to Pliny, Nepos 'divi Augusti principatu obiit' (*NH* ix 137; x 60). But he has failed to achieve *PIR*. [Atticus died in 32 B.C. (Nep. *Att.* 22, 3).]

be with the imperial family.[1] The paucity of anecdotes about one who acquired fame so early and lived so long is a remarkable fact. Of some half-dozen Livian opinions on questions of style preserved by the elder Seneca and by Quintilian, not one bears the stamp of verbal tradition. All of them look like quotations from his treatise on rhetoric.[2] Perhaps he was never long or frequently at the metropolis.[3] Were there enough books at Patavium? Enough, it should seem, for Livy's needs and methods as disclosed in what survives. But the narration of Augustus' reign would present problems of another order.

Livy set himself to write history in the manner enjoined by Cicero for that art: ample, smooth, and balanced—'genus orationis fusum atque tractum et cum lenitate quadam profluens.'[4] He did not achieve it all at once. The earlier books have an archaic and poetical colouring, especially Book i. That is due in large measure to the subject—but not entirely. A careful study of the development of Livy's prose style shows an increasing classicism.[5] As he goes on, the author drops certain vulgarisms, restricts the employment of frequentative verbs, and regularizes his usage. Book i may be described as 'modern' in execution as well as in style.[6] Subsequently there is a reversion to Ciceronianism, especially in the structure of sentences.

Livy was not only against the innovators. The Atticist tendency, | strongly 'anti-Ciceronian', continued to enjoy high credit. Pollio, retiring from war and politics after his campaign in Macedonia (39 B.C.), soon became the most powerful literary influence in Triumviral Rome. The advocates of the plain severe style appealed to Attic models—Lysias for the orators, Thucydides for the historian.[7] Also to Roman tradition and Roman qualities. Atticism tended to imply archaism, with its vices as well as its virtues—deliberate harshness, concision pushed to the extreme of obscurity, broken jerky rhythms and a predilection for old-fashioned words.[8] Livy in the epistle to his son spoke with distaste of the orators who affect *verba antiqua et sordida* and succumb to obscurity in the pursuit of austerity;[9] and he criticized one of Sallust's adaptations from Thucydides.[10]

Livy's enthusiasm for Cicero was political as well as literary. The

---

[1] Suetonius, *Divus Claudius* 41, 1.

[2] Seneca, *Controv.* ix 1, 14; 2, 26; Quintilian ii 5, 20; viii 2, 18; x 1, 39.

[3] That has been argued by V. Lundström, *Eranos* xxvii (1929), 1 ff. Against, Bayet, op. cit. viii.

[4] *De oratore* ii 54, cf. *Orator* 66.

[5] S. G. Stacey, *Archiv für lat. Lex.* x (1898), 17 ff. For criticism which corrects but does not invalidate Stacey's view see K. Gries, *Constancy in Livy's Latinity* (Diss. Columbia, 1959).

[6] Cf. Bayet, op. cit. lxiv.

[7] Orators who aped Thucydides moved Cicero to righteous anger (*Orator* 32).

[8] E. Norden, op. cit. 256 ff.   [9] Seneca, *Controv.* ix 2, 26.

[10] Ibid. ix 1, 14. The original was in fact a Demosthenic phrase.

municipia were in general held to be the firm strongholds of the old Roman morality—the Transpadane region especially, with Patavium first in repute.[1] Republican loyalties were emphatic. In the War of Mutina, Patavium stood by the Senate against Antonius;[2] and when Pollio held the Cisalpina for Antonius he imposed severe requisitions on that wealthy city.[3] All in all, Livy, the pride and glory of Augustan letters, should perhaps be claimed as the last of the Republican writers.[4]

The impact of change and revolution produced a lively interest in the study of history and left a permanent impress on the manner of its writing. Sallust is the supreme and convincing document. Contemporary or recent history exercised the strongest attraction. Sallust died in 35 B.C., leaving his two monographs and his unfinished *Histories* covering the years 78–67 B.C. Another retired politician, Pollio, inherited Sallust's literary adviser, the learned Ateius Philologus.[5] And Pollio soon took up the tale, narrating the fall of the Republic from the consulate of Metellus and Afranius (60 B.C.). The earliest and most vivid echo of Pollio's *Historiae* is the famous ode of Horace, 'motum ex Metello consule civicum'.[6] That poem admits of no close dating—yet it may be as early as 28 B.C.

Livy in his début can also be claimed for the 'Triumviral Period', if the term be extended to cover the years in which the heir of Caesar no longer bore the name and title of Triumvir, down to the return of 'normal government' in 28 and 27 B.C. If that be conceded, those fifteen years emerge as the most vital epoch in all the literature of the Latins.

Livy, in his *Preface*, enounces the justification for telling once again | the story of the past—superior accuracy or a style surpassing the ancients in elegance.[7] An adequate defence. But men are impelled by a variety of motives, among them discontent with the times—and discontent with history as it is written.

The style of Sallust was repellent to Livy.[8] Not less the man and his opinions—the turbulent politician expelled from the Senate but restored by Caesar and enriched by civil war; the comfortable author of a depressing history; the austere moralist of equivocal conduct.

Nor did Pollio inspire esteem everywhere. The profession of Republican sentiments had not prevented him from espousing the cause of Caesar and of Antonius; and his fine spirit of independence did not

---

[1] Martial xi 16; Pliny, *Ep.* i 14, 6. [2] Cicero, *Phil.* xii 10.
[3] Macrobius i 11, 22. [4] E. Norden, op. cit. 234 ff.
[5] Suetonius, *De gramm.* 10, 4. [6] *Odes* ii 1, 1.
[7] *Praef.* 2: 'dum novi semper scriptores aut in rebus certius aliquid allaturos se aut scribendi arte rudem vetustatem superaturos credunt.'
[8] Contrast and even aversion is deduced from the *Praefatio* by L. Amundsen, *SO* xxv (1947), 31.

counsel retirement from affairs until he had accumulated the handsome gains of a successful career. Wealth, station, honours, and security, all were his. Yet Pollio was a harsh and bitter man. His hostility towards Cicero was maintained beyond the grave; and he scorned the panegyrists of the great orator.[1] Pollio was later to express disapproval of Livy, denouncing him for *Patavinitas*.[2] No evidence survives of any retort from Patavium to Teate of the Marrucini. Livy's earliest experience of the methods of Pollio cannot have created a friendly predisposition—if, as may well be, his family was among the good citizens of Patavium penalized by the proconsul. No tradition, fable, or false erudition produces calamities in or after the Proscriptions such as are alleged to have befallen Virgil. The reason is clear. The poet attracted scholiasts, but not the historian.

Repulsion from Sallust and Pollio, the enemies of Cicero, may have reinforced Livy in his sentiments and helped to determine the tone and colour of his writing; and Livy in his turn may have served as a foil to later historians. The ex-consul L. Arruntius (*cos.* 22 B.C.) narrated the First Punic War in a manner that was fanatically Sallustian.[3]

The deeper interest in history was not confined to recent events. It touched also the remote past. Varro had compiled massive stores of antiquarian erudition. Caesar, who had an expert's taste for ritual, encouraged such studies, for personal and for political reasons.[4] With Caesar's heir, the government intervenes deliberately to revive ancient practices and institutions. The policy antedated by many years the systematic Augustan programme of a moral and religious reformation—it goes back before the War of Actium.

Various tendencies converged—scholarship, romanticism, official exploitation. While the dynasts paraded like monarchs in the theatre of the world, emulating Alexander and the rulers in his succession, it | could be foretold, in the narrower sphere of Rome's history, that the age of the Kings was coming back. Etruscan predictions or theories of cosmic cycles corresponded with the facts.

On a conventional view, *rex* and *regnum* were names of abomination. A friendlier estimate was not excluded.[5] Not all of the Seven Kings had been tyrannical. Some, indeed, were irreproachable—Numa the Sabine, who ordained the religion of the early state; Servius Tullius, the author

---

[1] Seneca, *Suas.* vi 27.   [2] For the meaning of *Patavinitas*, below, p. 453.
[3] Seneca, *Ep.* 114, 17.
[4] At least, Varro dedicated the *Antiquitates* to him (Augustine, *Civ. dei* vii 35). But too much is made of the monarchic motive in Caesar's policy by J. Carcopino, *Histoire romaine* ii (1936), 996 ff.
[5] Cf. A. Alföldi, *MH* viii (1951), 190 ff.

of a timocratic constitution, and also the friend of the Roman plebs. They could suitably be commended as virtuous *novi homines*.[1]

It would be strange if the young Caesar did not annex and exploit the myth of Romulus the Founder.[2] When he seized the consulate on 19 August 43 B.C., the omen of the twelve vultures was seen in the sky, so it was alleged (how soon, it is not clear).[3] An odd and neglected item registered under the year 38 might have some significance. The hut of Romulus on the Palatine caught fire as the result of some ritual operations (unspecified) that the *pontifices* were there performing.[4]

It is asseverated that the victor of Actium would have liked to have 'Romulus' for *cognomen*, but in fact adopted 'Augustus'. That choice, according to Florus (who may be reproducing Livy), was 'sanctius et reverentius'[5] —and it also conveyed a strong suggestion of Romulus who founded the City 'augusto augurio'.[6] The name, it could have been added, was also 'tutius'. The Founder, in favour with soldiers and populace, was not altogether liked by the Senate. Livy, reporting the Assumption of Romulus, discloses a rumour: the Founder had been massacred by the *patres*.[7]

That was only, so Livy comments, a 'perobscura fama'. The Romans loudly acclaimed their ruler as 'deum deo natum regem parentemque urbis Romanae'. Similarly Camillus, the second founder. Like Romulus, he foreshadows the third, who is 'Caesar, divi filius'.[8] Camillus was hailed as 'Romulus ac parens patriae conditorque alter urbis'.[9]

The formula applied to Romulus by Livy is solemn and even liturgical. It will be noted that early in the year 29 the name of the victorious *Divi filius* was added to the hymn of the Salii, the priests of Mars.[10]

Rome in the years before and after Actium furnished an abundance of spectacles to incite and inspire a historian—the triumphs, the ancient monuments rebuilt, the old rituals revived. In 28 no fewer than eighty-two temples were restored.[11] That is the claim of Augustus. Yet there had been considerable activity before that year. The generals of the Triumvirs had devoted war-booty to the embellishment of the City; and the interest in the Temple of Juppiter Feretrius also lies some years back.[12] |

When war was declared against a foreign enemy, the Queen of Egypt, in 32, the thing was advertised as a *bellum iustum piumque* through the ritual of the *Fetiales*.[13] That venerable confraternity had not been heard of for more than a century. Then, after victory, Janus was closed in 29 (that

---

[1] iv 3, 17 (the speech of Canuleius): 'optimis regum, novis hominibus.' For later exploitation of the plebeian King, Servius Tullius, by the *novus homo* Sejanus, cf. *Hermes* lxxxiv (1956), 257 ff. [= pp. 309 ff., above].
[2] Cf. J. Gagé, *Mélanges d'archéologie et d'histoire* xlvii (1930), 138 ff.
[3] Suetonius, *Divus Aug.* 95. [4] Dio xlviii 43, 4. [5] Florus ii 34, 66.
[6] Ennius, quoted by Varro, *Res rusticae* iii 1, 2. [7] i 16, 4. [8] Above, p. 423.
[9] v 49, 7. [10] *Res Gestae* 10, cf. Dio li 20, 1. [11] *Res Gestae* 20.
[12] Above, p. 420. [13] Dio l 4, 5.

had happened only once before since Romulus). And the *Augurium Salutis*, a ceremony recently in abeyance, was brought back.[1]

Livy was no antiquarian—he lacked the passion for facts or the collector's mania. Nor did he exploit, as he might have, the rich stores of Varronian learning.[2] But the earliest history demanded a certain veneer of antiquarianism—and a style in keeping, with an archaic formula here and there to suggest the immemorial past. There were also curious or picturesque episodes to be exploited, and legends that adhered to certain of the Roman monuments, such as the story of the Curiatii. Livy adduces the formula of trials for *perduellio*.[3] Also the ritual of the *Fetiales*, now of contemporary interest.[4] Cataloguing the institutions of Numa, however, he reveals no trace of the *Fratres Arvales*. They had not yet been resuscitated by the ruler.[5]

In one of its aspects, Book i is a colourful and eloquent guide-book. Perhaps the first intention of Livy was to satisfy the growing public interest in the Roman past by producing what was beyond the capacity of professional scholars, a readable and lively account of early Rome.[6] Perhaps Book i in its original form was composed and published separately, some years before the books on the infant Republic, success inducing the author to conceive a larger design, and, as he was later to realize, much more than he had bargained for.

Yet it is likely enough that the plan of a general history of Rome, down to his own time, was present to him from the outset. In the *Preface* Livy acknowledges his affection for the most ancient history: it enables him to turn aside from contemplating 'the calamities which for so long our time has witnessed'. But, he adds, the public will be impatient for the recent and ruinous history.[7] Despite the protestations of historians, such disturbed and deplorable periods offer the widest scope for their talents—and they sometimes avow it.

Livy proposed to sweep the annalists off the board; to transcend mere antiquarianism; to honour famous men, but not as a biographer; and to assert a nobler view of human nature than was found in the pages of

---

[1] Dio li 20, 4. Last recorded in 63 B.C. (xxxvii 24, 2).

[2] It is not perhaps important that he should ignore that scholar's view of the *spolia opima* —'M. Varro ait opima spolia esse, etiam si manipularis miles detraxerit, dummodo duci hostium' (Festus p. 204 L). [The passage, as we have it, is corrupt and difficult to interpret.] But it appears that he was unaware of the cycle of 110 years for the *Ludi Saeculares*; cf. the evidence of Censorinus, who cites *commentarii* and Horace's hymn against Livy (*De die natali* 17, 9).

[3] i 25, 6 ff.   [4] i 24, 4 ff.

[5] The *Arvales* are not in Dionysius either. Hence a clue to the value of the sources they employ.

[6] His account of Numa does not therefore reflect even partially 'die Reformbestrebungen des Augustus', as G. Stübler claims (*Die Religiosität des Livius* (1941), 34).

[7] *Praef.* 4: 'festinantibus ad haec nova quibus iam pridem praevalentis populi vires se ipsae conficiunt.'

Sallust. His *Res Romanae* were to be moral, patriotic, and edifying, an exhortation, supported by the examples of the glorious past, to that rebirth of Rome which, when he wrote his *Preface*, was not yet even a programme but only an aspiration.

The significance of the Triumviral Period for Roman historiography | becomes evident, both in general and with reference to three men, Sallust, Pollio, and Livy. The eldest, Sallust, is in certain respects the most modern, for all the archaism of his vocabulary. The youngest is an anomalous figure. Sallust and Pollio were bitter and pessimistic; but Livy seems comparatively untouched by the era of tribulation. The Ciceronian features of his style make him something of a stranger in his own generation. His mind was formed before the Battle of Actium, his history begun before *pax et princeps* was firmly established.[1] Yet that history turns out to be the enduring monument of the spirit and the majesty of Augustan Rome. As with Virgil, Augustus was very lucky.

Ancient legends and the new monarchy—both Virgil and Livy illuminate their age. Virgil, who might have composed epics about the Kings (Alban or Roman) or a verse panegyric on the life and exploits of Caesar's heir, found in the *Aeneid* a subtle and superior device for linking the origins and destiny of the imperial city to the glorious present; and Livy narrated the annals of Rome from the beginning to their culmination with the establishment of the monarchy.

Did either influence the other? It appears not. They are independent, using the same material in much the same spirit.[2] Moreover, by time of writing the priority belongs to Livy, with Book i at least to his credit while Virgil was still completing the *Georgics*.

Livy (it has been said) is a kind of prose Virgil. A helpful conception. But the legends and fictions of regal Rome and of the early Republic are only a small portion of his achievement. A large question remains: how did Livy manage the history of his own time, the *municipalis eques* taking up the challenge of the senators Sallust and Pollio?

III. *The Reign of Augustus*

When the historian, having brought to completion the narrative of the Second Punic War, paused for a moment and looked ahead, he was

---

[1] The concept of 'Augustan' requires careful definition and restrained handling. Cf. above, p. 401, and *JRS* xxxv (1945), 104 [= pp. 172 f., above]. Also A. Momigliano, ibid. 142 ff. and A. H. McDonald in *Fifty Years of Classical Scholarship* (ed. M. Platnauer, 1954), 397, referring to 'the higher interpretation of his Augustan sentiment'.

[2] A. Rostagni, *Scritti minori* ii 2 (1956), 201 ff.

filled with dismay. An ocean threatened to engulf him.[1] His apprehensions were well grounded. He had found his style, hence ease of composition, once the material had been grasped and digested. But the material kept expanding. Livy was slow to distinguish a good from a bad historian. His account of the period from Zama to Pydna does not reveal a master's hand in the manipulation of historical sources, or any gift for structure.

His predicament got worse and worse as he advanced towards his | own day. The record became abundant and intricate, perplexing and hazardous. It was no longer enough to stand by a single annalist, noting the more important variants, or, using several, to strike a mean of general probability and glide with graceful scepticism over the harmonies or discordances of fable and invention. The safe and venerable annals of the Roman past gave place to real history, alive and recalcitrant.

Such was Asinius Pollio's history of his own time. It was acclaimed by Horace with due sense of the peculiar hazards attendant on the task. It was in truth 'periculosae plenum opus aleae'.[2] Pollio was promenading his Muse across the ash and lava of a recent eruption—'per ignes / suppositos cineri doloso'. The ground was firmer when Livy, some twenty years later, came to tell of the fall of the Republic.

Many of the traps and pitfalls had been removed, or at least explained away. The professions of the victorious party underwent a rapid metamorphosis. Having abolished the Republic, Octavianus pretended to restore it; and Caesar's heir came to terms with Caesar's enemies. There ensued a certain rehabilitation of Pompeius—and even of Cato. It was therefore possible for Livy to write as a *Pompeianus* without fear of any reproach from Caesar Augustus.[3] The Princeps himself could approve of Cato as a good citizen who (like himself) did not wish the law and the constitution to be subverted.[4] Caesar was the 'divine' parent of Octavianus, avenged and honoured by the *pietas* of his son. Hence a double advantage. The deification of Caesar rendered it easy to depersonalize him, to dissociate *Divus Julius* from *Dictator Caesar*. Of Caesar the Dictator there is scant mention in Augustan literature: blame rather than praise.[5] Livy debated whether Caesar's birth were not a greater curse than blessing to the world.[6] The testimony of Virgil is parallel—and convincing. No place for Caesar in the ancestry of Caesar Augustus. He is thrown out of that context and introduced later, only to be exhorted in solemn tones to disarm before Pompeius. Neither is named, but they are

---

[1] xxxi 1, 5: 'iam provideo animo, velut qui proximis litori vadis inducti mare pedibus ingrediuntur, quidquid progredior, in vastiorem me altitudinem ac velut profundum invehi, et crescere paene opus quod prima quaeque perficiendo minui videbatur.'
[2] *Odes* ii 1, 6.   [3] Tacitus, *Ann.* iv 34, 3.
[4] Macrobius ii 4, 18 (in answer to Strabo, i.e. Seius Strabo).
[5] Cf. *Rom. Rev.* (1939), 317 f.; *Tacitus* (1958), 432 ff.
[6] Seneca, *NQ* v 18, 4.

designated as *socer* and *gener* in a political and matrimonial compact that had lapsed.[1]

Pompeius and Cato were conveniently out of the way before Octavianus appeared on the scene. Therefore freedom of treatment was not merely permitted but encouraged by Augustus. Very different was the history after 44 B.C. What was to be said of the career of Caesar's heir— treachery and violence, proscription and murder? Many of the actors in that tragedy were still alive.

A member of the imperial family was incited to the study of history by the example and the counsels of Livy. It was the young Claudius, | the son of Drusus.[2] Unfortunate, however, in his first choice of a subject. He wanted to write about the Civil Wars. His mother, Antonia, and his grandmother, Livia, frightened him off, so he fell back upon the years of peace, the reign of Caesar Augustus.

The government was unable to suppress the entire truth about the revolutionary period. Too many of the opponents of Octavianus, both Republicans and Antonians, were extant, some of them occupying positions of profit and eminence in the new order. As was pertinently remarked, the victor recruited his friends and allies from the ranks of his adversaries.[3] The national and patriotic front that won the War of Actium was a peculiar conglomeration. Many of the adherents of Octavianus had a past to live down: traitors to every cause, such as Munatius Plancus. Some kept silent. Others were not ashamed of the part they had played. The eloquent and patrician Messalla Corvinus was proud to have fought at Philippi, under Brutus and Cassius.[4] And rightly. Men of lesser station would be no less eager to affirm that they had been there, when *Virtus* was shattered and the Republic went down before the Caesarian armies. If Messalla (and other Republicans) had not written their memoirs and recalled their loyalties, there was the redoubtable Pollio, Caesarian and Antonian in allegiance, Republican in spirit, and, before all else, ferociously independent.

Furthermore, despite victory, peace, and restored Republic, the new dispensation was precarious and insecure. Caesar Augustus could not rule without the consent and support of the nobility. Some rallied to the government. Hence, in a year of crisis (23 B.C.), Cn. Piso, a Republican, appointed consul, and L. Sestius, once quaestor of M. Brutus. At the same time, the heroes and the ideals of the Republic were accorded especial honour by the heir of Caesar. It is easy enough for a government to filch and furbish up the forms and phrases of its adversaries, and Caesar Augustus operated with dexterity. There was also a genuine and tangible revival

---

[1] *Aen.* vi 826 ff.   [2] Suetonius, *Divus Claudius* 41, 1.
[3] Seneca, *De clem.* i 10, 1.   [4] Tacitus, *Ann.* iv 34, 4.

of the Republic—the old houses came back, to public honour and perhaps to hopes of power. The emergence of the *nobiles* is significant. Not for some time after Actium, despite certain aristocratic partisans already in the alliance of the victor, such as Messalla Corvinus and Paullus Aemilius Lepidus. Twelve or fifteen years elapsed; and, a little later, several families became very important in the period when, Agrippa dead and Tiberius in exile at Rhodes, Augustus, frail and decrepit, needed the alliance of the aristocracy to safeguard the dynasty and to secure the succession for his grandsons, Gaius and Lucius.[1] |

For these reasons a historian might, if he chose, fortified by illustrious examples—and perhaps by the favour of families in the *nobilitas*—narrate the history of the Civil Wars from a Republican or Pompeian point of view, without risk or censure. Ostensible independence might well be profit and advantage. There was an easier path. The Republican and the Caesarian versions might be combined. Why not? The heir of Caesar blended Caesarism with the Republic in his *novus status*.

Livy was able to benefit from the official version of Triumviral history. It can be recovered in various ways. On epigraphic record, the *Res Gestae* of Augustus preserve the outline. The *Autobiography* of the Princeps was more explicit. Its influence can be traced in many details, surviving in subsequent historians, where the actions of Octavianus called for apology. Livy, and later writers, whether they drew on Livy or not, provide adequate evidence.[2] The general argument of the *Autobiography* can be summed up—*pietas, necessitudo rei publicae*, and *clementia*. The claims of *pietas*, neglected by Antonius (the disloyal Caesarian who was ready to come to terms with Brutus and Cassius) enforced the duty of revenge against the assassins of Caesar. There was no alternative to armed action; it was justified by patriotism; and the victor was merciful.[3]

Further, to save the faces of old enemies—and new associates—various scapegoats were available. Sex. Pompeius was displayed as a pirate, Lepidus as a decayed and pretentious relic, Marcus Antonius as a voluptuary, the slave and victim of the strange woman. The War of Actium was not a civil war but a crusade against a foreign enemy. 'Nefas, Aegyptia coniunx.'[4]

The blame for the proscriptions might be laid upon the other Triumvirs, Antonius and Lepidus. Yet the murder of Cicero was most awkward. Young Octavianus had flattered and honoured him, had called him by the name of 'father'.[5] The cardinal virtues of *pietas* and *clementia* ought to have intervened to save the great orator. They did not avail. Cicero

[1] Cf. *Rom. Rev.* (1939), 373; 419 ff.
[2] See the detailed study of F. Blumenthal, *WS* xxxv (1913), 113 ff.; xxxvi (1914), 84 ff. For the fragments, E. Malcovati, *Imperatoris Caesaris Augusti Operum Fragmenta*⁵ (1969), 84 ff.   [3] Cf. Tacitus, *Ann.* i 9.   [4] *Aen.* viii 688.
[5] Brutus to Atticus (*Ad M. Brutum* 25, 5 = i 17, 5, cf. Plutarch, *Cicero* 45).

perished. Caesar Augustus might revive, from interested motives, the memory of Pompeius Magnus and of Cato. Cicero, like Brutus, remained under a cloud, a fact which should perplex those who prefer to see their Roman history through the eyes of both Cicero and Augustus, with no thought of all the Romans who distrusted both of them. The style of Cicero quickly became unfashionable. Nor is it easy to believe that his political ideals were studied, admired, and adopted by Caesar's heir and his associates in power. There is cited, to be sure, an improving anecdote. 'A great writer and a great patriot', so Augustus said to one of the young princes, his | grandsons.[1] That is not enough. More instructive is the cool judgement which Livy, who was a fervent admirer of Cicero, passed on the last actions and tragic end of his hero. Cicero (he pointed out) suffered from his enemies only what he would have done to them had he prevailed.[2]

An official version of recent history thus facilitated the task of Livy. The paths of duty and of inclination coincided, for the victorious cause, by liberating Rome from the threat of foreign domination, by establishing peace, order, and concord, had shown itself to be the 'better cause'.

Unfortunately, the material difficulty subsisted. The story was rich and complex—and so was the written record. The chief history available was that of Asinius Pollio. No doubt sound on facts, but not of a suitable 'tendency'. The *Historiae* of the eminent consular, which probably ended with the Battle of Philippi, were critical and subversive. As for memoirs, the Princeps' *Autobiography* led the field. Dominant all through for the interpretation of events, it was perhaps the sole available source for such matters as the campaigns in Illyricum in 35 and 34 B.C. Further, Agrippa, Messalla, the ex-Antonian Q. Dellius—and no doubt many other authors —had their contributions to make. Biographies were also written of illustrious Romans in the recent past—friends, relatives, and clients left their memorials of Marcus Brutus.[3] Again, it might be necessary to consult letters, speeches, or despatches for information not otherwise available. For example, the oration which Sallust composed for the great Ventidius may have been an important source for the eastern wars in 40–38 B.C.[4] Above all, the literature of propaganda and abuse, ranging from the missives interchanged between Octavianus and Antonius to such *curiosa* as Antonius' *De ebrietate sua*, or the erotic correspondence between Q. Dellius and the Queen of Egypt (entertaining but not perhaps authentic).[5]

---

[1] Plutarch, *Cicero* 49.
[2] Quoted by Seneca, *Suas.* vi 22: 'omnium adversorum nihil ut viro dignum erat tulit praeter mortem, quae vere aestimanti minus indigna videri potuit quod a victore inimico nihil crudelius passurus erat quam quod eiusdem fortunae compos victo fecisset.'
[3] Plutarch, *Brutus* 2; 13; 23; 48.   [4] O. Hirschfeld, *Kl. Schriften* (1913), 781 ff.
[5] For the propaganda war, K. Scott, *MAAR* xi (1933), 7 ff.; M. P. Charlesworth, *CQ* xxvii (1933), 172 ff.

Patent partisans and the grosser fabrications need not have given much trouble. But there was room almost everywhere for slight and subtle misrepresentation, especially in the order and interaction of events. The years 44 and 43 B.C. were especially complex, if they were to be narrated as political history (and not, as happens so often in modern times, as a part of the biography of Cicero). Even now it is difficult to disentangle the truth about such matters as the allotment of provinces before and after Caesar's death, though here (it must be admitted) some of the confusion may be due to the errors or misrepresentations of historians later than Livy.[1] The actors were numerous, their evolutions | intricate. For example, when was the important meeting of the Senate to have occurred about which Cicero was informed at Leucopetra (near Rhegium) early in August of 44: on the first day of August or on the first day of September?[2] Or, when did Brutus decide to take possession of Macedonia? After Octavianus' march on Rome (he entered the city on 10 November), or after the session of the Senate on 28 November?[3] To avoid error, perpetual vigilance was necessary, a steady consultation and comparison of documents. It would not look well for a historian with a world-wide reputation to confess doubt or ignorance about facts which could be ascertained by the exercise of care and diligence.

Livy narrated the story of the years 44 to 29 in great abundance of detail. From the advent of Octavianus to the Battle of Philippi no fewer than eight books were needed (cxvii–cxxiv); and nine more down to the triumph of Octavianus (cxxv–cxxxiii). Not the easiest, but, along with the appendix on the reign of Augustus, surely the most difficult section of the whole work.

It remains to examine the last nine books (cxxxiv–cxlii), the guiding theme of which was presumably *res publica restituta*. From the outbreak of the war between Pompeius Magnus and Caesar, the history of Livy was the history of his own time: he now had to deal with events that had occurred since he began his work.

At first sight, a welcome change of subject after the long years of confusion and calamity. The dangers that threatened to destroy Rome and shatter the *imperium* of the Roman People had been arrested; certain unsatisfactory persons had been eliminated; others were converted to political sanity. Morality returned to public life—or at least a firm and central control. The *res publica restituta* was a blessing for a historian. History itself, like the Roman State, had been brought back into the right and

---

1 That was not properly cleared up before the studies of Schwartz and Sternkopf, *Hermes* xxxiii (1898), 185 ff.; xlvii (1912), 321 ff.

2 *Ad Att.* xvi 7, 1; *Phil.* i 8. Cf. *Rom. Rev.* (1939), 117 f.

3 Gelzer (*RE* x, col. 1000) suggests that Brutus did not move until he learned of that session. Probably too late.

traditional path. In the briefest of Roman definitions, the Republic consisted in the government of annual consuls, chosen by election. And the Republic subsisted until such election was abolished: in fact, until A.D. 14. After long labours and wanderings Livy could revert to the annalistic method—'annos a consule nomen habentes'.[1]

The material now grouped itself around the proper activities of Senate, People, and magistrates. Free elections returned, but managed (one presumes). There were some electoral contests (in 22–19 B.C.), until such an exercise of *libertas* was seen to be pernicious or futile. Comitial legislation came back, dignified by a Princeps bringing before | the sovereign People a programme of moral reform and social regeneration. The majesty of the Roman name was advertised when ambassadors brought gifts and homage from distant peoples, from the Scythians, from the lands towards the Caucasus, from India; the *patres* heard with pride the reports of victorious proconsuls and voted them honours; and petitions from the Hellenic cities recalled the grants and dispositions of the imperial Republic that had broken and abased the monarchs in the succession of Alexander.

Above all, the antiquarian operations of the government provided rich material for an annalistic record of the accepted scope and content— games and ceremonies, temples dedicated or restored, ancient observances brought back to life. The celebration of the *Ludi Saeculares*, or the choice of a *flamen Dialis* (the first for seventy-five years), demanded learned digressions, combining, for an artistic historian, the claims of tradition and variety. Further, the installation of Augustus as *pontifex maximus* and the dedication of the *Ara Pacis* were important acts of public policy.

The private beliefs of the educated were irrelevant to the ritual and the fabric of the state religion. They cannot still have believed in portents and prodigies. But such manifestations had not abated in the last age of the Republic. A shower of bricks fell from the heavens when Milo was prosecuted; and a mule giving birth foretold civic dissensions.[2] Livy, it is true, deplored the fact that faith had vanished in his own day, that there were no more *prodigia* on official record or in the pages of historians.[3] His regrets disclose his ignorance, or a thoughtless reverence for pious antiquity. When he came to narrate the reign of Augustus, he was not disappointed. Portents continued duly to be reported, as is shown not merely by Cassius Dio but by a writer who took his examples from Livy.[4] Fire, flood, and pestilence were not infrequent visitations.[5] With the record of such matters, and with the deaths of illustrious men (loyal servants of the Republic and the dynasty), the annals of each year might find a suitable termination.[6]

[1] Lucan vii 441.   [2] Pliny, *NH* ii 147; Obsequens 65 (50 B.C.).   [3] xliii 13, 1.
[4] Obsequens 70 (17 B.C.).   [5] Notably in the winter of 23–22 B.C. (Dio liii 33, 5).
[6] For Tacitus' practice, cf. *AJP* lxxix (1958), 18 ff. [= *Ten Studies in Tacitus* (1970), 79 ff.].

So far the structure. The rest was not at all easy. A later writer, Cassius Dio, reveals the truth about imperial history.[1] Hitherto, he says, the more important transactions came to public notice and passed into historical record; the truth, even though deformed by favour or prejudice, could more or less be ascertained. Now, however, secrecy began to envelop the acts of the government, and the published account of events was naturally suspect, as being the official version. The facts were unknown, fiction and variants everywhere rampant. In any case the very magnitude of the Empire and the complexity of its | government tended to debar from exact knowledge anybody not directly concerned.

When Livy began to set down in writing the annals of *res publica restituta* (perhaps towards A.D. 6),[2] he had few, if any, predecessors. Livy appears to have the field largely to himself. His previous achievement was enough to deter competitors from encroaching; and it had earned him the rank of the official Roman historian.

What other writers were there? Despite the interest in history aroused by the revolutionary age, the Principate of Augustus can show few historians. Apart from Livy, they are little more than names, and hardly any of them seem to have dealt with the years of peace and order after the end of the Civil Wars.

The consular historians L. Arruntius (*cos.* 22 B.C.) and C. Clodius Licinus (*cos. suff.* A.D. 4) dealt with an earlier period, perhaps in emulation of Livy.[3] A certain Cornutus has been disinterred, who appears to have written about the Civil Wars: surely of slight importance.[4]

For the rest, in the list of historians contemporary with Livy (apart from mere biographers or scholars), only three names deserve any consideration, and they can quickly be dismissed. The *Historiae Philippicae* of the learned Narbonensian, Pompeius Trogus, reached the reign of Augustus in two of its sections, the Spanish wars and Parthian history. The latest event to be mentioned was the surrender of prisoners, military standards, and hostages by the King of Parthia.[5] Trogus' work was universal in scope, and it conceived history from the Macedonian, not the Roman, point of view. The date of its publication is uncertain, perhaps before 2 B.C.[6] It is doubtful whether Livy needed, or cared, to use it. When Trogus wrote, something (and perhaps a lot) of Livy had already been published, for Trogus criticized Livy's practice of inserting speeches in direct discourse.[7]

T. Labienus, a *Pompeianus* of a very different breed from Livy, was not only a famous speaker. He wrote histories, parts of which he refused to make public.[8] Labienus was an irreconcilable adherent of the defeated

---

[1] Dio liii 19. 　　　　[2] Below, p. 448. 　　　　[3] *PIR*[2], A 1129; C 1167.
[4] Cichorius, *Römische Studien* (1922), 261 ff. 　　　　[5] Justin xlii 5, 11 f.
[6] R. Helm, *RE* xxi, col. 2301. 　　　　[7] Justin xxxviii 3, 11.
[8] Seneca, *Controv.* x, *praef.* 4 ff.

cause: surely of no use to Livy, even had he narrated the later years, of which there is no evidence. The same tendency was represented, perhaps in a milder form, by A. Cremutius Cordus, prosecuted in A.D. 25 'because he had praised Brutus and called Cassius the last of the Romans'.[1] Further, Seneca, in a treatise to his daughter, asseverates that he damned the authors of the Proscriptions to eternal infamy.[2] However, it is stated that Augustus had been present at recitations of his work.[3] Cordus dealt also with the beginnings of the reign. He is quoted by Suetonius for an incident in 18 B.C., hardly of a | kind to commend itself to Augustus: on the occasion of the *lectio senatus*, senators were only admitted to the Curia one by one, and after bodily search.[4] The completed work may not, in fact, have been given to the world before, or much before, A.D. 25. It may—or may not—have been an important source for later writers.[5] In any case, there is no evidence that Cordus' account of the years after Actium was composed before Livy's epilogue.

Nor would Roman pride descend to the use of Greek sources if it could be helped. Livy had not, it appears, consulted Posidonius for the Gracchan period.[6] Nor is it likely that he drew upon certain inferior competitors or successors of Polybius for contemporary affairs—Strabo, Nicolaus, and Timagenes. As for Strabo's *History*, it probably ended at 30 B.C. when Alexandria fell, the last of the Ptolemies perished, and the last of the Hellenistic kingdoms lapsed to the empire of the Romans.[7] Nicolaus, however, fluent in 144 books, went down to 4 B.C.[8]

Nicolaus and Strabo were of about the same age as Livy. Timagenes of Alexandria was a little older. The influence of his work, invoked by some scholars for another section of Livy, the geographical digressions on Gaul and Germany in Books ciii–civ, is not easy to ascertain.[9] Timagenes was an objectionable fellow, anti-Roman in spirit—'felicitati urbis inimicus'.[10] Cast off by the Princeps, he was harboured by Pollio. If his name lurks under the disdainful plural of the 'levissimi ex Graecis' in an early book of Livy, who extolled the fame of Alexander and favoured the Parthians against Rome, it is irrelevant to the present inquiry.[11]

---

1 Tacitus, *Ann.* iv 34, 1.
2 Seneca, *Ad Marciam* 26, 1: 'proscribentes in aeternum ipse proscripsit.'
3 Suetonius, *Tib.* 61, 3; Dio lvii 24, 3 [reading ἐκείνῳ for the MSS. ἐκεῖνος; Tacitus (loc. cit.) does not seem to know of this tradition]. 4 Suetonius, *Divus Aug.* 35, 2.
5 Kornemann argued that he was the main source of Appian's *Bella civilia* (*Klio* xvii (1921), 33 ff.). Against, W. Ensslin, *Klio* xx (1926), 463 ff.
6 E. Meyer, *Kl. Schriften* i (1910), 421.
7 The terminal date of 27 B.C., assumed by Honigmann (*RE* iv A, col. 90) and others, can hardly be correct. 8 Jacoby, *FGrH* ii C 229.
9 For a discussion, strongly negative, see R. Laqueur, *RE* vi A, coll. 1063 ff.
10 Seneca, *Ep.* 91, 13.
11 ix 18, 6. For Timagenes, R. Laqueur, *RE* vi A, coll. 1063 ff.; P. Treves, *Il mito di Alessandro e la Roma d'Augusto* (1953), 39 ff. [There is no reason to think that Timagenes expressed this view or is here intended.]

Livy was therefore compelled to collect, digest, and shape the material for himself—official documents, verbal information, and his own reminiscences. That useful guide, the *Memoirs* of Caesar Augustus, ended very soon, with the campaign of the Spanish wars which was conducted by the Princeps in person, namely the *Bellum Cantabricum* of 26 B.C.[1] That fact had a perceptible effect on the tradition. Augustus in the *Autobiography* narrated only his own exploits.[2] Therefore the operations of the column of invasion commanded by the Princeps in 26 B.C. were recorded in detail.[3] Little or nothing was said about the other two columns of the army of Hispania Citerior, or about the other army, that of Hispania Ulterior.[4] For the campaigns of the next year, historians had to use other sources—and were probably guilty of a serious error about the order of events, namely the capture of the town of Lancia by P. Carisius, Augustus' legate in Hispania Ulterior. That action is narrated at the end of 25 B.C. It clearly belongs to the beginning of a campaign, probably that of 26 B.C.[5] |

The *acta senatus* provided the kind of material that Livy needed, a pretty full account of official business. One of the ruler's earliest acts had been to suppress the publication of this record.[6] Yet access would not perhaps have been denied to an approved person such as Livy, although he was not a senator. In the Senate's archives stood, among other things, the speeches of Augustus and other pronouncements of significance for public policy. About military events, provincial governors in their dispatches furnished detailed evidence, often with an eye to honours. According to Cassius Dio (under the year 19 B.C.), many proconsuls not only aspired to triumphs but celebrated them, for no other merit than suppression of brigandage or the establishment of internal order in the cities of the Empire.[7] That is an exaggeration. After Sex. Appuleius (January 26 B.C.), the only proconsuls to be voted triumphs were Sempronius Atratinus and Cornelius Balbus, both from Africa (21 and 19 B.C.). Nor was the Princeps silent about the successes achieved in the wide territories of his own *provincia*. Later, however, as the imperial system developed, the Senate came to learn less and less about the provinces of Caesar; and certain military operations, failing to find public record, might easily escape the

---

[1] Suetonius, *Divus Aug.* 85, 1: *Cantabrico tenus bello nec ultra.* [In fact, 25 B.C.: see p. 848 below.]

[2] Appian, *Ill.* 15.

[3] As is clear from the accounts in Orosius v 21, 1–5; Florus ii 33.

[4] Failure to allow for the second army impairs the value of D. Magie's study (*CP* xv (1920), 323 ff.). Cf. observations pp. [837 f. below]. Schulten's elaborate work is very useful (*Los Cántabros y Astures y su guerra con Roma*, 1943), but contains errors, e.g. his notion that Lucus (Lugo, in Callaecia) was in Roman hands before the war (p. 177).

[5] Cf. [pp. 835; 844 ff. below].

[6] Suetonius, *Divus Aug.* 36.

[7] Dio lv 25, 1.

notice of history. For the time of Augustus, certain geographical information goes back to the *acta senatus*, for example the full record of towns and
tribes traversed by Balbus in his march to the land of the Garamantes, in
the far south, in Fezzan.[1] Similarly, curiosity is excited by Pliny's brief
notice about the tribe of the Homonadenses in the Taurus, Homana their
capital, and their forty-four *castella*.[2] This may well derive from the record
of a grant of *ornamenta triumphalia* to the legate P. Sulpicius Quirinius for
his successful campaign (of unknown date).[3]

To supplement or elucidate official documents, it might be expedient
for an historian who was not a senator to question those who knew. Livy
was on terms of amity with the household of the Princeps, as witness
Augustus' decisive revelation about the *spolia opima*, and the interest shown
in the historical studies of young Claudius. Otherwise there is a singular
absence of evidence about patrons and friends.

Without the *acta senatus*, he would have been in a sorry plight. The case
of Strabo is in point: the city or cities where he wrote (and revised) his
Geography seem to have put him out of touch with information about
contemporary wars. One example will suffice. Balbus' march to the land
of the Garamantes was sheer delight for a geographer. Strabo knows
nothing of it.[4]

Livy may have had access to the *acta senatus*. A large part of his narrative
was devoted to wars—from choice, for it recalled an earlier | and happier
period, and from necessity, to avoid awkward topics and fill space.
Whereas the two books of which the *Periochae* are missing (cxxxvi and
cxxxvii) appear to have covered the years 24 to 17 B.C. inclusive, and the
next carried the record to the beginning of 12 B.C. (cxxxviii, mentioning
the death of Agrippa), the last four books embrace the four years of
Tiberius' and Drusus' campaigns in Illyricum and Germany (12–9 B.C.).
A splendid theme. As a later historian was mournfully to remark, his
Republican predecessors had all the luck—'ingentia illi bella, expugna-
tiones urbium, fusos captosque reges.'[5] Livy on the campaigns of the two
Claudii did his best to put himself back in the atmosphere of the foreign
wars in the great age.

This was the culmination of the grandiose Augustan plan of conquest
in central Europe. Many diverse operations had prepared the way; and
almost every other region of the Empire had been subjected to a process
of methodical consolidation, especially Spain, the Alpine lands, and the
Balkans. Noteworthy, for example, is the variety of campaigns chron-
icled by Cassius Dio in resumptive sections, under 25 B.C. and 16 B.C.

[1] Pliny, *NH* v 35 f. [2] *NH* v 94.
[3] Tacitus, *Ann.* iii 48, 1; Strabo xii 6, 5, p. 569.
[4] Though Cn. Piso (*cos.* 7 B.C.), a former proconsul, told him something about African
geography (ii 5, 33, p. 130).
[5] Tacitus, *Ann.* iv 32, 1.

(the latter covering the events of 19–16 B.C.).[1] It follows that military operations of the period 28–9 B.C., having been recounted in Livy's annals, stood a better chance of surviving in the literary tradition than certain campaigns subsequent to 9 B.C. Later writers, whether they had drawn on Livy or not, tend to be thin and inadequate for the military history of the next dozen years. This is partly, but not wholly, due to the fact that Livy stopped at 9 B.C. It must be recalled that Velleius makes deliberate omissions for political reasons; and the text of Dio is defective in the period 6 B.C.–A.D. 4.[2]

The veteran historian had had plenty of practice at military narration, but the geography should have given him some trouble. In the subjugation of the north-west of Spain, the legions of Augustus penetrated to regions untouched by the armies of the Republic. New ground was also broken in central Europe. Drusus reached the Elbe; and Tiberius extended the bounds of Illyricum to the Danube. It must be conceded, however, that exact and up-to-date geographical knowledge was not demanded of Roman historians.[3]

Tacitus' account of the campaigns of Germanicus (perhaps designed to recall Livy to his readers) shows how much could be done. Yet even the writing of military history, innocuous theme, could not be entirely free from preoccupation in the time of Augustus. The prestige of Princeps and dynasty was paramount. The official version celebrated the Spanish campaigns of 26 and 25 B.C. as the final conquest, justifying Augustus' second closing of the temple of Janus. Yet there was serious | fighting in 24 and 22 B.C.; and in 19 B.C. Agrippa completed the subjugation of the north-west. In fact, there is good cause for speaking of a ten years' war in Spain.[4] It was easy enough for a dishonest writer like Velleius Paterculus—profound peace in Spain, not even disturbed by brigandage after Augustus left the peninsula.[5] A scrupulous annalist had to record the detail of the wars in Spain, to the end. At the same time, bright colour and high relief for the Princeps' campaign in 26 B.C.

Nor was it desirable that the exploits of his stepsons should be clouded by a too emphatic commemoration of other generals. All students of the *Odes* of Horace know that the Alpine lands were conquered in 15 B.C. by the swift and convergent campaign of the two Claudii, Tiberius and Drusus.[6] The preliminary and necessary operations have all but lapsed

---

[1] Dio liii 25, 3 ff.; liv 20, 1 ff.

[2] These two factors must always be allowed for when there is obscurity or dispute about the dates of certain military operations. Cf. *CQ* xxvii (1933), 146 [= *Danubian Papers*, 31]; *Klio* xxvii (1934), 138; *JRS* xxiv (1934), 121 ff. [= *Danubian Papers*, 48 ff.].

[3] Some of the information had been supplied previously, in the digression on Germany (*Per.* civ); perhaps also in the account of Octavianus' campaigns in Illyricum in 35 and 34 B.C. (cxxxi and cxxxii). Fresh knowledge had accrued.

[4] Cf. *AJP* lv (1934), 314 [and pp. 825; 849 below].   [5] Velleius ii 90, 4.

[6] *Odes* iv 4 and 14.

from record. From the side of northern Italy P. Silius Nerva prepared the way for Drusus: one source only records his activities.[1] In Gaul the predecessor of Tiberius was M. Lollius. Partisan history, best represented by Velleius, saddles him with a serious disaster.[2] A milder and better tradition, however, has been preserved.[3] Velleius' version can easily be explained. Lollius was a bitter enemy of Tiberius, if not now, at least later.

Again, Tiberius' conquests in Illyricum (12–9 B.C.) were prepared and facilitated by the operations of M. Vinicius, proconsul of Illyricum (14–13 B.C.), and by Agrippa himself (his last achievement) in the winter of 13/12 B.C.[4] If, as every theory assumes, Livy was narrating these events after A.D. 4, discretion was required of the historian. Agrippa was long dead, but Vinicius was one of the generals employed in high commands during the period of Tiberius' exile at Rhodes—and like others, dropped after A.D. 4.[5]

If the foreign wars of the restored Republic demanded circumspection, what of internal affairs? The truth could not be told, even if it could be ascertained. When Tacitus was composing his *Histories*, civil war and despotism the theme, he professed to reserve for his old age the history of that happy and contemporaneous epoch, the reigns of Nerva and Trajan. He did not carry out his promise (not that it should so be regarded), but turned back to the period of the Julii and the Claudii. For a number of good reasons. A similar difficulty confronted Livy. The new order, the *felicissimus status*, was not all that it seemed to be. What was he to say about such episodes as the alleged conspiracy of Varro Murena in 23 B.C.? A consul had to be discarded and destroyed, one of the leading partisans of Augustus, no less than the brother-in-law of Maecenas. Moreover, there was the whole | dynastic policy of Augustus, his ambitions for Marcellus, and the secret struggle for power in that year when Augustus seemed close to death.

No historian gives a satisfactory account of those transactions—let alone an interpretation. It is a suspicious fact that in the narrative of Dio the conspiracy should be postdated and put in 22 B.C., not 23.[6] Nor does any ancient source explicitly record the grant to Agrippa of a share in the provincial *imperium* of Caesar Augustus. It only emerges indirectly.[7]

By eschewing high politics and keeping anxiously to a dry and annalistic record, it was still possible for Livy to write a history of the years 28–9 B.C. that should not be an uneasy amalgam of adulation and mendacity, like Velleius'. But he could not go much further.

[1] Dio liv 20, 1. [See D. van Berchem, *MH* xxv (1968), 1 ff.] [2] Velleius ii 97, 1.
[3] Dio liv 20, 4 ff. (under 16 B.C.). Obsequens 71 has 17 B.C., presumably the true date.
[4] Velleius ii 96, 3; Florus ii 24, 8; Dio liv 24, 3 (without any general's name).
[5] *Rom. Rev.* (1939), 435. [6] Dio liv 3.
[7] *Rom. Rev.* (1939), 427. [See now *ZPE* v (1970), 217 ff. and vi (1970), 227 ff.]

The real history is secret history. If that were not implicit in the new dispensation from the outset, it was revealed and demonstrated by the events of the years 6 B.C.–A.D. 4. Tiberius abruptly refused to support and facilitate the dynastic policy of Augustus, insistent for the succession of his grandsons Gaius and Lucius. Then came the scandal and disgrace of Julia, the Princeps' daughter—or rather the "conspiracy of the five *nobiles*"; and the young Caesars, inadequate bearers of a great name and unworthy of their parentage, passed away. Augustus was constrained first to permit the return of Tiberius and then to adopt him, with a share of the imperial powers. The Claudian was now *vindex custosque imperii* (A.D. 4).[1] Internal and domestic politics had suffered a revolutionary change. It was not merely that one plan of succession had failed, to be replaced by another. An important nexus of noble houses, standing behind the dynasty in those difficult years, saw its high ambitions frustrated. The enemies and the rivals of Tiberius were now displaced; and a new group of families came to the fore, some with Pompeian blood, many with Pompeian allegiance.[2] More trouble for the historian, many occasions for giving personal offence, not least if he tried to be impartial. Yet impartiality was out of the question.

It required the peculiar talents of Velleius Paterculus to do justice to these transactions.[3] The departure of Tiberius shook the whole world—the Germans rebelled and the Parthians seized Armenia. His return meant that Rome's rule would be eternal. Peace, tranquillity, security, salvation dawned for mankind; the sanctity of the family and of property was guaranteed. Only loyalty to Augustus had induced Tiberius to go away to Rhodes—'mira quaedam et incredibilis atque inenarrabilis pietas.' He did not want to stand in the way of the young princes, but such was Tiberius' modesty that he concealed the reason. Patriotism brought him back. |

On the other side stood the unsatisfactory Julia and her depraved paramours; and, as a scapegoat for the conduct of Gaius Caesar, his guide and counsellor, M. Lollius, who fell from favour and was removed by a providential death, to the general rejoicing. Tiberius was indispensable to the Empire. Nobody else was of any use. Hence, in Velleius, silence about the exploits of Roman generals at this time, with one exception (M. Vinicius, who was the grandfather of his patron). This is one of the most obscure decades of imperial history.

Velleius, it is true, wrote nearly a generation later than Livy. His work reveals the rapid growth of adulation; it is almost a caricature of the methods imposed by the new system of government on the writing of contemporary history. Velleius takes to himself credit for *candor*, that is,

---

[1] Velleius ii 104, 2.   [2] *Rom. Rev.* (1939), 424 f.; 450.   [3] Velleius ii 100–4.

a flattering portraiture of the right kind of people.[1] Livy was prone to benevolent appraisals.[2] But Livy is held an honest man, though disquieting signs can be discovered in the earlier books of patriotic expurgations, of the remodelling of incidents for a moral or didactic purpose.[2] How was Livy to proceed? Politics could perhaps be avoided (though only by the exercise of great skill) in the narration of the early years of the Augustan Principate, for the government had been able in a large measure to suppress the evidence of internal discord. The period 6 B.C.–A.D. 4 unfolded a series of terrible revelations. How was Livy to write of these matters? He had to stop. The year 9 B.C. was the ideal date.

The occasion was melancholy—the death of Drusus in Germany, returning from the campaign that took him to the river Elbe. But it called for proud commemoration of Rome's imperial task, of the achievement of the dynasty, of the *virtus* of the Claudii. Funeral laudations were suitably delivered by Augustus and by Tiberius. The poet Horace had celebrated the exemplary qualities of the young Claudii—aristocratic breeding reinforced by moral training. The bright promise had been amply fulfilled; and there were just reasons for acclaiming the *pietas* of Tiberius, who, learning of his brother's mishap, hastened by forced marches to the scene, crossing the Alps and the Rhine.[4] A splendid example of the traditional Roman virtues—and a refutation of the 'solita fratrum odia' that tend to disfigure the history of dynasties. The obsequies of Drusus will have provided a subject congenial to the talents of the historian—pageantry, the evocation of generals of the Republic, and the generous comments of sagacious men.

The wars of Tiberius and Drusus in 12–9 B.C. were the high epoch of the Augustan conquests. To advertise the achievement, the *pomerium* of the city of Rome was extended in 8 B.C.[5] Further, in the years 7–2 | B.C., a large number of soldiers were released from service and furnished with bounties in money.[6] Janus should surely have been closed—and so the Senate had voted—after the campaigns of 11 B.C., but a Dacian incursion frustrated the proposal.[7] Yet Janus was in fact closed a third time by Augustus. The only indication of date (2 B.C.) comes from the confused

---

[1] Velleius ii 116, 5: 'neque enim iustus sine mendacio candor apud bonos crimini est.' [For a different estimate of Velleius, see G. V. Sumner, *HSCP* lxxiv (1970), 257 ff.]

[2] Quintilian ii 5, 19: 'candidissimus'; xi 101: 'mirae iucunditatis clarissimique candoris'.

[3] H. Nissen, *Kritische Untersuchungen über die Quellen der 4. und 5. Dekade des Livius* (1863), 29 ff. On 'Livy as Scripture' cf. M. Hadas, *AJP* lxi (1940), 445 ff.; on improving distortions, P. G. Walsh, *AJP* lxxvi (1955), 369 ff.

[4] Observe especially the emotional and adulatory expressions of Valerius Maximus v 5, 3: 'eodemque tempore et fraternae maiestati cessit et vita excessit. his scio equidem nullum aliud quam Castoris et Pollucis specimen consanguineae caritatis convenienter adici posse.'

[5] Dio lv 6, 6. Not in the *Res Gestae*.

[6] *Res Gestae* 16.

[7] Dio liv 36, 2.

narrative of Orosius, which presents considerable perplexities.[1] However, if the third closing of Janus took place subsequent to 9 B.C., it could still have been mentioned somewhere by Livy in his epilogue (and hence have percolated to Orosius). Likewise the disaster of Varus, though much later (in A.D. 9). The manuscripts of the *Periochae* end with the phrase 'clades Quinctilii Vari'. It would be easy to suspect an interpolation—and quite unnecessary.[2]

Livy, though not a flatterer and a time-server, did not write his contemporary annals in utter oblivion of political considerations. His account of the years down to 9 B.C. must have been coloured by the fact that, despite vicissitudes, Tiberius had in A.D. 4 turned out to be the destined successor of Augustus. The catastrophe of Varus was a severe shock. It was expedient to exculpate the government—not so very easy, for Varus was a 'political' appointment, being the husband of one of the great-nieces of the Princeps, Claudia Pulchra. It may be conjectured that Livy's brief notice of the *clades Variana* tended to exalt by contrast the successes of Tiberius in Germany—and elsewhere. Varus took the blame. Velleius' narrative duly gives the explanation—the personal incompetence of that corrupt and slothful character.[3] In truth, a better general than Varus might well have come to grief.

The year 9 B.C. therefore appears to be both a necessary and an attractive terminal date. At some time or other Livy had decided to go on after 29 B.C. as far as that year. Perhaps there was a short interval in his activity after he had completed the books on the Civil Wars. Who shall tell? Perhaps by A.D. 1 he had reached the end of Book cxxxiii, a reasonable output for some thirty years of steady labours, though more recently the task had grown more difficult and more complex. The political change in A.D. 4 may have encouraged him to continue, for it indicated what was the proper and safe treatment of the years 28–9 B.C. The composition of the appendix (Books cxxxiv–cxlii) may belong to the years A.D. 6–10.

If the statement attached to the *Periocha* of Book cxxi is to be accorded credence, it could be argued that Books cxxi–cxlii were not published until after the death of Augustus.[4] That is possible. | The writing of contemporary history was delicate as well as laborious. Moreover, the death of the Princeps might provoke a crisis in Roman politics. Anxious rumours were current. In fact, though certain of the formalities at Rome

---

[1] Orosius' date of 2 B.C. is explicitly, and naturally, that of the Nativity (vi 22, 1; cf. i 1, 6; vii 2, 16). Mommsen argued plausibly for a date between 8 and 1 B.C. (*Res Gestae Divi Augusti* (1883), 50). A third closing of Janus in 13 B.C. has been proposed by I. S. Ryberg, *MAAR* xix (1949), 92 f. It is attractive at first sight, but not easy to accept.

[2] Schanz–Hosius, op. cit. 300, assumes an interpolation. O. Rossbach defends the passage in his edition (Teubner, 1910), xv. He appeals to the phrase with which the derivative *Liber prodigiorum* terminates—'multitudo Romanorum per insidias subiecta est'. That is, a reference to the *clades Variana*.   [3] Velleius ii 117, 2.   [4] Above, p. 412.

might cause friction, the government was ready for the emergency, being in proper control of provinces and armies. The decision had been made long ago, in A.D. 4. Still, an historian might prefer to take no chances.

Despite the fair prospect announced by Velleius Paterculus, the last ten years of Augustus' reign were not a happy period—disasters abroad, insecurity at home, scandal in the dynasty.[1] One symptom was the suppression of offensive literature. Bonfires were decreed by vote of the Senate. The histories of the Pompeian Labienus were among the condemned books. Labienus took the manuscript with him to the family mausoleum and there committed suicide.[2] Livy was in no danger. That very fact may have moved him—it was invidious to publish in security when others were penalized for their freedom of speech.

Another reason might be invoked, of a technical and literary character. Livy's history would contain speeches by Augustus. To insert the original documents would be a sin against the artistic canons of ancient historiography. Instead, he would have to compose orations in his own style and manner. Yet there might be something awkward and incongruous in the publication of speeches attributed to a person still living—especially if he were the head of the State. Sallust had not done so, or, so far as is known, Pollio. A speech was meant not only to expound a policy but to express, in a vivid and direct fashion, a character; and Roman historians did not insert character-studies of the living.

So far a hypothesis, based on the 'dicitur' in the *Periocha* of Book cxxi. The fragility of this testimony will be borne in mind.[3] It might be merely a 'tradition', or a scholastic inference, deriving from the notion that the twenty-two books in question could never have been given to the world while Augustus yet lived. It may be, indeed, that the final nine were only published after A.D. 14. But there is something else. Discarding defective evidence, one can argue that Livy himself predeceased the Princeps. He may have died not in A.D. 17 but about A.D. 12.[4] However that may be, it is likely enough that the writing of his epilogue falls in the period A.D. 4–10.

An approximate date for the composition of the last portion of Livy's history has been suggested. It is tempting to speculate about his treatment of the reign of Augustus. What were Books cxxxiv–cxlii | really like? The meagre *Periochae* and other scraps give little guidance. Florus and Orosius are remarkable for their full and concordant accounts of the Cantabrian campaign of 26 B.C., certainly deriving from an abbreviation of Livy and ultimately from the *Autobiography* of Caesar Augustus.[5] Otherwise, however, those authors are an occasion of much perplexity.

---

[1] Cf. Pliny, *NH* vii 149: 'iuncta deinde tot mala', etc.   [2] Seneca, *Controv*. x, *praef*. 5.
[3] Above, pp. 412 f.   [4] Above, pp. 414 ff.   [5] Above, p. 442.

A brief indication must suffice. Orosius sandwiches the campaigns of Drusus in the Alps and in Germany and the African war of Cossus Cornelius Lentulus (A.D. 6) into the period of Augustus' sojourn in Spain.[1] Then, after Augustus' return, follows a string of anachronistic wars introduced by the words 'quibus etiam diebus, multa per se multaque per duces et legatos bella gessit', ranging from a campaign of Piso against the Vindelici (which may never have happened) to the disaster of Varus, ending with Agrippa's operations in the Black Sea (14 B.C.), the surrender of standards and hostages by the Parthians—and the third closing of Janus.[2]

At first sight Florus appears to preserve a more logical order.[3] He narrates the wars of the period in thirteen sections. Yet his arrangement is peculiar—he begins with the conquest of the Alpine lands (15 B.C.), and, after narrating the Spanish War, concludes with a mention of peace with Parthia, the closing of Janus (apparently that of 29 B.C.), and the conferment of the name 'Augustus'. In detail, Florus is confused (as in his account of the Spanish War); the German wars pass at once from Drusus to Varus, with no mention there or anywhere else of Tiberius; and, like Orosius, he mentions several matters subsequent to 9 B.C.[4] The elucidation of Florus and Orosius presents a pretty problem for *Quellenkritik*.

Cassius Dio no doubt read Livy to the end; but his account of this period does not appear to reflect Livy in any way after 29 B.C.[5] It could be argued that his full account of the campaigns of M. Crassus in Thrace is Livian. Dio narrates them under 29 B.C. In Livy, however, they do not appear until 27 B.C., after Augustus' departure to the provinces of the West, to judge by the *Periochae*.[6] Crassus' triumph, celebrated in July of that year, was therefore the justification for that arrangement of events— which was skilful. It took Crassus' exploits, and especially his claim to the *spolia opima*, out of the chronological sequence that led up to the 'constitutional settlement' of January 27 B.C. The affair of Crassus was perhaps a factor of some moment.[7]

In fact, Dio can be invoked as negative testimony, to show how Livy did not write—and could not write: secret politics, scandal, anecdote, and

[1] Orosius, vi 21, 1–21.   [2] Ibid. 22–9.   [3] Florus ii 22–34.

[4] Of wars subsequent to 9 B.C., Orosius mentions the *Bellum Gaetulicum* of Cossus Lentulus, Tiberius' operations in Germany and Illyricum (taken from Suetonius and Eutropius, erroneously conflated), and the disaster of Varus. Florus has Cossus Lentulus, the Varian disaster, C. Caesar in Armenia, also Vibius in Dalmatia (ii 23, presumably C. Vibius Postumus operating in A.D. 9). Further, of uncertain date, Sulpicius Quirinius against the Marmaridae (?c. 14 B.C.), Lentulus (the Augur) against Dacians and Sarmatians (which might be in 9 B.C.).

[5] E. Schwartz, *RE* iii, col. 1698. At what point did Dio desert Livy? M. A. Levi suggests a new source in 27 B.C., at liii 17 (*Il tempo di Augusto* (1951), 426; 433). The beginning of Book lii, however, in 29 B.C., looks attractive.

[6] *Per.* cxxxiv. But they also occur in *Per.* cxxxv, followed by Augustus' war in Spain and the conquest of the Salassi. [See P. G. Walsh, *PACA* iv (1961), 34 f.]

[7] Above, pp. 418 ff.

depreciation of the government. It will suffice briefly to examine a short section of Dio's work, covering the years 18–16 B.C. Take the | following items:[1] incidents in the purging of the Senate, such as Augustus' wearing of a cuirass; the opprobrious treatment of Lepidus, the *pontifex maximus*; Antistius Labeo's spirited and witty refusal to belong to a bodyguard for the protection of the Princeps; awkward episodes in the moral legislation, such as the malicious insistence of senators that Augustus should tell them what rules of conduct he enjoined upon his own consort; the anecdote about the actors Bathyllus and Pylades; the gossip about Augustus' relations with Terentia, the wife of Maecenas.

Livy's treatment of the period 28–9 B.C. was a reversion to Republican annals. Like the Princeps in his public utterances, the historian asserted continuity with the Republican past. It was the fashion. But it was more than that. Livy was following the bent of his own nature and the tradition of his birthplace. But the men from northern Italy had also a strong imperial patriotism. The two loyalties were not inconsistent.[2] Livy, like others of his class and sentiments, the non-political order in society, rescued and preserved by the new dispensation, acclaimed the rule of Caesar Augustus without feeling dishonest. The Romans were conscious of long development in the history of their state, they knew the need for change and innovation. Livy makes the tribune Canuleius state this axiom of Rome's destiny—'quis dubitat quin in aeternum urbe condita, in immensum crescente, nova imperia, sacerdotia, iura gentium hominumque instituantur?'[3] Livy's argument was adopted by his pupil, the Emperor Claudius, to justify a revolutionary innovation in the recruitment of the Roman Senate.[4]

Referring to *nova imperia*, Livy had recent or present developments in mind. To seek to reconstruct Livy's justification for the new political order would not be an idle or ambitious speculation. In brief, three arguments: the Empire is so large that it can only be preserved by a single ruler; the establishment of the Principate had been accompanied by violence—but only such as was inevitable; the result is liberty without licence, discipline without despotism.

Those pleas are put forward by one set of *prudentes* at the obsequies of Caesar Augustus, in Tacitus' presentation.[5] They also occur in the parallel passage in Cassius Dio which (it is plain) derives likewise from one of the earlier historians.[6] Nothing precludes the notion that formulations of this kind went back a long way—even to contemporaries.[7]

---

[1] Dio liv 13, 1–19, 4.   [2] Cf. G. E. F. Chilver, *Cisalpine Gaul* (1941), 208 ff.   [3] iv 4, 4.
[4] *ILS* 212 (Lugdunum); Tacitus, *Ann.* xi 24. Cf. A. Momigliano, *Claudius. The Emperor and his Achievement* (1934), 17 f.
[5] *Ann.* i 9, 4 f.   [6] Dio lvi 43 f., on which cf. *Tacitus* (1958), 272 f.
[7] Cf. Florus ii 14, 5 f. (possibly deriving from Livy): 'perculsum undique ac perturbatum ordinavit imperii corpus, quod haud dubie numquam coire et consentire potuisset nisi unius praesidis nutu quasi anima et mente regeretur.'

Such, in outline, may have been Livy's annals of *res publica restituta*. Some may have fancied that his narrative of those years was destined to | be decisive in its influence on later historians. That expectation is not borne out by the facts. Except for Censorinus, nobody appeals to Livy as the authority for any detail or opinion: that is the only quotation from Books cxxxiv–cxlii that happens to have survived.[1] Dio's procedure is significant. For Augustus he goes to historians who wrote under his successors. They are little more than names. The prosecution and suicide of Cremutius Cordus may have earned a publicity that his work was far from deserving. But impressive testimony asserts the merits of Aufidius Bassus and M. Servilius Nonianus (*cos.* A.D. 35).[2] This is not the place to raise the question of Dio's main source for the reign of Augustus. Perhaps, as some argue, Aufidius Bassus.[3] It may be that these historians disregarded Livy completely or used him only for the outline of events, and for such matters as the campaigns of Tiberius and Drusus. Aufidius also published a separate monograph on the *Bella Germaniae*, which may have been a continuation of the wars after the death of Drusus, embracing the period down to the triumph of Germanicus in A.D. 17. As for annalistic history, Livy's sources were available to Aufidius and Servilius, and they perhaps wished to write a very different kind of history.

Livy's style was obsolescent, his sentiments distasteful or irrelevant. The bright promise—or the skilful camouflage—of Augustus faded before the suspicion that *principatus* meant in fact *dominatus*. When it is not adulation, imperial history tends to be an attack, open or covert, on the imperial system. The person of Augustus, the founder of the dynasty of Julii and Claudii, was more or less protected: but the history of his reign gave opportunities for unfriendly portrayal. Livy's annals did not provide the material, for he had not been able to record the real and secret history of the dynasty.

Livy's annals of Augustus were written in joyful acceptance of the new order, in praise of the government and its achievements. Their tone was moral, their colouring benevolent. Unlike most earlier historians, he set out to provide, not only guidance for the politician, but models for the conduct of the common man.[4] The direction which the Principate had taken justified a return to the sombre and pessimistic conception of politics and of human nature that Sallust had made classical. In sentiment as in style, Livy does not fit into the development of Roman historiography that links Sallust to Tacitus.

---

[1] Censorinus, *De die natali* 17, 9 = fr. 56 Weissenborn.
[2] Quintilian x 1, 102; Tacitus, *Dial.* 23, 4.
[3] e.g. F. A. Marx, *Klio* xxvi (1933), 323 ff.; xxix (1936), 202 ff. For this historian see now *Tacitus* (1958), 274 ff.; 697 ff. A proper investigation into Dio's treatment of the reign of Augustus is sorely needed.
[4] R. Heinze, *Vergils epische Technik*[3] (1914), 475 f.

From that line of succession a further reason debars him. The writing of history was regarded as a proper occupation for the statesman in retirement: it was not a career and a profession in itself. Livy began to write history without having learned how history is made. |

If Cassius Dio can be taken as a guide, Livy, canonical for Republican history, was less influential for the history of the Triumviral period—and little regarded for the reign of Caesar Augustus. Indeed, at an earlier stage, when Dio had the choice between Livy and Sallust as sources for the campaigns of Lucullus, he chose Sallust.[1]

The reasons are not far to seek. It will be asked: was Livy at his best in Books cxxxiii–cxlii? May not those contemporary annals have exposed some of his characteristic weaknesses—his docility, his benevolence, his disinclination to grapple with historical problems, his lack of political penetration?

As is natural, the opinions of ancient critics about Livy bear upon his style, rather than his qualities as a historian. Yet the ancients would not have admitted a sharp distinction between form and substance. Certain literary judgements that have been preserved go deeper than style and execution. Pollio, so it is stated by Quintilian, blamed Livy for *Patavinitas*. An enigmatic utterance, and responsible for interminable discussion. What does it mean—style and colour, syntax, vocabulary, or even orthography? The context in which Quintilian records this observation suggests a criticism of words and idiom—Transpadane expressions comparable to the solecisms of Etruria, Praeneste, or the Sabine land.[2]

Quintilian, however, does not seem to be positive or explicit enough. He cites no examples, he neither admits nor rejects the allegation. Perhaps it was 'a tradition of the schools'. The opprobrious word uttered by the disdainful consular may have been meant to convey much more than a reproof for the use of local idiom. Rather a general lack of *urbanitas*.[3] Or perhaps something deeper. Patavium was a smug, opulent *municipium*. *Patavinitas* might be taken to connote the rich and ample discourse of an improving publicist.[4] In short, all that history should not be.

Caligula, spurning the classics of Augustan Rome and the literary models of his uncle Claudius, declared that Livy was careless and verbose.[5] Caligula is no guide to orthodox opinion. Yet the verdict of a scholarly and authoritative critic is disquieting. Quintilian's description, 'lactea

---

[1] Th. Reinach, *Mithridate Eupator* (1890), 449 f.
[2] Quintilian i 5, 56: 'taceo de Tuscis et Sabinis et Praenestinis quoque: nam ut eorum sermone utentem Vettium Lucilius insectatur, quemadmodum Pollio reprehendit in Livio Patavinitatem, licet omnia Italica pro Romanis habeam.' The other passage (viii 1, 12) adds nothing.
[3] K. Latte, *CP* xxxv (1940), 56; A. H. McDonald, *JRS* xlvii (1957), 172.
[4] As suggested in *Rom. Rev.* (1939), 485 f.   [5] Suetonius, *Cal.* 34, 6.

ubertas', 'a rich creaminess', was not produced in praise of an historian.¹ In another place, with sensible remarks about the education of the young, he says that Livy is a diet for boys, Sallust for men: Sallust is the *maior auctor*.²

POSTSCRIPT. For help, and for various improvements, I owe a great debt to Professor Mason Hammond and to Mr. R. M. Ogilvie.

---

¹ Quintilian x 1, 32: 'neque illa Livii lactea ubertas satis docebit eum qui non speciem expositionis sed fidem quaerit.'

² ii 5, 19: 'ego optimos quidem et statim et semper, sed tamen eorum candidissimum quemque et maxime expositum velim, ut Livium a pueris magis quam Sallustium; et hic historiae maior est auctor.'

33

Missing Persons II

To continue. Among the shortcomings of Pauly-Wissowa viii A, Part I, was omission. Forty-one names were briefly registered in *Historia* v (1956), 204 ff. [= pp. 315 ff. above], of which no fewer than thirteen had stood on record these long years in the *Prosopographia Imperii Romani*. The second part is now to hand ('P. Vergilius Maro bis Vindeleia'), and it is gratifying to observe that twelve of the missing forty-one items find entry in the *Nachträge*. Among them are Vatienus (the husband of 'Cornelia L. Scipionis f.'), Veranius, the friend of Catullus, and the Prefect of Egypt, Cn. Vergilius Capito. Welcome, and a voice from the grave, is the article on Vatienus—it bears the name, one could add the signature, of Münzer. As for Capito, an unpublished inscription from Miletus (*Didyma* II, no. 149), is cited, which, showing the tribe Falerna, indicates his ultimate origin.

Not, indeed, that the new instalment is everywhere good enough or up to date. There will be sundry disappointments. Thus the article on the eminent consular Vestricius Spurinna betrays no awareness of the piece of the *Fasti Ostienses* which, first published in 1939, brought his *praenomen* 'Titus' and his second consulate in 98 (*FO* xiv [= *Inscr. It.* xiii 1, 194–5]): the discussion about Spurinna's movements and occupations in 97 and 98 is therefore obsolete. Again, older information has not always been utilized. The article on M. Vettius Bolanus (*cos. suff.* 66) ignores the inscription at Deuriopus in Macedonia which records an annual festival to commemorate his birthday (noted in *PIR*[1], V 323).

Nor has the propensity to leave out people been overcome. On the contrary. Forty items of the 160 in the parallel stretch of *PIR* (V 280–439) are absent. That is grave—and there is no sign of awareness, no indication that these items have been reserved for treatment later on.

Among the omissions are four characters in Tacitus, viz. Verulanus Severus, legate under Corbulo and consul *c.* 66; Verulana Gratilla, 'insignis femina', perhaps the wife of Junius Rusticus; Vibennius Rufinus, an equestrian; Vibilius, the king of the Hermunduri.

Also Vibia Sabina, the consort of Hadrian, and a number of consuls. None of the Vettuleni is there, that Sabine family which rose with Vespasian and through alliance with the Ceionii became attached to the family tree of the Antonine dynasty. *PIR* had three consular Vettuleni, viz. the two *suffecti* of Vespasian's reign who governed Moesia in succession (V 351 f.) and Pompeianus, the consul of 136 (V 353). There is also the consul of 106—and the consul of 157 whom a recent epigraphic discovery shows to have been a Vettulenus, not a Ceionius (see below). |

It would take too much space to catalogue those forty individuals from *PIR*. What follows is a supplement of twenty-eight names, Republican as well as imperial, belonging to various classes. It may be worth stating in justification that the list includes two Gallic chieftains from Caesar; two characters in Catullus (Victius and Victor); a person Vidius mentioned by Cicero, who may be identical with P. Vedius; two of the proscribed; no fewer than six consuls; a writer on the ritual of the Etruscans.

The list does not claim to be exhaustive, and it does not draw upon the newest epigraphic discoveries (with one exception, M. Vettulenus Civica Barbarus, the consul of 157). Furthermore, a restriction. Recent issues of *RE* have been generous to excess. Going beyond the practice of *PIR*, Roman knights with nothing higher than military service have been admitted. Not all, however, and not with proper discrimination. A number of persons have been left out, remarkable for one reason or another. Thus the *praefectus equitum* Sex. Verteblasius Victor, son of a magistrate at Lambaesis (*CIL* viii 2776). The *gentilicium* 'Verteblasius' is unique, not registered in the repertory of Wilhelm Schulze—and it might have taxed his categories and resources. Again, and more remunerative, L. Versenus Aper, prefect of a cohort in Dacia Superior in 157 or 158 (*CIL* xvi 107), prefect of an *ala* at Petavonium near Asturica (*AE* 1937, 166). His family belongs to Hispellum in Umbria, as emerges from the dedication he set up in honour of his brother (who was also an equestrian officer) at Perusia (*CIL* xi 1937); and they were styled 'Versenus' or 'Versinius', indiscriminately.

Addenda about such knights would be lengthy (and not always very instructive). The following catalogue will take in only two of them, for special reasons (a Vibius Pansa and a Vettius Priscus). And, for the other categories, though names and persons may open up various paths of inquiry, annotation and bibliography has been cut to the minimum.

P. Vergilius M. f. Pontianus. Curator of the Tiber in the board of five, the president being C. Antistius Vetus (*cos.* 23): *AE* 1922, 95 = *CIL* xiv 4707.

Ti. Vergilius Ti. f. Rufus. In the same function as the preceding.

Vergilia Florentina. Styled 'C. f.', wife of the consular Julius Fortunatianus (*AE* 1917/18, 52: Lambaesis). Her husband's name is to be restored in *CIL* viii 2797, which honours a governor of Numidia, for the dedicants of the two inscriptions are identical: cf. E. Birley, *JRS* xl (1950), 66. Julius Fortunatianus (*suff. c.* 262) is not in Degrassi's *Fasti consolari* (1952).

VERTISCUS. The aged and heroic *princeps* of the Remi, commanding their cavalry and killed in a skirmish with the Bellovaci. [Caesar] (i.e. Hirtius), *BG* viii 12, 4 f.

VERUCLOATIUS. Helvetian nobleman: Caesar, *BG* i 7, 3. |

A. VETTIUS PRISCUS. Styled 'leg. Aug.' on the inscription painted on the neck of an amphora found at Vindonissa (*Gesellschaft Pro Vindonissa, Jahresbericht* 1951/2, 52, with photograph, whence *AE* 1953, 248b). For Vettii Prisci, cf. the full catalogue and discussion by E. Birley, ibid. 55 f. Observe further that the Vettius Priscus in Pliny (*Ep.* vi 12, 2), a friend of his *prosocer* L. Calpurnius Fabatus of Comum, is assumed by the latest editor (M. Schuster, Teubner, 1933) to be a 'Bittius Priscus'. That reading is accepted in *RE* viii A, col. 1861. It is tempting, compare 'Bittius Proculus' in ix 13, 13, whose *gentilicium* is independently attested, and who is Q. Fulvius Gillo Bittius Proculus, *suff.* ? 98 (*PIR*², F 544). But the man might be a Vettius Priscus after all. The next item is therefore relevant, indistinctive though the nomenclature may be. [See *JRS* lviii (1968), 137 f. = pp. 698 f. below.]

C. VETTIUS PRISCUS. Prefect commanding Ala I Ituraeorum in Dacia in 110: *CIL* xvi 57.

VETTIUS SALASSUS. One of the proscribed, whom his wife betrayed: Valerius Maximus ix 11, 7; cf. Appian, *BC* iv 24, 98, who has only the *cognomen*. For that *cognomen* among contemporaries, note the two brothers, P. Curtius (Salassus) and Q. Curtius Salassus (*RE* iv, coll. 1865, 1891): the former killed by the son of Pompeius in Spain, the latter, an officer of Antonius, burned alive at Aradus in Syria. They are patently from Canusium; cf. *CIL* ix 326 = *ILS* 3316. There is also a Salassus *duumvir* at Lilybaeum (M. Grant, *From Imperium to Auctoritas* (1946), 196).

C. VETTLAEUS C. F. RUFUS. *Pontifex* at Nursia (*CIL* i² 1893 [= *ILLRP* 632]). The *nomen* appears to be found nowhere else; cf. W. Schulze, *LE* 379.

VETTO. The subject of an epigram of Cicero, 'in quodam ioculari libello' (Quintilian viii 6, 73).

SEX. VETTO. An early inscription at Sextantio near Montpellier, 'litteris optimis et magnis', has two aediles, C. Pedo and Sex. Vetto (*CIL* xii 4190 = i² 2281): noted in *RE* xix, col. 45. The name 'Vetto' is not registered in *LE*.

VET(T)ULENUS. One of the proscribed: gathering a force (compare the

actions of Lucilius Hirrus and of Arruntius), he was able to get his companions and his son across the Strait of Messina, but was himself killed
near Rhegium (Appian, *BC* iv 25, 104 f.). The *nomen* is patently Sabine
by its local distribution; cf. R. Syme, *Athenaeum* xxxv (1957), 313
[= p. 330 above]; and a senator of the early Empire, T. Vettulenus P. f.
Quadratus (*CIL* vi 31773), has in fact the tribe Quirina.

SEX. VETTULENUS CIVICA CERIALIS. *Cos.* 106. A piece of the *Fasti Ostienses*
discovered and published in 1940 (*FO* xix [= *Inscr. It.* xiii 1, 196–7])
reveals the full nomenclature of the Cerialis who was *ordinarius* in 106
with L. Ceionius Commodus and supplies the link between the two
Vettuleni consuls suffect under Vespasian (Sex. Vettulenus Cerialis and
C. Vettulenus Civica Cerialis) and Sex. Vettulenus Civica Pompeianus,
consul in 136 (*PIR*[1], V 353).

M. VETTULENUS SEX. F. CIVICA BARBARUS. *Cos.* 157. This consul, M. Civica
Barbarus, the uncle of L. Verus, was naturally and universally believed to
be a | Ceionius (*PIR*[2], C 602). But the *gentilicium*, filiation, and the tribe
Quirina, have been disclosed by a Greek inscription at Argos published
by P. Charneux, *BCH* lxxxi (1957), 121 ff. For further observations on
identities and relationships see *Athenaeum* xxxv (1957), 306 ff. [= pp.
325 ff. above].

CN. VETURIUS. Defended by C. Aurelius Cotta (*cos.* 75 B.C.), whose
oration is quoted Charisius p. 284, 10; cf. H. Malcovati, *ORF*[3] 291.

C. VIBIUS MARINUS PI[. Described as 'v.c.' on an inscription at Thamugadi
(*AE* 1901, 195).

C. VIBIUS T. F. CLU. PANSA. Described as 'tr. mil. bis' on an inscription
of the early Empire (*CIL* vi 3542). Notable for homonymy with the
consul of 43 B.C.—whose town, however, is surely Perusia, with the tribe
Tromentina (cf. *Rom. Rev.* (1939), 90: doubted in *RE* viii A, col. 1954).

L. VIBIUS L. F. ROM. VARUS APPIANUS. Benefactor and patron of Hiero-
caesarea (*IGR* iv 1353: Hyrcanis).

VI]BUSIUS L. F. *Xvir stlitibus iudicandis* and tribune of either I or II Adiutrix
(*AE* 1937, 132: Spoletium). The *nomen* is very uncommon; cf. *LE* 71.
It is patently indigenous at Spoletium; cf. *CIL* xi 4818 (= *ILS* 6637);
4820; 4937. Further, 5006 (Trebia) shows a Sabine man, married to a
Vibusia, holding a magistracy at Spoletium.

VICELLIUS. Brontoscopic writer cited by Lydus, *De ostentis* 54. Noted in
Schanz–Hosius, *Gesch. der röm. Lit.* i[4] (1927), 603: subsequent, however,
to Ptolemy; cf. S. Weinstock, *PBSR* xviii (1950), 47. For 'Vicellius',
'Vigellius' (and kindred *nomina*) cf. *LE* 102; 261. They are put under the
same rubric in *CIL* vi, where the large total of *liberti* justifies the registra-

tion of a M. Vigellius as *PIR¹*, V 433: 'homo si non nobilis at certe dives.'
That Vigellius is noted in *RE* viii A, col. 2569.

VICENN[IA]. Wife of a senator in A.D. 204: *AE* 1932, 70.

A. VICIRIUS PROCULUS. *Cos. suff.* 89. Revealed by the *Fasti Potentini* (*AE*
1949, 23). Patently close kin to A. Vicirius Martialis, *suff.* 98 (*PIR¹*,
V 428). The *nomen* points to Etruria or Campania: observe *CIL* i² 2623
(Caere); 2239 [= *ILLRP* 748] (Delos—a *magister Mercurialium*); x 1440
(Herculaneum—Viciria A. f. Archais, mother of the senator M. Nonius
Balbus); xi 1806 (Saena—a local notable, praetor of Etruria and honoured
with a public funeral).

P. VICRIUS [. *Cos. suff.* 145 (*FO* XXVII [= *Inscr. It.* xiii 1, 204–5]). For the
nomen, *LE* 102. In *CIL* vi there are only three Vicrii as against twenty-six
Vicirii. Amiternum in the Sabine country has an early instance of a
Vicrius (*CIL* i² 1889).

C. VICRIUS RUFUS. *Cos. suff.* 145: *CIL* xvi 91, cf. *FO* XXVII.

VICTIUS. Derided by Catullus (98, 1: 'putide Victi'; 5: 'Victi'). It was an
easy guess that the *nomen* was really 'Vettius', and Achilles Statius in his
commentary (Venice, 1566) suggested that the person is identical with the
notorious informer L. Vettius, the Picentine. However, the manuscripts
are concordant, and modern editions (to cite only the latest, that of
R. A. B. Mynors, Oxford, | 1958) retain 'Victi'. The name 'Victius' is
not attested for the period of the Republic—and (apparently) not more
than once subsequently (*CIL* vi 28902). For a discussion of the problem,
and consideration of other *gentilicia*, see C. L. Neudling, *A Prosopography
to Catullus* (*Iowa Studies in Classical Philology* xii, 1935), 186. Add 'Vicrius'
as a possibility; also 'Vitius' in view of 'Vitia, Fufii Gemini mater' (Tacitus,
Ann. vi 10, 1), which might be corrupt but ought to be retained; cf.
R. Syme, *JRS* xxxix (1949), 18 [= *Ten Studies in Tacitus* (1970), 77 f.].
Finally, however, let it be noted that a Vettius happens to occur among
the alleged lovers of Clodia; cf. Cicero, *Pro Caelio* 71: 'nempe quod
eiusdem mulieris dolorem et iniuriam Vettiano sunt stupro persecuti. ergo
ut audiretur Vetti nomen in causa, ut illa vetus aeraria fabula referretur'
etc. This Vettius, the subject of some scandalous anecdote concerning
Clodia, is not verifiable. He is registered in *RE* viii A, col. 1844, but was
not noted by C. L. Neudling (op. cit. 186). He may be identical with
(Vettius) Scato, a Marsian, an adherent of Clodia's brother (Cicero, *De
domo sua* 116), a dealer in real estate; cf. *Rom. Rev.* (1939), 91.

VICTOR. Person referred to in a poem addressed by Catullus to Gellius
(i.e. L. Gellius Poplicola, who was to be consul in 36 B.C.)—'clamant
Victoris rupta miselli / ilia' (80, 7 f.). For a discussion see C. L. Neudling
(op. cit. 187), who, observing the fact that the *cognomen* 'Victor' does not

occur on inscriptions of Republican date, wonders whether the name be not a pseudonym in Catullus. That is not necessary. A Victor is mentioned in a letter of Cicero of 27 April 44 B.C.: Cicero expects that this man, along with Sempronius Rufus, will be recalled from exile by Marcus Antonius (*Ad Att.* xiv 14, 2: this item 'Victor' is registered in *RE* viii A, col. 2058). Therefore a historical character—and there will be no need to invoke the *nomen* 'Vitorius', first emerging with a municipal magistrate at Anagnia (*CIL* i² 1520 [= *ILLRP* 534]) and ultimately signalized by M. Vitorius Marcellus (*suff.* 105), to whom Quintilian dedicated the *Institutio*.

VIDIUS. Mentioned by Cicero in a friendly letter to Dolabella at the very end of 46 (*Ad fam.* ix 10, 1, cited by Suetonius, *De gramm.* 14). No news to report, says Cicero, unless it be his acting as arbiter in a philological dispute 'inter Niciam nostrum et Vidium'. Now Curtius Nicias (*RE* iv, col. 1868) is the remarkable character who later, in the Antonian period, turns up as tyrant of Cos, as demonstrated on the basis of unpublished inscriptions by R. Herzog, *HZ* cxxv (1922), 190 ff.: cf. A. Stein in *RE* xvii, col. 334. Who might Vidius be? He has failed to elicit any kind of comment from Tyrrell and Purser. The name (not registered in *LE*, but attested, e.g. *CIL* vi 36550) ought to be corrected to 'Vedius' or better, to the other and older form, 'Veidius'. Compare P. Veidius, a candidate at Pompeii (*CIL* i² 1671), or indeed the notorious friend of Caesar Augustus who styles himself 'P. Veidius P. f. Pollio' on the *Caesareum* he erected at Beneventum (*ILS* 109) [on this and what follows, see pp. 518–29 ff. below].

One is then impelled irresistibly towards that 'magnus nebulo', P. Vedius, a friend of Pompeius Magnus: travelling in Asia Minor in the spring of 50, he | left his baggage with Pompeius Vindullus at Laodicea— and in it were discovered wax effigies (*imagunculae*) of five society ladies (*Ad Att.* vi 1, 25). Let it be recalled that Curtius Nicias had once been a friend of Magnus—'haesit Cn. Pompeio et C. Memmio: sed cum codicillos Memmi ad Pompei uxorem de stupro pertulisset, proditus ab ea Pompeium offendit domoque ei interdictum est' (Suetonius, *De gramm.* 14). The pair go well together: polite letters, low origin, and high life.

VILIUS MILIONIUS. Proconsul of Cyprus under Nero: *AE* 1953, 166 (Soli), cf. 167 (Paphus), which certifies the *nomen* and further supplies the two brothers of the proconsul, one of whom was *legatus*.

34

Proconsuls d'Afrique sous Antonin le Pieux[1]

Les gouverneurs d'Afrique et d'Asie peuvent surgir au détour de problèmes fort divers. D'abord, ceux de simple chronologie: la date d'un proconsulat peut aider à fixer, de façon plus ou moins précise, celle du consulat correspondant. Puis, le système réglant l'avancement dans les charges: au bout de combien de temps l'ancien consul peut-il accéder à ces postes? Quel avantage y a-t-il à être *consul ordinarius* ou bien à avoir des enfants? Enfin, et surtout, la structure des classes supérieures dans la société romaine: quels sont les consulaires à qui l'on donne ces postes et pour quelles raisons? (On remarque que les grands chefs militaires sont rarement de leur nombre.)

Les proconsulats consulaires illustrent le fonctionnement régulier d'un système. Ils fournissent aussi des indications précieuses sur l'histoire sociale et politique. En outre, les proconsuls d'Afrique et d'Asie, avec les problèmes qui les concernent, ne sont pas sans interférer avec l'histoire de la littérature. Les dernières années d'Antonin le Pieux en fournissent un exemple: un personnage connu (et de fâcheuse notoriété), Apulée de Madaure, fut accusé pour magie et autres procédés répréhensibles devant le proconsul Claudius Maximus (*suff.* ?143 ou 144); et Apulée dans son discours fait allusion au prédécesseur de celui-ci en cette charge, à savoir Lollianus Avitus (qui fut *consul ordinarius* en 144).[2] Dans d'autres ouvrages, dans ses *Florida*, l'éloquent Africain parle en termes élogieux de deux proconsuls, postérieurs de quelques années, à savoir Cocceius Honorinus (*suff.* 147) et Salvidienus Orfitus (*cos.* 149).[3]

Autre exemple: les proconsuls d'Asie entre 140 et 150 ne sont pas étrangers aux mouvements et aux maladies du sophiste de Smyrne, Aelius Aristide. Trois de ceux qu'il mentionne sont Pollio, | Severus et Quadratus, dans cet ordre chronologique, mais peut-être pas pendant des

---

[1] [Compare the lists in Bengt E. Thomasson, *Die Statthalter der römischen Provinzen Nordafrikas von Augustus bis Diocletianus* (1960)—not, of course, able to use this article, but not always familiar with other recent interpretations and the evidence of other provinces: see E. Birley, *JRS* lii (1962), 219 ff.]

[2] Apulée, *Apol.* 94.

[3] *Florida* 9; 17.

8143672   H h

années consécutives.[1] Qui sont-ils? Un bref examen du problème, en écartant une identification généralement admise, aide à supposer un nouveau consulaire Pollio. Non pas Vitrasius Pollio qui avait épousé une cousine de Marc-Aurèle et qui fut consul pour la seconde fois en 176, mais un Pollio antérieur: peut-être celui que l'on suppose son père, le légat de Lyonnaise, qui a pu être consul vers 137.[2] Severus peut être identifié avec C. Julius Severus d'Ancyre (*suff. c.* 138). Mais on pourrait avoir des doutes en ce qui concerne Quadratus. Est-il certain que ce soit L. Statius Quadratus (*cos.* 142)? Et, pour parachever nos incertitudes, quelle est l'année de Statius Quadratus, c'est-à-dire l'année qui a vu le martyre du vieillard Polycarpe?[3] On accepte en général la date de 154/5,[4] ce qui donnerait un laps de temps anormalement court depuis son consulat (douze ans).

Les documents présentent des variations notables et il y a de grandes lacunes. Même lorsque les proconsuls connus sont mentionnés, un grand nombre de points douteux subsiste. Et il y a des éléments troublants. L'intervalle entre le consulat et le proconsulat d'un sénateur varie, bien qu'à l'intérieur de certaines limites. Maintenu à dix ans environ par Vespasien, cet intervalle atteint quatorze ans à la fin du règne de Domitien. Il va jusqu'à dix-sept ans avant la mort de Trajan, mais est rapidement réduit par son successeur. Un intervalle de quatorze ou quinze ans peut être considéré comme normal au cours de la période suivante, bien qu'il ait pu s'en présenter de plus longs pour une raison quelconque, et quelquefois peut-être parce que l'intéressé avait une autre charge quand son tour arrivait. Voilà pour la limite supérieure. Quant à la limite inférieure, on peut, semble-t-il, affirmer qu'aucun exemple net d'un intervalle inférieur à treize ans n'est attesté entre 103/4 (où on a un proconsulat daté) et l'accession au pouvoir de Marc-Aurèle en 161.

Qu'un fait nouveau apparaisse et il démolira les tentatives les plus raisonnables ou les plus méthodiques pour dater un consulat ou un proconsulat. Il peut arriver aussi que quelque fait négligé | jusque-là, ou mal interprété, entre en jeu. Il en résulte une mise au point, et aussi un progrès. L'on peut ajouter un nom, compléter une série de proconsuls, confirmer, éventuellement, quelque conjecture antérieure. Le but de la présente enquête est limité: elle vise à restituer un proconsul ignoré et à rétablir ainsi fermement une suite de huit gouverneurs pendant les dernières

---

[1] Pour les références, voir Hüttl, *Antoninus Pius* ii (1933), 50 ss. [See now C. A. Behr, *Aelius Aristides and the Sacred Tales* (1968), 131 ff. (with references to discussion in his commentary)—not entirely reliable; and Barnes (n. 3 below).]

[2] Vitrasius Pollio, légat de Lyonnaise (*Dig.* XXVII 1, 15, 17), a été distingué du *cos. II* par A. Stein, *Die Legaten von Moesien* (1940), 73 s. Pour les conséquences à en tirer, cf. R. Syme, *JRS* xliii (1953), 159 [= pp. 251 f. above]: compte-rendu de A. Degrassi, *I fasti consolari* (1952).

[3] *PIR*[1], S 640. [See T. D. Barnes, *JThS* xviii (1967), 433 ff.]

[4] Hüttl, op. cit. 52; D. Magie, *Roman Rule in Asia Minor* ii (1950), 1584.

années d'Antonin le Pieux et les premières de son successeur (de 157/8 à 164/5).

Cependant, ce sera une bonne occasion pour mentionner en même temps les autres proconsuls d'Afrique sous Antonin le Pieux. Très peu d'entre eux, cinq seulement, sont certains. Une chance s'offre de proposer une courte série, reposant sur des conjectures, au début du règne d'Antonin.

I

Proconsuls de 139/40 à 142/3. Les quatre noms suivants sont admissibles:

139/40	Minicius	*suff.* ? 124 ou 125
140/1	T. Prifernius Sex. f. Paetus Rosianus Geminus	*suff.* ? 125
141/2	? Sex. Julius Maior	*suff.* 126
142/3	P. Tullius Varro	*suff.* 127

Une inscription fragmentaire de Thagora fait connaître l'existence du proconsul Minicius à l'époque de la seconde *tribunicia potestas* d'Antonin le Pieux: donc en 138/9 ou 139/40.[1] Le plus sûr est de supposer qu'il s'agit d'un consul suffect de 124 ou 125, inconnu par ailleurs. Il serait hasardeux de l'identifier avec le fameux et valeureux Cn. Minicius Faustinus Sex. Julius Severus (*suff.* 127), légat de quatre provinces consulaires consécutivement (Mésie inférieure, Bretagne, Judée, Syrie) qui avait reçu les *ornamenta triumphalia* pour ses services pendant la guerre juive.[2]

La carrière de Prifernius Paetus n'est mentionnée nulle part d'une manière directe et explicite. Questeur en 100, il subit une longue éclipse et accéda tard au consulat. Deux faits dans le cursus de son gendre, P. Pactumeius Clemens, révèlent son existence et permettent de le dater approximativement.[3] Prifernius fut proconsul d'Achaïe avec Pactumeius comme légat (après la questure | de ce dernier). Ses fonctions de gouverneur doivent se placer aux environs de 123. Pactumeius lorsqu'il était légat en Cilicie, pendant l'été de 138, détint les *fasces* par intérim. Son poste suivant fut celui de légat en Afrique sous le père de sa femme. Le proconsulat de ce vieillard pourrait donc être fixé sans trop d'inquiétude en 140/1. Il a dû être consul suffect vers 125.

Vient ensuite Sex. Julius Maior. Une inscription d'Épidaure montre qu'il a été proconsul ou d'Afrique ou d'Asie.[4] Avant son consulat il était légat de Numidie. Ces fonctions, croyait-on, se plaçaient entre 129 et 133; il aurait donc été consul en 132 ou 133. Et, allant plus loin, on admettait (peut-être avec un peu trop d'assurance) que l'on possédait une série bien établie de proconsuls d'Asie entre 145/6 et 152/3, ce qui ne laissait pas de

---

[1] *CIL* viii 4643.
[2] *ILS* 1056 (Burnum), cf. *AE* 1904, 9; 1950, 45 (Aequum). [See Additional Note, p. 469 below.]   [3] *ILS* 1067 (Cirta).
[4] *IG* iv 1179+1510. [See *PIR*[2], I 397, undecided. But see E. Birley's review of Thomasson (above, p. 461, n. 1), firm for Africa.]

place pour Julius Maior.[1] Ces dates et ces arguments sont maintenant périmés. Des documents fixent son commandement de Numidie—en 125 à Timgad, en 126 à Gemellae.[2] Il est évident qu'il succède à P. Metilius Secundus (*suff.* ? 123); et qu'il précède Q. Fabius Catullinus (*cos.* 130). Il a dû détenir les *fasces* au cours de l'année 126, puisqu'il n'y a pas place pour lui en 127 ou 128. Si l'Afrique et non l'Asie était la province proconsulaire de Julius Maior (et la question n'est pas résolue), 141/2 conviendrait comme date de sa charge. Jusqu'à maintenant il ne peut être démontré qu'un autre légat de Numidie sous Hadrien et Antonin ait terminé sa carrière par l'un de ces proconsulats.[3]

En dernier lieu, le proconsulat de P. Tullius Varro (*suff.* 127).[4] On peut le placer en 142/3. Deux postes dans la carrière de son fils (ou neveu), L. Dasumius Tullius Tuscus (*suff.* 152), concordent parfaitement.[5] D'abord, Tuscus servit comme tribun militaire dans la IV Flavia, légion de la Mésie supérieure: Varron était *legatus Augusti pro praetore* de cette province, sans doute vers 135. Puis Tuscus, après avoir été questeur et avant d'être tribun du peuple, est légat auprès d'un proconsul d'Afrique: la date de 142/3 convient.|

II

Proconsuls entre 143/4 et 156/7. Au cours de ces quatorze années deux gouverneurs seulement sont mentionnés.

D'abord, le mystérieux Ennius Proculus (si le nomen a été correctement transmis) qui est attesté sous Antonin par un passage du *Digeste*.[6] Aucun indice de date ou d'identité.

En second lieu, L. Minicius Natalis Quadronius Verus. Son consulat était en général fixé au voisinage immédiat de 133. Sa carrière rendait cette date plausible. Alors qu'il était questeur (et en fait *quaestor Augusti*) il servit en Afrique pendant le proconsulat de son père, L. Minicius Natalis (*suff.* 106), dont les fonctions, à en juger d'après la suite connue et complète des proconsuls d'Asie de 120/1 à 126/7, peuvent se placer en 121/2.[7] De plus, lorsqu'il gagna une victoire dans la course de chars à Olympie, en 129, il avait déjà le rang prétorien.[8] On aurait pu croire que ce jeune homme était destiné à parvenir rapidement au consulat—et son père avait commandé la grande province militaire de Pannonie supérieure à l'époque

---

[1] Hüttl, op. cit. 22.   [2] *AE* 1950, 58; 1954, 149.

[3] En outre, contre l'hypothèse de l'Afrique, noter que tout associe Julius Maior à l'Orient (*RE* x, col. 666 ss.). Ajouter ce détail important concernant sa carrière: il était gouverneur de Syrie, succédant à Bruttius Praesens, dans les dernières années du règne d'Hadrien (*AE* 1938, 137: Palmyre). [Denied by Eck, *Senatoren von Hadrian bis Vespasian* (1970), 232.]

[4] *ILS* 1047 (Tarquinii).   [5] *ILS* 1081 (ibid.).   [6] *Dig.* l 6, 6, 1.

[7] *ILS* 1029 (Barcino), le père; 1061 (Tibur), le fils. Le proconsulat de Q. Pompeius Falco (*suff.* 108), maintenant fixé à 123/4 (*AE* 1957, 17), confirme la série tout entière.

[8] *SIG*[3] 840.

critique de l'accession d'Hadrien au pouvoir.[1] Cependant il dut attendre jusqu'en 139, comme nous le révèle maintenant un diplôme de cette année-là.[2] Le proconsulat doit donc se placer seulement en 153 ou 154.

Il peut être opportun ici de mentionner brièvement les noms de deux proconsuls de l'époque antonine qui pourraient appartenir à cette période. D'abord le Marcellus, dont le décret est reproduit sur une inscription d'Aunobaris près de Thugga.[3] Ce pourrait être, ou non, le même personnage que le Marcellus attesté à Lepcis.[4] Tant de facteurs demeurent incertains qu'il ne vaut guère la peine de spéculer sur les personnes et les dates. Il est vrai qu'on a suggéré les noms de C. Quinctius Certus Publicius Marcellus (*suff.* 120) et de Q. Pomponius Rufus Marcellus (*suff.* 121). Le premier peut être éliminé. L'inscription d'Aquilée, qui rappelle ses provinces consu|laires, qualifie Hadrien de 'divus';[5] et il est peu probable que ce personnage, étant donné la date de son consulat, soit entré en possession d'une charge en Afrique après la mise en place de l'inscription. Le second, en revanche, pourrait très bien avoir gouverné l'Afrique dans les dernières années du règne d'Hadrien.

En second lieu, et plus considérable, le proconsul ']rius Severus', dont le *cursus* est fourni par une inscription de Thubursicu.[6] Il accéda au consulat après trois postes de rang prétorien: la charge d'une route en Italie, le commandement d'une légion et le gouvernement de la Lycie-Pamphylie; par la suite, il fut légat d'une des Germanies. Le dater et l'identifier ne semblait pas folle espérance. On a pensé à C. Valerius Severus (*suff.* 124), attesté comme légat de Lycie-Pamphylie.[7] Mais celui-ci avait aussi été proconsul d'Achaïe, poste qui n'est pas mentionné dans l'inscription.[8] Peut-être alors un autre Valerius Severus. Mais le *gentilicium* n'est pas forcément 'Valerius'. Ce proconsul aurait pu être un Sertorius, un Elufrius ou un Veturius. Il y avait un sénateur prétorien du nom de Sertorius Severus à l'époque de Domitien.[9] Un L. Elufrius Severus fut proconsul de Crète en 100;[10] et cette mention revient dans la nomenclature de l'*ordinarius* polyonyme de 114.[11] Il y a encore un consul, dont on ne connaît pas la date, du nom d'Arrianus Afer Veturius Severus.[12] De plus et pour en finir, ce *cognomen* est si répandu qu'on peut difficilement attendre

---

[1] *ILS* 1029.   [2] *CIL* xvi 175.   [3] *Inscriptions latines d'Afrique*, 591.
[4] *IRT* 304. Cf. A. Merlin dans son supplément minutieux et indispensable aux Fastes proconsulaires, *Mém. de la Soc. nat. des Antiquaires de France* lxxxiii (1954), 29.
[5] *AE* 1934 231. [Pomponius Marcellus now seems to have governed Asia: see *AJA* lxxviii (1974), 122.]
[6] *Inscriptions latines de l'Algérie* i 1283. [The traces of the *nomen* have now been read MIO and he has been identified with C. Septimius Severus: see *AE* 1967, 536. If this is correct, the discussion based on the old reading is no longer relevant.]
[7] *IGR* iii 739, col. iv, 16 (Rhodiapolis). Les indications données à son sujet dans *RE* viii A, col. 223 ss. ne sont pas exactes.
[8] *IG* ix 1, 61 (Daulis).   [9] Pline, *Ep.* v 1.   [10] *AE* 1933, 7.
[11] *ILS* 1044 (Tibur).   [12] *PIR*² , A 1080.

quelque lumière d'une recherche parmi tous les consuls non identifiés appelés 'Severus'.

Cependant, les données que l'on possède sur les gouverneurs de Lycie-Pamphylie (province généralement conservée pendant trois ans et menant à un consulat) pourraient permettre de réduire les limites chronologiques.[1] Il n'y a pas de place libre au début du règne d'Hadrien jusqu'à et y compris C. Valerius Severus (*suff.* 124). De plus les années 139–52 semblent complètes. Il y a un trou | entre 124 et 139,[2] où il n'y a que deux ou trois gouverneurs connus à insérer. Donc le consulat de ']rius Severus' devrait se situer ou bien entre 126 et 140, ou bien après 154. Il faut en rester là. Il se peut que des témoignages indirects se présentent et permettent, en les associant à d'autres, de dater assez précisément la carrière de ce personnage. Elles pourraient aussi modifier légèrement et rectifier l'ordre des proconsuls suggéré ci-dessus pour les années 139–43.

III

Les huit proconsuls de 157/8 à 164/5. Une étude des sénateurs de cette période a donné une liste de sept proconsuls, à partir de 158/9.[3] La voici:

158/9	L. M[
159/60	L. Lollianus Avitus
160/1	Claudius Maximus
161/2	Sex. Cocceius Severianus Honorinus
162/3	Q. Voconius Saxa Fidus
163/4	Ser. Cornelius Scipio Salvidienus Orfitus
164/5	M. Antonius Zeno.

Cette liste présentait certains points vulnérables. De nouvelles découvertes, révisions ou conjectures exigent qu'on la remanie complètement.

Tout d'abord, L. Lollianus Avitus (*cos.* 144), dont le nom complet est L. Hedius Rufus Lollianus Avitus. Une étude serrée montre que son proconsulat peut être décalé de deux ans et placé, non en 159/60, mais en 157/8.[4] Le théâtre de Lepcis fut dédié ou achevé sous son proconsulat: deux inscriptions portant son nom appartiennent à cet édifice.[5] Il y en a encore une autre, un fragment sans le nom, mais avec une date, 157

---

[1] Pour la liste la plus récente, voir D. Magie, *Roman Rule in Asia Minor* ii (1950). Mais il subsiste de nombreux problèmes; cf. R. Syme, *JRS* xlviii (1958), 2 s. [= pp. 379 ff. above]. Par exemple, le gouverneur Calestrius Tiro (*IGR* iii 704: Rhodiapolis) devrait être dissocié de T. Calestrius Tiro, consul suffect en 122 (*CIL* xvi 169). Ce dernier serait alors le contemporain et l'ami de Pline le Jeune. [M. Flavius Aper is now attested in 125: see W. Eck, *Senatoren von Vespasian bis Hadrian* (1970), 197 f. On the Calestrii Tirones, see pp. 779 ff. below.]

[2] [Now reduced to 126–37.]

[3] P. Lambrechts, *La composition du Sénat romain de l'accession au trône d'Hadrien à la mort de Commode* (1936), 221.

[4] J. Guey, *REL* xxix (1951), 307 ss.; noté dans *AE* 1952, 177.   [5] *IRT* 533 s.

d'après la titulature impériale.[1] Donc 157/8 pour Lollianus.[2] Un laps de temps de treize années seulement depuis le consulat est facilement admissible. Lollianus étant un *ordinarius*, il peut avoir joui d'un traitement de faveur.

Une conséquence importante en découlait.[3] Le discours d'Apu|lée et le proconsulat de Claudius Maximus (*suff.* 143 ou 144) doivent se situer en 158/9 et non, comme on le croyait communément, en 160/1.

Nouvelle incertitude: le cas du proconsul dont la nomenclature est incomplète, placé en 158/9. La réunion adroite de deux fragments trouvés à Avitta Bibba a donné '[? Q.] Egrilio Plariano / L. M['.[4] En outre une inscription de Rome atteste l'existence du couple de *suffecti*, L. Aemilius et Q. Egrilius.[5] Dans le premier on peut reconnaître L. Aemilius Carus dont nous possédons le *cursus*. Il fut légat d'Arabie, passant de là au consulat; et sa présence est attestée en Arabie précisément en 142/3.[6] Ce couple consulaire peut donc se placer en 143 ou 144.[7] Voyons maintenant l'année du proconsulat d'Egrilius; ce n'est pas forcément 158/9; l'année suivante est tout aussi admissible; c'est celle que nous adopterons ici.

En troisième lieu, un proconsul ignoré peut être ramené au jour et introduit ici avec pour résultat d'ajouter un huitième nom à la liste, en modifier l'ordre et en resserrer l'enchaînement, confirmant ainsi la nouvelle date de l'*Apologie* d'Apulée.

Une inscription de Rome révèle l'existence d'un proconsul d'Afrique: '[T. Prifer]nio T. f. [Paeto Ro]siano Gemino'.[8] Ce témoignage a été négligé, ou, qui pis est, mal interprété. Deux personnages appelés chacun 'T. Prifernius Paetus' et vivant sous le règne d'Antonin le Pieux posaient des problèmes embarrassants par certains côtés, mais il était possible de ne pas les confondre. Tous deux se trouvent sur une liste de sénateurs patrons d'une corporation d'Ostie, en 140, le père à la première place, le fils à la quatrième.[9] Une autre liste, de 152, comporte le père seulement, 'Sex.

---

[1] *IRT* 372.

[2] Les doutes récemment exprimés dans *PIR²*, H 40, n'ont pas de bases solides. [Guey is more hesitant in his conclusion than appears in *AE* 1954. It rests on a conjecture regarding the reference in *IRT* 372, suggested (but never fully established) by Caputo. Thomasson (op. cit. 75) reports an observation by K. Hanell, strengthening the case.]

[3] Cela a été solidement établi par J. Guey [following Caputo's suggestion].

[4] *CIL* viii 800+1177, réunies par A. Merlin, *CRAI* 1941, 235 ss., d'où *AE* 1942/3, 85; *Inscriptions latines de Tunisie*, 672.

[5] *CIL* vi 30868.

[6] *ILS* 1077 (Rome), cf. *AE* 1909, 237 (Gerasa).

[7] Cf. R. Syme, *JRS* xxxvi (1946), 167: compte-rendu de A. Stein, *Die Reichsbeamten von Dazien* (1944) [= *Danubian Papers* (1971), 171 f., cf. 176, opting for 144].

[8] *CIL* vi 1449. [But B. E. Thomasson has very plausibly suggested a new restoration for this inscription (*Eranos* lxvii (1969), 175 ff.—already proposed, without full discussion, *Statthalter* ii 71), which does away with the proconsulate of the son and makes him merely his father's legate.]

[9] *CIL* xiv 246.

f.'.[1] Et une troisième, non datée, le fils seulement, 'T. f.', avec l'indication de sa tribu, la Quirina.[2]

En ce qui concerne les proconsulats d'Afrique, le père a été identifié grâce au *cursus* de son gendre, P. Pactumeius Clemens (*suff.* 138), d'où il ressort qu'il fut consul suffect *c.* 125, proconsul | peut-être en 140/1 (comme il est indiqué ci-dessus). Quant à son fils, l'inscription de Rome montrait qu'un Prifernius Paetus, 'T. f.', fut proconsul d'Afrique. Puis un fragment des *Fasti Ostienses*, publié pour la première fois en 1934, a montré qu'un certain T. Prifernius Paetus se trouvait parmi les *suffecti* de 146.[3] Il s'agissait évidemment du fils déjà connu, grâce aux deux inscriptions, sur les listes de *patroni* à Ostie. Jusque-là tout va bien. Mais on a fait valoir que, si Prifernius le Jeune était proconsul d'Afrique, son mandat devait se placer aux alentours de 161, époque pour laquelle la liste serait complète. Par conséquent le *suffectus* de 146 ne peut pas avoir été proconsul; il y aurait donc une erreur dans la filiation donnée par l'inscription romaine: il faudrait lire 'Sex. f.' au lieu de 'T. f.'.[4]

Le procédé était extrême, la confiance prématurée. On peut situer ce proconsul d'une manière précise et satisfaisante en 160/1, année d'où Claudius Maximus a été écarté. La liste corrigée comportant huit proconsuls en ordre suivi de 157/8 à 164/5 se présentera ainsi:

157/8	L. Hedius Rufus Lollianus Avitus	*cos.* 144
158/9	Claudius Maximus	*suff.* ? 143 ou 144
159/60	[Q.] Egrilius Plarianus L. M[	*suff.* ? 144
160/1	T. Prifernius T. f. Paetus Rosianus Geminus	*suff.* 146
161/2	Q. Voconius Saxa Fidus	*suff.* 146
162/3	Sex. Cocceius Severianus Honorinus	*suff.* 147
163/4	Ser. Cornelius Scipio Salvidienus Orfitus	*cos.* 149
164/5	M. Antonius Zeno	*suff.* 148

Le cas de quatre de ces proconsuls a déjà été étudié, à savoir: Lollianus Avitus, Claudius Maximus, Egrilius Plarianus et Prifernius Paetus. Les données essentielles pour dater les autres peuvent être exposées brièvement.

1. Voconius Saxa. Des inscriptions de Gigthis et de Carthage fournissent la seconde *tribunicia potestas* de L. Verus, c'est-à-dire 162. On peut donc le placer en 161/2, et non, comme on le faisait jusqu'à maintenant, en 162/3.[5]

2. Cocceius Honorinus. Une inscription de Thagora le situe entre | 161 et 163, puisque 'Armeniacus' manque dans l'énumération des titres de L. Verus.[6] De même une inscription de Carthage n'est pas postérieure à 163.[7] Par conséquent 162/3 est admissible au lieu de 161/2.[8]

[1] *CIL* xiv 250 = *ILS* 6174.	[2] *CIL* xiv 247.
[3] *NSA* 1934, 247, maintenant *FO* xxvii [*Inscr. It.* xiii 1, 204–5].
[4] Lambrechts, op. cit. 90, suivi dans *RE* xxii, col. 1969 (de 1954): l'article n'est pas bon.
[5] *AE* 1949, 27; *CIL* viii 22691.	[6] *Inscriptiones latines de l'Algérie* i 1030.
[7] *CIL* viii 24535.	[8] *PIR*², C 1230 suggérit 161/2.

3. Salvidienus Orfitus. La date de son mandat est fixée par une inscription d'Oea, comportant 'Armeniacus' pour L. Verus, mais non pour M. Aurelius.[1]

4. Antonius Zeno. L'unique témoignage, une inscription de Thugga, ne fournit aucune date.[2]

Cette série de huit proconsuls est la bienvenue. Il est très regrettable que l'Asie ne puisse fournir une liste parallèle. Les documents sont rares pour la dernière décade du règne d'Antonin le Pieux, qui est également empoisonnée par le problème des proconsuls cités par Aelius Aristide. Les résultats exposés ci-dessus ne sont d'aucun secours dans ce domaine, mais ils ont une utilité, si modeste soit-elle. Ils permettent de situer trois proconsuls dans le triennium 160–3 au lieu de 161–4, à savoir P. Mummius Sisenna Rutilianus (*suff.* 146), Q. Cornelius Proculus (*suff.* 146) et C. Popilius Carus Pedo (*suff.* 147).[3]

[1] *CIL* viii 24 = *IRT* 232: *PIR*[2], C 1447 donne 163/4, à juste titre.

[2] *CIL* viii 1480. Donc *PIR*[2], A 883 donne 'quinto decimo fere anno post consulatum'. [The date and identification here adopted must be abandoned in the light of the combination of several new fragments with this inscription by Cl. Poinssot, to give 184/5 as the date of Zeno's proconsulate. See *AE* 1966, 511.]

[3] La liste la plus récente, celle de Magie, peut être modifiée sur plusieurs points. Comparer, pour les proconsuls de 103/4 à 120/1, avec R. Syme, *Tacitus* (1958), 664 f. Magie place Rutilianus après 166 (op. cit. 1584): cette hypothèse (trouvée dans *RE* xvi, col. 532) a été détruite par la découverte de son année consulaire (146). Magie ne propose pas de date pour Popilius Carus, alors que *RE* xxii, col. 67, avance avec assurance 163/4. Il vaut peut-être la peine de noter que Rutilianus est important pour l'étude de Lucien—Rutilianus, ami, gendre et fauteur du prophète Alexandre d'Abonotichos.

[*Additional Note.* Minicius turns out to be T. Salvius Rufinus Minicius Opimianus, revealed by a diploma as consul in August 123 (W. Eck, *Historia* xxiv (1975), 324 ff.). Eck would put his proconsulate in 138/9, moving M'. Acilius Glabrio (if accepted) to 139/40.]

35

Roman Historians and Renaissance Politics

THE day and occasion we celebrate is the birth of Shakespeare. The present discourse, while not concerned with Shakespeare or even with his Roman dramas, will evoke before it ends another playwright, Ben Jonson, who not only followed Roman historians closely in his *Catiline* and his *Sejanus* but was so fanatically addicted to practices of erudition that he equipped the second piece with elaborate annotation. Indeed, an attempt can be made to utilize Jonson as a means of linking together, in more ways than one, two potent and portentous names: Tacitus and Machiavelli.

History among the Romans took its origin in the governing class, and it tended for a long time to be the monopoly of senators. They wrote after experience of affairs, some in retreat or in revulsion, frustrated, angry, and censorious. Thus Sallust at least, after disappointments in his political life: he confesses the folly of ambition and proclaims that he is glad to be out of the turmoil. Tacitus had no personal cause to complain, and he continued in the career of honours; but Tacitus turned aside from public elo|quence (its function was finished) and, as though estranged from his own time, composed the sombre annals of despotism.

Livy, in sundry respects, falls outside the main line of Roman historiography. He was not a senator; his tone is benevolent and edifying. Yet Livy had a political theme: to praise ancient virtue and justify Rome's dominion over the nations. The style, by its opulence and splendour, and the sentiments (moral, patriotic, and republican) exercised a long and pervasive influence on the humanist writers of history in the Italian cities. But Livy was not an abiding force in the sixteenth century and subsequently: he succumbed to a sharp decline for reasons in no way mysterious.

So did the humanist historians themselves, and they have suffered much depreciation in modern times. Their rhetorical and dramatic fashion of writing found no favour; and it was alleged that they were deficient in political insight. A juster estimate will discover signal merits, notably in the Florentines. And, as they furnish much of the intellectual background of Machiavelli and Guicciardini, they ought not to be neglected.

Society and History in the Renaissance. A Report of a Conference held at the Folger Library on April 23 and 24, 1960 (1960), 3–12.

In the year 1512 Machiavelli, who had served the Florentine republic for fourteen years, was thrown out of employment when the Medici came back. Not only that. They affected to believe that he had been conspiring, and he was put to torture. The ex-secretary displayed fortitude—and resilience. Like a Roman in retirement, like Sallust 'ex multis miseriis atque periculis', he turned for consolation to study and writing. Experience of affairs and the ancient classics were his guides. As he says, 'con una lunga esperienza delle cose moderne et con una continua lezione delle antique.'

His reflections soon bore fruit. He had already begun a political commentary on the first ten books of Livy, the *Discorsi*, so it is generally but not perhaps correctly held, when he allowed himself to be diverted into composing a short monograph, the | *Prince* (or rather *De principatibus*). That book was completed before the end of 1513.

Prince and *Discorsi*, their comparative influences and significance are a problem, and a paradox. As for the *Prince*, it might well be asked whether that one of the Medici to whom it was dedicated ever cared to read it. The publication created no stir. The fame of Machiavelli, or rather his obloquy, is posthumous.

For posterity Machiavelli is the author of the *Prince*, the personification of its doctrine. By contrast, the *Discorsi* are eclipsed and have been little studied. The two works have a common theme, however, which can be defined as political stability. The *Discorsi* counsel a republic how to be strong and how to survive, ancient Rome being the model. And is not this the real Machiavelli—who is seen elsewhere, for example, in his fervour for citizen militias?

Machiavelli took Livy as text for a kind of Biblical exegesis in a pagan spirit. Why Livy especially, and not some writer of greater penetration? An answer can be given. Livy was no doubt familiar to him from his early education. Moreover, Machiavelli avows a hostility towards the Caesars and the empire. In the *Discorsi* (i 10) he affirms that Caesar was worse than Catilina; and he furnishes a catalogue of the disasters of the imperial period (based on Tacitus, *Hist.* i 2).

Yet one might ask why he was not drawn to Sallust. Surely the plain hard language appealed, and the trenchant aphorisms on men and government, likewise the disillusion about party and the sophisticated political argumentation. And certain opinions were highly congenial. Speaking in his own person or in the oration of Caesar, the historian affirms that 'fortuna' holds domination everywhere; yet he denounces sloth or resignation and preaches a gospel of energy, 'virtus' being its name.

Sallust, who might have served as a valuable foil or corrective to Livy, is mentioned or quoted only three times in all the | *Discorsi*. Others were fascinated by his style and manner, in the forefront Rucellai, whose narration of the French invasion of 1494, the *De bello Italico*, is a splendid and classic performance. Not only literature but life—there was a *Catilinarismo* of the Renaissance, a cult of criminal or heroic energy. It is perhaps relevant that Sallust was known and notorious as the narrator of a conspiracy against a republican government, whereas Machiavelli is all for order, stability, and civil government.

It is natural to think next of Tacitus. He is named and quoted three times in the *Discorsi*; there are also a quotation without the name and three passages where he has clearly been used. That is all. One of the quotations from Tacitus is singled out by Machiavelli as a 'sentenza . . . aurea'. It comes from the oration of the opportunistic politician Eprius Marcellus: 'One may admire the past, but one should keep in step with the present; pray that a virtuous ruler be vouchsafed, but submit to what you get' (*Hist.* iv 8). The maxim might be labelled typically 'Machiavellian', in the conventional sense.

Tacitus and Machiavelli, the confrontation is inevitable. What emerges? The ingenious Toffanin came forward with a bold theory and many assumptions (*Machiavelli e il Tacitismo*, 1921). The *Discorsi* are dedicated to two men of republican sentiments. Now Machiavelli was an advocate of monarchy, and so (Toffanin lightly assumes) was Tacitus. Therefore Machiavelli, instead of holding discourse on Tacitus, chooses amiably and artfully to spare the feelings of his friends by employing a republican writer, Livy.

This notion is elaborate, flimsy, and false. Machiavelli is straight and above-board in the *Discorsi*. There appears to be no deception; he expounds, as he says, 'quanto io so'. Nor is there any sign that the Florentine thinker is anywhere deeply in the debt of Cornelius Tacitus.

A matter of literary chronology here comes into the reckoning. The *editio princeps* of Tacitus appeared in 1470. It com|prised only the *Historiae* and *Annales* xi–xvi. Books i–vi were not published until 1515. This, for various reasons the most Tacitean part of Tacitus, came too late to influence the *Prince*; and there is no trace of it in the *Discorsi*, save possibly in a single passage (iii 19,1), where some scholars detected a confused reminiscence of *Ann.* iii 55, 4.

Those books, it might seem, would have had an irresistible appeal for the author of the *Prince*—if they had been available. They depicted Tiberius Caesar as a master in the art of dissimulation. It is a common assumption that the historian traduced the emperor. Rather perhaps did he fall under the spell of that sombre, sagacious, and suspicious monarch, conceiving no small admiration. The Roman senator knew the ways of men and governments. How did a ruler survive and hold the power for twenty-three years, baffling his enemies and avoiding many a hazard, if not by deep dissembling?

'Qui nescit dissimulare, nescit regnare.' That was a maxim familiar to the sixteenth century. It was commonly attributed to Louis XI of France, who is reckoned by Francis Bacon as one of the three Magi (the others are Henry VII and Ferdinand of Aragon).

The story of Tiberius' reign exhibited in dramatic form an archetypal theme—the relation between the monarch and his minister. Distrustful towards all others, Tiberius surrendered his confidence to Sejanus—and came in the end to repent of it. Sejanus was crafty, but he met his match. If Sejanus formed a plot, the only conspiracy that can clearly be demonstrated is that whereby Tiberius Caesar contrived the destruction of his minister.

Conspiracies were not alien to the interests of Machiavelli. By far the longest chapter in the *Discorsi* (iii 6) is devoted to that theme. He there touches briefly on Sejanus, drawing his information from Cassius Dio. (It should be added that even if he had *Annales* i–vi before him, he could not there have read the climax of the drama, for Book v is missing.) |

It was some time before Tacitus came into his own. Not all Latinists could like or tolerate the style, although as early as 1517 Alciati was ready to proclaim the demotion of Livy—'sed et nobis prae Tacito sordescet Livius.' The decisive impulsion was given by Justus Lipsius, who published his views in his oration at Jena in 1572 and in the preface to his commentary in 1581. It was not merely the style that ravished him, but the sharp and immediate relevance of Tacitus to life as it was lived in the epoch of wars and despotism. The Roman writer was nothing less than 'theatrum hodiernae vitae'.

In the meantime the Florentine had emerged into notoriety. They put him on the Index in 1552. And now Tacitus and Machiavelli come together in a close nexus. Machiavelli was scandalous and immoral, but Tacitus was a classic and could therefore more safely be exploited by students of political science. Lipsius, it will be noted, paid a high tribute to Machiavelli—'unius tamen Machiavelli ingenium non contemno, acre, subtile, igneum'. But he went on to express disapproval of the *Prince* (in the preface of his *Politicorum libri sex* of 1589). Lipsius had already been explicit: he would not write any political commentary on Tacitus. This in 1581. Others, however, were quick to take up the challenge: Paschali (1581), Scipione Ammirato (1594), the Spaniard Alamos de Barrientos (after 1590). The prudent Lipsius was perhaps deterred from risky projects by the painful recollection of his own vicissitudes.

Tacitus was now in vogue, and history surpassed itself in reproducing Tacitus. Philip II, whom the Spaniards know as 'El Prudente', offers various analogies to Tiberius Caesar. Enslaved to a sense of duty, rigorous and pedantic in his application to state business and official papers, he was prone to hesitations and suspicions. And he fell into a predicament like that of Tiberius: he found the indispensable helper. An insinuating courtier earned his trust in 1568 (a year of troubles and perplexity) and held it for ten years, not only as a confidential secretary, but as a minister and | a friend. This was Antonio Pérez, whose intrigues and adventures would fill a volume. Let it suffice to say that, involved in tortuous negotiations with people in Flanders, he contrived the murder of Escobedo, the envoy of Don Juan, that brilliant and expansive person who outshone the King, his half-brother. That deed was not ordered by Philip, but he may have known about it—and he soon conceived doubt and scruples. Pérez was arrested. An inconclusive inquiry followed and long delays, from 1579 to 1590, after which Pérez evaded Castilian justice by a flight to Aragon, where he stirred up trouble. In the end, escaping, he visited various European courts and died in Paris in 1611.

Pérez, an accomplished Latinist and a lover of Tacitus, composed his memoirs, which he published in 1593 (he was then in England), with a dedication to Essex. He saw himself in a double role—as a Sejanus who had got away, and as the equivalent of the classic historian. He modestly avers, 'I cannot give assurance that there will not be a Tacitus for this century as for the other.'

Antonio Pérez also helped to enrich the Tacitean dossier indirectly. His friend Alamos de Barrientos, enlisted in his defence, was sent to prison. He assuaged the eight years of his confinement by translating the works of Tacitus—with aphorisms in the margin. In a letter to Pérez he says that he 'touched, under the names of Tiberius and Sejanus, many points of history'.

So much for Pérez, 'this Spanish traitor', as Elizabeth called him. England in due course produced its contribution to the classic theme: Charles and his favourite, the Duke of Buckingham. In his speech of 10 May 1626, Sir John Eliot, moving the impeachment of Buckingham, was enboldened to quote Tacitus on the character and ambitions of Sejanus (*Ann.* iv 1). The King took the point. He exclaimed, 'implicitly he must intend me for Tiberius.' Eliot was put under arrest the next day.

Tacitus already enjoyed high esteem in England among the understanding, as witness his use by Bacon. He was also feared as sinister and subversive, as an incident of the same year demon|strates. A refugee from Holland, Isaac Dorislaus, secured appointment as professor of history at Trinity College, Cambridge. He started to lecture on Tacitus. They stopped him before he had got any further than the first chapter of the *Annales*.

The earliest translation of this author had been published in the 1590s. The eminent Sir Henry Saville undertook the first four books of the *Histories*. The rest of Tacitus was dealt with by Richard Grenewey—not so well. At least in the opinion of Ben Jonson, as delivered to Drummond, *Ann.* i–iv were 'ignorantly done into English'.

Jonson needed no such aids, and he could allow himself the luxury of contempt—a fine scholar who had been educated at St. Paul's under the best of masters. It was none other than William Camden, whom he salutes with gratitude in the dedication to *Cynthia's Revels*—'alumnus olim, aeternum amicus'. Jonson was also a friend of Saville. The poem which he addresses to Saville suitably carries an echo of one of the Latin historians (Sallust, as it happens, not Tacitus)—'from hope, from fear, from fancy free'.

It may be observed in passing, and not irrelevant, that Saville and Camden entered into an amicable and beneficent competition. The translator of Tacitus established at Oxford chairs of astronomy and geometry. Camden, however, chose ancient history (in 1622). He had his own ideas about the subject—not on any account ecclesiastical history. He even enjoined a topic: the Camden professor was to lecture on Florus. The choice of an elementary and miserable compiler (Florus is condensed Livy) might occasion surprise and doubts about William Camden, a historian in his own right and a correspondent of Justus Lipsius. Perhaps he was careful and cautious. What happened to Dorislaus at Cambridge only four years later speaks for Camden's prescience.

However that may be, one of Camden's old pupils had acquired a passionate interest in Rome of the Caesars. In 1603 he produced his *Sejanus*. It was not a success. Certain of the defects are patent. The author does not rise to his subject and exploit the | opportunities presented by the characters of Tiberius and Sejanus. Further, as can happen with Roman history in whatever medium portrayed, the plethora of characters is an embarrassment. None the less, there are several items of high achievement. One is due to Tacitus: the author renders in blank verse with hardly a change the oration in defence of free speech which Tacitus invented and put into the mouth of a Roman historian, Cremutius Cordus (*Ann.* iv 34 f.). Another success is all Jonson's own. Tiberius Caesar in a long, deceitful, and tortuous missive from Capreae to the Senate announced the doom of his friend and minister. Tacitus no doubt exercised his talent on the document—he was waiting for it. But this portion of Tacitus is not extant. Jonson essays the 'verbosa et grandis epistula' on hints from Juvenal, Suetonius, and Dio.

The *Sejanus* is a venture on a 'Machiavellian' theme. Jonson uses Tacitus and his own imagination to create a drama of tyranny and conspiracy. He did not stand in any need of Machiavelli. But Machiavelli crops up elsewhere, in a subdued and vulgar fashion.

The repute of Machiavelli in Elizabethan England is a subject that has attracted and rewarded the attention of literary critics. The Florentine was barely known as an author, and much time was to elapse before he could be translated and published. He made his début as a character in literature, the type and model of craft and crime. Thus, as most familiar, in the prologue of Marlowe's *Jew of Malta*:

> Admired I am of those that hate me most.
> Though some speak openly against my books
> Yet they will read me and thereby attain
> To Peter's Chair.

To this notion, French hostility to Catherine de' Medici and a book written by the French Protestant Gentillet contributed efficaciously. The debased and criminal Machiavelli came in handy for all manner of caricatures. National conceit did its worst, and the alarming accounts of virtuous tourists from the northern lands, | concentrating under one name the variegated manifestations of Italian depravity. Machiavelli stands for the Jesuit or the atheist, the political scientist or the subtle poisoner—

> 'Tis not the first time I have killed a man:
> I learned in Naples how to poison flowers.
> (*Edward II*, 1594; Malone Soc. Reprint, 1925, ll. 2539 f.)

It is therefore appropriate that only four years after the high and classic tragedy of *Sejanus* Ben Jonson should go on and write a Machiavellian comedy. His *Volpone* is built up around a standard theme of imperial Rome. It is *captatio*, the cumulated devices whereby artful men beguile the childless opulent, to be named in their testaments—or themselves to be baffled and cheated—encountering a superior practitioner who is not the victim but the victor. Into that traditional comedy of deception Jonson brings the English tourist. He is a student of political science, half-learned and gullible, Sir Politick Would-be. His fitting consort is a wife with literary interests. The play happens to mention political theorists by name.

> Nic. Machiavel and Monsieur Bodin, both
> Were of this mind.

It also descends to the ridiculous by importing the fancy (credulously taken up) that mountebank doctors command secret and sagacious influence—

> They are the only knowing men of Europe
>
> . . .
>
> And cabinet counsellors to the greatest princes.

Jonson discovered a congenial subject of delight in Italian comedy. There was another side also to Machiavelli. Jonson will not have ignored the *Mandragola*, a farce that showed up moral pretence, sex, and the duplicity of the clergy. With Jonson, imperial Rome and contemporary Italy converge and blend: political diagnosis and social satire. Those elements might also be discovered in the historian Tacitus.

Date Due

BJJJ